WITHDRAWN

Index to
BOOK REVIEWS
IN
HISTORICAL PERIODICALS
1974

by

John W. Brewster

and

Joseph A. McLeod

The Scarecrow Press, Inc.
Metuchen, N.J.   1975

Ref
Index/
Abstr,
D
1
B73

ISBN: 0-8108-0818-8
LC: 75-18992

DEDICATION

To Carol and Pam

INTRODUCTION

The Index to Book Reviews in Historical Periodicals has developed out of a recognized need among the students at North Texas State University for aid in locating reviews of books assigned for class readings. The present volume includes 97 of the better known scholarly journals and historical society organs. Although the reviews concentrate more heavily upon U.S. history, an effort has been made to include materials relating to other countries as well. The index includes only English-language periodicals. Books written in foreign languages are included if the review is in English. The original title is indicated except where a translation is given, in which case the English version is used. In some periodicals, works are included which stress other disciplines as well as history. These are included for the sake of completeness; such entries comprise a very small minority of the total index.

In most cases, the complete title of the work is indicated although in the case of an exceptionally long title, an abridged form may appear. In all cases, the policy has been to include enough of the title to enable the researcher to identify the work. In regard to imprint, the editors have endeavored to provide enough information to identify the work clearly. Well-known publishers whose works appear frequently are cited by abbreviations (a key to academic press abbreviations appears before the beginning of the Index proper). States are included only when needed to identify a city.

Although designed primarily as a tool for locating book reviews, because the index includes some 5000 titles, most of which are current publications, it may also serve as a bibliographic guide in history. As nearly as possible, the editors have used the format of the University of Chicago Style Manual. Standardized abbreviations for months and seasons are used.   In cases where reviewers' entries conflict, <u>Books in Print</u> has been followed.

The editors present this work with the belief that it will be a useful tool for the scholar, the student, and the general reader with an interest in history.

John W. Brewster
Joseph A. McLeod

Denton, Texas
April 1975

ACKNOWLEDGMENTS

The authors of the index recognize that their efforts have been made much easier by the indulgence and cooperation of others. Not least among those who have made the task easier were the families of the authors who bore with good grace and a minimum of complaint the cluttering of their homes with file cards, trays, and volumes of periodicals. In addition they have rendered valuable assistance in the compilation, typing, and proof-reading and in offering timely suggestions.

Besides members of their immediate families, the authors express appreciation to members of the library staffs in the Fort Worth-Dallas-Denton metroplex. At North Texas State University, special mention should be made of the encouragement given by Director of Libraries, Dr. David A. Webb and Assistant Director, Central Services, George D. Mitchell. Indeed it was Mr. Mitchell who first made the observation which led to the compilation of the index. Valuable assistance also came from William B. Floyd and his staff of the Social Science division of the North Texas State University Library. Dr. Gustave L. Seligman, Jr. of the NTSU history faculty offered helpful suggestions.

PERIODICALS INDEXED (1974)

A & W	Arizona and the West
AfAf	African Affairs
Africa	Africa
AH	American Heritage
AHR	The American Historical Review
AI	Annals of Iowa
AJA	American Journal of Archaeology
AlaHQ	The Alabama Historical Quarterly
AlaRe	The Alabama Review
AmAnt	American Antiquity
AmArc	The American Archivist
Antiquity	Antiquity
Archaeology	Archaeology
Archives	Archives
ArkHQ	The Arkansas Historical Quarterly
BHR	Business History Review
CH	Church History
ChOk	Chronicles of Oklahoma
CHQ	California Historical Quarterly
CHR	The Canadian Historical Review
CoMag	Colorado Magazine
Commentary	Commentary
CR	China Report
Crisis	The Crisis
CurH	Current History
CWH	Civil War History
CWTI	Civil War Times Illustrated
EEQ	East European Quarterly

EHR	English Historical Review
ESR	European Studies Review
ETHJ	East Texas Historical Journal
FCHQ	Filson Club Historical Quarterly
FHQ	Florida Historical Quarterly
GHQ	Georgia Historical Quarterly
GPJ	Great Plains Journal
GR	The Georgia Review
HAHR	The Hispanic American Historical Review
H & T	History and Theory
Historian	The Historian: A Journal of History
History	History
HJ	Historical Journal
HRNB	History: Reviews of New Books
HT	History Teacher
HTo	History Today
IMH	Indiana Magazine of History
InHi	The Indian Historian
JAAS	Journal of Asian and African Studies
JAfH	The Journal of African History
JAH	The Journal of American History
JAmS	The Journal of American Studies
JAriH	The Journal of Arizona History
JAS	The Journal of Asian Studies
JEH	The Journal of Economic History
JIH	The Journal of Interdisciplinary History
JISHS	The Journal of the Illinois State Historical Society
JLAS	Journal of Latin American Studies
JMAS	The Journal of Modern African Studies
JMH	Journal of Modern History
JMiH	Journal of Mississippi History
JNH	Journal of Negro History
JOW	Journal of the West
JSH	The Journal of Southern History
LaH	Louisiana History

Mankind	Mankind
MAS	Modern Asian Studies
MHM	Maryland Historical Magazine
MHR	Missouri Historical Review
MiA	Mid America
MichH	Michigan History
MinnH	Minnesota History
NCHR	North Carolina Historical Review
NDH	North Dakota History
NEQ	New England Quarterly
NMHR	New Mexico Historical Review
NYH	New York History
NYHSQ	New York Historical Society Quarterly
OH	Ohio History
OrHQ	Oregon Historical Quarterly
PH	Pennsylvania History
PHR	Pacific Historical Review
PNQ	Pacific Northwest Quarterly
RKHS	Register of the Kentucky Historical Society
RQ	Renaissance Quarterly
SCHM	South Carolina Historical Magazine
SCQ	Southern California Quarterly
SWHQ	The Southwestern Historical Quarterly
TAm	The Americas
T & C	Technology and Culture
THQ	The Tennessee Historical Quarterly
Texana	Texana
UHQ	Utah Historical Quarterly
VH	Vermont History
VMHB	Virginia Magazine of History and Biography
WHQ	Western Historical Quarterly
WMH	The Wisconsin Magazine of History
WMQ	William and Mary College Quarterly--3rd Series.
WVH	West Virginia History

ABBREVIATIONS OF PUBLISHERS

Standard abbreviations are used for commercial publishers ("& Sons," "Co.," "Inc.," and the like are
omitted). The following abbreviations are used for
university presses and educational presses:

Cam U Press	Cambridge University Press, Cambridge, England
Cath U Amer Press	Catholic University of America Press, Washington, D. C.
Coll and U Press	College and University Press, New Haven, Conn.
Cor U Press	Cornell University Press, Ithaca, N. Y.
CWRU Press	Case Western Reserve University Press, Cleveland, Ohio
Edin U Press	Edinburgh University Press, Edinburgh, Scotland
Har U Press	Harvard University Press, Cambridge, Mass.
Heb Union Coll Press	Hebrew Union College Press, Cincinnati, Ohio
Huntington	Huntington Library, San Marino, California
Ia St U Press	Iowa State University Press, Ames, Ia.
Ind U Press	Indiana University Press, Bloomington, Indiana
JHU Press	Johns Hopkins University Press, Baltimore, Md.
La St U Press / LSU Press	Louisiana State University Press, Baton Rouge, La.
MHS	Maryland Historical Society, Baltimore, Maryland
MIT Press	Massachusetts Institute of Technology Press, Cambridge, Mass.
N Ill U Press	Northern Illinois University Press, DeKalb, Ill.
NW St U La Press	Northwest State University of Louisiana, Natchitoches, La.

NWU Press	Northwestern University Press, Evanston, Illinois
NYU Press	New York University Press, New York, N.Y.
Ox U Press	Oxford University Press, New York, N.Y.
PHMC	Pennsylvania Historical and Museum Commission
Prin U Press	Princeton University Press, Princeton, N.J.
S Ill U Press / So Ill U Press	Southern Illinois University Press, Carbondale, Ill.
Stan U Press	Stanford University Press, Stanford, California
Syr U Press	Syracuse University Press, Syracuse, N.Y.
TCU Press	Texas Christian University Press, Ft. Worth, Texas
U and Coll Press Miss	University and College Press of Mississippi, Hattiesburg, Mississippi
UBC Press	University of British Columbia Press, Vancouver, B.C.
U Cal Press	University of California Press, Berkeley and Los Angeles
U Chi Press	University of Chicago Press, Chicago, Illinois
U Ga Press	University of Georgia Press, Athens, Georgia
U Ia Press	University of Iowa Press, Iowa City, Iowa
U Ill Press	University of Illinois Press, Urbana, Ill.
U Kan Press / U Ks Press	University of Kansas Press, Lawrence, Kansas
U Mich Press	University of Michigan Press, Ann Arbor, Michigan
U Minn Press	University of Minnesota Press, Minneapolis, Minn.
U Mo Press	University of Missouri Press, Columbia, Mo.
U Mont Press	University of Montana Press, Missoula, Mont.
UNC Press	University of North Carolina Press, Chapel Hill, N.C.
UNM Press	University of New Mexico Press, Albuquerque, N.M.
U Ok Press / U Okla Press	University of Oklahoma Press, Norman, Oklahoma
U Press Ky	University Press of Kentucky, Lexington, Ky.
U Press NE	University Press of New England, Hanover, Vt.

U Press Va	University Press of Virginia, Charlottesville, Va.
USC Press / USCar Press	University of South Carolina Press, Columbia, S. C.
USNI	United States Naval Institute, Annapolis, Md.
U Tenn Press	University of Tennessee Press, Knoxville, Tenn.
U Tex Press / U Tx Press	University of Texas Press, Austin, Texas
U Tor Press	University of Toronto Press, Toronto
U Utah Press	University of Utah Press, Salt Lake City, Utah
U Wash Press	University of Washington Press, Seattle, Washington
U Wis Press	University of Wisconsin Press, Madison, Wisconsin
Van U Press	Vanderbilt University Press, Nashville, Tenn.
W St U Press	Wayne State University Press, Detroit, Mich.
Wes U Press	Wesleyan University Press, Middletown, Conn.

THE INDEX: 1974

Aaron, Daniel. The Unwritten War: American Writers and the Civil War. New York: Knopf, 1973. Rev. by L. Marshall, JAH, 61(Sep 1974):487-8; R. B. Nye, JSH, 40(Aug 1974): 486-7.

Abbas, Ibrahim Muhammad Ali. The British, Slave Trade, and Slavery in the Sudan, 1820-1881. Khartoum: Khartoum U Press, 1972. Rev. by R. Gray, JAfH, 15(Num 3 1974):497-8.

Abbas, S. A. see Brecher, Irving

Abbiateci, A. and F. Billaçois, eds. Crimes et Criminalité en France sous l'Ancien Regime, 17e-18e siècles.... Paris: Armand Colin, 1972. Rev. by W. F. Church, AHR, 79(Je 1974):789-90; C. Tilly, CHR, 55(Mar 1974):113-4; O. Hufton, EHR, 89(Ja 1974):192-3.

Abbott, Richard H. Cobbler in Congress: The Life of Henry Wilson, 1812-1875. Lexington, Ky.: U Press Ky, 1972. Rev. by S. H. Strom, AHR, 79(Oct 1974):1268-70.

Abell, Tyler, ed. Drew Pearson: Diaries, 1949-1959. New York: Holt, Rinehart and Winston, 1974. Rev. by E. L. Schapsmeier, HRNB, 2(Mar 1974):131.

Abella, Irving Martin. Nationalism, Communism, and Canadian Labour: The CIO, the Communist Party, and the Canadian Congress of Labour, 1936-1956. Toronto: U Tor Press, 1973. Rev. by R. N. Kottman, JAH, 61(Je 1974):259-60.

Abernathy, David B. The Political Dilemma of Popular Education: An African Case. Stanford, Cal.: Stan U Press, 1969. Rev. by A. H. M. Kirk-Greene, Africa, 44(Apr 1974):263-4.

Abraham, Henry J. Freedom and the Court: Civil Rights and Liberties in the United States. New York: Ox U Press, 1972. Rev. by R. E. Fisher, Historian, 36(May 1974):573-4.

Abshire, David M. and Michael A. Samuels, eds. Portuguese Africa: A Handbook. New York: Praeger, 1969. Rev. by W. C. Opello, Jr., JMAS, 12(Sep 1974):487-91.

1

Acheson, A. K. L., J. F. Chant, and M. F. J. Prachowny, eds.
Bretton Woods Revisited. Toronto: U Tor Press, 1972. Rev.
by J. Helliwell, CHR, 55(Je 1974):204-5.

Acheson, Dean. This Vast External Realm. New York: Norton,
1973. Rev. by T. M. Leonard, HRNB, 2(Feb 1974):92.

Acomb, Frances. Mallet Du Pan (1749-1800): A Career in Political
Journalism. Durham, N. C.: Duke U Press, 1973. Rev. by
R. Birn, AHR, 79(Oct 1974):1188-9; R. M. Isherwood, HRNB,
2(Ja 1974):81.

Acton, Harold. Tuscan Villas. London: Thames and Hudson, n.d.
Rev. by S. Harcourt-Smith, HTo, 24(Mar 1974):207-8.

Acuña, Rodolfo F. Occupied America: The Chicano's Struggle toward Liberation. San Francisco: Canfield, 1972. Rev. by
M. T. Gracia, PHR, 43(Feb 1974):123-5.

_____. Sonoran Strong Man: Ignacio Pesqueira and His Times.
Tucson: U Ariz Press, 1974. Rev. by F. MacD. Spindler,
HRNB, 3(Nov/Dec 1974):39-40.

Adair, Douglass. Fame and the Founding Fathers. New York:
Norton, 1974. Rev. by M. R. Zahniser, HRNB, 3(Oct 1974):
3.

Adam, Heribert. Modernizing Racial Domination: South Africa's
Political Dynamics. Berkeley: U Cal Press, 1971. Rev. by
L. Frank, JMAS, 12(Mar 1974):137-41.

Adam, Jean-Paul. Instauration de la politique des chemins de fer
France. Paris: Presses Universitaires de France, 1972.
Rev. by C. E. Freedeman, AHR, 78(Dec 1973):1478.

Adamovich, Laszlo and Oszkar Sziklai. Foresters in Exile: The
Sopron Forestry School in Canada. Vancouver: U BC ...
1970. Rev. by N. F. Dreisziger, CHR, 55(Mar 1974):96-7.

Adams, Alexander B. Sitting Bull: An Epic of the Plains. New
York: Putnam's, 1973. Rev. by D. Youngkin, CoMag, 51
(Sum 1974):264-5.

Adams, Arthur E. and Jan Steckelberg Adams. Men Versus Systems: Agriculture in the U S S R, Poland and Czechoslovakia.
New York: Free Press, 1971. Rev. by W. W. Hagen, AgH,
47(Ja 1973):86-7; G. D. Jackson, Jr., AHR, 79(Apr 1974):
551-2.

Adams, Francis. History of the Elementary School Contest in England. Brighton: Harvester, 1972. Rev. by D. M. Thompson,
History, 59(Feb 1974):124-5.

Adams, Henry H. Years to Victory. New York: David McKay,
    1973. Rev. by B. F. Cooling, HRNB, 2(Feb 1974):98.

Adams, Robert M. Proteus: His Lies, His Truth. New York:
    Norton, 1973. Rev. by L. H. Peer, GR, 28(Sum 1974):357-
    60.

Adams, Willena C. see Cottner, Robert C., et al. Texas Cit-
    ies....

Adams, William H. The Whig Party of Louisiana. Lafayette: U
    SW La Press, 1973. Rev. by H. C. Dethoff, ETHJ, 12(Fall
    1974):94; V. P. Bernhard, JSH, 40(Nov 1974):657-8; R. G.
    Lowe, SWHQ, 78(Jl 1974):97-8.

Adamson, Alan H. Sugar Without Slaves: The Political Economy
    of British Guiana, 1838-1904. New Haven, Conn.: Yale U
    Press, 1972. Rev. by B. L. Moore, HAHR, 54(May 1974):
    321-2.

Adamson, J. H. and H. F. Folland. Sir Henry Vane: His Life
    and Times (1613-1662). Boston: Gambit, 1973. Rev. by
    C. R. Boxer, HTo, 24(Aug 1974):583; D. B. Rutman, NEQ,
    47(Mar 1974):158-61; F. C. McLaughlin, 57(Jl 1974):321-4.

Adas, Michael. European Imperialism in Asia. St. Charles, Mo.:
    Forum Press, 1974. Rev. by M. P. McCarthy, HT, 8(Nov
    1974):109-10.

Adeleye, R. A. Power and Diplomacy in Northern Nigeria, 1804-
    1906: the Sokoto Caliphate and Its Enemies. London: Long-
    mans, 1971. Rev. by D. E. Allyn, AfAf, 72(Ja 1973):84-5;
    D. F. McCall, AHR, 79(Oct 1974):1228-9.

Adelson, H. L., ed. Studies in Medieval and Renaissance History.
    Vol. IX. Lincoln: U Neb Press, 1972. Rev. by A. V.
    Autonovics, History, 59(Feb 1974):95-6.

Adler, Jacob and Gwynn Barrett, eds. The Diaries of Walter Mur-
    ray Gibson, 1886-1887. Honolulu: U Press Hawaii, 1973.
    Rev. by M. Tate, AHR, 79(Apr 1974):597; J. M. McCutcheon,
    JAH, 60(Mar 1974):1155-6; D. E. Livingston-Little, JOW, 13
    (Apr 1974):127; D. D. Johnson, PNQ, 65(Oct 1974):188-9.

Ady, Peter, ed. Private Foreign Investment and the Developing
    World. New York: Praeger, 1971. Rev. by A. Van Dam,
    JMAS, 12(Sep 1974):510-11.

Affeeck, Edward Lloyd. Sternwheelers, Sandbars and Switchbacks:
    A Chronicle of Steam Transportation in the British Columbia
    Waterways of the Columbia River System, 1865-1965. Van-
    couver, B. C.: Alexander Nicholls Press, 1973. Rev. by B.
    Mitchell, PNQ, 65(Oct 1974):191.

Afigbo, A. E. The Warrant Chiefs. Indirect Rule in Southeastern Nigeria 1891-1929. New York: Humanities, 1972. Rev. by P. Manning, JAAS, 9(Ja & Apr 1974):125-7.

Agar, Herbert. The Darkest Year: Britain Alone, June 1940-June 1941. Garden City, N.Y.: Doubleday, 1973. Rev. by W. T. Deininger, HRNB, 2(Ja 1974):85-6.

Ageron, Charles-Robert. Politiques coloniales au Maghreb. Paris: Presses Universitaires de France, 1972. Rev. by R. M. Brace, AHR, 79(Feb 1974):208-9.

Agpalo, Remigio E. The Political Elite and the People: A Study of Politics in Occidental Mindoro. Manila: U Philippines, 1972. Rev. by K. G. Machado, JAS, 33(May 1974):503-5.

Los agraviados de Cataluña. 4 vols. Pamplona: Ediciones Universidad de Navarra ... 1972. Rev. by H. V. Livermore, AHR, 79(Je 1974):794-6.

Aguilar, Luis E. Cuba 1933, Prologue to Revolution. Ithaca, N.Y.: ... Cornell U Press, 1972. Rev. by R. Carr, EHR, 89(Apr 1974):466-7; A. R. Millett, TAm, 30(Apr 1974):549-50.

Agulhon, Maurice. Pénitents et francs-maçons de l'ancienne Provence. Paris: Fayard, 1968. Rev. by T. W. Margadant, JIH, 5(Sum 1974):119-30.

_____. La République au village. Paris: Plon, 1970. Rev. by T. W. Margadant, JIH, 5(Sum 1974):119-30.

_____. La vie sociale en Provence intérieure au lendemain de la Révolution. Paris: Société des Études Robespierristes, 1970. Rev. by T. W. Margadant, JIH, 5 (Sum 1974):119-30.

_____. Une Ville ouvrière au temps du socialisme utopique. Toulon de 1815 à 1851. Paris: Mouton, 1970. Rev. by T. W. Margadant, JIH, 5(Sum 1974):119-30.

Ahern, Emily M. The Cult of the Dead in a Chinese Village. Stanford, Cal.: Stan U Press, 1973. Rev. by G. Aijmer, JAS, 34(Nov 1974):232-3.

Ahlstrom, Sydney E. A Religious History of the American People. New Haven, Conn.: Yale U Press, 1972. Rev. by J. W. Grant, CHR, 55(Sep 1974):341-2; W. R. Ward, EHR, 89(Ja 1974):122-5; W. R. Hutchison, JIH, 5(Aut 1974):313-18; J. B. Boles, MHM, 69(Sum 1974):241; P. J. Greven, Jr., NYHSQ, 58(Ja 1974):65-7; P. A. Carter, WHQ, 5(Oct 1974):478-8.

Ajayi, J. F. A. and Michael Crowder, eds. History of West Africa. Vol. 1. n.p.: Longman, 1971. Rev. by D. H. Jones, AfAf, 73(Apr 1974):235.

_____ and _____, eds. History of West Africa. Vol. 2.
New York: Columbia U Press, 1974. Rev. by V. M. Smith,
HRNB, 2(Sep 1974):251.

Akamatsu, Paul. Meiji 1868: Revolution and Counter-Revolution in
Japan. London: Allen and Unwin, 1972. Rev. G. Daniels,
History, 59(Je 1974):320.

Akenson, Donald Harman. Education and Enmity: The Control of
Schooling in Northern Ireland, 1920-50. New York: Barnes
and Noble, 1973. Rev. by J. M. Curran, Historian, 36(May
1974):547-8.

Alba, Victor. The Horizon Concise History of Mexico. New York:
American Heritage, 1973. Rev. by M. Stuart, RKHS, 72(Ja
1974):77-9.

Albert, William. The Turnpike Road System in England 1663-1840.
Cambridge: Cam U Press, 1972. Rev. by G. E. Mingay,
EHR, 89(Ja 1974):187-8; D. A. Baugh, JIH, 5(Sum 1974):155-
8.

Albertin, Lothar. Liberalismus und Demokratie am Anfang der
Weimarer Republik: Eine vergleichende Analyse der Deutschen
Demokratischen Partei und der Deutschen Volkspartei. Düssel-
dorf: Droste Verlag, 1972. Rev. by G. Braunthal, AHR, 79
(Feb 1974):175-6; C. M. Kimmich, JMH, 46(Je 1974):361-2.

Alberts, Robert C. The Good Provider: H. J. Heinz and His 57
Varieties. Boston: Houghton Mifflin, 1973. Rev. by T. A.
Comp, BHR, 48(Sum 1974):260-1; M. Y. Kujovich, JAH, 61
(Sep 1974):508-9; J. Markowitz, WPHM, 57(Ja 1974):107-9.

Albion, Robert G. Naval and Maritime History: An Annotated Bib-
liography. Mystic, Conn.: Marine Historical Assn., 1973.
Newton Abbott: David and Charles, 1973. Rev. by J. S.
Bromley, EHR, 89(Apr 1974):475.

_____, William A. Baker, Benjamin W. Labaree, and Marion V.
Brewington, Picture Ed. New England the Sea. Middletown,
Conn.: Wesleyan U Press, 1972. Rev. by W. R. Higgins,
NYH, 55(Apr 1974):242-3.

Alcock, Leslie. Arthur's Britain: History and Archaeology, AD
367-634. New York: St. Martin's, 1972. Rev. by D. A.
White, AHR, 79(Je 1974):769-70.

_____. 'By South Cadbury Is That Camelot...': Excavations at
Cadbury Castle 1966-70. London: Thames and Hudson, 1972.
Rev. by B. Hope-Taylor, Antiquity, 48(Mar 1974):72-3.

Alden, Dauril, ed. Colonial Roots of Modern Brazil: Papers of
the Newberry Library Conference. Berkeley: U Cal Press,

1973. Rev. by R. M. Morse, HAHR, 54(Feb 1974):127-30;
F. Safford, HRNB, 2(Feb 1974):101-2; A. J. R. Russell-Wood,
JLAS, 6(May 1974):173-5.

Alden, John Richard. Robert Dinwiddie: Servant of the Crown.
Charlottesville: U Press Va for Colonial Williamsburg Foundation, 1973. Rev. by R. B. Davis, NCHR, 51(Sum 1974):337-
9; J. L. Anderson, VMHB, 82(Oct 1974):492-3.

Alderman, Geoffrey. The Railway Interest. Leicester: U Leicester Press, 1973. Rev. by N. A. Ferguson, Historian, 36
(Aug 1974):767-8; J. Brown, History, 59(Je 1974):286.

Alderson, J. Michael see Alderson, Jo Bartels

Alderson, Jo Bartels and J. Michael. The Man Mazzuchelli; Pioneer Priest. Madison, Wisc.: Wisc. House, 1974. Rev. by
R. N. Hamilton, WMH, 58(Aut 1974):56-7.

Aldred, Cyril. Akhenaten and Nefertiti. New York: Viking, 1973.
Rev. by H. Goedicke, AJA, 78(Jl 1974):300-1.

Alexander, J. J. G. see Pächt, Otto

Alexander, John. Yugoslavia Before the Roman Conquest. New
York: Praeger, 1972. Rev. by B. Jovanovic, EEQ, 8(Sum
1974):231-4.

Alexander, Robert J. Latin American Political Parties. New York:
Praeger, 1973. Rev. by D. A. Chalmers, HAHR, 54(Feb
1974):170-1.

_____. Trotskyism in Latin America. Stanford, Cal.: Hoover
Institution Press, 1973. Rev. by E. H. Hyman, HAHR, 54
(Nov 1974):729-31; J. M. Hart, TAm, 31(Oct 1974):218-19.

_____, ed. and trans. Aprismo: The Ideas and Doctrines of
Victor Raúl Haya de la Torre. Kent, Ohio: Kent St U Press,
1973. Rev. by P. F. Klarén, HAHR, 54(Feb 1974):150-1.

Alexander, Thomas B. and Richard E. Beringer. The Anatomy of
the Confederate Congress: A Study of the Influences of Member Characteristics on Legislative Voting Behavior, 1861-1865.
Nashville: Van U Press, 1972. Rev. by R. P. Swierenga,
AHR, 79(Je 1974):869-70.

Alexander, Thomas G., ed. Essays on the American West, 1972-
73. Provo, Utah: BYU Press, n.d. Rev. by L. L. Morrison, JOW, 13(Apr 1974):106-7.

Alföldi-Rosenbaum, Elisabeth. The Necropolis of Anemurium. An-
kara: Turk Tarih Kurumu Basimevi, 1971. Rev. by C. Ver-
menle, AJA, 78(Jl 1974):312-13.

Al-Idrisi. Opus Geographicum sine "Liber adeorum delectationem
    qui terras peragrare studeant". Naples, Rome: n.p., 1970-
    1972. Rev. by B. Lewis, 15(Num 1 1974):150-2.

Allain, Mathé and Glenn R. Conrad, ed. France and North Amer-
    ica: Over Three Hundred Years of Dialogue. Lafayette: The
    U of SW La, 1973. Rev. by G. Reinecke, LaH, 15(W 1974):
    90-1.

Allen, Gay Wilson. Carl Sandburg. Minneapolis: U Minn Press.
    Rev. by J. Stronks, JISHS, 67(Je 1974):342-3.

Allen, James B. see Hill, Marvin S.

Allison, Graham T. Essence of Decision: Explaining the Cuban
    Missile Crisis. Boston: Little, Brown, 1971. Rev. by
    L. D. Langley, HAHR, 54(Feb 1974):181-2.

Allum, P. A. Italy-Republic Without Government? New York:
    Norton, 1974. Rev. by S. Saladino, HRNB, 2(Sep 1974):244.

Allworth, Edward, ed. The Nationality Question in Soviet Central
    Asia. New York: Praeger, 1973. Rev. by M. Rossabi,
    JAS, 33(Feb 1974):323.

Almaraz, Felix D., Jr. Tragic Cavalier: Governor Manuel Sal-
    cedo of Texas, 1808-1813. Austin: U Tx Press, 1971. Rev.
    by R. W. Gronet, TAm, 30(Ja 1974):421-3.

Altholz, Josef L., et al., eds. The Correspondence of Lord Acton
    and Richard Simpson. Volume 2. New York: Cam U Press,
    1973. Rev. by G. Himmelfarb, AHR, 79(Feb 1974):149-50.

Altmann, Alexander. Moses Mendelssohn: A Biographical Study.
    University, Ala.: U Ala Press, n.d., Rev. by J. Katz, Com-
    mentary, 58(Aug 1974):82-4.

Alvarez del Vayo, Julio. Give Me Combat: The Memoirs of Julio
    Alvarez del Vayo. Boston: Little, Brown, 1973. Rev. by
    L. H. Nelson, HRNB, 2(Ja 1974):84.

Alzinger, Wilhelm and Anton Bammer. Das Monument des C. Mem-
    mius. Vienna: Österreichisches Archäologisches Institut,
    1971. Rev. by Diana E. E. Kleiner and Fred S. Kleiner,
    AJA, 78(Jl 1974):312.

Ambler, Effie. Russian Journalism and Politics, 1861-1881: The
    Career of Aleksei S. Suvorin. Detroit: Wayne St U Press,
    1972. Rev. by D. M. O'Flaherty, AHR, 79(Oct 1974):1218-
    20.

Ambrose, Stephen E. and James A. Barber, ed. The Military and
    American Society. New York: Free Press, n.d. Rev. by

D. Lindsey, Mankind, 4(Apr 1974):64-5.

American West. The Great Northwest: the Story of a Land and its People. Palo Alto, Calif.: American West Pub. Co., 1973. Rev. by W. O. Douglas, PNQ, 65(Apr 1974):85; R. P. Collier, UHQ, 42(Spr 1974):205-6.

_____. The Magnificent Rockies: Crest of a Continent. Palo Alto, Calif.: American West Pub. Co., 1973. Rev. by G. M. Leonard, UHQ, 42(W 1974):88-9.

Ameringer, Charles D. The Democratic Left in Exile: The Anti-dictatorial Struggle in the Caribbean, 1945-1959. Coral Gables, Fla.: U Miami Press, 1974. Rev. by R. M. Malek, HRNB, 3(Oct 1974):8.

Ames, Susie M., ed. County Court Records of Accomack-North-ampton, Virginia, 1640-1645. Charlottesville: U Press Va, 1973. Rev. by R. S. Klein, JSH, 40(Aug 1974):456-8; W. S. Price, Jr., NCHR, 51(Spr 1974):230; E. S. Morgan, VMHB, 82(Apr 1974):191-3.

Ames, William E. A History of the National Intelligencer. Chapel Hill: UNC Press, 1972. Rev. by J. E. Walsh, AHR, 79(Je 1974):856-7.

Amfitheatrof, Erik. The Children of Columbus: An Informal History of the Italians in the New World. Boston: Little, Brown, 1973. Rev. by R. G. Vecoli, JAH, 60(Mar 1974):1085-6.

Amiet, Pierre. Glyptique Susienne, des Origines à l'Époque des Perses Achéménides Cachets, Sceaux-Cylindres et Empreintes Antiques Decouvertes à Suse de 1913 à 1967. Vols. I-II. Paris: Mémoires de la Délégation Archéologique en Iran ... 1972. Rev. by B. Buchanan, AJA, 78(Apr 1974):187.

Ammon, Harry. The Genet Mission. New York: Norton, 1973. Rev. by G. C. Rogers, FHQ, 53(Jl 1974):83-4; P. P. Hill, JAH, 61(Je 1974):172-3; G. H. Warren, JSH, 40(Feb 1974): 132-3; L. S. Kaplan, WMQ-3, 31(Apr 1974):336-7.

Ammons, A. R. Collected Poems, 1951-1971. New York: Norton, 1972. Rev. by D. Jenkins, GR, 28(Spr 1974) 156-9.

Ampuero D., Raúl. La izquierda en punto muerto. Santiago: Editorial Orbe, 1969. Rev. by S. Collier, JLAS, 4(May 1974): 182-5.

Amsler, Robert W. see Boren, Carter E.

Anastaplo, George. The Constitutionalist: Notes on the First Amendment. Dallas: SMU Press, 1971. Rev. by R. W. Bland, JAH, 61 (Dec 1974):850-1.

Anderson, B. R. O'G. Java in a Time of Revolution: Occupation and Resistance, 1944-1946. Ithaca: Cor U Press, 1972. Rev. by C. S. Kessler, MAS, 8(Ja 1974):134-9.

————, ed. see Holt, C.

Anderson, Donald F. William Howard Taft: A Conservative's Conception of the Presidency. Ithaca, N.Y.: Cornell U Press, 1973. Rev. by H. S. Merrill, AHR, 79(Oct 1974):1277-8; J. D. Baker, JAH, 61(Sep 1974):513-14; D. C. Roller, JSH, 40(Aug 1974):499-500.

Anderson, Eric A. and George F. Earle, eds. Design and Aesthetics in Wood. Albany: St U N Y Press, 1973. Rev. by I. M. G. Quimby, T & C, 15(Ja 1974):132-5.

Anderson, J. K. Xenophon. New York: Scribner's, 1974. Rev. by C. G. Starr, HRNB, 2(May/Je 1974):174.

Anderson, John Q., ed. Brokenburn: The Journal of Kate Stone, 1861-1868. Baton Rouge: La St U Press, 1972. Rev. by A. P. McDonald, LaH, 15(W 1974):84-5.

Anderson, M. S. The Ascendency of Europe: Aspects of European History, 1815-1914. London: Longman, 1972. Rev. by R. Anstey, EHR, 89(Ja 1974):209-10.

Anderson, Malcolm. Conservative Politics in France. London: George Allen and Unwin, 1974. Rev. by T. Judt, HJ, 17 (Num 3 1974):668-70.

Anderson, Richard Lloyd. Joseph Smith's New England Heritage: Influences of Grandfathers Solomon Mack and Asael Smith. Salt Lake City: Deseret, 1971. Rev. by J. Shipps, Historian, 36(Feb 1974):354-5; J. Shipps, Historian, 36(May 1974):567-8.

Anderson, William. Castles of Europe from Charlemagne to the Renaissance. London: Elek, 1970. Rev. by R. A. Brown, History, 59(Feb 1974):84-5.

Andics, Erzsébet. Metternich und die Frage Ungarns. Budapest: Akadémiai Kiadó, 1973. Rev. by R. D. Billinger, Jr., AHR, 79(Je 1974):809; K. W. Rock, EEQ, 8(Fall 1974):380-2.

Andreano, R. L. see Wiesbrod, B. A.

Andrews, Clarence A. A Literary History of Iowa. Iowa City: U Iowa Press, 1972. Rev. by J. Stranks, Jr., WMH, 57(Win 1973-74):157-8.

Andrist, Ralph K., ed. George Washington: A Biography in His Own Words. New York: Harper & Row, 1973. Rev. by H. A. Ohline, PH, 41(Ja 1974):102-3.

Andronicos, Emmanuel, John Kakrides, Basil Karageorge, Demetri Lasarides, Nicholas Papahatzes, Chryses Pelekides, Demetri Petropoulos, Evangelos Roussos, Michael Sakellariou, John Theodoracopoulos, and Constantine Trypanis. A History of the Greek States. Athens: Ekodtike of Athens, 1971. Rev. by P. Karavites, AJA, 78(Apr 1974):194-5.

Angell, Alan. Politics and the Labour Movement in Chile. Oxford: Ox U Press ... 1972. Rev. by T. S. Di Tella, JLAS, 6(May 1974):181-2.

Annual Studies of America, 1972. Moscow: Nauka, 1972. Rev. by R. F. Byrnes, JAH, 61(Je 1974):145-6.

Anthony, Earl see King, Woodie

Antiken aus dem Akademischen Kunstmuseum Bonn. Düsseldorf: Rheinland-Verlag, 1971. Rev. by D. K. Hill, AJA, 78(Ja 1974):99.

Antler, Joyce see Fuchs, Elinor

Antoine, Charles. Church and Power in Brazil. Maryknoll, N. Y.: Orbis Books, 1973. Rev. by M. T. Williams, HAHR, 54 (Nov 1974):735-6.

Antoine, Michel. Le Conseil du Roi sous le Regne de Louis XV. Paris: Droz, 1970. Rev. by B. Behrens, HJ, 17(Num 3 1974):631-43.

Antonini, Gustavo A., ed. Public Policy and Urbanization in the Dominican Republic and Costa Rica. Gainesville: ... U Fla, 1972. Rev. by H. Wood, HAHR, 54(Aug 1974):545.

Aptheker, Herbert, ed. The Correspondence of W. E. B. DuBois. Volume I: Selections, 1877-1934. Amherst: U Mass Press, 1973. Rev. by S. D. Jackson, AmArc, 37(Oct 1974):595-6; S. Stuckey, JAH, 61(Dec 1974):746-7; C. G. Contee, JSH, 40 (Aug 1974):498-9.

Arai, Tsuguo, ed. Alaska and Japan: Perspectives of Past and Present. Anchorage: Alaska Methodist U Press, 1972. Rev. by S. Okamoto, JAH, 61(Je 1974):231-2.

Arató, Endre. The History of Eastern Europe in the First Half of the 19th Century. Budapest: Akadémiai Kiadó, 1971. Rev. by I. Deak, AHR, 79(Feb 1974):186-7.

_____. Kelet-Europa Története a 19. szazad elsö felében. Budapest: Akadémiai Kiadó, 1971. Rev. by J. Komlos, EEQ, 7(Ja 1974):459-61.

Archambault, Paul. Seven French Chroniclers: Witnesses to His-

tory. Syracuse: Syr U Press, 1974. Rev. by W. T. Deininger, HRNB, 2(Sep 1974):237.

Archer, Jules. Chou En-lai. New York: Hawthorn, 1973. Rev.
by E. Lubot, HT, 8(Nov 1974):138-9.

_____. The Plot to Seize the White House. New York: Haw-
thorn, 1973. Rev. by J. E. Sargent, HT, 8(Nov 1974):151-2;
D. Carter, Mankind, 4(Feb 1974):24, 59.

Archer, Leonard C. Black Images in the American Theatre:
NAACP Protest Campaigns--Stage, Screen, Radio and Tele-
vision. Brooklyn, N.Y.: Pageant-Poseidon, 1973. Rev. by
J. B. Kirby, JSH, 40(Aug 1974):500-2.

Archer, Margaret Scotford see Vaughan, Michaline

Architecture of Middle Tennessee: the Historic American Buildings
Survey. Ed. by Thomas B. Brumbaugh, Martha I. Strayhorn,
and Gary G. Gore. Nashville: Vanderbilt U Press, 1974.
Rev. by H. L. Harper, THQ, 33(Fall 1974):347-8.

Archives Procedural Manual, Washington University School of Medicine Library. Seattle: Wash U School of Medicine Library,
1974. Rev. by F. L. Williams, AmArc, 37(Jl 1974):
462-3.

L'Archivo Storico del Banco de Napoli. Una fonte preziosa per la
Storia economica sociale sociale e artistica del Mezzogiorno
d'Italia. Naples: n.p., 1972. Rev. by T. W. Blomquist,
JEH, 34(Je 1974):502-3.

Armbruster, Adolf. Romanitatea Românilor: Istoria unei idei.
Bucureşti: Editura Academiei Republicii Socialiste România,
1972. Rev. by K. Hitchins, JMH, 46(Je 1974):368-9.

Armstrong, Edward A. Saint Francis: Nature Mystic. The Deri-
vation and Significance of the Nature Stories in the Franciscan
Legend. Berkeley: U Cal Press, 1973. Rev. by D. Burr,
CH, 43(Mar 1974):105-6.

Armstrong, F. H., H. A. Stevenson, and J. D. Wilson, eds. Aspects of Nineteenth-Century Ontario: Essays Presented to
James J. Talman. Toronto: U Tor Press ... 1974. Rev.
by R. A. Preston, HRNB, 2(Jl 1974):199-200.

Arnold, Emmett L. Gold Camp Drifter, 1906-1910. Reno: U Nev
Press, 1973. Rev. by W. Parker, JOW, 13(Jl 1974):132.

Arnold, Joseph L. The New Deal in the Suburbs: A History of the
Greenbelt Town Program, 1935-1954. Columbus, Ohio: Ohio
St U Press, 1971. Rev. by B. McKelvey, AHR, 79(Apr 1974):
607-8.

Arnold-Foster, Mark. The World at War. New York: Stein and
    Day, 1973. Rev. by H. A. Arnold, HRNB, 2(Ja 1974):84.

Arnott, Peter. The Byzantines and Their World. New York: St.
    Martin's, 1973. Rev. by P. Henry, CH, 43(Dec 1974):532-3;
    P. Charanis, HRNB, 2(Ja 1974):72-3.

Aron, Jean-Paul, Paul Dumont, Emmanuel Le Roy Ladurie. An-
    thropologie du conscrit français d'après les comptes numériques
    et sommaires du recrutement de l'armée (1819-1826).... Par-
    is: Mouton, 1972. Rev. by E. Shorter, CHR, 55(Sep 1974):
    352-4.

Aron, Raymond. Histoire et Dialectique de la Violence. Paris:
    Gallimard, 1973. Rev. by M. Poster, H & T, 13(Num 3
    1974):326-35.

The Art of Romare Bearden: The Prevalence of Ritual. New York:
    Harry N. Abrams, 1973. Rev. by W. Marr, II, Crisis, 81
    (Mar 1974):106.

Arthos, John. Shakespeare: the Early Writings. Totowa, N.J.:
    Rowman and Littlefield, 1972. Rev. by A. Covatta, RQ, 27
    (Spr 1974):102-3.

Artola, Miguel. La burguesiá revolucionaria (1808-1869). Madrid:
    Alianza Editorial Alfaguara, 1973. Rev. by R. Herr, AHR,
    79(Oct 1974):1196.

Ascher, Abraham. Pavel Axelrod and the Development of Menshev-
    ism. Cambridge, Mass.: Har U Press, 1972. Rev. by L.
    Gerstein, AHR, 79(Feb 1974):200.

Ashley, Maurice. The Age of Absolutism, 1648-1775. London:
    Weidenfeld and Nicolson, n.d. Rev. by J. Richardson, HTo,
    24(Je 1974):437-8.

Asiegbu, Johnson U. J. Slavery and the Politics of Liberation,
    1787-1861: A Study of Liberated African Emigration and Brit-
    ish Anti-Slavery Policy. London: Longmans, Green, 1969.
    Rev. by M. J. Echenberg, JAAS, 9(Ja & Apr 1974):123-5.

Asihene, E. V. Introduction to Traditional Art of Western Africa.
    London: Constable, 1972. Rev. by G. I. Jones, Africa, 44
    (Apr 1974):210-12.

Astaf'ev, I. I. Russian-German Diplomatic Relations, 1905-1911
    (From the Peace of Portsmouth to the Potsdam Agreement).
    Moscow: Izdatel'stvo Moskovskogo Universiteta, 1972. Rev.
    by H. Ragsdale, AHR, 79(Apr 1974):541-2.

Atanda, J. A. The New Oyo Empire: Indirect Rule and Change in
    Western Nigeria 1894-1934. London: Longman, 1973. Rev.

by R. C. C. L. , JAfH, 15(Num 2 1974):330-2.

Athearn, Robert G. Union Pacific Country. Chicago: Rand Mc-
Nally, 1971. Rev. by W. E. Lass, NDH, 41(W 1974):26.

Atherton, Herbert M. Political Prints in the Age of Hogarth: A
Study in the Ideographic Representation of Politics. New York:
Ox U Press, 1974. Rev. by T. M. Kemnitz, HRNB, 3(Nov/
Dec 1974):25-6; M. Greenhalgh, HTo, 24(Sep 1974):662-4.

Atherton, Lewis E. The Frontier Merchant in Mid-America. Columbia: U Mo Press, 1971. Rev. by W. B. Wheeler, NDH,
41(Spr 1974):30.

Atkinson, G. and A. C. Keller. Prelude to the Enlightenment.
London: Macmillan, 1971. Rev. by H. V. Wardman, ESR,
4(Ja 1974):91-2.

Attman, Artur. The Russian and Polish Markets in International
Trade, 1500-1650. Göteborg: Gothenburg U, 1973. Rev. by
W. J. Kelly, JEH, 34(Sep 1974):785-6.

Atwood, Elijah Francis. Ye Atte Wode Annals. Sisseton, S. D. :
Atwood, 1929. Rev. by K. B. Haas, WPHM, 57(Ja 1974):120-
1.

Aubert, Hippolyte. Correspondance de Théodore de Bèze. Volume
7: 1566. Geneva: Librairie Droz, 1973. Rev. by J. Raitt,
CH, 43(Dec 1974):544-5.

Ault, Warren O. Open-Field Farming in Medieval England: A
Study of Village By-Laws. New York: Barnes and Noble,
1972. Rev. by D. O. Whitten, JEH, 34(Je 1974):503-4.

Aurand, Harold W. From the Molly Maguires to the United Mine
Workers: The Social Ecology of an Industrial Union, 1869-
1897. Philadelphia: Temple U Press, 1971. Rev. by H. W.
Currie, AHR, 79(Apr 1974):593-4; H. B. Powell, PH, 41(Ja
1974):103-4.

Austin, Herbert H. With Macdonald in Uganda. London: Dawsons
of Pall Mall, 1973. Rev. by J. Tosh, JAfH, 15(Num 3 1974):
522-3.

Austin, R. W. J. , trans. and ed. Sufis of Andalusia: The Rūh
alquds and al-Durrat al fākhirah of Ibn'Arabi. Berkeley: U
Cal Press, 1971. Rev. by J. Kritzeck, AHR, 79(Feb 1974):
206-7.

Autenrieth, Johanne and Franz Brunholzl, eds. Festschrift Bernhard Bischoff. Stuttgart: Anton Hiersemann, 1971. Rev. by
J. M. Wallace-Hadrill, EHR, 89(Ja 1974):145-6.

Avi-hai, Avraham. Ben Gurion, State-Builder: Principles and Pragmatism 1948-1963. New York: Wiley, 1974. Rev. by D. E. Specter, HRNB, 3(Oct 1974):16.

Avrich, Paul. Kronstadt, 1921. Princeton, N.J.: Prin U Press, 1970. Rev. by J. Lively, History, 59(Feb 1974):149-50.

_____. Russian Rebels 1600-1800. New York: Schocken, 1972. Rev. by D. L. Ransel, AHR, 79(Apr 1974):533-4; P. Pomper, Historian, 36(May 1974):541-2; R. O. Crummey, JMH, 46 (Mar 1974):131-2.

Aydelotte, William O. Quantification in History. London: Addison-Wesley, 1971. Rev. by T. J. Nossiter, History, 59(Feb 1974):158-9.

_____, Allan G. Bogue, and Robert William Fogel, eds. The Dimensions of Quantitative Research in History. Princeton, N.J.: Prin U Press, 1972. Rev. by R. Forster, JIH, 5 (Aut 1974):303-12; P. Kleppner, JISHS, 67(Nov 1974):562-3.

Ayling, Stanley. George the Third. New York: Knopf, 1972. Rev. by J. Cannon, History, 59(Je 1974):281-2; R. Middleton, JAH, 60(Mar 1974):1098-9.

Aylmer, G. E. The Interregnum: The Quest for Settlement, 1646-1660. London: Macmillan, 1972. Rev. by K. H. D. Haley, EHR, 89(Ja 1974):185-6; B. Manning, History, 59(Feb 1974): 108-9; B. Worden, HJ, 17(Mar 1974):216-17.

_____. The State's Servants. London: Routledge and Kegan Paul, n.d. Rev. by M. Ashley, HTo, 24(Ja 1974):63.

Babbitt, Bruce E. Color and Light: The Southwest Canvases of Louis Akin. Flagstaff, Ariz.: Northland, 1973. Rev. by P. A. Rossi, JAriH, 15(Aut 1974):309-10.

Babín, María Teresa. The Puerto Ricans' Spirit: Their History, Life, and Culture. New York: Collier-Macmillan, 1971. Rev. by L. E. Agrait, HAHR, 54(Feb 1974):157-9.

Bacciocco, Edward J., Jr. The New Left in America: Reform to Revolution, 1956-1970. Stanford, Cal.: Hoover Institution Press, 1974. Rev. by I. Unger, JAH, 61(Dec 1974):849-50.

Bachrach, Bernard S. A History of the Alans in the West: From Their First Appearance in the Sources of Classical Antiquity through the Early Middle Ages. Minneapolis: U Minn Press, 1973. Rev. by T. D. Barnes, AHR, 79(Apr 1974):501; J. M. Wallace-Hadrill, EHR, 89(Jl 1974):649-50.

_____. Merovingian Military Organization, 481-751. Minneapolis: U Minn Press, 1972. Rev. by N. P. Brooks, History,

59(Feb 1974):84; C. W. Hollister, JIH, 5(Aut 1974):320-3.

Backer, Dorothy Anne Liot. Precious Women: A Feminist Phenomenon in the Age of Louis XIV. New York: Basic Books,
   1974. Rev. by C. R. Francois and M. E. Francois, HRNB,
   3(Nov/Dec 1974):30.

Backmund, Norbert. Die mittelalterlichen Geschichtsschreiber des
   Pramonstratenserordens. Avenbode: Bibliotheca Analectorum
   Praemonstratensium, 1972. Rev. by M. D. Knowles, EHR,
   89(Jl 1974):656.

Badian, E. Publicans and Sinners: Private Enterprise in the Service of the Roman Republic. Ithaca, N.Y.: Cornell U Press,
   1972. Rev. by R. E. Mitchell, AHR, 79(Feb 1974):120;
   M. W. Frederiksen, EHR, 89(Apr 1974):410-11.

Baelde. De domeingoederen van de vorst in de Nederlanden omstreeks het midden van de zestiende eeuw, 1551-1559. Brussels: Academie Royale de Belgique, 1971. Rev. by A. Duke,
   EHR, 89(Apr 1974):431-2.

Bagchi, Amiya Kumar. Private Investment in India 1900-1939.
   Cambridge: Cam U Press, 1972. Rev. by M. D. Morris,
   MAS, 8(Oct 1974):535-55.

Bagley, J. J. Historical Interpretation. Volume 1, Sources of
   English Medieval History, 1066-1540; volume 2, Sources of
   English History, 1540 to the Present Day. New York: St.
   Martin's, 1973. Rev. by W. H. Dunham, Jr., AHR, 79(Apr
   1974):510.

Bagliani, Agostino Paravicini. Cardinali di Curia e "familiae"
   cardinalizie dal 1227 al 1254. 2 vols. Padua: Editrice Antenore, 1972. Rev. by P. A. Linehan, EHR, 89(Jl 1974):
   620-2.

Bailey, D. R. Shackleton. Cicero. New York: Scribner's, 1971.
   Rev. by G. M. Paul, AHR, 79(Oct 1974):1157.

Bailey, David C. ¡Riva Cristo Rey! The Cristero Rebellion and
   the Church-State Conflict in Mexico. Austin: U Tx Press,
   1974. Rev. by C. A. Astiz, HRNB, 2(Aug 1974):224.

Bailey, Jackson H., ed. Listening to Japan: A Japanese Anthology.
   New York: Praeger, 1973. Rev. by A. D. Coox, Historian,
   36(Aug 1974):751.

Bailey, M. Thomas. Reconstruction in Indian Territory: A Story
   of Avarice, Discrimination, and Opportunism. Port Washington, N.Y.: Kennikat, 1972. Rev. by L. L. Gould, AHR, 79
   (Je 1974):876; H. E. Fritz, JAH, 61(Je 1974):201-2; C. Bolt,
   JAmS, 8(Apr 1974):117-19.

Bailey, William A. Bill Bailey Came Home. Ed. by Austin Fife and Alta Fife. Logan: Utah St U Press, 1973. Rev. by S. Bennett, UHQ, 42(W 1974):94-5.

Bailyn, Bernard. The Ordeal of Thomas Hutchinson. Cambridge, Mass.: Har U Press, 1974. Rev. by J. P. Greene, HRNB, 2(May/Je 1974):158; J. A. Schutz, JAH, 61(Dec 1974):771-2; J. Catanzariti, NEQ, 47(Sep 1974):459-61.

Bainton, Roland H. and Eric W. Gritsch. Bibliography of the Continental Reformation: Materials Available in English. Hamden, Conn.: Shoe String, 1972. Rev. by M. Grossmann, CH, 43(Dec 1974):542-3.

Baird, Jesse Hays. Land of the Pilgrim's Pride. Richmond, Va.: John Knox Press, 1973. Rev. by D. Wells, JOW, 13(Jl 1974): 118.

Baker, Alan R. H., ed. Progress in Historical Geography. Newton Abbot, Eng.: David and Charles, 1972. Rev. by H. R. Merrens, JIH, 5(Sum 1974):145-50.

_____ and Robin A. Butlin, eds. Studies of Field Systems in the British Isles. New York: Cam U Press, 1973. Rev. by W. O. Ault, AHR, 79(Je 1974):771-2.

Baker, Derek, ed. Sanctity and Secularity: The Church and the World. New York: Barnes and Noble, 1973. Rev. by R. G. Clouse, CH, 43(Dec 1974):548-9.

Baker, Jean H. The Politics of Continuity: Maryland Political Parties from 1858-1870. Baltimore: JHU Press, 1973. Rev. by R. P. Formisano, CWH, 20(Mar 1974):65-7; H. Hamilton, JAH, 60(Mar 1974):1128-9; M. C. Kahl, MHM, 69(Sum 1974): 233-5.

Baker, Leonard. John Marshall: A Life in Law. New York: Macmillan, 1974. Rev. by D. O. Dewey, HRNB, 3(Oct 1974): 3-4.

Baker, Lindsay T., Steven R. Rae, Joseph E. Minor and Seymour V. Connor. Water for the Southwest: Historical Survey and Guide to Historic Sites. New York: American Soc. of Civil Engineers, 1973. Rev. by J. B. Frantz, T & C, 15(Jl 1974): 501-2; D. B. Gracy, II, ETHJ, 12(Fall 1974):87-8.

Baker, Robert A. The Southern Baptist Convention and Its People, 1607-1972. Nashville: Broadman Press, 1974. Rev. by R. G. Gardner, CH, 43(Dec 1974):550.

Baker, Ronald L. Folklore in the Writings of Rowland E. Robinson. Bowling Green, Ohio: Bowling Green U Press, 1973. Rev. by W. H. Soule, VH, 42(Spr 1974):174-6.

Baker, Thomas Harrison. The Memphis "Commercial Appeal": The
   History of a Southern Newspaper. Baton Rouge: LSU Press,
   1971. Rev. by L. H. Parsons, AHR, 79(Oct 1974):1242-4.

Baker, William A. see Albion, Robert G.

Bakey, L. The Treatment of Head Injuries in the Thirty Years'
   War (1618-1648); Joannis Scultetus and His Age. Springfield,
   Ill.: C. C. Thomas, 1971. Rev. by P. S. Miller, AmAnt,
   39(Apr 1974):391-2.

Balán, Jorge, Harley L. Browning and Elizabeth Jelin. Men in a
   Developing Society: Geographic and Social Mobility in Monterrey, Mexico. Austin: U Tx Press, 1973. Rev. by J. Walton, HAHR, 54(Feb 1974):175-8.

Baldwin, Donald N. The Quiet Revolution: Grass Roots of Today's
   Wilderness Preservation Movement. Boulder, Colo.: Pruett,
   1972. Rev. by R. H. Adams, CoMag, 51(Win 1974):78-9;
   W. W. Biddle, WHQ, 5(Ja 1974):59-60.

Baldwin, J. W. and R. A. Goldthwaite, eds. Universities in Politics: Case Studies from the Late Middle Ages and Early Modern Period. Baltimore: JHU Press, 1972. Rev. by D. M.
   Nicol, EHR, 89(Jl 1974):660-1; G. Leff, History, 59(Feb 1974):
   99.

Baldwin, John W. The Scholastic Culture of the Middle Ages, 1000-
   1300. Lexington, Mass.: D. C. Heath, 1971. Rev. by
   W. J. Courtenay, CH, 43(Mar 1974):98-9.

Balfour, Michael and Julian Frisby. Helmuth von Moltke: A Leader Against Hitler. New York: St. Martin's, 1972. Rev. by
   E. Hahn, JMH, 46(Mar 1974):160-1.

Balke, W. Calvijn en de Doperse Radikalen. Amsterdam: Uitge-
   verij Ton Bolland, 1973. Rev. by J. H. Primus, CH, 43
   (Sep 1974):405.

Ball, Johnson. William Caslon: Master of Letters. Kineton, War-
   wickshire: Roundwood Press, 1973. Rev. by H. J. Haden,
   T & C, 15(Apr 1974):329-32.

Baluev, B. P. The Political Reaction of the 1880s and Russian
   Journalism. Moscow: Izdatel'stvo Moskovskogo Universiteta,
   1971. Rev. by D. M. O'Flaherty, AHR, 79(Oct 1974):1218-
   20.

Balwin, R. E. see Wiesbrod, B. A.

Bamford, Paul W. Fighting Ships and Prisons: The Mediterranean
   Galleys of France in the Age of Louis XIV. Minneapolis: U
   Minn Press, 1973. Rev. by J. B. Wolf, JMH, 46(Je 1974):
   352-3.

BAMMER 18

Bammer, Anton see Alzinger, Wilhelm

Bangert, William V. A History of the Society of Jesus. St. Louis:
Institute of Jesuit Sources, 1972. Rev. by D. G. Thompson,
CHR, 55(Sep 1974):348-9.

Barash, Asher. Pictures from a Brewery. Indianapolis: Bobbs-
Merrill, n.d. Rev. by D. Stern, Commentary, 58(Nov 1974):
88, 90-2.

Barber, James. South Africa's Foreign Policy, 1945-1970. London:
Ox U Press, 1973. Rev. by J. E. Spence, JAfH, 15(Num 3
1974):524.

Barber, James A., ed. see Ambrose, Stephen E., ed.

Barber, Noel. The Sultans. New York: Simon and Schuster, 1973.
Rev. by R. H. Davison, HRNB, 2(Ja 1974):74-5.

Barbour, Hugh and Arthur O. Roberts, eds. Early Quaker Writings,
1650-1700. Grand Rapids, Mich.: Eerdmans, 1973. Rev. by
T. L. Underwood, CH, 43(Mar 1974):116.

Barbour, Roger W. see Wharton, Mary E.

Barclay, Glen. Struggle for a Continent: The Diplomatic History
of South America 1917-1945. New York: NYU Press, 1972.
Rev. by J. S. Tulchin, TAm, 30(Apr 1974):543-4.

Barfield, Lawrence. Northern Italy Before Rome. New York:
Praeger, 1972. Rev. by R. E. A. Palmer, AHR, 79(Je 1974):
765.

Barker, Bernard, ed. Ramsay MacDonald's Political Writings.
New York: St. Martin's, 1972. Rev. by C. A. Cline, AHR,
79(Feb 1974):153.

Barker, Danny see Buerkle, Jack V.

Barker, Dudley. G. K. Chesterton: A Biography. New York:
Stein and Day, 1973. Rev. by P. Misner, CH, 43(Sep 1974):
414.

Barker, Elisabeth. Austria, 1918-1972. Coral Gables, Fla.: U
Miami Press, 1973. Rev. by K. Forster, HRNB, 2(Ja 1974):
85.

Barker, Nancy Nichols. The French Legation in Texas. Volume 2.
Mission Miscarried. Austin: Texas State Historical Assn.,
1973. Rev. by S. V. Connor, AHR, 79(Je 1974):861-2; M.
Henson, ETHJ, 12(Spr 1974):56-7; B. Procter, JAH, 60(Mar
1974):1115; G. H. Warren, JSH, 40(May 1974):309-10; J. A.

Stout, Jr., NMHR, 49(Ja 1974):80-2; J. M. Nance, SWHQ, 78
(Jl 1974):93-5.

Barlow, William and Peter Shapiro. An End to Silence: The San
Francisco State College Student Movement in the '60s. New
York: Pegasus, 1971. Rev. by W. L. O'Neill, AHR, 79(Je
1974):911-12.

Barnea, Ion and Stefan Stefanescu. Bizantini Romani si Bulgari la
Dunarea de jos. Bucharest: Editura Academi Republicii Socialiste Romania, 1971. Rev. by D. Dvoichenko-Markov, AHR,
79(Apr 1974):491.

Barnes, Robert, comp. Marriages and Deaths from the Maryland
Gazette, 1727-1839. Baltimore: Genealogical Publishing Co.,
1973. Rev. by J. H. Livezey, MHM, 69(Sum 1974):228.

Barnes, Timothy David. Tertullian: A Historical and Literary
Study. New York: Ox U Press, 1971. Rev. by M. Smith,
AHR, 79(Je 1974):768.

Barnet, Richard J. Roots of War. New York: Atheneum, 1972.
Rev. by B. J. Bernstein, AHR, 79(Apr 1974):618-19.

Barnett, Franklin. Dictionary of Prehistoric Indian Artifacts of
the American Southwest. Flagstaff, Ariz.: Northland,
1973. Rev. by E. N. Ferdon, Jr., JAriH, 15(Sum 1974):
191-2.

Barney, William L. The Road to Secession: A New Perspective
on the Old South. New York: Praeger, 1972. Rev. by H.
Hamilton, AHR, 79(Apr 1974):583-4; R. A. Wooster, CWH,
20(Je 1974):173-4.

_____. The Secessionist Impulse: Alabama and Mississippi in
1860. Princeton, N.J.: Prin U Press, 1974. Rev. by F. N.
Boney, CWH, 20(Sep 1974):276-7; J. A. Hodges, HRNB, 2
(Jl 1974):198; R. E. Corlew, JMiH, 36(Nov 1974):390-2.

Barnhart, John D. and Dorothy L. Riker. Indiana to 1816: The
Colonial Period. Indianapolis: Ind Historical Bureau and Ind
Historical Society, 1971. Rev. by W. E. Foley, AHR, 79(Je
1974):843-4.

Barnie, John. War in Medieval English Society: Social Values in
the Hundred Years War 1337-99. Ithaca, N.Y.: Cornell U
Press, 1974. Rev. by C. T. Marshall, HRNB, 3(Nov/Dec
1974):24-5.

Barnikol, Ernst. Bruno Bauer: Studien und Materialien. Assen:
Van Gorcum, 1972. Rev. by E. Tenner, JMH, 46(Mar 1974):
148-9.

Barns, William D. The West Virginia State Grange: the First Century. Morgantown, W. Va.: Morgantown Printing and Binding Co., 1973. Rev. by O. K. Rice, WVH, 35(Jl 1974):319-20.

Barr, Pat. To China With Love: The Lives and Times of Protestant Missionaries in China, 1860-1900. Garden City, N.Y.: Doubleday, 1973. Rev. by D. H. Bays, HT, 8(Nov 1974):138.

Barraclough, Solon, ed. Agrarian Structure in Latin America: A Resume of the CIDA Land Tenure Studies of Argentina, Brazil, Chile, Colombia, Ecuador, Guatemala, Peru. Lexington, Mass.: D. C. Heath, 1973. Rev. by H. J. Bruton, HAHR, 54(Nov 1974):733-5.

Barrett, David. Catalogue of the Wardrop Collection and of Other Georgian Books and Manuscripts in the Bodleian Library. Oxford: ... Ox U Press, 1973. Rev. by E. Kasinec, AmArc, 37(Apr 1974):295-6.

Barrett, Glen, ed. Mackinaws Down the Missouri. Logan, Utah: Western Text Society, Utah St U Press, 1973. Rev. by M. Gilman, N H, 55(Sum 1974):294-6.

Barrett, Gwynn see Adler, Jacob

Barron, Gloria J. Leadership in Crisis: FDR and the Path to Intervention. Port Washington, N.Y.: Kennikat, 1973. Rev. by C. W. Johnson, AHR, 79(Je 1974):902-3; A. E. Campbell, HJ, 17(Num 2 1974):443-7; A. Yarnell, HT, 8(Nov 1974):152; W. S. Cole, JAH, 61(Je 1974):248-9; V. A. Lapomarda, MiA, 56(Ja 1974):62-4; J. Mc.V. Haight, Jr., PHR, 43(Nov 1974):626-7.

Barrow, G. W. S. The Kingdom of the Scots: Government, Church and Society from the Eleventh to the Fourteenth Century. New York: St. Martin's, 1973. Rev. by J. W. Ferguson, HRNB, 2(Mar 1974):118-19.

_____, ed. The Acts of William I, King of Scots, 1165-1214. Chicago: Aldine, 1971. Rev. by W. L. Warren, AHR, 79 (Oct 1974):1167-8.

Barry, Boubacar. Le royaume du Waalo. Le Senegal avant le conquête. Paris: Francois Maspero, 1972. Rev. by C. Quinn, JAfH, 15(Num 2 1974):326-8.

Barry, Elaine. Robert Frost. New York: Frederick Ungar, 1973. Rev. by R. Foster, NEQ, 47(Sep 1974):469-72.

_____. Robert Frost on Writing. New Brunswick, N.J.: Rutgers U Press, 1973. Rev. by R. Foster, NEQ, 47(Sep 1974):469-72.

Barry, James P. Ships of the Great Lakes: 300 Years of Naviga-
    tion. Berkeley, Calif.: Hamell-North, 1973. Rev. by R. J.
    Wright, WMH, 58(Aut 1974):58-9.

Barry, Mary J. A History of Mining on the Kenai Peninsula. An-
    chorage: Alaska Northwest Publishing Co., 1973. Rev. by
    J. H. Cash, JAH, 61(Dec 1974):792-3; M. Walsh, JAmS, 8
    (Aug 1974):267-70; A. Probert, JOW, 13(Apr 1974):111; M.
    Sherwood, PHR, 43(Nov 1974):608-9.

Bartley, Russell H. and Stuart L. Wagner. Latin America in Basic
    Historical Collections: A Working Guide. Stanford, Cal.:
    Hoover Institution Press, 1972. Rev. by N. L. Benson, HAHR,
    54(Aug 1974):499-500.

Bartram, William. Travels Through North and South Carolina,
    Georgia, East and West Florida. Savannah, Ga.: Beehive,
    1973. Rev. by L. De Vorsey, Jr., GHQ, 58(Sum 1974):286-
    7; W. S. Powell, NCHR, 51(Spr 1974):229.

Barzun, Jacques. Clio and the Doctors: Psycho-History, Quanto-
    History, and History. Chicago: U Chi Press, 1974. Rev. by
    B. Noggle, HRNB, 3(Nov/Dec 1974):22.

Basic Problems of the History of the USA in American Historiogra-
    phy from the Colonial Period to the Civil War, 1861-1865.
    Moscow: "Nauka," 1971. Rev. by E. L. Perkins, JAH, 61
    (Dec 1974):755-7.

Basin, Thomas. Histoire de Louix XI. Vol. V. Paris: Les
    belles Lettres, 1972. Rev. by P. S. Lewis, EHR, 89(Apr
    1974):424-5.

Basin, V. I. Russia and the Kazakh Khanates in the 16th to 18th
    Centuries (Kazakhstan and the System of Foreign Politics of
    the Russian Empire). Alma Ata: Izdatel'stvo "Nauka" Kaza-
    khskoi SSR, 1971. Rev. by F. Kazemzadeh, AHR, 79(Feb
    1974):195-6.

Basler, Roy P. A Touchstone for Greatness: Essays, Addresses
    and Occasional Pieces About Abraham Lincoln. Westport,
    Conn.: Greenwood, 1973. Rev. by R. A. Heckman, CWH,
    20(Je 1974):174-6; B. D. Ledbetter, MiA, 56(Jl 1974):202.

Bassett, Margaret. Abraham and Mary Todd Lincoln. New York:
    Crowell, 1973. Rev. by C. B. Strozier, JISHS, 67(Feb 1974):
    124-5.

Bastid, Marianne. Aspects de la réforme de l'enseignement en
    Chine au début du XXe siècle, d'après des écrits de zhang
    Jian. The Hague: Mouton, 1971. Rev. by M. Gewurtz, AHR,
    79(Feb 1974):211-12.

Bates, Charles Francis and Francis Roe. Custer Engages the Hostiles. Fort Collins, Colo.: Old Army Press, 1973. Rev. by
R. D. Edmonds, ChOk, 52(Fall 1974):377-8.

Bateson, Mary Catherine. Our Own Metaphor: a Personal Account
of a Conference on the Effects of Conscious Purpose of Human
Adaptation. New York: Knopf, 1972. Rev. by W. D. Lewis,
T & C, 15(Ja 1974):146-50.

Batho, G. R. Calendar of the Shrewsbury and Talbot Papers. Vol.
VII: Talbot Papers in the College of Arms. London: H.M.-
S.O., 1972. Rev. by D. M. Loades, History, 59(Je 1974):
273.

Baughman, James P. The Mallorys of Mystic: Six Generations in
Maritime Enterprise. Middletown, Conn.: Wes U Press,
1972. Rev. by H. W. Scheiber, CWH, 20(Je 1974):164-6;
E. S. Bruchey, NYH, 55(Apr 1974):250-2.

Baxendall, Michael. Painting and Experience in Fifteenth-Century
Italy: A Primer in the Social History of Pictorial Style. Ox-
ford: Clarendon Press, 1972. Rev. by J. R. Hale, EHR, 89
(Jl 1974):663-4; J. White, History, 59(Feb 1974):96-7.

Baxter, Maurice G. The Steamboat Monopoly: Gibbons v. Ogden,
1824. New York: Knopf, 1972. Rev. by J. Teaford, AHR,
79(Oct 1974):1257-8.

Baydo, Gerald. A Topical History of the United States. Englewood
Cliffs, N.J.: Prentice-Hall, 1974. Rev. by S. T. McSeveney, HRNB, 2(Jl 1974):193-4.

Beaglehole, J. C. The Life of Captain James Cook. Stanford,
Cal.: Stan U Press, 1974. Rev. by R. G. Smolka, HRNB,
2(May/Je 1974):170.

Beals, Alan R., ed. see Siegel, Bernard J., ed.

Beasley, William G. The Meiji Restoration. Stanford, Cal.:
Stan U Press, 1972. Rev. by P. Duus, CHR, 55(Je 1974):
183-5.

Beaumont, Gustave de. Lettres d'Amérique 1831-1832. Paris:
Presses Universitaires de France, 1973. Rev. by H. Brogan,
JAmS, 8(Apr 1974):119-21.

Beaver, Daniel R. Newton D. Baker and the American War Effort,
1917-1919. Lincoln: U Neb Press, 1966. Rev. by E. C.
Blackorby, Historian, 36(May 1974):578-9.

Becatti, Giovanni. L'arte dell'età classica. Florence: Sansoni,
1971. Rev. by H. Bloch, Archaeology, 27(Ja 1974):143,146.

_____. Scavi di Ostia VI: Edificio con opus sectile fuori Porta
Marina. Rome: Instituto Paligrafico Dello Stato, Librerio
Stato, 1969. Rev. by H. Bloch, Archaeology, 27(Ja 1974):75.

Beck, John Jacob. MacArthur and Wainwright: Sacrifice of the
Philippines. Albuquerque: U NM Press, 1974. Rev. by
B. F. Cooling, HRNB, 2(Sep 1974):257-8; D. Lindsey, Man-
kind, 4(Oct 1974):54-5, 65.

Becker, Carl A. "What Is the Good of History?": Selected Letters
of Carl L. Becker, 1900-1945. Ed. by Michael Kammen.
Ithaca: Cor U Press, 1973. Rev. by B. Wilkins, MHM, 69
(Fall 1974):334-6; R. A. Billington, NYH, 55(Ja 1974):115-16;
R. R. Locke, PHR, 43(May 1974):260-1.

Becker, Winfried. Der Kurfürstenrat: Grundzüge seiner Entwicklung
in der Reichsverfassung und seine Stellung auf dem Westfälischen Friedenskongress. Münster: Verlag Aschendorff, 1973.
Rev. by H. Gross, JMH, 46(Sep 1974):555-6.

Bedinger, Margery. Indian Silver: Navajo and Pueblo Jewelers.
Albuquerque: U NM Press, 1973. Rev. by C. L. Tanner,
JAriH, 15(Aut 1974):306-7.

Beer, Barrett L. Northumberland: The Political Career of John
Dudley, Earl of Warwick and Duke of Northumberland. Kent,
Ohio: Kent St U Press, 1974. Rev. by H. S. Reinmuth, Jr.,
HRNB, 2(Aug 1974):229-30.

Beer, Stafford. Brain of the Firm: the Managerial Cybernetics of
Organization. London: Penquin Press, 1972. Rev. by W. L.
Casey, Jr., T & C, 15(Ja 1974):129-31.

Beers, Paul B. Profiles from the Susquehanna Valley. Harrisburg:
Stackpole Books, 1973. Rev. by R. L. Bloon, PH, 41(Ja
1974):111-12.

Beever, E. A. Launceston Bank for Savings, 1835-1970: A History
Australia's Oldest Savings Bank. Melbourne: Melbourne U
Press, 1972. Rev. by A. Barnard, BHR, 48(Sum 1974):235-7.

Beezley, William H. Insurgent Governor: Abraham González and
the Mexican Revolution in Chihuahua. Lincoln: U Neb Press,
1973. Rev. by F. Katz, HAHR, 54(Aug 1974):530-1; S. R.
Ross, HRNB, 2(Ja 1974):71-2; K. J. Grieb, HT, 7(Feb 1974):
312; P. J. Vanderwood, SCQ, 56(Sum 1974):204-6; A. Bryan,
SWHQ, 78(Oct 1974):219-20.

Befu, Harumi. Japan: An Anthropological Introduction. San Francisco: Chandler, 1971. Rev. by J. B. Cornell, JAS, 33(Aug
1974):708-10.

Beijbom, Ulf. Swedes in Chicago: A Demographic and Social Study

of the 1846-1860 Immigration. Växjö, Sweden: Uppsala U;
Chicago: Chicago Historical Society, 1971. Rev. by O. H.
Zabel, JISHS, 67(Je 1974):344-5.

Beitzell, Robert. The Uneasy Alliance: America, Britain, and
Russia, 1941-1943. New York: Knopf, 1972. Rev. by M. O.
Gustafson, AHR, 79(Je 1974):757-8; B. B. Gilbert, Historian,
36(Feb 1974):335; J. D. Doenecke, JAH, 60(Mar 1974):1181-2.

Beling, Willard A., ed. The Middle East: Quest for an American
Policy. Albany: SUNY Press, 1973. Rev. by D. Lindsey,
Mankind, 4(Apr 1974):62, 64.

Bell, Hershel M. Rangeland Management for Livestock Production.
Norman: U Ok Press, 1973. Rev. by J. M. Skaggs, ChOk,
52(Spr 1974):115-16.

Bell, Leland V. In Hitler's Shadow: The Anatomy of American
Nazism. Port Washington, N. Y.: Kennikat, 1973. Rev. by
S. M. Stern, AHR, 79(Apr 1974):609; J. F. Paul, HT, 7(Feb
1974):317-18; S. A. Diamond, JAH, 60(Mar 1974):1179-81.

Bell, Michael see Miller, Alfred J.

Bell, Rudolph M. Party and Faction in American Politics: The
House of Representatives, 1789-1801. Westport, Conn.:
Greenwood, 1974. Rev. by R. Ketcham, HRNB, 2(Jl 1974):
196-7.

Bell, Sidney. Righteous Conquest. Woodrow Wilson and the Evolution of the New Diplomacy. Fort Washington, N. Y.: Kennikat, 1972. Rev. by F. B. Misse, Historian, 36(May 1974):
581-2; A. E. Campbell, HJ, 17(Num 2 1974):443-7.

Bellamy, John. Crime and Public Order in England in the Late
Middle Ages. London: Routledge and Kegan Paul, 1973. Rev.
by M. M. Lomax, Historian, 36(Feb 1974):312-13.

Bellanger, Claude, et al., eds. Histoire générale de la presse
française. Vol. III. De 1871 a 1940. Paris: Presses Universitaires de France, 1972. Rev. by J. Colton, AHR, 79
(Feb 1974):167-9; N. Hampson, EHR, 89(Ja 1974):223-4.

Bence-Jones, Mark. Clive of India. London: Constable, n. d.
Rev. by W. Seymour, HTo, 24(Aug 1974):578-9.

Bene, Eduard, ed. Les Lumières en Hongrie, en Europe centrale
et en Europe orientale: Actes du colloque de Mátrafüred, 3-5
novembre 1970. Budapest: Akademiai Kiado, 1971. Rev. by
D. Stone, AHR, 79(Feb 1974):136-7.

Benedict, Michael Les. The Impeachment and Trial of Andrew Johnson. New York: Norton, 1973. Rev. by I. Dilliard, AHR,

79(Je 1974):837-40; S. H. Rye, AI, 42(Fall 1974):460-1; W. M.
Armstrong, HRNB, 2(Ja 1974):64; G. M. Linden, JSH, 40(Feb
1974):150-1; W. S. McFeely, JAH, 60(Mar 1974):1137-8; R. D.
Bridges, OH, 83(Spr 1974):147-8; P. T. Echols, WMH, 58
(Aut 1974):60-1.

Benevolo, Leonardo. History of Modern Architecture. Volume 1,
The Tradition of Modern Architecture. Volume 2, The Modern
Movement. Cambridge, Mass.: M I T Press, 1971. Rev.
by D. Hoffman, AHR, 79(Feb 1974):108.

Ben Israel, Mannesseh see Israel, Manesseh Ben

Bennett, Geoffrey. Nelson: the Commander. New York: Scribner's, 1972. Rev. by R. Callahan, AHR, 79(Oct 1974):1178-9.

Bennett, Marj. Patchwork Poetry. Oklahoma City: Petite, 1973.
Rev. by L. A. McRill, ChOk, 52(Fall 1974):379.

Bennett, Noël. The Weaver's Pathway: A Clarification of the
"Spirit Trail" in Navajo Weaving. Flagstaff, Ariz.: Northland, 1974. Rev. by M. Link, JAriH, 15(Aut 1974):308-9.

Bénot, Yves. Idéologies des indépendances Africaines. Paris:
Maspero, 1972. Rev. by J.-F. Bayart, AfAf, 73(Apr 1974):
233-4.

Bensell, Royal N. All Quiet on the Yamhill: The Civil War in
Oregon. Eugene: U Oregon Books, 1959. Rev. by J. I.
Robertson, CWH, 20(Sep 1974):279-81.

Benson, Don and David Miles. The Upper Thames Valley: an
Archaeological Survey of the River Gravels. Oxford: Oxford-
shire Archaeological Unit Survey, 1974. Rev. by G. Webster,
Antiquity, 48(Sep 1974):246-7.

Benson, Elizabeth P. The Maya World. New York: Crowell, 1972.
Rev. by P. W. Burch, JOW, 13(Ja 1974):145-6.

Benson, J. L. Bamboula at Kourion. The Necropolis and the Finds.
Excavated by J. F. Daniel. Philadelphia: U Pa Press, 1972.
Rev. by R. S. Merrillees, AJA, 78(Jl 1974):302-3.

_____. The Necropolis at Kaloriziki Excavated by J. F. Daniel
and G. H. McFadden for the University Museum, University
of Pennsylvania, Philadelphia. Philadelphia: U Pa Press,
1973. Rev. by R. S. Merrillees, AJA, 78(Jl 1974):302-3.

Benton, Minnie M. Boomtown: A Portrait of Burkburnett. Wichita
Falls, Tx.: Nortex Offset, 1973. Rev. by D. L. Hofsommer,
ChOk, 52(Sum 1974):259.

Berend, Iván T. and György Ránki. Economic Development in East-

Central Europe in the 19th and 20th Centuries. New York: Columbia U Press, 1974. Rev. by G. J. Cavanaugh, HRNB, 2(Aut 1974):228-9.

Berg, Arne, et al. Architecture in Wood: A History of Wood Building and Its Techniques in Europe and North America. New York: Viking, 1971. Rev. by L. K. Eaton, AHR, 79(Oct 1974):1141.

Berg, Roger, et al. Histoire des Juifs en France. Toulouse: Edouard Privat, Editeur, 1972. Rev. by L. J. Apt, AHR, 79(Feb 1974):157-8.

Berger, Carl. The Sense of Power: Studies in the Ideas of Canadian Imperialism, 1867-1914. Toronto: U Tor Press, 1971. Rev. by A. F. McC. Madden, EHR, 89(Ja 1974):221-2.

Berger, Kermit C. Sun, Soil, and Survival: An Introduction to Soils. Norman: U Ok Press, 1972. Rev. by E. L. Schapsmeier, JOW, 13(Ja 1974):151.

Berger, Mark L. The Revolution in the New York Party Systems, 1840-1860. Port Washington, N. Y.: Kennikat, 1973. Rev. by E. R. Barkan, AHR, 79(Apr 1974):576-7; M. F. Holt, JAH, 60(Mar 1974):1124-6; P. O. Weinbaum, NYHSQ, 58(Ja 1974):70-1.

Berger, Raoul. Impeachment: The Constitutional Problems. Cambridge, Mass.: Har U Press, 1973. Rev. by I. Dilliard, AHR, 79(Je 1974):837-40; M. L. Benedict, JAH, 60(Mar 1974): 1088-90.

Bergeron, Paul H. see Weaver, Herbert

_____, ed. see Polk, James K.

Berghahn, V. R. Germany and the Approach of War in 1914. New York: St. Martin's, 1973. Rev. by J. R. Dukes, HRNB, 2 (Mar 1974):116.

Beringer, Richard see Alexander, Thomas B.

Berkeley, Edmund and Dorothy Smith Berkeley. John Beckley: Zealous Partisan in a Nation Divided. Philadelphia: American Philosophical Society, 1973. Rev. by W. H. Masterson, JSH, 40(Aug 1974):470-1; R. F. Jones, NYSHQ, 58(Oct 1974): 322-3; A. Shaffer, VMHB, 82(Apr 1974):197-8; R. R. Beeman, WMQ-3, 31(Jl 1974):519-21; L. H. Johnson, III, WVH, 36 (Oct 1974):66-7.

Berle, Beatrice Bishop and Travis Beal Jacobs, eds. Navigating the Rapids, 1918-1971: From the Papers of Adolf A. Berle. New York: Harcourt Brace Jovanovich, 1973. Rev. by E. W.

Hawley, AHR, 79(Apr 1974):603-4; B. M. Russett, JAH, 60 (Mar 1974):1171-2.

Bernard, H. Russell and Pertti J. Pelto, eds. Technology and Social Change. New York: Macmillan, 1972. Rev. by S. Lieberstein, T & C, 15(Ja 1974):144-6.

Berry, Mary Frances. Black Resistance/White Law: A History of Constitutional Racism in America. New York: Appleton-Century-Crofts, 1971. Rev. by A. H. Kelly, AHR, 79(Apr 1974):567-8.

Berry, Ralph. Shakespeare's Comedies. Princeton: Prin U Press, 1972. Rev. by P. G. Phialas, RQ, 27(Fall 1974):361-4.

Berschin, Walter. Bonizo of Sutri, Leben und Werk. Berlin: de Gruyter, 1972. Rev. by M. Gibson, EHR, 89(Jl 1974):653-4.

Bertelli, Sergio. Ribelli, Libertini e Ortodossi Nella Storiografia Barocca. Florence: La Nuova Italia, 1973. Rev. by W. J. Bouwsma, H & T, 13(Num 3 1974):305-14.

Berthoud, Gabrielle. Antoine Marcourt: Réformateur et Pamphlétaire du "Livre des Marchans" aux Placards de 1534. Geneva: Librairie Droz, n.d. Rev. by C. L. Salley, CH, 43(Mar 1974):108.

Berthrong, Donald T. The American Indian: From Pacifism to Activism. St. Charles, Mo.: Forum Press, 1973. Rev. by M. P. McCarthy, HT, 8(Nov 1974):109-10.

Bertrand, Kenneth J. Americans in Antarctica, 1775-1948. New York: National Society Foundation, 1971. Rev. by W. L. Berg, AHR, 79(Oct 1974):1246.

Beshoar, Barron B. Hippocrates in a Red Vest: The Biography of a Frontier Doctor. Palo Alto, Cal.: American West, 1973. Rev. by C. Bancroft, CoMag, 51(Sum 1974):244-5; W. Rundell, Jr., HRNB, 2(Ja 1974):68; D. A. Smith, JAH, 61(Sep 1974): 499-500; N. C. Bledsoe, JAriH, 15(Apr 1974):91-2; A. W. Spring, NH, 55(Spr 1974):157-9.

Beskrovnyi, D. L. The Russian Army and Navy in the 19th Century: Russia's Military-Economic Potential. Moscow: Izdatel'stvo "Nauka," 1973. Rev. by J. S. Curtiss, AHR, 79(Oct 1974): 1220-1.

Bethell, Leslie. The Abolition of the Brazilian Slave Trade: Britain, Brazil and the Slave Trade Question, 1807-1869. Cambridge: Cam U Press, 1970. Rev. by M. J. Echenberg, JAAS, 9(Ja & Apr 1974):123-5.

Beynon, H. and R. M. Blackburn. Perceptions of Works: Varia-

tions within a Factory. New York: Cambridge U Press, 1972.
Rev. by R. L. Ehrlich, T & C, 15(Jl 1974):527-9.

Bezou, Henry C. Metairie: A Tongue of Land to Pasture. Gretna,
La.: Pelican, 1973. Rev. by T. H. Matheny, CH, 43(Sep
1974):423; C. G. Griffith, LaH, 15(W 1974):316-7.

Bianco, Lucien. Origins of the Chinese Revolution, 1915-1949.
Tr. by Muriel Bell. Stanford, Calif.: Stan U Press, 1971.
Rev. by B. A. Lee, MAS, 8(Apr 1974):270-1.

Bibliography Committee, Adirondack Mountain Club, Dorothy A.
Plum, chrm., comp. Adirondack Bibliography Supplement,
1956-1965. Blue Mountain Lake, N.Y.: Adirondack Museum,
1973. Rev. by C. Z. Stiverson, AmArc, 37(Apr 1974):302-3.

Bicanic, Rudolf. Economic Policy in Socialist Yugoslavia. London:
Cam U Press, 1973. Rev. by R. C. Amacher, EEQ, 8(Sum
1974):244-6.

Biddle, Arthur W. and Paul A. Eschholz, ed. The Literature of
Vermont: A Sampler. Hanover, N.H.: U Press of New Eng-
land, 1973. Rev. by R. C. Barret, NEQ, 47(Je 1974):315-8;
E. Urie, VH, 42(Win 1974):62-5.

Bidwell, Robin. Morocco under Colonial Rule: French Administration of Tribal Areas, 1912-1956. London: Frank Cass, 1973.
Rev. by E. Burke, III, JMH, 46(Dec 1974):722-4.

Bierlaire, F. see Erasmus

Bierley, Paul E. John Philip Sousa: American Phenomenon. New
York: Appleton-Century-Crofts, 1973. Rev. by P. F. Erwin,
HRNB, 2(Ja 1974):61.

Bietenholz, Peter G. Basle and France in the Sixteenth Century:
The Basle Humanists and Printers in their Contacts with
Francophone Culture. Geneva: Librairie Droz ... 1971. Rev.
by A. Santosuosso, CHR, 55(Mar 1974):114-15.

Bigler, Robert M. The Politics of German Protestantism: The
Rise of the Protestant Church Elite in Prussia, 1815-1848.
Berkeley: U Cal Press, 1972. Rev. by F. Eyck, CHR, 55
(Je 1972):234-5; W. Carr, History, 58(Je 1974):294-5.

Billaçois, F. see Abbiateci, A.

Billias, George Athan see Vaughan, Alden T.

Billikopf, David Marshall. The Exercise of Judicial Power, 1789-
1864. New York: Vantage, 1973. Rev. by H. M. Hollings-
worth, JAH, 61(Sep 1974):472.

Billingsley, Andrew and Jeanne M. Giovannoni. Children of the
    Storm. New York: Harcourt, Brace Jovanovich, 1972. Rev.
    by T. D. Perry, N H B, 37(Aug/Sep 1974):295.

Billington, Ray Allen. Frederick Jackson Turner: Historian, Schol-
    ar, Teacher. New York: Ox U Press, 1973. Rev. by L. S.
    Sage, AI, 42(Spr 1974):300-2; J. P. Bloom, AmArc, 37(Ja
    1974):86-7; C. Strout, H & T, 13(Num 3 1974):315-25; T. Col-
    bourn, NEQ, 47(Je 1974):302-4; J. T. Hubbell, MHM, 69(Sum
    1974):237-40; M. E. Nackman, MiA, 56(Ja 1974):70; W. T.
    Jackson, SCQ, 56(Sum 1974):201-2; J. Burt, THQ, 33(Sum
    1974):234-5; C. Earle, WMQ-3, 31(Ja 1974):146-8.

_____, ed. People of the Plains and Mountains: Essays in the
    History of the West Dedicated to Everett Dick. Westport,
    Conn.: Greenwood, 1973. Rev. by F. C. Luebke, A & W,
    16(Spr 1974):86-8; R. W. Paul, AHR, 79(Apr 1974):565-6;
    L. R. Hafen, CoMag, 51(Sum 1974):261-2; D. A. Smith, His-
    torian, 36(May 1974):568-9; J. B. Frantz, JAH, 61(Je 1974):
    207-8; G. E. Moulton, JOW, 13(Jl 1974):121; J. Caughey, PHR,
    43(Feb 1974):130-1; T. A. Larson, WHQ, 5(Jl 1974):355-6.

_____. Western Expansion: A History of the American Frontier.
    New York: Macmillan, 1974. Rev. by L. E. Oliva, HRNB,
    2(Jl 1974):191.

Binford, Lewis R. An Archaeological Perspective. New York:
    Seminar Press, 1972. Rev. by B. R. Butler, AmAnt, 39(Oct
    1974):646-7.

Bining, Arthur Cecil. Pennsylvania Iron Manufacture in the Eight-
    eenth Century. Harrisburg: Pa Historical Museum Commis-
    sion, 1973. Rev. by R. E. Carlson, PH, 41(Jl 1974):357-9;
    F. A. Zahrosky, WPHM, 57(Ja 1974):121-2.

Biobaku, S. O., ed. Sources of Yoruba History. Oxford: Claren-
    don Press, 1973. Rev. by B. Awe, JAfH, 15(Num 3 1974):
    490-1.

Biographical Directory of the South Carolina House of Representatives,
    Volume I: Session Lists, 1692-1973. Ed. by Walter B. Ed-
    gar, researched by Inez Watson. Columbia: U SC Press,
    1974. Rev. by J. I. Waring, SCHM, 75(Jl 1974):192.

Birchall, Ann see Crossland, R. A.

Birket-Smith, Kaj. Eskimos. New York: Crown, 1971. Rev. by
    W. Fitzhugh, AHR, 79(Oct 1974):1137-8.

Birmingham, Judy see Cambitoglou, Alexander

Bischofberger, Otto. The Generation Classes of the Zanaki (Tan-
    zania). Fribourg: U Fribourg Press, 1972. Rev. by T. O.

Beidelman, Africa, 44(Apr 1974):206-7.

Bishop, A. S. The Rise of a Central Authority for English Education. Cambridge: Cam U Press, 1971. Rev. by G. Sutherland, EHR, 89(Ja 1974):218-19.

Black, R. D. Collison, A. W. Coats, and Crawford D. W. Goodwin, eds. The Marginal Revolution in Economics: Interpretation and Evaluation. Durham, N.C.: Duke U Press, 1973. Rev. by H. D. Woodman, JIH, 5(Aut 1974):295-301.

Blackburn, R. M. see Beynon, H.

Blackman, D. J., ed. Marine Archaeology. Hamden, Conn.: Archon, 1973. Rev. by L. Casson, Archaeology, 27(Jl 1974): 218.

Blake, Marion Elizabeth. Roman Construction in Italy from Nerva through the Antonines. Philadelphia: American Philosophical Society, 1973. Rev. by M. Hammond, AHR, 79(Feb 1974): 120-1.

Blake, William. Cross and Flame in Wisconsin: the Story of United Methodism in the Badger State. Sun Prairie, Wisc.: Wisconsin Conference, United Methodist Church, 1973. Rev. by J. E. Kalas, WMH, 58(Aut 1974):57.

Blakemore, Harold. British Nitrates and Chilean Politics 1886-1896: Balmaceda and North. London: Athlone, 1973. Rev. by W. F. Sater, TAm, 31(Jl 1974):113-14.

Blakey, Arch Frederic. The Florida Phosphate Industry: A History of the Development and Use of a Vital Mineral. Cambridge, Mass.: Wertheim Committee, Har U, 1973. Rev. by W. Flynt, FHQ, 53(Oct 1974):199-201; A. R. Stoesen, GHQ, 58 (Fall 1974):377; J. E. Stealey, III, JSH, 40(Nov 1974):682-3.

Blanco, Hugo. Land or Death: The Peasant Struggle in Peru. New York: Pathfinder Press, 1972. Rev. by J. D. Powell, TAm, 31(Jl 1974):117-18.

Bland, Randall W. Private Pressure on Public Law: The Legal Career of Justice Thurgood Marshall. Port Washington, N.Y.: Kennikat, 1973. Rev. by S. B. Hand, HT, 8(Nov 1974):146-7; J. S. Auerbach, JAH, 61(Je 1974):253-4.

Blank, David Eugene. A Country Study: Politics in Venezuela. Boston: Little, Brown, 1973. Rev. by P. B. Taylor, HAHR, 54(Aug 1974):546-7.

Blanning, T. C. W. Reform and Revolution in Mainz 1743-1803. New York ...: Cam U Press, 1974. Rev. by W. J. Brunhumer, HRNB, 3(Nov/Dec 1974):29-30.

31   BLASSINGAME

Blassingame, John W. Black New Orleans, 1860-1880. Chicago:
    U Chi Press, 1973. Rev. by R. A. Fisher, CWH, 20(Mar
    1974):76-7; D. R. Colburn, FHQ, 53(Oct 1974):216-17; A. H.
    Spear, GHQ, 58(Fall 1974):372-4; H. W. Raper, Historian, 36
    (Aug 1974):780-1; B. A. Brownell, JNH, 59(Apr 1974):203-5;
    B. L. Turpen, JOW, 13(Jl 1974):130; J. J. Jackson, JSH, 40
    (May 1974):314-16; J. H. Dormon, NCHR, 51(Spr 1974):231-
    2; R. M. Lapp, PNQ, 65(Jl 1974):151-2.

_____. In Search of America see Fowler, David H.

_____. The Slave Community: Plantation Life in the Antebellum
    South. New York: Ox U Press, 1972. Rev. by M. S. Miller,
    Crisis, 81(Apr 1974):139-40; F. N. Boney, GR, 28(Spr 1974):
    147-50; L. B. De Graaf, Historian, 36(Feb 1974): 341-2; T. P.
    Govan, MHM, 69(Spr 1974):106-7.

Blegen, Carl W., Marion Rawson, Lord William Taylour, William
    P. Donovan. The Palace of Nestor at Pylos in Western Mes-
    senia. Volume III: Acropolis and Lower Town, Tholoi and
    Grave Circle and Chamber Tombs. Discoveries Outside the
    Citadel. Princeton, N.J.: Prin U Press, 1973. Rev. by
    O. T. P. K Dickinson, Antiquity, 48(Je 1974):147-8; J. W.
    Shaw, Archaeology, 27(Ja 1974):141,143.

Blet, Pierre, et al., eds. Le Saint Siège et les victimes de la
    guerre, mars 1939-décembre 1940. Vatican City: Libreria
    Editrice Vaticana, 1972. Rev. by G. O. Kent, AHR, 79(Apr
    1974):508-10.

_____, et al., eds. Le Saint Siège et la guerre mondiale, no-
    vembre 1942-décembre 1943. Vatican City: Libreria Editrice
    Vaticana, 1973. Rev. by G. O. Kent, AHR, 79(Apr 1974):
    508-10.

Bleuel, Hans Peter. Sex and Society in Nazi Germany. New York:
    Lippincott, 1973. Rev. by D. E. Showalter, HRNB, 2(Mar
    1974):117.

Blevins, Winfred. Give Your Heart to the Hawks: a Tribute to
    the Mountain Men. Los Angeles: Nash Pub. Co., 1973. Rev.
    by R. C. Poulsen, UHQ, 42(W 1974):93-4.

Blewett, N. The Peers, the Parties and the People: The General
    Election of 1910. London: Macmillan, 1972. Rev. by P. J.
    Waller, EHR, 89(Ja 1974):230-2.

Blickenstorfer, Christian. Die Haltung der englischen Regierung
    wahrend der mandschurischen Krise (1931-1933). Zurich:
    Juris Druck Verlag, 1972. Rev. by H. R. Winkler, AHR,
    79(Feb 1974):117-18.

Blinkenberg, Lars. India-Pakistan: The History of Unsolved Conflicts. Copenhagen: Munksgaard, 1972. Rev. by R. L. Park, JAS, 33(Aug 1974):725.

Blit, Lucjan. The Origins of Polish Socialism: The History and Ideas of the First Polish Socialist Party, 1878-1886. Cambridge: Cam U Press, 1971. Rev. by N. M. Naimark, EEQ, 7(Ja 1974):461-6; R. F. Leslie, ESR, 4(Ja 1974):97-8.

Bliven, Bruce, Jr. Under the Guns: New York: 1775-1776. New York: Harper & Row, 1972. Rev. by R. J. Koke, NYHSQ, 58(Ja 1974):63-5.

Bloom, John Porter, ed. The American Territorial System. Athens, Ohio: Ohio U Press, 1974. Rev. by R. P. Swierenga, HRNB, 2(May/Je 1974):165; G. M. Dennison, JAH, 61(Dec 1974):773-4; N. Lederer, JOW, 13(Oct 1974):141-2; V. Westphall, NMHR, 49(Oct 1974):332-3; H. N. Scheiber, PHR, 43 (Aug 1974):413-15; D. L. Smith, RKHS, 72(Oct 1974):423-6; H. P. Hinton, SWHQ, 78(Oct 1974):222-4; W. D. Aeschbacher, UHQ, 42(Fall 1974):390-1.

Blue, Frederick J. The Free Soilers: Third Party Politics, 1848-54. Urbana: U Ill Press, 1973. Rev. by G. H. Mayer, AHR, 79(Je 1974):862-3; C. F. Van Deventer, CWH, 20(Mar 1974): 64-5; P. Riddleberg, IMH, 70(Mar 1974):84-5; R. O. Curry, JAH, 60(Mar 1974):1126-7; C. Trafzer, JOW, 13(Oct 1974): 137; K. J. Brauer, JSH, 40(May 1974):310-11; J. H. Schroeder, MHM, 69(Fall 1974):332-3; V. B. Howard, OH, 83(W 1974):76-7; J. B. Ginsberg, WMH, 57(W 1973/74):159-60.

Bluhm, William T. Building an Austrian Nation: The Political Integration of a Western State. New Haven, Conn.: Yale U Press, 1973. Rev. by J. Dreijmanis, EEQ, 8(Mar 1974):120-2.

Blum, John Morton, ed. The Price of Vision: The Diary of Henry A. Wallace, 1942-1946. Boston: Houghton Mifflin, 1973. Rev. by F. H. Schapsmeier, AHR, 79(Oct 1974):1287-8; A. L. Hamby, JAH, 61(Sep 1974):534-5.

Blumberg, Arnold. The Diplomacy of the Mexican Empire, 1863-1867. Philadelphia: American Philosophical Society, 1971. Rev. by H. Blakemore, EHR, 89(Jl 1974):684-5.

Blumenson, Martin. The Patton Papers. Volume 1, 1885-1940. Boston: Houghton Mifflin, 1972. Rev. by J. K. Mahon, AHR, 79(Apr 1974):596-7.

Blunt, C. E. and R. H. M. Dolley, eds. Sylloge of Coins of the British Isles, Part 18, National Museum, Copenhagen, IV; Anglo-Saxon Coins from Harold I and Anglo-Norman Coins. London: Ox U Press, 1972. Rev. by D. M. Metcalf, EHR, 89(Ja 1974):149.

Blunt, Wilfrid. On Wings of Song. A Biography of Felix Mendelssohn. London: H. Hamilton, n.d. Rev. by J. Richardson,
HTo, 24(Oct 1974):731-2.

Boase, T. S. R. Kingdoms and Strongholds of the Crusaders. Indianapolis: Bobbs-Merrill, 1971. Rev. by C. L. Tipton, AHR,
79(Feb 1974):131-2.

Boatner, Mark A., III. Landmarks of the American Revolution: a
Guide to Locating and Knowing What Happened at the Sites of
Independence. Harrisburg, Pa.: Stackpole, 1973. Rev. by
E. P. Alexander, VMHB, 82(Oct 1974):494-5.

Bode, Carl, comp. and ed. Midcentury America: Life in the 1850's.
Carbondale: S Ill U Press, 1972. Rev. by I. B. Holley, Jr.,
JISHS, 67(Je 1974):350-1.

Bodnar, John E., ed. The Ethnic Experience in Pennsylvania.
Lewisburg, Pa.: Bucknell U Press, 1973. Rev. by P. S.
Klein, JAH, 61(Je 1974):228-9; J. F. Marszalek, Jr., PH,
41(Oct 1974):478-9.

Body, Paul. Joseph Eötvös and the Modernization of Hungary, 1840-
1870. Philadelphia: American Philosophical Society, 1972.
Rev. by R. A. Kann, CHR, 55(Mar 1974):115-16; M. Fenyo,
EEQ, 8(Mar 1974):111-12.

Boehringer, Erich, ed. Pergamon, Gesammelte Aufsätze. Berlin:
Walter de Gruyter, 1972. Rev. by H. A. and D. A. Thompson, AJA, 78(Jl 1974):310-12.

Boesch, Bruno, ed. German Literature: A Critical Survey. London: Methuen, 1971. Rev. by M. C. Ives, ESR, 4(Ja 1974):
93-5.

Bogle, Donald. Toms, Coons, Mulattoes, Mammies, and Bucks:
An Interpretative History of Blacks in American Films. New
York: Viking, 1973. Rev. by J. W. Ivy, Crisis, 81(Feb
1974):63.

Bogolinbov, Aleksee. Un heroe espanol del progreso: Agustin de
Betancourt. Madrid: Seminarios y Ediciones, 1973. Rev.
by T. F. Glick, T & C, 15(Ja 1974):97-8.

Bogue, Allan G. Dimensions of Quantitative Research. see
Aydelotte, William O.

Bohr, Paul Richard. Famine in China and the Missionary: Timo-
thy Richard as Relief Administrator and Advocate of National
Reform, 1876-1884. Cambridge, Mass.: Har U Press, 1972.
Rev. by J. G. Lutz, AHR, 79(Oct 1974):1232-3.

Boicu, L. and Al Zub, eds. A. D. Xenopol: Studies in His Life

and <u>Works</u>. Bucharest: Editura Academiei Republicii Socialiste România, 1972. Rev. by K. Hitchins, AHR, 79(Je 1974):
813-14.

Boles, John B., ed. <u>America, the Middle Period: Essays in Hon-</u>
<u>or of Bernard Mayo</u>. Charlottesville: U Press Va, 1973.
Rev. by D. A. Harris, GHQ, 58(Sum 1974):296-7; G. L. Se-
ligmann, Jr., HRNB, 2(Feb 1974):95-6; N. E. Cunningham,
Jr., JAH, 61(Sep 1974):477-8; W. G. Morgan, JSH, 40(Nov
1974):655-6; P. J. Coleman, NCHR, 51(Sum 1974):351-2;
J. L. Bugg, Jr., VMHB, 82(Oct 1974):486-7.

Bolitho, Harold. <u>Treasures Among Men: The Fudai Daimyo in</u>
<u>Tokugawa Japan</u>. New Haven: Yale U Press, 1974. Rev. by
A. W. Burks, HRNB, 2(Jl 1974):203.

Bollens, John C. and Grant B. Geyer. <u>Yorty: Politics of a Con-</u>
<u>stant Candidate</u>. Pacific Palisades, Cal.: Palisades, 1973.
Rev. by F. M. Brodie, JAH, 60(Mar 1974):1187-9; D. R.
Berman, PHR, 43(Feb 1974):131-2; R. C. Post, PNQ, 65
(Apr 1974):92.

Bolster, Evelyn (Sister Mary Angela). <u>A History of the Diocese of</u>
<u>Cork from the Earliest Times to the Reformation</u>. New York:
Barnes and Noble, 1972. Rev. by J. T. McNeill, CH, 43
(Dec 1974):533-4.

Bolton, G. <u>Roman Century, 1870-1970</u>. London: H. Hamilton,
1970. Rev. by C. H. Church, ESR, 4(Ja 1974):95-7.

Bolus, Malvina, ed. <u>People and Pelts: Selected Papers of the</u>
<u>Second North American Fur Trade Conference</u>. Winnipeg:
Peguis, 1972. Rev. by J. L. Clayton, PHR, 43(May 1974):
267.

Bon, Antoine. <u>The Ancient Civilization of Byzantium</u>. London:
Barrie and Jenkins, 1972. Rev. by K. Snipes, Antiquity, 48
(Mar 1974):69-70.

Bonachea, Ramón L. and Marta San Martín. <u>The Cuban Insurrec-</u>
<u>tion 1952-1959</u>. New Brunswick, N.J.: Transaction Books,
1974. Rev. by R. H. Chilcote, HRNB, 3(Oct 1974):8.

Bonachea, Rolando E. and Nelson P. Valdés, eds. <u>Che: Selected</u>
<u>Works of Ernesto Guevara</u>. Cambridge, Mass.: M I T
Press, 1969. Rev. by M. Zeitlin, HAHR, 54(Nov 1974):715-
18.

Bonavia, David <u>see</u> Heren, Louis

Bondanella, Peter E. <u>Machiavelli and the Art of Renaissance His-</u>
<u>tory.</u> Detroit: Wayne St U Press, 1973. Rev. by De L. Jen-
sen, HRNB, 2(May/Je 1974):183-4.

Boney, F. N., ed. Slave Life in Georgia: A Narrative of the Life, Sufferings, and Escape of John Brown, a Fugitive Slave. Savannah, Ga.: Beehive, 1972. Rev. by W. A. Low, JNH, 59(Ja 1974):91-2.

Bonner, James C. Georgia's Last Frontier: The Development of Carroll County. Athens, Ga.: U Ga Press, 1971. Rev. by S. Gurr, AHR, 79(Je 1974):840.

Bonsal, Philip W. Cuba, Castro and the United States. Pittsburgh: U Pittsburgh Press, 1971. Rev. by R. M. Schneider, TAm, 31(Jl 1974):116-17.

Bontemps, Arna. Free at Last: The Life of Frederick Douglass. New York: Dodd, Mead, 1971. Rev. by C. E. Wynes, AHR, 79(Apr 1974):580-1.

_____. The Poetry of the Negro. see Hughes, Langston

Boone, Sylvia Ardyn. West African Travels: A Guide to People and Places. New York: Random House, 1974. Rev. by W. Marr, II, Crisis, 81(Aug-Sep 1974):246.

Boorstin, Daniel J. The Americans: The Democratic Experience. New York: Random House, 1973. Rev. by T. C. Cochran, JAH, 61(Je 1974):220-1; J. L. Loos, JSH, 40(May 1974):325-6; R. A. Gerber, PHR, 43(Aug 1974):409-10.

Borah, Woodrow see Cook, Sherburne F.

Borchardt, Frank L. German Antiquity in Renaissance Myth. Baltimore ...: JHU Press, 1971. Rev. by H. J. Cohn, EHR, 89(Apr 1974):427-8.

Borchhardt, Jürgen. Homerische Helme. Helmformen der Ägäis in ihren Beziehungen in der Bronze-und Frühen Eisenzeit. Mainz am Rhein: Verlag Philipp von zabern, 1972. Rev. by J. C. Waldbaum, AJA, 78(Ja 1974):93-5.

Bordes, Francois. A Tale of Two Caves. New York: Harper and Row, 1972. Rev. by E. Anati, Archaeology, 27(Apr 1974): 146.

Boren, Carter E., Robert W. Amsler, Audra L. Prewitt and H. Wayne Morgan. Essays on the Gilded Age. Austin: U Tx Press, 1973. Rev. by H. Humphreys, ETHJ, 12(Apr 1974): 68-9; J. Braeman, JAH, 61(Je 1974):218-19.

Borg, Alan. Architectural Sculpture in Romanesque Provence. Oxford: Ox U Press, 1972. Rev. by G. Zarnecki, History, 59 (Feb 1974):88-9.

Borg, Dorothy and Shumpei Okamoto, eds. Pearl Harbor as History:

Japanese-American Relations, 1931-1941. New York: Columbia U Press, 1973. Rev. by R. Dingman, AHR, 79(Je 1974): 756-7.

Borgese, Elisabeth Mann, ed. Pacem in Maribus. New York: Dodd, Mead, 1973. Rev. by V. Cox, Mankind, 4(Aug 1974): 6, 8.

Bork, Albert William and Georg Maier. Historical Dictionary of Ecuador. Metuchen, N.J.: Scarecrow, 1973. Rev. by J. E. Rodríguez O., HAHR, 54(Nov 1974):696-7.

Bose, A. C. Indian Revolutionaries Abroad, 1905-1922. Patna: Bharati Bhamian, 1971. Rev. by J. Brown, EHR, 89(Apr 1974):463-4.

Bosher, J. F., ed. French Government and Society 1500-1850. London: Athlone, 1973. Rev. by J. M. Roberts, EHR, 89 (Ja 1974):191-2; N. Hampson, History, 59(Je 1974):264-5.

Boss, Valentin. Newton and Russia: The Early Influence, 1698-1796. Cambridge, Mass.: Har U Press, 1972. Rev. by M. Raeff, AHR, 79(Feb 1974):196-7.

Botello, Arthur P., trans. Don Pio Pico's Historical Narrative. Glendale, Cal.: Arthur H. Clark, 1973. Rev. by M. M. Smith, JOW, 13(Apr 1974):120; F. E. Balderama, PHR, 43 (Aug 1974):426-7.

Bothwell, Robert and Michael Cross, eds. Policy by Other Means: Essays in honour of C. P. Stacey. see Cross, Michael and Robert Bothwell, eds. Policy by Other Means....

Bottigheimer, K. S. English Money and Irish Land. The Adventurers in the Cromwellian Settlement of Ireland. Oxford: Clarendon, Press, 1971. Rev. by J. P. Cooper, EHR, 89(Ja 1974):182-3.

Bourgeon, Jean-Louis. Les Colbert avant Colbert: Destin d'une famille marchande. Paris: Universitaires de France, 1973. Rev. by N. L. Roelker, AHR, 79(Apr 1974):518-19.

Bouvier, Pierre. Fanon. Paris: Editions universitaires, 1971. Rev. by F. F. Clairmonte, JMAS, 12(Mar 1974):154-7.

Bowden, Henry Warner. Church History in the Age of Science: Historiographical Patterns in the United States, 1876-1918. Chapel Hill: UNC Press, 1971. Rev. by M. E. Marty, AHR, 79(Apr 1974):591-2.

Bowden, J. J. Spanish and Mexican Land Grants in the Chihuahuan Acquisition. El Paso: Texas Western Press, U Tx, 1971. Rev. by W. A. Beck, AHR, 79(Je 1974):842-3.

Bowen, Ashley. The Journals of Ashley Bowen (1728-1813) of Mar-
blehead. Ed. by Philip Chadwick Foster Smith. Portland,
Maine: Peabody Museum of Salem, 1973. Rev. by G. A.
Billias, NEQ, 47(Mar 1974):140-3.

Bowie, Theodore, M. C. Subhadradis Diskul, and A. B. Griswold.
The Sculpture of Thailand. New York: Asia Society, 1972.
Rev. by P. M. Young, JAS, 33(Aug 1974):733-5.

Bowles, Samuel. Our New West: Records of Travel Between the
Mississippi River and the Pacific Ocean, Over the Plains;
Over the Mountains, Through the Great Interior Basin, Over
the Sierra Nevadas, to and Up and Down the Pacific Coast.
n. p., 1869 Reprint. Rev. by D. A. Smith, CoMag, 51(Spr
1974):157-9.

Bowman, Albert Hall. The Struggle for Neutrality: Franco-Ameri-
can Diplomacy During the Federalist Era. Knoxville: U Tenn
Press, 1974. Rev. by G. B. Ostrower, HRNB, 2(Jl 1974):
195.

Bowman, Amos see Marsh, Andrew J. Reports....

Bowser, Frederick P. The African Slave in Colonial Peru, 1524-
1650. Stanford, Cal.: Stan U Press, 1974. Rev. by P. E.
Kuhl, HRNB, 2(Apr 1974):153-4.

Boyce, D. G. Englishmen and Irish Troubles: British Public Opinion and the Making of Irish Policy, 1918-1922. Cambridge,
Mass.: M I T Press, 1972. Rev. by H. F. Mulvey, AHR,
79(Feb 1974):155; G. A. Cahill, Historian, 36(Feb 1974):328-9;
D. W. Savage, JIH, 5(Aut 1974):324-5.

Boyce, George A. When the Navajos Had Too Many Sheep: the
1940's. n. p.: Indian Historian Press, 1974. Rev. by Staff,
InH, 7(Win 1974):51.

Boyd, Gavin see Wilcox, Wayne

Boyd, Julian P., et al., eds. The Papers of Thomas Jefferson.
Volume 18, 4 November 1790-24 January 1791. Princeton,
N. J.: Prin U Press, 1971. Rev. by M. Brant, AHR, 79
(Je 1974):852-3.

Boyer, Paul and Stephen Nissembaum. Salem Possessed: The Social Origins of Witchcraft. Cambridge, Mass.: Har U Press,
1974. Rev. by M. B. Akin, CH, 43(Sep 1974):418. J. T.
Main, HRNB, 2(Aug 1974):221-2; N. Salisbury, NEQ, 47(Sep
1974):472-5.

Boyer, Richard O. The Legend of John Brown: A Biography and
a History. New York: Knopf, 1973. Rev. by J. L. Thomas,
AHR, 79(Feb 1974):231-3; J. J. Cardoso, CWH, 20(Je 1974):

159-63; E. H. Berwanger, Historian, 36(Feb 1974):344-5;
V. B. Howard, VMHB, 82(Oct 1974):506-7.

Boylan, Brian Richard. Benedict Arnold: The Dark Eagle. New
York: Norton, 1973. Rev. by L. Gerlach, JSH, 40(Feb 1974):
125-6; R. R. Alexander, WVH, 35(Ja 1974):163-4.

Boyle, J. A., ed. The Cambridge History of Iran. Vol. V. The
Seljuq and Mongol Periods. Cambridge: Cam U Press, 1968.
Rev. by B. Lewis, History, 59(Je 1974):315-16.

Boyle, John Hunter. China and Japan at War, 1937-1945: The
Politics of Collaboration. Stanford, Cal.: Stan U Press, 1972.
Rev. by R. L. Sims, History, 59(Je 1974):321-2.

Boyle, Leonard E. A Survey of the Vatican Archives and of its
Medieval Holdings. Toronto: Pontifical Institute of Medieval
Studies, 1972. Rev. by C. M. D. Crowder, CHR, 55(Je 1974):
229-31.

Bracey, John H., Jr., August Meier and Elliott Rudwick, eds. The
Rise of the Ghetto. Belmont, Cal.: Wadsworth, 1971. Rev.
by J. L. Arnold, JNH, 59(Apr 1974):196-203.

Bradeen, Donald William and Malcom Francis McGregor. Studies
in Fifth-Century Attic Epigraphy. Norman: U Ok Press, 1974.
Rev. by O. W. Reinmuth, HRNB, 2(May/Je 1974):174.

Bradford, Ernle. Christopher Columbus. New York: Viking, 1973.
Rev. by W. E. Washburn, AHR, 79(Oct 1974):1172; T. Floyd,
HAHR, 54(Nov 1974):706-7.

Brading, David A. Los orígenes del nacionalismo mexicano. México: SepSetentas, 1973. Rev. by D. M. Ladd, HAHR, 54
(Aug 1973):525-8.

Braeman, John. Albert J. Beveridge: American Nationalist. Chicago: U Chi Press, 1971. Rev. by C. J. Phillips, JAH, 61
(Je 1974):236-8.

Braider, Donald. Solitary Star: A Biography of Sam Houston. New
York: Putnam's, 1974. Rev. by D. W. Whisenhunt, JSH, 40
(Nov 1974):658-9.

Brancourt, Jean-Pierre. Le duc de Saint-Simon et la monarchie.
Paris: Éditions Cujas, 1971. Rev. by A. N. Hamscher, AHR,
79(Je 1974):790-1.

Brand, Oscar. Songs of '76: a Folksinger's History of the Revolution. New York: M. Evans, 1972. Rev. by R. A. Brown,
55(Ja 1974):117.

Brandon, James R., ed. On Thrones of Gold: Three Javanese

Shadow Plays. Cambridge, Mass.: Har U Press, 1970. Rev.
by P. R. Goethals, JAAS, 9(Ja & Apr 1974):107-8.

Brandon, William. The Lost Americans: The Indian in American
Culture. New York: McGraw-Hill, 1974. Rev. by P. Oaks,
JAriH, 15(Aut 1974):297-8; L. R. Hafen, UHQ, 42(Fall 1974):
388-9; D. A. Grinde, Jr., WPHM, 57(Jl 1974):318-19.

Brandt, Vincent. A Korean Village, Between Farm and Sea. Cambridge, Mass.: Har U Press, 1971. Rev. by H. R. Bar-
ringer, JAAS, 9(Ja & Apr 1974):100-1.

Branigan, Keith. The Foundations of Palatial Crete: A Survey of
Crete in the Early Bronze Age. New York: Praeger, 1970.
Rev. by J. E. Coleman, Archaeology, 27(Ja 1974):66, 68.

_____. Town and Country: the Archaeology of Verulamium and
the Roman Chilterns. Bourne End: Spurbooks, 1973. Rev.
by J. S. Wacher, Antiquity, 48(Je 1974):154.

Brant, Irving. Impeachment: Trials and Errors. New York:
Knopf, 1972. Rev. by I. Dilliard, AHR, 79(Je 1974):837-40.

Brathwaite, Edward. Creole Society in Jamaica 1770-1820. London: Ox U Press, 1971. Rev. by A. Bryan, TAm, 30(Ja
1974):418-19.

Braudel, Fernand. Capitalism and Material Life, 1400-1800. New
York: Harper and Row, 1973. Rev. by J. W. Baldwin,
HRNB, 2(Ja 1974):74.

_____. The Mediterranean and the Mediterranean World in the
Age of Philip II. Vol. 1. New York: Harper and Row, 1972.
Rev. by T. F. Glick, HAHR, 54(Feb 1974):159-61; C. R.
Boxer, HTo, 24(Apr 1974):285-7.

Braunfels, Wolfgang. Monasteries of Western Europe: The Architecture of the Orders. London: Thames and Hudson, 1972.
Rev. by C. N. L. Brooke, History, 59(Feb 1974):86-7.

Bravo, Enrique R. An Annotated, Selected Puerto Rican Bibliography. New York: Urban Center, Columbia U, 1972. Rev. by
L. E. Agrait, HAHR, 54(Feb 1974):157-9.

Breach, R. W. and R. M. Hartwell, eds. British Economy and
Society, 1870-1970: Documents, Descriptions, Statistics. Oxford: Oxford U Press, 1972. Rev. by T. C. Barker, History,
59(Feb 1974):147.

Brecher, Irving and S. A. Abbas. Foreign Aid and Industrial Development in Pakistan. Cambridge: Cam U Press, 1972.
Rev. by A. Robinson, MAS, 8(Apr 1974):263-6.

Brecher, Jeremy. Strike! San Francisco: Straight Arrow Books,
     1972. Rev. by H. W. Currie, AHR, 79(Apr 1974):593-4.

Breck, Allen D. and Wolfgang Yourgrau, eds. Biology, History,
     and Natural Philosophy. New York: Plenum Press, 1972.
     Rev. by T. H. Levere, CHR, 55(Je 1974):177-8.

Bree, Germaine. Women Writers in France: Variations on a
     Theme. New Brunswick, N.J.: Rutgers U Press, 1973.   Rev.
     by G. Downum, HRNB, 2(Mar 1974):114.

Breese, Gerald, ed. Urban Southeast Asia: A Selected Bibliogra-
     phy. New York: Seadag, 1973. Rev. by A. Howard, JAS,
     33(Feb 1974):328.

Bremer, Arthur H. Arthur H. Bremer. An Assassin's Diary.
     n. p.: Harper's Magazine Press, n. d. Rev. by S. Gershgor-
     en, Mankind, 4(Je 1974):6, 64, 66.

Brennan, Louis A. Beginner's Guide to Archaeology: The Modern
     Digger's Step-by-Step Introduction to the Expert Ways of Un-
     earthing the Past. Harrisburg, Pa.: Stackpole, 1973. Rev.
     by J. L. Cotter, Archaeology, 27(Ja 1974):76.

Brenneman, Bill. Miracle on Cherry Creek: An Informal History
     of the Birth and Rebirth of a Neighborhood. Denver: World
     Press, 1973. Rev. by S. J. Leonard, CoMag, 51(Sum 1974):
     254-5.

Brenner, Louis. The Shehus of Kukawa: A History of the Al-
     Kanemi Dynasty of Bornu. Oxford: Clarendon Press, 1973.
     Rev. by M. Last, Africa, 44(Apr 1974):216; J. Spaulding,
     JAfH, 15(Num 3 1974):501-3.

Brent, Peter. God Men of India. New York: Quadrangle, 1972.
     Rev. by R. J. Fornaro, JAS, 33(May 1974):497-8.

Brentano, Robert. Rome Before Avignon: A Social History of Thir-
     teenth-Century Rome. New York: Basic Books, 1974. Rev.
     by P. N. Bebb, HRNB, 2(Sep 1974):240-1.

Bresc, Henri, ed. La correspondance de Pierre Ameilh, arché-
     veque de Naples puis d'Embrun (1363-1369). Paris: Éditions
     du Centre National de la Recherche Scientifique, 1972. Rev.
     by B. G. Kohl, AHR, 79(Je 1974):775.

Brettell, Richard R. Historic Denver: the Architects and the
     Architecture, 1858-1893. Denver: Historic Denver Inc., 1973.
     Rev. by M. D. Lester, UHQ, 42(Fall 1974):393-4.

Bretton, Henry L. Power and Politics in Africa. Chicago: Aldine,
     1973. Rev. by P.-K. Tunteng, JMAS, 12(Mar 1974):152-4.

Brewington, Marion V. see Albion, Robert G.

Bridenbaugh, Carl and Roberta. No Peace Beyond the Line: The
    English in the Caribbean 1624-1690. New York: Ox U Press,
    1972. Rev. by G. Williams, EHR, 89(Apr 1974):441-2; K. R.
    Andrews, RQ, 27(Sum 1974):231-3.

Bridge, F. R. From Sadowa to Sarajevo. The Foreign Policy of
    Austria-Hungary, 1866-1914. London: Routledge and Kegan
    Paul, 1972. Rev. by C. A. Macartney, EHR, 89(Jl 1974):
    686; R. F. C. Okey, ESR, 4(Jl 1974):283-6.

_____. Great Britain and Austria-Hungary, 1906-1914: A Diplo-
    matic History. London: Weidenfeld and Nicolson, 1972. Rev.
    by K. Robbins, ESR, 4(Jl 1974):281-3; P. W. Schroeder, JMH,
    46(Je 1974):344-5.

Bridgers, Henry C., Jr. East Carolina Railway: Route of the Yel-
    lowhammer. Tarboro, N.C.: T & E Publishers of Louisville,
    1973. Rev. by C. L. Price, NCHR, 51(Spr 1974):227-8.

Bridgewater, Dorothy W. see Willcox, William B.

Briggs, Asa. Victorian People: A Reassessment of Persons and
    Themes, 1851-67. Chicago: U Chi Press, 1973. Rev. by
    J. C. D'Oronzio, HT, 8(Nov 1974):142-3.

Briggs, John and Ian Sellers, eds. Victorian Nonconformity. New
    York: St. Martin's, 1974. Rev. by R. A. Rempel, HRNB,
    2(Sep 1974):236.

Brilliant, Richard. Roman Art: From the Republic to Constantine.
    London: Phaidon, n.d. Rev. by M. Grant, HTo, 24(Nov
    1974):732-4.

Brinkworth, E. R. C. Shakespeare and the Bawdy Court of Strat-
    ford. Chichester: Phillimore, 1972. Rev. by A. L. Rowse,
    EHR, 89(Apr 1974):430-1.

Brinton, Howard H. The Religious Philosophy of Quakerism: The
    Beliefs of Fox, Barclay, and Penn as Based on the Gospel of
    John. Wallingford, Pa.: Pendle Hill, 1973. Rev. by T. L.
    Underwood, CH, 43(Je 1974):273-4.

Briscoe, John. A Commentary on Livy, Books XXXI-XXXIII. New
    York: Ox U Press, 1973. Rev. by R. K. Sherk, AHR, 79
    (Oct 1974):1157-8.

Broadbent, John. Paradise Lost, Introduction. Cambridge: Cam-
    bridge U Press, 1972. Rev. by J. A. Wittreich, Jr., RQ,
    27(Sum 1974):258-61.

Brock, Peter. Pacifism in Europe to 1914. Princeton, N.J.:

Prin U Press, 1973. Rev. by A. J. A. Morris, History, 59 (Je 1974):293.

Brock, P. W. and Basil Greenhill. Steam and Sail in Britain and North America. Princeton, N.J.: Prin U Press, 1973. Rev. by C. G. Reynolds, T & C, 15(Oct 1974):644-5.

Brock, William R. Conflict and Transformation: The United States, 1844-1877. Baltimore: Penguin, 1973. Rev. by K. I. Polakoff, HT, 7(Aug 1974):633-4.

Brodhaus, Michael J. A Soldier-Scientist in the American Southwest: Being a Narrative of the Travels of Brevet Captain Elliott Coues, Assistant Surgeon, U.S.A..... Tucson: Arizona Hist. Soc., 1973. Rev. by R. C. Post, PHR, 43(May 1974):272-3.

Brodhead, Michael J. A Soldier-Scientist in the American Southwest ... 1864-1865. Tucson: Ariz Historical Society, 1973. Rev. by W. E. Hollon, JAH, 61(Dec 1974):785-6.

Brodie, Fawn M. Thomas Jefferson: An Intimate History. New York: Norton, 1974. Rev. by D. H. Donald, Commentary, 58(Jl 1974):96-8; H. A. Barnes, HRNB, 2(Jl 1974):190-1; R. M. McBride, THQ, 33(Fall 1974):349-50; J. M. Cooper, Jr., WMH, 58(Aut 1974):63-4; S. H. Hockman, WVH, 36(Oct 1974):65-6.

Broesamle, John J. William Gibbs McAdoo: a Passion for Change, 1863-1917. Port Washington, N.Y.: Kennikat, 1974. Rev. by B. I. Kaufman, WMH, 57(Sum 1974):322-3.

Bromke, Adam and John W. Strong, eds. Gierek's Poland. New York: Praeger, 1973. Rev. by Z. Gitelman, HRNB, 2(Ja 1974):80.

Bromlei, I. V., et al., eds. The Slavs and Russia: For the 70th Birthday of S. A. Nikitin. Moscow: Izdatel'stvo "Nauka," 1972. Rev. by A. Gleason, AHR, 79(Oct 1974):1217-18.

Brooke, Christopher. Medieval Church and Society: Collected Essays. New York: NYU Press, 1972. Rev. by J. Dahmus, AHR, 79(Feb 1974):123-4.

Brooke, John. King George III. London: Constable, 1972. Rev. by P. Langford, EHR, 89(Ja 1974):196-7; J. J. Hecht, NEQ, 47(Mar 1974):161-3.

_____ and Mary Sorensen, eds. The Prime Ministers' Papers: W. E. Gladstone, I. Autobiographical Memoranda. London: H. M. S. O., 1971-3. Rev. by N. Gash, EHR, 89(Apr 1974): 400-2.

Brooke-Rose, Christine. A ZBC of Ezra Pound. Berkeley: U Cal
    Press, 1972. Rev. by V. Miller, GR, 28(Sum 1974):354-7.

Brooks, George E., Jr. The Kru Mariner in the Nineteenth Cen-
    tury: An Historical Compendium. Newark, Del.: Liberian
    Studies Assn in America, 1972. Rev. by E. Tonkin, JAfH, 15
    (Num 2 1974):332-4.

Brooks, Juanita. Frontier Tales: True Stories of Real People.
    Logan: Western Text Soc., 1972. Rev. by N. E. Lambert,
    UHQ, 42(Spr 1974):202-3.

_____. On the Ragged Edge: The Life and Times of Dudley
    Leavitt. Salt Lake City: Utah Historical Society, 1973. Rev.
    by C. Trafzer, JOW, 13(Oct 1974):146-7.

Brooks, Lester see Parris, Guichard

Broome, Harvey. Faces of the Wilderness. Missoula: Mountain
    Men, 1972. Rev. by E. Richardson, PNQ, 65(Jan 1974):42-3.

Brophy, A. Blake. Foundlings on the Frontier: Racial and Reli-
    gious Conflict in Arizona Territory, 1904-1905. Tucson: U
    Ariz Press, 1972. Rev. by H. M. Ward, JOW, 13(Ja 1974):
    149.

Brose, Olive J. Frederick Denison Maurice: Rebellious Conform-
    ist. Athens, Ohio: Ohio U Press, 1971. Rev. by S. Meach-
    am, AHR, 79(Apr 1974):514-15.

Brötel, D. Französischer Imperialismus in Vietnam. Die koloniale
    Expansion und die Errichtung des Protektorates Annam-Tonking
    1880-1885. Zurich: Atlantis, 1972. Rev. by D. J. Buncan-
    son, EHR, 89(Ja 1974):224-7.

Broué, Pierre and Emile Témine. The Revolution and the Civil
    War in Spain. Cambridge, Mass.: M I T Press, 1972. Rev.
    by T. Kaplan, AHR, 79(Oct 1974):1198-9.

Brown, Anne S. K. see Rice, Howard C., Jr.

Brown, Harry James and Frederick D. Williams, eds. The Diary
    of James A. Garfield. Volume III: 1875-1877. East Lansing:
    Mich St U Press, 1973; Rev. by A. Peskin, CWH, 20(Je
    (1974):179-80; H. C. Miner, Historian, 36(Aug 1974):787-8;
    T. H. Williams, JSH, 40(Aug 1974):496-8.

Brown, J. Douglas. An American Philosophy of Social Security:
    Evolution and Issues. Princeton, N.J.: Prin U Press, 1972.
    Rev. by R. Lubove, AHR, 79(Oct 1974):1244-5; R. H. Brem-
    ner, JAH, 60(Mar 1974):1175-6.

Brown, John A. see Ruby, Robert H.

Brown, Judith M. Gandhi's Rise to Power: Indian Politics 1915-
1922. Cambridge: Cam U Press, 1972. Rev. by P. G.
Robb, History, 59(Je 1974):318-19; H. Spodek, JAAS, 9(Ja &
Apr 1974):114-15.

Brown, Lloyd A., ed. Revolutionary War Journals of Henry Dearborn, 1775-1783. New York: Da Capo, 1971. Rev. by F. C.
McLaughlin, WPHM, 57(Ja 1974):116-17.

Brown, R. Allen. Origins of English Feudalism. New York:
Barnes and Noble, 1973. Rev. by C. W. Hollister, AHR, 79
(Feb 1974):124-5; C. V. Graves, Historian, 36(Aug 1974):739-
40.

_____. The Origins of Modern Europe. London: Constable,
1972. Rev. by P. Wormald, EHR, 89(Apr 1974):413-14; D.
Luscombe, History, 59(Je 1974):250.

Brown, Stuart Gerry. The Presidency on Trial: Robert Kennedy's
1968 Campaign and Afterwards. Honolulu: U Press Hawaii,
1972. Rev. by H. F. Bedford, AHR, 79(Je 1974):910-11.

Brown, Truesdell S. The Greek Historians. Lexington, Mass.:
D. C. Heath, 1973. Rev. by W. P. Kaldis, HRNB, 2(Ja 1974):
72.

Brown, W. Norman. The United States and India, Pakistan, Bangladesh. Cambridge: Harvard U Press, 1972. Rev. by D. R.
SarDesai, PHR, 43(Feb 1974):142-3.

Browne, Jefferson B., ed. Key West: The Old and the New.
Gainesville: U Fla Press, 1973. Rev. by H. S. Marks,
RKHS, 72(Ja 1974):70-1.

Browne, Lina Fergusson see Huning, Franz

Brownell, Blaine A. and Warren E. Stickle, eds. Bosses and Reformers: Urban Politics in America 1880-1920. Boston:
Houghton, 1973. Rev. by E. D. Schmiel, HT, 7(Aug 1974):
634-5; A. Hoffman, JOW, 13(Oct 1974):138.

Browning, Harley L. see Balán, Jorge

Bruce, Robert V. Beli: Alexander Graham Bell and the Conquest
of Solitude. Boston: Little, Brown, 1973. Rev. by J. F.
Wall, 48(Spr 1974):132-3; H. A. Meier, JAH, 60(Mar 1974):
1148-9; H. I. Sharlin, T & C, 15(Apr 1974):334-6.

Bruegel, J. W. Czechoslovakia Before Munich: The German Minority Problem and British Appeasement Policy. New York:
Cam U Press, 1973. Rev. by R. Szporluk, AHR, 79(Oct
1974):1214-15.

Brumbaugh, Thomas B., ed. see Architecture of Middle Tennessee

Brundage, Burr Cartwright. A Rain of Darts: The Mexica Aztecs.
Austin: U Tx Press, 1973. Rev. by E. E. Calnek, TAm, 30
(Apr 1974):554-5.

Brundage, James A. Richard Lion Heart. New York: Scribner's,
1974. Rev. by F. Frankfort, HRNB, 3(Oct 1974):9-10.

Bruneau, Philippe. Exploration Archeologique de Délos Faite par
l'Ecole Française d'Athens.... Paris: Editions E. de Boccard, 1972. Rev. by D. J. Smith, AJA, 78(Ja 1974):307-8.

_____. Mosaïques de Delos. Paris: Editions E. de Boccard,
1973. Rev. by D. J. Smith, AJA, 78(Jl 1974):307-8.

Bruneau, Thomas C. The Political Transformation of the Brazilian
Catholic Church. New York: Cam U Press, 1974. Rev. by
D. J. Mabry, HRNB, 2(Jl 1974):201-2.

Bruner, James E., Jr. The American Experience. New York:
Benziger, 1972. Rev. by J. W. Larner, Jr., HT, 7(Aug 1974):
632-3; H. S. Alexander, HT, 8(Nov 1974):127-8.

Brunholzl, Franz see Autenrieth, Johanne

Brunhouse, Robert L. In Search of the Maya: The First Archaeologists. Albuquerque: U NM Press, 1973. Rev. by M. J.
Becker, AHR, 79(Je 1974):913-14; C. Corson, AmAnt, 39(Jl
1974):517-18; R. E. W. Adams, HAHR, 54(Aug 1974):548-50.

Brunn, Gerhard. Deutschland und Brasilien, 1889-1914. Cologne:
Böhlau-Verlag, 1971. Rev. by E. Stolls, HAHR, 54(Nov 1974):
718-20.

Brusher, Joseph H. Consecrated Thunderbolt: Father Yorke of
San Francisco. Hawthorne, N.J.: Joseph F. Wagner, 1973.
Rev. by F. J. Weber, SCQ, 56(Fall 1974):309-10.

Bryan, Frank M. Yankee Politics in Rural Vermont. Hanover,
N.H.: U Press of New England, 1974. Rev. by R. M. Judd,
VH, 42(Spr 1974):170-4.

Bryant, Clifton D. and J. Gipson Wells. Deviancy and the Family.
Philadelphia: F. A. Davis, 1973. Rev. by J. W. Ivy, Crisis,
81(Ja 1974):32.

Bryant, Stella Vinson. Pioneers of Yesteryear, Pleasant Mound
"Public" Cemetery and Memorial Park, 1848-1973. Dallas:
privately printed, 1974. Rev. by H. B. Simpson, Texana, 11
(W 1974):91.

Bryant, Will. The Big Lonesome. Garden City, N.Y.: Doubleday, 1971. Rev. by P. Bonnifield, ChOk, 52(Sum 1974):255-6.

Bucchioni, Eugene and Francesco Cordasco. The Puerto Rican Experience: A Sociological Sourcebook. see Cordasco, Francesco and Eugene Bucchioni. The Puerto Rican Experience....

Buchholz, Hans-Günter and Vassos Karageorghis. Prehistoric Greece and Cyprus: An Archaeological Handbook. London: Phaidon, 1973. Rev. by F. H. Stubbings, Antiquity, 48(Sep 1974):243-4.

Buck, Lawrence P. and Jonathan W. Zophy, eds. The Social History of the Reformation. In Honor of Harold J. Grimm. Columbus, Ohio: Ohio St U Press, 1972. Rev. by B. Pullan, HJ, 17(Mar 1974):209-13; F. Fillespie, RQ, 27(Sum 1974):209-11.

Buckland, Patrick. Irish Unionism. Volume 1, The Anglo-Irish and the New Ireland, 1885-1922. New York: Barnes and Noble, 1972. Rev. by M. Waters, AHR, 79(Feb 1974):156-7; F. S. L. Lyons, History, 59(Feb 1974):131-2; A. T. Q. Stewart, History, 59(Je 1974):298.

Budhraj, Vijay Sen. Soviet Russia and the Hindustan Subcontinent. Columbia, Mo.: South Asia Books, 1973. Rev. by L. J. Williams, HRNB, 2(Mar 1974):116.

Buel, Richard, Jr. Securing the Revolution: Ideology in American Politics, 1789-1815. Ithaca, N.Y.: Cornell U Press, 1972. Rev. by L. H. Harrison, AHR, 79(Je 1974):850-1; R. H. Brown, JIH, 5(Sum 1974):163-7.

Bueler, William M. U. S. China Policy and the Problem of Taiwan. Boulder: Colorado Associated U Press, 1971. Rev. by F. H. Harrington, AHR, 79(Oct 1974):1287.

Buell, Lawrence. Literary Transcendentalism: Style and Vision in the American Renaissance. Ithaca, N.Y.: Cornell U Press, 1973. Rev. by C. Albanese, CH, 43(Je 1974):281; F. Murphy, NEQ, 47(Je 1974):304-6.

Buenker, John D. Urban Liberalism and Progressive Reform. New York: Scribner's, 1973. Rev. by D. P. Thelen, JAH, 61(Dec 1974):818-19.

Buerkle, Jack V. and Danny Barker. Bourbon Street Black: The New Orleans Black Jazzman. New York: Ox U Press, 1973. Rev. by G. A. Boeck, AHR, 79(Apr 1974):619-20; A. W. Adkins, LaH, 15(Sum 1974):307-8.

Buhite, Russell D. Patrick J. Hurley and American Foreign Policy. Ithaca, N.Y.: Cornell U Press, 1973. Rev. by J. K. Fair-

bank, AHR, 79(Feb 1974):250-1; A. E. Campbell, JAmS, 8
(Aug 1974):272-4; S. J. Kneeshaw, MiA, 56(Jl 1974):206-7;
W. W. Tozer, PHR, 43(Feb 1974):136-7.

Buitenhuis, Peter. The Grasping Imagination: The American Writings of Henry James. Toronto: U Tor Press, 1970. Rev.
by H. Daniels, JAmS, 8(Apr 1974):126-7.

Bulgaru, Maria Matilda Alexandrescu-Dersca. Nicolae Iorga: A
Romanian Historian of the Ottoman Empire. Bucharest:
Academy of Social and Political Sciences of the Socialist Re-
public of Romania, 1972. Rev. by S. D. Spector, AHR, 79
(Feb 1974):189-90; H. Inalcik, JMH, 46(Mar 1974):110-12.

Bulletin philologie et historique du comite des travaux historiques
et scientifiques. 2 vols. Paris: Bibliothèque nationale, 1972.
Rev. by P. Rycroft, EHR, 89(Ja 1974):156-7.

Bullough, D. A. and R. L. Storey, eds. The Study of Medieval
Records: Essays in Honour of Kathleen Major. Oxford:
Clarendon Press, 1971. Rev. by C. A. F. Meekings, EHR,
89(Ja 1974):147-8.

Bullough, Donald. The Age of Charlemagne. London: Paul Elek,
n.d. Rev. by P. Q., HTo, 24(Apr 1974):287-8.

Bullough, Vern L. The Subordinate Sex: A History of Attitudes
Toward Women. Urbana: U Ill Press, 1973. Rev. by G.
Lerner, AHR, 79(Oct 1974):1138-9; J. Sochen, IMH, 70(Sep
1974):269-70.

Bumsted, J. M. Henry Alline. Toronto: U Tor Press, 1971.
G. A. Rawlyk, EHR, 89(Jl 1974):671-2.

Bunche, Ralph J. The Political Status of the Negro in the Age of
F. D. R. Chicago: U Chi Press, 1973. Rev. by E. Rudwick,
AHR, 79(Je 1974):899; N. Lederer, GHQ, 58(Supp 1974):214-
15; L. Ruchames, JAH, 61(Je 1974):244; J. M. Matthews,
JSH, 40(Feb 1974):156-8; J. H. Cartwright, THQ, 33(Spr 1974):
106-8; C. E. Wynes, VMHB, 82(Ja 1974):122-3.

Bunnag, Jane. Buddhist Monk, Buddhist Layman: A Study of Urban
Monastic Organization in Central Thailand. Cambridge: Cam
U Press, 1973. Rev. by A. T. Kirsch, JAS, 33(Feb 1974):
334-5.

Burckhardt, Titus. Moorish Culture in Spain. New York: McGraw-
Hill, 1972. Rev. by T. F. Glick, HAHR, 54(May 1974):334-5.

Burdick, Charles B. Ralph H. Lutz and the Hoover Institution.
Stanford, Cal.: Hoover Institution Press, 1974. Rev. by
A. A. Ekirch, Jr., HRNB, 2(Sep 1974):256.

_____. Unternehmen Sonnenblume: Der Entschluss zum Afrika-
Feldzug. Neckargemünd: Kurt Vowinckel Verlag, 1972. Rev.
by A. W. Turney, JMH, 46(Mar 1974):162-3.

Burggraaff, Winfield J. The Venezuelan Armed Forces in Politics,
1935-1959. Columbia, Mo.: U Mo Press, 1972. Rev. by
D. H. Levine, HAHR, 54(Feb 1974) 146-8; G. E. Carl, JLAS,
6(May 1974):179-80.

Burke, John. Buffalo Bill: The Noblest Whiteskin. New York:
Putnam, 1973. Rev. by N. S. Yost, N H, 55(Sum 1974):313-
17.

Burke, Peter. Culture and Society in Renaissance Italy, 1420-1540.
London: Batsford, 1972. Rev. by J. Hook, ESR, 4(Apr 1974):
178-81.

_____, ed. A New Kind of History: From the Writings of Lu-
cien Febvre. London: Routledge and Kegan Paul, 1973. Rev.
by J. Bossy, History, 59(Je 1974):327-8.

Burkhardt, Johannes. Die Entstehung der modernen Jahrhundertrechnung. Goppingen: Alfred Kummerle, 1971. Rev. by A.
Witschi-Bernz, H & T, 13(Num 2 1974):181-9.

Burland, C. A. Montezuma: Lord of the Aztecs. London: Weidenfeld and Nicolson, 1973. Rev. by N. Hammond, Antiquity,
48(Je 1974):155.

Burnett, John, ed. Annals of Labour: Autobiographies of British
Working-Class People 1820-1920. Bloomington: Ind U Press,
1974. Rev. by R. J. Plowman, HRNB, 3(Nov/Dec 1974):26.

Burnette, Robert and John Koster. The Road to Wounded Knee.
n.p.: Bantam, 1974. Rev. by Staff, InH, 7(Spr 1974):51.

Burns, E. L. M. A Seat at the Table. Toronto/Vancouver: Clarke,
Irwin, 1972. Rev. by J. W. Holmes, CHR, 55(Je 1974):207-9.

Burns, Norman T. Christian Mortalism from Tyndale to Milton.
Cambridge, Mass.: Harvard U Press, 1972. Rev. by C. A.
Patrides, RQ, 27(Fall 1974):375-6.

Burns, Robert Ignatius. Islam Under the Crusaders: Colonial Survival in the Thirteenth-Century Kingdom of Valencia. Princeton: Prin U Press, 1974. Rev. by R. Brilliant, HRNB, 3
(Oct 1974):9.

Burns, Ruby. Josephine Clardy Fox: Traveler, Opera-Goer, Collector of Art, Benefactor. El Paso: Texas Western Press,
1973. Rev. by R. L. Davis, SWHQ, 78(Jl 1974):105-6.

Burnside, Wesley M. Maynard Dixon: Artist of the West. Provo,

Utah: BYU Press, 1972.   Rev. by E. F. Sanguinetti, JAriH,
15(Win 1974):397-8.

Burroughs, Peter.   The Canadian Crisis and British Colonial Policy,
1828-1841.   Toronto: Macmillan, 1972.   Rev. by W. Ormsby,
CHR, 55(Je 1974):189-90.

Burston, W. H.   James Mill on Philosophy and Education.   London:
Athlone, 1973.   Rev. by W. Thomas, History, 59(Je 1974):
287-9.

Burt, Jesse and Robert B. Ferguson.   Indians of the Southeast:
Then and Now.   Nashville, Tenn.:   Abingdon Press, 1973.
Rev. by M. LeBreton, ETHJ, 12(Fall 1974):75-6.

Burt, Roger, ed.   Corning Mining: Essays on the Organization of
Cornish Mines and the Cornish Mining Economy.   North Pom-
fret, VT: David & Charles, 1969.   Rev. by D. G. C. Allan,
T & C, 15(Oct 1974):633-4.

Burton, David H.   Theodore Roosevelt.   New York: Twayne, 1972.
Rev. by H. R. Grant, HT, 7(Aug 1974):637; M. I. Urofsky,
JAH, 61(Je 1974):236; D. Crosson, MiA, 56(Jl 1974):200-1.

_____.   Theodore Roosevelt and His English Correspondents: A
Special Relationship of Friends.   American Philosophical So-
ciety, The Transactions, new series, vol. 63, part 2, 1973.
Rev. by D. Crosson, MiA, 56(Jl 1974):200-1.

Burton, Robert E.   Democrats of Oregon: The Pattern of Minority
Politics, 1900-1956.   Eugene: U Ore Press, 1970.   Rev. by
R. Jensen, AHR, 79(Apr 1974):600.

Burts, Robert Milton.   Richard Irvine Manning and the Progressive
Movement in South Carolina.   Columbia, S. C.:   U SCar Press,
1974.   Rev. by D. M. McFarland, HRNB, 3(Oct 1974):6-7.

Bury, J. P. T.   Gambetta and the Making of the Third Republic.
London: Longmans, n. d.   Rev. by J. Richardson, HTo, 24
(Ja 1974):60-1.

Bush, Robert, ed.   Grace King of New Orleans: A Selection of
Her Writings.   Baton Rouge: LSU Press, 1973.   Rev. by
M. M. Sibley, CWH, 20(Je 1974):189-90; D. K. Texada, LaH,
15(Sum 1974):313-14.

Bushnell, Eleanore.   The Nevada Constitution: Origin and Growth.
Reno: U Nev Press, 1972.   Rev. by I. K. Smemo, JAH, 61
(Dec 1974):793-4.

Butler, Jon.   Religion and Witchcraft in Early American Society.
St. Charles, Mo.:   Forum Press, 1974.   Rev. by M. P. Mc-
Carthy, HT, 8(Nov 1974):109-10.

Butler, Marilyn. Maria Edgeworth: A Literary Biography. Oxford: Clarendon Press, 1972. Rev. by E. A. Smith, EHR, 89(Ja 1974):199-200.

Butlin, Robin A. see Baker, Alan R. H.

Butt, J. and I. F. Clarke, eds. The Victorians and Social Protest: A Symposium. Hamden, Conn.: Archon, 1973. Rev. by T. R. Tholfsen, AHR, 79(Feb 1974):149; P. Hollis, History, 59(Je 1974):289-90.

Butterfield, L. H. and Marc Friedlander, eds. The Adams Papers. Adams Family Correspondence. Vols. 3 and 4. Cambridge, Mass.: Belknap Press of Har U Press, 1973. Rev. by J. A. Hodge, HTo, 24(Mar 1974):209-10; D. F. Hawke, NYHSQ, 58 (Jl 1974):242-4; J. E. Cooke, PH, 41(Oct 1974):467-9; J. Hutson, WMQ-3, 31(Apr 1974):326-7.

Byers, William N. and John H. Kellom. Handbook to the Gold Fields of Nebraska and Kansas: Being a Complete Guide to the Gold Regions of the North and South Platte, and Cherry Creek. n.p.: 1859 (reprint). Rev. by D. A. Smith, CoMag, 51(Apr 1974):157-9.

Byron, Brian. Loyalty in the Spirituality of St. Thomas More. Nieuwkoop: B. De Graaf, 1972. Rev. by L. P. Fairfield, CH, 43(Sep 1974):400; J. B. Trapp, EHR, 89(Apr 1974):428-9.

Cadbury, Henry J. John Woolman in England, 1772: A Documentary Supplement. London: Friends Historical Soc., 1971. Rev. by L. Gara, PH, 41(Apr 1974):227-8.

Cadenhead, Ivie E., Jr. Benito Juárez. New York: Twayne, 1973. Rev. by T. G. Powell, HAHR, 54(Nov 1974):714-15.

Cahill, Susan and Thomas. A Literary Guide to Ireland. New York: Scribner's, 1973. Rev. by A. O Doire, E-I, 9(Spr 1974):159.

Cahm, Eric. Péguy et le nationalisme français. Paris: L'Amitié Charles Péguy, 1972. Rev. by J. M. Roberts, EHR, 89(Jl 1974):690-1; M. J. M. Larkin, History, 59(Feb 1974):155-6.

Cain, Louis P. and Paul J. Uselding, eds. Business Enterprise and Economic Change: Essays in Honor of Harold F. Williamson. Kent, Ohio: Kent St U Press, 1973. Rev. by G. D. Nash, BHR, 48(Spr 1974):120-1; R. S. Maxwell, Historian, 36(Aug 1974):739; A. M. Johnson, JAH, 61(Je 1974):148-9.

Caizzi, Bruno. L'economia lombarda durante la Restaurazione (1814-1859). Milan: Banca Commerciale Italiana, 1972. Rev. by S. B. Clough, AHR, 79(Feb 1974):182-3.

Caldwell, Malcolm and Lek Tan. Cambodia in the Southeast Asian War. New York: Monthly Review Press, 1973. Rev. by J. F. Cady, AHR, 79(Je 1974):831-2.

Caldwell, Mary French. Tennessee: The Dangerous Example; Watauga to 1849. Nashville: Aurora, 1974. Rev. by O. N. Meredith, THQ, 33(Fall 1974):345.

Caldwell, Oliver J. A Secret War: Americans in China, 1944-1945. Carbondale: So Ill U Press, 1972. Rev. by W. W. Tozer, PHR, 43(May 1974):289-90.

Calhoon, Robert McCluer. The Loyalists in Revolutionary America, 1760-1781. New York: Harcourt Brace Jovanovich, 1973. Rev. by K. Coleman, FHQ, 53(Oct 1974):207-8; G. M. Meroney, GHQ, 58(Sum 1974):291-2; C. B. Smith, HRNB, 2(Mar 1974):133; R. A. Overfield, JSH, 40(Aug 1974):462-4; F. C. Meyers, NCHR, 51(Spr 1974):232-3; R. D. Brown, NEQ, 47 (Je 1974):344-5; P. U. Bonomi, NYH, 55(Jl 1974):350-1; D. V. J. Bell, WMQ-3, 31(Jl 1974):495-6.

Calhoun, Daniel. The Intelligence of a People. Princeton, N.J.: Prin U Press, 1973. Rev. by P. A. Kalisch, AHR, 79(Je 1974):845-6; R. Welter, JAH, 61(Sep 1974):474-5; N. Harris, NYHSQ, 58(Jl 1974):239-40; R. D. Brown, WMQ-3, 31(Jl 1974): 496-8.

Calhoun, John C. The Papers of John C. Calhoun. Volume VII: 1822-1823. Ed. by W. Edwin Hemphill. Columbia: U SC Press, 1973. Rev. by J. H. Moore, NCHR, 51(Jan 1974):98-9; W. J. Fraser, Jr., SCHM, 75(Apr 1974):125-6.

Callahan, North. George Washington: Soldier and Man. New York: Morrow, 1972. Rev. by C. H. Hall, JAH, 61(Dec 1974):768-9.

Callahan, William J. Honor, Commerce and Industry in Eighteenth-Century Spain. Boston: Harvard Graduate School of Business Administration, 1972. Rev. by A. A. Sicroff, CHR, 55(Je 1974):232-4; D. Ringrose, HAHR, 54(Feb 1974):162-4.

Callaway, Joseph A. The Early Bronze Age Sanctuary at Ai. London: Bernard Quaritch, 1972. Rev. by A. E. Glock, AJA, 78(Apr 1974):187-8.

Calvert, Robert A. see Rosaldo, Renato

Calvocoressi, Peter and Guy Wint. Total War: The Story of World War II. New York: Pantheon, 1972. Rev. by E. Andrade, Jr., Historian, 36(Feb 1974):336-7.

Cambitoglou, Alexander, J. J. Coulton, Judy Birmingham and J. R. Green. Zagora I. Excavation Season 1967; Study Season

CAMARILLO 52

1968-9. Sydney: Sydney U Press, 1971. Rev. by J. M.
Davison, AJA, 78(Jl 1974):304-5.

Camarillo, Albert, ed. see Castillo, Pedro, ed.

Cameron, James K., ed. The First Book of Discipline. Edinburgh:
Saint Andrew Press, 1972. Rev. by S. A. Burrell, CH, 43
(Sep 1974):408-9.

Campbell, Charles S. From Revolution to Rapprochement: The
United States and Great Britain, 1783-1900. New York: Wiley,
1974. Rev. by W. J. Baker, HRNB, 2(May/Je 1974):158.

Campbell, Thomas M. Masquerade Peace: America's UN Policy,
1944-1945. Tallahassee: Fla St U Press, 1973. Rev. by
W. F. Kimball, JAH, 61(Dec 1974):837-9.

Camporeala, Salvatore I. Lorenzo Valla, umanesimo e teologia.
Florence: Istituto Nazionale di Studi sul Rinascimento, 1972.
Rev. by C. Trinkaus, RQ, 27(Spr 1974):43-45.

Camporesi, Cristiano. Il marxismo teorico negli USA, 1900-1945.
Milan: Feltrinelli Editore, 1973. Rev. by J. P. Diggins,
AHR, 79(Je 1974):889-90.

Canadian Public Figures on Tape. Toronto: Ontario Institute for
Studies in Education, 1972, 1973. Rev. by M. Bliss, CHR,
55(Sep 1974):323-5.

Cancian, Frank. Another Place: Photographs of a Maya Community. San Francisco: Scrimshaw, n.d. Rev. by Staff, InH,
7(Spr 1974):50.

Cannon, Carl L., ed. Scout and Ranger: Being the Personal Adventures of James Pike of the Texas Rangers in 1859-60.
New York: Da Campo, 1972. Rev. by D. L. DeBerry, JOW,
13(Apr 1974):108.

Cannon, John. Parliamentary Reform, 1640-1832. Cambridge:
Cam U Press, 1973. Rev. by J. R. Dinwiddy, History, 59
(Je 1974):283-4; W. A. Speck, JMH, 46(Sep 1974):544-6.

Canton, Dario. Elecciones y partidos políticos en la Argentina.
Historia, interpretación y balance: 1910-1966. Buenos Aires:
Siglo XXI Argentina Editores, 1973. Rev. by P. Snow, HAHR,
54(May 1974):331-2.

Cantrell, Dallas. Youngers' Fatal Blunder. San Antonio: Naylor,
1973. Rev. by P. T. Nolan, JOW, 13(Oct 1974):127.

Caponetto, Salvatore, ed. Benedetto da Mantova, Il Beneficio di
Criso con le versioni del secolo XVI. Documenti e testimoni-
anze.... Chicago: Newberry Library, 1972. Rev. by W. J.

Bouwsma, CH, 43(Sep 1974):401-2.

_____, ed. Il beneficio di Cristo. Florence and Chicago: San-
soni and the Newberry Library, 1972. Rev. by D. Hay, EHR,
89(Apr 1974):426-7.

Capps, B. S. The Fifth Monarchy Men. London: Faber & Faber,
1972. Rev. by I. Roots, EHR, 89(Ja 1974):184-5.

Capps, Benjamin. The Warren Wagontrain Raid. New York: Dail,
1974. Rev. by W. Gard, SWHQ, 78(Jl 1974):102-3.

Carageorge, Ted and Thomas J. Gilliam, eds. Proceedings of the
Gulf Coast History and Humanities Conference, Volume IV,
Gulf Coast Politics in the Twentieth Century. Pensacola, Fla.:
Historic Pensacola Preservation Board, 1973. Rev. by W. I.
Hair, FHQ, 53(Oct 1974):202-4; J. M. Richardson, LaH, 15
(Spr 1974):205-6; G. Green, SWHQ, 78(Oct 1974):224-5.

Cardenal, Ernesto. Homage to the American Indians. Baltimore:
JHU Press, 1973. Rev. by D. S. Gaus, TAm, 31(Jl 1974):
109-10.

Cardona, George, Henry M. Hoenigswald, and Alfred Senn, eds.
Indo-European and Indo-Europeans. Philadelphia: U Pa
Press, 1970. Rev. by J. H. Jasanoff, JIH, 5(Sum 1974):139-
45.

Carleton, Mark T. Politics and Punishment: The History of the
Louisiana State Penal System. Baton Rouge: LSU Press,
1971. Rev. by P. D. Jordan, AHR, 79(Oct 1974):1260-2;
J. A. Carrigan, CWH, 20(Mar 1974):78-9.

Carlisle, Rodney P. Prologue to Liberation. New York: Appleton-
Century-Crofts, 1972. Rev. by T. D. Perry, N H B, 37(Je/
Jl 1974):273.

Carmack, Robert. Quichean Civilization: The Ethnohistoric, Ethnographic, and Archaeological Sources. Berkeley: U Cal Press,
1973. Rev. by R. Wauchope, HAHR, 54(Feb 1974):165-6.

Carnicelli, D. D., ed. Lord Morley's Tryumphes of Fraunces
Petrarcke: The First English Translation of the Trionfi.
Cambridge: Harvard U Press, 1971. Rev. by J. L. Lievsay,
RQ, 27(Spr 1974):89-91.

Carpenter, Jesse Thomas. Competition and Collective Bargaining
in the Needle Trades, 1910-1967. Ithaca, N.Y.: ... Cornell

U Press, 1972. Rev. by L. Stein, AHR, 79(Feb 1974):243-4.

Carpenter, L. P. G. D. H. Cole: An Intellectual Biography. New York: Cam U Press, 1973. Rev. by L. Bisceglia, HRNB, 2 (Mar 1974):120; B. Sacks, JMH, 46(Dec 1974):715-16.

Carr, John Laurence. Robespierre. London: Constable, 1972. Rev. by N. Temple, History, 59(Feb 1974):133-4.

Carr, Lois Green and David William Jordan. Maryland's Revolution of Government, 1689-1692. Ithaca: Cornell U Press, 1974. Rev. by J. Sosin, HRNB, 2(May/Je 1974):167-8; J. C. Morton, JSH, 40(Nov 1974):643-4; M. G. Hall, MHM, 69(Fall 1974): 327-8.

Carr, Raymond, ed. The Republic and the Civil War in Spain. New York: St. Martin's, 1971. Rev. by T. Kaplan, AHR, 79(Oct 1974):1198-9.

Carr, William. Arms, Autarky and Aggression: A Study in German Foreign Policy, 1933-1939. New York: Norton, 1973. Rev. by H. A. Arnold, AHR, 79(Oct 1974):1208; T. W. Mason, History, 59(Feb 1974):152-3.

Carretero, Andrés M. Los Anchorena. Política y negocios en el siglo XIX. Buenos Aires: Ediciones de la 8a década, 1970. Rev. by M. Falcoff, HAHR, 54(Aug 1974):533-5.

Carrière, Gaston. Histoire documentaire de la Congrégation des Missionnaires Oblats de Marie-Immaculée dans l'Est du Canada. 2e Partie: Dans la Seconde Moitié du XIXe Siècle (1861-9000), Tome X. Ottawa: Editions de l'Université d'Ottawa, 1972. Rev. by M. Wade, CHR, 55(Je 1974):191-2.

Carrithers, Gale H., Jr. Donne at Sermons. Albany: St UNY Press, 1972. Rev. by W. Schleiner, RQ, 27(Fall 1974):373-5.

Carroll, Charles F. The Timber Economy of Puritan New England. Providence, R. I.: Brown U Press, 1973. Rev. by J. P. Greene, BHR, 48(Win 1974):544-5; J. Judd, T & C, 15(Jl 1974):494-6.

Carroll, Daniel B. Henri Mercier and the American Civil War. Princeton, N. J.: Prin U Press, 1971. Rev. by R. O. Curry, AHR, 79(Apr 1974):589.

Carroll, John M. Buffalo Soldiers West. Fort Collins, Colo.: Old Army Press, 1971. Rev. by L. G. Griffin, III, ChOk, 52(Sum 1974):253-4.

_____, ed. The Black Military Experience in the American West. New York: Liveright Pub Co., 1971. Rev. by W. H. Leckie,

55   CARRUTH

NDH, 41(Sum 1974):39.

Carruth, Gorton and Associates, eds. The Encyclopedia of American Facts and Dates. New York: Crowell, 1972. Rev. by
D. L. Hofsommer, JOW, 13(Apr 1974):109.

Carson, Clarence B. The Rebirth of Liberty: The Founding of the
American Republic, 1760-1800. New Rochelle, N.Y.: Arlington, 1973. Rev. by J. May, HRNB, 2(Ja 1974):66-7.

Carson, Edward. The Ancient and Rightful Customs: A History of
the English Customs Service. Hamden, Conn.: Archon, 1972.
Rev. by A. M. Burton, AHR, 79(Feb 1974):143.

Carson, Morris E. Pablo Neruda: regresó el caminante (aspectos
sobresalientes en la obra y la vida de Pablo Neruda). New
York: Plaza Mayor Ediciones, 1971. Rev. by D. A. Yates,
HAHR, 54(Aug 1974):550-1.

Carson, R. A. G., ed. Mints, Dies and Currency: Essays Dedicated to the Memory of Albert Baldwin. New York: Barnes
and Noble, 1971. Rev. by H. C. Boren, AHR, 79(Oct 1974):
1140-1.

Carsten, F. L. Revolution in Central Europe, 1918-1919. Berkeley: U Cal Press, 1972. Rev. by J. C. Campbell, AHR, 79
(Oct 1974):1212-13.

Carswell, John. From Revolution to Revolution: England, 1688-
1776. New York: Scribner's, 1973. Rev. by R. J. Sinner,
HRNB, 2(Mar 1974):119; V. M. Prince, Jr., HT, 8(Nov 1974):
112-13.

_____. Kütahya Tiles and Pottery from the Armenian Cathedral
of St. James, Jerusalem. 2 vols. Oxford: Clarendon Press,
1972. Rev. by B. Gray, Antiquity, 48(Je 1974):144-5.

Carter, Alice Clare. The Dutch Republic in Europe in the Seven
Years' War. Coral Gables, Fla.: U Miami Press, 1971.
Rev. by G. D. Homan, AHR, 79(Feb 1974):172.

Carter, Boyd G. and Mary Eileen, eds. Manuel Gutiérrez Nájera:
Escritos inéditos de sabor satírico "Plato del Día." Columbia, Mo.: U Mo Press, 1972. Rev. by J. W. Robb, HAHR,
54(Feb 1974):174-5.

Carter, Francis W. Dubrovnik (Ragusa) A Classic City-State.
New York: Seminar Press, 1972. Rev. by G. W. Hoffman,
EEQ, 8(Fall 1974):372-3.

Carter, Kathryn Turner. Stagecoach Inns of Texas. Waco, Tx.:
Texian Press, 1972. Rev. by C. G. James, ETHJ, 12(Fall
1974):81.

Carter, Paul A. The Spiritual Crisis of the Gilded Age. DeKalb:
    N Ill U Press, 1971. Rev. by W. S. Hudson, CH, 43(Sep
    1974):426.

Carter, Samuel, III. Cowboy Capital of the World: The Saga of
    Dodge City. Garden City, N. Y.: Doubleday, 1973. Rev. by
    W. B. Shillingberg, N H, 55(Sum 1974):312-3.

_____. The Siege of Atlanta, 1864. New York: St. Martin's,
    1973. Rev. by S. Sternlicht, HRNB, 2(Feb 1974):93; G. W.
    King, JSH, 40(Aug 1974):494-5.

Cartwright, William H. and Richard L. Watson, Jr., eds. The
    Reinterpretation of American History and Culture. Washing-
    ton: National Council for Social Studies, 1973. Rev. by D.
    Perkins, JAH, 61(Dec 1974):753.

Caruthers, J. Wade. American Pacific Ocean Trade: Its Impact
    of Foreign Policy and Continental Expansion, 1784-1860. New
    York: Exposition Press, 1973. Rev. by R. W. VanAlstyne,
    PHR, 43(Nov 1974):622-23.

Casares, Gabriel Tortella. Los Origenes del Capitalismo en Es-
    pana. Banca Industria y Ferrocarriles en el siglo XIX. Ma-
    drid: Editorial Tecnos, 1973. Rev. by R. W. Kern, JEH,
    34(Sep 1974):786-7.

Cash, Joseph H. Working the Homestake. Ames: Ia St U Press,
    1973. Rev. by J. R. Conlin, A & W, 16(Spr 1974):88-9;
    H. P. Hinton, AHR, 79(Je 1974):880-1; R. W. Paul, Historian,
    36(Aug 1974):783-4; W. Parker, JAH, 60(Mar 1974):1146-7;
    M. Walsh, JAmS, 8(Aug 1974):267-70; A. Probert, JOW, 13
    (Jl 1974):119-20; J. M. Dykshorn, WHQ, 5(Apr 1974):217-8.

Cash, Philip. Medical Men at the Siege of Boston, April, 1775
    April, 1776: Problems of the Massachusetts and Continental
    Armies. Philadelphia: American Philosophical Society, 1973.
    Rev. by J. H. Cassedy, NEQ, 47(June 1974):326-8.

Castillo, Carmin see Mattelart, Armand

Castillo, Leonardo see Mattelart, Armand

Castillo, Pedro and Albert Camarillo, eds. Furia y Muerte: Los
    Gandidos Chicanos. Los Angeles: U Cal, Chicano Studies
    Center, 1973. Rev. by M. T. Garcia, PHR, 43(Nov 1974):
    611-13.

Castillo F., Victor M. Estructura Economica del Sociedad Mexica.
    Mexico: Universidad Nacional Autonoma de Mexico, 1972.
    Rev. by C. Gibson, TAm, 30(Ja 1974):412.

Catalano, Pierangelo. Tribunato e resistenza. Turin: G. B.

Paravia, 1971. Rev. by H. C. Mansfield, Jr., JMH, 46(Mar 1974):130-1.

Catanach, I. J. Rural Credit and the Cooperative Movement in the Bombay Presidency, 1875-1930. Berkeley: U Cal Press, 1970. Rev. by C. J. Dewey, MAS, 8(Oct 1974):566-8.

Catlin, George. Letters and Notes on the Manners, Customs, and Conditions of North American Indians; Written During Eight Years' Travel (1832-1939) Amongst the Wildest Tribes of Indians in North America. 2 vols. New York: Dover, 1973. Rev. by B. A. Storey, CoMag, 51(Sum 1974):251.

Catton, Bruce. Gettysburg: The Final Fury. Garden City, N.Y.: Doubleday, 1974. Rev. by I. G. Blake, RKHS, 72(Oct 1974): 404-6; J. I. Robertson, Jr., NCHR, 51(Sum 1974):350-1.

Caudill, Harry M. The Senator from Slaughter County. Boston: Little, Brown, 1973. Rev. by N. L. Dawson, FCHQ, 48(Oct 1974):362-3.

Cavanagh, Gerald F. see Purcell, Theodore V.

Cecil, David. The Cecils of Hatfield House. Boston: Houghton Mifflin, 1973. Rev. by S. Harcourt-Smith, HTo, 24(Ja 1974): 59; S. W. Jackman, NEQ, 47(Je 1974):340-2.

Ceram, C. W. The First Americans: A Story of North American Archaeology. New York: Harcourt Brace Jovanovich, 1971. Rev. by T. R. Hester, AHR, 79(Apr 1974):568-9.

Cernovodeanu, P. England's Trade Policy in the Levant and Her Exchange of Goods with the Romanian Countries under the Latter Stuarts (1660-1714). Bucarest: Publishing House of the Academy of the Socialist Republic of Romania, 1972. Rev. by R. Davis, JMH, 46(Je 1974):345-6.

Cervantes' Christian Romance: A Study of Persiles u Sigismunda. Princeton: Prin U Press, 1972. Rev. by S. L. Guyler, RQ, 27(Fall 1974):355-7.

Cervenka, Zdenek. The Nigerian War 1967-1970. Frankfurt am Main: Bernard & Graefe Verlag, 1971. Rev. by A. H. M. Kirk-Greene, Africa, 44(Apr 1974):216-17.

Chadwick, John see Ventris, Michael

Chafe, William Henry. The American Woman: Her Changing Social, Economic, and Political Roles, 1920-1970. New York: Ox U Press, 1972. Rev. by J. S. Lemons, AHR, 79(Apr 1974): 604-5.

Chai, Winberg, ed. The Foreign Relations of the People's Republic of China. New York: Putnam's, 1972. Rev. by B. D. Larkin, JAS, 33(May 1974):475-6.

Chaitanya, Krishna. A History of Malayalam Literature. New Delhi: Orient Longman, 1971. Rev. by R. E. Asher, JAS, 34 (Nov 1974):254-5.

Challener, Richard D. Admirals, Generals, and American Foreign Policy, 1898-1914. Princeton, N.J.: Prin U Press, 1973. Rev. by A. T. Ford, WMH, 57(Win 1973-1974):164-5.

Chamberlain, John. The Enterprising Americans: A Business History of the United States. New York: Harper and Row, 1974. Rev. by T. V. Di Bacco, HRNB, 2(Mar 1974):131.

Chamberlin, E. R. The Fall of the House of Borgia. New York: Dial, 1974. Rev. by S. Ross, Mankind, 4(Aug 1974):60-1.

Chambers, Clarke A. Paul U. Kellogg and the Survey: Voices for Social Welfare and Social Justice. Minneapolis: U Minn Press, 1971. Rev. by A. A. Ekirch, Jr., AHR, 79(Oct 1974):1280.

Chancellor, Sir Christopher, ed. An Englishman in the American Civil War: The Diaries of Henry Yates Thompson, 1863. New York: NYU Press, 1971. Rev. by L. P. Simpson, JISHS, 67(Je 1974):357-8.

Chandler, Billy Jaynes. The History of a Family and a Community in Northeast Brazil, 1700-1930. Gainesville: U Fla Press, 1972. Rev. by W. R. Crawford, AHR, 79(Oct 1974):1296-7.

Chandler, David. The Art of Warfare on Land. n.p.: Hamlyn, n.d. Rev. by C. C. Trench, HTo, 24(Aug 1974):581.

_____. Marlborough as Military Commander. New York: Scribner's, 1973. Rev. by S. B. Baxter, AHR, 79(Apr 1974):513-14; S. E. Lehmberg, Historian, 36(Aug 1974):762; A. Bakshian, Jr., Mankind, 4(Oct 1974):65.

Chandler, David P. The Land and People of Cambodia. Philadelphia: Lippincott, 1972. Rev. by Mrs. J. M. Jacob, JAS, 33(Feb 1974):335-6.

Chang, Hao. Liang Ch'i-ch'ao and Intellectual Transition in China, 1890-1907. Cambridge, Mass.: Har U Press, 1971. Rev. by Ping-Chia Kuo, AHR, 79(Oct 1974):1233.

Chang, Chung-Li see Michael, Franz

Chang Yü-Fa. Constitutionalists of the Ch'ing Period. Taipei: Institute of Modern History..., 1971. Rev. by D. D. Buck, JAS, 33(Feb 1974):303.

Chant, J. F., A. K. L. Acheson, and M. F. J. Prachowny, eds.
Bretton Woods Revisited. see Acheson, A. K. L., J. F.
Chant, and M. F. J. Prachowny, eds. Bretton Woods Re-
visited.

Chaplin, David, ed. Population Policies and Growth in Latin America. Lexington, Mass.: D. C. Heath, 1971. Rev. by M. M.
Ortega, HAHR, 54(Feb 1974):173-4.

Chaplin, Raymond E. The Study of Animal Bones from Archaeological Sites. New York: Seminar Press, 1971. Rev. by J. L.
Angel, Archaeology, 27(Apr 1974):147,149.

Chapman, Paul H. The Man Who Led Columbus to America. Atlanta: Judson Press, 1973. Rev. by J. D. L. Holmes, ETHJ,
12(Fall 1974):74.

Chappell, Gordon S. Logging Along the Denver and Rio Grande:
Narrow Gauge Logging Railroads of Southwestern Colorado and
Northern New Mexico. Golden, Colo.: Colorado Railroad
Museum, 1971. Rev. by T. J. Noel, CoMag, 51(Win 1974):
72-5.

Charron, Pierre. Renée Kogel. Geneva: Droz, 1972. Rev. by
R. J. Knecht, History, 59(Je 1974):275.

Charvet, John. The Social Problem in the Philosophy of Rousseau.
New York: Cam U Press, 1974. Rev. by W. T. Deininger,
HRNB, 3(Nov/Dec 1974):22-3.

Chase, James S. The Emergence of the Presidential Nominating
Convention, 1789-1832. Urbana: U Ill Press, 1974. Rev.
by N. K. Risjord, ArkHQ, 33(Aut 1974):262-3.

Chase-Sardi, Miguel. La Situación Actual de los Indígenas en el
Paraguay. Asunción, Paraguay: Centro de Estudios Anthro-
pologicos de la Universidad Católica ... 1972. Rev. by D. J.
Vodarsik, TAm, 30(Ja 1974):410-11.

Chassagne, Serge. La Manufacture de Toiles Imprimees de Tourne-
Mine-Les-Angers (1752-1820): Etude d'une Enterprise et
d'une Industrie au XVIIIe siecle. Paris: Klincksieck, 1971.
Rev. by F. Jequier, BHR, 48(Win 1974):584-6.

Chatfield, Charles. For Peace and Justice. Pacifism in America,
1914-1941. Knoxville: U Tenn Press, 1971. Rev. by A. E.
Campbell, HJ, 17(Num 2 1974):443-7.

_____, ed. Peace Movements in America. New York: Schock-
en, 1973. Rev. by M. J. Yavenditti, HT, 8(Nov 1974):143.

Chatterji, Nikshoy C. Muddle of the Middle East. Volumes I and
II. New York: Humanities Press, 1973. Rev. by A. G.

Gerteiny, HRNB, 2(Apr 1974):147-8.

Chaudhuri, K. N., ed. The Economic Development of India under
    the East India Company, 1814-1858: A Selection of Contem-
    porary Writings. Cambridge: Cam U Press, 1971. Rev. by
    A. W. Heston, JAS, 33(Feb 1974):325-6.

Chaunu, Pierre. L'Espagne de Charles Quint. 2 vols. Paris:
    Société d'édition d'enseignment supérieur, 1973. Rev. by
    C. J. Bishko, HAHR, 54(May 1974):335-6.

Chavez, Fray Angelico. Origins of New Mexico Families in the
    Spanish Colonial Period.... Albuquerque: U Albuquerque,
    1973. Rev. by B. A. Glasrud, JOW, 13(Oct 1974):147-8.

Chazan, Robert. Medieval Jewry in Northern France: A Political
    and Social History. Baltimore: JHU Press, 1973. Rev. by
    C. T. Marshall, HRNB, 2(May/Je 1974):179-80.

Checkland, S. G. The Gladstones: A Family Biography, 1764-1851.
    Cambridge: Cam U Press, 1971. Rev. by J. M. Prest, EHR,
    89(Ja 1974):206-7.

Cheetham, Sir Nicolas. A Short History of Mexico. New York:
    Crowell, 1971. Rev. by N. B. Stern, JOW, 13(Jl 1974):128-
    9.

Cheetham, Russell J. see Kelley, Allen C.

Chejne, Anwar G. Muslim Spain: Its History and Culture. Min-
    neapolis: U Minn Press, 1974. Rev. by A. R. Lewis, HRNB,
    2(May/Je 1974):180-1.

Chen, John Hsueh-ming. Vietnam: A Comprehensive Bibliography.
    Metuchen, N.J.: Scarecrow, 1973. Rev. by P. T. Chau,
    JAS, 33(Feb 1974):337-8.

Chen, Phillip M. Law and Justice: The Legal System in China,
    2400 B.C. to 1960 A.D. New York: Dunellen, 1974. Rev.
    by J. W. Dardess, HRNB, 2(Feb 1974):105.

Chenery, H. B., ed. Studies in Development Planning. Cambridge,
    Mass.: Har U Press, 1971. Rev. by A. F. Ewing, JMAS,
    12(Sep 1974):507-10.

Cheney, C. R. Medieval Texts and Studies. New York: Ox U
    Press, 1973. Rev. by R. W. Pfaff, CH, 43(Sep 1974):390.

Cheney, Thomas E. The Golden Legacy: A Folk History of J.
    Golden Kimball. Santa Barbara and Salt Lake City: Pere-
    grine Smith, 1973. Rev. by P. Bailey, UHQ, 42(Spr 1974):
    197-9.

61   CHENHALL

Chenhall, Robert. Computers in Anthropology and Archeology [sic]
n. p.: International Business Machines, Branch Offices, 1971.
Rev. by D. Green, AmAnt, 39(Jl 1974):517.

Cherrington, John. Mission on the Fraser. Vancouver: Mitchell,
1974. Rev. by H. A. Fleming, JOW, 13(Jl 1974):123.

Cheshire, N. M. see Quinn, D. B.

Chesneaux, Jean. Peasant Revolts in China, 1840-1949. New York:
Norton, 1973. Rev. by E. S. Laffey, AHR, 79(Oct 1974):
1231-2.

_____. The Political and Social Ideas of Jules Verne. London:
Thames and Hudson, 1972. Rev. by E. Cahm, History, 59
(Feb 1974):136-7.

Chester, Edward W. Radio, Television and American Politics.
New York: Sheed and Ward, 1969. Rev. by S. Marcus, JAH,
61(Dec 1974):845-6.

Chevalier, Louis. Labouring Classes and Dangerous Classes in
Paris During the First Half of the Nineteenth Century. Lon-
don: Routledge and Kegan Paul, n. d. Rev. by T. J. Clark,
History, 59(Je 1974):294.

Chevallier, Raymond. Les voies Romaines. Paris: Armand Colin,
1972. Rev. by R. Agache, Antiquity, 48(Je 1974):153-4.

Chiappelli, Fredi. Studi sul linguaggio del Petrarca: La canzone
delle visioni. Fierenze: Leo S. Olschki, 1971. Rev. by
A. S. Bernardo, RQ, 27(Spr 1974):36-40.

Chibnall, Marjorie, ed. and trans. The Ecclesiastical History of
Orderic Vitalis. Volume 3: Books 5 and 6. New York: Ox
U Press, 1972. Rev. by J. K. Yost, CH, 43(Sep 1974):391-
2; D. J. A. Matthew, History, 59(Feb 1974):87-8.

_____, ed. and trans. The Ecclesiastical History of Orderic
Vitalis. Volume 4: Books 7 and 8. New York: Ox U Press,
1973. Rev. by J. K. Yost, CH, 43(Sep 1974):391-2.

Chilcote, Ronald H. The Brazilian Communist Party: Conflict and
Integration, 1922-1972. New York: Ox U Press, 1974. Rev.
by F. D. McCann, HRNB, 2(Aug 1974):223.

_____, ed. Protest and Resistance in Angola and Brazil. Berke-
ley: U Cal Press, 1972. Rev. by C. M. MacLachlan, TAm,
30(Apr 1974):559.

Childs, David. Germany Since 1918. London: Batsford, 1971.
Rev. by H. P. von Strandman, History, 59(Feb 1974):153-4.

_____ . Marx and the Marxists: An Outline of Practice and Theory. London: Ernest Benn, 1973. Rev. by J. Barber, History, 59(Je 1974):327.

Chodorow, Stanley A. Christian Political Theory and Church Politics in the Mid-Twelfth Century: The Ecclesiology of Gratian's Decretum. London: U Cal Press, 1972. Rev. by M. Wilks, History, 59(Feb 1974):90-1.

Chrimes, S. B., C. D. Ross, and R. A. Griffiths, eds. Fifteenth-Century England 1399-1509. Manchester: Manchester U Press, 1972. Rev. by J. K. McConica, CHR, 55(Je 1974):210-11; K. G. Madison, Historian, 36(May 1974):535-7; C. F. Richmond, History, 59(Feb 1974):98-9.

Christensen, Aristéa Papanicolaou and Charlotte Friis Johansen. Hama. Fouilles et Recherches de la Fondation Carlsberg, 1931-1938, III, 2.... Copenhagen: National Museum, 1971. Rev. by F. O. Waage, AJA, 78(Apr 1974):188-9.

Christensen, Mildred H. see Jones, Vincent L.

Christman, Albert B. Sailors, Scientists, and Rockets: Origins of the Navy Rocket Program and of the Naval Ordnance Test Station, Inyokern. Washington: Naval History Division, 1971. Rev. by L. H. Brune, AHR, 79(Apr 1974):607.

Christoff, Peter K. An Introduction to Nineteenth-Century Russian Slavophilism. Volume 2, I. V. Kireevskij. The Hague: Mouton, 1972. Rev. by M. Raeff, AHR, 79(Apr 1974):534-5; G. Florovsky, CH, 43(Je 1974):275-6.

Chudodeev, Yu V. see Nepomnin, O. E. and Yu V. Chudodeev, comps.

Chung, Joseph Sang-Hoon. The North Korean Economy: Structure and Development. Stanford, Cal.: Hoover Institution Press, 1974. Rev. by Y. Lim, JAS, 34(Nov 1974):237-9.

Church, William F. Richelieu and Reason of State. Princeton, N.J.: Prin U Press, 1972. Rev. A. L. Moote, AHR, 79 (Feb 1974):161-2.

Churchill, Winston S. Great Contemporaries. Chicago: U Chi Press, 1974. Rev. by J. T. Covert, HRNB, 2(Apr 1974): 139.

Churchman, Michael. The Kent School, 1922-1972. Englewood, Colo.: Kent School, 1972. Rev. by R. C. Black, III, CoMag, 51(Win 1974):66-7.

Churchward, L. G. The Soviet Intelligentsia. London: Routledge and Kegan Paul, 1973. Rev. by R. W. Pethybridge, EHR, 89 (Jl 1974):693.

Chyet, Stanley F. see Marcus, Jacob R.

Ciechanowski, Jan M. The Warsaw Rising of 1944. New York: Cam U Press, 1974. Rev. by J. Held, HRNB, 2(May/Je 1974):182.

Cieplak, Tadeusz N. Poland Since 1956. New York: Twayne, 1972. Rev. by W. J. Wagner, EEQ, 8(Fall 1974):386-7.

Cillinan, Gerald. The United States Postal Service. New York: Praeger, 1973. Rev. by R. H. Jones, Historian, 36(Aug 1974):792-3.

Cintas, Pierre. Manuel d'Archéologie Punique, I: Histoire et Archéologie Comparées; Chronologie des Temps Archaiqués de Carthage et des Villes Phéniciennes de l'Ouest. Paris: A. & J. Picard, 1970. Rev. by J. G. Pedley, Archaeology, 27(Ja 1974):68-9.

Cioranesco, George, et al. Aspects des relations russo-roumaines: Rétrospectives et orientations. Etudes. Paris: Minard, 1967. Rev. by S. Fischer-Galati, AHR, 79(Je 1974):814.

_____, et al. Aspects des relations soviéto-roumaines, 1967-1971: Sécurité européenne. Etudes. Paris: Minard, 1971. Rev. by S. Fischer-Galati, AHR, 79(Je 1974):814.

Cipolla, Carlo, ed. Instruction et developpement économique au XIXeme siecle. Padua: U Padua, 1971. Rev. by C. R. Day, T & C, 15(Jl 1974):518-20.

Cipolla, Carlo M., ed. The Fontana Economic History of Europe. Volume 1, The Middle Ages. London: Collins/Fontana Books, 1972. Rev. by K. F. Drew, AHR, 79(Apr 1974):491-2.

_____, ed. The Fontana Economic History of Europe. Volume 3. The Industrial Revolution; volume 4, The Emergence of Industrial Societies.... London: Collins/Fontana Books, 1973. Rev. by S. G. Checkland, AHR, 79(Je 1974):752-5; S. Pollard, EHR, 89(Ja 1974):125-7.

Clammer, David. The Zulu War. New York: St. Martin's, 1973. Rev. by J. A. Casada, Historian, 36(Aug 1974):744-5.

The Clamorous Malcontents: Criticisms and Defenses of the Colony of Georgia, 1741-1743. Introduced by Trevor R. Reese. Savannah, Ga.: Beehive, 1973. Rev. by M. Ready, GHQ, 58(Supp 1974):202-4.

Clark, Alan. Aces High. New York: Ballantine Books, n.d. Rev. by R. Smedley, Mankind, 4(Oct 1974):6,54.

Clark, Dennis. The Irish in Philadelphia: Ten Generations of

Urban Experience. Philadelphia: Temple U Press, 1973.
Rev. by P. Gleason, CH, 43(Sep 1974):423-4; R. A. Mohl,
JAH, 61(Dec 1974):799-800.

Clark, G. Kitson. Churchmen and the Condition of England, 1832-
1885: A Study in the Development of Social Ideas and Practice
from the Old Regime to the Modern State. London: Methuen,
1973. Rev. by R. W. Greaves, AHR, 79(Feb 1974):148-9;
B. Harrison, EHR, 89(Jl 1974):678-9; B. B. Schnorrenberg,
Historian, 36(Feb 1974):325-6; O. Anderson, History, 59(Je
1974):290.

Clark, Sir George, ed. Sir William Temple's Observations Upon
the United Provinces of the Netherlands. Oxford: Ox U Press,
1972. Rev. by H. Dunthorne, History, 59(Je 1974):275-6.

Clark, Harry. A Venture in History: The Production, Publication,
and Sale of the Works of Hubert Howe Bancroft. Berkeley:
U Cal Press, 1973. Rev. by B. Draper, CoMag, 51(Sum 1974):
257-8; J. Monaghan, JAH, 61(Je 1974):210-11; H. E. Mills,
OrHQ, 75(Mar 1974):79-80; H. M. Goodwin, Jr., PHR, 43
(May 1974):278-9.

Clark, J. Desmond. Kalambo Falls Prehistoric Site. Vol. II:
The Later Prehistoric Cultures. Cambridge: Cam U Press,
1974. Rev. by M. Posnansky, Antiquity, 48(Sep 1974):241-2.

Clark, James A. and Michel T. Halbouty. The Last Boom. New
York: Random House, 1972. Rev. by B. H. Johnson, ETHJ,
12(Fall 1974):88-9.

Clark, Peter and Paul Slack, eds. Crisis and Order in English
Towns, 1500-1700. London: Routledge and Kegan Paul, 1972.
Rev. by A. Woolrych, EHR, 89(Ja 1974):172-3; V. Pearl,
History, 59(Je 1974):265-6.

Clark, Terry Nichols. Prophets and Patrons: The French Univer-
sity and the Emergence of the Social Sciences. Cambridge,
Mass.: Har U Press, 1973. Rev. by D. Lacapra, AHR, 79
(Apr 1974):517; F. K. Ringer, JMH, 46(Dec 1974):719-22.

Clark, Thomas D. Helm Bruce, Public Defender: Breaking Louisville's Gothic Political Ring, 1905. Louisville: Filson Club,
n.d. Rev. by T. L. Wolford, FCHQ, 48(Apr 1974):189-92.

_____. Indiana University: Midwestern Pioneer. Volume II,
In Mid-Passage. Bloomington: Ind U Press, 1973. Rev. by
P. A. Graham, IMH, 70(Je 1974):180-2; D. W. Hollis, JAH,
61(Sep 1974):515-16.

_____, ed. The South Since Reconstruction. Indianapolis: Bobbs-
Merrill, 1973. Rev. by J. E. Fickle, JSH, 40(Feb 1974):153.

Clark, William Leslie and Walker D. Wyman. Charles Round Low
Cloud: Voice of the Winnebago. River Falls: U Wisc R F
Press, 1973. Rev. by F. A. O'Neil, WHQ, 5(Ja 1974):78-9.

Clarke, David L., ed. Models in Archaeology. London: Methuen,
1972. Rev. by C. Renfrew, Antiquity, 48(Je 1974):156-8;
R. M. Rowlett, Archaeology, 27(Jl 1974):212.

Clarke, I. F. see Butt, J.

Clarke, Kenneth W. Uncle Bud Long: The Birth of a Kentucky
Folk Legend. Lexington, Ky.: U Press Ky, 1973. Rev. by
D. T. Cullen, FCHQ, 48(Apr 1974):194-5; L. Anderson, RKHS,
72(Oct 1974):417-18.

Clasen, Peter-Claus. Anabaptism, a Social History, 1525-1618:
Switzerland, Austria, Moravia, South and Central Germany.
Ithaca, N.Y.: ... Cornell U Press, 1972. Rev. by B. Pul-
lan, HJ, 17(Mar 1974):209-13.

Clausner, Marlin D. Rural Santo Domingo: Settled, Unsettled, and
Resettled. Philadelphia: Temple U Press, 1973. Rev. by
B. Calder, HAHR, 54(Nov 1974):694-6.

Clay, Floyd Martin. Coozan Dudley Le Blanc: From Huey Long
to Hadacol. Gretna, La.: Pelican, 1973. Rev. by H. P.
Jones, JMiH, 36(Aug 1974):313-14; M. J. Schott, JSH, 40
(Nov 1974):674-5.

Clayton, Bruce. The Savage Ideal: Intolerance and Intellectual
Leadership in the South, 1890-1914. Baltimore: JHU Press,
1972. Rev. by H. D. Graham, AHR, 79(Feb 1974):238-9.

Cleaveland, Norman. The Morleys- Young Upstarts on the South-
west Frontier. By Norman Cleaveland with George Fitzpatrick.
Albuquerque: Calvin Horn, 1971. Rev. by L. R. Murphy,
NMHR, 49(Jl 1974):258-60.

Clebsch, William A. American Religious Thought: A History.
Chicago: U Chi Press, 1973. Rev. by P. Ramsey, CH, 43
(Sep 1974):420-1; T. D. Bozeman, JSH, 40(Aug 1974):512-13.

Clecak, Peter. Radical Paradoxes: Dilemmas of the American
Left, 1945-1970. New York: Harper and Row, 1973. Rev.
by W. L. O'Neill, JAH, 61(Sep 1974):543-4.

Clemens, Samuel L. see Marsh, Andrew J. Reports....

Clemoes, Peter, ed. Anglo-Saxon England. 1. Cambridge: Cam
U Press, 1973. Rev. by R. W. Pfaff, CH, 43(Mar 1974):97-
8; J. L. Nelson, History, 59(Feb 1974):85-6.

_____ ed. Anglo-Saxon England. 2. Cambridge: Cam U Press,

1973. Rev. by D. Whitelock, Antiquity, 48(Je 1974):162-3;
R. W. Pfaff, CH, 43(Sep 1974):389-90.

Clifford, John Garry. The Citizen Soldiers: The Plattsburg Training Camp Movement, 1913-1920. Lexington, Ky.: U Press
Ky, 1972. John W. Chambers, AHR, 79(Je 1974):892-4; J. J.
Hudson, JISHS, 67(Sep 1974):452-3; C. L. Christman, MiA,
56(Ja 1974):57-8; J. P. Finnegan, NYH, 55(Ja 1974):106-7.

Clinch, Nancy Gager. The Kennedy Neurosis. New York: Gros-
set and Dunlap, 1973. Rev. by J. M. McCarthy, Mankind, 4
(Apr 1974):65; H. Hamilton, RKHS, 72(Ja 1974):63-4.

Clissold, Stephen. Latin America: New World, Third World. New
York: Praeger, 1972. Rev. by A. B. Edwards, AHR, 79(Apr
1974):620.

Clive, John. Macaulay: The Shaping of the Historian. New York:
Knopf, 1973. Rev. by G. K. Clark, H & T, 13(Num 2 1974):
145-64; A. M. Wilson, JMH, 46(Dec 1974):688-90.

Clopton, Robert W. and Tsuin-Chen Ou, trans. and eds. John
Dewey: Lectures in China, 1919-1920. Honolulu: U Hawaii
Press, 1973. Rev. by V. N. Kobayashi, JAAS, 9(Ja & Apr
1974):109-10; C. W. Hayford, JAS, 33(Aug 1974):695-6.

Clowse, Converse D. Economic Beginnings in Colonial South Carolina, 1670-1730. Columbia, S.C.: USC Press, 1971. Rev.
by R. A. Becker, WMQ-3, 31(Jl 1974):512-13.

Coale, Ansley J. The Growth and Structure of Human Populations:
A Mathematical Investigation. Princeton, N.J.: Prin U Press,
1972. Rev. by M. A. Vinovskis, JIH, 5(Aug 1974):319-20.

Coarelli, Filippo. Rome, Monuments of Civilization. London:
Cassells, n.d. Rev. by S. Harcourt-Smith, HTo, 24(Je 1974):
433.

Coats, A. W. see Black, R. D. Collison

Cobb, Richard. Reactions to the French Revolution. Oxford: Ox
U Press, 1972. Rev. by O. Hufton, History, 59(Feb 1974):
132-3.

Coben, Stanley, ed. Reform, War, and Reaction, 1912-1932. Columbia, S.C.: USCar Press, 1973. Rev. by L. D. Hill,
GHQ, 58(Supp 1974):213.

Cochell, Shirley Holmes. Land of the Coyote. Ames: Ia St U
Press, 1972. Rev. by W. Parker, JOW, 13(Apr 1974):134;
E. Bern, NDH, 41(Fall 1974):35.

Cochran, Thomas C. American Business in the Twentieth Century.

Cambridge, Mass.: Har U Press, 1972. Rev. by L. Galam-
bos, AHR, 79(Apr 1974):598-9; G. C. Fite, JAH, 60(Mar
1974):1162-3.

Cochrane, Eric. Florence in the Forgotten Centuries, 1527-1800:
Florence and the Florentines in the Age of the Grand Dukes.
Chicago: U Chi Press, 1973. Rev. by G. Symcox, HT, 7
(Feb 1974):310; J. H. Whitfield, RQ, 27(Sum 1974):215-18.

Cockburn, J. S. A History of English Assizes, 1558-1714. Cambridge: Cambridge U Press, 1971. Rev. by A. H. Smith,
RQ, 27(Spr 1974):82-6.

Codex Vaticanus 3773 (Codex Vaticanus B), Biblioteca Apostólica
Vaticana. Vol. XXXVI. Graz, Austria: Akademische Druck-
u. Verlagsanstalt, 1972. Rev. by C. Gibson, HAHR, 54(Feb
1974):122-5.

Coffin, Tristram P. and Henning Cohen, eds. Folklore: From the
Working Folk of America. Garden City, N.Y.: Doubleday,
1973. Rev. by F. Crossen, CoMag, 51(Win 1974):76-8.

Cogan, Sara G., comp. The Jews of San Francisco and the Greater Bay Area, 1859-1919. Berkeley, Cal.: Western Jewish
History Center, 1973. Rev. by C. Wollenberg, CHQ, 53(Spr
1974):88-9.

Cohen, Daniel. Shaka: King of the Zulus. A Biography. Garden
City, N.Y.: Doubleday, 1973. Rev. by J. W. Ivy, Crisis,
81)Ja 1974):32.

Cohen, David W. and Jack P. Greene, eds. Neither Slave Nor
Free: The Freedman of African Descent in the Slave Societies
of the New World. Baltimore: JHU Press, 1972. Rev. by
G. Shepperson, JAfH, 15(Num 1 1974):170; R. S. Dunn, JAH,
60(Mar 1974):1116-17; D. R. Leet, JEH, 34(Je 1974):504-5;
D. R. Murray, JLAS, 6(May 1974):175-7.

Cohen, David William. The Historical Tradition of Busaga. Oxford: Clarendon Press, 1972. Rev. by K. Ingham, JAfH, 15
(Num 1 1974):154-6.

Cohen, Edward E. Ancient Athenian Maritime Courts. Princeton,
N.J.: Prin U Press, 1973. Rev. by J. P. Cavarnos, HRNB,
2(Apr 1974):144.

Cohen, Henning see Coffin, Tristram P.

Cohen, Henry. Business and Politics in America from the Age of
Jackson to the Civil War: The Career Biography of W. W.
Corcoran. Westport, Conn.: Greenwood, 1971. Rev. by W.
Haller, Jr., JEH, 34(Sep 1974):786-7.

Cohen, I. Bernard. Introduction to Newton's "Principia". Cambridge, Mass.: Har U Press, 1971. Rev. by A. Thackery, AHR, 79(Feb 1974):104-7; R. Olson, JMH, 46(Mar 1974):116; N. Swerdlow, JMH, 46(Mar 1974):117-19.

_____. Isaac Newton's "Philosophiae.... see Koyré, Alexandre

Cohen, Martin A., ed. The Jewish Experience in Latin America: Selected Studies from the Publications of the American Jewish Historical Society. 2 vols. New York: KTAV, 1971. Rev. by I. Bar-Lewaw, HAHR, 54(Feb 1974):120-1.

Cohen, Warren I. America's Response to China: An Interpretative History of Sino-American Relations. New York: Wiley, 1971. Rev. by B. F. Beers, AHR, 79(Oct 1974):1239-40.

Cohen, William B. Rulers of Empire: The French Colonial Service in Africa. Stanford, Cal.: Hoover Institution Press, 1971. Rev. by A. S. Trickett, Historian, 36(Aug 1974):745-8.

Cohn, Rubin G. To Judge With Justice: History and Politics of Illinois Judicial Reform. Urbana: U Ill Press, 1973. Rev. by I. Dilliard, JISHS, 67(Apr 1974):238-40.

Coldstream, J. N. Knossos: The Sanctuary of Demeter. London: ... Thames and Hudson, 1973. Rev. by R. S. Stroud, AJA, 78(Apr 1974):193-4; E. M. Varney, Antiquity, 48(Sep 1974): 239-40.

Cole, Herbert M. see Fraser, Douglas

Cole, Hubert. Fouché: The Unprincipled Patriot. London: Eyre and Spottiswoode, 1971. Rev. by J. M. J. Rogister, History, 59(Feb 1974):134.

Cole, Martin and Henry Welcome, eds. Don Pío Pico's Historical Narrative. Glendale, Cal.: Arthur H. Clark, 1973. Rev. by C. A. Hutchinson, HAHR, 54(Nov 1974):711-12.

_____, ed. see Botello, Arthur P., tr.

Cole, Robert E. Japanese Blue Collar. The Changing Tradition. Berkeley: U Cal Press, 1971. Rev. by S. Broadbridge, MAS, 8(Oct 1974):565-6.

Colección documental de la Independencia del Perú. Lima: Comisión Nacional del Sesquicentenario de la Independencia del Perú, 1971-1972. Rev. by Frank Safford, HAHR, 54(Aug 1974) 522-4.

Coleman, Peter J. Debtors and Creditors in America: Insolvency, Imprisonment for Debt, and Bankruptcy, 1607-1900. Madison: State Historical Society of Wisconsin, 1974. Rev. by T. V.

DiBacco, HRNB, 3(Oct 1974):7.

Coleman, Terry. Going to America. Garden City, N.Y.: Anchor/
Doubleday, 1973. Rev. by N. Lederer, E-I, 9(Spr 1974):152-
3; J. E. L. Robertson, RKHS, 72(Ja 1974):71-3.

Coles, Robert. The Old Ones of New Mexico. Albuquerque: U
NM Press, 1973. Rev. by C. L. Briggs, NMHR, 49(Oct 1974):
344-5.

Coletta, Paolo E. The Presidency of William Howard Taft. Lawrence: U Press Kan, 1973. Rev. by J. T. Patterson, AHR,
79(Apr 1974):601-2; G. W. McFarland, Historian, 36(Aug 1974):
788-9; J. A. Garraty, JAH, 60(Mar 1974):1162-3; L. L. Gould,
PNQ, 65(Apr 1974):89.

The Collected Writings of John Maynard Keynes. Vol. VII. The
General Theory. London: Macmillan, 1973. Rev. by P. F.
Clarke, History, 59(Je 1974):302.

_____. Vol. VIII. Treatise on Probability. London: Macmil-
lan, 1973. Rev. by P. F. Clarke, History, 59(Je 1974):302.

_____. Vol. IX. Essays in Persuasion. London: Macmillan,
1972. Rev. by P. F. Clarke, History, 59(Je 1974):302.

_____. Vol. X. Essays in Biography. London: Macmillan,
1972. Rev. by P. F. Clarke, History, 59(Je 1974):302.

_____. Vols. XIII and XIV. The General Theory and After.
London: Macmillan, 1973. Rev. by P. F. Clarke, History,
59(Je 1974):302.

Colliander, Roland, et al. Spokane Sketchbook. Seattle: U Wash
Press, 1974. Rev. by D. E. Livingston-Little, JOW, 13(Oct
1974):125.

Collier, Jane Fishburne. Law and Social Change in Zinacantan.
Stanford, Cal.: Stan U Press, 1973. Rev. by H. F. Sala-
mini, TAm, 31(Oct 1974):227-8.

Collier, John and Ira Moskowitz. American Indian Ceremonial
Dances: Navajo--Pueblo--Apache--Zuni. New York: Crown,
1972. Rev. by H. F. Dobyns, A & W, 16(Spr 1974):66-7.

Collier, Peter. When Shall They Rest? New York: Holt, Rinehart, and Winston, 1973. Rev. by Staff, InH, 7(Win 1974):51.

Collins, Chase. The Country Guide for City People. New York:
Stein and Day, n.d. Rev. by B. Hughes, Mankind, 4(Apr
1974):65.

Colonne, Guido delle. Historia Destructionis Troiae. Bloomington:

Ind U Press, 1974. Rev. by W. P. Kaldis, HRNB, 2(May/Je 1974):184.

Colvin, H. M. Building Accounts of King Henry III. New York: Ox U Press, 1971. Rev. by G. P. Cuttino, AHR, 79(Apr 1974):496-7.

Comaroff, John L., ed. The Boer War Diary of Sol T. Plaatje: An African at Mafeking. Johannesburg: Macmillan, 1973. Rev. by P. L. Bonner, JAfH, 15(Num 2 1974):341-3.

Comeaux, Malcolm L. Atchafalaya Swamp Life: Settlement and Folk Occupations, Vol. II. Baton Rouge: La St U School of Geoscience, 1972. Rev. by R. M. Crisler, LaH, 15(W 1974): 88-9.

Comfort, Howard see Oxe, August

Commager, Henry Steele, ed. Britain Through American Eyes. New York: McGraw-Hill, 1974. Rev. by W. J. Baker, HRNB, 3(Oct 1974):3; B. Clayton, WPHM, 57(Oct 1974):452-4.

Commynes, Philippe de. Memoirs: The Reign of Louis XI, 1461-83. Harmondsworth: Penguin, 1972. Rev. by P. Spufford, History, 59(Je 1974):261.

Comparato, Frank E. Books for the Millions: A History of the Men Whose Methods and Machines Packaged the Printed Word. Harrisburg, Pa.: Stackpole, 1971. Rev. by J. M. Adams, T & C, 15(Jl 1974):503-5.

Comstock, Mary and Cornelius Vermeule. Greek, Etruscan and Roman Bronzes in the Museum of Fine Arts, Boston. Greenwich, Conn.: N Y Graphic Society, 1971. Rev. by C. Rolley, AJA, 78(Ja 1974):98-9.

Conacher, J. B. The Peelites and the Party System, 1846-52. Newton Abbot, Devon: David and Charles ... 1972. Rev. by F. A. Dreyer, CHR, 55(Mar 1974):101-2; H. C. G. Matthew, EHR, 89(Apr 1974):459-60.

Conaway, James. Judge: The Life and Times of Leander Perez. New York: Knopf, 1973. Rev. by L. H. Harrison, Historian, 36(Aug 1974):782-3.

Condit, Carl W. Chicago 1910-29: Building, Planning, and Urban Technology. Chicago: U Chi Press, 1973. Rev. by C. E. Clark, Jr., HRNB, 2(Ja 1974):67; D. Hoffmann, IMH, 70(Sep 1974):265-6; J. Burchard, JAH, 61(Sep 1974):522-3; M. H. Rose, MiA, 56(Apr 1974):134-6; R. H. Baylor, T & C, 15 (Apr 1974):342-3.

_____. Chicago 1930-70: Building, Planning, and Urban

Technology. Chicago: U Chi Press, 1974. Rev. by F. I.
Olson, HRNB, 2(Jl 1974):196; W. J. Doherty, IMH, 70(Dec
1974):365-7; R. H. Baylor, T & C, 15(Apr 1974):648-9.

Confederación Perú-Boliviana, 1835-1839. Lima: Ministerio de
Relaciones Exteriores del Perú, 1972. Rev. by R. W. Delaney,
HAHR, 54(Aug 1974):531-3.

Confino, Michael. Violence dans la violence: Le débat Bakounine-
Nečaev. Paris: François Maspero, 1973. Rev. by P. Avrich,
AHR, 79(Apr 1974):536-7; J. Joll, EHR, 89(Apr 1974):459.

Conklin, Henry. Through "Poverty's Vale": A Hardscrabble Boyhood in Upstate New York, 1832-1862. Syracuse: Syr U
Press, 1974. Rev. by J. L. Wakelyn, HRNB, 2(Aug 1974):
215-16.

Connell-Smith, Gordon and Howell A. Lloyd. The Relevance of
History. London: Heinemann ..., 1972. Rev. by L. D.
Stephens, HT, 7(Feb 1974):304-5.

Connelley, Thomas Lawrence. Autumn of Glory: The Army of
Tennessee, 1862-1865. Baton Rouge: LSU Press, 1971. Rev.
by R. Hartje, AHR, 79(Oct 1974):1266-7.

_____ and Archer Jones. The Politics of Command: Factions
and Ideas in Confederate Strategy. Baton Rouge: LSU Press,
1973. Rev. by J. L. Morrison, Jr., CWH, 20(Mar 1974):
45-7; R. A. Wooster, ETHJ, 12(Spr 1974):60-1; N. D. Brown,
Historian, 36(May 1974):564-5; E. B. Long, JAH, 60(Mar
1974):1133-4; H. Bridges, JSH, 40(Feb 1974):146-8; R. M.
McMurry, NCHR, 51(Ja 1974):104-5; R. H. Johnson, III,
VMHB, 82(Apr 1974):211-13.

Connor, Seymour V. and Odie B. Faulk. North America Divided:
The Mexican War, 1846-1848. New York: Ox U Press, 1971.
Rev. by S. R. Ross, AHR, 79(Je 1974):862.

_____. Water for the Southwest. see Baker, T. Lindsay

Connors, Richard J. A Cycle of Power: The Career of Jersey
City Mayor Frank Hague. Metuchen, N.J.: Scarecrow, 1971.
Rev. by S. J. Mandelbaum, AHR, 79(Oct 1974):1279-80.

Conquest, Robert. The Great Terror: Stalin's Purge of the Thirties. New York: Collier, 1973. Rev. by R. D. Warth,
RKHS, 72(Ja 1974):82-4.

_____. V. I. Lenin. New York: Viking, 1972. Rev. by R.
Thompson, AHR, 79(Apr 1974):543-5.

Conrad, Agnes C., ed. see Gast, Ross H.

Conrad, Glenn R., ed. see Allain, Mathé

Conrad, Robert. The Destruction of Brazilian Slavery, 1850-1888.
     Berkeley: U Cal Press, 1972. Rev. by E. V. da Costa,
     HAHR, 54(Feb 1974):140-4; D. R. Murray, JLAS, 6(May 1974):
     175-7; T. D. Schoonover, JSH, 40(May 1974):311-12; A. J. R.
     Russell-Wood, TAm, 31(Jl 1974):111-13.

Conrotto, Eugene L. Miwok Means People: The Life and Fate of
     the Native Inhabitants of the California Gold Rush Country.
     Fresno, Cal.: Valley Publishers, 1973. Rev. by L. J. Bean,
     CHQ, 53(Sum 1974):185-6; Staff, InH, 7(Win 1974):51; F. J.
     Johnston, JOW, 13(Ja 1974):150; S. D. Beckham, WHQ, 5(Jl
     1974):347-8.

Conroy, Hilary and T. Scott Miyakawa, eds. East Across the Pa-
     cific: Historical and Sociological Studies of Japanese Immigra-
     tion and Assimilation. Santa Barbara, Cal.: Clio, 1972.
     Rev. by D. D. Johnson, AHR, 79(Oct 1974):1240-1.

Constable, G. and B. Smith, eds. and trans. The Orders and
     Callings of the Church. Oxford: Clarendon Press, 1972
     Rev. by M. D. Knowles, EHR, 89(Ja 1974):151-2; R. Hill,
     History, 59(Feb 1974):89.

Constantiniu, Florin. Agrarian Relations in Wallachia in the 18th
     Century. Bucharest: Editura Academiei Republicii Socialiste
     România, 1972. Rev. by S. Fischer-Galaţi, AHR, 79(Apr
     1974):530.

_____. Relatile agrare din tara Românească în secolul al XVIII-
     lea. Bucharest: Editura Academiei Republicii Socialiste Ro-
     mânia, 1972. Rev. by J. Tucker, JMH, 46(Je 1974):369-71.

Conte, Carmelo. Il Sudan come nazione. Milan: Guiffrè, 1970.
     Rev. by G. N. Sanderson, Africa, 44(Apr 1974):217.

The Contemporary Scientific-Technical Revolution. Moscow: Nauka,
     1970. Rev. by S. Lieberstein, T & C, 15(Apr 1974):354-6.

Conwell, Russell H. Magnolia Journey: A Union Veteran Revisits
     the Former Confederate States. University, Ala.: U Ala
     Press, 1974. Rev. by S. F. Roach, CWH, 20(Sep 1974):285-
     6; J. E. Sefton, HRNB, 2(Aug 1974):218; A. W. Trelease,
     NCHR, 51(Sum 1974):344-5.

Conyngham, William J. Industrial Management in the Soviet Union:
     The Role of the CPSU in Industrial Decision-Making, 1917-
     1970. Stanford, Calif.: Hoover Inst. Press, 1973. Rev. by
     L. Lieberstein, T & C, 15(Ja 1974):121-2.

Cook, Adrian. The Armies of the Streets: The New York City
     Draft Riots of 1863. Lexington, Ky.: U Press Ky, 1974.

Rev. by R. J. Imholt, CWH, 20(Sep 1974):266-7; R. Lane, JAH, 61(Dec 1974):783-4.

Cook, Blanche Wiesen. Dwight David Eisenhower: Antimilitarist in the White House. St. Charles, Mo.: Forum Press, 1973. Rev. by M. P. McCarthy, HT, 8(Nov 1974):109-10.

Cook, Cecil see Rehder, Denny

Cook, Harold E. Shaker Music: A Manifestation of American Folk Culture. Lewisburg, Pa.: Bucknell U Press, 1973. Rev. by M. W. Clarke, FCHQ, 48(Oct 1974):363-5.

Cook, J. M. The Troad. An Archaeological and Topographical Study. Oxford: Ox U Press, 1973. Rev. by J. L. Caskey, AJA, 78(Jl 1974):303-4.

Cook, Richard I. Jonathan Swift as a Tory Pamphleteer. Seattle: U Wash Press, 1967. Rev. by S. N. Bogorad, E-I, 9(Spr 1974):153-5.

Cook, Robert M. Greek Art: Its Development, Character and Influence. New York: Farrar, Strauss, Giroux, 1972. Rev. by I. K. Raubitschek, AJA, 78(Ja 1974):95-6; D. G. Mitten, Archaeology, 27(Oct 1974):284.

Cook, Sherburne F. and Woodrow Borah. Essays in Population History: Mexico and the Caribbean. Berkeley: U Cal Press, 1971. Rev. by R. Carr, EHR, 89(Apr 1974):472.

Cook, Warren L. Flood Tide of Empire: Spain and the Pacific Northwest, 1543-1819. New Haven, Conn.: Yale U Press, 1973. Rev. by C. R. Arena, AHR, 79(Apr 1974):569-70; P. Rodriguez, CoMag, 51(Apr 1974):161-3; C. A. Hutshinson, HAHR, 54(Aug 1974):507-8; D. B. Quinn, JAmS, 8(Aug 1974):261-2; I. W. Engstrand, JOW, 13(Apr 1974):127-8; W. M. Mathes, NMHR, 49(Ja 1974):79-81; B. E. Bobb, PHR, 43(May 1974):263-4; D. C. Cutter, WHQ, 5(Apr 1974):187-8.

Cooke, A. M. A History of the Royal College of Physicians of London. Oxford: Ox U Press, 1972. Rev. by R. S. Roberts, History, 59(Je 1974):335-6.

Cooke, James J. New French Imperialism, 1880-1910: The Third Republic and Colonial Expansion. Hamden, Conn.: Archon, 1973. Rev. by J. E. Freifort, Historian, 36(Aug 1974):757.

Cooling, Benjamin Franklin. Benjamin Franklin Tracy: Father of the Modern American Fighting Navy. Hamden, Conn.: Archon, 1973. Rev. by G. T. Edwards, CWH, 20(Je 1974):186-8; R. W. Turk, JAH, 61(Dec 1974):802-3; J. G. Clifford, NYH, 55(Jl 1974):357-8.

Cooper, Arthur, trans. <u>Li Po and Tu Fu.</u> London: Penguin, 1973.
Rev. by K. C. Leung, JAS, 33(Feb 1974):295-6.

Cooper, J. P., ed. <u>Wentworth Papers, 1597-1628.</u> London: Royal
Historical Society, 1973.   Rev. by L. Stone, AHR, 79(Je 1974):
781-3; G. E. Aylmer, EHR, 89(Apr 1974):387-9.

————. <u>see</u> Thirsk, Joan

Cooper, Wayne, ed. <u>The Passion of Claude McKay: Selected Po-</u>
<u>etry and Prose,</u> 1912-1948. New York: Schocken, 1973. Rev.
by D. G. Nielson, JAH, 61(Sep 1974):516-17.

Cope, Robert S. <u>Carry Me Back: Slavery and Servitude in Seven-</u>
<u>teenth-Century Virginia.</u> Pikeville, Ky.:   Pikeville College
Press, ... 1973. Rev. by L. S. Butler, JSH, 40(May 1974):
294-5.

Copleston, F. C. <u>A History of Medieval Philosophy.</u> London:
Methuen, 1972. Rev. by M. Wilks, History, 59(Feb 1974):
83-4.

Coppola, Carlo, Surjit S. Dulai and C. M. Naim, eds. <u>Journal of</u>
<u>South Asian Literature: Fall and Winter,</u> 1973. East Lansing:
Mich St U ... 1973. Rev. by R. O. Swan, JAS, 34(Nov 1974):
253-4.

Cordasco, Francesco and Eugene Bucchioni. <u>The Puerto Rican Ex-</u>
<u>perience: A Sociological Sourcebook.</u> Totowa, N.J.: Little-
field, Adams & Co., 1973. Rev. by L. E. Agrait, HAHR,
54(Feb 1974):157-9.

Corder, Jim W. <u>More Than a Century.</u> Ft. Worth: Tx. Christian
U Press, 1973. Rev. by H. B. Simpson, Texana, 11(W 1974):
91.

Cordier, Andrew W. and Wilder Foote, eds. <u>Public Papers of the</u>
<u>Secretaries-General of the United Nations.</u> Vol. III. <u>Dag</u>
<u>Hammarskjöld, 1956-1957.</u> New York: Columbia U Press,
1973. Rev. by J. F. Green, HRNB, 2(Feb 1974):103; W. F.
Kuehl, JAH, 61(Sep 1974):442-3.

Córdova, Arnaldo. <u>La ideología de la Revolución Mexicana.</u> Mexico: Ediciones Era, 1973. Rev. by L. B. Hall, HAHR, 54(May
1974):323-4.

Corning, Howard McKinley. <u>Willamette Landings: Ghost Towns of</u>
<u>the River.</u> Portland, Ore.: Ore Hist Soc, 1973. Rev. by
G. T. Edwards, PNQ, 65(Jl 1974):150-1.

Cortada, James W. <u>United States-Spanish Relations, Wolfram and</u>
<u>World War II.</u> Barcelona: Manuel Pareja, 1971. Rev. by
L. L. Cummins, Historian, 36(Aug 1974):791-2.

Cortner, Richard C. The Jones and Laughlin Case. New York:
    Knopf, 1970. Rev. by J. Teaford, AHR, 79(Oct 1974):1257-
    8; J. G. Rayback, JAH, 61(Je 1974):245-6.

Coser, Lewis A. Greedy Institutions: Patterns of Undivided Com-
    mitment. New York: Free Press, 1974. Rev. by W. J.
    Gilmore, HRNB, 2(Jl 1974):207-8.

Cotner, Robert C., et al. Texas Cities and the Great Depression.
    Austin: Texas Memorial Museum, 1973. Rev. by D.
    McComb, ETHJ, 12(Fall 1974):89-90; B. A. Brownell, JAH,
    61(Sep 1974):527-8; I. M. May, Jr., JSH, 40(May 1974):322-
    3.

Cotran, Eugene. Restatement of African Law: The Law of Mar-
    riage and Divorce: Kenya (Vol I). London: Sweet and Max-
    well, 1968. Rev. by G. Ferraro, Africa, 44(Apr 1974):205-
    6.

Coulter, E. Merton. Daniel Lee, Agriculturist: His Life North
    and South. Athens, Ga.: U Ga Press, 1972. Rev. by C. O.
    Cathey, AHR, 79(Je 1974):865.

Coulter, Wayne Burns. Vermont Obsolete Notes and Script. Iola,
    Wisc.: Krause, 1972. Rev. by A. N. Nuquist, VH, 42(Spr
    1974):177-9.

Coulton, J. J. see Cambitoglou, Alexander

Council on Economic Priorities. The Price of Power: Electric
    Utilities and the Environment. Cambridge, Mass.: MIT Press,
    1973. Rev. by T. A. Camp, T & C, 15(Ja 1974):127-9.

Cowan, L. Gray. The Cost of Learning: The Politics of Primary
    Education in Kenya. New York: Columbia U Teachers Col-
    lege Press, 1970. Rev. by J. Adwere-Boamah, JMAS, 12
    (Je 1974):349-52.

Cowdrey, H. E. J. The Epistolae Vagantes of Pope Gregory VII.
    Oxford: Clarendon Press, 1972. Rev. by E. John, EHR, 89
    (Jl 1974):655-6.

Cowley, Malcolm. A Second Flowering, Works and Days of the Lost
    Generation. New York: Viking, 1973. Rev. by F. C. Mc-
    Laughlin, WPHM, 57(Oct 1974):458-61.

Cox, Joseph W. Champion of Southern Federalism: Robert Goodloe
    Harper of South Carolina. Port Washington, N.Y.: Kennikat,
    1972. Rev. by B. Wyatt-Brown, AHR, 79(Je 1974):854-5.

Cox, Virginia D. and Willis T. Weathers. Old Houses of King and
    Queen County, Virginia. Richmond: Whitter and Shepperson,
    1973. Rev. by V. Dabney, VMHB, 82(Oct 1974):503-4.

Coy, Owen C. California County Boundaries. Berkeley: Cal Historical Commission; Fresno, Cal.: Valley Publishers, 1973.
Rev. by W. W. Corday, JOW, 13(Apr 1974):118.

Cracraft, James. The Church Reform of Peter the Great. Stanford, Cal.: Stan U Press, 1971. Rev. by A. Blane, AHR,
79(Feb 1974):197-8.

Crane, Diana. Invisible Colleges: Diffusion of Knowledge in Scientific Communities. Chicago: U Chi Press, 1972. Rev. by
N. W. Storer, T & C, 15(Ja 1974):139-42.

Crane, Robert I. A History of South Asia. Washington: American
Historical Assn., 1973. Rev. by A. Lipski, HT, 7(Feb 1974):
305-6.

Crane, Silvia E. White Silence: Greenough, Powers and Crawford,
American Sculptors in the Nineteenth-Century Italy. Coral
Gables, Fla.: U Miami Press, 1972. Rev. by G. Proske,
NYHSQ, 58(Ja 1974):75-7.

Cranston, Fumiko E. and Edwin A. see Rosenfield, John M.

Crapanzano, Vincent, comp. The Fifth World of Forster Bennett:
Portrait of a Navajo. New York: Viking, 1972. Rev. by
H. F. Dobyns, JAriH, 15(Sum 1974):194-5.

Crapol, Edward P. America for Americans: Economic Nationalism
and Anglophobia in the Late Nineteenth Century. Westport,
Conn.: Greenwood, 1973. Rev. by R. H. Werking, BHR, 48
(Sum 1974):264-5; W. J. Baker, HRNB, 2(Ja 1974):59; P. C.
Nagel, JAH, 61(Sep 1974):503-4; B. Perkins, PHR, 43(Aug
1974):434-5; W. W. Savage, Jr., WHQ, 5(Oct 1974):477-8.

Crary, Katherine S., ed. The Price of Loyalty: Tory Writings
from the Revolutionary Era. New York: McGraw-Hill, 1973.
Rev. by G. M. Meroney, FHQ, 53(Jl 1974):81-3; J. Sosin,
IMH, 70(Mar 1974):82-3; L. W. Seegers, NCHR, 51(W 1974):
112-13; A. Oliver, NYHSQ, 58(Apr 1974):151-2; L. R. Gerlach, RKHS, 72(Apr 1974):183-5.

Crathorne, Nancy. Tennant's Stalk: The Story of the Tennants of
the Glen. London: Macmillan, 1973. Rev. by K. H. Wolff,
BHR, 48(Win 1974):583-4.

Crawford, Ann Fears and Jack Keever. John B. Connally: a Portrait in Power. Austin: Jenkins Pub. Co., 1973. Rev. by
H. L. Klevar, SWHQ, 78(Oct 1974):225-6.

Crawford, Charles W., ed. Cal Alley. Memphis: Memphis St U
Press, 1973. Rev. by J. S. Chase, ArkHQ, 33(Aut 1974):263-
5; J. C. Vinson, GHQ, 58(Sum 1974):295-6; T. H. Baker,
JMiH, 36(Aug 1974):315-17; C. O. Bissell, THQ, 33(Spr 1974):
103-5.

Creare, A. E. A Word-Index to the Poetic Works of Rousard.
    Leeds: W. S. Maney, 1972. Rev. by I. Silver, RQ, 27(Sum
    1974):235-7.

Creigh, Dorothy Weyer. Adams County. 2 vols. Hastings, Neb.:
    Adams County-Hastings Centennial Commission, 1972. Rev.
    by H. E. Socolofsky, JAH, 60(Mar 1974):1144-5.

Creighton, Wilbur F., Jr. A Page From Nashville's History: The
    Foster-Creighton Story. Nashville: the author, 1974. Rev.
    by J. G. Shahlman, THQ, 33(Fall 1974):348-9.

Cripe, Helen. Thomas Jefferson and Music. Charlottesville: U
    Press Va, 1974. Rev. by C. Covey, JSH, 40(Nov 1974):648-
    9; J. W. Molnar, VMHB, 82(Oct 1974):499-500.

Crocker, Mary Wallace. Historic Architecture in Mississippi.
    Jackson: U and Coll Press Miss, 1973. Rev. by J. R.
    Skates, JMiH, 36(Nov 1974):387-8.

Crockett, David. A Narrative of the Life of David Crockett of the
    State of Tennessee. Knoxville: U Tenn Press, 1973. Rev.
    by E. M. Coffman, RKHS, 72(Jl 1974):285-7; R. E. Dalton,
    THQ, 33(Spr 1974):102-3.

Cronon, E. David, ed. Great Lives Observed: Marcus Garvey.
    Englewood Cliffs, N.J.: Prentice-Hall, 1973. Rev. by G. E.
    Osborne, Crisis, 81(Nov 1974):317-18; J. J. Jackson, His-
    torian, 36(Aug 1974):779; J. A. Hodges, HRNB, 2(Mar 1974):
    129; W. H. Daniel, HT, 8(Nov 1974):131-2.

Crosby, Alfred W., Jr. The Columbian Exchange: Biological and
    Cultural Consequences of 1492. Westport, Conn.: Greenwood,
    1972. Rev. by R. Chardkoff, ETHJ, 12(Spr 1974):77-8.

Crosby, Sumner McK. The Apostle Bas-Relief at Saint-Denis. New
    Haven, Conn.: Yale U Press, 1972. Rev. by J. D. Brady,
    AHR, 79(Oct 1974):1169.

Cross, Anthony, ed. Russia Under Western Eyes, 1517-1825. Lon-
    don: Elek, 1971. Rev. by M. S. Anderson, ESR, 4(Ja 1974):
    89-91.

Cross, Frank Moore. Canaanite Myth and Hebrew Epic: Essays in
    the History of the Religion of Israel. Cambridge, Mass.:
    Har U Press, 1973. Rev. by C. H. Gordon, AHR, 79(Oct
    1974):1149.

Cross, Michael and Robert Bothwell, eds. Policy by Other Means:
    Essays in honour of C. P. Stacey. Toronto/Vancouver:
    Clark, Irwin, 1972. Rev. by J. W. Holmes, CHR, 55(Je
    1974):187-8.

Crossland, R. A. and Ann Birchall, eds. Bronze Age Migration in the Aegean. Totowa, N.J.: Rowman and Littlefield, 1973. Rev. by J. Rutter, Archaeology, 27(Oct 1974):283.

Crossley, Robert N. Luther and the Peasants' War: Luther's Actions and Reactions. New York: Exposition, 1974. Rev. by D. J. Wilcox, HRNB, 3(Nov/Dec 1974):31.

Crossman, Carl L. The China Trade: Export Paintings, Furniture, Silver and Other Objects. Princeton, N.J.: Pyne, 1972. Rev. by R. B. Haas, AHR, 79(Je 1974):840-1.

Crowder, Michael. Revolt in Bussa: A Study of British "Native Administration" in Nigerian Bargu, 1902-1935. London: Faber and Faber, 1973. Rev. by D. C. Dorward, JAfH, 15 (Num 3 1974):511-13.

_____ and J. F. Ade Ajayi, eds. The History of West Africa, Volume I. see Ajayi, J. F. Ade and Michael Crowder, eds. The History of West Africa....

_____. History of West Africa. Vol. II see Ajayi, J. F. A.

Crowell, Pamela A. see Tuohy, Donald R.

Crowley, F. K. Forrest, 1847-1918. Volume 1, 1847-91: Apprenticeship to Premiership. St. Lucia: U Queensland Press, 1971. Rev. by S. C. McCulloch, AHR, 79(Apr 1974):561-2.

Crowson, P. S. Tudor Foreign Policy. New York: St. Martin's, 1973. Rev. by S. E. Lehmberg, HRNB, 2(Apr 1974):140.

Crucial American Elections: Symposium Presented at the Autumn General Meeting of the American Philosophical Society, November 10, 1972. Memoirs of the American Philosophical Society, Volume 99. Philadelphia: American Philosophical Society, 1973. Rev. by J. M. Belohlavek, JSH, 40(Aug 1974): 473-4; G. B. Tindall, NCHR, 51(Sum 1974):353-4.

Cruden, Robert. The War that Never Ended: The American Civil War. Englewood Cliffs, N.J.: Prentice-Hall, 1973. Rev. by C. P. Roland, CWH, 20(Je 1974):157-9.

Crummey, Donald. Priests and Politicians: Protestant and Catholic Missions in Orthodox Ethiopia, 1830-1868. Oxford: Clarendon Press, 1972. Rev. by T. Tamrat, JAfH, 15(Num 1 1974):156-8.

Cuff, Robert D. The War Industries Board: Business-Government Relations During World War I. Baltimore: JHU Press, 1973. Rev. by R. F. Himmelberg, JAH, 60(Mar 1974):1165-6.

Culbert, T. Patrick, ed. The Classic Maya Collapse. Albuquerque:

U NM Press, 1973. Rev. by D. M. Pendergast, HAHR, 54 (May 1974):336-7.

Cullen, L. M. An Economic History of Ireland Since 1660. London: Batsford, 1972. Rev. by C. O. Gráda, JEH, 34(Je 1974):505-7.

Cullinan, Gerald. United States Postal Service. New York: Praeger, 1973. Rev. by R. H. Jones, Historian, 36(Aug 1974): 792-3.

Culmsee, Carlton. Utah's Black Hawk War: Lore and Reminiscences of Participants. Logan: Utah St U Press, 1973. Rev. by G. C. Thompson, UHQ, 42(Fall 1974):386-7.

Culotta, Charles A. Respiration and the Lavoisier Tradition: Theory and Modification, 1777-1850. Philadelphia: American Philosophical Society, 1972. Rev. by F. L. Holmes, AHR, 79(Je 1974):755.

Culp, Edwin D. Stations West, the Story of the Oregon Railways. Caldwell, Idaho: Caxton, 1972. Rev. by V. G. Ferriday, OrHQ, 75(Mar 1974):85-6.

Cumberland, Charles C. Mexican Revolution: The Constitutionalist Years. Austin: U Tx Press, 1972. Rev. by H. E. Davis, AHR, 79(Feb 1974):253-4; W. H. Beezley, TAm, 30(Ja 1974): 420-1.

Cumming, John. A Guide for the Writing of Local History. Lansing, Mich.: American Revolution Bicentennial Commission, 1974. Rev. by J. H. Moore, AmArc, 37(Jl 1974):463-4.

Cummins, D. Duane and William G. White. The American Frontier. New York: Benziger, 1972. Rev. by J. W. Larner, Jr., HT, 7(Aug 1974):632-3; H. S. Alexander, HT, 8(Nov 1974):127-8.

_____ and _____. The Origins of the Civil War. New York: Benziger, 1972. Rev. by J. W. Larner, Jr., HT, 7(Aug 1974):632-3; H. S. Alexander, HT, 8(Nov 1974): 127-8.

Cunliffe, Barry. The Regni. London: Duckworth, 1973. Rev. by J. S. Wacher, Antiquity, 48(Mar 1974):76-7.

Cunliffe, Marcus. The Age of Expansion, 1848-1917. London: Weidenfeld and Nicolson, n.d. Rev. by J. Richardson, HTo, 24(Je 1974):437-8.

_____. Soldiers and Civilians: The Martial Spirit in America, 1775-1865. New York: Free Press, 1973. Rev. by H. F. Rankin, HRNB, 2(May/Je 1974):160.

Cunningham, Robert E. Perry, Pride of the Prairie. Stillwater:
Frontier Printers, 1973. Rev. by C. N. Tyson, ChOk, 52
(Sum 1974):251.

Curato, Federico, ed. Le ralazione diplomatiche fra il governo
provvisorio siciliano e la Francia (31 marzo 1848-18 aprile
1849).... Rome: Istituto Storico Italiano ... 1971. Rev.
by D. Koenig, AHR, 79(Je 1974):810-11; A. Ramm, EHR, 89
(Ja 1974):214-15.

_____, ed. Le relazioni diplomatiche fra il governo provvisorio
sicilano e la Gran Bretagna (14 aprile 1848-10 aprile 1849)....
Rome: Istituto Storico Italiano ... 1971. Rev. by D. Koenig,
AHR, 79(Je 1974):810-11.

_____, ed. Le relazioni diplomatiche fra la Gran Bretagna e il
Regno di Sardegna. First Series, 1814-1830. ... Rome: Is-
tituto Storico Italiano ... 1971. Rev. by D. Koenig, AHR, 79
(Je 1974):810-11.

Curran, Stuart and Joseph A. Wittreich, eds. Blake's Sublime Allegory: Essays on the Four Zoas, Milton, Jerusalem. Madison: U Wis Press, 1973. Rev. by M. P. Baine, GR, 28
(Spr 1974):146-7.

Current-Garcia, Eugene, ed. Shem, Ham and Japheth: The Papers
of W. O. Tuggle, Comprising His Indian Diary, Sketches and
Observations, Myths and Washington Journal, in the Territory
and at the Capital, 1879-1882. Athens, Ga.: U Ga Press,
1973. Rev. by Editor, AI, 42(Win 1974):235; W. W. Savage,
Jr., ChOk, 52(Sum 1974):262; J. Jelen, ETHJ, 12(Spr 1974):
67-8; A. R. Sunseri, JAH, 61(Je 1974):217.

Currey, Cecil B. Code Number 72/Ben Franklin: Patriot or Spy?
Englewood Cliffs, N.J.: Prentice-Hall, 1972. Rev. by R. B.
Morris, AHR, 79(Apr 1974):573-4; F. McDonald, WMQ-3, 31
(Ja 1974):150-2.

Curry, Lerond. Protestant-Catholic Relations in America: World
War I through Vatican II. Lexington, Ky.: U Press Ky, 1972.
Rev. by R. M. Miller, AHR, 79(Je 1974):883-4.

Curtin, Philip D., ed. Africa and the West: Intellectual Responses
to European Culture. Madison: U Wis Press, 1972. Rev. by
J. Sales, CH, 43(Je 1974):277-8.

Curtiss, Richard D. Thomas E. Williams & the Fine Arts Press.
Los Angeles: Dawson's Book Shop, 1973. Rev. by W. Ritchie,
SCQ, 56(Fall 1974):310-11.

Cutten, George Barton. Silversmiths of North Carolina, 1696-1850.
Revised by Mary Reynolds Peacock. Raleigh: North Carolina
Division of Archives and History, 1973. Rev. by J. Bivins,

Jr., NCHR, 51(Sum 1974):334-5.

Cuttino, G. P. English Diplomatic Administration, 1259-1339. Oxford: Clarendon Press, 1971. Rev. by F. A. Cazel, Jr.,
Historian, 36(Aug 1974):740-1.

Cuyler, Louise. The Emperor Maximilian I and Music. London:
Oxford U Press, 1973. Rev. by M. Picker, RQ, 27(Spr
1974):45-7.

Cwiekowski, Frederick J. The English Bishops and the First Vatican Council. Louvain: Publications Universitaires de Louvain,
1971. Rev. by J. L. Altholz, CH, 43(Je 1974):274.

D'Addario, Arnaldo. Aspetti della Controriforma a Firenze. Rome:
the Ministero, 1972. Rev. by C. K. Pullapilly, AHR, 79(Feb
1974):181-2; A. D. Wright, EHR, 89(Apr 1974):438.

Dahm, Bernard. History of Indonesia in the Twentieth Century.
London: Pall Mall, 1971. Rev. by A. Short, History, 59
(Je 1974):324.

Dahmus, Joseph. Seven Medieval Queens. Garden City, N. Y.:
Doubleday, 1972. Rev. by J. T. Rosenthal, AHR, 79(Oct 1974):
1163.

Daim, Wilfried. Christianity, Judaism and Revolution. n. p.:
Frederick Ungar, n. d. Rev. by J. Hitchcock, Commentary,
58(Nov 1974):92, 94, 96.

Dakin, D. Documents on British Foreign Policy. see Medlicott,
W. N.

Dakin, Douglas. The Greek Struggle for Independence, 1821-1833.
Berkeley: U Cal Press, 1973. Rev. by L. S. Stavrianos,
AHR, 79(Feb 1974):190-2; W. St. Clair, ESR, 4(Apr 1974):
185-7.

Dalven, Rae. Anna Comnena. New York: Twayne, 1972. Rev.
by C. M. Brand, AHR, 79(Je 1974):777.

Dalzell, Robert F., Jr. Daniel Webster and the Trial of American
Nationalism, 1843-1852. Boston: Houghton Mifflin, 1973. Rev.
by P. C. Nagel, JSH, 40(Feb 1974):140-1; J. L. Crouthamel,
NYH, 55(Apr 1974):243-5; S. Penney, NYHSQ, 58(Apr 1974):
156-8.

Damachi, Ukandi Godwin. Nigerian Modernization: The Colonial
Legacy. New York: Third Press, Joseph Okpaku, 1972.
Rev. by H. I. Ajegbu, JMAS, 12(Sep 1974):496-8.

Dane, Hendrik. Die wirtschaftlichen Beziehungen Deutchlands zu
Mexiko und Mittelamerika im 19. Jahrhundert. Köln: Böhlau

Verlag, 1971. Rev. by T. Schoonover, TAm, 31(Jl 1974):
119-20.

Danelski, David J. and Joseph S. Tulchin, eds. The Autobiographical Notes of Charles Evans Hughes. Cambridge, Mass.: Har
U Press, 1973. Rev. by E. W. Tucker, AHR, 79(Je 1974):
896-7.

Daniel, Pete. The Shadow of Slavery: Peonage in the South 1901-
1969. Urbana: U Ill Press, 1972. Rev. by A. T. Gilmore,
NHB, 37(Je/Jl 1974):273-4.

Daniels, Roger. The Bonus March: An Episode of the Great Depression. Westport, Conn.: Greenwood, 1971. Rev. by
D. E. Conrad, AHR, 79(Je 1974):897-8.

_____ and Harry H. L. Kitano. American Racism: Exploration
of the Nature of Prejudice. Englewood Cliffs, N.J.: Prentice-
Hall, 1970. Rev. by P. L. van den Berghe, PNQ, 65(Apr
1974):92-3.

Danker, Kathleen M. Winnebago Clothing Styles. Macy, Nebraska:
Nebraska Indian Press, 1973. Rev. by M. J. Schneider,
N H, 55(Sum 1974):317-8.

Dannett, Sylvia G. L. The Yankee Doodler: Music, Theater, and
Fun in the American Revolution. South Brunswick, N.J.:
A. S. Barnes, 1973. Rev. by J. J. Heslin, NYHSQ, 58(Apr
1974):152-3.

Darby, H. C., ed. A New Historical Geography of England. [Cam-
bridge:] Cam U Press, 1973. Rev. by D. J. Gregory, HJ,
17(Num 3 1974):652-4; W. A. Moffett, HRNB, 2(Feb 1974):
107-8.

_____ and I. B. Terrett, eds. The Domesday Geography of Midland England. New York: Cam U Press, 1971. Rev. by
W. O. Ault, AHR, 79(Je 1974):771-2.

Dardess, John W. Conquerors and Confucians: Aspects of Political
Change in Late Yüan China. New York: Columbia U Press,
1973. Rev. by W. Eberhard, AHR, 79(Oct 1974):1229-30;
J. D. Langlois, Jr., JAS, 34(Nov 1974):218-20.

Dargo, George. Roots of the Republic: A New Perspective on
Early American Constitutionalism. New York: Praeger, 1974.
Rev. by G. L. Seligmann, Jr., HRNB, 2(Aug 1974):218-19.

Darmon, Jean-Jacques. Le Colportage de librairie en France sous
le Second Empire. Paris: Plon, 1972. Rev. by R. D. Anderson, EHR, 89(Apr 1974):458-9; W. H. C. Smith, History,
59(Feb 1974):136.

Davidson, Basil. Black Star: A View of the Life and Times of Kwame Nkrumah. London: Allen Lane, 1973. Rev. by R. D. Jeffries, AfAf, 73(Apr 1974):237-8.

Davidson, Chalmers Gaston. The Last Foray: The South Carolina Planters of 1860. A Sociological Study. Columbia, S. C.: U SCar Press ... 1971. Rev. by T. G. Edelstein, AHR, 79 (Je 1974):866-7.

Davidson, Chandler. Biracial Politics: Conflict and Coalition in the Metropolitan South. Baton Rouge: LSU Press, 1972. Rev. by J. J. Cardoso, AHR, 79(Je 1974):906-7.

Davies, J. F. Athenian Propertied Families, 600-300 B. C. New York: Ox U Press, 1971. Rev. by C. G. Starr, AHR, 79 (Feb 1974):119.

Davies, K. G. The North Atlantic World in the Seventeenth Century. Minneapolis: U Minn Press, 1974. Rev. by W. D. Jones, HRNB, 3(Nov/Dec 1974):41-2.

_____, ed. Documents of the American Revolution, 1770-1783. (Colonial Office Series). Volume I: Calendar, 1770-1771; Volume II: Transcripts, 1770; Volume III: Transcripts, 1771. Shannon, Ireland: Irish U Press, 1972. Rev. by R. D. Higginbotham, JSH, 40(Aug 1974):465-6.

Davies, Nigel. The Aztecs. n. p.: Putnam's, n. d. Rev. by R. F. Locke, Mankind, 4(Aug 1974):41, 60.

Davies, Norman. White Eagle-Red Star: The Polish-Soviet War 1919-1920. London: MacDonald, 1972. Rev. by J. Piekalkiewicz, EEQ, 8(Fall 1974):383-6; L. P. Morris, History, 59 (Je 1974):300-1.

Davies, P. N. The Trade Makers: Elder Dempster in West Africa, 1852-1972. Hemel Hempstead: George Allen and Unwin, 1973. Rev. by S. Marriner, BHR, 48(Sum 1974):237-8; A. G. H., JAfH, 15(Num 3 1974): 516-7.

Davies, Thomas M., Jr. Indian Integration in Peru: A Half Century of Experience, 1900-1948. Lincoln: U Neb Press, 1974. Rev. by P. E. Kuhl, HRNB, 2(Sep 1974):252-3.

Davis, Allen F. and Mark H. Haller, eds. The Peoples of Philadelphia: A History of Ethnic Groups and Lower-Class Life, 1790-1940. Philadelphia: Temple U Press, 1973. Rev. by M. Rischin, JAH, 61(Dec 1974):775-6; J. E. Bodnar, PH, 41 (Oct 1974):469-70.

Davis, Carl L. Arming the Union: Small Arms in the Civil War. Port Washington, N. Y.: Kennikat, 1973. Rev. by A. C. Aimone, CWH, 20(Sep 1974):277-8; J. A. Carpenter, HRNB,

2(Aug 1974):216-17.

Davis, Douglas. Art and the Future. New York: Praeger, 1973.
Rev. by L. Vaczek, T & C, 15(Apr 1974):360-2.

Davis, Harold Eugene. Latin American Thought: A Historical Introduction. Baton Rouge: LSU Press, 1972. Rev. by F.
Macd. Spindler, AHR, 79(Je 1974):913.

_____, et al. Revolutionaries, Traditionalists, and Dictators in
Latin America. New York: Cooper Square, 1973. Rev. by
H. M. Hamill, Jr., HAHR, 54(Feb 1974):138-39; J. R. Bara-
ger, TAm, 30(Ja 1974):413-14.

Davis, Lance E., et al. American Economic Growth: An Economist's History of the United States. New York: Harper and
Row, 1972. Rev. by S. L. Engerman, AHR, 79(Feb 1974):
214-15; M. Rothstein, JAH, 61(Je 1974):147-8.

Davis, Lawrence B. Immigrants, Baptists, and the Protestant Mind
in America. Urbana: U Ill Press, 1973. Rev. by L. Schel-
bert, AHR, 79(Je 1974):881-2; G. E. Pozzetta, FHQ, 53(Jl
1974):94-6; J. Findlay, JAH, 60(Mar 1974):1147-8; J. J.
Thompson, Jr., MHM, 69(Sum 1974):235-6; I. V. Brown, PH,
41(Ja 1974):105-6.

Davis, Michael. The Image of Lincoln in the South. Knoxville:
U Tenn Press, 1971. Rev. by R. F. Weigley, AHR, 79(Feb
1974):233-4.

Davis, Norman and Colin M. Kraay. The Hellenistic Kingdoms:
Portrait Coins and History. London: Thames and Hudson,
1973. Rev. by M. H. Crawford, Antiquity, 48(Je 1974):154-5.

Davis, Ralph. The Rise of the Atlantic Economies. Ithaca, N.Y.:
Cornell U Press, 1973. Rev. by M. Wolfe, AHR, 79(Oct
1974):1142.

Davis, Richard Beale. Literature and Society in Early Virginia,
1608-1840. Baton Rouge: LSU Press, 1973. Rev. by R. D.
Jacobs, JSH, 40(Feb 1974):122-3; J. A. Leo Lemay, VMHB,
82(Ja 1974):115-17; O. K. Rice, WVH, 35(Apr 1974):245-6.

Davis, Richard W. Political Change and Continuity, 1760-1885: A
Buckinghamshire Study. Hamden, Conn.: Archon, 1972. Rev.
by J. Vincent, History, 59(Feb 1974):117-18; R. J. Helmstad-
ter, JMH, 46(Je 1974):347-8.

Davison, Kenneth E. The Presidency of Rutherford B. Hayes.
Westport, Conn.: Greenwood, 1972. Rev. by S. W. Brown,
WVH, 35(Apr 1974):238-9.

Davisson, William I. Information Processing: Applications in the

Social and Behavioral Sciences. New York: Appleton-Century-
Crofts, 1970. Rev. by P. Peebles, AHR, 79(Je 1974):751-2.

Davydov, M. I. The Struggle for Bread: The Food Policy of the
    Communist Party and the Soviet State During the Time of the
    Civil War (1917-1920). Moscow: Izdatel'stvo "Mysl'," 1971.
    Rev. by G. D. Jackson, Jr., AHR, 79(Apr 1974):551-2.

Dawn, C. Ernest. From Ottomanism to Arabism, Essays on the
    Origins of Arab Nationalism. Urbana: U Ill Press, n.d.
    Rev. by S. Gershgoren, Mankind, 4(Feb 1974):65.

Daws, Gavan. Holy Man: Father Damien of Molokai. New York:
    Harper and Row, 1973. Rev. by J. B. McGloin, S.J., PHR,
    43(Nov 1974):614-5.

Dawson, Philip. Provincial Magistrates and Revolutionary Politics
    in France, 1789-1795. Cambridge, Mass.: Har U Press,
    1972. Rev. by T. F. Sheppard, AHR, 79(Feb 1974):165-6;
    A. Forrest, 89(Jl 1974):673; P. Lucas, JMH, 46(Mar 1974):
    128-30.

D-Day: The Normandy Invasion in Retrospect. Lawrence: U Press
    Kan, 1971. Rev. by R. G. O'Connor, AHR, 79(Je 1974):779-
    80.

Deagan, Kathleen A. see Hemmings, E. Thomas

Dean, Jill and Susan Smith, eds. Wisconsin: A State for All Sea-
    sons. Madison: Wis Tales and Trails, 1972. Rev. by J. J.
    Newman, IMH, 70(Dec 1974):363-5.

Dean, Jill see Mead, Howard

Deasy, Liam. Towards Ireland Free. Cork: Mercier Press, 1973.
    Rev. by R. T. Reilly, E-I, 9(Spr 1974):144-5.

Deaton, Charles. The Year They Threw the Rascals Out. Austin,
    Tx.: Shoal Creek Publishers, 1973. Rev. by J. E. Ericson,
    ETHJ, 12(Fall 1974):92-3; B. Proctor, SWHQ, 78(Jl 1974):
    107-8.

de Bernardi Ferrero, Daria. Teatri Classici in Asia Minore. Ci-
    byra, Selge, Hieropolis. Rome: "L'Erma" di Bretschneider,
    1966. Rev. by E. R. Gebhard, AJA, 78(Ja 1974):99-100.

De Bertier, Guillaume de Souvigny. Metternich et la France Après
    le Congrès de Vienne. Paris: Presses Continentales, 1971.
    Rev. by A. Ramm, EHR, 89(Ja 1974):210-11.

DeBoe, David C., Van Mitchell Smith, Elliott West, and Norman A.
    Graebner. Essays on American Foreign Policy. Austin: U
    Tx Press, 1974. Rev. by W. F. Kimball, HRNB, 3(Nov/Dec

1974):46-7; R. Eubanks, SWHQ, 78(Oct 1974):227-8.

Debray, Régis. Conversations with Allende. Socialism in Chile.
London: N L B, 1971. Rev. by S. Collier, JLAS, 6(May
1974):183-5.

Debus, Allen G. , ed. Science, Medicine and Society in the Renaissance: Essays to Honor Walter Pagel. 2 vols. London:
Heinemann, 1972. Rev. by P. M. Heiman, History, 59(Je
1974):267-8.

Decker, Leslie E. and Robert Seager II, eds. America's Major
Wars: Crusaders, Critics and Scholars. Reading, Mass.:
Addison-Wesley, 1973. Rev. by B. L. Turpin, HT, 7(Feb
1974):296.

D'Eercole, G. and A. M. Stickler, eds. Comunione interecclesiale,
collegialita, primato ecumenismo. Rome: ... Librerio Ateneo
Salesiano, 1972. Rev. by H. E. J. Cowdrey, EHR, 89(Apr
1974):411-12.

Defoe, Daniel. A General History of the Pyrates. Ed. by Manuel
Schonhorn. Columbia: U SC Press, 1972. Rev. by H. F.
Rankin, NCHR, 51(Jan 1974):109-10.

De Frede, Carlo. La Restaurazione Cattolica in Inghilterra sotto
Maria Tudor. Naples: Libreria Scientifica Editrice, 1971.
Rev. by D. Fenlon, EHR, 89(Apr 1974):430.

Degler, Carl N. Neither Black nor White: Slavery and Race Relations in Brazil and the United States. New York: Macmillan, 1971. Rev. by D. Ramios, TAm, 30(Ja 1974):414-15.

_____. The Other South: Southern Dissenters in the Nineteenth
Century. New York: Harper and Row, 1974. Rev. by B.
Procter, HRNB, 2(Apr 1974):149; S. W. Wiggins, JAH, 61(Dec
1974):798-9; S. Hackney, JSH, 40(Nov 1974):631-6; J. T.
Moore, VMHB, 82(Oct 1974):507-8.

_____, ed. see Potter, David M.

de Kadt, Emanuel, ed. Patterns of Foreign Influence in the Caribbean. London: Ox U Press ... 1972. Rev. by D. A. G.
Waddell, JLAS, 6(May 1974):191-2.

Dekker, George and John P. McWilliams, eds. Fenimore Cooper:
The Critical Heritage. Boston: Routledge and Kegan Paul,
1973. Rev. by C. Swann, JAmS, 8(Apr 1974):124-6.

de la Garza, Rudolph, Z. Anthony Kruszewski, Tomas A. Arciniega,
ed. Chicanos and Native Americans: The Territorial Minorities. Englewood Cliffs, N. J.: Prentice-Hall, 1973. Rev.
by R. H. Vigil, NMHR, 49(Apr 1974):161-3.

de la Mare, A. C. The Handwriting of Italian Humanists, Vol. 1,
    fascicule 1. Oxford: U Press for the Assn. Internationale de
    Bibliophilie, 1973. Rev. by R. Nash, RQ, 27(Fall 1974):338-
    9.

de la Maziere, Christian. The Captive Dreamer. n. p. : Saturday
    Review Press/Dutton, n. d. Rev. by P. Shaw, Commentary,
    58(Nov 1974):84-6, 88.

Delaney, Norman C. John McIntosh Kell of the Raider Alabama.
    University, Ala. : U Ala Press, 1973. Rev. by R. Seager,
    II, AHR, 79(Oct 1974):1265-6; R. E. Johnson, CWH, 20(Mar
    1974):72-3; W. S. Hoole, FHQ, 53(July 1974):89-91; R. W.
    Daly, JAH, 60(Mar 1974):1132-3; M. Abbott, RKHS, 72(Ja
    1974):55-6.

Delaney, Robert W. see Jefferson, James

de la Roncière, Charles M. Un Changeur Florentin du Trecento:
    Lippi di Fede del Sega (1285 env.-1363 env.). Paris:
    S. E. V. P. E. N., 1973. Rev. by T. W. Blomquist, BHR,
    48(Win 1974):579-81.

de la Taille, Jean. Dramatic Works. Ed. by Kathleen M. Hall
    and C. N. Smith. London: Athlone Press, 1972. Rev. by
    N. B. Spector, RQ, 22(Fall 1974):348-52.

Delavenay, Emile. D. H. Lawrence, the Man and His Work: The
    Formative Years, 1885-1919. Carbondale: S Ill U Press,
    1972. Rev. by J. E. Stoll, GR, 28(Sum 1974):370-1.

Delery, Simone de la. Napoleon's Soldiers in America. Gretna,
    La. : Pelican Pub. Co. , 1972. Rev. by M. Allain, LaH, 15
    (W 1974):87-8.

de Madariaga, Salvador see Madariaga, Salvador de

Demiéville, Paul. Choix d'Études Bouddhiques. Leiden: E. J.
    Brill, 1973. Rev. by E. H. Schafer, JAS, 33(Aug 1974):688-
    91.

_____. Choix d'Études Sinologiques. Leiden: E. J. Brill, 1973.
    Rev. by E. H. Schafer, JAS, 33(Aug 1974):689-91.

de Miroschedji, Pierre R. L'Époque pré-Urbaine en Palestine.
    Paris: Galbalda, 1971. Rev. by K. M. Kenyon, Antiquity,
    48(Sep 1974):235-6.

DeMolen, Richard L. , ed. The Meaning of the Renaissance and
    Reformation. Boston: Houghton Mifflin, 1974. Rev. by J. C.
    Troust, CH, 43(Sep 1974):399; K. H. Dannenfeldt, HRNB, 2
    (Mar 1974):117-18.

_____, ed.   One Thousand Years: Western Europe in the Middle
Ages.   Boston: Houghton Mifflin, 1974.   Rev. by J. J.
Smith, CH, 43(Sep 1974):398-9; J. L. Shneidman, HRNB, 2
(Apr 1974):141.

Demos, John ed.   Remarkable Providences, 1600-1760.   New York:
Geo. Braziller, 1972.   Rev. by R. D. Cohen, HT, 8(Nov
1974):126-7.

Dempsey, Hugh A.   Crowfoot, Chief of the Blackfeet.   Normañ: U
Ok Press, 1972.   Rev. by M. B. Husband, JOW, 13(Apr 1974):
120; D. E. Livingston-Little, WHQ, 5(Ja 1974):77-8.

Deng, Francis Mading.   The Dinka and Their Songs.   Oxford: Clarendon Press, 1973.   Rev. by R. Gray, JAfH, 15(Num 3 1974):
497-8.

Denholm, Anthony.   France in Revolution, 1848.   Sydney Australia:
Wiley, 1972.   Rev. by R. W. Lougee, Historian, 36(May 1974):
545; R. D. Anderson, History, 59(Feb 1974):135.

Dennis, Austin.   Politics in Ghana, 1946-1960.   New York: Oxford
U Press, 1970.   Rev. by C. G. Contee, N H B, 37(Feb/Mar
1974):229-30.

Dennis, Frank Allen, ed.   Kemper County Rebel: The Civil War
Diary of Robert Masten Holmes, C. S. A.   Jackson, Miss.:   U
and Coll Press Miss, 1973.   Rev. by G. T. Chappell, AlaHQ,
36(Spr 1974):823; J. Barnett, CWH, 20(Sep 1974):281-3; J. I.
Robertson, Jr., GHQ, 58(Supp 1974):216-17; W. M. Drake,
JMiH, 36(Feb 1974):121-2.

Dennis, Peter.   Decision by Default: Peacetime Conscription and
British Defence, 1919-39.   Durham, N. C.:   Duke U Press,
1972.   Rev. by A. Gollin, AHR, 79(Oct 1974):1184; J. O.
Stubbs, CHR, 55(Sep 1974):329-30; B. Bond, EHR, 89(Ja 1974):
236-7; J. Gooch, History, 59(Feb 1974):145.

Denoon, Donald.   Southern Africa Since 1800.   London: Longman,
1972.   Rev. by S. M., JAfH, 15(Num 3 1974):491-3.

DeNovo, John A., ed.   The Gilded Age and After.   New York:
Scribner's, 1972.   Rev. by E. D. Schmiel, HT, 7(Aug 1974):
634-5.

Dent, Anthony.   Lost Beasts of Britain.   London: Harrap, n. d.
Rev. by A. Haynes, HTo, 24(Sep 1974):661-2.

Dent, Julian.   Crisis in Finance: Crown, Financiers, and Society
in Seventeenth-Century France.   New York: St. Martin's,
1973.   Rev. by D. Koenig, HRNB, 2(Mar 1974):114; A. N.
Hamscher, JMH, 46(Dec 1974):718-19.

den Tex, Jan. Oldenbarnvelt. 2 vols. New York: Cam U Press, 1973. Rev. by H. H. Rowen, AHR, 79(Feb 1974):171-2; J. Tanis, CH, 43(Mar 1974):113-14; G. N. Clark, EHR, 89(Jl 1974):633-5.

Denzer, Horst, ed. Jean Bodin: Verhandlungen der internationalen Bodin Tagung in München. Munich: Verlag C. H. Beck, 1973. Rev. by M. L. Daniels, AHR, 79(Je 1974):788-9.

de Oliveira Marques, A. H. History of Portugal. Vol. II: From Empire to Corporate State. New York: Columbia U Press, 1972. Rev. by S. C. Schneider, HAHR, 54(Aug 1974):540-2; R. H. Mattoon, Jr., TAm, 31(Jl 1974):105-6.

Deresiewicz, Janusz, ed. Historical-Economic Studies of Western Poland. Poznań: Poznańskie Towarzystwo Przyjaciól Nauk, 1971. Rev. by Z. J. Gasiorowski, AHR, 79(Je 1974):812-13.

Derry, T. K. A History of Modern Norway. Oxford: Clarendon Press, 1973. Rev. by R. E. Lindgren, HT, 7(Feb 1974):308-9.

Derykolenko, O. I., et al., eds. History of the Cities and Villages of the Ukranian SSR--Chernigov Province. Kiev: Institut Istorii Akademii Nauk URSR, 1972. Rev. by J. Armstrong, 79 (Feb 1974):193-4.

de St. Jorre, John. The Brothers' War: Biafra and Nigeria. Boston: Houghton Mifflin, 1972. Rev. by D. F. McCall, AHR, 79(Oct 1974):1228-9.

Desaive, J.-P., et al. Médecins, Climat, et epidemies à la fin du XVIIIe siècle. Paris: Mouton, 1972. Rev. by G. Ellis, EHR, 89(Apr 1974):389-93.

Desborough, V. R. d'A. The Greek Dark Ages. New York: St. Martin's, 1972. Rev. by P. A. Alin, AJA, 78(Apr 1974):198; R. Hamilton, AHR, 79(Je 1974):761.

De Sens, Odorannus. Opera Omnia. Paris: Éditions du Centre National de la Recherche Scientifique, 1972. Rev. by M. Chibnall, AHR, 79(Je 1974):774.

Des Forges, Roger V. Hsi-liang and the Chinese Revolution. New Haven, Conn.: Yale U Press, 1973. Rev. by P. A. Cohen, JAS, 33(May 1974):466-8; P. B. Cares, HRNB, 2(Feb 1974): 104-5.

des Gagniers, Jean see Gagniers, Jean des

de Silva, Chandra Richard. The Portuguese in Ceylon, 1617-1638. Colombo: H. W. Cave, 1972. Rev. by C. R. Boxer, AHR, 79(Je 1974):828-9.

Despinis, G. I.   A Contribution to the Study of Agorakritos.   Athens: Hermes Press, 1971.   Rev. by N. Bookidis, AJA, 78(Ja 1974): 96-7.

Dessen, Alan C. , ed.   see   Schoenbaum, S.

Detsicas, Alec, ed.   Current Research in Romano-British Coarse Pottery.   London: Council for British Archaeology, 1973. Rev. by M. G. Jarrett, Antiquity, 48(Je 1974):161-2.

Deutsch, Harold C.   Hitler and His Generals: The Hidden Crisis, January-June 1938.   Minneapolis: U Minn Press, 1974.   Rev. by P. H. Silfen, HRNB, 2(Sep 1974):243.

The Development of a Revolutionary Mentality: Papers Presented at the First Symposium, May 5 and 6, 1972, Library of Congress Symposium on the American Revolution.   Washington: Library of Congress, 1972.   Rev. by R. S. Dunn, JSH, 40(Feb 1974): 126-8;   L. R. Gerlach, NYHSQ, 58(Apr 1974):165-9.

deVillier, Gladys.   The Opelousas Post: A Compendium of Church Records Relating to the First Families of Southwest Louisiana, 1776-1806.   Cottonport, La.:   Polyanthos, 1972.   Rev. by R. R. Fontenot, LaH, 15(W 1974):83-4.

Devine, George.   Liturgical Renewal: An Agonizing Reappraisal. Staten Island, N. Y.:   Alba House, 1973.   Rev. by G. H. Bricker, CH, 43(Sep 1974):429-30.

Devon, Francis.   Mr. Piper and His Cubs.   Ames: Ia St U Press, 1973.   Rev. by R. Higham, BHR, 48(Sum 1974):274-5.

Devonshire Jones, Rosemary.   Francesco Vettori: Florentine Citizen and Medici Servant.   London: Athlone, 1972.   Rev. by G. A. Brucker, AHR, 79(Apr 1974):528-9;   D. M. Buena de Mesquita, EHR, 89(Jl 1974):665-6;   C. B. Clough, ESR, 4(Apr 1974):175-8;   J. Hook, History, 59(Feb 1974):100-1;   R. A. Goldthwaite, JIH, 5(Aug 1974):323.

De Vooght, Paul.   Jacobellus de Stríbro: Premier Théologien du Hussitisme.   Louvain: Publications Universitaires de Louvain, 1972.   Rev. by W. R. Cook, CH, 43(Sep 1974):397-8.

De Vos, George A.   Socialization for Achievement: Essays on the Cultural Psychology of the Japanese.   Berkeley: U Cal Press, 1973.   Rev. by D. W. Plath, JAS, 34(Nov 1974):193-200.

Dewey, Donald O.   Marshall versus Jefferson: The Political Background of Marbury v. Madison.   New York: Knopf, 1970. Rev. by J. Teaford, AHR, 79(Oct 1974):1257-8.

DeWindt, Edwin Brezette.   Land and People in Holywell-cum-Needingworth.   Toronto: Pontifical Institute of Medieval Studies, 1972.

Rev. by E. Searle, CHR, 55(Sep 1974):326-7; R. H. Hilton,
EHR, 89(Apr 1974):422; P. D. A. Harvey, History, 59(Feb
1974):93; J. A. Corbett, JEH, 34(Je 1974):507-8.

Dial, Adolph and David Eliades. The Only Land I Know: A History
of the Lumbee Indians. San Francisco: Indian Historian Press,
1974. Rev. by Staff, InH, 7(Sum 1974):59.

Díaz-Alejandro, Carlos F. Essays on the Economic History of the
Argentine Republic. New Haven, Conn.: Yale U Press, 1970.
Rev. by M. Mamalakis, JLAS, 6(May 1974):185-6.

Di Bona, Joseph E. Change and Conflict in the Indian University.
Durham, N.C.: Duke U Press, 1969. Rev. by M. L. Cormack, JAS, 33(May 1974):500.

Dicey, Edward. Spectator of America. London: Gollancz, 1972.
Rev. by R. Belflower, JAmS, 8(Apr 1974):121-2.

Dick, William M. Labor and Socialism in America: The Gompers
Era. Port Washington, N.Y.: Kennikat, 1972. Rev. by
G. N. Grob, BHR, 48(Sum 1974):257-8; D. E. Schob, JISHS,
67(Sep 1974):453-4.

Dickens, A. G. The Age of Humanism and Reformation: Europe in
the Fourteenth, Fifteenth and Sixteenth Centuries. Englewood
Cliffs, N.J.: Prentice-Hall, 1972. Rev. by M. Jones, History, 59(Feb 1974):100.

Dickey, John W., David M. Glancy, and Ernest M. Jennelle. Technology Assessment. Lexington, Mass.: Heath-Lexington, 1973.
Rev. by V. L. Ferwerda, T & C, 15(Jl 1974):529-34.

Diener, Hermann. Die Grossen Registerserien im Vatikanischen
Archiv (1378-1523). Tubingen: Max Niemeyer Verlag, 1972.
Rev. by C. R. Cheney, EHR, 89(Ja 1974):163.

Dierdorff, John. How Edison's Lamp Helped Light the West. Portland, Ore.: Pacific Light and Power, 1971. Rev. by R. J.
Tosiello, BHR, 48(Spr 1974):138-40.

Diggins, John P. The American Left in the Twentieth Century.
New York: Harcourt Brace Jovanovich, 1973. Rev. by K. E.
Hendrickson, Jr., HT, 8(Nov 1974):148-9; M. Zanger, JAH,
61(Je 1974):232-3.

d'Igny, Guerric. Sermons. Volume 2. Paris: Les Editions du
Cerf, 1973. Rev. by J. Crawford, CH, 43(Sep 1974):393.

Dillard, Annie. Pilgrim at Tinker Creek. n.p.: Harper's Magazine, n.d. Rev. by E. Hoffman, Commentary, 58(Oct 1974):
87-8, 90-1.

Dillon, Richard. Burnt-Out Fires. Englewood Cliffs, N.J.: Prentice-Hall, 1973. Rev. by V. E. Ray, WHQ, 5(Ja 1974):79-81.

Dinnerstein, Leonard and Mary Dale Palsson, eds. Jews in the
South. Baton Rouge: LSU Press, 1973. Rev. by R. V.
Haynes, ETHJ, 12(Spr 1974):69-70; A. J. Going, Historian,
36(May 1974):563; L. A. Berman, LaH, 15(Sum 1974):305-6.

Diop, Cheikh Anta. The African Origin of Civilization: Myth or
Reality. New York: Lawrence Hill, 1974. Rev. by D. F.
McCall, JAAS, 9(Ja & Apr 1974):91-7.

Diskul, M. C. Subhadradis see Bowie, Theodore

Divine, Robert A., ed. The Cuban Missile Crisis. Chicago: Quadrangle, 1971. Rev. by L. D. Langley, HAHR, 54(Feb 1974):
181-2.

Dmitrenko, V. P. The Trade Policy of the Soviet State After the
Transition to N E P, 1921-1924. Moscow: Izdatel'stvo "Nauk-
a," 1971. Rev. by D. Mulholland, AHR, 79(Oct 1974):1224-5.

Dobbin, Christine. Urban Leadership in Western India: Politics
and Communities in Bombay City, 1840-1885. New York: Ox
U Press, 1972. Rev. by S. Gujral, AHR, 79(Je 1974):828.

Dobbs, Farrell. Teamster Power. New York: Monad Press, 1973.
Rev. by H. Berman, MinnH, 44(Spr 1974):34-5.

Dobie, J. Frank. Out of the Old Rock. Boston: Little, Brown,
1972. Rev. by W. L. Richter, GPJ, 13(Spr 1974):211.

Dobson, Narda. A History of Belize. London...: Longman Caribbean, 1973. Rev. by R. L. Woodward, Jr., HAHR 54(May
1974):307-8.

Dobson, R. B. Durham Priory, 1400-1450. New York: Cam U
Press, 1973. Rev. by R. W. Pfaff, AHR, 79(Je 1974):773-4;
J. F. Kelly, CH, 43(Mar 1974):107-8.

_____, ed. The Peasants' Revolt of 1381. London: Macmillan,
1970. Rev. by J. Gillingham, History, 59(Je 1974):257-8.

Dobyns, Henry F. and Robert C. Euler. The Navajo People. Phoenix: Indian Tribal Series, 1972. Rev. by L. C. Kelly, A & W,
16(Spr 1974):69-70.

_____. The Hopi People. see Euler, Robert C.

Dodd, Donald B. and Wynelle S. Historical Statistics of the South,
1790-1970. University, Ala.: U Ala Press, 1973. Rev. by
B. Cresap, AlaR, 27(Oct 1974):288-9; R. J. Jensen, HRNB,

2(Ja 1974):63-4; J. C. Kiger, JMiH, 36(Feb 1974):120-1; R. W.
Twyman, JSH, 40(May 1974):293-4; J. C. Robert, VMHB, 82
(Apr 1974):204.

Dodds, Gordon B. Hiram Martin Chittenden: His Public Career.
Lexington, Ky: U Press Ky, 1973. Rev. by K. A. Murray,
A & W, 16(Spr 1974):89-91; R. G. Dunbar, AHR, 79(Je 1974):
891-2; R. Deming, HT, 8(Nov 1974):149-50; J. L. Bates,
JAH, 61(Je 1974):224-5; R. A. Bartlett, PHR, 43(Aug 1974):
423-4; B. Proctor, PNQ, 65(Oct 1974):187-8; P. A. Kalisch,
RKHS, 72(Apr 1974):189-90; M. Sherwood, T & C, 15(Apr
1974):341-2; B. Le Roy, WHQ, 5(Apr 1974):213-14.

Dodge, Ernest S. The Polar Rosses: John and James Clark Ross
and Their Explorations. New York: Barnes and Noble, 1973.
Rev. by J. E. Caswell, AHR, 79(Oct 1974):1180.

Doenecke, Justus D. The Literature of Isolationism: A Guide to
Non-Interventionist Scholarship, 1930-1972. Colorado Springs,
Colo.: Ralph Myles, 1972. Rev. by A. Yarnell, HT, 8(Nov
1974):152; T. A. Krueger, JISHS, 67(Sep 1974):446-7.

Dollar, Charles M. and Richard J. Jensen. Historian's Guide to
Statistics: Quantitative Analysis and Historical Research.
New York: Holt, Rinehart and Winston, 1971. Rev. by P.
Peebles, AHR, 79(Je 1974):751-2.

Dollar, George W. A History of Fundamentalism in America.
Greenville, S. C.: Bob Jones U Press, 1973. Rev. by
E. R. Sandeen, CH, 43(Sep 1974):426-7.

Dolley, R. H. M. see Blunt, C. E.

D'Ombrain, Nicholas. War Machinery and High Policy: Defence
Administration in Peacetime Britain, 1902-1914. New York:
Ox U Press, 1973. Rev. by P. Guinn, HRNB, 2(Ja 1974):82.

Domes, Jürgen. The Internal Politics of China, 1949-1972. New
York: Praeger, 1973. Rev. by J. K. Kallgren, HRNB, 2(Ja
1974):76; K. Lieberthal, JAS, 33(Aug 1974):701-3.

Domínguez Ortiz, Antonio. El Antiguo Régimen: Los reyes católicos y los Austrias. Madrid: Alianza Editorial Alfaguara,
1973. Rev. by P. J. Hauben, AHR, 79(Je 1974):793-4.

_____. The Golden Age of Spain, 1516-1659. New York: Basic
Books, 1971. Rev. by P. J. Hauben, AHR, 79(Je 1974):793-4.

Domros, M. see Schweinfurth, U.

Donaghy, Thomas J. Liverpool & Manchester Railway Operations
1831-1845. Newton Abbot: David and Charles, 1972. Rev. by
T. R. Gourvish, History, 59(Feb 1974):123-4.

Donaldson, Gordon. Battle for a Continent: Quebec 1759. Toronto: Doubleday Canada, 1973. Rev. by C. B. Cone, RKHS, 72(Jl 1974):292-4.

Donnan, Christopher B. Moche Occupation of the Santa Valley, Peru. Berkeley: U Cal Press, 1973. Rev. by D. A. Proulx, TAm, 31(Jl 1974):110-11.

Donno, Elizabeth Story, ed. Andrew Marvell: the Complete Poems. Harmondsworth-Baltimore: Penguin Books, 1972. Rev. by K. S. Datta, RQ, 27(Spr 1974):114-17.

Donovan, Timothy Paul. Historical Thought in America: Postwar Patterns. Norman: U Ok Press, 1973. Rev. by D. R. Jamieson, HRNB, 2(Feb 1974):91; D. W. Noble, JSH, 40(May 1974):291-3.

Donovan, William P. see Blegen, Carl W.

Doolin, Dennis J. see Ridley, C. P.

_____ and Charles P. Ridley. A Chinese-English Dictionary of Communist Chinese Terminology. Stanford, Cal.: Hoover Institution, Stan U Press, 1973. Rev. by J. J. Wrenn, JAS, 33(May 1974):468-9.

Dore, Ronald. British Factory--Japanese Factory: The Origins of National Diversity in Industrial Relations. Berkeley: U Cal Press, 1973. Rev. by K. Taira, JAS, 33(May 1974):487-9.

Dorsett, Lyle W. The Early American City. St. Charles, Mo.: Forum Press, 1973. Rev. by M. P. McCarthy, HT, 8(Nov 1974):109-10.

Dorsey, John and James D. Dilts. A Guide to Baltimore Architecture. Cambridge, Md.: Tidewater Publishers, 1973. Rev. by C. F. Black, MHM, 69(Fall 1974):336-7.

Dorson, Richard M. America in Legend: Folklore from the Colonial Period to the Present. New York: Pantheon, 1973. Rev. by W. D. Wyman, MinnH, 44(Spr 1974):35.

_____, ed. Folklore and Folklife: An Introduction. Chicago: U Chi Press, 1972. Rev. by S. Stein, PHR, 43(May 1974): 262.

Dorwart, Reinhold August. The Prussian Welfare State Before 1740. Cambridge, Mass.: Harvard U Press, 1972. Rev. by H. J. Cohn, History, 59(Je 1974):277-8.

Dosa, Marta L. Libraries in the Political Scene: Georg Leyh and German Librarianship, 1933-1953. Westport, Conn.: Greenwood, 1974. Rev. by G. Strauss, HRNB, 3(Nov/Dec 1974):31.

Dos Passos, John. <u>The Fourteenth Chronicle: Letters and Diaries</u> <u>of John Dos Passos.</u> Ed. by Townsend Ludington. Boston: Gambit Inc., 1973. Rev. by H. A. Larrabee, NEQ, 47(Sep 1974):461-7.

Dostian, I. S. <u>Russia and the Balkan Question: On the History of</u> <u>Russian-Balkan Political Relations in the First Third of the</u> <u>19th Century.</u> Moscow: Izdatel'stvo "Nauka," 1972. Rev. by N. E. Saul, AHR, 79(Apr 1974):535-6.

Douglas, Henry Kyd. <u>The Douglas Diary: Student Days at Franklin</u> <u>and Marshall College.</u> Lancaster, Pa.: Franklin and Mar- shall College, 1973. Rev. by J. I. Robertson, CWH, 20(Sep 1974):279-81.

Douglas, Kenneth, tr. <u>see</u> Wagner, Jean

[Douglas, Paul H.] <u>In the Fulness of Time: The Memoirs of Paul</u> <u>H. Douglas.</u> New York: Harcourt Brace Jovanovich, 1972. Rev. by O. L. Graham, Jr., AHR, 79(Je 1974):889-901.

Dowd, Douglas F. <u>The Twisted Dream: Capitalist Development in</u> <u>the United States Since 1776.</u> Cambridge, Mass.: Winthrop, 1974. Rev. by M. N. Rothbard, BHR, 48(Win 1974):547-8.

Downard, William L. <u>The Cincinnati Brewing Industry: A Social</u> <u>and Economic History.</u> Athens, Ohio: Ohio U Press, 1973. Rev. by J. W. Lozier, BHR, 48(Sum 1974):256-7; P. L. Si- mon, OH, 83(W 1974):77-8.

Downes, Ferne <u>see</u> Skaggs, Jimmy M. <u>Chronicles.</u>

Downey, Fairfax and J. N. Jacobsen. <u>The Red Bluecoats: The In-</u> <u>dian Scouts.</u> Fort Collins, Colo.: Old Army, 1973. Rev. by S. B. Brinckerhoff, JAriH, 15(Aut 1974):301-2; H. H. Lang, SWHQ, 78(Jl 1974):101-2.

Dowty, Alan. <u>The Limits of American Isolation: The United States</u> <u>and the Crimean War.</u> New York: NYU Press, 1971. Rev. by H. Jones, JAH, 61(Je 1974):193-4.

Doxiadis, C. A. <u>Architectural Space in Ancient Greece.</u> Cambridge, Mass.: M I T Press, 1972. Rev. by R. Brilliant, AHR, 79 (Oct 1974):1152-4.

Drachkovitch, Milorad M. and Branko Lazitch. <u>Lenin and the Com-</u> <u>intern.</u> Volume I. <u>see</u> Lazitch, Branko and Milorad M. Drachkovitch. <u>Lenin and the Comintern.</u>

Dragnich, Alex H. <u>Serbia, Nikola Pasic, and Yugoslavia.</u> New Brunswick, N.J.: Rutgers U Press, 1974. Rev. by J. F. Zacek, HRNB, 3(Oct 1974):13.

Dreifort, John E. Yvon Delbos at the Quai d'Orsay: French Foreign
    Policy During the Popular Front, 1936-1938. Lawrence: U
    Press Kan, 1973. Rev. by H. F. Lewis, AHR, 79(Oct 1974):
    1194; R. Stromberg, HRNB, 2(Ja 1974):87.

Drinnon, Richard. White Savage: The Case of John Dunn Hunter.
    New York: Schocken, 1972. Rev. by W. Fenton, AHR, 79
    (Oct 1974):1258-60; L. J. White, JOW, 13(Apr 1974):121.

Droz, Jacques, ed. Histoire générale du socialisme. Volume I.
    Des origines à 1875. Paris: Universitaires de France, 1972.
    Rev. by C. Landauer, AHR, 79(Feb 1974):110-11; J. Joll,
    History, 59(Je 1974):292-3.

Drury, Clifford M. Marcus and Narcissa Whitman and the Opening
    of Old Oregon. 2 vols. Glendale, Cal.: Arthur H. Clark,
    1973. Rev. by H. J. Gilkey, AI, 42(Win 1974):230-1; R. H.
    Keller, Jr., CH, 43(Mar 1974):120-1; B. Procter, HRNB, 2
    (Ja 1974):64-5; R. J. Loewenberg, JAH, 61(Sep 1974):482-3;
    N. M. Walker, OrHQ, 75(Mar 1974):77-8; M. W. Wells, UHQ,
    42(Spr 1974):204-5; K. A. Murray, WHQ, 5(Apr 1974):212-13.

Du, Nguyen. The Tale of Kieu. New York: Random House, 1973.
    Rev. by M. Ross, JAS, 33(Aug 1974):743-4.

Dua, R. P. Anglo-Japanese Relations During the First World War.
    New Delhi: S. Chand, 1972. Rev. by P. Lowe, AHR, 79
    (Feb 1974):115.

Duby, Georges. The Early Growth of the European Economy: War-
    riors and Peasants from the Seventh to the Twelfth Century.
    Ithaca, N.Y.: Cornell U Press, 1974. Rev. by M. B. Beck-
    er, HRNB, 2(Jl 1974):208.

Duc de San-Simon. Historical Memoirs, Volume III, 1715-1723.
    New York: McGraw-Hill, 1972. Rev. by G. Symcox, HT, 8
    (Feb 1974):311.

Dudley, B. J. Instability and Political Order: Politics and Crisis
    in Nigeria. Ibadan: Ibadan U Press, 1973. Rev. by E.
    Osagie, JMAS 12(Sep 1974):500-1.

Dudley, Edward and Maximillian E. Novak, eds. The Wild Man
    Within. An Image in Western Thought from the Renaissance
    to Romanticism. Pittsburgh: U Pittsburgh Press, 1972, 1973.
    Rev. by C. Bolt, JAmS, 8(Apr 1974):117-9; M. J. Leaf, JMH,
    46(Je 1974):341-3.

Dudley, Guilford A. A History of Eastern Civilization. New York:
    Wiley, 1973. Rev. by H. P. French, Jr., JAS, 34(Nov 1974):
    211-12.

Dudley, W. R. Bahlman, ed. The Diary of Edward Walter Hamilton,

1880-1885. 2 vols. New York: Ox U Press, 1972. Rev. by P. Marsh, AHR, 79(Feb 1974):150-1.

Duffy, Christopher. The Army of Frederick the Great. Newton Abbot: David and Charles, n.d. Rev. by D. G. Chandler, HTo, 24(Oct 1974):726-8.

Duffy, John J., ed. Coleridge's American Disciples: The Selected Correspondence of James Marsh. Amherst: U Mass Press, 1973. Rev. by S. H. Wurster, CH, 43(Je 1974):282; R. B. Stein, JAH, 61(Sep 1974):479-81; E. Cassara, VH, 42(W 1974): 68-70.

Duignan, Peter, ed. Guide to Research and Reference Works on Sub-Saharan Africa. Stanford, Cal.: Hoover Institution Press, 1972. Rev. by G. Shepperson, JAfH, 15(Num 3 1974):525-6.

_____ and L. H. Gann. Colonialism in Africa, 1870-1960: Volume 5, A Bibliographical Guide to Colonialism in Sub-Saharan Africa. New York: Cam U Press, 1974. Rev. by J. A. Casada, HRNB, 2(May/Je 1974):171-2.

Duke, Benjamin C. Japan's Militant Teachers: A History of the Left-Wing Teachers' Movement. Honolulu: U Press Hawaii, 1973. Rev. by J. Singleton, JAS, 33(Feb 1974):321-3.

Dulai, Surjit S. see Coppola, Carlo

Dülffer, Jost. Weimar, Hitler und die Marine: Reichspolitik und Flottenbau, 1920-1939. Düsseldorf: Droste Verlag, 1973. Rev. by K. W. Bird, AHR, 79(Feb 1974):177-8.

Dulles, Foster Rhea. American Policy Toward Communist China, 1949-1969. New York: Crowell, 1972. Rev. by B. F. Beers, AHR, 79(Oct 1974):1239-40.

Dulles, John W. F. Anarchists and Communists in Brazil, 1900-1935. Austin: U Tx Press, 1973. Rev. by C. E. Lida, HRNB, 2(Jl 1974):201; M. M. Hall, TAm, 31(Oct 1974):219-21.

Dumbarton Oaks Papers, Number 26. Washington: Dumbarton Oaks Center for Byzantine Studies ... 1972. Rev. by R. Cormack, AHR, 79(Feb 1974):132-4.

Dumézil, Georges. The Destiny of a King. Chicago: U Chi Press, 1973. Rev. by J. Jochens, AHR, 79(Oct 1974):1149-51.

_____. The Destiny of the Warrior. Chicago: U Chi Press, 1970. Rev. by J. Jochens, AHR, 79(Oct 1974):1149-51.

_____. From Myth to Fiction: The Saga of Hadingus. Chicago: U Chi Press, 1973. Rev. by J. Jochens, AHR, 79(Oct 1974): 1149-51.

_____. Heur et malheur du guerrier: Aspects mythiques de la fonction guerrière chez les Indo-Européens. Paris: Presses Universitaires de France, 1969. Rev. by J. Jochens, AHR, 79(Oct 1974):1149-51.

Dumont, Paul see Aron, Jean-Paul

Duncan, Francis see Hewlett, Richard G.

Duncan, James S. Not a One-Way Street: The Autobiography of James S. Duncan. Toronto/Vancouver: Clarke, Irwin, 1971. Rev. by M. Bliss, CHR, 55(Mar 1974):90-1.

Duncan, Joseph E. Milton's Earthly Paradise: A Historical Study of Eden. Minneapolis: U Minn Press, 1972. Rev. by B. K. Lewalski, CH, 43(Dec 1974):546-7.

Duncan, T. Bentley. Atlantic Islands, Madeira, The Azores, and the Cape Verdes in Seventeenth-Century Commerce and Navigation. Chicago: U Chi Press, 1972. Rev. by C. R. Boxer, JAfH, 15(Num 1 1974):169; P. D. Curtin, RQ, 27(Sum 1974): 233-5.

Duncan-Jones, Richard. The Economy of the Roman Empire: Quantitative Studies. New York: Cam U Press, 1974. Rev. by F. S. Lear, BHR, 48(Win 1974):577-9; C. G. Starr, HRNB, 2 (May/Je 1974):173-4; D. Jones, HTo, 24(May 1974):359-60.

Dungen, P. H. M. The Punjab Tradition: Influence and Authority in Nineteenth-Century India. London: Allen and Unwin, 1972. Rev. by E. Stokes, History, 59(Je 1974):316-17.

Dunham, Dows and William Kelly Simpson. The Mastaba of Queen Mersyankh III. Boston: Museum of Fine Arts, 1974. Rev. by J. D. Cooney, AJA, 78(Oct 1974):433.

Dunn, John. Modern Revolutions: An Introduction to the Analysis of a Political Phenomenon. Cambridge: Cam U Press, 1972. Rev. by E. Ions, History, 59(Feb 1974):164.

_____ and A. F. Robertson. Dependence and Opportunity: Political Change in Ahafo. New York: Cam U Press, 1974. Rev. by J. R. Hooker, HRNB, 2(Mar 1974):123-4.

Dunnell, Robert C. Systematics in Prehistory. New York: Free Press, 1971. Rev. by A. C. Spaulding, AmAnt, 39(Jl 1974): 513-16.

Dunning, R. W. and T. D. Tremlett, eds. Bridgwater Borough Archives, V, 1468-1485. Yeovil: Somerset Record Society, 1971. Rev. by J. Youings, EHR, 89(Ja 1974):165-6.

Dupre, Flint. Hap Arnold: Architect of American Air Power. New

York: Macmillan, 1972. Rev. by R. F. Futrell, AHR, 79(Oct 1974):1284-5.

Dupree, Louis. Afghanistan. Princeton, N. J. Prin U Press, 1973. Rev. by D. N. Wilber, Archaeology, 27(Oct 1974):283-4; R. G. Landen, HRNB, 2(Apr 1974):146.

Durand, Yves. Le Fermiers Generaux au Dix huitieme Siecle. Paris: Presses Universitaires de France, 1971. Rev. by B. Behrens, HJ, 17(Num 3 1974):631-43.

Durden, Robert F. The Gray and the Black: The Confederate Debate on Emancipation. Baton Rouge: LSU Press, 1972. Rev. by T. J. Pressly, AHR, 79(Oct 1974):1267-8; C. L. Mohr, GR, 28(Spr 1974):163-5; K. B. Shover, Historian, 36(Feb 1974):343; W. D. Reeves, LaH, 15(Sum 1974):308-9.

Durham, Walter T. A College for This Community. A History of the Local Colleges Antecedent to Volunteer State Community College, Galatin, Tennessee. Galatin, Tenn.: Sumner County Public Library Board, 1974. Rev. by R. E. Dalton, THQ, 33(W 1974):454-5.

Dussell, Enrique D. Historia de la iglesia en America Latina. Barcelona: Editorial Nova Terra, 1972. Rev. by M. E. Crahan, HAHR, 54(Feb 1974):118-19.

Duster, Alfreda M., ed. Crusade for Justice: The Autobiography of Ida B. Wells. Chicago: U Chi Press, 1970. Rev. by B. Quarles, AHR, 79(Feb 1974):237-8.

Dvornik, Francis. Origins of Intelligence Services: The Ancient Near East, Persia, Greece, Rome, Byzantium, the Arab Muslim Empires, the Mongol Empire, China, Muscovy. New Brunswick, N.J.: Rutgers U Press, 1974. Rev. by O. W. Reinmuth, HRNB, 3(Oct 1974):19.

Dyer, Alan D. The City of Worcester in the Sixteenth Century. Leicester: Leicester U Press, 1973. Rev. by P. Slack, History, 59(Je 1974):266-7.

Dyer, James. Discovering Archaeology in Denmark. Aylesbury: Shire Publications, 1972. Rev. by B. Gilman, Antiquity, 48 (Je 1974):148-9.

_____. Southern England: An Archaeological Guide. London: Faber, 1973. Rev. by C. W. Phillips, Antiquity, 48(Sep 1974): 236.

Dykhuizen, George. The Life and Mind of John Dewey. Carbondale: S Ill U Press, 1973. Rev. by R. H. Elias, JAH, 61 (Dec 1974):809-10; W. P. Kroliowski, MiA, 56(Ja 1974):71-2; M. Curti, VH, 42(W 1974):65-6.

Dyos, H. J. and Michael Wolff, eds. The Victorian City: Images
    and Realities. 2 volumes. London: Routledge and Kegan
    Paul, 1973. Rev. by N. Harris, JMH, 46(Dec 1974):709-13.

Eakin, Terry Clay. Students and Politics: A Comparative Study.
    Bombay: Popular Prakashan, 1972. Rev. by M. L. Cormack,
    JAS, 33(May 1974):500.

Eakle, Arlene H. see Jones, Vincent L.

Earle, George F., ed. see Anderson, Eric A.

Earle, Peter, ed. Essays in European Economic History, 1500-
    1800. New York: Ox U Press, 1974. Rev. by D. P. Res-
    nick, HRNB, 3(Oct 1974):14-15.

_____. Robert E. Lee. New York: Saturday Review Press,
    1973. Rev. by F. N. Boney, JSH, 40(Nov 1974):665-6.

Earnshaw, Deanne. Castle Rock--West of Skyline. Los Altos:
    Sempervirens Fund, 1973. Rev. by J. H. Engbeck, Jr., CHQ,
    53(Sum 1974):186-7.

Eason, Ruth P. History of the Town of Glen Burnie. Glen Burnie,
    Md.: The Kuethe Library, Inc., 1972. Rev. by M. N.
    Schatz, MHM, 63(Spr 1974):114-5.

Easton, Stewart C. The Heritage of the Past: Earliest Times to
    1500. New York: Holt, Rinehart and Winston, 1970. Rev.
    by A. W. Godfrey, HT, 8(Nov 1974):110-11.

_____. The Western Heritage from Earliest Times to the
    Present. New York: Holt, Rinehart and Winston, 1970.
    Rev. by E. Y. Enstam, HT, 7(May 1974):483-5; L. Wilson,
    HT, 7(May 1974):484-5.

Eaton, Leonard K. American Architecture Comes of Age: European
    Reaction to H. H. Richardson and Louis Sullivan. Cambridge,
    Mass.: M I T Press, 1972. Rev. by N. Harris, AHR, 79
    (Je 1974):886-7; M. H. Rose, MiA, 56(Apr 1974):135-6.

Eayrs, James. In Defence of Canada. III: Peacemaking and De-
    terrence. Toronto: U Tor Press, 1972. Rev. by J. L.
    Granatstein, CHR, 55(Je 1974):205-6.

Eber, Dorothy, ed. Pitselak: Pictures out of My Life. Seattle:
    U Wash Press, 1971. Rev. by E. Gunther, PNQ, 65(Ja 1974):
    41-2.

Eby, Cecil. "That Disgraceful Affair," The Black Hawk War. New
    York: Norton, 1973. Rev. by R. N. Satz, JAH, 61(Je 1974):
    183-4; V. J. Vogel, JISHS, 67(Apr 1974):237-8; R. L. Nichols,
    WMH, 58(Aut 1974):60; E. M. Coffman, WVH, 35(Apr 1974):
    241-2.

Eccles, W. J. France in America. New York: Harper and Row,
1972. Rev. by L. S. Fallis, AHR, 79(Je 1974):842; J. Sosin,
CHR, 55(Sep 1974):313-15; J. P. Donnelly, JAH, 61(Sep 1974):
455; J. P. Greene, LaH, 15(W 1974):94.

Eckert, Allan W. The Court-Martial of Daniel Boone. Boston:
Little, Brown, 1973. Rev. by E. W. Bentley, FCHQ, 48(Ja
1974):67-8.

Eckert, Edward K. The Navy Department in the War of 1812.
Gainesville: U Fla Press, 1973. Rev. by R. E. Johnson,
AlaHQ, 36(Spr 1974):81-2; W. N. Still, Jr., FHQ, 53(Oct
1974):211; R. V. Haynes, NCHR, 51(W 1974):114-15.

The Economic Commission for Latin America, The United Nations.
Income Distribution in Latin America. New York: The United
Nations, 1971. Rev. by R. A. Berry, HAHR, 54(Aug 1974):
542-4.

Edelstein, Sidney M. Historical Notes on the Wet-processing Industry. New York: Dexter Chemical Corp., 1972. Rev. by
M. Gorman, T & C, 15(Apr 1974):328-9.

Edgar, Walter B., ed. see Biographical Directory of the South
Carolina House of Representatives

Edge, Charles see Harper, Howard M., Jr.

Edwardes, Michael. Ralph Fitch, Elizabethan in the Indies. New
York: Barnes and Noble, 1973. Rev. by P. S. McGarry,
Historian, 36(Aug 1974):743-4.

_____. A Season in Hell. New York: Taplinger, 1973. Rev.
by M. Nadis, AHR, 79(Feb 1974):213.

Edwards, I. E. S., et al., eds. The Cambridge Ancient History.
Volume 2, part 1, History of the Middle East and the Aegean
Region c. 1800-1380 B.C. New York: Cam U Press, 1973.
Rev. by T. B. Jones, AHR, 79(Je 1974):760-1.

Edwards, J. A., comp. Historical Farm Records. Reading, England: U Reading, 1973. Rev. by H. T. Pinkett, AmArc, 37
(Apr 1974):290-1.

Edwards, Jerome E. The Foreign Policy of Col. McCormick's
Tribune, 1929-1941. Reno: U Nev Press, 1971. Rev. by
T. A. Bailey, AHR, 79(Apr 1974):608-9.

Edwards, O. C., Jr. How It All Began: Origins of the Christian
Church. New York: Seabury, 1973. Rev. by E. P. Y. Simpson, CH, 43(Sep 1974):385-6.

Edwards, Samuel. Rebel! A Biography of Tom Paine. New York:

Praeger, 1974. Rev. by J. B. Whisker, HRNB, 3(Nov/Dec 1974):45.

Edwards, Stewart. The Paris Commune, 1871. Chicago: ... Quadrangle, 1971. Rev. by R. L. Williams, Historian, 36(Feb 1974):326-7.

Egami, Namio. The Beginnings of Japanese Art. New York and Tokyo: Weatherhill/Heibonsha, 1973. Rev. by J. E. Kidder, Archaeology, 27(Apr 1974):149-50.

Egerton, John. The Americanization of Dixie: The Southernization of America. New York: Harper's Magazine Press, 1974. Rev. by M. Billington, JSH, 40(Nov 1974):641-2.

Eggert, Gerald G. Richard Olney: Evolution of a Statesman. University Park, Pa.: Pa St U Press, 1974. A. Hoogenboom, HRNB, 3(Oct 1974):4.

Egret, Jean. Louis XV et l'Opposition Parlementaire. Paris: Armand Colin, 1970. Rev. by B. Behrens, HJ, 17(Num 3 1974):631-43.

Ehrenkreutz, Andrew S. Saladin. Albany: SUNY Press, 1972. Rev. by H. Nierman, AHR, 79(Apr 1974):501-2; A. A. Heggoy, HT, 7(Feb 1974):307.

Eide, Ingvard Henry. Oregon Trail. Chicago: Rand McNally, 1973. Rev. by M. J. Mattes, NDH, 41(Spr 1974):33-4.

Eighmy, John Lee. Churches in Cultural Captivity: A History of the Social Attitudes of Southern Baptists. Knoxville: U Tenn Press, 1972. Rev. by W. J. Gribbin, AHR, 79(Apr 1974): 566-7; H. C. Davis, AlaHQ, 36(Spr 1974):85-7.

Ekundare, R. Olufemi. An Economic History of Nigeria, 1860-1960. London: Methuen, 1973. Rev. by A. J. H. Latham, History, 59(Je 1974):307; T. R. DeGregori, T & C, 15(Ja 1974):150.

Elazar, Daniel J. Cities of the Prairie: The Metropolitan Frontier and the American Politics. New York: Basic Books, 1970. Rev. by H. R. Lamar, JAH, 61(Sep 1974):501-3.

Elcock, Howard. Portrait of a Decision: The Council of Four and the Treaty of Versailles. London: Eyre Methuen, 1972. Rev. by K. Robbins, History, 59(Feb 1974):150-1.

Eldridge, C. C. England's Mission: The Imperial Idea in the Age of Gladstone and Disraeli, 1868-1880. Chapel Hill: UNC Press, 1974. Rev. by J. A. Casada, HRNB, 2(Apr 1974):138.

Elegant, Robert S. Mao's Great Revolution. London: Weidenfeld & Nicolson, 1971. Rev. by A. J. Watson, MAS, 8(Apr 1974): 273-5.

Eliades, David <u>see</u> Dial, Adolph

Elias, Robert H. "Entangling Alliances with None": An Essay on
the Individual in the American Twenties. New York: Norton,
1973. Rev. by C. Forcey, JAH, 60(Mar 1974):1172-3.

Elias, T. O. Africa and the Development of International Law.
Dobbs Ferry, N.Y.: Oceana, 1972. Rev. by R. A. Akindele,
JMAS, 12(Je 1974):323-6.

Elkins, Stanley and Eric McKitrick, eds. The Hofstadter Aegis:
A Memorial. New York: Knopf, 1974. Rev. by T. V. Di-
Bacco, HRNB, 3(Oct 1974):4-5.

Elkinton, Amelie <u>see</u> Fink, Augusta. Adobes in the Sun.

[Ellington, Edward Kennedy]. Music is My Mistress: Edward Kennedy Ellington. Garden City, N.Y.: Doubleday, 1973. Rev.
by G. G. Current, Crisis, 81(Apr 1974):139.

Elliott, Philip. The Sociology of the Professions. New York: Mc-
Graw-Hill, 1972. Rev. by E. A. Krause, T & C, 15(Jl 1974):
524-6.

Elliott, Russell R. History of Nevada. Lincoln: U Neb Press,
1973. Rev. by W. Bean, JAH, 60(Mar 1974):1145-6; L. P.
James, JOW, 13(Apr 1974):111-12; G. M. Ostrander, WHQ,
5(Ja 1974):67-8.

Ellis, G. M., trans. Boso's Life of Alexander III. Totowa, N.J.:
Rowman and Littlefield, 1973. Rev. by B. McGinn, CH, 43
(Mar 1974):100-1.

Ellis, John. Armies in Revolution. New York: Ox U Press, 1974.
Rev. by J. P. Smaldone, HRNB, 2(May/Je 1974):169-70.

Ellis, Joseph J. The New England Mind in Transition: Samuel
Johnson of Connecticut, 1696-1772. New Haven, Conn.: Yale
U Press, 1973. Rev. by S. J. Stein, CH, 43(Sep 1974):419-
20; R. A. Gleissner, HRNB, 2(Ja 1974):64; D. H. Flaherty,
JAH, 61(Dec 1974):759-60; S. S. Cohen, NYHSQ, 58(Jl 1974):
238-9; N. S. Fiering, WMQ-3, 31(Apr 1974):314-18.

Ellison, James Whitfield. The Summer After the War. New York:
Dodd, Mead, 1972. Rev. by W. Maier, VH, 42(Sum 1974):
245.

Ellison, Mary. Support for Secession: Lancashire and the American Civil War. Chicago: U Chi Press, 1972. Rev. by C.
Bolt, AHR, 79(Je 1974):868-9; N. B. Ferris, CWH, 20(Mar
1974):67-9; K. J. Brauer, JAH, 60(Mar 1974):1131-2; B. D.
Ledbetter, MiA, 56(Apr 1974):127-8; J. A. Carpenter, NYHSQ,
58(Ja 1974):71-2.

Ellsworth, Lucius F., ed. The Americanization of the Gulf Coast: 1803-1850. Pensacola, Fla.: Historic Pensacola Preservation Board, 1972. Rev. by D. W. Curl, CWH, 20(Sep 1974):267-8.

_____. see Taylor, George Rogers

Ellsworth, S. George. Dear Ellen: Two Mormon Women and Their Letters. Salt Lake City: U Utah Library, 1974. Rev. by B. Beeton, UHQ, 42(Sum 1974):296-8.

Ellwood, Robert S. The Feast of Kingship: Accession Ceremonies in Ancient Japan. Tokyo: Sophia U, 1973. Rev. by A. Bloom, JAS, 33(May 1974):481-3.

Elrington, C. R. The Registers of Roger Martival Bishop of Salisbury, 1315-1330. Vol. ii (bis): the Register of Divers Letters. (Second Half.) n.p.: Canterbury and York Society, 1972. Rev. by F. R. H. Du Boulay, EHR, 89(Apr 1974):420.

Elsmere, Jane Shaffer. Henry Ward Beecher, the Indiana Years, 1837-1847. Indianapolis: Ind Historical Society, 1973. Rev. by J. C. Dann, FCHQ, 48(Oct 1974):365-6; W. W. Wimberly II, IMH, 70(Je 1974):189-90; C. E. Clark, Jr., JAH, 61(Je 1974):184-5; J. H. Rodabaugh, RKHS, 72(Oct 1974):420-2.

Elson, Robert T. The World of Time, Inc.: The Intimate History of a Publishing Enterprise. Volume 2, 1941-1960. New York: Atheneum, 1973. Rev. by R. A. Rutland, AHR, 79(Apr 1974): 611-12.

Elton, G. R. Policy and Police: The Enforcement of the Reformation in the Age of Thomas Cromwell. Cambridge: Cam U Press, 1972. Rev. by J. C. Spalding, CH, 43(Mar 1974): 111-12; M. E. James, History, 59(Je 1974):270-3.

_____. Reform and Renewal: Thomas Cromwell and the Common Weal. New York: Cambridge U Press, 1973. Rev. by L. B. Smith, AHR, 79(Feb 1974):140-1; J. C. Spalding, CH, 43(Mar 1974):111-12; M. E. James, History, 59(Je 1974): 270-3.

_____. Studies in Tudor and Stuart Politics and Government: Papers and Reviews, 1946-1972. New York: Cam U Press, 1974. Rev. by S. Hanft, HRNB, 3(Sep 1974):235-6.

Elvin, Mark. The Pattern of the Chinese Past. Stanford, Cal.: Stan U Press, 1973. Rev. by C. Dietrich, AHR, 79(Feb 1974): 209-10; J. S. Major and D. C. Major, T & C, 15(Jl 1974): 511-14.

Embleton, Gerry see Windrow, Martin

Emerson, Dorothy. Among the Mescalero Apaches: The Story of

Father Albert Braun, O. F. M.   Tucson: U Ariz Press, 1973.
Rev. by P. F. Blankenship, CH, 43(Je 1974):283-4; R. N.
Ellis, ChOk, 52(Fall 1974):389-90; M. H. Wilson, NMHR, 49
(Oct 1974):334-5; M. B. Cooley, WHQ, 5(Jl 1974):348.

Emmanuel, Arghiri.   Unequal Exchange: A Study of the Imperialism of Trade.   New York: Monthly Review Press, 1972.   Rev.
by B. Stuckey, JMAS, 12(Mar 1974):148-50.

Emmerich, J. Oliver.   The Two Faces of Janus: The Saga of Deep
South Change.   University, Miss.:   U and Coll Press Miss,
1973.   Rev. by R. Jenkins, AlaHQ, 36(Spr 1974):88-91; G. C.
Osborn, GHQ, 58(Supp 1974):213-24; E. C. Johnson, NCHR,
51(Jan 1974):107-8.

Emmitt, Robert.   The Last War Trail: The Utes and the Settlement
of Colorado.   Norman: U Okla Press, 1972.   Rev. by J.
Cornelison, N H, 55(Sum 1974):303-4.

Emy, H. V.   Liberals, Radicals and Social Politics, 1892-1914.
New York: Cam U Press, 1973.   Rev. by P. P. Poirier,
AHR, 79(Feb 1974):151-2; H. Pelling, EHR, 89(Apr 1974):
405-7.

Endy, Melvin B., Jr.   William Penn and Early Quakerism.   Princeton, N.J.:   Prin U Press, 1973.   Rev. by J. W. Frost, CH,
43(Sep 1974):418-19; R. T. Vann, JAH, 61(Sep 1974):459-60.

Engel, Beth Bland.   The Middleton Family....   Jesup, Ga.:   Jesup
Sentinel, 1972.   Rev. by B. D. Stanley, GHQ, 58(Supp 1974):
219.

Engerman, Stanley L.   see   Fogel, Robert William

Enloe, Cynthia H.   Ethnic Conflict and Political Development.   Boston: Little, Brown, n.d.   Rev. by M. Friedman, Commentary,
58(Jl 1974):98-9.

Ennen, Edith.   Die Europaische stadt des mittelalters.   Göttingen:
Vanderhoeck and Ruprecht, 1972.   Rev. by T. H. Lloyd, History, 59(Feb 1974):82-3.

Enterline, James Robert.   Viking America: The Norse Crossings
and Their Legacy.   Garden City, N.Y.:   Doubleday, 1972.
Rev. by A. R. Lewis, AHR, 79(Oct 1974):1247-8.

Epstein, David G.   Brasilia, Plan and Reality: A Study of Planned
and Spontaneous Urban Development.   Berkeley: U Cal Press,
1973.   Rev. by F. Violich, HAHR, 54(May 1974):343-4.

Epstein, T. Scarlett.   South India: Yesterday, Today and Tomorrow.   New York: Holmes and Meier, 1973.   Rev. by G.
Rosen, JAS, 33(Aug 1974):727-9.

Erasmus. The Comparation of a Virgin and a Martyr (1523). Tr. by Thomas Raynell. Ed. by William James Hirten. Gainesville, Fla.: Scholars' Facsimiles and Reprints, 1970. Rev. by H. T. Mandeville, RQ, 27(Spr 1974):57-60.

_____. Opera omnia, recognita et adnotatione critica instructa notisque illustrata. Ed. by L. E. Halkin, F. Bierlaire, and R. Hoven. Amsterdam: North-Holland Pub. Co., 1972. Rev. by C. R. Thompson, RQ, 27(Sum 1974):196-8.

Erickson, Arvel B. and Wilbur Devereux Jones. The Peelites, 1846-1857. see Jones, Wilbur Devereux and Arvel B. Erickson. The Peelites....

Erickson, Charlotte. Invisible Immigrants: The Adaptation of English and Scottish Immigrants in Nineteenth-Century America. Coral Gables, Fla.: U Miami Press, 1972. Rev. by G. T. Morgan, Jr., ETHJ, 12(Spr 1974):63-4; P. A. M. Taylor, JAmS, 8(Aug 1974):265-6; B. P. Sherman, JOW, 13(Oct 1974): 125; R. J. Vecoli, MHM, 69(Spr 1974):109-11; T. M. Pitkin, NYHSQ, 58(Ja 1974):73-5; T. Saloutos, PHR, 43(Feb 1974): 129-30; D. J. Jeremy, T & C, 15(Jl 1974):497-8; F. C. McLaughlin, WPHM, 57(Ja 1974):118-19.

Erikson, Erik H. Dimensions of a New Identity: The 1973 Jefferson Lectures in the Humanities. New York: Norton, 1974. Rev. by W. T. Deininger, HRNB, 2(Aug 1974):222.

Erlanger, Philippe. Margaret of Anjou: Queen of England. Coral Gables, Fla.: U Miami Press, 1971. Rev. by J. Dahmus, AHR, 79(Oct 1974):1167.

Erlich, Walter, ed. Presidential Impeachment: An American Dilemma. St. Charles, Mo.: Forum Press, 1974. Rev. by A. Burke, HT, 7(Aug 1974):639-41.

Ernst, Joseph Albert. Money and Politics in America, 1755-1775. Chapel Hill: UNC Press, 1973. Rev. by G. M. Walton, BHR, 48(Sum 1974):245-6; J. E. Fickle, HRNB, 2(Apr 1974):152; J. H. Soltow, JAH, 61(Dec 1974):765-7; H. M. Ward, JSH, 40 (Aug 1974):460-2; M. L. M. Kay, NCHR, 51(Sum 1974):347-8; J. A. Schutz, NEQ, 47(Sep 1974):489-90; J. G. Smith, WPHM, 57(Jl 1974):324-5.

Eschholz, Paul A., ed. see Biddle, Arthur W., ed.

Esherick, Joseph W., ed. Lost Chance in China: The World War II Despatches of John S. Service. New York: Random House, 1974. Rev. by K. E. Shewmaker, HRNB, 3(Nov/Dec 1974): 36-7.

Esin, B. I. Russian Prerevolutionary Newspapers 1702-1917: A Brief Essay. Moscow: Izdatel'stvo Moskovskogo Universiteta,

1971.   Rev. by D. M. O'Flaherty, AHR, 79(Oct 1974):1218-
20.

Essame, H. Patton: A Study in Command. New York: Scribner's,
1974. Rev. by S. Sternlicht, HRNB, 2(Jl 1974):194-5.

Etter, Don D. Denver University Park: Four Walking Tours. Denver: Graphic Impressions, 1974. Rev. by B. A. Storey,
CoMag, 51(Spr 1974):169-70.

Ettinghausen, Henry. Francisco de Quevedo and the Neostoic Movement. New York: Oxford U Press, 1972. Rev. by J. Vinci,
RQ, 27(Sum 1974):207-9.

Euler, Robert C. The Navajo People. see Dobyns, Henry F.

_____ and Henry F. Dobyns. The Hopi People. Phoenix: Indian Tribal Series, 1971. Rev. by L. C. Kelly, A & W, 16
(Spr 1974):69-70.

Evans, Carol see Johnson, Walter. The Papers of Adlai E.
Stevenson, Vol. III.

Evans, Eli N. The Provincials: A Personal History of the Jews
in the South. New York: Atheneum, 1973. Rev. by L. Berg,
Commentary, 81(Jl 1974):94-6; J. A. Isaacs, JSH, 40(May
1974):348-9.

Evans, J. G. Land Snails in Archaeology. London...: Seminar
Press, 1972. M. P. Kerney, Antiquity, 48(Mar 1974):75-6.

Evans, John X., ed. The Works of Sir Roger Williams. Oxford:
Ox U Press, 1972. Rev. by H. Dunthorne, History, 59(Je
1974):275-6.

Evans, W. McKee. To Die Game: The Story of the Lowry Band,
Indian Guerrillas of Reconstruction. Baton Rouge: LSU Press,
1971. Rev. by J. R. Kirkland, AHR, 79(Je 1974):876-7.

Everitt, Alan. The Pattern of Rural Dissent: The Nineteenth Century. Leicester: Leicester U Press, 1972. Rev. by D. M.
Thompson, EHR, 89(Ja 1974):208-9.

_____, ed. Perspectives in English Urban History. New York:
Macmillan, n.d. Rev. by A. L. Rowse, HTo, 24(Mar 1974):
211-12.

Evers, Alf. The Catskills: From Wilderness to Woodstock. Garden City, N.Y.: Doubleday, 1972. Rev. by W. Tripp, Historian, 36(Feb 1974):352-3.

Eversley, D. C., ed. Third International Conference on Economic
History, Munich, 1965: Section VII, Demography and Economy.

Paris and The Hague: Mouton, 1972. Rev. by R. Mitchison, History, 59(Feb 1974):162-3.

Faber, J. A. Drie eeuwen Friesland economische en sociale ont- wikkelingen van 1500 tot 1800. 2 vols. Wageningen: Land- bouwhogeschool, 1972. Rev. by J. L. Price, History, 59 (Feb 1974):110-11.

Faber, M. L. O. and J. G. Potter. Towards Economic Indepen- dence: Papers on the Nationalisation of the Copper Industry in Zambia. London: Cam U Press, 1971. Rev. by C. Ehr- lich, AfAf, 73(Jl 1974):378-9.

Faber, Mike and Dudley Seers, eds. The Crisis in Planning. 2 vols. London: Chatto and Windus, 1972. Rev. by A. F. Ewing, JMAS, 12(Sep 1974):507-10.

Fafunwa, A. Babs. A History of Nigerian Higher Education. Lagos: Macmillan, 1971. Rev. by A. H. M. Kirk-Greene, Africa, 44(Apr 1974):203-4.

Fagan, Patricia W. Exiles and Citizens: Spanish Republicans in Mexico. Austin: U Tx Press, 1973. Rev. by M. Kenny, TAm, 30(Ja 1974):424-8.

Fages, Pedro. A Historical, Political, and Natural Description of California. Ramona, Cal.: Ballena, 1972. Rev. by W. W. Cordray, JOW, 13(Oct 1974):129.

Fagg, W. The Living Arts of Nigeria. London: Studio Vista, 1971. Rev. by G. I. Jones, Africa, 44(Apr 1974):210-12.

Falcon, Walter P. and Gustav F. Papanek, ed. Development Policy II: The Pakistan Experience. Cambridge: Har U Press, 1971. Rev. by A. Robinson, MAS, 8(Apr 1974):263-6.

Fallas, Marco Antonio. La Factoría de Tobacos de Costa Rica. San José, C. R.: Editorial Costa Rica, 1972. Rev. by H. Pérez Brignoli, TAm, 30(Apr 1974):550.

Faraday, M. A. Herfordshire Militia Assessments of 1663. Lon- don: Royal Historical Society, 1972. Rev. by D. Allen, EHR, 89(Apr 1974):442-3.

Farley, Rawle. The Economics of Latin America: Development Problems in Perspective. New York: Harper and Row, 1972. Rev. by R. A. Berry, HAHR, 54(May 1974):542-4.

Farmer, Judith A. with Daniel B. Karnes, G. Thomas Babich, and Thompson P. Porterfield. Historical Atlas of Early Oregon. Text by Kenneth L. Holmes. Portland: Historical Cartograph- ic Publications, 1973. Rev. by E. P. Thatcher, PNQ, 65(Jl 1974):150.

Farmer, Margaret Pace. One Hundred Fifty Years in Pike County,
   Alabama, 1821-1971. Anniston, Ala.: Higginbotham, 1973.
   Rev. by C. J. Coley, AlaR, 27(Oct 1974):287-8.

Farnham, Emily. Charles Demuth: Behind a Laughing Mask. Norman: U Ok Press, 1971. Rev. by F. C. Jaher, AHR, 79
   (Feb 1974):243.

Farr, Finis. Chicago: A Personal History of America's Most
   American City. New Rochelle, N.Y.: Arlington House, 1973.
   Rev. by G. M. Danzer, JISHS, 67(Sep 1974):445.

Farrington, S. Kip, Jr. The Santa Fe's Big Three: the Life Story
   of a Trio of the World's Greatest Locomotives. New York:
   David McKay, 1972. Rev. by W. S. Greever, NMHR, 49(Ja
   1974):84-5.

Fathy, Hassan. Architecture for the Poor: An Experiment in Rural
   Egypt. Chicago: U Chi Press, 1973. Rev. by C. W. Condit,
   T & C, 15(Apr 1974):343-5.

Fatout, Paul. Indiana Canals. West Lafayette, Ind.: Purdue U
   Studies, 1972. Rev. by R. D. Gray, Historian, 36(Feb 1974):
   351; B. Anson, JISHS, 67(Sep 1974):450-1.

Faulk, Odie B. Destiny Road: The Gila Trail and the Opening of
   the Southwest. New York: Ox U Press, 1973. Rev. by S. V.
   Connor, ChOk, 52(Spr 1974):116-17; G. L. Seligmann, Jr.,
   HRNB, 2(Ja 1974):62-3; R. C. Carriker, JAH, 61(Sep 1974):
   484; A. Wallace, JAriH, 15(Sum 1974):186-7; M. E. Nackman,
   JSH, 40(May 1974):349-50; R. N. Ellis, NMHR, 49(Jl 1974):
   261-2; W. T. Jackson, PHR, 43(Aug 1974):419-20; L. L. Peterson, WHQ, 5(Jl 1974):352-3.

_____. North America Divided.... see Connor, Seymour V.

Fearon, Peter and Derek H. Aldcroft, eds. British Economic Fluctuations, 1790-1939. see Aldcroft, Derek H. and Peter Fearon, eds. British Economic Fluctuations....

Fedorov, M. G. Russian Progressive Thought of the 19th Century:
   From Geographic Determinism to Historical Materialism.
   Novosibirsk: Izdatel'stvo "Nauka," 1972. Rev. by J. L.
   Black, AHR, 79(Je 1974):819.

Fehrenbach, T. R. Fire and Blood: A History of Mexico. New
   York: Macmillan, 1973. Rev. by M. C. Meyer, HAHR, 54
   (Nov 1974):693-4.

Fehrenbacher, Don E., ed. History and American Society: Essays
   of David M. Potter. New York: Ox U Press, 1973. Rev.
   by M. Kammen, JIH, 5(Sum 1974):109-18; G. M. Capers, LaH,
   15(Sum 1974):317-18.

Feierman, Steven. The Shambaa Kingdom: A History. Madison: U Wis Press, 1974. Rev. by H. G. Soff, HRNB, 2(Aug 1974): 226-7.

Feinstein, Alan. African Revolutionary: The Life and Times of Nigeria's Aminu Kano. New York: Quadrangle, 1973. Rev. by D. F. McCall, AHR, 79(Oct 1974):1228-9.

Feinstein, Estelle F. Stamford in the Gilded Age: The Political Life of a Connecticut Town, 1868-1893. Stamford, Conn.: Stamford Historical Society, 1974. Rev. by H. A. Barnes, HRNB, 2(Mar 1974):130-1.

Feldback, Ole. Dansk neutralpolitik under krigen 1778-1783. Copenhagen: G. E. C. Gads Forlag, 1971. Rev. by M. Roberts, EHR, 89(Ja 1974):194-5.

Feldman, Leon A., ed. Ancient and Medieval Jewish History: Essays by Salo Wittmayer Baron. New Brunswick, N.J.: Rutgers U Press, 1972. Rev. by M. Wasserman, HT, 7(Feb 1974):306-7.

Fellman, Michael. The Unbounded Frame: Freedom and Community in Nineteenth-Century American Utopianism. Westport, Conn.: Greenwood, 1973. Rev. by H. Y. Vanderpool, CH, 43 (Sep 1974):424-6; C. Crowe, CWH, 20(Je 1974):168-9; H. Bridges, HRNB, 2(Ja 1974):61-2; L. Breslow, IMH, 70(Sep 1974):255-7; F. C. Jaher, JAH, 61(Je 1974):174.

Fellmeth, Robert C., et al. Politics of Land: Ralph Nader's Study Group Report on Land Use of California. New York: Grossman, 1973. Rev. by P. S. Taylor, PHR, 43(May 1974):284-5.

Felperin, Howard. Shakespearean Romance. Princeton, N.J.: Prin U Press, 1972. Rev. by J. H. P. Pafford, RQ, 27(Spr 1974):105-7.

Fenlon, Dermot. Heresy and Obedience in Tridentine Italy: Cardinal Pole and the Counter Reformation. Cambridge: Cam U Press, 1972. Rev. by J. H. Forse, Historian, 36(May 1974):538-9; J. K. McConica, RQ, 27(Spr 1974):62-4.

Fenno, Richard, ed. The Yalta Conference. Lexington, Mass.: D. C. Heath, 1972. Rev. by A. Yarnell, HT, 8(Nov 1974): 152.

Fenyo, Mario D. Hitler, Horthy and Hungary; German-Hungarian Relations, 1941-1944. New Haven, Conn.: Yale U Press, 1972. Rev. by N. Nagy-Talavera, EEQ, 8(Sum 1974):242-4; N. Stone, History, 59(Feb 1974):154.

Ferguson, E. James. The American Revolution: A General History, 1763-1790. Homewood, Ill.: Dorsey, 1974. Rev. by

J. E. Selby, JAH, 61(Dec 1974):769-70.

_____, et al., eds. see Morris, Robert. The Papers of Robert
Morris.

Ferguson, John. English Diplomacy, 1422-61. Oxford: Ox U Press,
1972. Rev. by M. G. A. Vale, History, 59(Je 1974):260.

_____, ed. Treaty Rolls Preserved in the Public Record Office.
London: H. M. S. O., 1972. Rev. by J. J. N. Palmer,
EHR, 89(Jl 1974):661-2.

Ferguson, Robert B. see Burt, Jesse

Fergusson, Edna. New Mexico: A Pageant of Three Peoples. Albuquerque: U NM Press, 1970. Rev. by G. R. Cruz, JOW,
13(Ja 1974):152-3.

Fernandes, Florestan. Comunidade e sociedade no Brasil. São
Paulo: Companhia Editora Nacional, 1972. Rev. by R. M.
Levine, HAHR, 54(May 1974):345-7.

Ferris, Robert G., ed. Signers of the Declaration: Historic Places
Commemorating the Signing of the Declaration of Independence.
Washington, D. C.: ... National Park Service, 1973. Rev. by
J. H. Broussard, RKHS, 72(Oct 1974):403-4; J. F. Sefcik,
WPHM, 57(Oct 1974):451-2.

Ferro, Marc. The Russian Revolution of February 1917. London:
Routledge and Kegan Paul, 1972. Rev. by J. Barber, History,
59(Je 1974):299-300.

Fetherling, Dale. Mother Jones, the Miners' Angel: A Portrait.
Carbondale: S Ill U Press, 1974. Rev. by H. S. Weast,
HRNB, 2(Mar 1974):128; J. R. Conlin, JAH, 61(Dec 1974):
826-8; N. Lederer, THQ, 33(Spr 1974):110-12; F. A. Zabro-
sky, WPHM, 57(Jl 1974):326-7; G. J. Tucker, WVH, 35(Jl
1974):320-1.

Fichtenau, Heinrich. Das Urkundenwesen in Österreich vom 8. bis
zum früben 13. Jahrhundert. Wien-Köln-Graz: Hermann Böhlaus Nachf., 1971. Rev. by T. A. Reuter, EHR, 89(Jl 1974):
651.

Fiechter, Georges-André. La régime modernisateur de Brésil,
1964-1972. Genève: A. W. Sijthoff-Leiden, 1972. Rev. by
R. H. Chilcote, HAHR, 54(May 1974):341-3.

Fieldhouse, D. K. Economics and Empire, 1830-1914. Ithaca,
N. Y.: Cornell U Press, 1974. Rev. by W. D. Jones, HRNB,
2(Apr 1974):143-4.

Fife, Alta, ed. see Bailey, William A.

Fife, Austin, ed. see Bailey, William A.

Fifield, Russell H. Americans in Southeast Asia: The Roots of Commitment. New York: Crowell, 1973. Rev. by J. F. Paul, HT, 7(Feb 1974):319; J. F. Cady, Historian, 36(May 1974):583-4.

Filesi, Teobaldi. China and Africa in the Middle Ages. London: Frank Cass, 1972. Rev. by J. E. G. Sutton, AfAf, 73(Apr 1974):238-9; D. B. Larkin, JAS, 33(May 1974):475-6.

Fillmore, Clyde. Prisoner of War. Quanah, Tx.: Nortex Offset, 1973. Rev. by V. Ming, ETHJ, 12(Spr 1974):74-5.

Finberg, H. P. R., ed. The Agrarian History of England and Wales. Vol. 1, Part 2. A. D. 43-1042. New York: Cam U Press, 1972. Rev. by W. O. Ault, AHR, 79(Oct 1974): 1163-4; H. R. Loyn, History, 59(Feb 1974):80-2.

Finch, Christopher. The Art of Walt Disney. New York: Abrams, n.d. Rev. by C. D. Anderson, Mankind, 4(Aug 1974):62-3.

Findlay, George. Dr. Robert Broom: Palaeontologist and Physician, 1866-1951. Cape Town: A. A. Balkema, 1972. Rev. by J. T. Robinson, Antiquity, 48(Sep 1974):242-3.

Fine, Lenore and Jesse A. Remington. The Technical Services-the Corps of Engineers: Construction in the United States. Washington: G. P. O., 1973. Rev. by L. G. Callahan, T & C, 15(Ja 1974):114-16.

Finegan, Jack. The Archaeology of the New Testament: The Life of Jesus and the Beginning of the Early Church. Princeton, N.J.: Prin U Press, 1969. Rev. by H. C. Kee, Archaeology, 27(Ja 1974):72, 74-5.

Fink, Augusta. Monterey: The Presence of the Past. San Francisco: Chronicle Books, 1972. Rev. by H. M. Ward, JOW, 13(Apr 1974):117.

_____ and Amelie Elkinton. Adobes in the Sun: Portraits of a Tranquil Era. San Francisco: Chronicle Books, 1972. Rev. by N. E. Ramirez, JOW, 13(Apr 1974):115-16.

Fink, Gary M. Labor's Search for Political Order: The Political Behavior of the Missouri Labor Movement, 1890-1940. Columbia, Mo.: U Mo Press, 1974. Rev. by J. E. Fickle, HRNB, 2(Jl 1974):197-8; W. Houf, MHR, 69(Oct 1974):115-17.

Finlay, John L. Social Credit: The English Origins. Montreal: McGill-Queens U Press, 1972. Rev. by C. B. MacPherson, JMH, 46(Je 1974):351-2.

Finley, Ian. Celtic Art: An Introduction. Park Ridge, N. J.:
    Noyes, 1973. Rev. by J. E. Keefe, AJA, 78(Oct 1974):445-
    6; M. Simpson, Antiquity, 48(Je 1974):146-7.

Finley, Joseph E. The Corrupt Kingdom: The Rise and Fall of the
    United Mine Workers. New York: Simon and Schuster, 1972.
    Rev. by J. R. Sperry, PH, 41(Oct 1974):477-8.

Finley, M. I. The Ancient Economy. Berkeley: U Cal Press,
    1973. Rev. by L. Casson, AHR, 79(Oct 1974):1151-2; F. S.
    Lear, BHR, 48(Win 1974):577-9; C. C. Smith, HRNB, 2(Jl
    1974):205-6; D. Jones, HTo, 24(May 1974):359-60.

Finnegan, Ruth. Oral Literature in Africa. Oxford: Clarendon
    Press, 1970. Rev. by J. R. Rayfield, JAAS, 9(Ja & Apr
    1974):120-1.

_____. see Horton, Robin

Finney, Ben R. Big-Men and Business: Entrepreneurship and
    Economic Growth in the New Guinea Highlands. Honolulu: U
    Press Hawaii, 1973. Rev. by P. Hill, BHR, 48(Sum 1974):
    242-3.

Firth, J. J. Francis, ed. Liber Poenitentialis. Toronto: Pon-
    tifical Institute of Medieval Studies, 1971. Rev. by M. D.
    Knowles, EHR. 89(Ja 1974):114.

Fischer, Louis. The Road to Yalta: Soviet Foreign Relations,
    1941-1945. New York: Harper and Row, 1972. Rev. by P.
    Roley, AHR, 79(Feb 1974):200-1.

Fish, Peter Graham. The Politics of Federal Judicial Administra-
    tion. Princeton: Prin U Press, 1973. Rev. by E. Dum-
    bauld, JAH, 61(Je 1974):240-1.

Fish, Stanley E. Self-Consuming Artifacts· the Experience of
    Seventeenth-Century Literature. Berkeley-Los Angeles: U
    Calif Press, 1972. Rev. by B. Vickers, RQ, 27(Spr 1974):
    117-22.

Fishbein, Meyer H., ed. The National Archives and Statistical Re-
    search. Athens, Ohio: Ohio U Press, 1973. Rev. by R. P.
    Formisano, JAH, 61(Dec 1974):751-3; J. R. Ross, JSH, 40
    (Aug 1974):455-6; N. C. Burckel, HRNB, 2(May/Je 1974):
    162-3; G. T. White, PHR, 43(Nov 1974):600-1.

Fisher, Allan G. B. and Humphrey J. Slavery and Muslim Society
    in Africa: The Institution of Saharan and Sudanic Africa and the
    Trans-Saharan Trade. London: C. Hurst, 1970. Rev. by
    J. D. Fage, History, 59(Je 1974):309-10.

Fiszman, Joseph R. Revolution and Tradition in People's Poland.

Education and Socialization. Princeton, N.J.: Prin U Press, 1972. Rev. by A. Bromke, EEQ, 8(Mar 1974):122-4.

Fite, Gilbert C. and Jim E. Reese. An Economic History of the United States. Boston: Houghton Mifflin, 1973. Rev. by J. E. Fickle, JOW, 13(Jl 1974):112.

Fitting, James E. The Archaeology of Michigan: A Guide to the Prehistory of the Great Lakes Region. Garden City, N.Y.: Natural History Press, 1970. Rev. by J. A. Brown, AmAnt, 39(Apr 1974):395-6.

Fitzgerald, C. P. see Heren, Louis

FitzGerald, Garret. Towards a New Ireland. London: Charles Knight, 1972. Rev. by R. T. Reilly, E-I, 9(Spr 1974):146-7.

Fitzgerald, Richard. Art and Politics: Cartoonists of the Masses and Liberator. Westport, Conn.: Greenwood, 1973. Rev. by H. W. Morgan, HRNB, 2(Aug 1974):227-8.

Fitzhugh, Lester Newton, ed. Cannon Smoke: The Letters of Captain John J. Good, Good-Douglas Texas Battery, CSA. Hillsboro, Tx.: Hill Jr. Coll Press, 1971. Rev. by M. Darst, ETHJ, 12(Spr 1974):63.

Fladeland, Betty. Men and Brothers: Anglo-American Anti-Slavery Cooperation. Urbana: U Ill Press, 1972. Rev. by J. A. Rawley, CWH, 20(Mar 1974):60-4; J. E. Mooney, NEQ, 47 (Je 1974):318-21.

Flanagan, Sue. Sam Houston's Texas. Austin: U Tx Press, 1973. Rev. by S. E. Siegel, ETHJ, 12(Fall 1974):79-80; A. C. Ashcraft, JOW, 13(Oct 1974):131.

Flannery, Kent V. see MacNeish, Richard S. The Prehistory of the Tehuacan Valley, Volume Three.

Fleischer, Helmut. Marxism and History. New York: Harper and Row, 1974. Rev. by M. Berger, HRNB, 2(May/Je 1974):169.

Fleischer, Martin, ed. Machiavelli and the Nature of Political Thought. London: Croom Helm, 1973. Rev. by W. H. Greenleaf, History, 59(Je 1974):263-4; E. G. Gleason, RQ, 27(Fall 1974):322-4.

Fleming, Macklin. The Price of Perfect Justice: The Adverse Consequences of the Current Legal Doctrine of the American Courtroom. New York: Basic Books, n.d. Rev. by J. W. Bishop, Jr., Commentary, 58(Jl 1974):101-4.

Fleming, Thomas, ed. Benjamin Franklin: a Biography in His Own Words. New York: Harper & Row, 1972. Rev. by J. W.

Hutson, PH, 41(Jl 1974):355-7.

Fleming, W. G. Education: Ontario's Preoccupation. Toronto:
    U Tor Press, 1972. Rev. by J. Daly, CHR, 55(Je 1974):
    209-10.

Flint, John E. and Glyndwr Williams, eds. Perspectives of Empire:
    Essays Presented to Gerald S. Graham. London: Longman,
    1973. Rev. by R. T. Shannon, History, 59(Je 1974):331-2.

The Flint Mammoth Cave System, Mammoth Cave National Park,
    Kentucky, U.S.A. Columbus, Ohio: ... Cave Research Founda-
    tion, 1973. Rev. by A. I. George, FCHQ, 48(Apr 1974):199.

Flohn, H. see Schweinfurth, U.

Flores Caballero, Romeo. Counterrevolution: The Role of the
    Spaniards in the Independence of Mexico, 1804-38. Lincoln:
    U Neb Press, 1974. Rev. by D. M. Pletcher, HRNB, 2(Aug
    1974):224-5.

Floto, Inga. Colonel House in Paris: A Study of American Policy
    at the Paris Peace Conference, 1919. Aarhus, Denmark:
    Universitetsforlaget I Aarhus, 1973. Rev. by L. E. Gelfand,
    JAH, 61(Dec 1974):814-15; J. M. Carroll, MiA, 56(Ja 1974):
    61-2.

Floud, Roderick. An Introduction to Quantitative Methods for His-
    torians. Princeton, N.J.: Prin U Press, 1973. Rev. by P.
    Peebles, AHR, 79(Je 1974):751-2; R. O. Davis, CoMag, 51
    (Sum 1974):253-4; R. R. Locke, Historian, 36(Aug 1974):737-
    8; T. J. Nossiter, History, 59(Je 1974):326; E. R. Coover,
    IMH, 70(Mar 1974):88-9; T. B. Alexander, JAH, 60(Mar
    1974):1084-5; C. M. Dollar, JSH, 40(Feb 1974):119-20; W. G.
    Robbins, PHR, 43(May 1974):260-1.

_____, ed. Essays in Quantitative Economic History. New
    York: Ox U Press, 1974. Rev. by J. E. Fickle, HRNB, 3
    (Nov/Dec 1974):22.

Floyd, Troy S. The Columbus Dynasty in the Caribbean, 1492-1526.
    Albuquerque: U NM Press, 1973. Rev. by U Lamb, HAHR,
    54(Nov 1974):703-6; P. E. Kuhl, HRNB, 2(Sep 1974):258.

Fodale, Salvatore. Comes et Legatus Siciliae: Sul privilegio di
    Urbano II e la pretesa Apostolica Legazia dei Normanni di
    Sicilia. Palermo: U Manfredi Editore, 1970. Rev. by M. W.
    Baldwin, AHR, 79(Oct 1974):1170-1.

Fogel, Robert William and Stanley L. Engerman. Time on the
    Cross: The Economics of American Negro Slavery. Boston:
    Little, Brown, 1974. Rev. by N. Glazer, Commentary, 58
    (Aug 1974):70-2; R. A. Gerber, HRNB, 2(Jl 1974):199; J. H.

FOGEL   116

Pruett and R. M. McColley, JSH, 40(Nov 1974):636-9; R. B.
Campbell, SWHQ, 78(Oct 1974):215-7.

Fogel, Robert William. Dimensions of Quantitative Research. see
Aydelotte, William O.

Fois, Mario. Il pensiero cristiano di Lorenzo Valla nel quadro
storico-culturale del suo ambiente. Rome: Gregorian U
Press, 1969. Rev. by C. Trinkaus, RQ, 27(Spr 1974):43-5.

Foley, William E. A History of Missouri. Vol. I, 1673 to 1820.
Columbia, Mo.: U Mo Press, 1971. Rev. by D. Riker, AHR,
79(Oct 1974):1249-50.

Folland, H. F. see Adamson, J. H.

Folz, R., A. Guillou, L. Musset, D. Sourdel. Dé L'Anliquite au
Monde Médieval. Paris: Presses Universitaires de France,
1971. Rev. by P. A. B. Llewellyn, History, 49(Feb 1974):
79.

Folz, Robert. The Coronation of Charlemagne: December 25, 800.
London: Routledge and Kegan Paul, n.d. Rev. by J. Richardson, HTo, 24(Dec 1974):881-2.

Foner, Jack D. Blacks and the Military in American History: A
New Perspective. New York: Praeger, 1974. Rev. by J. F.
Marszalek, Jr., HRNB, 2(Sep 1974):256-7.

Foner, Philip S. Organized Labor and the Black Worker, 1619-1973.
New York: Praeger, 1974. Rev. by J. M. Gowaskie, BHR,
48(Win 1974):548-50; D. Hereshoff, HRNB, 2(Mar 1974):135.

_____. The Spanish-Cuban-American War and the Birth of Amer-
ican Imperialism, 1895-1902. 2 vols. New York: Monthly
Review Press, 1972. Rev. by K. J. Hagan, AHR, 79(Feb
1974):240-1; W. B. Gatewood, Jr., FHQ, 53(Oct 1974):217-19.

_____. The Voice of Black America: Major Speeches by Negroes
in the United States. New York: Simon & Schuster, 1972.
Rev. by N. R. McMillen, HT, 7(Feb 1974):316.

Foot, Michael. Aneurin Bevan: A Biography. Volume II. 1945-
1960. New York: Atheneum, 1973. Rev. by J. Lukacs,
HRNB, 2(Aug 1974):231; S. Koss, JMH, 46(Dec 1974):716-18.

Foote, Wilder see Cordier, Andrew W.

Forbes, Calvin. Blue Monday. Middletown, Conn.: Wes U Press,
1974. Rev. by D. Huddle, GR, 28(Fall 1974):535-40.

Forbis, William H. The Cowboys. New York: Time-Life Books,
1973. Rev. by H. Mothershead, CoMag, 51(Sum 1974):237-8.

Forbush, Bliss. A History of Baltimore Yearly Meeting of Friends.
    Three Hundred Years of Quakerism in Maryland, Virginia, the
    District of Columbia, and Central Pennsylvania. Sandy Spring,
    Md.: Baltimore Yearly Meeting of Friends, 1973. Rev. by
    K. L. Carroll, MHM, 63(Spr 1974):113-4.

Forcione, Alban K. Cervantes' Christian Romance: A Study of
    Persiles y Sigismunda. Princeton, N.J.: Prin U Press, 1972.
    Rev. by T. Niehaus, HAHR, 54(Feb 1974):161-2. S. L. Guy-
    ler, RQ, 27(Fall 1974):355-7.

Ford, Hugh, ed. The Left Bank Revisited: Selections from the
    Paris Tribune, 1917-1934. University Park: Pa St U Press,
    1972. Rev. by D. J. Harvey, Historian, 37(Feb 1974):330-1.

Ford, Nick Aaron. Black Studies: Threat or Challenge? Port
    Washington, N.Y.: Kennikat, 1973. Rev. by W. G. Paul,
    HT, 8(Nov 1974):135; T. D. Perry, NHB, 37(Je/Jl 1974):273.

Foreign Relations of the United States: The Conference at Quebec,
    1944. Washington: Government Printing Office, 1972. Rev.
    by R. W. Leopold, JAH, 60(Mar 1974):1077-8.

Foreign Relations of the United States, 1946. Volume 1, General;
    The United Nations. Washington: Government Printing Office,
    1972. Rev. by W. C. Clemens, Jr., AHR, 79(Apr 1974):614-
    15.

Foreign Relations of the United States, 1946, Volume 8, The Far
    East; 1947, Volume 6, The Far East. Washington: Govern-
    ment Printing Office, 1971, 1972. Rev. by R. D. Buhite,
    AHR, 79(Apr 1974):613-14.

Foreign Relations of the United States, 1946. Vols. 9 and 10. The
    Far East; China. Washington: Government Printing Office,
    1972. Rev. by J. Mirsky, AHR, 79(Feb 1974):249-50.

Foreign Relations of the United States, 1947. Vol. I: General;
    The United Nations. Washington: Government Printing Office,
    1973. Rev. by W. F. Kuehl, JAH, 61(Je 1974):143-4.

Foreign Relations of the United States, 1947. Vol. 3. The British
    Commonwealth; Europe. Washington: Government Printing Of-
    fice, 1972. Rev. by R. E. Bunselmeyer, AHR, 79(Oct 1974):
    1288-9; R. H. Ferrell, JAH, 61(Je 1974):144-5.

Foreign Relations of the United States, 1947. Volume 4, Eastern
    Europe; The Soviet Union. Washington: Government Printing
    Office, 1972. Rev. by W. W. Kulski, AHR, 79(Apr 1974):615-
    17.

Foreign Relations of the United States, 1947. Vol. 5. The Near
    East and Africa. Washington: Government Printing Office,

1971. Rev. by J. A. DeNovo, JAH, 60(Mar 1974):1079-80.

Foreign Relations of the United States, 1947. Vol. 6: The Far
    East. Washington: Government Printing Office, 1972. Rev.
    by R. W. Leopold, JAH, 60(Mar 1974):1080-1.

Foreign Relations of the United States, 1947. Vol. 7. The Far
    East: China. Washington: Government Printing Office, 1972.
    Rev. by J. Mirsky, AHR, 79(Feb 1974):249-50; R. W. Leopold,
    JAH, 60(Mar 1974):1080-1; R. G. O'Connor, PHR, 43(May
    1974):290-1.

Foreign Relations of the United States, 1947. Volume 8, The Amer-
    ican Republics. Washington: Government Printing Office,
    1972. Rev. by R. J. Bartlett, AHR, 79(Je 1974):905-6.

Foreign Relations of the United States, 1948. Vol. 7. The Far
    East: China. Washington: Government Printing Office, 1973.
    Rev. by J. Mirsky, AHR, 79(Oct 1974):1289-90.

Foreign Relations of the United States, 1948. Vol. 9. The West-
    ern Hemisphere. Washington: Government Printing Office,
    1972. Rev. by R. R. Trask, JAH, 60(Mar 1974):1082-3.

Forey, A. J. The Templars in the Corona de Aragon. New York:
    Ox U Press, 1973. Rev. by C. J. Bishko, AHR, 79(Feb
    1974):129-30; R. A. Fletcher, EHR, 89(Jl 1974):614-18.

Forman, Robert E. Black Ghettos, White Ghettos and Slums. En-
    glewood Cliffs, N.J.: Prentice-Hall, 1973. Rev. by J. L.
    Arnold, JNH, 59(Apr 1974):196-203.

Formisano, Ronald P. The Birth of Mass Political Parties: Mich-
    igan, 1827-1861. Princeton, N.J.: Prin U Press, 1971.
    Rev. by R. O. Davis, JISHS, 67(Je 1974):346-7.

Fornari, Harry. Bread Upon the Waters. A History of the United
    States Grain Exports. Nashville, Tenn.: Aurora, 1973. Rev.
    by J. G. Clark, BHR, 48(Spr 1974):140.

Forster, Colin and G. S. L. Tucker. Economic Opportunity and
    White American Fertility Ratios, 1800-1860. New Haven,
    Conn.: Yale U Press, 1972. Rev. by E. S. Lee, AHR, 79
    (Je 1974):857; S. J. Crowther, BHR, 48(Spr 1974):124-5;
    D. R. Leet, JIH, 5(Aut 1974):340-3.

Foskett, Daphne. Samuel Cooper. London: Faber, n.d. Rev. by
    P. Quennell, HTo, 24(Mar 1974):214-15.

Fossett, Frank. Colorado: Its Gold and Silver Mines, Farms and
    Stock Ranges, and Health and Pleasure Resorts. New York:
    Arno, 1973. Rev. by D. A. Smith, CoMag, 51(Spr 1974):157-
    9.

Foster, Elizabeth Read. The Painful Labour of Mr. Elsyng: Trans-
    actions American Philosophical Society, n. s., Vol. lxii, part
    8. Philadelphia: American Philosophical Society, 1972. Rev.
    by G. E. Aylmer, EHR, 89(Jl 1974):667-8.

Foster, Stephen. Their Solitary Way: The Puritan Social Ethic in
    the First Century of Settlement in New England. New Haven,
    Conn.: Yale U Press, 1971. Rev. by C. Brooks, EHR, 89
    (Ja 1974):177-8.

Fowler, Arlen L. The Black Infantry in the West, 1869-1891.
    Westport, Conn.: Greenwood, 1971. Rev. by S. N. Murray,
    NDH, 41(Spr 1974):31-2.

Fowler, David H., Eugene D. Levy, John W. Blassingame and Jac-
    quelyn S. Haywood, eds. In Search of America: Community,
    National Identity, Democracy. 2 vols. New York: Holt,
    Rinehart and Winston, 1972. Rev. by J. G. Buchanan, HT,
    8(Nov 1974):115-16; S. Markowitz and L. Madaras, HT, 8
    (Nov 1974):116-17.

Fowler, William M., Jr. William Ellery: a Rhode Island Politico
    and Lord of Admirality. Metuchen, N.J.: Scarecrow, 1973.
    Rev. by A. T. Klyberg, NEQ, 47(Je 1974):314-5; I. H. Poli-
    shook, WMQ-3, 31(Apr 1974):339-40.

Fox, E. R. James W. Connella, Pioneer Editor. Everett, Wash.:
    1972. Rev. by N. Clark, PNQ, 65(Ja 1974):42.

Fox, Robin Lane. Alexander the Great. London: Allen Lane and
    Longman, n. d. Rev. by M. Grant, HTo, 24(Feb 1974):135-6.

Franchere, Hoyt C., ed. and tr. The Overland Diary of Wilson
    Price Hunt. Ashland, Ore.: Oregon Book Soc., 1973. Rev.
    by L. R. Hafen, WHQ, 5(Oct 1974):459-60.

Francis, A. D. The Wine Trade. New York: Barnes and Noble,
    1973. Rev. by G. V. Scammell, BHR, 48(Spr 1974):113;
    J. L. Bolton, History, 59(Je 1974):279-80.

Francis, Michael J. La Victoria de Allende. Vista por un norte-
    americano.... Santiago, Chile: Editorial Francisco de
    Aguirre, 1972. Rev. by R. H. Dix, HAHR, 54(Feb 1974):
    153-5.

Franda, Marcus F. Radical Politics in West Bengal. Cambridge,
    Mass.: M I T Press, 1971. Rev. by A. Lipski, JAAS, 9
    (Ja & Apr 1974):110-11.

Frank, André Gunder. Lumpenbourgeoisie: Lumpendevelopment.
    Dependence, Class and Politics in Latin America. New York:
    Monthly Review Press, 1972. Rev. by J. M. Hunter, HAHR,
    54(May 1974):305-6.

Frankel, Francine R.   India's Green Revolution: Economic Gains
and Political Costs.   Princeton: Prin U Press, 1971.   Rev.
by B. H. Farmer, MAS, 8(Ja 1974):143-4.

Frankl, Paul.   Principles of Architectural History: The Four
Phases of Architectural Style, 1420-1900.   Cambridge, Mass.:
... M I T Press, 1973.   Rev. by E. R. DeZurko, GR, 28
(Sum 1974):341-5; A. Hoxie, HT, 7(Feb 1974):308.

Franklin, John Hope, ed.   Reminiscences of an Active Life: The
Autobiography of John Roy Lynch.   Chicago: U Chi Press,
1970.   Rev. by B. Quarles, AHR, 79(Feb 1974):237-8; J. E.
Gonzales, JMiH, 36(Nov 1974):388-9.

Franklin, Julian H.   Jean Bodin and the Rise of the Absolutist
Theory.   New York: Cam U Press, 1973.   Rev. by R. Major,
AHR, 79(Apr 1974):504-5.

Frantz, Joe B.   The Driskill Hotel.   Austin: Encino Press, 1973.
Rev. by P. Goeldner, WHQ, 5(Jl 1974):359-60.

Franz, Gunther.   Huberinus-Rhegius-Holbein: Bibliographische und
druckergeschichtliche Untersuchungen der verbreitesten Trost-
und Erbauungsschriften des 16. Jahrhunderts.   Nieuwkoop: B.
de Graaf, 1973.   Rev. by M. Grossmann, CH, 43(Dec 1974):
543-4.

Fraser, Colin.   Tractor Pioneer: The Life of Harry Ferguson.
Athens, Ohio: Ohio U Press, 1973.   Rev. by E. S. Ferguson,
BHR, 48(Win 1974):563-4.

Fraser, Derek.   The Evolution of the British Welfare State: A History of Social Policy Since the Industrial Revolution.   New
York: Barnes and Noble, 1973.   Rev. by D. R. Neat, Historian, 36(Aug 1974):765-6.

Fraser, Douglas and Herbert M. Cole.   African Art and Leadership.
Madison: U Wis Press, 1972.   Rev. by W. M. Robbins, JNH,
59(Ja 1974):96-9.

Fraser, P. M.   Ptolemaic Alexandria.   Volume 1, Text; Volume 2,
Notes; volume 3, Indexes.   New York: Ox U Press, 1972.
Rev. by S. Dow, AHR, 79(Je 1974):763-5.

Frech, Mary L., ed.   Chronology and Documentary Handbook of
the State of Colorado.   Dobbs Ferry, N.Y.:   Oceana, 1973.
Rev. by M. Benson, CoMag, 51(Spr 1974):172-3.

Fredrickson, George M.   The Black Image in the White Mind: The
Debate on Afro-American Character and Destiny, 1817-1914.
New York: Harper and Row, 1971.   Rev. by S. M. Stern,
AHR, 79(Je 1974):857-8; D. H. Fowler, JAH, 61(Sep 1974):
476-7; E. J. Keller, JMAS, 12(Mar 1974):158-60.

Freeberne, Michael see Heren, Louis

Freeland, J. M. Architect Extraordinary: The Life and Work of
   John Horbury Hunt, 1838-1904. Melbourne: Cassell Australia,
   1970. Rev. by J. M. Crook, History, 59(Je 1974):324-5.

Freeman-Grenville, G. S. P. Chronology of African History. London: Ox U Press, 1973. Rev. by R. C. C. L., JAfH, 15
   (Num 3 1974):489-90.

Freiberg, Malcolm, ed. see Massachusetts. House of Representatives. Journals....

Freidel, Frank. Franklin D. Roosevelt: Launching the New Deal.
   Boston: Little, Brown, 1973. Rev. by G. T. Blakey, HRNB,
   2(Feb 1974):90; D. W. Grantham, JAH, 61(Je 1974):242-4;
   R. A. Lee, JSH, 40(Aug 1974):505-6; H. Hamilton, RKHS, 72
   (Oct 1974):412-13; R. N. Kottman, NYHSQ, 58(Apr 1974):162-
   4.

French, Peter J. John Dee: The World of an Elizabethan Magus.
   London: Routledge and Kegan Paul, 1972. Rev. by A. J.
   Turner, EHR, 89(Apr 1974):434.

Frend, W. H. C. The Rise of the Monophysite Movement. Cambridge: Cam U Press, 1972. Rev. by P. A. B. Llewellyn,
   History, 59(Feb 1974):79-80.

Fribourg, Marjorie G. The U. S. Congress: The Men Who Steered
   Its Course, 1787-1867. Philadelphia: Macrae Smith, 1972.
   Rev. by G. W. Wolff, CWH, 20(Je 1974):163-4.

Fridenson, Patrick. Histoire des usines Renault. Volume 1: Naissance de la grande entreprise. Paris: Éditions du Seuil,
   1972. Rev. by W. B. Cohen, JMH, 46(Mar 1974):152-3.

Fridrichsen, Anton. The Problem of Miracle in Primitive Christianity. Minneapolis: Augsburg, 1972. Rev. by J. R. Copeland,
   CH, 43(Sep 1974):385.

Fried, Marc. The World of the Urban Working Class. Cambridge,
   Mass.: Harvard U Press, 1973. Rev. by R. M. Johnson,
   NEQ, 47(Je 1974):333-7.

Friedlander, Marc see Butterfield, L. H.

Friedman, Isaiah. The Question of Palestine, 1914-1918: British-
   Jewish-Arab Relations. New York: Schocken, 1973. Rev. by
   W. R. Polk, AHR, 79(Oct 1974):1226-7; J. Janowski, HRNB,
   2(Ja 1974):75.

Friedman, Lawrence M. A History of American Law. New York:
   Simon and Schuster, 1973. Rev. by J. E. Semonche, JAH,

60(Mar 1974):1087-8.

Friedman, Leon. The Wise Minority. New York: Dial, 1971.
Rev. by S. N. Katz, AHR, 79(Feb 1974):218-19.

Friedman, Saul S. No Haven for the Oppressed: United States
Policy Toward Jewish Refugees, 1938-1945. Detroit: Wayne
St U Press, 1973. Rev. by H. W. Currie, Historian, 36(May
1974):580-1; A. A. Offner, JAH, 61(Je 1974):247-8.

Friedmann, Yohanan, Shakyh Ahmad Sirhindi. Montreal: McGill
U Press, 1971. Rev. by A. Ahmad, JAAS, 9(Ja & Apr 1974):
127.

Frisby, Julian see Balfour, Michael

Fritz, Paul and David Williams, eds. The Triumph of Culture:
18th-Century Perspectives. Toronto: A. M. Hakkert, 1972.
Rev. by J. S. Bromley, EHR, 89(Apr 1974):444-5.

Fritze, Wolfgang H. Papst und Frankenkonig: Studien zu den
papstlich-frankischen Rechtsbeziehungen von 754 bis 824. Sig-
maringen: Jan Thorbecke Verlag, 1973. Rev. by B. D. Hill,
AHR, 79(Feb 1974):122; J. M. Wallace-Hadrill, EHR, 89(Apr
1974):414.

Froncek, Thomas, ed. Voices from the Wilderness: The Frontiersman's Own Story. New York: McGraw-Hill, 1974. Rev. by
G. M. Waller, IMH, 70(Dec 1974):350-1; C. G. Talbert, RKHS,
72(Oct 1974):413-15; R. E. Dalton, THQ, 33(Sum 1974):231-2;
H. Collins, WPHM, 57(Oct 1974):449.

Frost, J. William. The Quaker Family in Colonial America: A
Portrait of the Society of Friends. New York: St. Martin's,
1973. Rev. by D. E. Ball, JAH, 61(Sep 1974):458-9.

Fry, Michael G. Illusions of Security: North Atlantic Diplomacy,
1918-22. Toronto: U Tor Press, 1972. Rev. by T. E.
Hachey, AHR, 79(Oct 1974):1146-7; S. F. Wells, Jr., CHR,
55(Sep 1974):334-5; A. J. P. Taylor, EHR, 89(Ja 1974):236;
K. Bourne, History, 59(Feb 1974):151-2; A. E. Campbell, HJ,
17(Num 2 1974):443-7.

Fuchs, Elinor and Joyce Antler. Year One of the Empire: A Play
of American Politics, War, and Protest Taken from the Historical Record. Boston: Houghton Mifflin, 1973. Rev. by
T. R. Clark, PHR, 43(Nov 1974):625-6.

Fuller, Sara S. see Lentz, Andrea D.

Fuller, Wayne E. The American Mail: Enlarger of the Common
Life. Chicago: U Chi Press, 1972. Rev. by M. Heald, AHR,
79(Oct 1974):1241-2.

Fundamental Testaments of the American Revolution. Washington:
    Library of Congress, 1973. Rev. by E. Wright, IMH, 70(Dec
    1974):345-7; J. M. Poteet, JSH, 40(Aug 1974):466-8; R. M.
    Calhoon, NCHR, 51(Sum 1974):348-9.

Funigiello, Philip J. Toward a National Power Policy: The New
    Deal and the Electric Utility Industry, 1933-1941. Pittsburgh:
    U Pittsburgh Press, 1973. Rev. by T. K. McCraw, BHR,
    48(Spr 1974):136-8; J. T. Gay, HRNB, 2(Feb 1974):100; R. D.
    Cuff, JAH, 61(Dec 1974):832-3; J. B. Smallwood, Jr., JSH,
    40(Aug 1974):503-5.

Furer, Howard B., comp. and ed. The Scandinavians in America
    986-1970: A Chronology and Fact Book. Dobbs Ferry, N.Y.:
    Oceana, 1972. Rev. by N. Lederer, NDH, 41(Spr 1974):34.

Furet, Francois. 'Le Catechisme de la Revolution Francaise,' in
    Annales (Economies, Societes, Civilisations) March to April
    1971. n.p.: n.d. Rev. by B. Behrens, HJ, 17(Num 3 1974):
    631-43.

Furneaux, Rupert. The Pictorial History of the American Revolu-
    tion. Chicago: J. G. Ferguson, 1973. Rev. by S. Sprague,
    RKHS, 72(Ja 1974):75-7.

Fussell, G. E. The Classical Tradition in West European Farming.
    Newton Abbot: David and Charles, 1972. Rev. by G. A. J.
    Hodgett, History, 59(Feb 1974):163-4.

_____. Crop Nutrition: Science and Practice before Liebig.
    Lawrence, Kansas: Coronado Press, 1971. Rev. by F. W.
    Kohlmeyer, T & C, 15(Ja 1974):98-100.

_____. Jethro Tull: His Influence on Mechanized Agriculture.
    Reading, Berkshire: Osprey Pub. Ltd., 1973. Rev. by F. W.
    Kohlmeyer, T & C, 15(Ja 1974):98-100.

Gabert, Glen. In Hoc Signo? A Brief History of Catholic Parochial
    Education in America. Port Washington, N.Y.: Kennikat,
    1973. Rev. by S. K. Schultz, JAH, 61(Je 1974):229-30.

Gabor, Dennis. The Mature Society. New York: Praeger, 1972.
    Rev. by W. A. Blanpied, T & C, 15(Apr 1974):352-4.

Gabor, Sandorne. Austria and the Hungarian Republic of Councils.
    Budapest: Akademiai Kiado, 1969. Rev. by T. Spira, EEQ,
    8(Sum 1974):240-2.

Gadamer, Hans-Georg, ed. Truth and Historicity. The Hague:
    Martinus Nijhoff, 1972. Rev. by M. S. Gram, H & T, 13(Num
    1 1974):83-96.

Gaddis, John Lewis. The United States and the Origins of the Cold

War 1914-1947. New York: Columbia U Press, 1972. Rev. by J. Gimbell, CHR, 55(Sep 1974):336-41; P. G. Boyle, JAmS, 8(Apr 1974):123-4; W. H. McNeill, PHR, 43(May 1974):287-8; D. R. Millar, PNQ, 65(Ja 1974):45.

Gagniers, Jean des. L'Acropole d'Athenes. Portland, Ore.: International Scholarly Book Services, 1971. Rev. by R. Brilliant, AHR, 79(Oct 1974):1152-4.

Gainer, Bernard. The Alien Invasion: The Origins of the Aliens Act of 1905. London: Heinemann, 1972. Rev. by J. Harris, History, 59(Feb 1974):142.

Galai, Shmuel. The Liberation Movement in Russia, 1900-1905. Cambridge: Cam U Press, 1973. Rev. by W. G. Rosenberg, AHR, 79(Je 1974):822-4; M. Raeff, Historian, 36(Feb 1974): 329-30.

Galarza, Joaquín. Lienzos de Chiepetlan. Manuscrits pictographiques et manuscrits en caractères latins de San Miguel Chiepetlan, Guerrero, Mexique. Mexico: Mission Archeologique et Ethnologique Française au Mexique avec le concours du Centre National de la Recherche Scientifique, 1972. Rev. by E. R. Craine, HAHR, 54(Nov 1974):702-3.

Galbraith, J. S. Mackinnon and East Africa, 1878-1895: A Study in the New Imperialism. Cambridge: Cam U Press, 1972. Rev. by B. Porter, History, 59(Feb 1974):126.

Galbraith, John Kenneth. A China Passage. Delhi: Vikas, 1973. Rev. by G. D. Dishingkar, CR, 10(May-Je 1974):63-5.

Galeano, Eduardo. Open Veins of Latin America: Five Centuries of the Pillage of a Continent. New York: Monthly Review Press, 1973. Rev. by W. Dean, HAHR, 54(Nov 1974):691-2.

Gallaway, B. P., comp. and ed. The Dark Corner of the Confederacy: Accounts of Civil War Texas as Told by Contemporaries. Dubuque, Ia.: Kendall/Hunt, 1972. Rev. by N. H. Bowen, ETHJ, 12(Spr 1974):61-2.

Gallego Blanco, Enrique, ed. and trans. The Rule of the Spanish Order of St. James, 1170-1493. Leiden: E. J. Brill, 1971. Rev. by D. W. Lowman, EHR, 89(Ja 1974):153-4.

Gamble, Sidney D., ed. Chinese Village Plays from the Ting Hsien Region: A Collection of Forty-Eight Rural Plays as Staged by Villagers from Ting Hsien in Northern China. Amsterdam: Philco, 1970; New York: Abner Schram, 1972. Rev. by D. S. P. Yang, JAS, 34(Nov 1974):217-18.

Ganguli, B. N. Gandhi's Social Philosophy: Perspective and Relevance. New York: Wiley, 1973. Rev. by L. A. Gordon, JAS, 34 (Nov 1974):244-5.

Gann, L. H. see Duignan, Peter

Gannon, Franklin Reid. The British Press and Germany 1936-1939.
    Oxford: Clarendon Press, 1971. Rev. by K. Robbins, EHR,
    89(Apr 1974):467-8.

Ganzevoort, Herman, tr. A Dutch Homesteader on the Prairies:
    the Letters of Willem De Gelder. Toronto: U Toronto Press,
    1973. Rev. by N. R. Ball, T & C, 15(Jl 1974):499-501.

Garbacz, Christopher. Industrial Polarization Under Economic In-
    tegration in Latin America. Austin: ... U Tx Press, 1971.
    Rev. by W. P. Glade, HAHR, 54(Feb 1974):178-81.

Garber, D. W. Jedediah Strong Smith: Fur Trader from Ohio.
    Stockton, Calif.: U of Pacific, 1973. Rev. by T. I. Berens,
    UHQ, 42(Spr 1974):201-2.

García de Cortázar, J. A. Historia de España Alfaguara. Vol. II:
    La época medieval. Madrid: Alianza Editorial, 1973. Rev.
    by W. D. Phillips, Jr., HAHR, 54(Nov 1974):697-9.

García Laguardia, Jorge Mario. La Reforma Liberal en Guatemala:
    Vida Política y Orden Constitucional. Guatemala: Editorial
    Universitaria de Guatemala and Editorial Universitaria Centro-
    America, 1972. Rev. by T. Schoonover, TAm, 30(Ja 1974):
    416-17.

Gardner, Lloyd, ed. The Great Nixon Turnabout. New York:
    Watts, 1972. Rev. by E. N. Paolino, HT, 8(Nov 1974):147-8.

Gardner, Lloyd C., Walter F. La Feber and Thomas J. McCormick.
    Creation of the American Empire: U. S. Diplomatic History.
    Chicago: Rand McNally, 1973. Rev. by J. D. Doenecke, HT,
    7(Feb 1974):293-5; R. E. Darilek, HT, 7(Aug 1974):624-6;
    J. W. Moore, HT, 7(Aug 1974):626-9; J. D. Doenecke, HT,
    7(Aug 1974):629-31; P. E. Coletta, PHR, 43(May 1974):265-6;
    P. W. Kennedy, PNQ, 65(Ja 1974):43-4.

Gardner, Joseph L. Departing Glory: Theodore Roosevelt as Ex-
    President. N. Y.: Scribner's, 1973. Rev. by G. T. Blakey,
    HT, 8(Nov 1974):150-1; H. Hamilton, Historian, 36(May 1974):
    571-2.

Gardner, W. J., et al. A History of the University of Canterbury,
    1873-1973. Christchurch: U Canterbury, 1973. Rev. by
    H. T. Manning, AHR, 79(Oct 1974):1181-2.

Gargallo di Castel Lentini, Gioacchino. Storia della storiografia
    moderna: Il Settecento. Rome: Bulzoni Editore, 1972. Rev.
    by J. T. S. Wheelock, JMH, 46(Sep 1974):529-30.

Gargan, L. Lo studio teologico e la biblioteca dei Domenicani a

Padova nel tre e quattrocento. Padua: Antenore, 1971. Rev. by B. Smalley, EHR, 89(Ja 1974):159-60.

Garlake, P. S. Great Zimbabwe. London: Thames and Hudson, 1973. Rev. by K. S. R. Robinson, AfAf, 73(Apr 1974):241-2; M. S. Bisson, Archaeology, 27(Jl 1974):211.

Garnett, R. G. Cooperation and the Owenite Socialist Communities in Britain, 1825-45. Manchester: Manchester U Press, 1972. Rev. by C. H. Johnson, AHR, 79(Feb 1974):145-6.

Garrard, J. G., ed. The Eighteenth Century in Russia. Oxford: Ox U Press, 1971. Rev. by T. G. Starvou, HRNB, 2(Feb 1974):107; I. Gray, HTo, 24(Je 1974):433-5.

Garrard, John A. The English and Immigration, 1880-1910. Oxford: Ox U Press, 1971. Rev. by J. Howarth, History, 59 (Feb 1974):141-2.

Garraty, John A. see Rodnitzky, Jerome L.

Gartner, Lloyd P. see Vorspan, Max

Garrett, Julia Kathryn. Fort Worth: A Frontier Triumph. Austin: Encino Press, 1972. Rev. by R. G. Miller, WHQ, 5(Oct 1974):482-3.

Garst, John W. see Patterson, Daniel W.

Gascon, Richard. Grand Commerce et vie urbaine au XVIe siecle: Lyon et ses marchands.... 2 vols. Paris: Mouton, 1971. Rev. by N. Z. Davis, AHR, 79(Feb 1974):158-61.

Gash, Norman. Sir Robert Peel: The Life of Sir Robert Peel after 1830. Totowa, N.J.: Rowman and Littlefield, 1972. Rev. by F. C. Mather, EHR, 89(Ja 1974):127-31; E. G. Callieu, History, 59(Feb 1974):122-3; J. Clive, JMH, 46(Mar 1974): 141-2.

Gasratian, M. A., et al., eds. Modern History of Turkey. Moscow: Izdatel'stvo "Nauka," 1968. Rev. by A. W. Fisher, AHR, 79(Je 1974):825-6.

Gast, Ross H. Don Francisco de Paula Marin: A Biography. Honolulu: U Press Hawaii, 1973. Rev. by M. Tate, AHR, 79 (Feb 1974):222-3; J. H. Kemble, JAH, 60(Mar 1974):1109-10; C. N. Tyson, JOW, 13(Jl 1974):116; H. W. Bradley, PHR, 43(Feb 1974):119; E. A. Beilharz, SCQ, 56(Fall 1974):307-8.

Gates, John Morgan. Schoolbooks and Krags: The United States Army in the Philippines, 1898-1902. Westport, Conn.: Greenwood, 1973. Rev. by S. L. Falk, AHR, 79(Je 1974):886;

D. E. Showalter, Historian, 36(May 1974):577-8; R. F. Weigley, JAH, 60(Mar 1974):1157-8; W. A. Wiegand, MiA, 56(Ja 1974):60-1; H. W. Morgan, PHR, 43(Feb 1974):134-5.

Gates, Paul W. Landlords and Tenants on the Prairie Frontier: Studies in American Land Policy. Ithaca, N.Y.: Cornell U Press, 1973. Rev. by H. E. Socolofsky, CoMag, 51(Sum 1974): 265-6; E. L. Schapsmeier, JOW, 13(Apr 1974):118; G. B. Dodds, PHR, 43(Aug 1974):415-6; R. M. Alston, WHQ, 5(Apr 1974):192-3.

Gati, Charles, ed. Caging the Bear: Containment and the Cold War. Indianapolis: Bobbs-Merrill, 1974. Rev. by R. D. Landa, HRNB, 2(Sep 1974):260.

Gätje, Helmut. Koran und Koranexegese. Zurich. Artemis Verlag, 1971. Rev. by J. Waardenburg, AHR, 79(Feb 1974):202-3.

Gaustad, Edwin Scott. Dissent in American Religion. Chicago: U Chi Press, 1973. Rev. by B. Wyatt-Brown, JSH, 40(Aug 1974): 514-15.

Gay, Peter, ed. The Enlightenment: A Comprehensive Anthology. New York: Simon and Schuster, 1973. Rev. by W. J. Brunhumer, HRNB, 2(Ja 1974):81-2.

Gebhard, Elizabeth R. The Theatre at Isthmia. Chicago: U Chi Press, n.d. Rev. by O. A. W. Dilke, AJA, 78(Apr 1974): 200-1.

Geertz, Clifford. Islam Observed. New Haven, Conn.: Yale U Press, 1968. Rev. by A. Ahmad, JAAS, 9(Ja & Apr 1974): 128-9.

Geiger, Maynard, Intro. California Calligraphy: Identified Autographs of Personages Connected with the Conquest and Development of the Californias. Ramona, Cal.: Bellena Press, 1972. Rev. by G. Jewsbury, JOW, 13(Jl 1974):113.

Geiger, Maynard, tr. The Letters of Alfred Robinson to the De La Guerra Family of Santa Barbara, 1834-1873. Los Angeles: Zamorano Club, 1972. Rev. by T. F. Andrews, SCQ, 56 (Sum 1974):198-9.

Geiss, Imanuel and Bernd Jürgen Wendt, eds. Deutschland in der Weltpolitik des 19. und 20. Jahrhunderts.... Düsseldorf: Bertelsmann Universitätsverlag, 1973. Rev. by W. E. Mosse, EHR, 89(Jl 1974):644-6.

Geisse, Guillermo and Jorge E. Hardoy, eds. Latin American Urban Research. Vol. 2. Regional and Urban Development Policies: A Latin American Perspective. Beverly Hills, Cal.: Sage, 1972. Rev. by P. Ranis, HAHR, 54(Feb 1974):171-2.

Gelb, Barbara S. So Short a Time: a Biography of John Reed and
Louise Bryant. New York: Norton, 1973. Rev. by A. C.
Spencer, III, OrHQ, 75(Mar 1974):84-5.

Gelfand, Lawrence E., ed. Essays on the History of American
Foreign Relations. New York: Holt, Rinehart and Winston,
1972. Rev. by J. W. Moore, HT, 8(Nov 1974):122-3.

Gellman, Irwin F. Roosevelt and Batista: Good Neighbor Diplomacy
in Cuba, 1933-1945. Albuquerque: U NM Press, 1973. Rev.
by J. D. Doenecke, HRNB, 2(Apr 1974):152-3.

Gemzell, Carl-Axel. Organization, Conflict, and Innovation: A
Study of German Naval Strategic Planning, 1888-1940. Lund:
Esselte Studium, 1973. Rev. by D. M. Schurman, JMH, 46
(Dec 1974):731-2.

Gendzier, Irene. Frantz Fanon: A Critical Study. New York:
Pantheon, 1973. Rev. by F. F. Clairmonte, JMAS, 12(Mar
1974):154-7; R. M. Brace, JMH, 46(Sep 1974):542.

Generous, William T., Jr. Swords and Scales: The Development
of the Uniform Code of Military Justice. Port Washington,
N.Y.: Kennikat, 1973. Rev. by L. Morton, JAH, 61(Sep
1974):544-6.

Genovese, Eugene D. Plantation, Town, and Country. see Miller,
Elinor

Gentil, Pierre, ed. Derniers Chefs d'un Empire. Paris: Académie des Sciences d'Outre-Mer, 1972. Rev. by C. H. Alex-
androwicz, HJ, 17(Num 3 1974):670-2.

George, Carol V. R. Segregated Sabbaths: Richard Allen and the
Rise of Independent Black Churches, 1760-1841. New York:
Ox U Press, 1973. Rev. by W. B. Gravely, CH, 43(Je 1974):
282-3; R. L. Harris, Jr., JNH, 59(Ja 1974):93-4; F. J. Miller, NEQ, 47(Mar 1974):168-73. Note: JNH renders this
title: Segregated Sabbaths: Richard Allen and the Emergence
of Independent Black Churches, 1760-1841.

George, Isaac. Heroes and Incidents of the Mexican War. Greens-
burg, Pa.: Review Publishing, 1903; Hollywood, Cal.: Sun
Dance Press, 1971. Rev. by T. E. Kline, JOW, 13(Jl 1974):
123.

Gerbi, Antonello. The Dispute of the New World: The History of
a Polemic, 1750-1900. Pittsburgh: U Pittsburgh Press, 1973.
Rev. by M. Kammen, CHR, 55(Je 1973):180-2; D. Echeverria,
JAH, 60(Mar 1974):1096-7.

Gerhard, Peter. A Guide to the Historical Geography of New Spain.
New York: Cam U Press, 1972. Rev. by J. J. Parsons,

AHR, 79(Je 1974):914-15; L. G. Canedo, TAm, 31(Jl 1974): 103-4.

Gericke, Philip O., tr. and ed. Historical Notes on Lower California With Some Relative to Upper California Furnished to the Bancroft Library by Manuel C. Rojo, 1879. Los Angeles: Dawson's Book Shop, 1972. Rev. by H. P. Hinton, SCQ, 56 (Sum 1974):199-200.

Gerlach, Horst. Der Englische Bauernaufstand von 1381 und der Deutsche Bauernkrieg: Ein vergleich. Meisenheim am Glan: Verlag Anton Hain, 1969. Rev. by J. Gillingham, History, 59(Je 1974):257-8.

Gerstein, Linda. Nikolai Strakhov. Cambridge, Mass.: Har U Press, 1971. Rev. by M. Katz, AHR, 79(Je 1974):817-818.

Gerteis, Louis S. From Contraband to Freedman: Federal Policy Toward Southern Blacks, 1861-1865. Westport, Conn.: Greenwood, 1973. Rev. by C. Walker, CWH, 20(Mar 1974):81-2; M. F. Berry, JAH, 61(Sep 1974):491-2; L. S. Williams, JNH, 59(Oct 1974):400-1; J. M. McPherson, JSH, 40(May 1974): 319-20.

Gertz, Elmer. For the First Hours of Tomorrow: The New Illinois Bill of Rights. Urbana: U Ill Press, 1972. Rev. by I. Dilliard, JISHS, 67(Apr 1974):238-40.

Gessner, Robert. Massacre: A Survey of Today's Indians. New York: Da Capo, 1972. Rev. by R. L. Munkres, JOW, 13 (Ja 1974):144.

Gettleman, Marvin E. The Dorr Rebellion: A Study in American Radicalism: 1833-1849. New York: Random House, 1973. Rev. by R. J. Moore, Historian, 36(Aug 1974):774-5; J. A. Rawley, JAH, 60(Mar 1974):1114; P. T. Conley, NEQ, 47 (Mar 1974):143-5.

Geyer, Grant B. see Bollens, John C.

Ghali, Mirrit Boutros. Tradition for the Future. Oxford: Alden Press, 1972. Rev. by H. J. Muller, T & C, 15(Ja 1974): 82-6.

Gibb, Sir Hamilton. The Life of Saladin: From the Works of 'Imad ad-Din and Baha' ad-Din. New York: Ox U Press, 1973. Rev. by H. Nierman, AHR, 79(Apr 1974):501-2; J. M. Rogers, EHR, 89(Jl 1974):657-8.

Gibbon, Guy E. The Sheffield Site: An Oneota Site on the St. Croix River. St. Paul: Minn. Historical Society, 1973. Rev. by W. M. Hurley, MinnH, 44(Sum 1974):77-8.

Gibson, Arrell M. Wilderness Bonanza: The Tri-State District of
   Missouri, Kansas, and Oklahoma. Norman: U Ok Press,
   1972. Rev. by G. E. Moulton, ChOk, 52(Fall 1974):376-7;
   T. Wilson, GPJ, 13(Spr 1974):209-10; F. W. Schruben, PHR,
   43(May 1974):276-7; H. Mothershead, WHQ, 5(Ja 1974):70-1.

Gibson, Richard. African Liberation Movements: Contemporary
   White Minority Rule. Oxford: Ox U Press ... 1972. Rev.
   by M. Legassick, JAfH, 15(Number 1 1974):166-7.

Gies, Joseph. Crisis, 1918: The Leading Actors, Strategies, and
   Events in the German Gamble for Total Victory on the Western
   Front. New York: Norton, 1974. Rev. by G. E. Silberstein,
   HRNB, 2(May/Je 1974):177-8.

Giesey, Ralph E. see Hotman, François Francogallia

Gifford, Prosser and William Roger Louis, eds. France and Britain in Africa: Imperial Rivalry and Colonial Rule. New
   Haven, Conn.: Yale U Press, 1972. Rev. by A. S. Trickett,
   Historian, 36(Aug 1974):745-8; M. Crowder, JAfH, 15(Num 1
   1974):141-5.

Giglio, Carlo, ed. Inventario delle Fonti manoscritte relative alla
   Storia dell' Africa del Nord esistenti in Italia. 2 vols. Lei-
   den: E. J. Brill, 1971, 1972. Rev. by R. Gray, JAfH, 15
   (Num 2 1974):343-5.

_____ and Elio Lodolini, eds. Guida delle Fonti per la Storia
   dell' Africa a Sud del Sahara esistenti in Italia. Vol. I. Zug:
   Inter Documentation Co., 1973. Rev. by R. Gray, JAfH, 15
   (Num 2 1974):343-5.

Gilbert, Amy M. Executive Agreements and Treaties, 1946-1973:
   Framework of the Foreign Policy of the Period. Endicott,
   N.Y.: Thomas-Newell, 1973. Rev. by T. M. Campbell,
   JAH, 61(Sep 1974):538-9.

Gilbert, B. Miles. Mammalian Osteo-archaeology: North America.
   Colombia, Mo.: U Mo Press, 1973. Rev. by J. L. Angel,
   Archaeology, 27(Oct 1974):288-9.

Gilbert, Felix and Stephen R. Graubard, eds. Historical Studies
   Today. New York: Norton, 1972. Rev. by T. K. Rabb,
   JMH, 46(Je 1974):337-41.

Gilbreath, Kent. Red Capitalism: An Analysis of the Navajo Economy. Norman: U Ok Press, 1973. Rev. by C. Trafzer,
   ChOk, 52(Sum 1974):260; L. C. Kelly, NMHR, 49(Jan 1974):
   88.

Gilfillan, S. Colum. Supplement to the Sociology of Invention. San
   Francisco: San Francisco Press, 1971. Rev. by I. Taviss,

T & C, 15(Ja 1974):136-8.

Gilhooley, Leonard. Contradiction and Dilemma: Orestes Brownson and the American Idea. New York: Fordham U Press, 1972. Rev. by H. Schwartz, AHR, 79(Oct 1974):1262-3.

Gilio, María Esther. The Tupamaro Guerrillas. New York: Saturday Review Press, 1972. Rev. by R. H. McDonald, HAHR, 54(Feb 1974):184-6.

Gill, Harold B., Jr. The Apothecary in Colonial Virginia. Charlottesville: U Press Va, 1972. Rev. by J. Stannard, AHR, 79(Apr 1974):572-3.

Gillespie, Neal C. The Collapse of Orthodoxy: The Intellectual Ordeal of George Frederick Holmes. Charlottesville: U Press Va, 1972. Rev. by W. U. Solberg, AHR, 79(Oct 1974):1264-5.

Gilliam, Thomas J. see Carageorge, Ted

Gillis, John R. The Prussian Bureaucracy in Crisis 1840-1860. Stanford, Cal.: Stan U Press, 1971. Rev. by A. Ramm, EHR, 89(Ja 1974):213-14.

Gilman, Stephen. The Spain of Fernando de Rojas: The Intellectual and Social Landscape of "La Celestina." Princeton, N.J.: Prin U Press, 1972. Rev. by A. Mackay, History, 59(Je 1974):261-2; J. Casalduero, RQ, 27(Fall 1974):353-5.

Gilmore, Myron P., ed. Studies on Machiavelli. Florence: Sansoni, 1972. Rev. by H. C. Mansfield, Jr., RQ, 27(Fall 1974): 321-2.

Gilmour, James M. Spatial Evolution of Manufacturing: Southern Ontario 1851-1891. Toronto: U Tor Press, 1972. Rev. by T. W. Acheson, CHR, 55(Sep 1974):319-20.

Gilpin, Alec R. The Territory of Michigan [1805-1837]. East Lansing: Mich St U Press, 1970. Rev. by C. W. Vander Hill, AHR, 79(Apr 1974):575-6.

Gimbutas, Marija. The Gods and Goddesses of Old Europe: 7000 to 3500 B.C.: Myths, Legends and Cult Images. London: Thames Hudson, 1974. Rev. by A. Fleming, Antiquity, 48 (Sep 1974):246.

Gimbutas, Marija. The Slavs. New York: Praeger, 1971. Rev. by J. W. Strong, AHR, 79(Je 1974):759-60.

Gingrich, Arnold. The Joys of Trout. New York: Crown, n.d. Rev. by A. Cardona-Hine, Mankind, 4(Feb 1974):6, 24.

Giovanni Pico della Mirandola: Conclusiones sive theses DCCCC
   Romae anno 1486 publice disputandae, sed non admissae.
   Geneva: Librairie Droz, 1974. Rev. by H. L. Bond, CH,
   43(Sep 1974):396-7.

Giovannoni, Jeanne M. see Billingsley, Andrew

Girard, Augustin. Cultural Development: Experience and Policies.
   Paris and New York: UNESCO, 1972. Rev. by W. Goldstein,
   T & C, 15(Ja 1974):142-4.

Giraud, Marcel. A History of French Louisiana. Volume I, The
   Reign of Louis XIV, 1698-1715. Baton Rouge: LSU Press,
   1974. Rev. by J. L. Barnidge, ChOk, 52(Fall 1974):388-9;
   H. S. Marks, HRNB, 2(Sep 1974):240.

Gish, Lowell. Reform at Osawatomie State Hospital: Treatment
   of the Mentally Ill, 1866-1970. Lawrence: U Press Kan,
   1972. Rev. by B. G. Rosenkrantz, JAH, 60(Mar 1974):1150-
   2.

Giuntella, Vittorio E. Roma nel Settecento. Bologna: Licinio
   Capelli Editore, 1971. Rev. by E. Cochrane, JMH, 46(Sep
   1974):552-3.

Glancy, David M. see Dickey, John W.

Glanz, Rudolf. The Jew in Early American Wit and Graphic Humor.
   New York: KTAV Pub. House, 1973. Rev. by J. J. Appel,
   NYH, 55(Jl 1974):351-2.

Glaser, Lynn. Indians or Jews? Gilroy, Cal.: Boswell, 1973.
   Rev. by L. Huddleston, JAH, 61(Sep 1974):451; F. M.
   McKiernan, UHQ, 42(W 1974):92.

Glass, D. V. and Roger Revelle, eds. Population and Social Change.
   London: Edward Arnold, 1972. Rev. by R. S. Schofield, History, 59(Feb 1974):160-1.

Glass, E. L. N., comp. and ed. The History of the Tenth Cavalry, 1866-1921. Fort Collins, Colo.: Old Army Press, 1972.
   Rev. by L. G. Griffin, III, ChOk, 52(Sum 1974):353-4.

Glazer, Nathan. Remembering the Answers: Essays on the American Student Revolt. New York: Basic Books, 1970. Rev. by
   W. L. O'Neill, AHR, 79(Je 1974):911-12.

Gleason, Abbott. European and Muscovite: Ivan Kireevsky and the
   Origins of Slavophilism. Cambridge, Mass.: Har U Press,
   1972. Rev. by P. K. Christoff, AHR, 79(Je 1974):819-820.

Glines, Carroll V., Jr. The Compact History of the United States
   Air Force. New York: Hawthorn, 1973. Rev. by M. C.

Campion, HT, 7(Feb 1974):318.

Glob, P. V. The Mound People: Danish Bronze-Age Man Preserved.
    Ithaca, N. Y.: Cornell U Press, 1974. Rev. by R. Rinehart,
    HRNB, 2(Sep 1974):251-2.

Glover, Jeffrey A. see Kane, Ralph J.

Glover, Michael. The Peninsula War of 1807-1814: A Concise
    Military History. Newton Abbot: David and Charles, n. d.
    D. G. Chandler, HTo, 24(Aug 1974):579-81.

Glover, Richard. Britain at Bay: Defence Against Napoleon, 1803-
    14. London: Allen and Unwin, 1973. Rev. by P. K. Crim-
    min, History, 59(Je 1974):284.

Glubb, Sir John Bagot. Soldiers of Fortune: The Story of the Mam-
    luks. New York: Stein and Day, 1974. Rev. by D. W. Lit-
    tlefield, HRNB, 2(Apr 1974):147.

Godbold, E. Stanley, Jr. Ellen Glasgow and the Woman Within.
    Baton Rouge: LSU Press, 1972. Rev. by E. C. Bufkin, JAH,
    61(Dec 1974):822-3.

Godbout, Arthur. L'Origine des écoles françaises dans l'Ontario.
    Ottawa: Editions de l'Université d'Ottawa, 1972. Rev. by P.
    Oliver, CHR, 55(Sep 1974):322-3.

Godechot, Jacques. The Counter Revolution: Doctrine and Action
    1789-1804. London: Routledge and Kegan Paul, 1972. Rev.
    by O. Hufton, History, 59(Feb 1974):132-3.

Godwin, George. Town Swamps and Social Bridges. Leicester:
    Leicester U Press, 1972. Rev. by P. J. Waller, EHR, 89
    (Ja 1974):218.

Godwin, Paul H. B. see Ridley, C. P.

Goebel, Julius, Jr. History of the Supreme Court of the United
    States. Vol. I. Antecedents and Beginnings to 1801. New
    York: Macmillan, 1971. Rev. by R. M. Ireland, AHR, 79
    (Oct 1974):1250-1.

Goetze, Sigmund. Die Politik des schwedischen Reichkanzlers Axel
    Oxenstierna gegenüber Kaiser und Reich. Kiel: Kommission-
    verlag Mühlau, 1971. Rev. by R. M. Hatton, EHR, 89(Ja
    1974):181-2.

Goetzmann, William H., ed. The American Hegelians: An Intellec-
    tual Episode in the History of Western America. New York:
    Knopf, 1973. Rev. by J. V. Metzgar, Historian, 36(May
    1974):569-71.

Goff, John S. George W. P. Hunt and His Arizona. Pasadena,
     Cal.: Socio-Technical, 1973. Rev. by J. H. Krenkel, JAH,
     61(Dec 1974):790-1; M. H. Wilson, JAriH, 15(Spr 1974):92-3;
     C. N. Tyson, JOW, 13(Oct 1974):129; W. H. Lyon, NMHR,
     49(Jl 1974):260-1; B. M. Fireman, PHR, 43(Nov 1974):616-18;
     C. S. Peterson, UHQ, 42(Fall 1974):394-5; J. J. Wagoner,
     WHQ, 5(Jl 1974):336-7.

Goitein, S. D. A Mediterranean Society: The Jewish Communities
     of the Arab World as Portrayed in the Documents of the Cairo
     Geniza. Volume 2, The Community. Berkeley: U Cal Press,
     1971. Rev. by F. Rosenthal, AHR, 79(Apr 1974):558-9.

Gold, Bela. Explorations in Managerial Economics. New York:
     Basic Books, 1971. Rev. by H. Freudenberger, T & C, 15
     (Apr 1974):351-2.

Goldenberg, Boris. Los sindicatos en América Latina. Hanover,
     Germany: Verlag für Literatur und Zeitgeschehen, 1964.
     Rev. by B. G. Burnett, HAHR, 54(May 1974):338.

Goldfield, David R. and James B. Lane, eds. The Enduring Ghet-
     to: Sources and Readings. Philadelphia: Lippincott, 1973.
     Rev. by J. L. Arnold, JNH, 59(Apr 1974):196-203.

Goldman, Albert. Ladies and Gentlemen--Lenny Bruce! New York:
     Random House, 1973. Rev. by D. Rabinowitz, Commentary,
     58(Oct 1974):96-8.

Goldman, Lucien. The Philosophy of the Enlightenment: The
     Christian Burgess and the Enlightenment. Cambridge, Mass.:
     M I T Press, 1974. Rev. by S. Hanft, HRNB, 2(Mar 1974):
     118.

Goldman, Marshall I. The Spoils of Progress: Environmental Pol-
     lution in the Soviet Union. Cambridge, Mass.: MIT Press,
     1972. Rev. by S. Lieberstein, T & C, 15(Ja 1974):125-7.

Goldman, Michael. Shakespeare and the Energies of Drama.
     Princeton: Prin U Press, 1972. Rev. by N. Rabkin, RQ,
     27(Sum 1974):247-9.

Goldstrom, J. M. The Social Content of Education, 1808-1870: A
     Study of the Working Class School Reader in England and Ire-
     land. Shannon: Irish U Press, 1972. Rev. by H. Perkin,
     EHR, 89(Jl 1974):677.

Goldthwaite, R. A. see Baldwin, J. W.

Goldwater, Leonard J. Mercury: A History of Quicksilver. Balti-
     more: York Press, 1972. Rev. by R. P. Multhauf, T & C,
     15(Ja 1974):91-2.

135 GOMBRICH

Gombrich, E. H. Symbolic Images. Studies in the Art of the Rennaissance, Vol. II. London: Phaidon Press, 1972. Rev. by K. Langedijk, RQ, 22(Fall 1974):336-7.

Gomez, David F. Somos Chicanos: Strangers in Our Own Land. Boston: Beacon, 1973. Rev. by A. Hoffman, PNQ, 65(Apr 1974):93.

Gonidec, P.-F. Les Systèmes politiques africains. Vol. 1, L'Evolution, la scène politique, l'intégration nationale. Paris: Librairie génerále de droit et de jurisprudence, 1971. Rev. by K. Lawson, JMAS, 12(Je 1974):331-3.

Good, Robert C. U D I: the International Politics of the Rhodesian Rebellion. London: Faber and Faber, 1973. Rev. by K. Good, AfAf, 73(Apr 1974):243-4.

Goodhart, C. A. E. The Business of Banking, 1891-1914. New York: Hilary House, 1972. Rev. by J. K. Horsefield, BHR, 48(Sum 1974):240-2.

Goodin, George, ed. The English Novel in the Nineteenth Century: Essays on the Literary Mediation of Human Values. Urbana: U Ill Press, 1972. Rev. by M. Baine, GR, 28(Sum 1974):333-5.

Goodman, Allan E. Politics in War: The Bases of Political Community in South Vietnam. Cambridge, Mass.: Har U Press, 1973. Rev. by J. F. Cady, AHR, 79(Apr 1974):560-1.

Goodman, Paul and Frank Otto Gatell. America in the Twenties: The Beginnings of Contemporary America. New York: Holt, Rinehart and Winston, 1972. Rev. by T. P. Kallman, HT, 7 (Feb 1974):302-3.

Goodspeed's History of Hamilton, Knox, and Shelby Counties of Tennessee. Nashville: Charles and Randy Elder Booksellers, 1974. Rev. by R. M. McBride, THQ, 33(Sum 1974):237-8.

Goodwin, Craufurd D. W. The Image of Australia: British Perception of the Australian Economy From the Eighteenth to the Twentieth Century. Durham, N.C.: Duke U Press, 1974. Rev. by P. J. Coleman, HRNB, 2(Spr 1974):245.

_____. see Black, R. D. Collison

Goodwin, Grenville. Western Apache Raiding and Warfare. Tucson: U Ariz Press, 1971. Rev. by J. R. Yakey, ChOk, 52(Fall 1974):381-2.

Goody, Jack. The Myth of the Bagre. Oxford: Clarendon, 1972. Rev. by R. Finnegan, Africa, 44(Apr 1974):214-5.

Gonnet, Paul. Un grand préfet de la Côte-d'Or sous Louis-Philippe: La correspondance d'Achille Chaper (1831-1840). Dijon: Société des Analecta Burgundica, 1970. Rev. by R. L. Williams, AHR, 79(Oct 1974):1190.

Gopal, S., ed. Selected Works of Jawaharlal Nehru. Vols. 1-3. New Delhi: Orient Longman, 1973. Rev. by J. M. Brown, EHR, 89(Apr 1974):407-9.

Gordon, Cyrus H. Riddles in History. New York: Crown, n. d. Rev. by R. Ashby, Mankind, 4(Aug 1974):8, 41.

Gordon, Dudley. Charles F. Lummis: Crusader in Corduroy. Los Angeles: Cultural Assets, 1972. Rev. by D. M. Powell, A & W, 16(Spr 1974):85-6; D. R. Culton, PHR, 43(May 1974): 279-80.

Gordon, Harold J., Jr. Hitler and the Beer Hall Putsch. Princeton, N.J.: Prin U Press, 1972. Rev. by K. Schönhoven, JMH, 46(Mar 1974):156-8.

Gordon, Leonard A. Bengal: The Nationalist Movement, 1876-1940. New York: Columbia U Press, 1974. Rev. by B. Farwell, HRNB, 2(May/Je 1974):176.

Gordon, Michael, ed. The American Family in Social-Historical Perspective. New York: St. Martin's Press, 1973. Rev. by J. B. Armstrong, NEQ, 47(Sep 1974):482-5.

Gordon, Suzanne. Black Mesa: The Angel of Death. New York: John Day, 1973. Rev. by A. T. Row, JAriH, 15(Spr 1974): 93-5.

Gore, Gary G., ed. see Architecture of Middle Tennessee

Gottesman, Ronald and Charles L. P. Silet. The Literary Manuscripts of Upton Sinclair. Columbus, Ohio: Ohio St U Press, 1972. Rev. by J. P. Putnam, SCQ, 56(W 1974):415-6.

_____. Upton Sinclair: An Annotated Checklist. Kent, Ohio: Kent St U Press, 1973. Rev. by J. K. Putnam, SCQ, 56 (W 1974):415-16.

Göttlicher, Arvid and Walter Werner. Schiffsmodelle in alten Agypten. Wiesbaden: Arbeitskreis Historicher Schiffbau, 1971. Rev. by P. Johnstone, Antiquity, 48(Je 1974):151.

Gottschalk, Louis and Donald Lach. Toward the French Revolution: Europe and America in the Eighteenth-Century World. New York: Scribner's, 1973. Rev. by C. A. Le Guin, Historian, 36(Feb 1974):322-3.

Gottschalk, Stephen. The Emergence of Christian Science in Amer-

ican Religious Life. Berkeley: U Cal Press, 1973. Rev. by
P. A. Carter, CH, 43(Sep 1974):424; E. S. Gaustad, JAH, 61
(Dec 1974):805-6.

Goubert, Pierre. L'Ancien Regime, vol. I, La Societe. Paris:
Armand Colin, 1969. Rev. by B. Behrens, HJ, 17(Num 3
1974):631-43.

_____. L'Ancien Regime. vol. II, Les Pouvoirs. Paris: Ar-
mand Colin, 1973. Rev. by B. Behrens, HJ, 17(Num 3 1974):
631-43.

Gough, Kathleen and Hari P. Sharma, eds. Imperialism and Revolution in South Asia. New York: Monthly Review Press, 1973.
Rev. by R. L. Park, JAS, 33(May 1974):496-7.

Gough, Michael. The Origins of Christian Art. London: Thames
and Hudson, 1973. Rev. by J. M. C. Toynbee, Antiquity, 48
(Mar 1974):70-1.

Gould, J. D. Economic Growth in History: Survey and Analysis.
London: Methuen, 1972. Rev. by W. N. Parker, AHR, 79
(Feb 1974):107; L. P. Cain, BHR, 48(Spr 1974):109-11.

Gould, Lewis L. Progressives and Prohibitionists: Texas Democrats in the Wilson Era. Austin: U Tx Press, 1973. Rev.
by H. C. Bailey, AHR, 79(Apr 1974):602-3; R. S. Maxwell,
ETHJ, 12(Spr 1974):71-2; P. E. Coletta, JAH, 60(Mar 1974):
1166-7; C. N. Tyson, JOW, 13(Oct 1974):124; A. S. Link,
JSH, 40(Feb 1974):154-5; R. C. McMath, Jr., SWHQ, 78(Jl
1974):108-10; G. N. Green, WHQ, 5(Apr 1974):206-7.

_____, ed. The Progressive Era. Syracuse, N.Y.: Syr U
Press, 1974. Rev. by J. J. Rumberger, HRNB, 2(Sep 1974):
258.

Goulden, Joseph C. Meany. New York: Atheneum, 1972. Rev.
by D. Brody, AHR, 79(Oct 1974):1293-4.

Goulder, Grace. John D. Rockefeller: The Cleveland Years.
Cleveland: Western Reserve Historical Society, 1972. Rev.
by R. J. Brugger, BHR, 48(Win 1974):561-2.

Gourvish, T. R. Mark Huish and the London and North Western
Railway: A Study of Management. Leicester: Leicester U
Press, 1972. Rev. by R. C. Overton, BHR, 48(Spr 1974):
118-20; S. Pollard, EHR, 89(Ja 1974):216-17; A. Slaven, History, 59(Je 1974):285-6.

Goy, Joseph et Emmanuel Le Roy Ladurie. Les Fluctuations du
produit de la dîme: Conjoncture décimale et domainiale de la
fin du Moyen Age au XVIIIe siècle. Paris/La Haye: Mouton,
1972. Rev. by T. J. A. Le Goff, CHR, 55(Mar 1974):111-13.

Grabar, Oleg. The Formation of Islamic Art. New Haven, Conn.:
Yale U Press, 1973. Rev. by N. Tolten, Archaeology, 27
(Ja 1974):75-6.

Grade, Chaim. The Agunah. Indianapolis: Bobbs-Merrill, n.d.
Rev. by D. Stern, Commentary, 58(Nov 1974):88, 90-2.

Grady, James. Architecture of Neel Reid in Georgia. Athens, Ga.:
U Ga Press, 1973. Rev. by T. F. Collum, GHQ, 58(Fall
1974):361-2.

Graebner, Norman A. see DeBoe, David C.

Graf, LeRoy P. and Ralph W. Haskins, eds. The Papers of Andrew Johnson: Volume 3: 1858-60. Knoxville: U Tenn
Press, 1972. Rev. by M. W. M. Hargreaves, JISHS, 67(Feb
1974):125-6; T. B. Alexander, JSH, 40(Feb 1974):144-5.

Graham, Gerald S. Tides of Empire: Discursions on the Expansion
of Britain Overseas. London: McGill-Queen's U Press, 1972.
Rev. by D. C. M. Platt, History, 59(Feb 1974):125.

Graham, John A. see Greene, Merle

Graham, John T. Donoso Cortés: Utopian Romanticist and Political
Realist. Columbia, Mo.: U Mo Press, 1974. Rev. by J. L.
Shneidman, HRNB, 3(Nov/Dec 1974):28.

Graham, Richard and Peter H. Smith, eds. New Approaches to
Latin American History. Austin: U Tx Press, 1974. Rev.
by J. L. Arbena, HRNB, 3(Nov/Dec 1974):40.

Graham, Otis L., Jr. The Great Campaigns: Reform and War in
America, 1900-1928. Englewood Cliffs, N.J.: Prentice-Hall,
1971. Rev. by A. E. Campbell, HJ, 17(Num 2 1974):443-7.

Graham, William Alexander. The Papers of William Alexander
Graham. Volume V: 1857-1863. Ed. by Max R. Williams
and J. G. de Roulhac Hamilton. Raleigh: North Carolina
Office of Archives and History, 1973. Rev. by T. H. Williams, NCHR, 51(Jan 1974):90-1.

Grant, Charles. The War Game. New York: St. Martin's, 1971.
Rev. by B. A. Guthrie, Jr., FCHQ, 48(Oct 1974):366-7.

Grant, Michael. The Army of the Caesars. New York: Scribner's,
1974. Rev. by O. W. Reinmuth, HRNB, 3(Nov/Dec 1974):
37; D. Jones, HTo, 24(Oct 1974):726.

_____. Herod the Great. New York: American Heritage, 1971.
Rev. by J. N. Claster, AHR, 79(Oct 1974):1158-9; S. Gersh-
goren, Mankind, 4(Apr 1974):8-9.

_____. The Jews in the Roman World. New York: Scribner's, 1973. Rev. by J. N. Claster, AHR, 79(Oct 1974):1158-9; W. Lewis, Mankind, 4(Feb 1974):65-6.

_____. Roman Myths. New York: Scribner's, 1971. Rev. by S. J. Simons, AHR, 79(Oct 1974):1156.

Gras, Christian. Alfred Rosmer (1877-1964) et le mouvement ré-volutionnaire international. Paris: Françoise Maspero, 1971. Rev. by E. Weber, AHR, 79(Feb 1974):169-70.

Gratus, Jack. The Great White Lie: Slavery, Emancipation and Changing Racial Attitudes. New York: Monthly Review Press, 1973. Rev. by R. R. Davis, Jr., AHR, 79(Je 1974):784-5; F. W. Knight, HAHR, 54(Aug 1974):524-5.

Graubard, Stephen R. see Gilbert, Felix

Gravely, William. Gilbert Haven, Methodist Abolitionist: A Study in Race, Religion, and Reform, 1850-1880. Nashville: Abing-don Press, 1973. Rev. by W. J. Gilmore, CWH, 20(Je 1974): 177-8; D. G. Mathews, GHQ, 58(Supp 1974):215-16; L. H. Fishel, Jr., JAH, 61(Je 1974):194-5; H. A. Barnes, JSH, 40 (Feb 1974):141-2.

Gray, C. S. Canadian Defence Priorities: A Question of Relevance. Toronto/Vancouver: Clarke, Irwin, 1972. Rev. by J. McLin, CHR, 55(Je 1974):206-7.

Graymont, Barbara, ed. Fighting Tuscarora: The Autobiography of Chief Clinton Rickard. Syracuse, N.Y.: Syr U Press, 1973. Rev. by R. Thornton, HRNB, 2(Feb 1974):96; W. E. Unrau, WHQ, 5(Oct 1974):463-4; M. R. Rubinoff, WPHM, 57(Apr 1974): 225-6.

Greehill, Basil see Brock, P. W.

Green, Barbara see Myres, J. N. L.

Green, Constance McLaughlin and Milton Lomask. Vanguard: A History. Washington: National Aeronautics and Space Adm., 1970. Rev. by R. C. Miller, AHR, 79(Oct 1974):1292-3.

Green, David. The Containment of Latin America. Chicago: Quad-rangle, 1971. Rev. by I. F. Gellman, CHR, 55(Je 1974):182-3.

_____. Queen Anne. London: Collins, 1970. Rev. by E. Gregg, ESR, 4(Jl 1974):269-74.

Green, Donald E. Land of the Underground Rain: Irrigation on the Texas High Plains, 1910-1970. Austin: U Tx Press, 1973. Rev. by J. H. Shideler, A & W, 16(Spr 1974):84-5; L. B.

Lee, AHR, 79(Oct 1974):1280-1; I. G. Clark, JAH, 61(Je
1974):235-6; M. W. M. Hargreaves, JSH, 40(Feb 1974):155-6;
R. G. Dunbar, PHR, 43(May 1974):283; J. B. Frantz, T & C,
15(Apr 1974):339-40; R. M. Webb, WHQ, 5(Apr 1974):205-6.

Green, Fletcher M. The Role of the Yankee in the Old South.
Athens, Ga.: U Ga Press, 1972. Rev. by L. Atherton, AHR,
79(Apr 1974):578; J. F. Marszalek, Jr., Historian, 36(May
1974):562.

Green, J. R. see Cambitoglou, Alexander

Green, Louis. Chronicle Into History: An Essay on the Interpretation of History in Florentine Fourteenth-Century Chronicles.
Cambridge: Cam U Press, 1972. Rev. by D. Waley, EHR,
89(Apr 1974):421; L. Martines, RQ, 27(Spr 1974):70-1.

Green, Martin. The von Richthofen Sisters: The Triumphant and
the Tragic Modes of Love. New York: Basic Books, 1974.
Rev. by W. J. McGill, HRNB, 2(May/Je 1974):168-9; E. Stans-
field, Mankind, 4(Dec 1974):70-1.

Green, Peter. Ancient Greece: An Illustrated History. New York:
Viking, 1973. Rev. by A. L. Boegehold, HRNB, 2(Ja 1974):
72.

Greenberg, Barbara L. The Spoils of August. Middletown, Conn.:
Wes U Press, 1974. Rev. by D. Huddle, GR, 28(Fall 1974):
535-40.

Greenblatt, Stephen J. Sir Walter Raleigh--The Renaissance Man
and His Roles. New Haven, Conn.: Yale U Press, 1973.
Rev. by F. S. Fussner, AHR, 79(Oct 1974):1176-7; G. F.
Lytle, HRNB, 3(Oct 1974):15; A. Haynes, HTo, 24(Ja 1974):
61-3.

Greene, Merle, Robert L. Rands, and John A. Graham. Maya
Sculpture. Berkeley, Cal.: Lederer, Street, and Zeus, 1972.
Rev. by D. M. Pendergast, Archaeology, 27(Ja 1974):76.

Greene, Jack P. see Cohen, David W.

Greenhalgh, P. A. L. Early Greek Warfare: Horseman and Chariots in the Homeric and Archaic Ages. New York: Cam U
Press, 1973. Rev. by M. L. Lang, AHR, 79(Feb 1974):118-
19; T. B. L. Webster, T & C, 15(Apr 1974): 325-6.

Greenough, Horatio. Letters of Horatio Greenough, American Sculptor. Ed. by Nathalia Wright. Madison: U Wisc Press, 1972.
Rev. by B. G. Proske, NYHSQ, 58(Ja 1974):75-7.

Greenwood, Roberta S. The Browne Site: Early Milling Stone Horizon in Southern California. Salt Lake City: Society for Amer-

ican Archaeology ... 1969. Rev. by T. King, AmAnt, 39(Apr 1974):392-4.

Greenwood, Val D. The Researcher's Guide to American Genealogy. Baltimore: Genealogical Pub'g Co., 1973. Rev. by J. R. Bentley, FCHQ, 48(Oct 1974):367.

Gregory, R. G. India and East Africa. Oxford: Clarendon Press, 1971. Rev. by J. M. Brown, EHR, 89(Ja 1974):228-9.

Greifenhagen, Adolf. Schmuckarbeiten in Edelmetall. Berlin: Gerbrüder Mann Verlag, 1970. Rev. by H. Hoffmann, AJA, 78 (Apr 1974):195-6.

Gressley, Gene M. West By East: The American West in the Gilded Age. Provo, Utah: BYU Press, 1972. Rev. by R. G. Athearn, CoMag, 51(Spr 1974):170-1; L. L. Morrison, JOW, 13(Apr 1974):106-7.

Grewal, J. S. Guru Nanak in History. Chandigarh: ... Panjab U, 1969. Rev. by B. Ramusack, JAS, 33(Aug 1974):721-2.

Grey, Ian. Boris Godunov: The Tragic Tsar. New York: Scribner's, 1973. Rev. by S. A. Zenkovsky, HRNB, 2(Ja 1974): 83.

Gribbin, William. The Churches Militant: The War of 1812 and American Religion. New Haven, Conn.: Yale U Press, 1973. Rev. by D. W. Howe, AHR, 79(Je 1974):848-9; B. M. Stephens, NEQ, 47(Je 1974):331-3; D. G. Mathews, WMQ-3, 31 (Jl 1974):518-19.

Grider, George see Wrobel, Sylvia

Gridley, Marion E. Contemporary American Indian Leaders. New York: Dodd, Mead, 1972. Rev. by R. H. Faust, JAriH, 15 (Sum 1974):197-8.

Griffith, Ernest S. A History of American City Government: The Conspicuous Failure 1870-1900. New York: Praeger, 1974. Rev. C. E. Clark, Jr., HRNB, 2(Sep 1974):256.

_____. A History of American City Government: The Progressive Years and Their Aftermath 1900-1920. New York: Praeger, 1974. Rev. by C. E. Clark, Jr., HRNB, 2(Sep 1974): 256.

Griffith, Kathryn. Judge Learned Hand and the Role of the Federal Judiciary. Norman: U Ok Press, 1973. Rev. by M. Cantor, HRNB, 2(Feb 1974):99-100; R. W. Bland, JAH, 61(Je 1974): 239-40.

Griffiths, B. Mexican Monetary Policy and Economic Development.

New York: Praeger, 1971. Rev. by M. S. Wionczek, JLAS, 6(May 1974):186-8.

Griffiths, J. F., ed. Climates of Africa. New York: Elsevier, 1972. Rev. by A. R. Waters, JMAS, 12(Sep 1974):506-7.

Griffiths, R. A. see Chrimes, S. B.

Grigoras, N. Institutii feudale din Moldava.... Bucharest: Editura Academici Republicii Socialiste România, 1971. Rev. by D. J. Deletant, EHR, 89(Apr 1974):423.

Grilliches, Zvi, ed. see Schmookler, Jacob

Grimshaw, Patricia. Women's Suffrage in New Zealand. Auckland: Auckland U Press, 1972. Rev. by B. Harrison, History, 59 (Je 1974):325.

Grimsted, David, ed. Notions of the Americans, 1820-1860. New York: George Braziller, 1970. Rev. by G. A. Danzer, HT, 7(Aug 1974):631-2.

Grimsted, Patricia Kennedy. Archives and Manuscript Repositories in the U S S R, Moscow and Leningrad. Princeton, N. J.: Prin U Press, 1972. Rev. by R. F. Byrnes, AmArc, 37(Ja 1974):73-5; J. Barber, Archives, 11(Spr 1974):187-8.

Grindle, Roger L. Quarry and Kiln: The Story of Maine's Lime Industry. Rockland, Me.: Courier-Gazette, 1971. Rev. by G. Porter, AHR, 79(Apr 1974):594-5.

Grinnell, George Bird. The Cheyenne Indians: Their History and Ways of Life. Lincoln: U Neb Press, 1972. Rev. by B. B. MacLachlan, JOW, 13(Apr 1974):122; W. Frantz, N H, 55(Spr 1974):159-60.

Grinstead, Marion C. The Life and Death of a Frontier Fort: Fort Craig, New Mexico, 1854-1885. Socorro, N. M.: Socorro County Historical Society, 1973. Rev. by C. E. Trafzer, JOW, 13(Jl 1974):111.

Griswold, A. B. see Bowie, Theodore

Gritsch, Eric W. see Bainton, Roland H.

Grob, Gerald N. Mental Institutions in America: Social Policy to 1875. New York: Free Press, 1973. Rev. by P. D. Jordan, AHR, 79(Oct 1974):1260-2; J. Waksmundski, Historian, 36 (May 1974):575-6.

Groh, Dieter. Negative Integration und revolutionärer Attentismus: Die deutsche Sozialdemokratie am Vorabend des Ersten Welt-krieges. Frankfurt am Main: Propyläen, 1973. Rev. by

V. L. Lidtke, AHR, 79(Apr 1974):523-4; D. K. Buse, JMH, 46(Dec 1974):732-5.

Groh, George. The Black Migration: The Journey to Urban America. New York: Weybright and Talley, 1972. Rev. by J. L. Arnold, JNH, 59(Apr 1974):196-203.

Groner, Alex, et al. The American Heritage History of American Business and Industry. New York: American Heritage, 1972. Rev. by G. E. Hopkins, JISHS, 67(Je 1974):353-4.

Grube, Oswald W. Industrial Buildings and Factories. Tr. by E. Rockwell. New York: Praeger, 1971. Rev. by C. W. Condit, T & C, 15(Ja 1974):112-13.

Gruber, Ira D. The Howe Brothers and the American Revolution. New York: Atheneum, 1972. Rev. by R. Buell, Jr., CHR, 55(Je 1974):220-2; G. Seed, EHR, 89(Apr 1974):446-7; D. C. Skaggs, OH, 83(W 1974):75-6; N. Callahan, PH, 41(Ja 1974): 98-100.

Gruen, Erich S. The Last Generation of the Roman Republic. Berkeley: U Cal Press, 1974. Rev. by J. E. Rexine, HRNB, 2(May/Je 1974):173.

Grunberger, Richard. Red Rising in Bavaria. New York: St. Martin's, 1973. Rev. by A. Bucholz, HRNB, 2(Mar 1974):116-17.

Grundiman, Claudia B., comp. Calendar of Continental Congress Papers. Richmond, Va St Library, 1973. Rev. by A. T. Dill, VMHB, 82(Apr 1974):195-6.

Gruner, Rebecca Brooks. An American History. New York: Appleton--Century--Crofts, 1972. Rev. by W. H. Ahern, HT, 8(Nov 1974):118-19.

Guest, Francis F., O.F.M. Fermin Francisco de Lasuen (1736-1803): A Biography. Washington, D.C.: Academy of American Franciscan History, 1973. Rev. by E. A. Beilharz, PHR, 43(Feb 1974):117-18.

Guhin, Michael A. John Foster Dulles: A Statesman and His Times. New York: Columbia U Press, 1972. Rev. by R. W. Pruessen, AHR, 79(Je 1974):907-8; D. Wrone, HT, 8(Nov 1974):145-6.

Guibert, Rita. Seven Voices: Seven Latin American Writers Talk to Rita Guibert. New York: Knopf, 1973. Rev. by D. A. Yates, HAHR, 54(Aug 1974):550-1.

Guicciardini, Francesco. Storia d'Italia. S. S. Menchi, ed. Torini: Einaudi, 1971. Rev. by M. Phillips, RQ, 27(Spr 1974): 72-3.

GUICE   144

Guice, John D. W. The Rocky Mountain Bench: The Territorial
Supreme Courts of Colorado, Montana, and Wyoming, 1861-
1890. New Haven, Conn.: Yale U Press, 1972. Rev. by
J. S. Goff, AHR, 79(Je 1974):865-6.

Guido, Margaret. Southern Italy: An Archaeological Guide. Park
Ridge, N. J.: Noyes Press, 1973. Rev. by B. S. Ridgway,
Archaeology, 27(Jl 1974):214-5.

Guillou, A. see Folz, R.

Guldbeck, Janet Sutherland. The Carriage and Harness Museum.
Cooperstown, N. Y. NY St Hist Soc, 1973. Rev. by D. H.
Berkebile, T & C, 15(Jl 1974):537-8.

Gulhati, N. D. Indus Waters Treaty: An Exercise in International
Mediation. Bombay: Allied, 1973. Rev. by C. H. Heimsath,
JAS, 34(Nov 1974):255-6.

Gulick, Edward V. Peter Parker and the Opening of China. Cambridge, Mass.: Har U Press, 1973. Rev. by D. Lindberg,
CH, 43(Dec 1974):558; J. W. Killigrew, HRNB, 2(Apr 1974):
146; R. J. Smith, JAS, 34(Nov 1974):220-2; J. M. Downs,
PHR, 43(Nov 1974):623-4.

Gulvin, Clifford. The Tweedmakers: A History of the Scottish
Fancy Woollen Industry 1600-1914. New York: Barnes and
Noble, 1973. Rev. by D. J. Jeremy, AHR, 79(Oct 1974):
1184-5.

Gumerman, George J., ed. The Distribution of Population Aggre-
gates. Prescott, Ariz.: Prescott Coll Press, 1971. Rev. by
R. B. Woodbury, AmAnt, 39(Apr 1974):399-400.

Gunnerson, Dolores A. The Jicarilla Apaches: A Study in Survival.
DeKalb: N Ill U Press, 1974. Rev. by H. A. Howard, JOW,
13(Apr 1974):128-9.

Gunter, A. Y. The Big Thicket: A Challenge to Conservation.
Austin, Tx.: Jenkins, 1971. Rev. by A. C. Keller, JOW,
13(Oct 1974):141.

Gunther, Erna. Ethnobotany of Western Washington: The Knowledge
and Use of Indigenous Plants by Native Americans. Seattle:
U Wash Press, 1973. Rev. by Staff, InH, 7(Spr 1974):49.

_____. Indian Life on the Northwest Coast of North America:
As Seen by the Early Explorers and Fur Traders During the
Last Decades of the Eighteenth Century. Chicago: U Chi
Press, 1972. Rev. by W. L. Cook, AHR, 79(Apr 1974):571-
2; JOW, 13(Jl 1974):121; F. L. Green, WHQ, 5(Apr 1974):
200-2.

145   GUPTA

Gupta, Brijen K. India in English Fiction, 1800-1970: An Anno-
    tated Bibliography. Metuchen, N.J.: Scarecrow, 1973. Rev.
    by K. B. Gauri, JAS, 34(Nov 1974):252-3.

Gurevich, A. Ia. Categories of Medieval Cultures. Moscow: Iz-
    datel 'stvo "Iskusstvo," 1972. Rev. by S. A. Zenkovsky,
    AHR, 79(Oct 1974):1162-3.

_____. The Free Peasantry of Feudal Norway. Moscow: Iz-
    datel 'stvo "Nauka," 1967. Rev. by H. E. Ellersieck, AHR,
    79(Feb 1974):173.

_____. The History and the Saga. Moscow: Izdatel 'stvo
    "Nauka," 1972. Rev. by S. A. Zenkovsky, AHR, 79(Oct 1974):
    1162-3.

Gustin, Lawrence R. Billy Durant, Creator of General Motors.
    Grand Rapids, Mich.: Eerdmans, 1973. Rev. by J. B. Rae,
    BHR, 48(Sum 1974):267-8; R. D. Gray, JAH, 61(Dec 1974):
    807-8.

Guterman, Simeon L. From Personal to Territorial Law: Aspects
    of the History and Structure of Western Legal-Constitutional
    Tradition. Metuchen, N.J.: Scarecrow, 1972. Rev. by
    A. M. Honoré, EHR, 89(Ja 1974):143-4.

Guthorn, Peter J. British Maps of the American Revolution. Mon-
    mouth Beach, N.J.: Philip Freneau Press, 1972. Rev. by
    D. W. Marshall, AmArc, 37(Apr 1974):300-2.

Gutman, Judith Mara. Is America Used Up? New York: Gross-
    man, 1973. Rev. by F. Peterson, NDH, 41(Fall 1974):32-3.

Gutmann, Joseph, ed. The Dura-Europos Synagogue: A Re-evalua-
    tion (1932-1972). n.p. Society of Biblical Literature, 1973.
    Rev. by M. A. R. Colledge, AJA, 78(Oct 1974):442-3.

Haas, Michael. International Organization: An Interdisciplinary
    Bibliography. Stanford, Cal.: Hoover Institution Press, 1971.
    Rev. by K. McKeough, AmArc, 37(Jl 1974):468-9.

Haase, Carl. Ernst Brandes, 1758-1810. Hildesheim: August Lax
    Verlagsbuchhandlung, 1973. Rev. by F. G. Nauen, AHR, 79
    (Oct 1974):1203.

Habermas, Jurgen. Theory and Practice. Boston: Beacon, 1973.
    Rev. by M. Bunge, T & C, 15(Jl 1974):539.

Hachey, Thomas E., ed. Anglo-Vatican Relations, 1914-1939: Con-
    fidential Annual Reports of the British Ministers to the Holy
    See. Boston: G. K. Hall, 1972. Rev. by J. J. Hughes, CH,
    43(Je 1974):275.

Hackensmith, Charles W. Biography of Joseph Neef, Educator in the Ohio Valley, 1809-1854. New York: Carlton, 1973. Rev. by W. B. Hendrickson, IMH, 70(Je 1974):182-4.

Hackett, Roger F. Yamagata Aritomo in the Rise of Modern Japan, 1838-1922. Cambridge, Mass.: Har U Press, 1971. Rev. by R. H. P. Mason, MAS, 8(Apr 1974):277-82.

Hafen, LeRoy R. Broken Hand: The Life of Thomas Fitzpatrick: Mountain Man, Guide and Indian Agent. Denver: Old West, 1973. Rev. by R. L. Munkres, JOW, 13(Jl 1974):125; D. J. Weber, NMHR, 49(Oct 1974):339-40; F. R. Gowans, UHQ, 42 (Sum 1974):301-2.

_____, ed. The Mountain Men and the Fur Trade of the Far West. Glendale, Cal.: Arthur H. Clark, 1972. Rev. by J. T. Bloom, CoMag, 51(Win 1974):71-2; A. M. Gibson, UHQ, 42(Sum 1974):300-1.

_____ and Ann W. The Joyous Journey of LeRoy R. and Ann W. Hafen: An Autobiography. Glendale, Cal.: Arthur H. Clark; Denver: Old West, 1973. Rev. by T. A. Larson, A & W, 16(Spr 1974):80-1; H. L. Carter, CoMag, 51(Spr 1974):165-6; W. R. Jacobs, JAH, 61(Je 1974):208-9; E. R. Bingham, JAriH, 15(Sum 1974):192-4; R. C. Post, JOW, 13(Apr 1974): 114; J. LeCompte, NMHR, 49(Apr 1974):183-4; A. Gutfield, PHR, 43(May 1974):280-1.

Haffner, Sebastian. Failure of a Revolution: Germany, 1918-19. La Salle, Ill.: Open Court, 1973. Rev. by G. F. Botjen, HRNB, 2(Feb 1974):110.

Hagan, Kenneth J. American Gunboat Diplomacy and the Old Navy, 1877-1889. Westport, Conn.: Greenwood, 1973. Rev. by W. H. Becker, BHR, 48(Sum 1974):263; J. E. Sefton, HRNB, 2(Feb 1974):93; M. Plesur, JAH, 61(Dec 1974):801-2.

Hager, Anna Marie, ed. see Janes, John F.

Hahn, Lili. White Flags of Surrender. Washington, D.C.: R. B. Luce, 1974. Rev. by D. E. Showalter, HRNB, 2(Sep 1974): 245-6.

Hair, Paul, ed. Before the Bawdy Court: Selections from Church Court and Other Records Relating to the Correction of Moral Offenses in England, Scotland and New England, 1300-1800. New York: Barnes and Noble, 1972. Rev. by S. B. Baxter, Historian, 36(Feb 1974):313-14.

Hakeda, Yoshita S. Kūkai: Major Works, Translated, with an Account of His Life and a Study of His Thought. New York: Columbia U Press, 1972. Rev. by S. Weinstein, JAS, 34 (Nov 1974):177-91.

Halberstam, David. The Best and the Brightest. New York: Random House, 1972. Rev. by T. A. Brindley, JAS, 33(Feb 1974):340-2.

Halbouty, Michel T. see Clark, James A.

Hale, J. R. Renaissance Europe: Individual and Society, 1480-1520. New York: Harper and Row, 1971. Rev. by R. D. Face, Historian, 36(Feb 1974):316-17.

_____, ed. Renaissance Venice. Totowa, N.J.: Rowman and Littlefield, 1973. Rev. by A. J. Schutte, CH, 43(Dec 1974): 539-41; D. M. Bueno de Mesquita, EHR, 89(Jl 1974):627-31.

Hale, Nathan G., Jr. Freud and the Americans: The Beginnings of Psychoanalysis in the United States, 1876-1917. New York: Ox U Press, 1971. Rev. by D. J. Kevles, AHR, 79(Je 1974): 881.

Halewood, William H. The Poetry of Grace: Reformation Themes and Structures in English Seventeenth-Century Poetry. New Haven, Conn.: Yale U Press, 1970. Rev. by K. S. Datta, RQ, 27(Spr 1974):114-17.

Haley, J. Evetts. Life on the Texas Range. Austin: U Tx Press, 1973. Rev. by R. H. Faust, JOW, 13(Ja 1974):155-6.

Haley, J. Evetts and William Curry Holden. The Flamboyant Judge, James D. Hamlin: A Biography. Canyon, Tx.: Palo Duro Press, 1972. Rev. by J. B. Frantz, NMHR, 49(Apr 1974): 182-3.

Haley, K. H. D. The Dutch in the Seventeenth Century. London: Thames and Hudson, 1972. Rev. by A. C. Carter, EHR, 89 (Apr 1974):439-40.

_____, ed. The Stuarts. New York: St. Martin's, 1973. Rev. by D. O. Fries, HRNB, 2(Mar 1974):121-2.

Haliburton, Gordon M. The Prophet Harris. London: Longman, 1971. Rev. by W. E. Phipps, JMAS, 12(Je 1974):329-31.

Halkin, L. E., ed. see Erasmus

Hall, Gwendolyn Mildo. Social Control in Slave Plantation Societies: A Comparison of St. Dominique and Cuba. Baltimore: JHU Press, 1971. Rev. by A. Bryan, Historian, 36(Feb 1974): 312.

Hall, H. Duncan. Commonwealth: A History of the British Commonwealth of Nations. London: Van Nostrand Reinhold, 1971. Rev. by M. Israel, JMH, 46(Je 1974):350-1.

Hall, Ivan Parker. Mori Arinori. Cambridge, Mass.: Har U Press, 1973. Rev. by P. Duus, JAS, 33(May 1974):483-4; F. G. Notehelfer, PHR, 43(Feb 1974):132-4.

Hall, Kathleen M., ed. see Taille, Jean de la

Hall, Marie Boas, Intro. The "Pneumatics" of the Hero of Alexander: A Facsimile of the 1851 Woodcroft Edition. New York: American Elsevier Pub., 1973. Rev. by C. Kreu, T & C, 15 (Apr 1974):326-8.

Hall, Thomas B. Medicine on the Santa Fe Trail. Dayton: Morningside, 1971. Rev. by M. S. Legan, JOW, 13(Jl 1974):117.

Haller, John S., Jr. and Robin M. The Physician and Sexuality in Victorian America. Chicago: U Chi Press, 1974. Rev. by J. F. Pacheco, HRNB, 2(Jl 1974):196.

Haller, Mark H. see Davis, Allen F.

Halperin, Maurice. The Rise and Decline of Fidel Castro: An Essay in Contemporary History. Berkeley: U Cal Press, 1972. Rev. by M. Zeitlin, HAHR, 54(Aug 1974):537-40.

Halperín-Donghi, Tulio. The Aftermath of Revolution in Latin America. New York: Harper and Row, 1973. Rev. by F. Safford, HAHR, 54(Nov 1974):709-11.

Halsey, A. H., ed. Trends in British Society Since 1900: A Guide to the Changing Social Structure of Britain. New York: St. Martin's, 1972. Rev. by J. M. Winter, AHR, 79(Win 1974):154-5.

Haltern, Utz. Die Londoner Weltausstellung von 1851. Munster: Verlag Ashendorff, 1971. Rev. by A. Briggs, EHR, 89(Ja 1974):217-18.

Hamarneh, Sami K. Temples of the Muses and a History of Pharmacy Museums. Tokyo: Naito Foundation, 1971. Rev. by P. A. Gerstner, T & C, 15(Ja 1974):156-7.

Hamby, Alonzo L. Beyond the New Deal: Harry S. Truman and American Liberalism. New York: Columbia U Press, 1973. Rev. by P. M. Buzanski, HRNB, 2(Feb 1974):91; G. Wolfskill, JAH, 61(Dec 1974):842-3; G. W. Reichard, JSH, 40 (Aug 1974):508-9.

Hamelin, Jean et Yves Roby. Histoire économique du Québec 1851-1896. Montreal: Fides, 1971. Rev. by J. E. Igartua, CHR, 55(Mar 1974):87-9.

Hamer, D. A. Liberal Politics in the Age of Gladstone and Rosebery. Oxford: Ox U Press, 1972. Rev. by R. M. Taylor,

HJ, 17(Mar 1974):221-3.

Hamerow, Theodore S. The Social Foundations of German Unification 1858-1871. Struggles and Accomplishments. Princeton,
N.J.: Prin U Press, 1972. Rev. by W. Carr, EHR, 89(Ja
1974):133-5; A. J. Nicholls, History, 59(Feb 1974):139.

Hamilton, Charles, ed. Cry of the Thunderbird: The American
Indian's Own Story. Norman: U Ok Press, 1972. Rev. by
B. A. Glasrud, JOW, 13(Ja 1974):152; L. Coates, WHQ, 5(Ja
1974):83-4.

Hamilton, Charles V. The Bench and the Ballot: Southern Federal
Judges and Black Voters. New York: Ox U Press, 1973.
Rev. by A. L. Yarnell, JSH, 40(May 1974):336-7.

Hamilton, Holman and Edward T. Houlihan. Meet Squire Coleman
(J. Winston Coleman, Jr.). Lexington, Ky.: n.p., 1973.
Rev. by R. E. McDowell, FCHQ, 48(Apr 1974):197.

Hamilton, J. G. deRoulhac. Papers of William Alexander Graham.
see Williams, Max R.

Hamilton, J. R. Alexander the Great. London: Hutchinson U Library, 1973. Rev. by T. S. Brown, AHR, 79(Je 1974):762-3.

Hamilton, Virginia Van der Veer. Hugo Black: The Alabama
Years. Baton Rouge: LSU Press, 1972. Rev. by I. A.
Newby, AHR, 79(Je 1974):896.

Hammer, Jefferson J., ed. Frederic Augustus James' Civil War
Diary: Sumter to Andersonville. Rutherford, N.J.: Fairleigh Dickinson U Press, 1973. Rev. by J. K. Folmar, CWH,
20(Mar 1974):74-6.

Hammond, George P., ed. A Guide to the Manuscript Collections
of the Bancroft Library. Vol. II. Berkeley: U Cal Press,
1972. Rev. by F. Morales, TAm, 30(Ja 1974):408-9.

Hammond, N. G. L. Studies in Greek History: A Companion Volume to A History of Greece to 322 B.C. New York: Ox U
Press, 1973. Rev. by W. G. Sinnigen, AHR, 79(Oct 1974):
1154-5.

Hammond, Norman, ed. South Asian Archaeology: Papers from
the First International Conference of South Asian Archaeologists
Held in the University of Cambridge. Park Ridge, N.J.:
Noyes, 1973. Rev. by W. A. Fairservis, Jr., Archaeology,
27(Jl 1974):212.

Hampden, John, ed. Francis Drake, Privateer: Contemporary Narratives and Documents. University, Ala.: U Ala Press, 1972.
Rev. by A. J. Loomie, HAHR, 54(Aug 1974):509-10; R. Harvey,

Historian, 36(Feb 1974):319; J. H. Kemble, PNQ, 65(Ja 1974): 40-1.

Hampton, H. Duane. How the U.S. Cavalry Saved Our National Parks. Bloomington: Ind U Press, 1971. Rev. by E. C. Bearss, JOW, 13(Oct 1974):143-4.

Hamshere, Cyril. The British in the Caribbean. Cambridge, Mass.: Har U Press, 1972. Rev. by K. R. Andrews, HAHR, 54(Feb 1974):121-2; J. J. TePaske, WMQ-3, 31(Apr 1974):334-6.

Hanan, Patrick. The Chinese Short Story: Studies in Dating, Authorship, and Composition. Cambridge, Mass.: Har U Press, 1973. Rev. by Y. W. Ma, JAS, 34(Nov 1974):213-15.

Handler, Jerome S. A Guide to Source Materials for the Study of Barbados History, 1627-1834. Carbondale: S Ill U Press, 1971. Rev. by J. S. Bromley, EHR, 89(Ja 1974):179.

_____. The Unappropriated People: Freedmen in the Slave Society of Barbados. Baltimore: JHU Press, 1974. Rev. by J. L. Arbena, HRNB, 2(Jl 1974):200.

Handy, Robert T. A Christian America: Protestant Hopes and Historical Realities. New York: Ox U Press, 1971. Rev. by M. E. Marty, AHR, 79(Apr 1974):591-2.

Hanke, Lewis, ed. History of Latin American Civilization. Boston: Little, Brown, 1973. Rev. by N. E. Ramirez, HT, 7(Feb 1974):292-3.

Hankins, John Erskine. Source and Meaning in Spencer's Allegory: A Study of the Faerie Queene. Oxford: Clarendon Press, 1971. Rev. by A. C. Hamilton, RQ, 27(Spr 1974):91-4.

Hanley, Mike. Owyhee Trails, the West's Forgotten Corner. Caldwell, Ida.: Caxton, 1973. Rev. by L. Skoog, OrHQ, 75(Sep 1974):293.

Hanley, Thomas O'Brien. The American Revolution and Religion: Maryland 1770-1800. Washington: Cath U of America Press, Consortium Press, 1971. Rev. by D. W. Howe, AHR, 79(Je 1974):848-9.

Hanna, Alfred Jackson and Kathryn Abbey Hanna. Napoleon III and Mexico: American Triumph Over Monarchy. Chapel Hill: U NC Press, 1971. Rev. by E. H. Moseley, JSH, 40(May 1974): 320-2.

Hansell, Haywood S., Jr. The Air Plan That Defeated Hitler. Atlanta: the Author, 1972. Rev. by R. F. Futrell, AHR, 79 (Oct 1974):1284-5.

Hansen, Gladys, ed. San Francisco: A Guide to the Bay and Its Cities. New York: Hastings House, 1973. Rev. by T. Knight, JOW, 13(Jl 1974):120.

Hansen, Hans Jürgen, ed. Architecture in Wood: A History of Wood-Building and Its Techniques in Europe and North America. New York: Viking, 1971. Rev. by C. W. Condit, T & C, 15(Oct 1974):637-9.

Harari, Ehud. The Politics of Labor Legislation in Japan. Berkeley: U Cal Press, 1973. Rev. by A. H. Cook, JAS, 33(Aug 1974):713-15.

Harbaugh, William H. Lawyer's Lawyer: The Life of John W. Davis. New York: Ox U Press, 1973. Rev. by L. M. Friedman, JAH, 61(Dec 1974):817-18; W. M. Bagby, JSH, 40(Aug 1974):502-3; R. M. Ireland, NEQ, 47(Sep 1974):475-7; O. K. Rice, WVH, 36(Oct 1974):68-70.

Harbert, Earl N. see Rees, Robert A.

Harbeson, John W. Nation Building in Kenya: The Role of Land Reform. n.p.: Northwestern U Press, 1973. Rev. by F. Furedi, JAfH, 15(Num 1 1974):165-6.

Hardin, Richard F. Michael Drayton and the Passing of Elizabethan England. Lawrence: U Press Kan, 1973. Rev. by W. G. Zeeveld, AHR, 79(Je 1974):781.

Harding, Alan. The Law Courts of Medieval England. New York: Barnes and Noble, 1973. Rev. by M. Hastings, AHR, 79(Apr 1974):494-5.

Hardoy, Jorge E. Pre-Columbian Cities. New York: Walker, 1973. Rev. by R. C. Padden, AHR, 79(Feb 1974):251-2.

————. see Geisse, Guillermo

Hardwick, Elizabeth. Seduction and Betrayal: Women and Literature. New York: Random House, n.d. Rev. by J. W. Aldridge, Commentary, 58(Aug 1974):75-8.

Hardy, Barbara. The Exposure of Luxury: Radical Themes in Thackeray. Pittsburgh: U Pittsburgh Press, 1972. Rev. by M. Greene, GR, 28(Sum 1974):345-7.

Hardy, P. The Muslims of British India. Cambridge: Cam U Press, 1972. Rev. by J. M. Brown, History, 59(Je 1974): 317-18; N. G. Barrier, JAS, 33(May 1974):498-500.

Hargreaves, Mary W. M. The Papers of Henry Clay. Vol. V. see Hopkins, James F.

Harlan, Louis R. Booker T. Washington--The Making of a Black
Leader, 1856-1901. New York: Ox U Press, 1972. Rev. by
R. B. Woods, ArkHQ, 33(Spr 1974):90-2; R. Gavins, MHM,
59(Sum 1974):236-7.

_____, Stuart B. Kaufman and Raymond W. Smock, eds. The
Booker T. Washington Papers. Vol. 3: 1889-95. Urbana:
U Ill Press, 1974. Rev. by J. B. Stewart, HRNB, 2(Sep
1974):259-60; N. Lederer, IMH, 70(Dec 1974):360-2; A. H.
Spear, JAH, 61(Dec 1974):748-9.

Harms-Baltzer, Kate. Die Nationalisierung der deutschen Einwanderer und ihrer Nachkommen in Brasilien als Problem der
deutsch-brasilianischen Beziehungen 1930-1938. Berlin: Col-
loquium Verlag Berlin, 1970. Rev. by T. E. Skidmore, HAHR,
54(Feb 1974):145-6.

Harnack, Curtis. We Have All Gone Away. New York: Doubleday,
1973. Rev. by J. McDonald, AI, 42(Spr 1974):297-9.

Harnetty, Peter. Imperialism and Free Trade: Lancashire and
India in the Mid-Nineteenth Century. Vancouver: U BC Press,
1972. Rev. by D. A. Farnie, History, 59(Feb 1974):125-6.

Harper, Howard M., Jr. and Charles Edge, eds. The Classic British Novel. Athens, Ga.: U Ga Press, 1972. Rev. by M.
Blaine, GR, 28(Sum 1974):333-5.

Harper, Norman, ed. Pacific Circle 2: Proceedings of the Third
Biennial Conference of the Australian and New Zealand American Studies Association. St. Lucia, Australia: U Queensland Press, 1972. Rev. by J. G. Banks, CWH, 20(Mar 1974):
80-1.

Harrell, David Edwin, Jr. A Social History of the Disciples of
Christ. Volume 1, Quest for a Christian America: The Dis-
ciples of Christ and American Society to 1866. Nashville:
Disciples of Christ Historical Society, 1966. Rev. by R. E.
Osborn, CH, 43(Dec 1974):551-2.

_____. A Social History of the Disciples of Christ. Volume 2,
The Social Sources of Division in the Disciples of Christ,
1865-1900. Atlanta and Athens, Ga.: Publishing Systems,
1973. Rev. by R. E. Osborn, CH, 43(Dec 1974):551-2; P. A.
Carter, JAH, 61(Dec 1974):806-7; W. B. Posey, JSH, 40(Nov
1974):678-9.

Harrington, Michael see Lindsay, T. F.

Harris, Frederick John. Andre Gide and Romain Rolland. New
Brunswick, N.J.: Rutgers U Press, n.d. Rev. by A. Cardona-Hine, Mankind, 4(Apr 1974):9.

Harris, James E. and Kent R. Weeks. X-Raying the Pharaohs. New York: Scribner's, 1973. Rev. by J. L. Angel, Archaeology, 27(Ja 1974):65-6.

Harris, José. Unemployment and Politics, a Study in English Social Policy, 1886-1914. Oxford: Clarendon Press, 1972. Rev. by D. Read, EHR, 89(Jl 1974):688; P. F. Clarke, History, 59 (Feb 1974):128-9.

Harris, Katherine, comp. Guide to Manuscripts. Iowa City: St Historical Soc of Iowa, 1973. Rev. by R. W. Richmond, AmArc, 37(Apr 1974):291-2.

Harris, Michael H., comp. Florida History: A Bibliography. Metuchen, N.J.: Scarecrow, 1973. Rev. by E. C. Williamson, AlaR, 27(Ja 1974):77.

Harris, Middleton. The Black Book. New York: Random House, 1974. Rev. by W. Marr, II, Crisis, 81(Je-Jl 1974):213.

Harris, Neil, ed. The Land of Contrasts, 1880-1902. New York: Geo. Braziller, 1970. Rev. by D. H. Culbert, HT, 8(Nov 1974):128-9.

_____. see Mann, Arthur. History and the Role of the City.

Harris, Sheldon H., ed. Paul Cuffe: Black American and the African Return. New York: Simon and Schuster, 1972. Rev. by F. J. Miller, NEQ, 47(Mar 1974):168-73.

Harrison, James Pinckney. The Long March to Power. A History of the Chinese Communist Party, 1921-72. New York: Praeger, 1972. Rev. by Hung-mao Tien, Historian, 36(Feb 1974): 309-10.

Harrison, John F. C. The Birth and Growth of Industrial England, 1714-1867. New York: Harcourt Brace Jovanovich, 1973. Rev. by E. H. Robinson, BHR, 48(Win 1974):588-9.

Harrison, Martin see Williams, Philip M.

Harrod, Howard L. Mission Among the Blackfeet. Norman: U Ok Press, 1971. Rev. by R. L. Whitner, PNQ, 65(Ja 1974):41.

Hart, Ansell. The Life of George William Gordon. Kingston: Institute of Jamaica, 1972. Rev. by T. Reese, EHR, 89(Ja 1974):219-20.

Hart, Cyril. The Verderers and Forest Laws of Dean. Newton Abbot: David and Charles, 1971. Rev. by D. Walker, EHR, 89(Ja 1974):160-1.

Hart, John Fraser, ed. Regions of the United States. New York:

Harper and Row, 1972. Rev. by F. H. Schapsmeier, JOW,
13(Oct 1974):134-5.

Hart, Katherine, trans. Alphonse in Austin: Being Excerpts from
the Official Letters Written to the French Foreign Ministry
by Alphonse Duboise de Saligny, Chargé d'Affaires of the Kingdom of France to the Republic of Texas, with Divers Notes
concerning the Pig War. Austin, Tex.: Encino, 1972. Rev.
by G. Theisen, JOW, 13(Oct 1974):124.

Hart, Mary L. see Willcox, William B.

Hartje, Robert G. Bicentennial USA: Pathways to Celebration.
Nashville: American Association for State and Local History,
1973. Rev. by P. Dodson, FHQ, 52(Jl 1974):100-1; G. M.
Waller, JAH, 61(Sep 1974):446-7; M. T. Smith, WHQ, 5(Oct
1974):476-7.

Hartley, Anthony. Gaullism: The Rise and Fall of a Political
Movement. London: Routledge and Kegan Paul, 1972. Rev.
by A. Adamthwaite, History, 59(Feb 1974):156-7.

Hartley, William and Ellen. Osceola: The Unconquered Indian.
New York: Hawthorn, 1973. Rev. by J. L. Wright, Jr.,
JSH, 40(Aug 1974):474-5.

Hartmann, Horst. Political Parties in India. Meerut: Meenakshi
Prakashan, 1971. Rev. by R. L. Park, JAS, 33(Aug 1974):
725.

Hartwell, R. M. The Industrial Revolution and Economic Growth.
London: Methuen, 1971. Rev. by A. J. Taylor, EHR, 89
(Ja 1974):207-8; M. E. Falkus, History, 59(Feb 1974):119-20.

_____, ed. see Breach, R. W.

Harvey, Nancy Lenz. Elizabeth of York: The Mother of Henry
VIII. New York: Macmillan, 1973. Rev. by R. Rinehart,
HRNB, 2(Feb 1974):109.

Haskins, James. Pinckney Benton Stewart Pinchback. New York:
Macmillan, 1973. Rev. by C. L. Mohr, GHQ, 58(Spr 1974):
122-4; W. Cheek, JAH, 61(Je 1974):200-1; R. C. McConnell,
JNH, 59(Oct 1974):396-9; D. C. Rankin, JSH, 40(May 1974):
347-8; E. G. Stewart, LaH, 15(Win 1974):91-2; T. D. Perry,
NHB, 37(Apr/May 1974):251.

Haskins, Ralph W. see Graf, LeRoy P.

Hassell, Cushing Biggs and Sylvester. History of the Church of
God, from the Creation to A.D. 1885; Including Especially the
History of the Kehukee Primitive Baptist Association. Conley,
Ga.: Old School Hymnal Co., 1973. Rev. by H. B. John-

son, NCHR, 51(Spr 1974):239-40.

Hassler, Warren H.   The President as Commander in Chief.   Menlo Park, Cal.: Addison-Wesley, 1971. Rev. by C. Reese,
JOW, 13(Oct 1974):136-8.

Hassrick, Peter H.   Frederick Remington.   Fort Worth: Amon
Carter Museum, 1973. Rev. by K. L. MacKay, UHQ, 42(Win
1974):89-90.

Hastings, Adrian. Christian Marriage in Africa. London: S P C K,
1973. Rev. by L. Mair, Africa, 44(Apr 1974):208.

_____. Wiriyami. n.p.: Search Press, 1974. Rev. by L. H.
Gann, AfAf, 73(Jl 1974):371-2.

Hastings, Robert J.   A Nickel's Worth of Skim Milk: A Boy's View
of the Great Depression. Carbondale: S Ill U Press, 1972.
Rev. by R. Stroud, JISHS, 67(Apr 1974):244-5.

Hatada, Takashi. Chinese Villages and Theories of Cooperative
Systems. Tokyo: Iwanami shoten, 1973. Rev. by R. H.
Myers, JAS, 34(Nov 1974):228-9.

Hatcher, John. English Tin Production and Trade Before 1550.
Oxford: Clarendon Press, n.d. Rev. by A. L. Rouse, HTo,
24(Feb 1974):136-7.

Hatting, Tove see Sørensen, Per

Hatton, R. M. Louis XIV and His World. New York: Putnam's,
1972. Rev. by G. Symcox, HT, 7(Feb 1974):311.

Hauck, Cornelius W. Narrow Gauge to Central and Silver Plume.
Golden, Colo.: Colorado Railroad Museum, 1972. Rev. by
L. Scamehorn, CoMag, 51(Spr 1974):163-4.

Haupt, Georges and Jean-Jacques Marie. Makers of the Russian
Revolution: Biographies of Bolshevik Leaders. Ithaca, N.Y.:
Cornell U Press, 1974. Rev. by S. M. Horak, HRNB, 3(Nov/
Dec 1974):32.

Hause, Earl Malcolm. Tumble-Down Dick: The Fall of the House
of Richard Cromwell. New York: Exposition, 1972. Rev.
by C. Hill, EHR, 89(Apr 1974):442; R. Ashton, History, 59
(Feb 1974):110.

Hauser, William B. Economic Institutional Change in Tokugawa
Japan: Osaka and the Kinai Cotton Trade. New York: Cam
U Press, 1974. Rev. by T. R. H. Havens, HRNB, 2(Jl 1974):
202.

Havard, William C., ed. The Changing Politics of the South.

Baton Rouge: LSU Press, 1972. Rev. by A. C. Ashcraft, JISHS, 67(Nov 1974):561-2; W. F. Winter, JMiH, 36(Feb 1974): 117-19.

Havelock, Christine Mitchell. Hellenistic Art: The Art of the Classical World from the Death of Alexander the Great to the Battle of Actium. Greenwich, Conn.: NY Graphic Society, 1971. Rev. by D. B. Thompson, Archaeology, 27(Ja 1974):70, 72.

Havran, Martin J. Caroline Courtier: The Life of Lord Cottington. London: Macmillan, 1973. Rev. by C. Russell, EHR, 89(Jl 1974):668-9.

Hawke, David Freeman. Paine. New York: Harper and Row, 1974. Rev. by W. O. Reichert, HRNB, 2(Aug 1974):221.

Hawkes, Christopher and Sonia, eds. Greeks, Celts and Romans: Studies in Venture and Resistance. London: Dent, 1973. Rev. by T. G. E. Powell, Antiquity, 48(Mar 1974):74-5.

Hawkes, Jacquetta. The First Great Civilizations: Life in Mesopotamia, the Indus Valley and Egypt. The History of Human Society. New York: Knopf, 1973. Rev. by S. Lloyd, Antiquity, 48(Je 1974):158-9.

Hawkins, Gerald S. Beyond Stonehenge. New York: Harper and Row, 1973. Rev. by R. M. Rowlette, Archaeology, 27(Jl 1974):218-20.

Hawkins, Hugh. Between Harvard and America: The Educational Leadership of Charles W. Eliot. New York: Ox U Press, 1972. Rev. by G. W. Pierson, AHR, 79(Feb 1974):234-5; P. R. Rulon, Historian, 36(May 1974):561-2; P. Borden, HT, 7(Feb 1974):315-16.

Haymond, Henry. History of Harrison County, West Virginia, from the Earliest Days of Northwestern Virginia to the Present. Parsons, W.Va.: McClain, 1973. Rev. by O. K. Rice, WVH, 36(Oct 1974):67-8.

Haynes, Richard F. The Awesome Power: Harry S. Truman as Commander in Chief. Baton Rouge: LSU Press, 1973. Rev. by R. A. Lee, JAH, 61(Sep 1974):537-8; R. W. Leopold, JSH, 40(Nov 1974):672-3; D. Stewart, MHR, 68(Apr 1974):368-70; R. N. Current, PHR, 43(Nov 1974):627-8.

Hayot, Emile. Les Gens de coleur libres du Fort Royal 1679-1823. Paris: ... Librairie P. Geunther, 1971. Rev. by J. S. Bromley, EHR, 89(Ja 1974):189-90.

Haywood, Jacquelyn S. see Fowler, David H.

Headlam-Morley, Agnes. A Memoir of the Peace Conference, 1919.

157   HEALY

London: Methuen, 1972. Rev. by R. Bullen, EHR, 89(Apr
1974):465-6.

Healy, Kathleen. Frances Warde: American Founder of the Sisters
of Mercy. New York: Seabury Press, 1973. Rev. by M. K.
Heavill, WPHM, 57(Apr 1974):228-31.

Heaps, Leo. Log of the Centurion: Based on the Original Papers
of Captain Philip Saumarez on Board [the] H M S Centurion,
Lord Anson's Flagship During His Circumnavigation 1740-44.
New York: Macmillan, 1974. Rev. by R. A. Courtemanche,
HRNB, 2(Sep 1974):239; R. Miller, HTo, 24(Aug 1974):581-3.

Heard, J. Norman. White Into Red: A Study of the Assimilation
of White Persons Captured by Indians. Metuchen, N.J.:
Scarecrow, 1973. Rev. by W. Fenton, AHR, 79(Oct 1974):
1258-60; W. D. Baird, JAH, 60(Mar 1974):1108-9; J. Suberi,
JOW, 13(Apr 1974):119; W. E. Unrau, WHQ, 5(Jl 1974):343-5.

Hearsey, John. Young Mr. Pepys. New York: Scribner's, n.d.
Rev. by A. Bakshian, Mankind, 4(Aug 1974):60, 62.

Heath, Shirley Brice. Telling Tongues: Language Policy in Mexico
Colony to Nation. New York: Teachers College Press, 1972.
Rev. by D. F. D'Amico, CH, 43(Je 1974):278.

Hébert, John R., comp. Panoramic Maps of Anglo-American Cities:
A Checklist of Maps in the Collections of the Library of Congress. Washington: Government Printing Office, 1974. Rev.
by L. L. Morrison, JOW, 13(Jl 1974):116-17.

Hecht, Marie B. John Quincy Adams: A Personal History of an
Independent Man. New York: Macmillan, 1972. Rev. by
W. R. Smith, PH, 41(Apr 1974):229-31.

Hedrick, Basil C., J. Charles Kelley and Carroll L. Riley, eds.
The Classic Southwest: Readings in Archaeology, Ethnohistory
and Ethnology. Carbondale: S Ill U Press, 1973. Rev. by
R. B. Spicer, JAriH, 15(Aut 1974):304-5; S. L. Meyers,
SWHQ, 78(Jl 1974):100-1.

Heeney, Arnold. The Things That Are Caesar's: Memoirs of a
Canadian Public Servant. Toronto: U Tor Press, 1972. Rev.
by C. P. Stacey, CHR, 55(Mar 1974):92-4.

Heer, Friedrich. Europe: Mother of Revolutions. New York:
Praeger, 1972. Rev. by R. Anchor, AHR, 79(Oct 1974):1173;
G. Best, History, 59(Feb 1974):164-5.

Heilbroner, Robert L. An Inquiry Into the Human Prospect. New
York: Norton, n.d. Rev. by R. Klein, Commentary, 58(Aug
1974):84-6.

Heimer, Franz-Wilhelm, ed. Social Change in Angola. Munich:
    Weltforum Verlag ... 1973. Rev. by D. Birmingham, JAfH,
    15(Num 3 1974):522.

Heller, Joseph. Something Happened. New York: Knopf, n.d.
    Rev. by E. Grossman, Commentary, 58(Nov 1974):80, 82-4.

Heller, L. G. Communicational Analysis and Methodology for His-
    torians. New York: NYU Press, 1972. Rev. by H. M.
    Hoenigswald, AHR, 79(Oct 1974):1137.

Hellie, Richard. Enserfment and Military Change in Muscovy. Chi-
    cago: U Chi Press, 1971. Rev. by C. B. O'Brien, AHR, 79
    (Feb 1974):194-5; H. W. Dewey, JMH, 46(Je 1974):371-2.

Helmreich, Paul C. From Paris to Sèvres: The Partition of the
    Ottoman Empire at the Peace Conference of 1919-1920. Colum-
    bus, Ohio: Ohio St U Press, 1974. Rev. by L. C. Rose,
    HRNB, 2(May/Je 1974):181.

Hemenway, Abby Maria. Abby Hemenway's Vermont. Ed. by
    Brenda C. Morrissey. Brattleboro, Vermont: Stephen Greene
    Press, 1972. Rev. by R. C. Barret, NEQ, 47(Je 1974):315-
    18.

Hemlow, Joyce, ed. The Journals and Letters of Fanny Burney.
    Oxford: Clarendon Press, 1973. Rev. by J. M. Roberts,
    EHR, 89(Apr 1974):452-3.

Hemmings, E. Thomas and Kathleen A. Deagan. Contributions of
    the Florida State Museum, Anthropology and History, Number
    18, Excavations on Amelia Island in Northeast Florida. Gaines-
    ville: Fla St Museum, 1973. Rev. by R. T. Grange, Jr.,
    FHQ, 53(Oct 1974):204-5.

Hemphill, W. Edwin, ed. The Papers of John C. Calhoun. Vol. V.
    1820-1821. Columbia, S.C.: U SCar Press, 1971. Rev. by
    J. A. Munroe, JAH, 61(Sep 1974):440-2.

_____, ed. The Papers of John C. Calhoun. Vol. VI. 1821-
    1822. Columbia, S.C.: U SCar Press, 1972. Rev. by J. A.
    Munroe, JAH, 61(Sep 1974):440-2; M. W. M. Hargreaves,
    JISHS, 67(Je 1974):355-6.

_____, ed. The Papers of John C. Calhoun. Vol. VII. 1822-
    1823. Columbia, S.C.: U SCar Press, 1973. Rev. by T. P.
    Govan, FHQ, 53(Jl 1974):84-6; J. A. Munroe, JAH, 61(Sep
    1974):440-2; H. Ammon, JSH, 40(May 1974):305-6; D. P.
    Jordan, VMHB, 82(Apr 1974):206-7.

Hencken, Hugh. The Earliest European Helmets. Bronze Age and
    Early Iron Age. Cambridge, Mass.: Har U Press, 1971.
    Rev. by C. Hawkes, AJA, 78(Ja 1974):92-3.

Henderson, David A. Men & Whales at Scammon's Lagoon. Los
Angeles: Dawson's Book Shop, 1972. Rev. by H. P. Hinton,
SCQ, 56(Fall 1974):319.

Henderson, Gregory, ed. Public Diplomacy and Political Change--
Four Case Studies: Okinawa, Peru, Czechoslovakia, Guinea.
New York: Praeger, 1973. Rev. by D. H. Mendel, Jr., JAS,
33(May 1974):489-90.

Henderson, Lenneal J., Jr., ed. Black Political Life in the United
States: A Fist as the Pendulum. San Francisco: Chandler,
1972. Rev. by E. J. Keller, JMAS, 12(Mar 1974):158-60.

Henderson, Moffitt Sinclair. A Long Day for November. Charlotte,
N.C.: n.p., 1972. Rev. by D. M. Vigness, ETHJ, 12(Fall
1974):78-9.

Henderson, Richard N. The King in Every Man: Evolutionary
Trends in Onitsha Ibo Society and Culture. New Haven, Conn.:
Yale U Press, 1972. Rev. by C. Onwubu, JMAS, 12(Je 1974):
333-6.

Hendrickson, Walter B. Forward in the Second Century of MacMur-
ray College: A History of 125 Years. Jacksonville, Ill.:
MacMurray College, 1972. Rev. by M. Brichford, JISHS, 67
(Je 1974):349-50.

_____. From Shelter to Self-Reliance: A History of the Illinois
Braille and Sight Saving School. Jacksonville, Ill.: Ill Braille
and Sight Saving School, 1972. Rev. by M. Z. Langzam, IMH,
70(Mar 1974):74-6; F. G. Davenport, JISHS, 67(Nov 1974):
563-4.

Henig, Gerald S. Henry Winter Davis: Antebellum and Civil War
Congressman from Maryland. New York: Twayne, 1973.
Rev. by F. Blue, CWH, 20(Sep 1974):271-2; R. N. Current,
HRNB, 2(Mar 1974):127-8; R. A. Gerber, JSH, 40(Nov 1974):
670-1; J. H. Baker, MHM, 69(Fall 1974):333-4; P. Kolchin,
WMH, 57(Sum 1974):319-20; J. F. Marszalek, Jr., WPHM,
57(Jl 1974):317-18.

Henig, Ruth B., ed. The League of Nations. New York: Barnes
and Noble, 1974. Rev. by W. J. Woolley, HRNB, 3(Oct 1974):
18-19.

Henle, Jane. Greek Myths: A Vase Painter's Notebook. Bloomington: Ind U Press, 1973. Rev. by M. E. Mayo, AJA, 78
(Oct 1974):440-1; R. M. Cook, Antiquity, 48(Sep 1974):249-50.

Hennock, E. P. Fit and Proper Persons: Ideal and Reality in
Nineteenth-Century Urban Government. London: Edward Arnold, 1973. Rev. by J. P. D. Dunbabin, EHR, 89(Apr 1974):
402-3; P. Thane, History, 59(Je 1974):291-2.

Henretta, James A. The Evolution of American Society, 1700-1815:
An Interdisciplinary Analysis. Lexington, Mass.: D. C.
Heath, 1973. Rev. by D. B. Rutman, HRNB, 2(Ja 1974):58-
9; R. M. Weir, JAH, 61(Sep 1974):465-6; M. Egnal, WMQ-3,
31(Jl 1974):510-11.

_____. "Salutary Neglect": Colonial Administration Under the
Duke of Newcastle. Princeton, N. J.: Prin U Press, 1972.
Rev. by I. D. Gruber, CHR, 55(Sep 1974):328-9; W. J. Gates,
PH, 41(Ja 1974):97-8.

Henry, Ruby Addison. The First West. Nashville: Aurora, 1972.
Rev. by C. G. Talbert, WHQ, 5(Apr 1974):191-2.

Heren, Louis, C. P. Fitzgerald, Michael Freeberne, Brian Hook,
and David Bonavia. China's Three Thousand Years: the
Story of a Great Civilization. New York: Collier Books,
1974. Rev. by J. W. Dardess, HRNB, 2(Jl 1974):204.

Herlihy, David. The Family in Renaissance Italy. St. Charles,
Mo.: Forum Press, 1972. Rev. by M. P. McCarthy, HT,
8(Nov 1974):109-10.

Herman, Donald L., ed. The Communist Tide in Latin America:
A Selected Treatment. Austin: U of Tex Press, 1973. Rev.
by E. H. Hyman, HAHR, 54(Nov 1973):729-30.

Hermann, Ruth. The Paiutes of Pyramid Lake: A Narrative Concerning a Western Nevada Indian Tribe. San Jose, Cal.:
Harlan-Young, 1972. Rev. by C. S. Fowler, WHQ, 5(Apr
1974):202-3.

Herndon, G. Melvin. William Tatham, 1752-1819: American Ver-
satile. Johnson City: E. Tenn St U, 1973. Rev. by J. F.
Roche, AHR, 79(Je 1974):846-7; G. W. Kyte, Historian, 36
(Feb 1974):338; P. J. Furlong, JAH, 60(Mar 1974):1093; C. G.
Talbert, RKHS, 72(Ja 1974):80-2; W. P. Cumming, NCHR, 51
(Ja 1974):100-1; J. M. Price, VMHB, 82(Apr 1974):202-3.

Herr, Richard. Spain. Englewood Cliffs, N. J.: Prentice-Hall,
1971. Rev. by G. Addy, AHR, 79(Oct 1974):1199-1201.

Herring, George C., Jr. Aid to Russia, 1941-1946: Strategy,
Diplomacy, the Origins of the Cold War. New York: Columbia U Press, 1973. Rev. by T. Buckley, Historian, 36(May
1974):552-3; R. A. Divine, JAH, 60(Mar 1974):1182-3; P. G.
Boyle, JAmS, 8(Apr 1974):123-4.

Herwig, Holger H. The German Naval Officer Corps: A Social
and Political History, 1890-1918. New York: Ox U Press,
1973. Rev. by S. C. Tucker, HRNB, 2(Apr 1974):142.

Herzog, James H. Closing the Open Door: American-Japanese

Negotiations, 1936-1941. Annapolis: Naval Institute Press, 1973. Rev. by F. C. Adams, JAH, 61(Dec 1974):834-5.

Heseltine, Nigel. Madagascar. New York: Praeger, 1971. Rev. by A. Southall, JAAS, 9(Ja & Apr 1974):132-4.

Hess, Gary R. America Encounters India, 1941-1947. Baltimore: JHU Press, 1971. Rev. by B. R. Babu, AHR, 79(Oct 1974): 1285-6.

Hess, Gunter. Deutsch-lateinische Narrenzunft. München: C. H. Beck'sche Verlagsbuchhandlung, 1971. Rev. by L. Bergel, RQ, 27(Spr 1974):68-70.

Hess, James W. Guide to Manuscripts and Archives in the West Virginia Collection. Morgantown: W Va Library, 1974. Rev. by E. Berkeley, Jr., AmArc, 37(Jl 1974):460-1.

Hesse, Eva, ed. New Approaches to Ezra Pound. Berkeley: U Cal Press, 1969. Rev. by V. Miller, GR, 28(Sum 1974): 354-7.

Hetzler, Stanley A. Applied Measures for Promoting Technological Growth. London: Routledge and Kegan Paul, 1973. Rev. by T. R. DeGregori, T & C, 15(Jl 1974):517-18.

Heuer, Kenneth. City of the Stargazers: The Rise and Fall of Ancient Alexandria. New York: Scribner's, 1972. Rev. by D. B. Thompson, Archaeology, 27(Jl 1974):215.

Hewes, Leslie. The Suitcase Farming Frontier: A Study in the Historical Geography of the Central Great Plains. Lincoln: U Neb Press, 1974. Rev. by P. D. Thomas, HRNB, 2(May/ Je 1974):161; M. B. Husband, JOW, 13(Oct 1974):145; B. Baltensperger, NH, 55(Sum 1974):292-4.

Hewitt, James, ed. Eye-Witnesses to Wagon Trains West. New York: Scribner's, 1974. Rev. by S. Ross, Mankind, 4(Dec 1974):6, 46, 70.

Hewitt, Margaret see Pinckbeck, Ivy

Hewlett, Richard G. and Francis Duncan. Atomic Shield: A History of the United States Atomic Energy Commission. Vol. 2 (1947-57). Washington: U.S. Atomic Energy Commission, 1972. Rev. by R. Sanders, T & C, 15(Jl 1974):506-8.

Hexter, J. H. The Vision of Politics on the Eve of Reformation: More, Machiavelli, and Seyssel. New York: Basic Books, 1973. Rev. by J. Hurstfield, AHR, 79(Oct 1974):1172-3.

Heywood, Ellis. Il Moro. Cambridge, Mass.: Har U Press, 1972. Rev. by H. S. Herbrüggen, RQ, 27(Spr 1974):86-9.

HIBBERT   162

Hibbert, Christopher. George IV: Prince of Wales, 1762-1811.
    London: Longman, 1972. Rev. by P. D. G. Thomas, History,
    59(Je 1974):282-3; G. B. Cooper, HRNB, 2(Mar 1974):119.

Hickin, Patricia, ed. see Reese, George, ed.

Hicks, Dave, ed. 1971 Brand Book: The Denver Westerners. Den-
    ver: Denver Westerners, 1972. Rev. by G. G. Suggs, Jr.,
    CoMag, 51(Spr 1974):175.

Higgs, David. Ultraroyalism in Toulouse: From Its Origins to the
    Revolution of 1830. Baltimore: JHU Press, 1973. Rev. by
    D. P. Resnick, AHR, 79(Feb 1974):166-7.

Higgs, E. S., ed. Papers in Economic Prehistory. London: Cam
    U Press, 1972. Rev. by J. Troels-Smith, Antiquity, 48(Je
    1974):163-4; P. E. Smith, Archaeology, 27(Ja 1974):65; M.
    Walker, T & C, 15(Ja 1974):86-9.

Higgs, Robert. The Transformation of the American Economy,
    1865-1914: An Essay in Interpretation. New York: Wiley,
    1971. Rev. by D. O. Whitten, CWH, 20(Mar 1974):55-6.

Higham, Robin. Air Power: A Concise History. New York: St.
    Martin's, 1972. Rev. by E. M. Emme, T & C, 15(Spr 1974):
    345-6.

_____, ed. Civil Wars in the Twentieth Century. Lexington,
    Ky.: U Press Ky, 1972. Rev. by L. W. Newton, FCHQ,
    48(Oct 1974):361-2.

Higonnet, Patrice L.-R. Pont-de-Montvert: Social Structure and
    Politics in a French Village, 1700-1914. Cambridge, Mass.:
    Har U Press, 1971. Rev. by D. D. Bien, JMH, 46(Mar 1974):
    112-15.

Hildebrand, Klaus. The Foreign Policy of the Third Reich. Berke-
    ley: U Cal Press, 1974. Rev. by R. E. Neil, HRNB, 2(Apr
    1974):142.

Hill, C. R. Chemical Apparatus. Oxford: Museum of the History
    of Science, 1971. Rev. by R. P. Multhauf, T & C, 15(Apr
    1974):365-7.

Hill, Christopher. The World Turned Upside Down. London:
    Temple Smith, 1972. Rev. by C. Cross, EHR, 89(Ja 1974):
    183-4.

Hill, Larry D. Emissaries to a Revolution: Woodrow Wilson's
    Executive Agents in Mexico. Baton Rouge: LSU Press, 1973.
    Rev. by R. E. Welch, Jr., HRNB, 2(Apr 1974):154; K. J.
    Grieb, JAH, 61(Dec 1974):813-14; M. T. Gilderhus, TAm, 31
    (Oct 1974):230-1; M. C. Meyer, NMHR, 49(Jl 1974):255-6.

Hill, Marvin S. and James B. Allen, eds. Mormonism and American Culture. New York: Harper and Row, 1972. Rev. by R. Flanders, CH, 43(Mar 1974):122-3; S. M. McMurrin, UHQ, 42(Win 1974):84-6.

Hill, Polly. Rural Hausa: A Village and a Setting. Cambridge: Cam U Press, 1972. Rev. by E. O. Akeredolu-Ale, JMAS, 12(Sep 1974):502-4.

Hill, W. Speed, ed. Studies in Richard Hooker: Essays Preliminary to an Edition of His Works. Cleveland: Press CWRU, 1972. Rev. by F. Shriver, CH, 43(Je 1974):271-2; R. W. Smith, Jr., RQ, 27(Fall 1974):358-9.

Hillerbrand, Hans J. The World of the Reformation. New York: Scribner's, 1973. Rev. by C. Garside, Jr., CH, 43(Dec 1974):541-2.

Hillgarth, J. N. Ramon Lull and Lullism in Fourteenth-Century France. New York: Ox U Press, 1971. Rev. by F. H. Peques, AHR, 79(Oct 1974):1169-70; H. S. Offler, EHR, 89 (Apr 1974):380-2.

Hilliard, Sam Bowers. Hog Meat and Hoecake: Food Supply in the Old South, 1840-1860. Carbondale: S Ill U Press, 1972. Rev. by R. E. Gallman, AHR, 79(Feb 1974):227-8; R. L. Troutman, CWH, 20(Mar 1974):52-3; J. A. Eisterhold, WHQ, 5(Jl 1974):357-8.

Hilton, Rodney. Bond Men Made Free: Medieval Peasant Movements and the English Rising of 1381. London: Temple Smith, 1973. Rev. by R. B. Dobson, History, 59(Je 1974): 258-9.

Himmelfarb, Gertrude. On Liberty and Liberalism: The Case of John Stuart Mill. New York: Knopf, n.d. Rev. by P. L. Berger, Commentary, 58(Oct 1974):80,82.

Himmelmann, Nikolaus. Das Akademische Kunstmuseum der Universität Bonn. Berlin: Gebr. Mann Verlag, 1972. Rev. by D. K. Hill, AJA, 78(Ja 1974):99.

Hinckley, Ted C. The Americanization of Alaska, 1867-1897. Palo Alto, Cal.: Pacific Books, 1972. Rev. by W. H. Wilson, AHR, 79(Oct 1974):1270-1; L. Kaufman, JOW, 13(Oct 1974):128.

Hind, R. J. Henry Labouchere and the Empire, 1880-1905. London: Athlone, 1972. Rev. by P. Smith, EHR, 89(Ja 1974): 227; B. Porter, History, 59(Feb 1974):126-7.

Hine, Robert V. The American West: An Interpretive History. Boston: Little, Brown, 1973. Rev. by W. S. Greener,

A & W, 16(Spr 1974):73-4; J. W. Caughey, CHQ, 53(Spr 1974): 90-91; P. J. Coleman, HRNB, 2(Apr 1974):150; R. W. Blew, HT, 8(Nov 1974):123-4; H. C. Miner, JAH, 61(Je 1974):205-6; J. Penick, Jr., JOW, 13(Apr 1974):113-14; R. J. Roske, PHR, 43(Feb 1974):125-8; B. Procter, PNQ, 65(Jl 1974):148-9.

_____ and Savoie Lottinville, eds. Soldier in the West: Letters of Theodore Talbot During His Services in California, Mexico, and Oregon, 1845-53. Norman: U Ok Press, 1972. Rev. by H. B. Simpson, Texana, 11(Spr 1974):198.

Hingley, Ronald. Joseph Stalin: Man and Legend. New York: Mc-Graw-Hill, 1974. Rev. by W. C. Clemens, Jr., HRNB, 3 (Nov/Dec 1974):32; M. Latey, HTo, 24(Jl 1974):511.

Hinnebusch, William A. The History of the Dominican Order. Volume 2: Intellectual and Cultural Life to 1500. Staten Island, N.Y.: Alba, 1973. Rev. by W. O. Paulsell, CH, 43(Sep 1974):393-4.

Hinrichs, Carl. Preussentum und Pietismus: Der Pietismus in Brandenburg-Preussen als religiös-soziale Reformbewegung. Göttingen: Vandenhoeck and Ruprecht, 1971. Rev. by R. Bireley, AHR, 79(Je 1974):801-2.

Hinsley, F. H. Nationalism and the International System. Dobbs Ferry, N.Y.: Oceana, 1973. Rev. by W. T. R. Fox, AHR, 79(Feb 1974):109-10; A. F. K. Organski, JMH, 46(Dec 1974): 708-9.

Hinton, Harold. An Introduction to Chinese Politics. New York: Praeger, 1973. Rev. by M. Bernal, JAS, 33(Aug 1974):701-3.

Hinz, Evelyn J. see Teunissen, John J.

Hirsch-Reich, Beatrice see Reeves, Marjorie

Hirschfelder, Arlene B., comp. American Indian and Eskimo Authors: A Comprehensive Bibliography. New York: Assn on American Indian Affairs, 1973. Rev. by L. J. White, JOW, 13(Apr 1974):125.

Hirst, David W. see Link, Arthur S.

Hirten, William James, ed. see Erasmus

Hiskett, Mervyn. The Sword of Truth: The Life and Times of Shehu Usuman dan Fodio. New York: Ox U Press, 1973. Rev. by L. Brenner, JIH, 5(Aut 1974):354-5.

History of Vietnam. Hanoi: Nhà Xuât Bán Khoa Hoc Xa Hôi, 1971. Rev. by K. Taylor, JAS, 33(Feb 1974):338-40.

Hitchcock, Henry-Russell, et al. The Rise of an American Architecture. New York: Praeger, 1970. Rev. by T. S. Hines, AHR, 79(Apr 1974):564-5.

Hitchcock, James. The Recovery of the Sacred. New York: Seabury Press, 1974. Rev. by H. Davies, CH, 43(Dec 1974): 558-9.

Hitchings, Sinclair see Whitehill, Walter Muir

Hitchman, James H. Leonard Wood and Cuban Independence 1898-1902. The Hague: Martinus Nijhoff, 1971. Rev. by A. E. Campbell, EHR, 89(Ja 1974):229-30; F. W. Knight, TAm, 31 (Jl 1974):114-16.

Hixson, William B., Jr. Moorfield Storey and the Abolitionist Tradition. New York: Ox U Press, 1972. Rev. by A. E. Strickland, Historian, 36(Feb 1974):338-9.

Ho, Alfred K. Japan's Trade Liberalization in the 1960's. White Plains, N. Y.: International Arts and Sciences Press, 1973. Rev. by R. S. Ozaki, JAS, 33(Aug 1974):715-16.

Hobbins, James M. see Reingold, Nathan

Hobbs, Joseph Patrick. Dear General: Eisenhower's Wartime Letters to Marshall. Baltimore: JHU Press, 1971. Rev. by R. W. Leopold, AHR, 79(Apr 1974):609-10.

Hoben, Allan. Land Tenure Among the Amhara of Ethiopia: The Dynamics of Cognatic Descent. Chicago: U Chi Press, 1973. Rev. by J. Markakis, JMAS, 12(Je 1974):341-5.

Hobsbawm, E. J. Revolutionaries: Contemporary Essays. New York: Pantheon, 1972. Rev. by W. B. Walsh, Historian, 36(Aug 1974):738-9.

Hobson, Fred C., Jr. Serpent in Eden: H. L. Mencken and the South. Chapel Hill: UNC Press, 1974. Rev. by W. Percy, GHQ, 58(Fall 1974):370-2; C. Dolmetsch, JAH, 61(Dec 1974): 823-5.

Hodges, Donald C., ed. Philosophy of the Urban Guerrilla: The Revolutionary Writings of Abraham Guillén. New York: Morrow, 1973. Rev. by R. H. McDonald, HAHR, 54(Feb 1974): 184-6.

Hoenigswald, Henry M. see Cardona, George

Hoerder, Dirk. Society and Government 1760-1780: The Power Structure in Massachusetts Townships. Berlin: Freie Universität Berlin, 1972. Rev. by A. Kulikoff, WMQ-3, 31(Jl 1974):513-14.

Hoffman, Abraham. Unwanted Mexican Americans in the Great Depression: Repatriation Pressures, 1929-1939. Tucson: U Ariz Press, 1974. Rev. by L. R. Murphy, HRNB, 2(May/Je 1974):162; M. Solomon, HRNB, 3(Nov/Dec 1974):41; N. Lederer, JAriH, 15(Sum 1974):188-9; M. M. Smith, JOW, 13(Oct 1974):142; M. Monteón, NMHR, 49(Oct 1974):341-3; M. Meier, PHR, 43(Nov 1974):619-21; J. S. Shockley, SWHQ, 78(Oct 1974):220-1.

Hoffman, Heinrich see Picker, Henry

Hoffman, Paul. Tiger in the Court. Chicago: Playboy Press, n.d. Rev. by S. Ross, Mankind, 4(Je 1974):6.

Hoffman, Robert L. Revolutionary Justice: The Social and Political Theory of P. J. Proudhon. Chicago: U Chi Press, 1972. Rev. by I. Collins, History, 59(Feb 1974):137.

Hoffman, Ronald. A Spirit of Dissension: Economics, Politics, and the Revolution in Maryland. Baltimore: JHU Press, 1974. Rev. by J. H. Flannagan, Jr., HRNB, 2(May/Je 1974):164-5; R. M. Jellison, JSH, 40(Nov 1974):649-51; R. O. Overfield, NCHR, 51(Sum 1974):341-2.

Hoffman, Ross J. S. The Marquis: A Study of Lord Rockingham, 1730-1782. New York: Fordham U Press, 1973. Rev. by R. M. Calhoon, VMHB, 82(Oct 1974):493-4; P. D. G. Thomas, WMQ-3, 31(Jl 1974):498-501.

Hoffmann, Donald. The Architecture of John Wellborn Root. Baltimore: JHU Press, 1973. Rev. by L. K. Eaton, AHR, 79 (Apr 1974):595-6.

Hoffmann, Herbert and A. E. Raubitschek. Early Cretan Armorers. Mainz: Von Zabern, 1972. Rev. by K. DeVries, AJA, 78(Ja 1974):95.

Hofstadter, Richard. People and a Nation. see Ver Steeg, Clarence L.

Hogarth, Paul. Artists on Horseback: The Old West in Illustrated Journalism, 1857-1900. New York: Watson-Guptil, 1972. Rev. by J. S. Ballard, JOW, 13(Apr 1974):108.

Hogg, James, ed. Late Fifteenth-Century Carthusian Rubrics for the Deacon and the Sacristan from the Ms. Valsainte 42/T.I.8. Salzburg: James Hogg, 1971. Rev. by W. O. Paulsell, CH, 43(Mar 1974):102-3.

Hogg, Peter C. The African Slave Trade and Its Suppression: A Classified and Annotated Bibliography of Books, Pamphlets, and Periodical Articles. Rev. by T. R. De Gregori, T & C, 15(Jl 1974):516-17.

Hohenthal, Helen, et al. Streams in a Thirsty Land: A History of the Turlock Region. Turlock, Cal.: Turlock Centennial Foundation, 1972. Rev. by A. Hoffman, A & W, 16(Spr 1974):71-2.

Holbrook, Clyde A. The Ethics of Jonathan Edwards: Morality and Aesthetics. Ann Arbor: U Mich Press, 1973. Rev. by S. E. Mead, AHR, 79(Je 1974):844-5; C. Cherry, CH, 43 (Mar 1974):118-19; R. A. Delattre, NEQ, 47(Mar 1974):155-8.

Holcombe, Lee. Victorian Ladies at Work: Middle-Class Working Women in England and Wales, 1850-1914. Hamden, Conn.: Archon, 1973. Rev. by J. W. Scott, JMH, 46(Dec 1974):713-15.

Holden, William Curry see Haley, J. Evetts

Holland, Norman N. Poems in Persons: An Introduction to the Psychoanalysis of Literature. New York: Norton, 1973. Rev. by H. G. McCurdy, GR, 28(Spr 1974):170-3.

Hollister, Ovando J. The Mines of Colorado. n.p.: 1867 (reprint). Rev. by D. A. Smith, CoMag, 51(Spr 1974):157-9.

Hollon, W. Eugene. Frontier Violence: Another Look. New York: Ox U Press, 1974. Rev. by C. Crowe, HRNB, 2(Aug 1974): 221; J. E. Suberi, JOW, 13(Oct 1974):143.

Holmes, Colin see Pollard, Sidney

Holmes, Geoffrey. The Trial of Doctor Sacheverell. London: Eyre Methuen, 1973. Rev. by J. M. Beattie, AHR, 79(Je 1974): 783-4.

Holsti, Ole R. Crisis, Escalation, War. Montreal: McGill-Queen's U Press, 1972. Rev. by P. W. Schroeder, JMH, 46(Sep 1974):537-40.

Holt, C., B. R. O'G. Anderson, J. Siegel, ed. Culture and Politics in Indonesia. Ithaca: Cor U Press, 1972. Rev. by C. S. Kessler, MAS, 8(Ja 1974):134-9.

Holt, P. M. Studies in the History of the Near East. London: Frank Cass, 1973. Rev. by R. S. O'Fahey, JAfH, 15(Num 2 1974):348-9.

Holton, Milne. Cylinder of Vision: The Fiction and Journalistic Writings of Stephen Crane. Baton Rouge: LSU Press, 1972. Rev. by D. Clough, JAmS, 8(Aug 1974):278-9.

Homan, Gerlof D. Jean-Francois. French Revolutionary, Patriot, and Director (1747-1807). The Hague: Martinus Nijhoff, 1971. Rev. by G. Ellis, EHR, 89(Apr 1974):449-50.

Homer, Rachel Johnston, ed.   The Legacy of Josiah Johnson Hawes:
19th-Century Photographs of Boston.   Barre, Mass.: Barre
Publishers, 1972.   Rev. by E. Lyon, AmArc, 37(Oct 1974):
592-4.

Honan, Park see Irvine, William

Hood, Graham.   Bonnin and Morris of Philadelphia: The First
American Porcelain Factory, 1770-1772.   Chapel Hill, UNC
Press, 1972.   Rev. by M. O'B. Quimby, BHR, 48(Spr 1974):
122-3.

Hook, Brian see Heren, Louis

Hook, Judith.   The Sack of Rome, 1527.   London: Macmillan, 1972.
Rev. by D. S. Chambers, History, 59(Feb 1974):102.

Hoole, W. Stanley.   According to Hoole: The Collected Essays and
Tales of a Scholar-Librarian and Literary Maverick.   Univer-
sity, Ala.: U Ala Press, 1973.   Rev. by O. B. Emerson,
AlaR, 27(Jl 1972):237-40.

Hoopes, Chad L.   What Makes a Man: The Annie E. Kennedy and
John Bidwell Letters, 1866-1868.   Fresno, Cal.: Valley Publishers, 1973.   Rev. by B. B. Jensen, JOW, 13(Apr 1974):137-
8; B. F. Gilbert, WHQ, 5(Oct 1974):461-2.

Hopkins, A. G.   An Economic History of West Africa.   London:
Longmans, 1973.   Rev. by P. E. Lovejoy, AfAf, 73(Apr 1974):
236-7; A. J. H. Latham, History, 59(Je 1974):305-6; V. M.
Smith, HRNB, 2(Ja 1974):74; C. C. Wrigley, JAfH, 15(Num 2
1974):323-5; T. R. De Gregori, T & C, 15(Jl 1974):514-16.

Hopkins, George E.   The Airline Pilots: A Study in Elite Unionization.   Cambridge, Mass.: Har U Press, 1971.   Rev. by J.
Grossman, AHR, 79(Je 1974):841.

Hopkins, James F. , et al. , eds.   The Papers of Henry Clay.   Vol.
IV.   Secretary of State, 1825.   Lexington, Ky.: U Press Ky,
1972.   Rev. by C. M. Wiltse, AHR, 79(Feb 1974):224; C. G.
Sellers, JSH, 40(Feb 1974):136-7.

_____   and Mary W. M. Hargreaves, eds.   The Papers of Henry
Clay.   Vol. V.   Secretary of State, 1826.   Lexington, Ky.:
U Press Ky, 1974.   Rev. by R. J. Cooke, HRNB, 2(Aug 1974):
219-20; D. F. Carmony, RKHS, 72(Oct 1974):418-20.

Horan, James D.   The McKenney-Hall Portrait Gallery of American
Indians.   New York: Crown, 1972.   Rev. by M. L. Heyman,
Jr. , JOW, 13(Apr 1974):113; W. G. Bell, WHQ, 5(Apr 1974):
197-9.

Horn, Rudolf.   Hellenistische Bildwerke auf Samos.   Bonn: Rudolf

169 HORNE

Habelt, 1972. Rev. by J. G. Pedley, AJA, 78(Apr 1974):
203-4.

Horne, Alistair. Small Earthquake in Chile: Allende's South America. New York: Viking, 1973. Rev. by R. H. Dix, HAHR,
54(Feb 1974):153-5.

Horne, Elinor Clark. Javanese-English Dictionary. New Haven,
Conn.: Yale U Press, 1974. Rev. by S. Wojowasito, JAS,
34(Nov 1974):260-1.

Hornung, Clarence P. Treasury of American Design. New York:
Abrams, 1972. Rev. by C. Scoon, NYHSQ, 58(Ja 1974):67-8.

Horrall, Stanley W. The Pictorial History of the Royal Canadian
Mounted Police. Toronto: McGraw-Hill Ryerson, 1973. Rev.
by R. E. Smith, RKHS, 72(Apr 1974):196-8.

Horrell, C. William, Henry Don Piper and John W. Voight. Land
Between the Rivers: The Southern Illinois Country. Carbondale: S Ill U Press, 1973. Rev. by J. W. Neilson, JISHS,
67(Apr 1974):245-6; J. H. Rodabaugh, RKHS, 72(Ja 1974):73-
4.

Horst, Irvin Buckwalter. The Radical Brethren: Anabaptism and
the English Reformation to 1558. Nieuwkoop: De Graaf, 1972.
Rev. by J. M. Stayer, RQ, 27(Spr 1974):65-7.

Horton, Louise. Samuel Bell Maxey: A Biography. Austin: U
Tx Press, 1974. Rev. by A. P. McDonald, CWH, 20(Sep
1974):269-71; R. N. Current, HRNB, 2(May/Je 1974):162;
L. L. Gould, SWHQ, 78(Oct 1974):226-7.

Horton, Robin and Ruth Finnegan, eds. Modes of Thought; Essays
on Thinking in Western and Non-Western Societies. London:
Faber and Faber, 1973. Rev. by T. Ranger, JAfH, 15(Num 1
1974):147-9.

Horward, Donald D. The French Revolution and Napoleon Collec-
tion at Florida State University: A Bibliographical Guide.
Tallahassee: Friends of Fla St U Library, 1973. Rev. by
J. Bowditch, AHR, 79(Apr 1974):521-2; H. C. Rice, Jr.,
AmArc, 37(Ja 1974):79-81.

Horwitz, Henry, ed. The Parliamentary Diary of Narcissus Luttrell 1691-1693. Oxford: Ox U Press, 1972. Rev. by W. A.
Speck, History, 59(Je 1974):278.

Hoshii, Iwao see Adams, T. F. M.

Hosking, Geoffrey A. The Russian Constitutional Experiment: Government and Duma, 1907-1914. New York: Cam U Press,
1973. Rev. by A. T. Anderson, Historian, 36(Aug 1974):

759-61; L. P. Morris, History, 59(Je 1974):298-9.

Hotman, François. Francogallia. Cambridge: Cam U Press, 1972. Rev. by R. J. Knecht, History, 59(Feb 1974):103-4; W. F. Church, RQ, 27(Spr 1974):75-7.

Houghton, Walter E., ed. The Wellesley Index to Victorian Periodicals, 1824-1900. Volume II: Tables of Contents and Identification of Contributors with Bibliographies of Their Articles and Stories and an Index of Initials and Pseudonyms. Toronto: U Tor Press; London: Routledge and Kegan Paul, 1972. Rev. by S. Eisen, CHR, 55(Je 1974):212-14.

Houlihan, Edward T. see Hamilton, Holman. Meet Squire Coleman.

Houston, Jeanne Wakatsuki and James D. Houston. Farewell to Manzanar: A True Story of Japanese American Experience During and After the World War II Internment. Boston: Houghton Mifflin, 1973. Rev. by R. A. Wilson, PHR, 43 (Nov 1974):621-22.

Hoven, R., ed. see Erasmus

Howard, Sir Albert. The Soil and Health: A Study of Organic Agriculture. New York: Schocken, 1972. Rev. by M. S. Legan, JOW, 13(Ja 1974):154-5.

Howard, Harold P. Sacajawea. Norman: U Ok Press, 1971, 1972. Rev. by C. Bolt, JAmS, 8(Apr 1974):117-9.

Howard, Michael. The Continental Commitment. London: Temple Smith, 1972. Rev. by D. Dilks, EHR, 89(Ja 1974):137-40.

_____. Grand Strategy. Vol. IV. August 1942-September 1943. London: H. M. S. O., 1970, 1972. Rev. by W. N. Medlicott, EHR, 89(Ja 1974):140-2; P. M. H. Bell, History, 59 (Feb 1974):146.

Howard, O. O. Nez Perce Joseph: An Account of His Ancestors, His Lands, His Confederates, His Enemies, His Murderers, His War, Pursuit and Capture. New York: Da Capo, 1972. Rev. by H. A. Howard, JOW, 13(Apr 1974):132-3.

Howard, Oliver O. My Live and Experiences Among Our Hostile Indians. New York: Da Capo, 1972. Rev. by R. N. Ellis, JISHS, 67(Je 1974):343-4.

Howarth, David. Sovereign of the Seas: The Story of British Sea Power. London: Collins, n.d. Rev. by D. Woodward, HTo, 24(Aug 1974):583-4.

Howat, G. M. D. Stuart and Cromwellian Foreign Policy. New

York: St. Martin's, 1974. Rev. by P. B. Cares, HRNB, 2
(Jl 1974):209-10.

Howe, C. Employment and Economic Growth in Urban China 1949-
1957. Cambridge: Cam U Press, 1971. Rev. by J. P. Emerson, MAS, 8(Ja 1974):126-34.

Howe, Christopher. Wage Patterns and Wage Policy in Modern
China 1919-1972. Cambridge: Cam U Press, 1973. Rev. by
C. Riskin, JAS, 34(Nov 1974):225-8.

Howe, John R. From the Revolution Through the Age of Jackson:
Innocence and Empire in the Young Republic. Englewood
Cliffs, N.J.: Prentice Hall, 1973. Rev. by F. O. Gatell,
HT, 7(Feb 1974):298-9; R. Buel, Jr., JAH, 61(Je 1974):166-7.

Hranicky, Jack, ed. Popular Archaeology Magazine (monthly). Arlington, Va.: n.p., n.d. Rev. by S. Terpning and J. R.
Cole, AmAnt, 39(Jl 1974):519.

Hsieh, Chiao-Min. Atlas of China. New York: McGraw-Hill, 1973.
Rev. by J. F. Williams, JAS, 33(May 1974):471-2.

Hsu, Immanuel C. Y., ed. Readings in Modern Chinese History.
New York: Ox U Press, 1971. Rev. by H. J. Beattie, MAS,
8(Apr 1974):268-70.

_____. The Rise of Modern China. New York: Ox U Press,
1970. Rev. by H. J. Beattie, MAS, 8(Apr 1974):268-70.

Huber, Hugo. Marriage and the Family in Rural Bukwaya. Fribourg: Fribourg U Press, 1973. Rev. by L. Mair, Africa,
44(Apr 1974):209.10.

Huber, Richard M. The American Idea of Success. New York:
McGraw-Hill, 1971. Rev. by C. A. Barker, JAH, 61(Dec
1974):757-8.

Hudson, A. B. Padju Epat: the Ma'anyan of Indonesian Borneo.
New York: Holt, Rinehart and Winston, 1972. Rev. by J. A.
Barnes, 559-60.

Hudson, Derek. Numby, Man of Two Worlds: The Life and Diaries
of Arthur J. Numby, 1828-1910. Boston: Gambit, 1972.
Rev. by B. Harrison, AHR, 79(Feb 1974):146-8.

Hudson, G. F., ed. Reform and Revolution in Asia. New York:
St. Martin's, 1973. Rev. by R. E. Bedeski, HRNB, 2(Ja
1974):76-7.

Hudson, Gladys W. Paradise Lost: A Concordance. Detroit:
Gale, 1971. Rev. by E. R. Weismuller, RQ, 27(Sum 1974):
255-7.

Hudson, Michael. Super Imperialism: The Economic Strategy of
American Empire. New York: Holt, Rinehart and Winston,
1972. Rev. by P. P. Abrahams, JEH, 34(Sep 1974):789-90.

Hudson, Michael C. see Taylor, Charles L.

Huerta, Gorgonio Gil. see MacNeish, Richard S. The Prehistory
of the Tehuacan Valley, Volume Four.

Huffman, Clifford Chalmers. Coriolanus in Context. Lewisburg,
Pa.: Bucknell U Press, 1972. Rev. by C. M. Shaw, RQ,
27(Spr 1974):103-5.

Hughes, Judith M. To the Maginot Line: The Politics of French
Military Preparation in the 1920's. Cambridge, Mass.: Har
U Press, 1971. Rev. by M. Hurst, AHR, 79(Feb 1974):170-1.

Hughes, Kathleen. Early Christian Ireland: Introduction to the
Sources. Ithaca, N. Y.: Cornell U Press, 1972. Rev. by
C. V. Graves, AHR, 79(Oct 1974):1168-9.

Hughes, Langston and Arna Bontemps, eds. The Poetry of the
Negro, 1746-1970. Garden City, N. Y.: Anchor Press/Dou-
bleday, 1973. Rev. by G. E. Osborne, Crisis, 81(Nov 1974):
317.

Hughes, Paul L. see Larkin, James F.

Hugins, Walter. The Reform Impulse, 1825-1850. Columbia, S. C.:
U SCar Press, 1972. Rev. by P. A. Kalisch, JISHS, 67(Sep
1974):456-7.

Huizinga, Johan. America: A Dutch Historian's Vision, From Afar
and Near. New York: Harper and Row, 1972. Rev. by
R. A. Waller, Historian, 36(Aug 1974):769-70.

Hull, P. L. The Caption of the Seisin of the Duchy of Cornwall.
n. p.: Devon and Cornwall Record Society ... 1971. Rev. by
B. Harvey, EHR, 89(Ja 1974):158-9.

Humboldt, Alexander von. Voyage aux Régions Equinoxiales du Nouveau Continent. Vols. XV-XVI.... New York: ... Da Capo,
1972. Rev. by W. Ruwet, HAHR, 54(Aug 1974):511-12.

Hunczak, Taras, ed. Russian Imperialism From Ivan the Great to
the Revolution. New Brunswick, N.J.: Rutgers U Press,
1974. Rev. by D. R. Papazian, HRNB, 3(Oct 1974):12.

Huning, Franz and Lina Fergusson Browne. Trader on the Santa Fe
Trail: Memoirs of Franz Huning. Albuquerque: U Albuquerque, 1973. Rev. by L. E. Oliva, WHQ, 5(Jl 1974):341-3.

Hunt, David. Parents and Children in History: The Psychology of

Family Life in Early Modern France. New York: Basic
Books, 1970. Rev. by C. Pletsch, JMH, 46(Mar 1974):124-6.

Hunt, Eva. see MacNeish, Richard S. The Prehistory of the
Tehuacan Valley, Volume Four.

Hunt, Michael H. Frontier Defense and the Open Door: Manchuria
in Chinese-American Relations, 1895-1911. New Haven, Conn.:
Yale U Press, 1973. Rev. by J. Israel, HRNB, 2(Ja 1974):
60-1; R. F. McClellan, JAH, 61(Sep 1974):510-11; J. Schreck-
er, JAS, 34(Nov 1974):222-4; M. B. Young, PHR, 43(Nov
1974):624-5.

Hunter, John Dunn. Memoirs of a Captivity Among the Indians of
North America. New York: Schocken, 1974. Rev. by D. C.
Cutter, HRNB, 2(Mar 1974):134.

Huntington, R. T. Hall's Breechloaders: John H. Hall's Invention
and Development of a Breechloading Rifle with Precision-Made
Interchangeable Parts, and Its Introduction into the United
States Service. York, Pa.: Geo. Shumway, 1972. Rev. by
E. A. Battison, AHR, 79(Oct 1974):1260.

Huntress, Keith, ed. Narratives of Shipwrecks and Disasters,
1586-1860. Ames: Ia St U Press, 1974. Rev. by R. G.
O'Connor, HRNB, 2(Sep 1974):247-8.

Hurd, D. J. see Irwin, H. T.

Hurst, James Willard. A Legal History of Money in the United
States, 1774-1970. Lincoln: U Neb Press, 1974. Rev. by
W. H. Becker, HRNB, 2(Apr 1974):148.

Hurstfield, Joel. Freedom, Corruption and Government in Eliza-
bethan England. Cambridge, Mass.: Har U Press, 1973.
Rev. by G. J. Cavanaugh, HRNB, 2(Ja 1974):78-9; L. L.
Peck, JMH, 46(Sep 1974):543-4.

_____, ed. The Tudors. New York: St. Martin's, 1973. Rev.
by T. Callahan, Jr., HRNB, 2(Feb 1974):108.

Hurwitz, Edith F. Politics and the Public Conscience: Slave Emancipation and the Abolition Movement in Britain. London:
George Allen and Unwin, 1973. Rev. by A. R. Meredith, CH,
43(Sep 1974):412.

Hurwicz, Leonid, ed. see Schmookler, Jacob

Hurwitz, Samuel J. and Edith F. Jamaica: A Historical Portrait.
New York: Praeger, 1971. Rev. by G. Knox, AHR, 79(Feb
1974):252-3.

Hurzhii, I. Friedrich Engels on Ukraine. Kiev: Vydavnytstvo

politychnoi literatury Ukrainy, 1970. Rev. by J.-P. Himka, EEQ, 8(Fall 1974):375-9.

Huston, James A. Out of the Blue: U. S. Army Airborne Operations in World War II. Lafayette, Ind., Purdue U Studies, 1972. Rev. by W. P. Newton, AHR, 79(Je 1974):903-4.

Hutchins, Francis G. India's Revolution: Ghandi and the Quit India Movement. Cambridge, Mass.: Har U Press, 1973. Rev. by R. E. Frykenberg, HRNB, 2(Ja 1974):77-8.

Hutchinson, William T. and William M. E. Rachal, eds. The Papers of James Madison. Volume 7, 3 May 1783-20 February 1784. Chicago: U Chi Press, 1971. Rev. by G. G. Van Deusen, AHR, 79(Je 1974):849-50.

Hutson, J. H. Pennsylvania Politics 1746-1770. Princeton, N.J.: Prin U Press, 1972. Rev. by H. G. Pitt, EHR, 89(Ja 1974): 197-8.

Hutson, James H. see Kurtz, Stephen G.

Hyam, Ronald. The Failure of South African Expansion, 1908-1948. New York: Africana, 1972. Rev. by A. Sillery, EHR, 89 (Apr 1974):464; S. Marks, History, 59(Je 1974):313-14; C. W. De Kiewiet, JMAS, 12(Sep 1974):512-13.

Hyde, Dayton O. The Last Free Man: The True Story Behind the Massacre of Shoshone Mike and His Band of Indians in 1911. New York: Dial, 1973. Rev. by E. B. McCluney, HRNB, 2 (Feb 1974):96; D. D. Fowler, WHQ, 5(Jl 1974):345-6.

Hyde, Francis E. Far Eastern Trade, 1860-1914. London: Adam and Charles Black, 1973. Rev. by G. Jackson, History, 59 (Je 1974):322.

_____. Liverpool and the Mersey: An Economic History of a Port 1700-1970. Newton Abbot: David and Charles, 1971. Rev. by R. Craig, History, 59(Je 1974):333-4.

Hyde, H. Montgomery. Baldwin: The Unexpected Prime Minister. n.p.: Hart-Davis, n.d. Rev. by A. O'Day, HTo, 24(Feb 1974):137.

Hyde, J. K. Society and Politics in Medieval Italy: The Evolution of the Civil Life, 1000-1350. New York: St. Martin's, 1973. Rev. by C. Zuckerman, HRNB, 2(Mar 1974):117.

Hyden, G., R. Jackson and J. Okumu, eds. Development Administration: the Kenyan Experience. Nairobi: Ox U Press, 1970. Rev. by C. Ehrlick, AfAf, 73(Jl 1974):378-9.

Hyman, Harold M. A More Perfect Union: The Impact of the Civil

War and Reconstruction on the Constitution. New York: Knopf, 1973. Rev. by D. E. Fehrenbacher, AHR, 79(Je 1974):872-4; D. H. Donald, JAH, 60(Mar 1974):1129-31; A. H. Kelly, JSH, 40(Aug 1974):487-9.

Hymans, J. L. Leopold Sedar Sengbor. An Intellectual Biography. Edinburgh: Edinburgh U Press, 1972. Rev. by A. H. M. Kirk-Greene, EHR, 89(Apr 1974):472-4.

Hynding, Alan. The Public Life of Eugene Semple: Promoter and Politician of the Pacific Northwest. Seattle: U Wash Press, 1973. Rev. by M. Clark, Jr., OrHQ, 75(Sep 1974):292-3; K. A. Murray, PNQ, 65(Oct 1974):187.

Inglis, Alex I. see Munro, John A.

Ingram, James C. Economic Change in Thailand, 1850-1970. Stanford, Calif.: Stan U Press, 1971. Rev. by R. C. Y. Ng, MAS, 8(Apr 1974):276-7.

Innis, Ben. Bloody Knife! Custer's Favorite Scout. Fort Collins, Colo.: Old Army Press, 1973. Rev. by M. E. Gerber, NCH, 41(Sum 1974):36-7.

Ireland, Robert M. The County Courts in Antebellum Kentucky. Lexington, Ky.: U Press Ky, 1972. Rev. by J. S. Goff, AHR, 79(Je 1974):865-6; R. Hartje, Historian, 36(Feb 1974): 345-6.

Iriye, Akira. The Cold War in Asia: A Historical Introduction. Englewood Cliffs, N.J.: Prentice-Hall, 1974. Rev. by G. R. Hess, HRNB, 2(May/Je 1974):175-6.

_____. Pacific Estrangement: Japanese and American Expansion 1897-1911. Oxford: Ox U Press, 1973. Rev. by E. W. Edwards, History, 59(Je 1974):320-1.

Irvine, Keith, ed. Encyclopedia of Indians of the Americas. Volume I: Conspectus and Chronology. Clair Shores, Mich.: Scholarly Press, 1974. Rev. in CurH, 67(Dec 1974):271.

Irvine, William and Park Honan. The Book, the Ring, and the Poet: A Biography of Robert Browning. New York: McGraw-Hill, 1974. Rev. by L. R. Bisceglia, HRNB, 3(Nov/Dec 1974):28.

Irwin, H. T., D. J. Hurd, and R. M. Lajeunesse. Description and Measurement in Anthropology. Pullman: Wash St U, 1971. Rev. by D. Green, AmAnt, 39(Jl 1974):517.

Isaacman, Allen F. Mozambique: The Africanization of a European Institution, the Zambezi prazos, 1750-1902. Madison: U Wis Press, 1972. Rev. by D. Birmingham, AfAf, 73(Jl 1974):

372-4; W. C. Opello, Jr., JMAS, 12(Sep 1974):487-91.

Isherwood, Robert M. Music in the Service of the King: France in the Seventeenth Century. Ithaca, N.Y.: Cornell U Press, 1973. Rev. by G. Ridout, CHR, 55(Je 1974):231-2.

Ishwaran, K., ed. Change and Continuity in India's Villages. New York: Columbia U Press, 1970. Rev. by M. Naidis, AHR, 79(Oct 1974):1234-5.

Isichei, Elizabeth. The Ibo People and the Europeans: The Genesis of a Relationship--to 1906. New York: St. Martin's, 1973. Rev. by B. Farwell, HRNB, 2(Mar 1974):124; A. J. H. Latham, JAfH, 15(Num 3 1974):510-11.

Isings, C. Roman Glass in Limburg. Groningen: Wolters-Noordhoff, 1971. Rev. by S. H. Auth, AJA, 78(Ja 1974):101-2.

Islam, A. K. M. Aminul. A Bangladesh Village: Conflict and Cohesion. Cambridge, Mass.: Schenkman, 1974. Rev. by P. J. Bertocci, JAS, 34(Nov 1974):245-7.

Israel, Manasseh Ben. Indians or Jews? Part II: The Hope of Israel. Gilroy, Cal.: Roy V. Boswell, 1973. Rev. by L. Huddleston, JAH, 61(Sep 1974):451; R. E. Greenleaf, NMHR, 49(Jl 1974):264.

Ivers, Larry E. British Drums on the Southern Frontier: The Military Colonization of Georgia, 1733-1749. Chapel Hill: UNC Press, 1974. Rev. by K. Coleman, GHQ, 58(Fall 1974): 362-4; L. R. Gerlach, HRNB, 2(May/Je 1974):168; J. H. O'Donnell, III, JAH, 61(Dec 1974):764-5; R. R. Rea, JSH, 40 (Nov 1974):645-6; S. King, 51(Sum 1974):340-1; R. M. Weir, SCHM, 75(Jl 1974):189; J. M. Gifford, THQ, 33(Sum 1974): 232-4.

Iyer, Raghavan N. The Moral and Political Thought of Mahatma Gandhi. New York: Ox U Press, 1973. Rev. by W. Spencer, HRNB, 2(Feb 1974):104.

Jack, R. Ian. Medieval Wales. London: ... Hodder and Stoughton, 1972. Rev. by D. Huws, Archives, 11(Spr 1974):181-2; G. Williams, EHR, 89(Jl 1974):652.

Jäckel, Eberhard. Hitler's Weltanshauung: A Blueprint for Power. Middletown, Conn.: Wes U Press, 1972. Rev. by G. W. F. Hallgarten, AHR, 79(Je 1974):806-7.

Jackson, Carlton. Zane Grey. New York: Twayne, 1973. Rev. by J. O. Steffen, RKHS, 72(Jl 1974):282-3.

Jackson, Donald. Custer's Gold. Lincoln: U Neb Press, 1972. Rev. by M. E. Gerber, NDH, 41(Sum 1974):36-7.

Jackson, Donald see Spence, Mary Lee

Jackson, Earl. Tumacacori's Yesterdays. Globe, Ariz.: Southwest Parks and Monuments Assn., 1973. Rev. by G. Eckert,
JAriH, 15(Spr 1974):90-1.

Jackson, Gordon. Hull in the Eighteenth Century: A Study in Economic and Social History. London: Ox U Press, 1972. Rev.
by A. Sutcliffe, EHR, 89(Apr 1974):443-4.

Jackson, John Brinckerhoff. American Space: The Centennial Years,
1865-1876. New York: Norton, 1972. Rev. by H. L. and
D. Horowitz, JIH, 5(Aut 1974):336-40.

Jackson, R. see Hyden, G.

Jackson, Robert. At War with the Bolsheviks: The Allied Intervention into Russia 1917-20. London: Tom Stacey, 1972.
Rev. by C. J. Bartlett, History, 59(Feb 1974):150.

Jacobs, Howard. Charlie the Mole and Other Droll Souls. Gretna,
La.: Pelican Pub. Co., 1973. Rev. by F. E. Hebert, LaH,
15(Win 1974):89-90.

Jacobs, Travis Beal see Berle, Beatrice Bishop

Jacobs, Wilbur R. Dispossessing the American Indian: Indians and
Whites on the Colonial Frontier. New York: Scribner's, 1972.
Rev. by R. R. Loder, CoMag, 51(Win 1974):63-5.

Jacobsen, J. N. see Downey, Fairfax

Jacobson, Jon. Locarno Diplomacy: Germany and the West, 1925-
1929. Princeton, N.J.: Prin U Press, 1972. Rev. by
G. E. Silberstein, AHR, 79(Feb 1974):138-9; A. J. Nicholls,
History, 59(Feb 1974):152.

Jacobstein, Helen L. The Segregation Factor in the Florida Democratic Gubernatorial Primary of 1956. Gainesville: U Fla
Press, 1972. Rev. by J. A. Tomberlin, FHQ, 53(Jl 1974):
79-80.

Jahan, Rounaq. Pakistan: Failure in National Integration. New
York: Columbia U Press, 1972. Rev. by R. L. Park, AHR,
79(Oct 1974):1236-7; L. D. Hayes, JAS, 33(Aug 1974):729-30.

Jaher, Frederic Cople, ed. The Rich, the Well-Born, and the
Powerful: Elites and Upper Classes in History. Urbana:
U Ill Press, 1974. Rev. by D. D. Braun, HRNB, 2(May/Je
1974):170-1; E. Pessen, NYH, 55(Jl 1974):345-7.

Jain, J. P. India and Disarmament: Vol. I, Nehru Era, An Analytical Study. Columbia, Mo.: South Asia Books, 1974.

Rev. by B. K. Gupta, HRNB, 3(Nov/Dec 1974):34-5.

Jairazbhoy, Rafique Ali. An Outline of Islamic Architecture. New
   York: Asia Publishing House, 1972. Rev. by C. W. Condit,
   T & C, 15(Oct 1974):636-7.

James, Bessie Rowland. Anne Royall's U.S.A. New Brunswick,
   N.J.: Rutgers U Press, 1972. Rev. by F. M. Rivers, MHM,
   69(Spr 1974):105-6; E. Cometti, WVH, 35(Ja 1974):165-7.

James, Edward T., et al., eds. Notable American Women. 3
   vols. Cambridge, Mass.: Belknap Press, Har U Press, 1971.
   Rev. by R. and V. Ginger, CHR, 55(Mar 1974):106-9.

James, Francis Godwin. Ireland in the Empire, 1688-1770: A His-
   tory of Ireland from the Williamite Wars to the Eve of the
   American Revolution. Cambridge, Mass.: Har U Press, 1973.
   Rev. by H. L. Calkin, AHR, 79(786-7).

James, Leonard F. Western Man and the Modern World. 5 vols.
   New York: Pergamon, 1973. Rev. by J. A. Davis, HT, 8
   (Nov 1974):111-12.

James, Mervyn. Family, Lineage and Civil Society ... in the Durham Region, 1500-1640. Oxford, Clarendon Press, n.d. Rev.
   by A. L. Rowse, HTo, 24(Oct 1974):730-1.

Janes, John F. The Adventures of Stickeen in Lower California.
   Ed. by Anna Marie Hager. Los Angeles: Dawson's Book
   Shop, 1972. Rev. by H. P. Hinton, SCQ, 56(Fall 1974):318-
   19.

Jansen, Henrik M. A Critical Examination of the Written and
   Archaeological Sources' Evidence Concerning the Norse Settlements in Greenland. Copenhagen: C. A. Reitzels Forlag,
   1972. Rev. by A. R. Lewis, AHR, 79(Je 1974):775-6.

Jantzen, Ulf, ed. Tiryns: Forschungen und Berichte, Band IV.
   Mainz: Philipp von Zabern, 1973. Rev. by E. French, Antiquity, 48(Sep 1974):251-3.

Jaques, Florence Page. Francis Lee Jaques: Artist of the Wilderness World. Garden City, N.Y.: Doubleday, 1973. Rev.
   by N. Searle, MinnH, 44(Spr 1974):33-4.

Jarausch, Konrad K. The Enigmatic Chancellor: Bethmann and
   the Hubris of Imperial Germany. New Haven, Conn.: Yale
   U Press, 1973. Rev. by L. E. Hill, CHR, 55(Sep 1974):
   354-6.

Jarchow, Merrill E. Private Liberal Arts Colleges in Minnesota:
   Their History and Contributions. St. Paul: Minn Historical
   Society, 1973. Rev. by G. W. Chessman, JAH, 61(Dec 1974):

812-13; T. R. Crane, MinnH, 44(Spr 1974):32.

Jardim, Anne. The First Henry Ford: A Study in Personality and Business Leadership. Cambridge, Mass.: M I T Press, 1970. Rev. by R. J. Brugger, BHR, 48(Win 1974):565-7.

Jarrett, Derek. The Begetters of Revolution: England's Involvement with France, 1759-1789. Totowa, N.J.: Rowman and Little-field, 1973. Rev. by L. G. Mitchell, EHR, 89(Ja 1974):197; G. Rudé, JMH, 46(Sep 1974):534-5.

Jay, Martin. The Dialectical Imagination: A History of the Frank-furt School and the Institute of Social Research, 1923-1950. Boston: Little, Brown, 1973. Rev. by M. Ermarth, JMH, 46(Sep 1974):559-62.

Jayawardena, Visakha Kumari. The Rise of the Labor Movement in Ceylon. Durham: Duke U Press, 1972. Rev. by C. S. Blackton, AHR, 79(Je 1974):829-30; T. Fernando, JAAS, 9(Ja & Apr 1974):104-5.

Jeanneney, Jules. Journal politique, septembre 1939-juillet 1942. Paris: Librairie Armand Colin, 1972. Rev. by E. A. Walk-er, AHR, 79(Oct 1974):1194-5.

Jefferson, James, Robert W. Delaney, and Gregory C. Thompson. The Southern Utes: a Tribal History. Ed. by Floyd A. O'Neil. Ignacio, Colo.: Southern Ute Tribe, 1972. Rev. by I. Sutton, PHR, 43(Feb 1974):121-2.

Jehasse, Jean and Laurence. La Nécropole Préromaine d'Aléria (1960-1968). Paris: Centre National de la Recherche Scien-tifique, 1973. Rev. by A. H. Ashmead, AJA, 78(Jl 1974): 309-10.

Jelavich, Barbara. The Ottoman Empire, the Great Powers, and the Straits Question, 1870-1887. Bloomington: Ind U Press, 1973. Rev. by C. E. Dawn, AHR, 79(Apr 1974):556-7.

_____. St. Petersburg and Moscow: Tsarist and Soviet Foreign Policy, 1814-1974. Bloomington: Ind U Press, 1974. Rev. by J. W. Long, HRNB, 3(Oct 1974):10-11.

Jelin, Elizabeth see Balán, Jorge

Jemnitz, J. The Danger of War and the Second International (1911). Budapest: Akadémiai Kiadó, 1972. Rev. by M. Richards, JMH, 46(Mar 1974):150-1.

Jen, Yu-Wen. The Taiping Revolutionary Movement. New Haven, Conn.: Yale U Press, 1973. Rev. by G. L. Beahan, His-torian, 36(Aug 1974):749-50; C. T. Hu, HRNB, 2(Ja 1974):77.

Jenkins, George D. see Post, Kenneth W. J.

Jenkins, J. Geraint, ed. The Wool Textile Industry in Great Britain. London: Routledge and Kegan Paul, 1972. Rev. by N. B. Harte, History, 59(Je 1974):332-3.

Jenkins, John H., ed. Papers of the Texas Revolution. Austin, Tx.: Presidial Press, 1973. Rev. by H. B. Simpson, Texana, 11(Spr 1974):197-8.

Jenkins, Trutenau, Johanson and Schlettwein, eds. Archivbeiträge, Volume 9: Mitteilungen der Basler Afrika Bibliographien. n. p.: n. d. Rev. by P. Hassing, CH, 43(Sep 1974):414-15.

Jennelle, Ernest M. see Dickey, John W.

Jennings, Gary. The Treasure of the Superstition Mountains. New York: Norton, 1973. Rev. by B. H. Granger, JAriH, 15 (Win 1974):399-400.

Jensen, Albert C. The Cod. New York: Crowell, 1972. Rev. by R. E. Eckles, AHR, 79(Apr 1974):484.

Jensen, De Lamar. Confrontation at Worms: Martin Luther and the Diet of Worms. Provo, Utah: BYU Press, 1973. Rev. by M. E. Francois, HRNB, 2(Apr 1974):141-2.

Jensen, John R. Journal and Letter Book of Nicholas Buckeridge, 1651-1654. Minneapolis: U Minn Press, 1973. Rev. by J. H. Gleason, HRNB, 2(Ja 1974):81.

Jensen, Richard J. see Dollar, Charles M.

Jensen, Vernon H. Strife on the Waterfront: The Port of New York Since 1945. Ithaca, N. Y.: Cornell U Press, 1974. Rev. by I. Bernstein, JAH, 61(Apr 1974):535-6.

Jenyns, Soame. Later Chinese Porcelain: the Ch'ing Dynasty (1644-1912). London: Faber & Faber, 1972. Rev. by M. Medley, MAS, 8(Ja 1974):143.

Jequier, François. Une Enterprise Horlogère du Val-de-Travers: Fleurier Watch Co. SA. Neuchâtel: Editions de la Baconnière, 1972. Rev. by J. M. Laux, BHR, 48(Spr 1974):108-9.

Jeter, Lorraine Bruce. Matagorda, Early History. Baltimore: Gateway, 1974. Rev. by H. B. Simpson, Texana, 11(Spr 1974):197.

Jewell, Helen M. English Local Administration in the Middle Ages. New York: Barnes and Noble, 1973. Rev. by M. Hastings, AHR, 79(Feb 1974):125; J. C. Russell, Historian, 36(May 1974):534-5.

Jewett, Robert. The Captain America Complex: The Dilemma of
    Zealous Nationalism. Philadelphia: Westminster Press, 1973.
    Rev. by R. T. Handy, CH, 43(Sep 1974):428.

Jha, Manoranjan. Civil Disobedience and After: The American Re-
    action to Political Development in India During 1930-1935.
    Columbia, Mo.: South Asia Books, 1973. Rev. by L. M.
    Simms, Jr., HRNB, 2(May/Je 1974):176-7.

Jodelle, Estienne. Le Recueil des inscriptions, 1558. Toronto:
    U Tor Press, 1972. Rev. by E. F. Rice, Jr., RQ, 27(Fall
    1974):344-6.

Joe, Wanne J. Traditional Korea: A Cultural History. Seoul:
    Chung'ang U Press, 1972. Rev. by J. C. Jamieson, JAS, 33
    (May 1974):493-5.

Joerger, Pauline King. To the Sandwich Islands on H M S Blonde.
    Honolulu: U Press Hawaii, 1971. Rev. by G. Williams, EHR,
    89(Ja 1974):204.

Johannsen, Robert W. Stephen A. Douglas. New York: Ox U
    Press, 1973. Rev. by J. A. Rawley, CoMag, 51(Sum 1974):
    240-1; J. G. Gambone, Historian, 36(Aug 1974):776-7; K. Jef-
    frey, JISHS, 67(Sep 1974):459-60; H. L. Trefousse, JAH, 60
    (Mar 1974):1123-4; J. E. Simpson, MiA, 56(Ja 1974):66-7;
    J. H. Schroeder, NYHSQ, 58(Apr 1974):158-60; P. S. Klein,
    PH, 41(Apr 1974):235-7; R. L. Hume, PNQ, 65(Apr 1974):
    85-6; H. Cohen, WHQ, 5(Ja 1974):75-6.

Johansen, Charlotte Friis see Christensen, Aristéa Papanicolaou

Johansen, Flemming. Reliefs en Bronze d'Etrurie. Copenhagen:
    Ny Carlsberg Glyptothek, 1971. Rev. by R. T. Scott, AJA,
    78(Apr 1974):205-6.

The John Carter Brown Library, Brown University: Annual Reports,
    1901-1966. Providence, R.I.: The John Carter Brown Li-
    brary, Brown U ..., 1972. Rev. by J. E. Pomfret, JAH,
    60(Mar 1974):1091-2; J. Gregory, NYHSQ, 58(Apr 1974):164-5.

John Norden's Manuscript Maps of Cornwall and Its Nine Hundreds.
    Exeter: U Exeter, n.d. Rev. by A. L. Rowse, HTo, 24
    (Aug 1974):579.

Johnson, A. Ross. The Transformation of Communist Ideology:
    The Yugoslav Case, 1945-1953. Cambridge, Mass.: M I T
    Press, 1972. Rev. by W. S. Vucinich, JMH, 46(Mar 1974):
    163-4.

Johnson, Bobby H. see Mohler, Stanley R.

Johnson, Chalmers, ed. Ideology and Politics in Contemporary China.

Seattle: U Wash Press, 1973. Rev. by M. Bernal, JAS, 33 (Aug 1973):701-3.

Johnson, Charles W. Indice de cuadros estadísticos socio-políticos sobre América Latina, 1946-1969. Vol. I and II. México: Instituto de Investigaciones Sociales, 1972. Rev. by R. H. Dolkart, HAHR, 54(Feb 1974):136-7.

Johnson, Dale L., ed. The Chilean Road to Socialism. Garden City, N.Y.: Anchor Press/Doubleday, 1973. Rev. by R. H. Dix, HAHR, 54(Feb 1974):153-5.

Johnson, David. Music and Society in Scotland in the Eighteenth Century. Oxford: Ox U Press, 1972. Rev. by N. T. Phillipson, History, 59(Feb 1974):112-13.

Johnson, Dorothy M. The Bloody Bozeman: The Perilous Trail to Montana's Gold. New York: McGraw-Hill, 1971. Rev. by E. Wallace, JAH, 61(Je 1974):212-13.

Johnson, E. A. J. The Foundations of American Economic Freedom: Government and Enterprise in the Age of Washington. Minneapolis: U Minn Press, 1973. Rev. by E. J. Ferguson, JAH, 61(Je 1974):170-1; H. J. Henderson, WMQ-3, 31(Apr 1974):330-2.

Johnson, Elden. The Arvilla Complex. St. Paul: Minn. Historical Society, 1973. Rev. by T. F. Kehoe, MinnH, 44(Spr 1974):34.

Johnson, Frederick see MacNeish, Richard S. The Prehistory of the Tehuacan Valley, Volume Four.

Johnson, G. Wesley, Jr. The Emergence of Black Politics in Senegal: The Struggle for Power in the Four Communes, 1900-1920. Stanford, Cal.: Stan U Press, 1971. Rev. by D. C. O'Brien, JAAS, 9(Ja & Apr 1974):121-2.

Johnson, Glenn L. and C. Leroy Quance, eds. The Overproduction Trap in U.S. Agriculture: A Study of Resource Allocation from World War I to the Late 1960's. Baltimore: JHU Press, 1972. Rev. by J. A. Shaw, JEH, 34(Je 1974):508-9.

Johnson, Gordon. Provincial Politics and Indian Nationalism: Bombay and the Indian National Congress, 1880-1915. New York: Cam U Press, 1974. Rev. by T. A. Timbery, HRNB, 2(May /Je 1974):176.

Johnson, Overton and William H. Winter. Route Across the Rocky Mountains. New York: Da Capo, 1972. Rev. by R. E. Smith, JOW, 13(Apr 1974):123.

Johnson, Patricia Givens. James Patton and the Appalachian Colonists. Verona, Va.: McClure, 1973. Rev. by G. G.

Shackelford, VMHB, 82(Ja 1974):193-4.

Johnson, Paul. Elizabeth: A Study in Power and Intellect. London: Weidenfeld and Nicolson, n.d. Rev. by A. Haynes, HTo, 24 (Jl 1974):514-15.

_____. The Offshore Islanders. London: Weidenfeld and Nicolson, 1972. Rev. by A. A. M. Duncan, History, 59(Je 1974): 330-1.

Johnson, Paul C., ed. The Early Sunset Magazine, 1898-1929. San Francisco: Cal Historical Society, 1973. Rev. by K. M. Johnson, JOW, 13(Jl 1974):130.

Johnson, Walter, ed. The Papers of Adlai E. Stevenson, Volume II: Washington to Springfield, 1941-1948. Boston: Little, Brown, 1973. Rev. by R. H. Bremner, JISHS, 67(Sep 1974): 447-8.

_____ and Carol Evans, eds. The Papers of Adlai E. Stevenson. Volume III. Governor of Illinois, 1849-1953. Boston: Little, Brown, 1973. Rev. by H. G. Nicholas, AHR, 79(Oct 1974): 1290-1.

Johnston, W. Ross. Sovereignty and Protection: A Study of British Jurisdictional Imperialism in the Late Nineteenth Century. Durham, N.C.: Duke U Press, 1973. Rev. by G. E. Silberstein, HRNB, 2(Ja 1974):83-4.

Johnston, William M. The Austrian Mind: An Intellectual and Social History, 1848-1938. Berkeley: U Cal Press, 1972. Rev. by H. P. Liebel, CHR, 55(Sep 1974):356-7; J. Joll, ESR, 4(Jl 1974):287-9; B. R. Holmes, EEQ, 8(Fall 1974):382.

Joll, James. Europe Since 1870. London: Weidenfeld and Nicolson, n.d. Rev. by W. J. Fishman, HTo, 24(Ja 1974):65.

Jones, Andrew. The Politics of Reform 1884. Cambridge: Cam U Press, 1972. Rev. by M. R. D. Foot, EHR, 89(Ja 1974): 227-8; A. B. Cooke, History, 59(Feb 1974):127-8.

Jones, Archer see Connelly, Thomas Lawrence

Jones, Charles Edwin. A Guide to the Study of the Holiness Movement. Metuchen, N.J.: Scarecrow, 1974. Rev. by D. W. Dayton, CH, 43(Dec 1974):552-3.

Jones, Emrys. Scenic Form in Shakespeare. Oxford: Clarendon Press, 1971. Rev. by B. Beckerman, RQ, 27(Spr 1974):96-8.

Jones, Gwyn. A History of the Vikings. London: Ox U Press, 1973. Rev. by R. E. Lindgren, HT, 7(Aug 1974):643.

Jones, Howard Mumford. Revolution and Romanticism. Cambridge:
    Harvard U Press, 1974. Rev. by N. Pettit, NEQ, 47(Sep
    1974):461-4.

Jones, J. Knox, Jr. see Dort, Wakefield, Jr.

Jones, J. R. The Revolution of 1688 in England. New York:
    Norton, 1974. Rev. by P.-A. Lee, HRNB, 2(Jl 1974):211.

Jones, James W. The Shattered Synthesis: New England Puritanism
    Before the Great Awakening. New Haven, Conn.: Yale U
    Press, 1973. Rev. by C. Wright, CH, 43(Mar 1974):117-18;
    R. Middlekauff, JAH, 61(Sep 1974):462-3; C. W. Akers,
    NYHSQ, 58(Oct 1974):318-21; J. W. Raimo, WMH, 57(Sum
    1974):315-16; J. M. Bumsted, WMQ-3, 31(Jl 1974):524-6.

Jones, Lewis Pinckney. Stormy Petrel: N. G. Gonzales and His
    State. Columbia, S.C.: USCar Press, 1973. Rev. by T.
    Graham, FHQ, 52(Jl 1974):96-7; W. H. Johnson Thomas,
    SCHM, 75(Apr 1974):126-7.

Jones, Lucille. History of Mineola. Quanah, Tx.: Nortex Offset,
    1973. Rev. by R. W. Glover, ETHJ, 12(Spr 1974):59-60.

Jones, P. J. The Malatesta of Rimini and the Papal State: A Po-
    litical History. New York: Cam U Press, 1974. Rev. by
    J. C. Moore, HRNB, 2(Jl 1974):209.

Jones, Robert B. Thai Titles and Ranks: Including a Translation
    of Traditions of Royal Lineage in Siam by King Chulalongkorn.
    Ithaca: Cor U Press, 1971. Rev. by J. H. Kemp, MAS, 8
    (Apr 1974):275-6.

Jones, Robert E. The Emancipation of the Russian Nobility, 1762-
    1785. Princeton, N.J.: Prin U Press, 1973. Rev. by
    J. T. Alexander, AHR, 79(Apr 1974):534.

Jones, Robert H. Disrupted Decades: The Civil War and Recon-
    struction Years. New York: Scribner's, 1973. Rev. by
    C. P. Roland, CWH, 20(Je 1974):157-9; P. Hubbard, Historian,
    36(Aug 1974):775-6; K. I. Polakoff, HT, 7(Feb 1974):301-2;
    D. E. Meerse, PH, 41(Oct 1974):473-5.

Jones, Robert Huhn. The Roads to Russia: United States Lend-
    Lease to the Soviet Union. Norman: U Ok Press, 1969.
    Rev. by M. O. Gustafson, AHR, 79(Je 1974):757-8.

Jones, Roger. The Rescue of Emin Pasha. London: Allison and
    Bushy, 1972. Rev. by C. Oliver, JAfH, 15(Num 2 1974):350.

Jones, Vincent L., Arlene H. Eakle, and Mildred H. Christensen.
    Genealogical Research--A Jurisdictional Approach. Salt Lake
    City: Publishers Press, 1972. Rev. by C. R. Ericson,

ETHJ, 12(Spr 1974):78-9.

Jones, Wilbur Devereux. The American Problem in British Diplomacy, 1841-1861. Athens, Ga.: U Ga Press, 1974. Rev. by J. B. Gidney, HRNB, 2(Jl 1974):195-6.

_____ and Arvel B. Erickson. The Peelites, 1846-1857. Columbus, Ohio: Ohio St U Press, 1972. Rev. by F. A. Dreyer, CHR, 55(Mar 1974):101-2.

Jones-Davies, Marie-Thérèse. Ben Jonson. Paris: Editions Seghers, 1973. Rev. by J. Carr, RQ, 27(Fall 1974):366-70.

Jongkees-Vos, M. F. Corpus Vasorum Antiquorum, The Netherlands III, Leyden I. Leiden: E. J. Brill, 1972. Rev. by M. M. Eisman, AJA, 78(Apr 1974):201-2.

Joralemon, Ira. Copper. Berkeley: Howell-North, 1973. Rev. by A. Probert, JOW, 13(Jl 1974):129; O. E. Young, Jr., WHQ, 5(Jl 1974):355-6.

Jorberg, Lennart. A History of Prices in Sweden, 1732-1914. 2 vols. Lund, Sweden: CWK Gleerup, 1972. Rev. by W. W. Rostow, BHR, 48(Sum 1974):234-5.

Jordan, David K. Gods, Ghosts, and Ancestors: The Folk Religion of a Taiwanese Village. Berkeley ...: U Cal Press, 1972. Rev. by H. G. Rohsenow, JAS, 33(May 1974):478-80.

Jordan, David William see Carr, Lois Green

Jordan, Jan. Give Me the Wind. Englewood Cliffs, N.J.: Prentice-Hall, 1974. Rev. by Staff, InH, 7(Sum 1974):57-8.

Jordan, Ruth. Sophie Dorothea. London: Constable, 1971. Rev. by R. Hatton, ESR, 4(Jl 1974):266-9.

Jordan, Weymouth T., Jr., comp. North Carolina Troops, 1861-1865: A Roster. Volume IV. Infantry. Raleigh: N C Office, Archives and History, 1973. Rev. by J. I. Robertson, Jr., CWH, 20(Mar 1974):71-2.

Jordan, Winthrop D. The White Man's Burden: Historical Origins of Racism in the United States. New York: Ox U Press, 1974. Rev. by J. A. Rawley, HRNB, 2(May/Je 1974):167.

Jordy, William H. American Buildings and Their Architects. Volume 3, Progressive and Academic Ideals at the Turn of the Twentieth Century; volume 4, The Impact of European Modernism in the Mid-Twentieth Century. Garden City, N.Y.: Doubleday, 1972. Rev. by T. S. Hines, AHR, 79(Je 1974):887-9.

Jorgensen, Joseph G. The Sun Dance Religion: Power for the Powerless. Chicago: U Chi Press, 1972. Rev. by J. D. Hughes, CoMag, 51(Sum 1973):266-8; F. A. O'Neil, VHQ, 42 (Sum 1974):305-6; M. P. Leone, WHQ, 5(Ja 1974):84-6.

Joseph, Peter. Good Times: An Oral History of America in the Nineteen Sixties. New York: Charterhouse, 1973. Rev. by D. McComb, CoMag, 51(Sum 1974):243-4.

Josephson, Matthew, ed. The Left Bank Revisited: Selections from the Paris Tribune, 1917-1934. University Park: Pa St U Press, 1972. Rev. by D. J. Harvey, Historian, 36(Feb 1974): 330-1.

Joslin, D. M. see Winter, J. M.

Journal of Glass Studies. Vol. 14. Corning, N. Y.: Corning Museum of Glass, 1972. Rev. by H. J. Haden, T & C, 15 (Apr 1974):367-9.

Joy, Richard J. Languages in Conflict. Toronto/Montreal: McClelland and Stewart, 1972. Rev. by H. B. Neatby, CHR, 55(Mar 1974):98-9.

Judd, Dennis R. and Robert E. Mendelson. The Politics of Urban Planning: The East St. Louis Experience. Urbana: U Ill Press, 1973. Rev. by J. A. Williams, JISHS, 67(Nov 1974): 565-6.

Judd, Jacob and Irwin H. Polishook, eds. Aspects of Early New York Society and Politics. Tarrytown, N.Y.: Sleepy Hollow Restorations, 1974. Rev. by J. F. Sefcik, HRNB, 2(Feb 1974):92; L. G. DePauw, JAH, 61(Sep 1974):456-7; R. C. Ritchie, NYHSQ, 58(Jl 1974):237-8.

Judd, Neil M. The Bureau of American Ethnology: A Partial History. Norman: U Ok Press, 1967. Rev. by F. A. O'Neil, UHQ, 42(Win 1974):92-3.

Jukes, Geoffrey. The Soviet Union in Asia. Berkeley: U Cal Press, 1973. Rev. by H. A. McFarlin, JAS, 33(Aug 1974): 691-2.

Julin, Suzanne and Stephen R. Ward, eds. The South Dakota Experience: An Oral History Collection of Its People. Volume 2. Pierre and Vermillion: S D Oral History Project, 1972-73. Rev. by D. McComb, 51(Spr 1974):168-9.

July, Robert W. A History of the African People. New York: Scribner's, 1974. Rev. by C. G. Contee, HRNB, 2(Jl 1974): 204-5.

Juston, Mary Carolyn Hollers. Alfred Giles: An English Architect in Texas and Mexico. San Antonio, Tx.: Trinity U Press, 1972. Rev. by V. Rainey, ETHJ, 12(Spr 1974):66.

Kabanov, P. I., et al. The Proletariat at the Head of the Liberation Movement in Russia (1895-1917). Moscow: Izdatel 'stvo "Mysl.", 1971. Rev. by W. G. Rosenberg, AHR, 79(Je 1974): 822-4.

Kabui, Joseph. The Coconut Girl. Nairobi: East Africa Pub. House, 1971. Rev. by H. Dinwiddy, AfAf, 73(Jl 1974):379-81.

Kabus-Jahn, Renate. Die Grimanische Figurengruppe in Venedig. Berlin: Verlag Gebr. Mann, 1972. Rev. by E. G. Pemberton, AJA, 78(Apr 1974):199-200.

Kaelble, Hartmut. Berliner Unternehmer während der fruhen Industrialisierung. Herkunft sozialer Status und politischer Einfluss. Berlin: Walter de Gruyter, 1972. Rev. by L. Schofer, JEH, 34(Sep 1974):790-1.

Kaestle, Carl F. The Evolution of an Urban School System: New York City, 1750-1850. Cambridge, Mass.: Har U Press, 1973. Rev. by P. A. Kalisch, AHR, 79(Je 1974):845-6; W. W. Cutler, III, JAH, 61(Je 1974):162-3; D. Ravitch, NYHSQ, 58(Jl 1974):246-8.

Kaeuper, Richard W. Bankers to the Crown: The Riccardi of Lucca and Edward I. Princeton, N.J.: Prin U Press, 1973. Rev. by T. W. Blomquist, BHR, 48(Sum 1974):228-30.

Kahil, Raouf. Inflation and Economic Development in Brazil, 1946-1963. New York: Clarendon Press, 1973. Rev. by J. H. Street, HAHR, 54(Feb 1974):182-4.

Kahlenberg, Friedrich P. Deutsche Archive in West und Ost: Zur Entwicklung des staatlichen archivwesens seit 1945. Düsseldorf: Droste Verlag, 1972. Rev. by G. R. Mork, AHR, 79 (Feb 1974):179; T. Scott, Archives, 11(Spr 1974):186-7.

Kahler, Erich. The Germans. Princeton, N.J.: Prin U Press, 1974. Rev. by F. Dumin, HRNB, 3(Nov/Dec 1974):30-1.

Kahn, Kathy. Hillbilly Women: Mountain Women Speak of Struggle and Joy in Southern Appalachia. New York: Doubleday, 1973. Rev. by R. Iobst, FHQ, 52(Jl 1974):98-9; H. W. Woelfel, GR, 28(Spr 1974):177-80; Q. B. Keen, RKHS, 72(Apr 1974):173-5.

Kakrides, John see Andronicos, Emmanuel

Kalmykow, Andrew D. Memoirs of a Russian Diplomat. Outposts of the Empire, 1893-1917. New Haven, Conn.: Yale U Press, 1971. Rev. by H. Hanak, EHR, 89(Ja 1974):232-3.

Kälvemark, Ann-Sofie. The Reaction Against Emigration: The Emigration Question in Swedish Discussion and Politics 1901-1904. Stockholm: Läromedelsförlagen, 1972. Rev. by F. D. Scott, AHR, 79(Je 1974):799-800.

Kammen, Michael. People of Paradox: An Inquiry Concerning the Origins of American Civilization. New York: Knopf, 1972. M. Curti, AHR, 79(Je 1974):832-4.

_____, ed. The History of the Province of New York. 2 vols. London: Ox U Press, 1972. Rev. by A. F. McC. Madden, EHR, 89(Apr 1974):445-6.

_____, ed. "What is the Good of History?" Selected Letters of Carl L. Becker, 1900-1945. Ithaca, N.Y.: Cornell U Press, 1973. Rev. by R. R. Locke, Historian, 36(Aug 1974):737-8; M. J. Morton, JAH, 61(Sep 1974):514-15; T. P. Donovan, JSH, 40(May 1974):290-1.

_____, ed. see Becker, Carl L.

Kampen, Michael Edwin. The Sculptures of El Tajin. Gainesville: U Fla Press, 1972. Rev. by N. Hammond, Antiquity, 48(Sep 1974):236-7; D. M. Pendergast, Archaeology, 27(Jl 1974):220.

Kane, Ralph J. and Jeffrey A. Glover, eds. Inquiry: U.S.A. Themes, Issues and Men in Conflict. New York: Globe, 1971. Rev. by J. S. Greene, III, HT, 8(Nov 1974):120.

Kane, William Everett. Civil Strife in Latin America. Baltimore: JHU Press, 1972. Rev. by D. Green, TAm, 30(Apr 1974): 555-7.

Kaneko, Erika and Herbert Melichar. Pura Mutuzuma: Archaeological Work on Miyako Island, Ryukyus. Honolulu: U Hawaii Press, 1972. Rev. by C. W. Meighan, JAAS, 9(Ja & Apr 1974):111-12.

Kann, Robert A. Kaiser Franz Joseph und der Ausbruch des Weltkrieges. Vienna: Herman Böhlaus Nachf., 1971. Rev. by J. Joll, ESR, 4(Jl 1974):287-9.

Kannegieter, J. Z. Geschiedenis van de Vroegere Quakergemeenschap te Amsterdam, 1656 tot begin negentiende eeuw. Amsterdam: Scheltma and Holkema, 1971. Rev. by A. C. Carter, EHR, 89(Apr 1974):441.

Kaplan, Harold. Democratic Humanism and American Literature. Chicago: U Chi Press, 1972. Rev. by L. Marx, AHR, 79 (Feb 1974):216-7.

Kaplan, Justin. Lincoln Steffens. New York: Simon and Schuster, n.d. Rev. by S. McCracken, Commentary, 58(Oct 1974):91-2.

189   KAPLAN

Kaplan, Sidney. The Black Presence in the Era of the American Revolution, 1770-1800. New York: Graphic Society, 1973. Rev. by W. M. Billings, NEQ, 47(Sep 1974):485-8.

Kaplow, Jeffry. The Names of Kings: The Parisian Laboring Poor in the Eighteenth Century. New York: Basic Books, 1972. Rev. by S. Lytle, AHR, 79(Feb 1974):162-3; N. M. Barker, Historian, 36(May 1974):543-4; S. L. Kaplan, JMH, 46(Je 1974):351-6.

Kapp, Robert A. Szechwan and the Chinese Republic: Provincial Militarism and Central Power, 1911-1938. New Haven, Conn.: Yale U Press, 1973. Rev. by E. Lubot, HRNB, 2(Feb 1974): 105; L. E. Eastman, JAS, 33(Aug 1974):696-8.

Karageorge, Basil see Andronicos, Emmanuel

Karageorghis, Vassos. Cypriote Antiquities in the Pierides Collection, Larnaca, Cyprus. Athens: Ekdotike Hellados, 1973. Rev. by R. S. Merrilees, Antiquity, 48(Je 1974):151-2.

_____. see Buchholz, Hans-Günter

Katz, Friedrich. The Ancient American Civilizations. New York: Praeger, 1972. Rev. by W. Borah, AHR, 79(Oct 1974):1295-6.

Katz, Jacob. Out of the Ghetto: The Social Background of Jewish Emancipation, 1770-1870. Cambridge, Mass.: Har U Press, 1973. Rev. by R. H. Popkin, AHR, 79(Apr 1974):505-6; V. D. Lipman, History, 59(Je 1974):292.

Katz, Jonathan. Resistance at Christiana: The Fugitive Slave Rebellion, Christiana, Pennsylvania, September 11, 1851; A Documentary Account. New York: Crowell, 1974. Rev. by L. M. Simms, Jr., HRNB, 2(Sep 1974):257.

Katz, Michael B., ed. Education in American History: Readings on the Social Issues. New York: Praeger, 1973. Rev. by W. U. Solberg, HRNB, 2(Ja 1974):69-70.

Katzman, David. Before the Ghetto: Black Detroit in the Nineteenth Century. Urbana: U Ill Press, 1973. Rev. by G. E. Osborne, Crisis, 81(Mar 1974):105-6; J. Richardson, CWH, 20(Je 1974):190-1; Z. L. Miller, IMH, 70(Mar 1974):76-7; M. W. Homel, JAH, 61(Sep 1974):475-6; M. G. Holli, JISHS, 67(Nov 1974):567-8; M. S. Miller, JNH, 59(Jl 1974):296-7.

Katznelson, Ira. Black Men, White Cities: Race, Politics, and Migration in the United States, 1900-30, and Britain, 1948-68. London: Ox U Press, 1973. Rev. by S. M. Scheiner, JAH, 60(Mar 1974):1160-1; C. N. Degler, JIH, 5(Aug 1974):330-3.

Kau, Ying-mao. The People's Liberation Army and China's Nation
Building. White Plains, N. Y. : International Arts and Sciences
Press, 1973. Rev. by J. C. Cheng, JAS, 34(Nov 1974):233-6.

Kaufman, Stuart Bruce. Samuel Gompers and the Origins of the
American Federation of Labor, 1848-1896. Westport, Conn. :
Greenwood, 1973. Rev. by D. Brody, BHR, 48(Win 1974):
550-2; G. N. Grob, JAH, 61(Sep 1974):507-8.

Kaufman, Stuart B. see Harlan, Louis R. The Booker T. Washington Papers.

Kavenagh, W. Keith, ed. Foundations of Colonial America: A
Documentary History. 3 vols. New York: Chelsea House,
1973. Rev. by L. R. Gerlach, WMQ-3, 31(Spr 1974):327-30.

Kay, G. B. , ed. The Political Economy of Colonialism in Ghana:
A Collection of Documents and Statistics, 1900-1960. Cam-
bridge: Cam U Press, 1972. Rev. by J. Mohan, JMAS, 12
(Mar 1974):145-8.

Kay, Robin, ed. The Australian-New Zealand Agreement, 1944.
Wellington: A. R. Shearer ... 1972. Rev. by C. S. Blackton, AHR, 79(Apr 1974):562-3.

Kealey, Edward J. Roger of Salisbury, Viceroy of England. Berkeley: U Cal Press, 1972. Rev. by H. E. J. Cowdrey, EHR,
89(Apr 1974):418.

Keats, John. Eminent Domain: The Louisiana Purchase and the
Making of America. New York: Charterhouse Books, 1973.
Rev. by M. Morgan, OrHQ, 75(Mar 1974):81.

Keddie, Nikki R. Sayyid Jamal ad-Din "al-Afghani. " A Political
Biography. Berkeley: U Cal Press, 1972. Rev. by R. A
McDaniel, Historian, 36(Feb 1974):308-9.

_____, ed. Scholars, Saints, and Sufis: Muslim Religious Insti-
tutions in the Middle East Since 1500. Berkeley: U Cal Press,
1972. Rev. by J. Kritzeck, AHR, 79(Feb 1974):206-7.

Kee, Robert. The Green Flag: A History of Irish Nationalism.
London: Weidenfeld and Nicolson, 1972. Rev. by A. T. Q.
Stewart, History, 59(Feb 1974):143.

Keeler, Mary Frear, ed. Bibliography of British History. Stuart
Period, 1603-1714. Oxford: Clarendon Press, 1970. Rev.
by J. P. Cooper, EHR, 89(Ja 1974):118-22.

Keen, Benjamin. The Aztec Image in Western Thought. New
Brunswick: Rutgers U Press, 1971. Rev. by C. A. Burland,
JLAS, 6(May 1974):170-2.

Keen, M. H. England in the Later Middle Ages: A Political History. London: Methuen, 1973. Rev. by A. R. Meyers, EHR, 89(Ja 1974):157-8.

Keene, Donald, ed. with Royall Tyler. Twenty Plays of the No Theatre. New York: Col U Press, 1970. Rev. by I. J. McMullen, MAS, 8(Oct 1974):563-4.

Keever, Jack see Crawford, Ann Fears

Kegan, Elizabeth Hamer, ed. Fundamental Testaments of the American Revolution. Washington: Library of Congress, 1973. Rev. by R. A. Rutland, VMHB, 82(Oct 1974):495-7.

Kelch, Ray A. Newcastle, a Duke Without Money: Thomas Pelham-Holles, 1693-1768. Berkeley: U Cal Press, 1974. Rev. by R. J. Chaffin, HRNB, 2(May/Je 1974):187.

Kelf-Cohen, R. British Nationalisation, 1945-1973. New York: St. Martin's, 1973. Rev. by J. M. Stopford, BHR, 48(Win 1974): 590-2; T. H. von Laue, HRNB, 2(May/Je 1974):184-5.

Kellam, Ida Brooks see Lennon, Donald R.

Keller, A. C. see Atkinson, G.

Keller, Werner. The Etruscans. New York: Knopf, 1974. Rev. by J. E. Seaver, HRNB, 2(Sep 1974):251.

Kelley, A. C. see Wiesbrod, B. A.

Kelley, Allen C., Jeffrey G. Williamson and Russell J. Cheetham. Dualistic Economic Development: Theory and History. Chicago: U Chi Press, 1972. Rev. by H. Patrick, JAS, 33(Feb 1974):319-21.

Kelley, Brooks Mather. Yale: A History. New Haven, Conn.: Yale U Press, 1974. Rev. by P. F. Erwin, HRNB, 2(Sep 1974):258-9; R. Middlekauf, JAH, 61(Dec 1974):760-1; J. D. Hoeveler, Jr., NEQ, 47(Sep 1974):467-9.

Kelley, Darwin. Milligan's Fight Against Lincoln. New York: Exposition Press, 1973. Rev. by L. S. Theisen, CWH, 20(Mar 1974):73-4; C. G. Summersell, JAH, 61(Sep 1974):490-1; D. E. Meerse, JISHS, 67(Feb 1974):126-7.

Kelley, J. Charles see Hedrick, Basil C.

Kelley, Joseph J., Jr. Life and Times in Colonial Philadelphia. Harrisburg, Pa.: Stackpole, 1973. Rev. by C. R. Allen, Jr., Historian, 36(May 1974):588-9.

Kellogg, Charles Flint. NAACP: A History of the National Associa-

tion for the Advancement of Colored People. Volume I, 1909-
1920. Baltimore: JHU Press, 1973. Rev. by A. E. Strickland, JNH, 59(Jl 1974):293-5.

Kellom, John H. see Byers, William N.

Kelly, Daniel T. The Buffalo Head: A Century of Mercantile Pioneering in the Southwest. Santa Fe: Vergara, 1972. Rev.
by C. C. Spence, NMHR, 49(Ja 1974):83-4.

Kelly, Lawrence C. Navajo Roundup: Selected Correspondence of
Kit Carson's Expedition Against the Navajo, 1863-1865. Boul-
der, Colo.: Pruett, 1970. Rev. by R. H. Faust, ChOk, 52
(Sum 1974):258-9.

Kemp, Tom. Economic Forces in French History: An Essay on the
Development of the French Economy, 1760-1914. London: Dennis Dobson, 1971. Rev. by J. Kaplow, AHR, 79(Feb 1974):
164-5.

Kempf, Nicholas. Tractatus de Mystica Theologica. 2 volumes.
Salzburg: Analecta Cartusiana, 1973. Rev. by J. P. Dolan,
CH, 43(Sep 1974):395-6.

Kenneally, Finbar. United States Documents in the Propaganda Fide
Archives: A Calendar. Washington, D. C.: Academy of Amer-
ican Franciscan History, 1971, 1973. Rev. by D. A. Johnson,
CH, 43(Je 1974):284.

Kennedy, Judith M. and James A. Reither, eds. A Theatre for
Spencerians. Toronto: U Tor Press, 1973. Rev. by A. W.
Satterthwaite, RQ, 27(Sum 1974):242-3.

Kennedy, Michael L. The Jacobin Club of Marseilles, 1790-1794.
Ithaca, N. Y.: Cornell U Press, 1973. Rev. by P. F. Riley,
Historian, 36(Aug 1974):753-4; S. T. Ross, HRNB, 2(Ja 1974):
86.

Kennedy, Paul P. The Middle Beat: A Correspondent's View of
Mexico, Guatemala, and El Salvador. New York: Teachers
College Press, Columbia U, 1971. Rev. by J. N. Goodsell,
HAHR, 54(Nov 1974):736-8.

Kennedy, Robert E., Jr. The Irish: Emigration, Marriage, and
Fertility. Berkeley: U Cal Press, 1973. Rev. by D. W.
Miller, JIH, 5(Aut 1974):326-7.

Kennedy, Susan Estabrook. The Banking Crisis of 1933. Lexington,
Ky.: U Press Ky, 1973. Rev. by N. L. Dawson, FCHQ, 48
(Jl 1974):284-6; P. P. Abrams, HRNB, 2(Mar 1974):135; E. W.
Hawley, JAH, 61(Dec 1974):830-1; P. A. Kalisch, RKHS, 72(Jl
1974):289-91.

Kent, H. S. K. War and Trade in Northern Seas: Anglo-Scandina-
    vian Economic Relations in the Mid-Eighteenth Century. Cam-
    bridge: Cam U Press, 1973. Rev. by W. Kirchner, BHR,
    48(Spr 1974):114.

Kent, Harold Winfield. Dr. Hyde and Mr. Stevenson: The Life of
    the Rev. Dr. Charles McEwen Hyde, Including a Discussion of
    the Open Letter of Robert Louis Stevenson. Rutland, Vt.:
    Tuttle, 1973. Rev. by M. Tate, AHR, 79(Je 1974):884-5; J.
    Findlay, JAH, 61(Je 1974):230-1; D. D. Johnson, PHR, 43(Nov
    1974):613-4.

Keppel, Sonia. The Sovereign Lady. A Life of Elizabeth, Third
    Lady Holland, with Her Family. London: H. Hamilton, n. d.
    Rev. by J. Richardson, HTo, 24(Aug 1974):577-8.

Kerby, Robert L. Kirby Smith's Confederacy: The Trans-Missis-
    sippi South, 1863-1865. New York: Columbia U Press, 1972.
    Rev. by J. Monaghan, AHR, 79(Apr 1974):587-9.

Keremitsis, Dawn. La industria textil mexicana en el siglo XIX.
    México: SepSetentas, 1973. R. A. Potash, HAHR, 54(Nov
    1974):712-14.

Kern, Robert, ed. The Caciques: Oligarchical Politics and the
    System of Caciquismo in the Luso-Hispanic World. Albuquer-
    que: U NM Press, 1973. Rev. by P. H. Smith, AHR, 79(Apr
    1974):620-1.

Kerr, Howard. Mediums, and Spirit-Rappers, and Roaring Radicals:
    Spiritualism in American Literature, 1850-1900. Urbana: U
    Ill Press, 1972. Rev. by D. J. Pivar, AHR, 79(Je 1974):864.

Kerr, Stanley E. The Lions of Marash: Personal Experiences with
    American Near East Relief 1919-1922. Albany: SUNY Press,
    1973. Rev. by K. L. Crose, CH, 43(Mar 1974):128-9.

Kershaw, Ian. Bolton Priory: The Economy of a Northern Monas-
    tery 1286-1325. Oxford: Ox U Press, 1973. Rev. by S.
    Raban, Archives, 11(Spr 1974):182-3; F. A. Underhill, CH,
    43(Sep 1974):392-3.

Kerst, Georg. Jacob Meckel: Sein Leben, sein Wirken in Deutsch-
    land und Japan. Göttingen: Musterschmidt-Verlag, 1970.
    Rev. by W. L. Spalding, Jr., AHR, 79(Feb 1974):212.

Kerwood, John R. see Reingold, Nathan

Ketcham, Ralph. James Madison: A Biography. New York: Mac-
    millan, 1971. Rev. by G. G. Van Deusen, AHR, 79(Apr 1974):
    574-5.

Ketchum, Richard M. The Winter Soldiers. Garden City, N. J.:

Doubleday, 1973. Rev. by D. Higginbotham, MHM, 69(Sum 1974):228-30.

Ketchum, Richard M. Will Rogers: His Life and Times. New York: American Heritage, 1973. Rev. by H. Hamilton, RKHS, 72(Apr 1974):187-8; R. Salisbury, WPHM, 57(Apr 1974):227-8.

Keyes, Roger S. and Keiko Mizushima. The Theatrical World of Osaka Prints: A Collection of Eighteenth and Nineteenth Century Japanese Woodblock Prints in the Philadelphia Museum of Art. Philadelphia: Philadelphia Museum of Art, 1973. Rev. by D. Jenkins, JAS, 33(May 1974):491-3.

Khan, Azizur Rahman. The Economy of Bangladesh. London: Macmillan, 1972. Rev. by A. Robinson, MAS, 8(Ja 1974):139-41.

Khan, Harold L. Monarchy in the Emperor's Eyes: Image and Reality in the Ch'ien-lung Reign. Cambridge, Mass.: Har U Press, 1971. Rev. by H. J. Beattie, MAS, 8(Ja 1974):142-3.

Khare, Ravindra S., James W. Kolka, and Carol A. Pollis, eds. Environmental Quality and Social Responsibility. Green Bay, Wis.: U Wis--Green Bay, 1972. Rev. by V. L. Ferwerda, T & C, 15(Jl 1974):529-34.

Khesin, S. S. The October Revolution and the Navy. Moscow: Izdatel'stvo "Nauka," 1971. Rev. by A. Rabinowitch, AHR, 79(Apr 1974):545-6.

Khilnani, N. M. British Power in the Punjab, 1839-1858. New York: Asia Pub. House, 1972. Rev. by M. Naidis, AHR, 79 (Je 1974):827-8.

Khonigsman, Ia. S. Penetration of the Economy of Western Ukraine by Foreign Capital in the Era of Imperialism (till 1918). Lvov: Vydavnytstvo L'vivs'koho Universytetu, 1971. Rev. by V. Holubnychy, AHR, 79(Oct 1974):1222-3.

Khrushchev, Nikita S. Khrushchev Remembers: The Last Testament. Boston: Little, Brown, 1974. Rev. by S. D. Spector, HRNB, 3(Nov/Dec 1974):32-3.

Kibler, Lillian Adele. The History of Converse College, 1889-1971. Spartanburg, S.C.: Converse College, 1973. Rev. by B. J. Brandon, JSH, 40(Aug 1974):515-16; M. L. Johnson, NCHR, 51(Sum 1974):336-7.

Kiessling, Rolf. Bürgerliche Gesellschaft und Kirche in Augsburg im Spätmittelalter: Ein Beitrag zur Strukturanalyse der oberdeutschen Reichsstadt. Augsburg: Verlag H. Muhlberger, 1971. Rev. by H. C. Erik Midelfort, AHR, 79(Feb 1974):130-1.

Kieszkowski, Bohdan. Giovanni Pico della Mirandola: Conclusiones

sive theses DCCCC Romae anno 1486 publice disputandae sed
non admissae.   Geneva: Librairie Droz, 1973.   Rev. by H. L.
Bond, CH, 43(Sep 1974):396-7.

Kieve, Jeffrey.   The Electric Telegraph in the U. K. :   A Social and
Economic History.   New York: Barnes and Noble, 1973.   Rev.
by H. I. Sharlin, AHR, 79(Je 1974):786; R. E. Tyson, History,
59(Je 1974):286-7; J. D. Tebo, T & C, 15(Apr 1974):332-4.

Kikuchi, Charles.   The Kikuchi Diary: Chronicle from an American
Concentration Camp.   Urbana: U Ill Press, 1973.   Rev. by
E. Uno, CHQ, 53(Sum 1974):184-5; M. Dubofsky, HRNB, 2(Ja
1974):60; D. Hata, JAH, 61(Dec 1974):835-6.

Killion, Ronald and Charles Waller, eds.   Slavery Time When I Was
Chillun Down on Marster's Plantation.   Savannah, Ga. :   Beehive, 1973.   Rev. by R. M. Miller, JSH, 40(Aug 1974):482-3.

Kilner, Colleen.   Kenilworth Tree Stories: History Woven Around
Its Trees.   Kenilworth, Ill. :   Kenilworth Historical Society,
1972.   Rev. by O. M. Robinson, JISHS, 67(Sep 1974):461-2.

Kim, C. I. Eugene, ed.   Korean Unification: Problems and Prospects.   Kalamazoo, Mich. :   Korea Research and Publications,
1973.   Rev. by B. C. Koh, JAS, 33(Aug 1974):716-19.

Kim, H. C. , ed.   The Gospel of Nicodemus.   Toronto: Center for
Medieval Studies, 1973.   Rev. by J. F. Kelly, CH, 43(Sep
1974):391.

Kim, Ilpyong J.   The Politics of Chinese Communism: Kiangsi under
the Soviets.   Berkeley: U Cal Press, 1973.   Rev. by L. P.
Van Slyke, JAS, 33(Aug 1974):698-701.

Kimambo, I. N.   see   Ranger, T. O.

Kimball, Arthur G.   Crisis in Identity and Contemporary Japanese
Novels.   Rutland, Vt. and Tokyo: Tuttle, 1973.   Rev. by
W. Sibley, JAS, 33(Feb 1974):317-19.

Kimball, Warren, ed.   Franklin D. Roosevelt and the World Crisis,
1937-1945.   Lexington, Mass. :   D. C. Heath, 1973.   Rev. by
A. L. Hamby, HRNB, 2(Mar 1974):130.

Kinchen, Oscar A.   Women Who Spied for the Blue and the Gray.
Philadelphia: Dorrance, 1972.   Rev. by L. S. Theisen, CWH,
20(Mar 1974):73-4.

Kindleberger, Charles P.   The World in Depression, 1929-1939.
Berkeley: U Cal Press, 1973.   Rev. by G. D. Green, BHR,
48(Sum 1974):271-3; P. Fearon, History, 59(Je 1974):301-2;
E. Wicker, JAH, 61(Sep 1974):526-7.

King, Edmund. Peterborough Abbey, 1086-1310: A Study in the Land Market. New York: Cam U Press, 1973. Rev. by G. Constable, AHR, 79(Apr 1974):495; R. W. Hays, CH, 43(Mar 1974):99.

King, P. D. Law and Society in the Visigothic Kingdom. New York: Cam U Press, 1972. Rev. by R. I. Burns, AHR, 79(Feb 1974): 129.

King, Woodie and Earl Anthony, eds. Black Poets and Prophets: The Theory, Practice and Esthetics of the Pan-Africanist Revolution. New York: New American Library, 1972. Rev. by L. Brownstein, JMAS, 12(Sep 1974):491-3.

Kingdon, Robert M., ed. Transition and Revolution: Problems and Issues of European Renaissance and Reformation History. Minneapolis: Burgess, 1974. Rev. by A. Tobriner, HRNB, 3 (Oct 1974):14.

Kinnamon, Kenneth. The Emergence of Richard Wright: A Study in Literature and Society. Urbana: U Ill Press, 1972. Rev. by R. E. Fleming, N H B, 37(Ja 1974):207.

Kinnear, Michael. The Fall of Lloyd George: The Political Crisis of 1922. London: Macmillan, 1973. Rev. by K. O. Morgan, History, 59(Je 1974):297-8.

Kinsbruner, Jay. Chile: A Historical Interpretation. New York: Harper and Row, 1974. Rev. by M. Grow, HRNB, 2(Jl 1974): 202.

Kintner, William R. and Robert L. Pfaltzgraff, Jr., ed. SALT: Implications for Arms Control in the 1970s. Pittsburgh: U Pitt Press, 1973. Rev. by C. L. Christman, MiA, 56(Ja 1974):57-8.

Kirk, Ruth. Desert: The American Southwest. Boston: Houghton Mifflin, 1973. Rev. by K. Black, JOW, 13(Oct 1974):144; H. P. Hinton, PNQ, 65(Oct 1974):192.

Kirkendale, Warren. L'Aria di Fiorenza, id est, Il Ballo del Gran Duca. Florence: L. S. Olschki, 1972. Rev. by L. Lockwood, RQ, 27(Spr 1974):48.

Kirkendall, Richard S., ed. The Truman Period as a Research Field: A Reappraisal, 1972. Columbia, Mo.: U Mo Press, 1974. Rev. by T. V. DiBacco, HRNB, 2(Apr 1974):151; R. A. Lee, JAH, 61(Dec 1974):841-2.

Kirk-Greene, A. H. M., ed. Gazetteers of the Northern Provinces of Nigeria. 4 vols. London: Cass, 1972. Rev. by M. Last, Africa, 44(Apr 1974):212-3.

Kirkpatrick, Jeanne. Leader and Vanguard in Mass Society: A
    Study of Peronist Argentina. Cambridge, Mass.: M I T
    Press, 1971. Rev. by R. D. Moseley-Williams, JLAS, 6(May
    1974):180-1.

Kirsch, A. Thomas. Feasting and Social Oscillation: Religion and
    Society in Upland Southeast Asia. Ithaca, N. Y.: ... Cornell
    U Press, 1973. Rev. by B. L. Foster, JAS, 33(Aug 1974):
    736-7.

Kisch, Guido. Judentaufen: Eine historisch-biographisch-psycholog-
    isch-soziologische Studie besonders für Berlin and Königsberg.
    Berlin: Colloquium Verlag, 1973. Rev. by J. J. Petuchow-
    ski, CH, 43(Sep 1974):430-1.

Kissinger, Henry. A World Restored. London: Gallancz, n. d.
    Rev. by M. Latey, HTo, 24(Ja 1974):61.

Kitano, Harry H. L. see Daniels, Roger

Kitskikis, Dimitri. Le Role des Experts à la Conference de la
    Paix de 1919. Ottawa: Editions de l'Universite de Ottawa,
    1972. Rev. by R. Bullen, EHR, 89(Apr 1974):465.

Kiwanuka, M. S. M. Semakula. A History of Buganda from the
    Foundation of the Kingdom to 1900. London: Longman, 1972.
    Rev. by A. D. Roberts, History, 59(Je 1974):311.

Kiyoshi, Haraguchi. The Boshin War. Tokyo: Hanawa Shobo, 1963.
    Rev. by C. D. Sheldon, JAS, 33(Feb 1974):314-16.

Ki-Zerbo, Joseph. Histoire de l'Afrique Noire. Paris: Hatier,
    1972. Rev. by A. D. R., JAfH, 15(Num 1 1974):149-50.

Klaassen, Walter. Anabaptism: Neither Catholic nor Protestant.
    Waterloo, Ontario: Conrad Press, 1973. Rev. by F. J. Wray,
    CH, 43(Sep 1974):406.

Klamkin, Lynn. Hello, Goodbye. New York: Dodd, Mead, 1973.
    Rev. by K. L. Bielenberg, VH, 42(Sum 1974):246.

Klarén, Peter F. Modernization, Dislocation, and Aprismo: Origins
    of the Peruvian Aprista Party, 1870-1932. Austin: ... U Tx
    Press, 1973. Rev. by S. Stein, HAHR, 54(Nov 1974):723-5;
    D. E. Worcester, HRNB, 2(Ja 1974):70-1.

Klasner, Lily. My Girlhood Among Outlaws. Tucson: U Ariz
    Press, 1972. Rev. by K. E. Anderson, JOW, 13(Apr 1974):
    112.

Klausner, Carla L. The Seljuk Vezirate: A Study of Civil Adminis-
    tration, 1055-1194. Cambridge, Mass.: Har U Press, 1973.
    Rev. by F. E. Peters, AHR, 79(Je 1974):776-7.

Klein, Maury. Edward Porter Alexander. Athens, Ga.: U Ga
    Press, 1971. Rev. by J. Monaghan, AHR, 79(Apr 1974):587-
    9.

_____. History of the Louisville and Nashville Railroad. New
    York: Macmillan, 1972. Rev. by I. D. Neu, JSH, 40(May
    1974):338-9.

Klement, Frank L. The Limits of Dissent: Clement L. Vallandig-
    ham and the Civil War. Lexington, Ky.: U Press Ky, 1970.
    Rev. by D. L. Lendt, AI, 42(Win 1974):229-30.

Klemperer, Klemens von. Ignaz Seipel: Christian Statesman in a
    Time of Crisis. Princeton, N.J.: Prin U Press, 1972. Rev.
    by A. Diamant, JMH, 46(Dec 1974):736-8.

Klinck, Carl F. and James J. Talman, eds. The Journal of Major
    John Norton, 1816. Toronto: Champlain Society, 1970. Rev.
    by W. Fenton, AHR, 79(Oct 1974):1258-60.

Kline, Mary-Jo, ed. Alexander Hamilton: A Biography in His Own
    Words. New York: Newsweek, Harper and Row, 1973. Rev.
    by R. G. Smolka, HRNB, 2(Feb 1974):94-5; T. S. Berry,
    VMHB, 82(Apr 1974):201-2.

Kluke, Paul. Die Stiftungsuniversitat Frankfurt am Main, 1914-1932.
    Frankfurt am Main: Waldemar Kramer, 1972. Rev. by R.
    Lenman, EHR, 89(Jl 1974):692-3.

Klumbach, Hans, ed. Spätrömische Gardehelme. Munich: C. H.
    Beck'sche, 1973. Rev. by K. S. Painter, Antiquity, 48(Je
    1974):145-6.

Knapp, Joseph G. The Advance of American Cooperative Enterprise:
    1920-1945. Danville, Ill.: Interstate Printers and Publishers,
    1973. Rev. by C. A. Chambers, AHR, 79(Je 1974):895-6;
    J. A. Shaw, JEH, 34(Sep 1974):791-3.

Knauth, Lothar. Confrontación transpacífica: El Japón y el Nuevo
    Mundo hispanico, 1542-1639. México: Universidad Nacional
    Autónoma de México, 1972. Rev. by J. L. Phelan, HAHR,
    54(May 1974):311-13.

Knight, Franklin W. The African Dimensions in Latin American
    Societies. New York: Macmillan, 1974. Rev. by G. Breathet
    HRNB, 2(Sep 1974):254.

Knight, Frida. Beethoven and the Age of Revolution. New York:
    International Publishers, 1973. Rev. by W. L. Woodfill, AHR,
    79(Apr 1974):506-7.

Knight, W. Nicholas. Shakespeare's Hidden Life: Shakespeare at
    Law 1585-1595. New York: Mason and Lipscomb, 1973. Rev

by R. Berman, RQ, 27(Spr 1974):99-100.

Knoerle, Jeanne. The Dream of the Red Chamber, A Critical Study.
Bloomington: Ind U Press, 1972. Rev. by J. Sailey, JAS,
33(Feb 1974):298-300.

Knoles, George H., ed. Essays and Assays: California History
Reappraised. San Francisco: Cal Historical Society, 1973.
Rev. by R. J. Roske, JAH, 61(Je 1974):206-7; J. H. Kemble,
PHR, 43(Aug 1974):425-6.

Knowles Middleton, W. E. The Experimenters: A Study of the Accademia del Cimento. Baltimore: JHU Press, 1971. Rev.
by C. Webster, EHR, 89(Apr 1974):436.

Knowlton, Evelyn H. see Larson, Henrietta M.

Koch, A. C. F. The Year of Erasmus' Birth. Utrecht: Dekker
and Gumbert, 1969. Rev. by H. I. Mandeville, RQ, 27(Spr
1974):57-60.

Koch, Albert C. Journey Through a Part of the United States of
North America in the Years 1844 to 1846. Carbondale: S Ill
U Press, 1972. Rev. by P. P. Mason, AmArc, 37(Ja 1974):
84-5; B. G. Ramsey, JAH, 61(Je 1974):188-9; P. Yoder, JISHS,
67(Apr 1974):242-3; M. A. Rockland, PH, 41(Apr 1974):233-5;
D. Bernstein, PHR, 43(May 1974):267-8; H. I. Mandeville,
RQ, 27(Spr 1974):57-60; R. L. Davis, WHQ, 5(Apr 1974):189-
91.

Koelsch, William A. see Rosenkrantz, Barbara Gutmann. American Habitat.

Kogel, Renée. Pierre Charron. Genèva: Librairie Droz, 1972.
Rev. by W. H. Beik, AHR, 79(Oct 1974):1187-8; M. C. Horowitz, RQ, 27(Fall 1974):346-8.

Kohler, A. see Lutz, H.

Kohlmeier, Louis M., Jr. "God Save This Honorable Court!"
New York: Scribner's, 1972. Rev. by J. W. Howard, Jr.,
AHR, 79(Oct 1974):1294-5.

Kolaukiewicz, George see Laue, David

Kolchin, Peter. First Freedom: The Responses of Alabama's
Blacks to Emancipation and Reconstruction. Westport, Conn.:
Greenwood, 1972. Rev. by C. M. Tarrant, CWH, 20(Mar
1974):77-8; T. B. Alexander, Historian, 36(May 1974):574-5;
R. F. Durden, JAH, 61(Je 1974):199-200.

Kolin, Ivo. Thermodynamics Atlas. Vol. 2: The Evolution of the

Heat Engine. London: Longman, 1973. Rev. by L. Bryant and A. R. Rogowski, T & C, 15(Oct 1974):641-4.

Kolinski, Charles J. Historical Dictionary of Paraguay. Metuchen, N. J.: Scarecrow, 1973. Rev. by J. H. Williams, HAHR, 54 (May 1974):309-10.

Kolka, James W. see Khare, Ravindra S.

Kolko, Joyce and Gabriel. The Limits of Power: The World and United States Foreign Policy, 1945-1954. New York: Harper and Row, 1972. Rev. by J. Gimbel, CHR, 55(Sep 1974):336-41.

Kolycheva, E. I. Bondage and Serfdom (End of the 15th-16th Century). Moscow: Izdatel'stvo "Nauka," 1971. Rev. by C. B. O'Brien, AHR, 79(Feb 1974):194-5.

Korbel, Josef. Deténte in Europe: Real or Imaginary? Princeton, N. J.: Prin U Press, 1972. Rev. by P. S. Wandycz, AHR, 79(Oct 1974):1148-9.

Korolenko, V. G. The History of My Contemporary. New York: Ox U Press, 1972. Rev. by J. D. Clarkson, AHR, 79(Je 1974):818.

Koss, Stephen. Fleet Street Radical: A. G. Gardiner and the Daily Press. Hamden, Conn.: Archon, 1973. Rev. by A. F. Havighurst, AHR, 79(Feb 1974):153-4.

_____, ed. The Pro-Boers: The Anatomy of an Antiwar Movement. Chicago: U Chi Press, 1973. Rev. by J. A. Casada, HRNB, 2(Ja 1974):75.

Koster, John see Burnette, Robert

Kostrowicki, Jerzy and Roman Szczesny. Polish Agriculture: Characteristics, Types, and Regions. n. p.: Hungarian Academy of Sciences, 1972. Rev. by N. J. G. Pounds, EEQ, 8(Mar 1974):124-6.

Kottman, Karl A. The Law and the Apocalypse: The Moral Thought of Luis de Leon (1527?-1591). The Hague: Nijhoff, 1972. Rev. by R. W. Truman, EHR, 89(Apr 1974):433.

Koury, Michael J. Arms for Texas: A Study of the Weapons of the Republic of Texas. Fort Collins, Colo.: Old Army, 1973. Rev. by J. Osborn, ETHJ, 12(Fall 1974):77-8.

Koyre, Alexandre. The Astronomical Revolution: Copernicus--Kepler--Borelli. Ithaca, N. Y.: Cornell U Press, 1973. Rev. by J. L. Heilbron, HRNB, 2(Ja 1974):73.

_____ and I. Bernard Cohen, eds. Isaac Newton's "Philosophiae Naturalis Principia Mathematica." Volumes 1 and 2.... Cambridge, Mass.: Har U Press, 1972. Rev. by A. Thackery, AHR, 79(Feb 1974):104-7; N. Swerdlow, JMH, 46(Mar 1974): 116-19.

Kozee, William C. Pioneer Families of Eastern and Southeastern Kentucky. Baltimore: Genealogical Publishing Co., 1973. Rev. by L. Anderson, RKHS, 72(Apr 1974):172-3.

Kozin, M. I., ed. Essays on the Economic History of Latvia, 1860-1900. Riga: Izdatel'stvo "Zinatne," 1972. Rev. by N. Balabkins, AHR, 79(Je 1974):814-15.

Kraay, Colin see Thompson, Margaret

Kraay, Colin M. see Davis, Norman

Krakel, Dean. End of the Trail: Odyssey of a Statue. Norman: U Ok Press, 1973. Rev. by J. Albright, CoMag, 51(Sum 1974):270-1.

Kramnick, Isaac, ed. Lord Bolingbroke: Historical Writings. Chicago: U Chi Press, 1973. Rev. by W. A. Speck, EHR, 89 (Jl 1974):669-70.

Krasheninnikov, Stepan Petrovich. Exploration of Kamchatka-North Pacific Scimitar: Opisanie Zemli Kamchatki: Report of a Journey Made to Explore Eastern Siberia in 1735-1741, by Order of the Russian Imperial Government. Tr. by E. A. P. Crownhart-Vaughan. Portland: Oregon Hist. Soc., 1972. Rev. by R. H. Fisher, PHR, 43(Feb 1974):116-7.

Krause, Clemens. Das Westtor, Ergebnisse der Augsrabungen, 1964-1968. Bern: Francke Verlag, 1972. Rev. by W. R. Biers, AJA, 78(Jl 1974):306-7.

Krauss, Friedrich. Das Theater von Milet. Vol. I: Das Hellenistische Theater der Romische zuschauerbau. Berlin: De Gruyter, 1973. Rev. by H. Plommer, Antiquity, 48(Sep 1974): 250-1.

Krausz, Michael, ed. Critical Essays on the Philosophy of R. G. Collingwood. New York: Ox U Press, 1972. Rev. by W. Dray, H & T, 13(Num 3 1974):291-305.

Kravchenko, E. A. The Popular Front in France, 1934-1938. Moscow: Izdatel'stvo "Nauka," 1972. Rev. by J. A. Armstrong, AHR, 79(Oct 1974):1193-4.

Kravchenko, G. S. The Economy of the USSR in the Years of the Great Fatherland War (1941-1945). Moscow: Ekonomika, 1970. Rev. by S. Lieberstein, T & C, 15(Ja 1974):122-5.

Kreissler, Félix. De la révolution à l'annexion: L'Autriche de 1918 à 1938. Paris: Presses Universitaires de France, 1971. Rev. by K. von Klemperer, AHR, 79(Feb 1974):179-81.

Krekic, Barisa. Dubrovnik in the 14th and 15th Centuries: A City Between East and West. Norman: U Ok Press, 1972. Rev. by K. Bangerter, EEQ, 8(Fall 1974):371-2.

Kreutzberger, Wolfgang. Studenten und Politik, 1918-1933: Der Fall Freiburg in Breisgau. Göttingen: Vandenhoeck and Ruprecht, 1972. Rev. by P. Loewenberg, JMH, 46(Mar 1974): 155-6.

Krichmar, Albert. The Women's Rights Movement in the United States, 1848-1970: A Bibliography and Sourcebook. Metuchen, N.J.: Scarecrow, 1972. Rev. by B. B. Jensen, CoMag, 51 (Spr 1974):160-1.

Kristeller, Paul Oskar. Renaissance Concepts of Man and Other Essays. London: Harper Torchbooks, 1972. Rev. by J. Larner, History, 59(Je 1974):262-3.

Kröll, Ulrich. Die internationale Buren-Agitation, 1899-1902. Munster: Verlag Regensberg, 1973. Rev. by L. H. Gann, AHR, 79(Oct 1974):1175.

Kruedener, Jürgen Freiherr von. Die Rolle des Hofes im Absolutismus. Stuttgart: Gustav Fischer Verlag, 1973. Rev. by J. A. Vann, AHR, 79(Je 1974):778-9.

Krüger, Peter. Deutschland und die Reparationen 1918/19: Die Genesis des Reparationsproblems in Deutschland zwischen Waffenstillstand und Versailler Friedensschluss. Stuttgart: Deutsche Verlags-Anstalt, 1973. Rev. by G. D. Feldman, JMH, 46(Sep 1974):558-9.

Kruszewski, Anthony. The Oder-Neisse Boundary and Poland's Modernization. New York: Praeger, 1972. Rev. by J. Piekalkiewicz, EEQ, 8(Sum 1974):234-7.

Kruszewski, Z. Anthony, ed. see de la Garza, Rudolph

Kübel, Paul. Schuld und Schicksal bei Origens, Gnostikern und Platonikern. Stuttgart: Calwer Verlag, 1973. Rev. by S. Laeuchli, CH, 43(Dec 1974):530.

Kubijovyc, Volodymyr, ed. Ukraine: A Concise Encyclopedia. Volume 2. Toronto: U Tor Press, ... 1971. Rev. by J. S. Reshetar, Jr., AHR, 79(Apr 1974):555-6.

Kubler, George. Portuguese Plain Architecture Between Spices and Diamonds, 1521-1705. Middletown, Conn.: Wes U Press, 1972. Rev. by J. D. Hoag, RQ, 27(Sum 1974):229-31.

Kuhn, Philip A.   Rebellion and Its Enemies in Late Imperial China:
Militarization and Social Structure, 1796-1864.   Cambridge,
Mass.: Har U Press, 1970.   Rev. by J. K. Leonard, AHR,
79(Oct 1974):1230-1.

Kuhns, William.   The Post-Industrial Prophets: Interpretations of
Technology.   New York: Harper and Row, 1973.   Rev. by
H. J. Muller, T & C, 15(Apr 1974):357-60.

Kuklick, Bruce.   Josiah Royce: An Intellectual Biography.   Indianapolis: Bobbs-Merrill, 1972.   Rev. by J. L. Blau, AHR, 79
(Apr 1974):597-8.

Kukulka, Józef.   France and Poland After the Versailles Treaty.
Warsaw: Ksiazka i Wiedza, 1970.   Rev. by S. Dabrowski,
EEQ, 7(Ja 1974):466-72.

Kulski, W. W.   The Soviet Union in World Affairs--A Documented
Analysis, 1964-1972.   Syracuse, N.Y.:   Syr U Press, 1973.
Rev. by A. Dallin, AHR, 79(Feb 1974):201-2.

Kurgan-Van Hentenryk, G.   Léopold II et les groups financiers
belges en Chine: la politique royale et ses prolongments (1895-
1914).   Brussels: Académie Royale de Belgique, 1972.   Rev.
by R. Anstey, EHR, 89(Jl 1974):689-90.

Kurland, Gerald.   Seth Low: The Reformer in an Urban and Industrial Age.   New York: Twayne, 1971.   Rev. by J. J.
Rumbarger, AHR, 79(Feb 1974):239.

Kuropiatnik, G. P.   The Farmers' Movement in the USA: From the
Grangers to the Populists, 1867-1896.   Moscow: Izdatel'stvo
"Nauka," 1971.   Rev. by R. V. Allen, AHR, 79(Je 1974):
877-8.

Kurtz, Stephen G. and James H. Hutson, eds.   Essays on the American Revolution.   Chapel Hill: UNC Press, 1973.   Rev. by
G. T. Miller, CH, 43(Mar 1974):119; B. W. Labaree, JAH,
60(Mar 1974):1099-1100; L. R. Gerlach, NYHSQ, 58(Apr 1974):
165-9; R. Detweiler, PH, 41(Ja 1974):100-2; G. B. Nash,
WMQ-3, 31(Apr 1974):311-14.

Kutakov, Leonid N.   Japanese Foreign Policy on the Eve of the
Pacific War: A Soviet View.   Tallahassee, Fla.:   Diplomatic
Press, 1972.   Rev. by G. R. Falconeri, AHR, 79(Apr 1974):
559-60.

Kuter, Laurence S. The Great Gamble: The Boeing 747.   University, Ala.:   Ala U Press, 1973.   Rev. by R. Higham, BHR,
48(Win 1974):573-5.

Kuttner, Stephan, ed.   The Proceedings of the Third International

Congress of Medieval Canon Law, Strasbourg, 3-6 September
1968. Volume 4. Vatican City: Biblioteca Apostolica Vaticana, 1971. Rev. by C. R. Cheney, EHR, 89(Jl 1974):
652-3.

Labaree, Benjamin see Albion, Robert G.

Lacey, Robert. Sir Walter Raleigh. London: Weidenfeld and Nicolson, n. d. Rev. by A. Haynes, HTo, 24(Ja 1974):61-3.

Lach, Donald see Gottschalk, Louis. Toward the French Revolution.

Lachica, Eduardo. The Huks: Philippine Agrarian Society in Revolt. New York: Praeger, 1971. Rev. by M. P. Fabella,
JAAS, 9(Ja & Apr 1974):103-4.

Lacombe, Américo Jacobina. Introdução ao estudo da História do
Brasil. Sao Paulo: Companhia Editora Nacional, 1974. Rev.
by B. W. Diffie, HAHR, 54(Aug 1974):503-4.

Ladurie, Emmanuel Le Roy. Le Territoire de L'Historien. Paris:
Gallimand, 1973. Rev. by R. Forster, BHR, 48(Sum 1974):
227-8.

_____ and Joseph Goy. Les Fluctuations du produit de la dîme:
Conjoncture décimale et domainiale de fin du Moyen Age au
XVIIIe siècle. see Goy, Joseph et Emmanuel Le Roy Ladurie.
Les Fluctuations....

Laeuchli, Samuel. Power and Sexuality: The Emergence of Canon
Law at the Synod of Elvira. Philadelphia: Temple U Press,
1972. Rev. by W. R. Schoedel, CH, 43(Sep 1974):388-9.

La Faye, Jacques, ed. Manuscrit Tovar Origines et Croyances des
Indiens du Mexique. Graz, Austria: Akademische Druck-un,
n. d. Rev. by W. Ruwet, AmAnt, 39(Jl 1974):518-19; C. Gibson, HAHR, 54(Feb 1974):122-5.

La Feber, Walter F. see Gardner, Lloyd C.

Lafon, Jacques. Les époux bordelais, 1450-1550: Régimes matrimoniaux et mutations sociales. Paris: S. E. V. P. E. N. , 1972.
Rev. by P. Viles, AHR, 79(Apr 1974):517-18; J. L. Gold-
smith, CHR, 55(Mar 1974):109-11; M. G. A. Vale, EHR, 89
(Apr 1974):424

Lajeunesse, R. M. see Irwin, H. T.

Lajugie, Joseph. Bordeaux au XXe Siècle. Bordeaux: Fédération
Historique du Sud-Ouest, 1972. Rev. by J. P. T. Bury, EHR,
89(Ja 1974):238.

Laird, M. A. Missionaries and Education in Bengal, 1793-1837.
 Oxford: Clarendon, 1972. Rev. by K. Ingham, MAS, 8(Oct
 1974):568-70.

Lambert, M. E. see Medlicott, W. N.

Lamson, Peggy. The Glorious Failure: Black Congressman Robert
 Brown Elliott and the Reconstruction in South Carolina. New
 York: Norton, 1973. Rev. by F. J. Miller, JAH, 60(Mar
 1974):1138-9.

Landfester, Rüdiger. Historia Magistra Vitae. ... Geneva: Droz,
 1972. Rev. by A. Witschi-Bernz, H & T, 13(Num 2 1974):
 181-9.

Landsberg, Melvin. Dos Passos' Path to U. S. A. : A Political Bi-
 ography, 1912-1936. Boulder: Colo Associated U Press, 1972.
 Rev. by R. Pells, JAH, 61(Sep 1974):520-2; G. W. Johnson,
 MHM, 69(Spr 1974):111-12.

Lane, Ann J. , ed. The Debate Over Slavery: Stanley Elkins and
 His Critics. Urbana: U Ill Press, 1971. Rev. by S. W.
 Mintz, HAHR, 54(Feb 1974):117-18.

Lane, Frederic C. Venice: A Maritime Republic. Baltimore:
 JHU Press, 1973. Rev. by P. N. Bebb, HRNB, 2(Feb 1974):
 105-6.

Lane, James B. The Enduring Ghetto. see Goldfield, David R.

_____ . Jacob A. Riis and the American City. Port Washington,
 N. Y. : Kennikat, 1974. Rev. by S. T. McSeveney, HRNB, 3
 (Nov/Dec 1974):43-4.

Lane, Mills. Savannah Revisited. Savannah, Ga. : Beehive, 1973.
 Rev. by E. Paris, GHQ, 58(Sum 1974):287-8.

Langbein, John H. Prosecuting Crime in the Renaissance: England,
 Germany, France. Cambridge, Mass. : Har U Press, 1974.
 Rev. by D. Bitton, HRNB, 2(Jl 1974):210.

Langdon, F. C. Japan's Foreign Policy. Vancouver, B. C. : U BC
 Press, 1973. Rev. by T. J. Pempel, JAS, 34(Nov 1974):242-
 4.

Langer, Paul F. Communism in Japan: A Case of Political Naturalization. Stanford, Cal. : Hoover Institution Press, 1972.
 Rev. by R. J. Gowen, AHR, 79(Oct 1974):1233-4.

Langer, Walter C. The Mind of Adolf Hitler: The Secret Wartime
 Report. New York: Basic Books, 1972. Rev. by D. Orlow,
 JIH, 5(Sum 1974):131-8.

Langford, Paul. The First Rockingham Administration, 1765-1766. New York: Ox U Press, 1973. Rev. by P. D. G. Thomas, WMQ-3, 31(Jl 1974):498-501.

Langley, J. Ayodele. Pan-Africanism and Nationalism in West Africa 1900-1945. A Study in Ideology and Social Classes. Oxford: Clarendon Press, 1973. Rev. by I. Duffield, AfAf, 73(Jl 1974):376-7; P. O. Esedebe, JAfH, 15(Num 3 1974):513-15.

Langley, Lester D. Cuba: A Perennial Problem in American Foreign Policy. St. Charles, Mo.: Forum Press, 1974. Rev. by M. P. McCarthy, HT, 8(Nov 1974):109-10.

Langsam, Walter E. Preservation: Metropolitan Preservation Plan, Falls of Ohio Metropolitan Council of Governments. Louisville: n. p., 1973. Rev. by Mrs. I. Abell, Jr., FCHQ, 48(Ja 1974): 63.

Lanham, Url. The Bone Hunters. New York: Columbia U Press, 1973. Rev. by J. E. Allen, OrHQ, 75(Mar 1974):78-9; M. E. Taylor, UHQ, 42(Fall 1974):389-90; R. A. Bartlett, WHQ, 5 (Oct 1974):486-7.

Lanier, Sidney. Florida: Its Scenery, Climate, and History. Gainesville: U Fla Press, 1973. Rev. by H. S. Marks, RKHS, 72(Ja 1974):69-71.

Lanning, John Tate. Pedro de la Torre: Doctor to Conquerors. Baton Rouge: LSU Press, 1974. Rev. by C. E. Lida, HRNB, 3(Nov/Dec 1974):39.

Lantis, Margaret, ed. Ethnohistory in Southwestern Alaska and the Southern Yukon: Method and Content. Lexington, Ky.: U Ky Press, 1970. Rev. by M. Zaslow, CHR, 55(Mar 1974):82-4.

Lantzeff, George V. and Richard A. Pierce. Eastward to Empire: Exploration and Conquest on the Russian Open Empire, to 1750. Montreal: McGill and Queen's U Press, 1973. Rev. by R. H. Fisher, PHR, 43(May 1974):264-5.

Lapp, Paul W. Biblical Archaeology and History. New York: World, 1969. Rev. by K. M. Kenyon, Antiquity, 48(Je 1974): 155-6.

Large, Stephen S. The Rise of Labor in Japan: The Yuaikai, 1912-19. Tokyo: Sophia University, 1972. Rev. by G. D. Allinson, AHR, 79(Je 1974):826.

Larkin, James F. and Paul L. Hughes, eds. Stuart Royal Proclamations: Vol. I, Royal Proclamations of King James I, 1603-1625. Rev. by R. E. Schrieber, HRNB, 2(Apr 1974):140.

Larson, Bruce L. Lindbergh of Minnesota: A Political Biography.
New York: Harcourt Brace Jovanovich, 1973. Rev. by J. M.
Cooper, Jr. , JAH, 61(Sep 1974):517-18; P. H. Argersinger,
MiA, 56(Jl 1974):204-5.

Larson, Charles R. The Emergence of African Fiction. Bloomington: Ind U Press, 1972. Rev. by H. Dinwiddy, AfAf, 73(Jl
1974):379-81; S. O. Iyasere, JMAS, 12(Mar 1974):160-3.

Larson, Henrietta M. , Evelyn H. Knowlton, and Charles S. Popple.
History of Standard Oil Company (New Jersey). Vol. III: New
Horizons, 1927-1950. New York: Harper and Row, 1971.
Rev. by C. C. Jones, JAH, 60(Mar 1974):1174-5.

Lasarides, Demetri see Andronicos, Emmanuel

Lasch, Christopher. The World of Nations: Reflections on Ameri-
can History, Politics and Culture. New York: Knopf, 1973.
Rev. by A. Theoharis, Historian, 36(May 1974):571; K. J.
Hansen, PHR, 43(Aug 1974):412-13.

Laslett, John H. M. and Seymour Martin Lipset, eds. Failure of
a Dream? Essays in History of American Socialism. Garden
City, N.Y. : Anchor Press/Doubleday, 1974. Rev. by F. I.
Olson, HRNB, 3(Oct 1974):5-6.

Laslett, P. , ed. Household and Family in Past Time. Cambridge:
Cam U Press, 1972. Rev. by R. Mitchison, History, 59(Feb
1974):162-3; J. Modell, PHR, 43(Feb 1974):114-16.

Lass, William E. From the Missouri to the Great Salt Lake: An
Account of Overland Freighting. Lincoln: Neb State Historical
Society ... 1972. Rev. by H. L. Carter, AHR, 79(Apr 1974):
577-8; S. G. Jackson, CoMag, 51(Sum 1974):246-7; H. C.
Miner, JAH, 61(Je 1974):191-2; M. B. Husband, JOW, 13(Ja
1974):156; W. T. Jackson, PHR, 43(May 1974):273-4; R. G.
Athearn, PNQ, 65(Jl 1974):151; L. E. Oliva, WHQ, 5(Apr 1974):
216-17.

La Terreur, Marc, ed. Dictionary of Canadian Biography. X:
1871 to 1880. Toronto: U Tor Press; Quebec: Les Presses
de l'Universite Laval, 1972. Rev. by P. Rutherford, CHR, 55
(Je 1974):197-9.

Latham, A. J. H. Old Calabar 1600-1891: The Impact of the In-
ternational Economy Upon a Traditional Society. Oxford:
Clarendon Press, 1973. Rev. by P. E. H. Hair, History, 59
(Je 1974):305; G. I. Jones, JAfH, 15(Num 2 1974):328-30.

Latham, Robert and William Matthews, eds. The Diary of Samuel
Pepys, Vol. VIII. London: G. Bell, n. d. Rev. by P. Q. ,
HTo, 24(Sep 1974):659-61.

Latour da Veiga Pinto, Françoise. La Portugal et le Congo au
XIXᵉ Siècle. Paris: Presses Universitaires de France, 1972.
Rev. by R. Anstey, JAfH, 15(Num 1 1974):158-60.

Laude, Jean. The Arts of Black Africa. London: U Cal Press,
1971. Rev. by G. I. Jones, 44(Apr 1974):210-12.

Laue, David and George Kolaukiewicz, eds. Social Groups in Polish
Society. New York: Columbia U Press, 1973. Rev. by R. F.
Byrnes, T & C, 15(Apr 1974):349-51.

Laugher, Charles T. Thomas Bray's Grand Design: Libraries of
the Church of England in America, 1695-1785. Chicago: ALA,
1973. Rev. by E. G. Breslaw, MHM, 69(Fall 1974):328-9;
D. T. Morgan, NCHR, 51(Sum 1974):345-6; R. B. Davis,
VMHB, 82(Oct 1974):489-91.

Laurenson, Diana T. and Alan Swingewood. The Sociology of Literature. New York: Schocken, 1972. Rev. by L. B. Cebik,
GR, 28(Sum 1974):337-41.

Lavallée, Daniele. Les Représentations Animales dans la Céramique
Mochica. Paris: Université de Paris ... 1970. Rev. by C.
Donnan, AmAnt, 39(Apr 1974):396-8.

Laya, Dioulde, ed. La Tradition orale: problématique et méthodologie des sources de l'histoire Africaine. Niamey: Centre
régional de documentation pour la tradition orale, 1972. Rev.
by D. P. Henige, JAfH, 15(Ja 1974):153-4.

Lazitch, Branko and Milorad M. Drachkovitch. Lenin and the Comintern. Volume I. Stanford, Cal.: Hoover Institution Press,
1972. Rev. by R. H. McNeal, CHR, 55(Mar 1974):117-18.

Le Clèrc, Bernard and Vincent Wright. Les préfets du Second Empire. Paris: Armand Colin, 1973. Rev. by T. Margadant,
AHR, 79(Oct 1974):1191-2.

Leach, Barry A. German Strategy Against Russia, 1939-1941. New
York: Ox U Press, 1973. Rev. by E. F. Ziemke, AHR, 79
(Je 1974):807.

Leach, Douglas Edward. Arms for Empire: A Military History of
the British Colonies in North America, 1607-1763. New York:
Macmillan, 1973. Rev. by L. Bowman, Historian, 36(Aug
1974):772-3; J. A. Huston, IMH, 70(Mar 1974):79-80; C. E.
Clark, JAH, 61(Je 1974):156-7; H. M. Ward, JISHS, 67(Sep
1974):449-50; J. M. Sosin, JSH, 40(Feb 1974):120-2; S. S.
Cohen, MiA, 56(Ja 1974):56; I. D. Gruber, NEQ, 47(Mar 1974):
148-50; P. M. Malone, NYH, 55(Apr 1974):246-7; L. M. Waddell, PH, 41(Oct 1974):462-4; M. Savelle, PHR, 43(Feb 1974):
112-14; R. R. Johnson, PNQ, 65(Ja 1974):40; W. D. Gilliam,
Jr., RKHS, 72(Ja 1974):59-61; J. Leland, SCHM, 75(Ja 1974):
58-9; W. J. Eccles, WMQ-3, 31(Jl 1974):501-3.

Lease, Benjamin. That Wild Fellow John Neal, and the American Literary Revolution. Chicago: U Chi Press, 1973. Rev. by M. Allen, JAmS, 8(Aug 1974):274-5.

LeBar, Frank M., ed. and comp. Ethnic Groups of Insular Southeast Asia. Volume 1: Indonesia, Andaman Islands and Madagascar. New Haven, Conn.: HRAF Press, 1973. Rev. by A. A. Yengoyan, JAS, 33(May 1974):500-1.

Lechner, Norbert. La democracia en Chile. Buenos Aires: Ediciones Signos, 1970. Rev. by S. Collier, JLAS, 6(May 1974): 182-5.

Ledbetter, Calvin R., Jr., et al. Politics in Arkansas: The Constitutional Experience. Little Rock: Academic Press, Ark, 1972. Rev. by J. E. Griner, ArkHQ, 33(Spr 1974):94-5.

Ledeen, Michael A. Universal Fascism. The Theory and Practice of the Fascist International: 1828-1936. New York: Howard Fertig, 1972. Rev. by S. Wilson, History, 59(Feb 1974):155; R. Vivarelli, HJ, 17(Num 3 1974):644-51.

Leder, Lawrence H. America--1603-1789: Prelude to a Nation. Minneapolis: Burgess, 1972. Rev. by R. S. Nelson, Jr., PH, 41(Apr 1974):221-2.

————, ed. The Colonial Legacy. Volume 1, Loyalist Historians; Volume 2, Some Eighteenth-Century Commentators. New York: Harper and Row, 1971. Rev. by A. O. Aldridge, AHR, 79 (Apr 1974):572.

————, ed. The Colonial Legacy: Vol. III, Historians of Nature and Man's Nature; Vol. IV, Early Nationalist Historians. New York: Harper and Row, 1974. Rev. by R. M. Johnson, HRNB, 2(Jl 1974):192.

Lee, Bradford A. Britain and the Sino-Japanese War, 1937-1939: A Study in the Dilemmas of British Decline. Stanford: Stan U Press, 1973. Rev. by C. Thorne, AHR, 79(Apr 1974):516-17; H. Conroy, Historian, 36(May 1974):549-50; F. E. Rogers, JAS, 34(Nov 1974):224-5.

Lee, C. M. A Cotton Enterprise 1795-1840: A History of McConnel and Kennedy, Fine Cotton Spinners. Manchester: Manchester U Press, 1972. Rev. by D. Bythell, EHR, 89(Apr 1974):455.

Lee, Hilda I. Malta 1813-1914: A Study in Constitutional and Strategic Development. Valletta: Progress, n.d. Rev. by R. Albrecht-Carrié, AHR, 79(Oct 1974):1173-4.

Lee, Joseph. The Modernisation of Irish Society, 1848-1918. Dublin: Gill and Macmillan, 1973. Rev. by J. C. Beckett, History, 59(Feb 1974):130-1.

Lee, Leo Ou-fan. The Romantic Generation of Modern Chinese
Writers. Cambridge, Mass.: Har U Press, 1973. Rev. by
F. P. Brandauer, JAS, 34(Nov 1974):215-17.

Lee, Maurice, Jr. , ed. Dudley Carleton to John Chamberlain 1603-
1624; Jacobean Letters. New Brunswick, N. J.: Rutgers U
Press, 1972. Rev. by G. E. Aylmer, EHR, 89(Jl 1974):666-
7.

Lee, Peter H. , comp. and trans. Poems from Korea: A Historical
Anthology. Honolulu: U Press Hawaii, 1974. Rev. by Doo
Soo Suh, JAS, 34(Nov 1974):207-10.

Lee, R. Alton. A History of Regulatory Taxation. Lexington, Ky.:
U Press Ky, 1973. Rev. by M. W. M. Hargreaves, FCHQ,
48(Jl 1974):278-9.

Leene, Jentina E. Textile Conservation. Washington, D. C.: Smithsonian Institution, 1972. Rev. by G. W. Cooper, T & C, 15
(Spr 1974):363-65.

Lefler, Hugh Talmage and Albert Ray Newsome. North Carolina:
The History of a Southern State. Chapel Hill: U NC Press,
1973. Rev. by R. N. Elliott, NCHR, 51(Jan 1974):92-3.

_____ and William S. Powell. Colonial North Carolina: A History. New York: Scribner's, 1973. Rev. by J. Levin, HRNB,
2(Feb 1974):95; R. M. Jellison, JAH, 61(Dec 1974):761-3;
J. L. Anderson, JSH, 40(Aug 1974):458-9; J. P. Greene,
NCHR, 51(Spr 1974):225-6; J. J. Nadelhaft, WMQ-3, 31(Jl
1974):507-9.

Lehmann, William C. Henry Home, Lord Kames and the Scottish
Enlightenment: A Study in National Character and in the His-
tory of Ideas. The Hague: Martinus Nijhoff, 1971. Rev. by
M. Lee, Jr. , AHR, 79(Apr 1974):514.

Lehning, Arthur. Michel Bakounine et ses relations avec Sergej
Necaev, 1870-1872: Ecrits et matériaux. Leiden: E. J.
Brill, 1971. Rev. by P. Avrich, AHR, 79(Apr 1974):536-7.

Leifer, Michael. Dilemmas of Statehood in Southeast Asia. Vancouver: U BC Press, 1972. Rev. by K. G. Machado, JAS,
33(Feb 1974):328-9.

Leighton, Albert C. Transport and Communication in Early Modern
Europe, A. D. 500-1100. Newton Abbot: David and Charles,
1971. Rev. by R. H. C. Davis, EHR, 89(Apr 1974):416.

Leisinger, Albert H. , Jr. A Study of the Basic Standards for Equipping, Maintaining, and Operating a Reprographic Laboratory in

Archives of Developing Countries. Brussels: International
Council on Archives ... 1973. Rev. by C. W. Nelson, AmArc,
37(Oct 1974):586-7.

Leiva Vivas, Rafael. Los Tratados Internacionales de Honduras.
Tegucigalpa: Universidad Nacional Autonoma de Honduras, 1971.
Rev. by T. Schoonover, TAm, 30(Apr 1974):551-2.

Lemarchand, Rene. Ruanda and Burundi. New York: Praeger,
1970. Rev. by Y. Saffu, JAAS, 9(Ja & Apr 1974):118-20.

Lemmon, Sarah McCulloh. Frustrated Patriots: North Carolina and
the War of 1812. Chapel Hill: UNC Press, 1973. Rev. by
R. F. Weigley, HRNB, 2(Feb 1974):93-4; R. H. Brown, JAH,
61(Dec 1974):776-7; J. H. Broussard, JSH, 40(May 1974):304-
5; J. K. Mahon, NCHR, 51(Ja 1974):91-2.

Lemons, J. Stanley. The Woman Citizen: Social Feminism in the
1920s. Urbana: U Ill Press, 1973. Rev. by B. Welter, AHR,
79(Je 1974):894-5; R. L. Pearson, Historian, 36(May 1974):
576-7; G. T. Blakey, HT, 7(Feb 1974):316-17; A. K. Harris,
JISHS, 67(Sep 1974):445-6.

Lennon, Donald R. and Ida Brooks Kellam, eds. The Wilmington
Town Book, 1743-1778. Raleigh: Div. Archives and History,
N.C. Dept. Cultural Resources, 1973. Rev. by D. M. Mc-
Farland, HRNB, 2(Ja 1974):67-8; R. N. Olsberg, JSH, 40(Aug
1974):459-60; A. D. Watson, NCHR, 51(Spr 1974):224-5; L.
Lee. SCHM, 75(Apr 1974):125.

Lens, Sidney. The Forging of the American Empire. New York:
Crowell, 1971. Rev. by R. M. Abrams, AHR, 79(Je 1974):
834-5.

Lensen, George Alexander. The Damned Inheritance: The Soviet
Union and the Manchurian Crises, 1924-1935. Tallahassee,
Fla.: Diplomatic Press, 1974. Rev. by E. Anderson, HRNB,
3(Oct 1974):10; J. J. Stephan, JAS, 34(Nov 1974):212-13.

_____. The Strange Neutrality: Soviet-Japanese Relations During
the Second World War, 1941-1945. Tallahassee, Fla.: Diplomatic Press, 1972. Rev. by G. R. Falconeri, AHR, 79(Apr
1974):559-60.

Lentz, Andrea D. and Sara S. Fuller, eds. A Guide to Manuscripts
at the Ohio Historical Society. Columbus: Ohio Historical
Society, 1972. Rev. by H. Finch, OH, 83(Spr 1974):149-50.

Leon, Christoph F. Die Bauornamentik des Trajansforums und ihre
Stellung in der Früh-und Mittelkaiserzeitlichen Architekturde-
koration Roms. Wien-Köln-Graz: n.p., 1971. Rev. by D.
White, AJA, 78(Apr 1974):209.

LEON 212

Léon, Pierre, et al., eds. L'industrialisation en Europe au XIXe siècle: Cartographie et typologie (Lyon 7-10 octobre 1970). Paris: the Centre, 1972. Rev. by P. N. Stearns, AHR, 79 (Oct 1974):1142-3.

Leon-Portilla, Miguel. Voyages of Francisco de Ortega, California, 1632-1636. Los Angeles: Dawson's Book Shop, 1973. Rev. by H. P. Hinton, SCQ, 56(Fall 1974):319-21.

Lerner, Gerda, ed. Black Women in White America. A Documentary History. New York: Pantheon, 1972. Rev. by E. L. Thornbrough, Historian, 36(Feb 1974):348-9.

_____. The Woman in American History. Menlo Park, Cal.: Addison-Wesley, 1971. Rev. by K. Xidis, HT, 8(Nov 1974): 124-5.

Lerner, Robert E. The Heresy of the Free Spirit in the Later Middle Ages. Berkeley: U Cal Press, 1972. Rev. by H. S. Offler, EHR, 89(Ja 1974):165; M. D. Lambert, History, 59(Feb 1974):92-3.

Lerner, Warren. Karl Radek: The Last Internationalist. Stanford, Cal.: Stan U Press, 1970. Rev. by H. J. Rogger, AHR, 79 (Apr 1974):553-4.

Lesky, Erna and Adam Wandrusza, eds. Gerard van Swieten und seine zeit.... Vienna: Verlag Hermann Böhlaus Nachf., 1973. Rev. by W. J. McGill, AHR, 79(Oct 1974):1208-9.

Leslie, Vernon E. Faces in Clay: The Archaeology and Early History of the Red Man in the Upper Delaware Valley. Middletown, N.Y.: T. Emmett Henderson, 1973. Rev. by R. F. W. Meader, NYH, 55(Ja 1974):107-8.

Lesy, Michael. Wisconsin Death Trip. New York: Pantheon, 1973. Rev. by D. E. Ball, JEH, 34(Je 1974):509-10; M. Hough, MiA, 56(Apr 1974):131-3; A. Allegretti, NDH, 41(Fall 1974):31-2.

Letarte, Jacques. Atlas d'histoire économique et sociale du Québec 1851-1901. Montreal: Fides, 1971. Rev. by J. E. Igartua, CHR, 55(Mar 1974):87-9.

Leuzinger, Elsy. The Art of Black Africa. London: Studio Vista, 1972. Rev. by G. I. Jones, Africa, 44(Apr 1974):210-12.

Levack, Brian P. The Civil Lawyers in England, 1603-1641: A Political Study. New York: Ox U Press, 1973. Rev. by C. Zinberg, AHR, 79(Oct 1974):1177-8; G. R. Elton, HJ, 17 (Mar 1974):213-16.

Levenstein, Harvey A. Labor Organizations in the United States and Mexico: A History of Their Relations. Westport, Conn.:

Greenwood, 1971. Rev. by G. N. Green, AHR, 79(Oct 1974):
1275-6.

Lever, Henry. The South African Voter: Some Aspects of Voting
Behavior.... Capetown: Juta, 1972. Rev. by S. J. Morse,
JMAS, 12(Mar 1974):141-3.

Levet, Richard H. Ambrose L. (Aqua Fortis) Jordan, Lawyer.
New York: Vantage, 1973. Rev. by I. T. Kelsay, NYH, 55
(Jl 1974):339-41.

Levi-Strauss, Claude. Tristes Tropiques. New York: Atheneum,
n. d. Rev. by F. Lipsius, Commentary, 58(Sep 1974):88, 90-1.

Levin, N. Gordon, Jr., ed. The Zionist Movement in Palestine and
World Politics, 1880-1918. Lexington, Mass.: D. C. Heath,
1973. Rev. by W. Spencer, HRNB, 2(Jl 1974):205.

Levine, Daniel H. Conflict and Political Change in Venezuela.
Princeton, N.J.: Prin U Press, 1973. Rev. by E. J. Stann,
HAHR, 54(Feb 1974):148-50.

Levine, Erwin L. Theodore Francis Green: The Washington Years,
1937-1960. Providence, R.I.: Brown U Press, 1971. Rev.
by P. L. Silver, AHR, 79(Je 1974):901-2.

Levine, Herbert S. Hitler's Free City: A History of the Nazi
Party in Danzig, 1925-39. Chicago: U Chi Press, 1973.
Rev. by B. B. Frye, HRNB, 2(Ja 1974):82-3.

Levtzion, Nehemia. Ancient Ghana and Mali. London: Methuen,
1973. Rev. by H. J. Fisher, History, 59(Je 1974):304.

Levy, David W. see Urofsky, Melvin I.

Levy, Eugene. James Weldon Johnson: Black Leader, Black Voice.
Chicago: U Chi Press, 1973. Rev. by A. Hornsby, Jr., JSH,
40(May 1974):346.

Levy, Eugene D. see Fowler, David H.

Levytsky, Borys, comp. The Stalinist Terror in the Thirties: Documentation from the Soviet Press. Stanford, Cal.: Hoover Institution Press, 1974. Rev. by L. J. Williames, HRNB, 2
(Sep 1974):243.

Lewalski, Barbara Kiefer. Donne's Anniversaries and the Poetry
of Praise. Princeton, N.J.: Prin U Press, 1973. Rev. by
W. G. Ingram, RQ, 27(Fall 1974):370-2.

Lewin, Günter. Die Ersten Fünfzig Jahre der Song-Dynastie in
China: Beitrag zu einer Analyse der sozialökonomischen Formation während der ersten fünfzig Jahre der chinesischen Song-

Dynastie (960-ca. 1010). Berlin: Akademie-Verlag, 1973.
Rev. by C. Schirokauer, JAS, 33(May 1974):461-2.

Lewin, Ronald. Churchill as Warlord. New York: Stein and Day,
1974. Rev. by A. J. Ward, HRNB, 2(May/Je 1974):186.

Lewis, Bernard. Islam in History: Ideas, Men and Events in the
Middle East. La Salle, Ill.: Open Court, 1973. Rev. by
L. C. Rose, HRNB, 2(Mar 1974):125.

Lewis, Henry T. Ilocano Rice Farmers: A Comparative Study of
Two Philippine Barrios. Honolulu: U Hawaii Press, 1971.
Rev. by A. A. Yengoyan, JAS, 33(May 1974):505.

Lewis, W. S., ed. Selected Letters of Horace Walpole. New
Haven, Conn.: Yale U Press, 1973. Rev. by A. A. Hansen,
HT, 8(Nov 1974):141-2.

Lewy, Guenter. Religion and Revolution. Oxford: Ox U Press,
n. d. Rev. by J. Hitchcock, Commentary, 58(Nov 1974):92,
94, 96.

Lhotsky, Alphons. Das Zeitalter des Hauses Österreich: Die ersten
Jahre der Regierung Ferdinands I. in Osterreich (1520-1527).
Vienna: Hermann Böhlaus Nachf, 1971. Rev. by F. G. Hey-
mann, 807-9.

Liang, Chin-Tung. General Stilwell in China, 1942-1944: The Full
Story. Jamaica, N. Y.: St. John's U Press, 1972. Rev. by
C. C. Tan, AHR, 79(Oct 1974):1286-7; R. F. Weigley, His-
torian, 36(May 1974):556-7.

Lichauco, Alejandro. The Lichauco Paper: Imperialism in the
Philippines. New York: Monthly Review Press, 1973. Rev.
by R. E. Welch, Jr., HRNB, 2(Jl 1974):204.

Lichtenstein, W. H. C. 1. Foundation of the Cape. 2. About
the Bechuanas. Capetown: A. A. Balkema, 1973. Rev. by
S. M., JAfH, 15(Num 2 1974):349.

Lichtheim, George. Europe in the Twentieth Century. London:
Weidenfeld and Nicolson, 1972. Rev. by S. Wilson, History,
59(Feb 1974):139-40.

Lida, Clara E. Anarquismo y revolución en la España del XIX.
Madrid: Siglo XXI de España Editores, 1972. Rev. by J. C.
Ullman, AHR, 79(Oct 1974):1196-7; E. Malafakis, HAHR, 54
(Nov 1974):739-40; M. Ackelsberg, JMH, 46(Mar 1974):147-8.

Liddell-Hart, B. H. Why Don't We Learn From History? London:
Allen and Unwin, 1972. Rev. by M. Howard, History, 59
(Feb 1974):160.

Liebknecht, Wilhelm. Briefwechsel mit deutschen Sozialdemokraten
    Vol. 1, 1862-1878. Assen: Van Gorcum, 1973. Rev. by
    V. L. Lidtke, AHR, 79(Oct 1974):1203-4.

Liechty, Edward E. The Plain People: Left Wing of the Reforma-
    tion. Berne, Ind.: Publisher's Printing House, 1973. Rev.
    by L. H. Zuck, CH, 43(Mar 1974):110-11.

Liège et Bourgogne: Actes du colloque tenu à Liège les 28, 29 et
    30 Octobre 1968. Paris: Société d'Edition "Les Belles Let-
    tres," 1972. Rev. by B. Lyon, AHR, 79(Apr 1974):498-9; M.
    Jones, History, 59(Je 1974):260-1.

Liehr, Reinhard. Stadrat und Stadlische Oberschicht von Puebla am
    enden der Kolonialzeit, 1787-1810. Wiesbaden: Frany Steiner
    Verlag, 1971. Rev. by J. Malagón, TAm, 30(Apr 1974):545-6.

Lievsay, John Leon. Venetian Phoenix: Paolo Sarpi and Some of
    His English Friends (1606-1700). Lawrence: U Press Kan,
    1973. Rev. by F. V. Mills, Sr., CH, 43(Sep 1974):407-9.

Lifshey, Earl. The Housewares Story--A History of the American
    Housewares Industry. Chicago: National Housewares Mfrs
    Assn, 1973. Rev. by M. J. Kinsman, FCHQ, 48(Ja 1974):65-
    6; S. Goldfarb, T & C, 15(Jl 1974):502-3.

Limbaugh, Ronald H. see Marquis, Thomas B.

Lincoln, C. Eric. The Black Muslims in America. Boston: Bea-
    con, 1973. Rev. by L. H. Fishel, Jr., JAH, 60(Mar 1974):
    1185-6.

Lindbeck, John M. China: Management of a Revolutionary Society.
    London: Allen and Unwin, 1971. Rev. by G. D. Deshingkar,
    CR, 10(May-Je 1974):63-5.

Linden, Ian and Jane. Catholics, Peasants and Chewa Resistance
    in Nyasaland 1889-1939. Berkeley: U Cal Press, 1974. Rev.
    by B. Fetter, HRNB, 3(Nov/Dec 1974):38.

Lindsay, Diana. Our Historic Desert: The Story of the Anza-Bor-
    rego Desert. San Diego: Copley Books, 1973. Rev. by R. G.
    Lillard, CHQ, 53(Sum 1974):183-4; R. Leadabrand, SCQ, 56
    (Fall 1974):315-16.

Lindsay, T. F. and Michael Harrington. The Conservative Party,
    1918-1970. New York: St. Martin's, 1974. Rev. by L. J.
    Satre, HRNB, 2(Sep 1974):237-8.

Lindsey, David. Americans in Conflict: The Civil War and Recon-
    struction. Boston: Houghton Mifflin, 1974. Rev. by N. A.
    Kuntz, HRNB, 2(Mar 1974):129.

Lings, Martin. A Sufi Saint of the Twentieth Century: Shaikh Ah-
      med al-'Alawi. His Spiritual Heritage and Legacy. Berkeley:
      U Cal Press, 1971. Rev. by J. Kritzeck, AHR, 79(Feb 1974):
      206-7.

Link, Arthur S. , David W. Hirst, John E. Little, Jean Maclachlan,
      M. Halsey Thomas, and John M. Mulder, eds. The Papers of
      Woodrow Wilson. Vol. 14. 1902-1903. Princeton, N. J. :
      Prin U Press, 1972. Rev. by R. L. Church, AHR, 79(Feb
      1974):242-3; D. W. Grantham, JAH, 60(Mar 1974):1075-7;
      V. A. Carrafiello, PH, 41(Ja 1974):106-8.

_____, et al. , eds. The Papers of Woodrow Wilson. Volume 15,
      1903-1905. Princeton, N. J. : Prin U Press, 1973. Rev. by
      H. Hawkins, AHR, 79(Apr 1974):600-1; D. W. Granthan, JAH,
      60(Mar 1974):1075-7; V. A. Carrafiello, PH, 41(Apr 1974):
      239-42.

_____, et al. , eds. The Papers of Woodrow Wilson. Vol. 16.
      1905-1907. Princeton, N. J. : Prin U Press, 1974. Rev. by
      A. Erlebacher, HRNB, 2(Mar 1974):134-5; P. Coletta, WVH,
      35(Jl 1974):321-3.

Lipset, Seymour Martin. Rebellion in the University. Boston: Lit-
      tle, Brown, 1972. Rev. by W. L. O'Neill, AHR, 79(Je 1974):
      911-12.

_____. see Laslett, John H. M.

Lissington, M. P. New Zealand and Japan, 1900-41. Wellington,
      N. Z. : Government Printer, 1972. Rev. by I. Nish, EHR, 89
      (Jl 1974):690.

Littell, Franklin H. and Hubert G. Locke, eds. The German
      Church Struggle and the Holocaust. Detroit: Wayne St U
      Press, 1974. Rev. by G. Lewy, CH, 43(Sep 1974):415-16;
      S. M. Bolkosky, HRNB, 2(May/Je 1974):178-9.

Little, John E. see Link, Arthur S.

Litvak, B. G. Russian Villages During the 1861 Reform: The
      Black-Soil Center, 1861-1895. Moscow: Izdatel'stvo "Nauka, "
      1972. Rev. by G. Yaney, AHR, 79(Oct 1974):1221-2.

Litvin, Martin, ed. Voices of the Prairie Land. Galesburg, Ill. :
      Log City Books, n. d. Rev. by M. V. Schulz, JISHS, 67(Apr
      1974):240-1.

Liu, James T. C. , ed. Political Institutions in Traditional China:
      Major Issues. New York: Wiley, 1974. Rev. by J. W.
      Dardess, HRNB, 3(Nov/Dec 1974):36.

Livermore, H. V. The Origins of Spain and Portugal. London:

George Allen and Unwin, 1971. Rev. by J. N. Hillgarth, AHR, 79(Apr 1974):499-500.

_____. Portugal: A Short History. Chicago: Aldine-Atherton, 1973. Rev. by G. Addy, AHR, 79(Oct 1974):1199-1201; T. Tortella-Casares, HAHR, 54(Nov 1974):699-702.

Livesay, Harold see Porter, Glenn. Merchants and Manufacturers.

Livingood, James W. see Raulston, J. Leonard.

Livingston, Jon, Joe Moore, and Felicia Oldfather, eds. Imperial Japan, 1800-1945. New York: Pantheon, 1974. Rev. by D. L. Spencer, HRNB, 2(Apr 1974):145-6.

Liyong, Taban lo, ed. Popular Culture of East Africa: Oral Literature. Nairobi: Longman, 1972. Rev. by A. Ricard, JMAS, 12(Mar 1974):163-5.

Lloyd, Alan. Marathon: The Story of Civilizations on Collison Course. New York: Random House, 1973. Rev. by B. C. P. Tsangadas, Historian, 36(May 1974):533-4.

Lloyd, Craig. Aggressive Introvert: A Study of Herbert Hoover and Public Relations Management, 1912-1932. Columbus, Ohio: Ohio St U Press, 1972. Rev. by R. K. Murray, AHR, 79(Apr 1974):606-7; A. R. Raucher, BHR, 48(Spr 1974):135-6; R. T. Reutten, Historian, 36(Aug 1974):789-90.

Lloyd, Howell A. The Rouen Campaign, 1590-1592: Politics: Warfare and the Early Modern State. New York: Ox U Press, 1973. Rev. by D. Bitton, HRNB, 2(Feb 1974):109.

_____. see Connell-Smith, Gordon

Locke, Hubert G. see Littell, Franklin H.

Locke, Robert R. French Legitimists and the Politics of Moral Order in the Early Third Republic. Princeton, N. J.: Prin U Press, 1974. Rev. by S. E. Cooper, HRNB, 2(Sep 1974): 234.

Lockhart, James. The Men of Cajamarca: A Social and Biographical Study of the First Conquerors of Peru. Austin: U Tx Press, 1972. Rev. by R. C. Padden, HAHR, 54(Feb 1974): 125-7; J. Fisher, JLAS, 6(May 1974):172-3.

Loeber, Dietrich A., ed. Diktierte Option: Die Umsiedlung der Deutsch-Balten aus Estland und Lettland, 1939-1941. Neumünster: Karl Wachholtz Verlag, 1973. Rev. by E. Anderson, AHR, 79(Feb 1974):187-8.

Loewenberg, Bert James. American History in American Thought.

Christopher Columbus to Henry Adams. New York: Simon and Schuster, 1972. Rev. by J. Higham, H & T, 13(Num 1 1974):78-83.

Loftis, Anne. California: Where the Twain Did Meet. New York: Macmillan, 1973. Rev. by C. Wollenberg, CHQ, 53(Spr 1974): 88-9; A. Rolle, PHR, 43(Feb 1974):122-3.

Logan, Oliver. Culture and Society in Venice, 1470-1790: The Renaissance and Its Heritage. London: Batsford, 1972. Rev. by P. J. Loven, History, 59(Feb 1974):106-7.

Logsdon, Joseph. Horace White, Nineteenth-Century Liberal. Westport, Conn.: Greenwood, 1971. Rev. by H. D. Shapiro, AHR, 79(Oct 1974):1273-4.

Logue, William. Léon Blum: The Formative Years, 1872-1914. De Kalb: N Ill U Press, 1973. Rev. by E. Weber, AHR, 79 (Je 1974):792-3.

Lomask, Milton see Green, Constance McLaughlin

Lombard, Maurice. Espaces et réseaux du haut Moyen Age. Paris: Mouton, 1972. Rev. by A. L. Udovitch, AHR, 79(Je 1974): 770.

_____. Monnaie et histoire d'Alexandre à Mahomet. Paris and the Hague: Mouton, 1971. Rev. by N. A. Stillman, JEH, 34 (Sep 1974):793-5.

Long, Ngo Vinh. Before the Revolution: The Vietnamese Peasants Under the French. Cambridge, Mass.: M I T Press, 1973. Rev. by J. F. Cady, HRNB, 2(May/Je 1974):175.

Longacre, Edward G. From Union Stars to Top Hat: A Biography of the Extraordinary General James Harrison Wilson. Harrisburg, Pa.: Stackpole, 1972. Rev. by J. Monaghan, AHR, 79 (Apr 1974):587-9.

Longford, Elizabeth. Wellington: Pillar of State. London: Weidenfeld and Nicolson, 1972. Rev. by I. R. Christie, History, 59 (Feb 1974):121.

Longworth, Philip. The Three Empresses: Catherine I, Anne and Elizabeth of Russia. New York: Holt, Rinehart and Winston, 1973. Rev. by J. T. Fuhrmann, AHR, 79(Feb 1974):198-9.

Looney, Ben Earl. Beau Sejour: Watercolors of the Louisiana Plantation Country. Baton Rouge, La.: Claitor's Pub. Div., 1972. Rev. by A. E. Simpson, LaH, 15(W 1974):83.

Lopez, Claude see Willcox, William B.

Lopez, R. S. The Commercial Revolution of the Middle Ages, 950-1350. Englewood Cliffs, N. J.: Prentice-Hall, 1971. Rev. by B. Harvey, EHR, 89(Ja 1974):148-9.

Lopez, Teofanes Egido. Opinion Publica y Oposicion al Poder en la Espana del Siglo XVIII (1713-1759). Valladolid: The University, 1971. Rev. by H. Kamen, EHR, 89(Jl 1974):670.

Lord, Walter. The Dawn's Early Light. New York: Norton, 1972. Rev. by M. M. LeBreton, LaH, 15(Spr 1974):204-5.

Lorenz, Alfred Lawrence. Hugh Gaine, a Colonial Printer's Odyssey to Loyalism. Carbondale: S Ill U Press, 1972. Rev. by P. C. Hoffer, NYH, 55(Ja 1974):102-3.

Lorwin, Val R. and Jacob M. Price, eds. The Dimensions of the Past: Materials, Problems, and Opportunities for Quantitative Work in History. New Haven, Conn.: Yale U Press, 1972. Rev. by C. M. Dollar, Historian, 36(Feb 1974):304-6; R. Floud, History, 59(Feb 1974):159.

Lotchin, Roger W. San Francisco, 1846-1856: From Hamlet to City. New York: Ox U Press, 1974. Rev. by W. H. Pease, HRNB, 2(Aug 1974):219; A. J. Moyer, SWHQ, 78(Oct 1974): 228-9.

Lottinville, Savoie see Hine, Robert V.

_____. see Wilhelm, Paul, Duke of Wurttemberg

Lötveit, Trygve. Chinese Communism, 1931-1934: Experience in Civil Government. Lund, Sweden: Studentlitteratur, 1973. Rev. by L. P. Van Slyke, JAS, 33(Aug 1974):698-701.

Loubère, Leo A. Radicalism in Mediterranean France: Its Rise and Decline, 1848-1914. Albany: SUNY Press, 1974. Rev. by G. Baer, HRNB, 3(Oct 1974):15.

Louis, William Roger see Gifford, Prosser

Love, Frank. Mining Camps and Ghost Towns: A History of Mining in Arizona and California Along the Lower Colorado. Los Angeles: Westernlore, 1974. Rev. by J. B. Harte, JAriH, 15 (Win 1974):395-6; H. P. Walker, UHQ, 42(Fall 1974):392-3.

Love, Paula McSpadden. The Will Rogers Book. Waco, Tx.: Texian, 1972. Rev. by J. A. Stout, Jr., ChOk, 52(Fall 1974): 386-7.

Lovejoy, David S. The Glorious Revolution in America. New York: Harper & Row, 1972. Rev. by S. S. Webb, MHM, 69(Spr 1974):98-100; H. M. Ward, NYH, 55(Jl 1974):348-50; G. Parkinson, WVH, 35(Apr 1974):244-5.

Loveland, Anne C. Emblem of Liberty: The Image of Lafayette in the American Mind. Baton Rouge: LSU Press, 1971. Rev. by M. W. Fishwick, AHR, 79(Je 1974):848.

Lovell, John, Jr. Black Song: The Forge and the Flame. New York: Macmillan, 1972. Rev. by H. H. Hudson, NYH, 55 (Apr 1974):249-50.

Lovett, Clara Maria. Carlo Cattaneo and the Politics of the Risorgimento, 1820-1860. The Hague: Martinus Nijhoff, 1972. Rev. by E. P. Noether, AHR, 79(Feb 1974):183; R. Grew, JMH, 46(Sep 1974):553-4.

Lowe, Alfonso. The Catalan Vengeance. Boston: Routledge and Kegan Paul, 1972. Rev. by A. Mackay, History, 59(Feb 1974): 96.

_____. La Serenissima: The Last Flowering of the Venetian Republic. London: Cassell, n. d. Rev. by S. Harcourt-Smith, HTo, 24(Sep 1974):657.

Lowe, E. A. Palaeographical Papers, 1907-1965. Oxford: Clarendon Press, 1970. Rev. by W. M. Stevens, CH, 43(Dec 1974): 536-7; P. H. Blair, EHR, 89(Ja 1974):111-13.

_____, ed. Codices Latini Antiquiores. Part 2: Great Britain and Ireland. Oxford: Clarendon Press, 1972. Rev. by L. Yeandle, AmArc, 37(Apr 1974):293-5; P. H. Blair, EHR, 89 (Ja 1974):111-13.

Lowenthal, Abraham F. The Dominican Intervention. Cambridge, Mass.: Har U Press, 1972. Rev. by I. F. Gellman, JAH, 61(Dec 1974):844-5; S. R. Ross, PHR, 43(Feb 1974):139-40.

Lowenthal, David. West Indian Societies. New York: Ox U Press, 1972. Rev. by J. S. Macdonald, JLAS, 6(May 1974):189-91.

Lower, Arthur R. M. Great Britain's Woodyard: British America and the Timber Trade, 1763-1867. Montreal: McGill-Queen's U Press, 1973. Rev. by R. G. Albion, AHR, 79(Apr 1974): 570-1.

Lowitt, Richard. George W. Norris: The Persistence of a Progressive, 1913-1933. Urbana: U Ill Press, 1971. Rev. by O. B. Faulk, JOW, 13(Oct 1974):130; D. W. Levy, WMH, 57 (Win 1973-74):162-3.

Lowy, Michael. The Marxism of Che Guevara: Philosophy, Economics, and Revolutionary Warfare. New York: Monthly Review Press, 1973. Rev. by M. Zeitlin, HAHR, 54(Nov 1974): 715-18.

Lucas, Colin. The Structure of the Terror: The Example of

Javogues and the Loire. New York: Ox U Press, 1973. Rev. by P. Dawson, AHR, 79(Oct 1974):1189-90; J. McManners, EHR, 89(Apr 1974):394-7.

Lucke, Mary M. *Gloriana: The Years of Elizabeth I.* New York: Coward, McCann and Geohegan, 1973. Rev. by R. E. Schreiber, HRNB, 2(Feb 1974):108.

Luckett, Richard. *The White Generals: An Account of the White Movement and the Russian Civil War.* New York: Viking, 1971. Rev. by J. A. White, AHR, 79(Apr 1974):549-51; H. Hanak, EHR, 89(Ja 1974):235-6.

Luckham, Robin. *The Nigerian Military: A Sociological Analysis of Authority and Revolt, 1960-67.* Cambridge: Cam U Press, 1971. Rev. by S. C. Sarkesian, JMAS, 12(Je 1974):338-41.

Luddington, Townsend, ed. *The Fourteenth Chronicle: Letters and Diaries of John Dos Passos.* Boston: Gambit, 1973. Rev. by R. J. Cooke, HRNB, 2(Ja 1974):70.

Ludmerer, Kenneth M. *Genetics and American Society: A Historical Appraisal.* Baltimore: JHU Press, 1972. Rev. by T. Dobzhansky, AHR, 79(Apr 1974):563-4; W. Stanton, JAH, 61 (Je 1974):225-6.

Lukacs, Georg. *Tactics and Ethics: Political Essays, 1919-1929.* New York: Harper and Row, 1974. Rev. by M. Berger, HRNB, 2(Sep 1974):247.

Lukken, G. M. *Original Sin in the Roman Liturgy.* Leiden: E. J. Brill, 1973. Rev. by H. Davies, CH, 43(Sep 1974):530-1.

Luschei, Martin. *The Sovereign Wayfarer: Walker Percy's Diagnosis of the Malaise.* Baton Rouge: LSU Press, 1972. Rev. by P. L. Gaston, GR, 28(Fall 1974):540-3.

Luscombe, D. E., ed. and trans. *Peter Abelard's Ethics.* Oxford: Ox U Press, 1971. Rev. by B. Smalley, EHR, 89(Ja 1974):154-5; C. J. Holdsworth, History, 59(Je 1974):252-3.

Lutz, G. *Kardinal Giovanni Francesco di Bagno. Politik und Religion im Zeitalter Richelieus.* Tübingen: Max Niemeyer Verlag, 1971. Rev. by J. W. Stoye, EHR, 89(Apr 1974):437-8.

Lutz, H. and A. Kohler, eds. *Das Reichslagsprotokoll des kaiserlichen Kommissars Felix Hornung von Ausburger Reichstag 1555.* Vienna: Böhlaus Nachf., 1971. Rev. by J. W. Stoye, EHR, 89(Ja 1974):170-1.

Lutz, Heinrich, ed. *Nuntiaturberichte aus Deutschland Nuniatur des Girolamo Muzzarelli, Sendung des Antonio Augustin Legation des Scipione Rebiba (1554-1556).* Tübingen: Max Niemeyer

Verlag, 1971. Rev. by J. Bossy, EHR, 89(Ja 1974):171-2.

Luvaas, Jay, ed. Dear Miss Em: General Eichelberger's War in the Pacific, 1942-1945. Westport, Conn.: Greenwood, 1972. Rev. by R. W. Leopold, AHR, 79(Apr 1974):609-10; L. Morton, CHR, 55(Je 1974):228-9.

Luza, Radomír see Mamatey, Victor S.

Lynch, John. The Spanish American Revolutions, 1808-1826. New York: Norton, 1973. Rev. by D. Bushnell, HAHR, 54(Aug 1974):512-14; D. E. Worcester, HRNB, 2(Apr 1974):154.

Lynd, Alice and Staughton, eds. Rank and File: Personal Histories of Working Class Organizers. Boston: Beacon, 1973. Rev. by D. Arnold, WMH, 57(Spr 1974):244-5.

Lynes, Russell. Good Old Modern: An Intimate Portrait of the Museum of Modern Art. New York: Atheneum, 1973. Rev. by L. B. Miller, AHR, 79(Apr 1974):599-600.

Lynn, Kenneth S. Visions of America: Eleven Literary Historical Essays. Westport: Greenwood Press, 1973. Rev. by W. G. Heath, Jr., NEQ, 47(Je 1974):309-11.

Lynton, Harriet Ronken and Mohini Rajan. The Days of the Beloved. Berkeley: U Cal Press, 1974. Rev. by R. G. Landen, HRNB, 2(Jl 1974):203-4; N. S. H. Safrani, JAS, 34(Nov 1974):251-2.

Lyon, Peter. Eisenhower: Portrait of the Hero. Boston: Little, Brown, 1974. Rev. by A. L. Hamby, HRNB, 2(Aug 1974): 215.

Lyovin, Anatole see Wang, William S.-Y.

Lyttelton, Adrian. The Seizure of Power: Fascism in Italy, 1919-1929. New York: Scribner's, 1973. Rev. by E. R. Tannenbaum, AHR, 79(Oct 1974):1209-10.

Lyttelton, Margaret. Baroque Architecture in Classical Antiquity. London: Thames and Hudson, n.d. Rev. by S. Harcourt-Smith, HTo, 24(Dec 1974):882-4.

Maass, John. The Glorious Enterprise: The Centennial Exhibition of 1876 and H. J. Schwarzmann, Architect-in-Chief. Watkins Glen, N.Y.: American Life Foundation, 1973. Rev. by R. L. Beisner, JAH, 61(Sep 1974):500; E. S. Ferguson, PH, 41(Oct 1974):475-7; M. S. Cohen, T & C, 15(Apr 1974):338-9.

Maass, Walter B. Assassination in Vienna. New York: Scribner's, 1972. Rev. by K. von Klemperer, AHR, 79(Feb 1974):180.

Mabry, Donald. Mexico's Acción Nacional: A Catholic Alternative

to Revolution. Syracuse, N.Y.: Syr U Press, 1973. Rev.
by K. J. Grieb, TAm, 31(Oct 1974):235-6.

McAfee, Ward. California's Railroad Era, 1850-1911. San Marino,
Cal.: Golden West Books, 1973. Rev. by H. R. Grant, BHR,
48(Win 1974):557-8; N. Tutorow, JAH, 61(Dec 1974):794-5.

McAlindon, T. Shakespeare and Decorum. New York: Barnes and
Noble, 1973. Rev. by M. Charney, RQ, 27(Fall 1974):360-1.

McBreaty, James C. American Labor History and Comparative
Labor Movements. Tucson: U Ariz Press, 1973. Rev. by
T. H. Coode, WPHM, 57(Apr 1974):219-20.

McCague, James. The Cumberland. New York: Holt, Rinehart
and Winston, 1973. Rev. by U. S. Beach, THQ, 33(Fall 1974):
346-7.

McCandless, Perry. A History of Missouri: Volume. II, 1820-1860.
Columbia, Mo.: U Mo Press, 1972. Rev. by D. Riker, AHR,
79(Oct 1974):1249-50; J. V. Mering, CWH, 20(Mar 1974):49-
50; R. E. Smith, JOW, 13(Jl 1974):134; D. Meyer, WHQ, 5
(Apr 1974):209-10.

McCann, Richard Dyer. The People's Films: A Political History
of U. S. Government Motion Pictures. New York: Hastings
House, 1973. Rev. by S. Dalton, WMH, 57(Win 1973-1974):
163-4.

McCarthy, Harold T. The Expatriate Perspective: American Nov-
elists and the Idea of America. Cranbury, N.J.: Fairleigh
Dickinson U Press, 1974. Rev. by J. D. Hoeveler, Jr.,
HRNB, 2(Sep 1974):260-1.

McCartney, John. Black Power: Past, Present, and Future. St.
Charles, Mo.: Forum Press, 1972. Rev. by M. P. McCarthy, HT, 8(Nov 1974):109-10.

McCaughey, Robert A. Josiah Quincy 1772-1864: The Last Federalist. Cambridge, Mass.: Har U Press, 1974. Rev. by
V. Sapio, HRNB, 3(Oct 1974):4.

McClelland, Donald H. The Central American Common Market.
London: Pall Mall Press, 1972. Rev. by D. Browning, JLAS,
6(May 1974):161-8.

McClelland, Vincent A. English Roman Catholics and Higher Education, 1830-1903. Oxford: Ox U Press, 1973. Rev. by
A. E. Firth, EHR, 89(Apr 1974):454-5; J. S. Hunt, History,
59(Je 1974):290-1.

McClinton, Katharine Morrison. The Chromolithographs of Louis
Prang. New York: Clarkson N. Potter, 1973. Rev. by A.

Fern, NYHSQ, 58(Oct 1974):334-5.

McCloskey, Donald M. Economic Maturity and Entrepreneurial Decline: British Iron and Steel, 1870-1913. Cambridge, Mass. :
Har U Press, 1973. Rev. by B. E. Supple, BHR, 48(Sum
1974):238-40; C. K. Hyde, JEH, 34(Sep 1974):795-6.

McCloskey, Donald N. , ed. Essays on a Mature Economy: Britain
After 1840. London ...: Methuen, 1971. Rev. by I. M.
Drummond, CHR, 55(Mar 1974):102-4; M. G. Morrissey, JMH,
46(Mar 1974):144-6.

McColley, Robert. Slavery and Jeffersonian Virginia. Urbana: U
Ill Press, 1973. Rev. by J. M. Gifford, GHQ, 58(Supp 1974):
209-10.

MacCormack, John R. Revolutionary Politics in the Long Parliament. Cambridge, Mass. : Har U Press, 1973. Rev. by
J. A. Casada, HRNB, 2(Ja 1974):79-80.

McCormick, Thomas J. see Gardner, Lloyd C.

McCoy, Donald R. and Richard T. Ruetten. Quest and Response:
Minority Rights and the Truman Administration. Lawrence:
U Press Kan, 1973. Rev. by M. H. Blewett, AHR, 79(Apr
1974):612-13; R. D. Younger, Historian, 36(Aug 1974):790-1;
R. Griffith, JAH, 61(Sep 1974):541-2; W. C. Berman, JSH,
40(May 1974):334-6; D. W. Detzer, MiA, 56(Ja 1974):65-6;
L. Ashby, PNQ, 65(Apr 1974):89.

McCoy, F. N. Robert Baillie and the Second Scots Reformation.
Berkeley: U Cal Press, 1974. Rev. by W. I. Hoy, CH, 43
(Sep 1974):409-10.

McCracken, Harold. The American Cowboy. Garden City, N. Y. :
Doubleday, 1973. Rev. by M. Simmons, NMHR, 49(Oct 1974):
347.

McCraw, Thomas K. TVA and the Power Fight, 1933-1939. Philadelphia: Lippincott, 1971. Rev. by R. Cuff, AHR, 79(Je
1974):901.

MacCurtain, Margaret. Tudor and Stuart Ireland. Dublin: Gill
and Macmillan, 1972. Rev. by H. F. Kearney, History, 59
(Feb 1974):101.

McDermott, John Francis. Seth Eastman's Mississippi: A Lost
Portfolio Recovered. Urbana: U Ill Press, 1973. Rev. by
L. M. Simms, Jr. , HRNB, 2(Ja 1974):62.

_____, ed. The Spanish in the Mississippi Valley, 1762-1804.
Urbana: U Ill Press, 1974. Rev. by D. C. Cutter, HRNB,
2(May/Je 1974):160-1; W. E. Foley, IMH, 70(Dec 1974):349-

50; G. C. Din, JMiH, 36(Aug 1974):317-19; J. T. Bloom, JSH, 40(Nov 1974):644-5; M. Bray, MinnH, 44(Sum 1974):78; J. Caughey, NMHR, 49(Jl 1974):254-5.

McDonald, Archie P. , ed. Make Me a Map of the Valley: The Civil War Journal of Stonewall Jackson's Topographer. Dallas: SMU Press, 1973. Rev. by R. J. Sommers, CWH, 20(Je 1974):184-5; Mrs. B. Davis, ETHJ, 12(Fall 1974):83-4; J. L. Wakelyn, HRNB, 2(May/Je 1974):160; B. F. Cooling, JSH, 40 (Aug 1974):489-90; J. I. Robertson, Jr., VMHB, 82(Apr 1974): 208-10; F. E. Vandiver, WVH, 36(Oct 1974):74-5.

McDonald, Forrest. The Presidency of George Washington. Lawrence: U Press Kan, 1974. Rev. by M. R. Zahniser, HRNB, 2(May/Je 1974):165-6; E. Cometti, WVH, 36(Oct 1974):63-4.

Macdonald, J. R. L. Soldiering and Surveying in East Africa, 1891-1894. London: Dawson's, Pall Mall, 1973. Rev. by J. Tosh, JAfH, 15(Num 3 1974):522-3.

McDonald, Lucile. Swan Among the Indians: Life of James G. Swan, 1818-1900. Portland: Binsford and Mort, 1972. Rev. by G. A. Frykman, PNQ, 65(Jl 1974):148.

MacDonald, Teresa. Union Catalogue of the Serial Publications of the Indian Government, 1858-1947. London: Mansell, 1973. Rev. by C. Dewey, MAS, 8(Oct 1974):571-3.

McDonald, William A. and George R. Rapp, Jr., eds. The Minnesota Messenia Expedition: Reconstructing a Bronze-Age Regional Environment. Minneapolis: U Minn Press, 1972. Rev. by L. V. Watrous, AJA, 78(Ja 1974):84-6; S. Diamant, Antiquity, 48(Mar 1974):77-8; E. Vermeule, JIH, 5(Sum 1974): 150-1.

McDowell, Bart. The American Cowboy in Life and Legend. Washington, D. C. : National Geographic Society, 1972. Rev. by A. W. Spring, CoMag, 51(Win 1974):67-8.

Macebuh, Stanley. James Baldwin: a Critical Study. New York: Third Press, 1973. Rev. by M. Perry, N H B, 37(Apr/May 1974):252.

McElrath, Damian. Richard Simpson 1820-1876: A Study in XIXth-Century English Liberal Catholicism. Louvain: Publications Universitaires de Louvain, 1972. Rev. by P. Misner, CH, 43(Je 1974):274-5.

McFarlane, K. B. The Nobility of Later Medieval England. Oxford: Clarendon Press, 1973. Rev. by G. P. Cuttino, AHR, 79(Feb 1974):126-7; J. S. Roskell, EHR, 89(Jl 1974):622-7; J. Catto, HJ, 17(Num 3 1974):655-6; A. Rogers, HTo, 24(Ja 1974):66-7.

McFaul, John M. The Politics of Jacksonian Finance. Ithaca, N. Y.:
Cornell U Press, 1972. Rev. by R. H. Keehn, BHR, 48(Spr
1974):128-30; T. P. Govan, NYHSQ, 58(Ja 1974):69-70; W. G.
Shade, PH, 41(Oct 1974):471-2.

McGaw, William Cochran. Savage Scene: The Life and Times of
James Kirker, Frontier King. New York: Hasting House,
1972. Rev. by W. L. Richter, GPJ, 13(Spr 1974):208-9;
D. J. Weber, NMHR, 49(Apr 1974):175-7.

McGiffert, Michael, ed. God's Plot: The Paradoxes of Puritan
Piety. Being the Autobiography and Journal of Thomas Shepard. Amherst: U Mass Press, 1972. Rev. by L. A. Loet-
scher, AHR, 79(Je 1974):844.

_____ and Robert Allen Skotheim, eds. American Social Thought:
Sources and Interpretations. 2 vols. Reading: Addison-Wesley, 1972. Rev. by S. C. Scholl, HT, 7(Feb 1974):296-7.

McGloin, John Bernard. Jesuits by the Golden Gate: The Society
of Jesus in San Francisco, 1849-1969. San Francisco: U
S F Press, 1972. Rev. by D. B. Nunis, Jr., JAH, 60(Mar
1974):1121-2.

McGrade, Arthur Stephen. The Political Thought of William of
Ockham: Personal and Institutional Principles. New York:
Cam U Press, 1974. Rev. by J. Muldoon, HRNB, 3(Nov/
Dec 1974):27.

McGrath, Sylvia Wallace. Charles Kenneth Leith: Scientific Adviser. Madison: U Wis Press, 1971. Rev. by M. M.
Vance, AHR, 79(Je 1974):894.

McGrath, William J. Dionysian Art and Populist Politics in Austria.
New Haven, Conn.: Yale U Press, 1974. Rev. by C. Keser-
ich, HRNB, 2(Sep 1974):241.

MacGregor, James A. A History of Alberta. Edmonton: Hurtig,
1972. Rev. by W. L. Morton, CHR, 55(Je 1974):202-3.

McGregor, Malcolm Francis see Bradeen, Donald William

McGuire, William, ed. The Freud/Jung Letters: The Correspondence
Between Sigmund Freud and C. G. Jung. Princeton, N. J.:
Prin U Press, 1974. Rev. by S. M. Bolkosky, HRNB, 3(Nov/
Dec 1974):23-4.

McHugh, Tom. The Time of the Buffalo. New York: Knopf, 1972.
Rev. by H. E. Socolosky, JOW, 13(Apr 1974):109; E. Wallace,
SWHQ, 78(Oct 1974):221-2.

McIntosh, Glenda Riley. The Origins of the Feminist Movement in
America. St. Charles, Mo.: Forum Press, 1973. Rev. by

M. P. McCarthy, HT, 8(Nov 1974):109-10.

McJimsey, George T. Genteel Partisan: Manton Marble, 1834-
1917. Ames: Ia St U Press, 1971. Rev. by E. B. Smith,
AHR, 79(Je 1974):874-5.

McKale, Donald M. The Nazi Party Courts: Hitler's Management
of Conflict in His Movement, 1921-1945. Lawrence: U Press
Kan, 1974. Rev. by R. E. Neil, HRNB, 3(Oct 1974):11-12.

McKay, Ernest. Henry Wilson: Practical Radical. A Portrait of
a Politician. Port Washington, N. Y.: Kennikat, 1971. Rev.
by S. H. Strom, AHR, 79(Oct 1974):1268-70.

Mackay, Ruddock F. Fisher of Kilverstone. New York: Ox U
Press, 1974. Rev. by P. Scherer, HRNB, 2(Jl 1974):210.

McKee, Christopher. Edward Preble: A Naval Biography 1761-
1807. Annapolis: Naval Institute Press, 1972. Rev. by L.
Morton, AHR, 79(Oct 1974):1256-7; E. S. Dodge, Historian,
36(May 1974):559-60; W. P. Strauss, WMQ-3, 31(Ja 1974):
159-60.

McKee, Jennie Starks. Throb of Drums in Tennessee, 1862-1865.
Philadelphia: Dorrance, 1973. Rev. by W. G. Eidson, IMH,
70(Mar 1974):72-3.

McKelven, James Lee. George III and Lord Bute: The Leicester
House Years. Durham, N. C.: Duke U Press, 1973. Rev.
by C. R. Ritcheson, AHR, 79(Feb 1974):144-5.

McKelvey, Blake. Rochester on the Genesee: The Growth of a
City. Syracuse, N. Y.: Syr U Press, 1973. Rev. by E. F.
Feinstein, JAH, 61(Dec 1974):804-5; R. J. Wechman, NYH, 55
(Je 1974):338-9.

McKelvey, James Lee. George III and Lord Bute: The Leicester
House Years. Durham, N. C.: Duke U Press, 1973. Rev.
by P. D. G. Thomas, WMQ-3, 31(Jl 1974):498-501.

Mackendrick, Paul. Roman France. New York: St. Martin's,
1972. Rev. by B. S. Bachrach, AHR, 79(Oct 1974):1159.

McKenney, Thomas L. Memoirs, Official and Personal. Lincoln:
U Neb Press, 1973. Rev. by R. Horsman, HRNB, 2(May/Je
1974):159; J. E. Sunder, IMH, 70(Je 1974):184-5; D. M.
Schockley, JOW, 13(Apr 1974):124.

_____. Sketches of a Tour to the Lakes, of the Character and
Customs of the Chippeway Indians, and of Incidents Connected
with the Treaty of Fond du Lac. Barre, Mass.: Imprint
Society, 1972. Rev. by P. P. Mason, AmArc, 37(Jan 1974):
84-5.

MacKenzie, David. The Lion of Tashkent: The Career of General
    M. G. Cherniaev. Athens, Ga.: U Ga Press, 1974. Rev.
    by N. E. Saul, HRNB, 3(Nov/Dec 1974):33-4.

Mackesy, Piers. The Strategy of Overthrow 1798-1799. London:
    Longman, n. d. Rev. by D. G. Chandler, HTo, 24(Sep 1974):
    658-9.

McKiernan, F. Mark, Alma R. Blair, and Paul M. Edwards, eds.
    The Restoration Movement: Essays in Mormon History. Law-
    rence, Kan.: Coronado Press, 1973. Rev. by R. C. Durham,
    Jr., UHQ, 42(Win 1974):91.

McKinzie, Richard D. The New Deal for Artists. Princeton, N. J.:
    Prin U Press, 1973. Rev. by G. M. Monroe, JAH, 60(Mar
    1974):1178-9.

McKitrick, Eric. The Hofstadter Aegis. see Elkins, Stanley

McKown, Dave R. The Dean: The Life of Julien C. Monnet. Nor-
    man: U Ok Press, 1973. Rev. by J. Short, JOW, 13(Oct
    1974):126.

McKown, Robin. Nkrumah: A Biography. Garden City, N. Y.:
    Doubleday, 1973. Rev. by J. W. Ivy, Crisis, 81(Ja 1974):
    32.

Mackrell, J. Q. C. The Attack on "Feudalism" in Eighteenth-Cen-
    tury France. Toronto: U Tor Press, 1973. Rev. by D.
    Koenig, HRNB, 2(May 1974):114-15.

McLachlan, James. American Boarding Schools: A Historical Study.
    New York: Scribner's, 1970. Rev. by K. V. Lottich, AHR,
    79(Oct 1974):1255-6.

Maclachlan, Jean see Link, Arthur M.

McLaughlin, Doris B. Michigan Labor: A Brief History from 1818
    to the Present. Ann Arbor: U Mich--Wayne St U, 1970. Rev
    by W. G. Shade, AHR, 79(Je 1974):858-9.

McLean, Antonia. Humanism and the Rise of Science in Tudor Eng-
    land. London: Heineman, 1972. Rev. by J. K. McConica,
    EHR, 89(Apr 1974):429; A. R. Hall, History, 59(Je 1974):268.

McLean, Malcolm D., comp. and ed. Papers Concerning Robert-
    son's Colony in Texas. Volume I, 1788-1822. Fort Worth:
    T C U Press, 1974. Rev. by R. P. Cross, THQ, 33(Win
    1974):456-8.

McLemore, Richard Aubrey, ed. A History of Mississippi. 2
    vols. Hattiesburg: U and Coll Press Miss, 1973. Rev. by
    A. H. DeRosier, Jr., CWH, 20(Mar 1974):51-2.

MacLeod, Murdo J. Spanish Central America: A Socioeconomic
    History, 1520-1720. Berkeley: U Cal Press, 1973. Rev. by
    D. Felix, BHR, 48(Sum 1974):231-2; C. Gibson, HAHR, 54
    (Aug 1974):505-7.

[McLoughlin, John]. John McLoughlin's Business Correspondence,
    1847-48. Seattle: U Wash Press, 1973. Rev. by J. A. Hus-
    sey, OrHQ, 75(Mar 1974):76-7; J. S. Galbraith, PHR, 43(Aug
    1974):418-19.

McManners, John. Church and State in France, 1870-1914. Lon-
    don: S. P. C. K., 1972. Rev. by J. P. T. Bury, History,
    59(Feb 1974):137-8.

McManus, Edgar J. Black Bondage in the North. Syracuse, N. Y.:
    Syr U Press, 1973. Rev. by A. Meier, AHR, 79(Oct 1974):
    1246-7; A. Tully, BHR, 48(Spr 1974):125-7; A. Zilversmit,
    JAH, 61(Je 1974):173-4; F. J. Miller, NEQ, 47(Mar 1974):
    168-73; B. Wyatt-Brown, NYHSQ, 58(Apr 1974):148-9; L. W.
    Brown, WMQ-3, 31(Apr 1974):337-9.

McMaster, Juliet. Thackeray: The Major Novels. Toronto: U
    Tor Press, 1971. Rev. by M. Greene, GR, 28(Sum 1974):
    345-7.

McMillen, Neil R. The Citizens' Council: Organized Resistance to
    the Second Reconstruction, 1954-64. Urbana: U Ill Press,
    1971. Rev. by K. L. Bryant, Jr., AHR, 79(Apr 1974):617-18.

MacMullen, Ramsay. Roman Social Relations: 50 B. C. to A. D.
    284. New Haven, Conn.: Yale U Press, 1974. Rev. by
    J. E. Seaver, HRNB, 2(Mar 1974):125-6.

McMullin, Phillip W., ed. Grassroots of America--A Computerized
    Index to the American State Papers: Land Grants and Claims
    (1789-1837) with Other Aids to Research. Salt Lake City:
    Gendata, 1972. Rev. by E. E. Hill, AmArc, 37(Ja 1974):87-
    9.

MacNamara, Ellen. Everyday Life of the Etruscan. New York:
    Putnam's, 1973. Rev. by R. Ling, Antiquity, 48(Sep 1974):
    240-1.

McNamara, Jo Ann. Gilles Aycelin: The Servant of Two Masters.
    Syracuse, N. Y.: Syr U Press, 1973. Rev. by J. E. Weak-
    land, CH, 43(Mar 1974):106-7; J. E. Wrigley, Historian, 36
    (Aug 1974):741-2.

McNeal, Robert H. Bride of the Revolution: Krupskaya and Lenin.
    Ann Arbor: U Mich Press, 1972. Rev. by R. Thompson,
    AHR, 79(Apr 1974):544-5; P. Dukes, History, 59(Je 1974):
    300.

McNeill, John T. The Celtic Churches: A History, A. D. 200 to
1200. Chicago: U Chi Press, 1974. Rev. by B. McGinn,
CH, 43(Je 1974):268; P. L. Hughes, HRNB, 2(Apr 1974):140.

McNeill, William H. The Shape of European History. New York:
Ox U Press, 1974. Rev. by J. L. Shneidman, HRNB, 2(Sep
1974):238-9.

_____. Venice: The Hinge of Europe, 1081-1797. Chicago: U
Chi Press, 1974. Rev. by F. L. Cheyette, HRNB, 2(Sep
1974):240.

MacNeish, Richard S. , Frederick A. Peterson, and Kent V. Flannery. The Prehistory of the Tehuacan Valley. Volume Three:
Ceramics. Austin: U Tx Press, 1970. Rev. by T. P. Culbert, AmAnt, 39(Oct 1974):644-5.

_____, Frederick Johnson, Karl A. Wittfogel, Richard B. Wood-
bury, James A. Neely, Gorgonio Gil Huerta, and Eva Hunt.
The Prehistory of the Tehuacan Valley. Volume Four: Chronology and Irrigation. Austin: U Tx Press, 1972. Rev. by
G. Vivian, AmAnt, 39(Oct 1974):643-4.

McNickle, D'Arcy. Native American Tribalism: Indian Survivals
and Renewals. New York: Ox U Press, 1973. Rev. by I.
Sutton, JOW, 13(Ja 1974):143; J. G. Jorgensen, WHQ, 5(Oct
1974):464-6.

McPheeters, Annie L. Negro Progress in Atlanta, Georgia, 1961-
1970. Atlanta: Annie L. McPheeters, n. d. Rev. by T. M.
Deaton; GHQ, 58(Supp 1974):204-5.

McSeveney, Samuel T. The Politics of Depression: Political Behavior in the Northeast, 1893-1896. New York: Ox U Press,
1972. Paul L. Murphy, AHR, 79(Je 1974):885-6; W. T. K.
Nugent, JAH, 60(Mar 1974):1156-7.

McWhiney, Grady. Southerners and Other Americans. New York:
Basic Books, 1973. Rev. by H. Cohen, AHR, 79(Apr 1974):
582-3; J. B. Scroggs, CWH, 20(Mar 1974):47-8; N. L. Dawson, FCHQ, 48(Apr 1974):200-1; R. B. Draughon, Jr. , GHQ,
58(Fall 1974):376-7; R. W. Johannsen, JAH, 61(Je 1974):177-8;
T. H. Baker, JMiH, 36(Feb 1974):119-20; J. G. Barrett,
RKHS, 72(Ja 1974):56-9; G. E. Moulton, THQ, 33(Spr 1974):
108-9; J. J. Halstead, WMH, 57(Spr 1974):241-2.

McWilliams, John P. see Dekker, George

McWilliams, John P. , Jr. Political Justice in a Republic: James
Fenimore Cooper's America. Berkeley: U Cal Press, 1972.
Rev. by C. Swann, JAmS, 8(Apr 1974):124-6; J. H. Pickering,
NYH, 55(Ja 1974):104-6; E. K. Spann, NYHSQ, 58(Ja 1974):
72-3.

McWilliams, Wilson Carey. The Idea of Fraternity in America.
    Berkeley: U Cal Press, 1973. Rev. by W. A. Clebsch, CH,
    43(Sep 1974):421-2; R. A. Gerber, HRNB, 2(Feb 1974):100;
    J. Higham, JAH, 61(Sep 1974):451-3; R. Berthoff, JSH, 40
    (Feb 1974):115-17.

Madariaga, Salvador de. Morning Without Noon. Memoirs. n. p. :
    Saxon House, n. d. Rev. by J. Richardson, HTo, 24(Mar
    1974):212-13.

Madden, Betty I. Art, Crafts, and Architecture in Early Illinois.
    Urbana: U Ill Press, 1974. Rev. by J. Y. Simon, JISHS,
    67(Nov 1974):559-60.

Maddox, Robert James. The New Left and the Origins of the Cold
    War. Princeton, N. J.: Prin U Press, 1973. Rev. by A. E.
    Campbell, HJ, 17(Num 2 1974):443-7; R. W. Leopold, JAH,
    60(Mar 1974):1183-5; N. A. Graebner, PHR, 43(Feb 1974):
    138-9.

Maenchen-Helfen, J. Otto. The World of the Huns: Studies in
    Their History and Culture. Berkeley: U Cal Press, 1973.
    Rev. by W. H. McNeill, CH, 43(Je 1974):269.

Maffei, Domenico. Il giovane Machiavelli banchiere con Berto Berti
    a Roma. Florence: ... Giunti-G. Barbera, 1973. Rev. by
    J. Kirshner, JMH, 46(Dec 1974):724-5.

Maguire, John. Marx's Paris Writings: An Analysis. New York:
    Barnes and Noble, 1973. Rev. by O. J. Hammen, AHR, 79
    (Feb 1974):137.

Mahar, J. Michael, ed. The Untouchables in Contemporary India.
    Tucson: U Ariz Press, 1972. Rev. by V. S. Parthasarathy,
    JAS, 33(Feb 1974):326-8.

Mahon, John K. The War of 1812. Gainesville: U Fla Press,
    1972. Rev. by C. P. Stacey, CHR, 55(Sep 1974):315-16;
    C. L. Christman, MiA, 56(Ja 1974):57-8; R. Glover, NYH,
    55(Ja 1974):110-12; S. R. Bright, Jr., PH, 41(Apr 1974):
    228-9; J. H. Harrison, Jr., VMHB, 82(Apr 1974):205-6; C. B.
    Brooks, WMQ-3, 31(Ja 1974):160-2.

Maier, Georg and Albert William Bork. Historical Dictionary of
    Ecuador. see Bork, Albert William and Georg Maier. His-
    torical Dictionary of Ecuador.

Maier, Pauline. From Resistance to Revolution: Colonial Radicals
    and the Development of American Opposition to Britain, 1765-
    1776. London: Routledge and Kegan Paul, 1973. Rev. by
    J. R. Pole, HJ, 17(Mar 1974):218-21.

Mails, Thomas E. Dog Soldiers, Bear Men and Buffalo Women: A

Study of the Societies and Cults of the Plains Indians. Englewood Cliffs, N. J.:   Prentice-Hall, 1973.   Rev. by R. M. Utley, ChOk, 52(Sum 1974):374; R. J. Demallie, CoMag, 51
(Sum 1974):268-70; J. C. Ewers, WHQ, 5(Oct 1974):466-7.

Main, Jackson Turner.   Political Parties Before the Constitution.
Chapel Hill: ... UNC Press, 1973.   Rev. by G. S. Wood,
CHR, 55(Je 1974):222-3; B. C. Wood, JAmS, 8(Apr 1974):116-
17; W. H. Nelson, JSH, 40(Feb 1974):128-30; R. E. Shalhope,
MHM, 69(Spr 1974):101-3; G. B. Warden, NYH, 55(Apr 1974):
245-6; S. R. Boyd, WMH, 57(Sum 1974):321-2.

_____. The Sovereign States, 1775-1783.   New York: New View-
points, 1973.   Rev. by L. L. Tucker, AHR, 79(Oct 1974):
1253-4; F. V. Mills, Sr., GHQ, 58(Supp 1974):211; M. Curti,
HT, 7(Feb 1974):297-8; C. L. Ver Steeg, JAH, 61(Je 1974):
167-8; R. Hoffman, JSH, 40(Feb 1974):130-2; R. B. Morris,
NCHR, 51(Win 1974):113-14; E. G. Burrows, NYHSQ, 58(Jl
1974):241-2; T. Thayer, PH, 41(Jl 1974):360-2; L. P. Jones,
SCHM, 75(Ja 1974):56-7; L. G. De Pauw, WMQ-3, 31(Apr
1974):319-20.

Mainga, Mutumba.   Bulozi Under the Luyana Kings.   London: Longman, 1973.   Rev. by A. Roberts, AfAf, 73(Apr 1974):242-3;
R. Fielder, JAfH, 15(Num 3 1974):495-6.

Makonnen, Ras.   Pan-Africanism from Within.   London: Ox U
Press, 1973.   Rev. by I. Duffield, AfAf, 73(Jl 1974):376-7;
R. J. Macdonald, JAfH, 15(Num 1 1974):171.

Makulu, H. F.   Education, Development and Nation-Building in Independent Africa.   London: S. C. M. Press, 1971.   Rev.
by J. Adwere-Boamah, JMAS, 12(Je 1974):349-52.

Malaise, Michel.   Les conditions de pénétration et de diffusion des
cultes Egyptiens en Italie.   n. p.:   n. d.   Rev. by R. I. Hicks,
AJA, 78(Jl 1974):315-16.

_____. Inventaire Préliminaire des documents Egyptiens, De-
couverts en Italie.   n. p.:   n. d.   Rev. by R. I. Hicks, AJA,
78(Jl 1974):315-16.

Maland, David.   Culture and Society in Seventeenth-Century France.
London: Batsford, 1970.   Rev. by J. H. Shennan, History,
59(Je 1974):278.

Malcolmson, Robert W.   Popular Recreations in English Society,
1700-1850.   New York: Cam U Press, 1973.   Rev. by D. C.
Itzkowitz, AHR, 79(Oct 1974):1178; L. F. Barmann, JMH, 46
(Sep 1974):547-9.

Maldonado-Denis, Manuel.   Puerto Rico: A Socio-Historic Interpretation.   New York: Random House, 1972.   Rev. by M. Han-

sen, AHR, 79(Je 1974):915.

Malecot, Georges. Les Voyageurs française et les relations entre
le France et l'Abyssinie de 1835 à 1870. Paris: Société
française d'Histoire d'Outre-Mer, 1972. Rev. by R. Gray,
EHR, 89(Apr 1974):458.

Mallett, Michael. Mercenaries and Their Masters. n. p. : Bodley
Head, n. d. Rev. by A. Haynes, HTo, 24(Apr 1974):289-90.

Malone, Dumas. Jefferson the President: Second Term, 1805-1809.
Boston: Little, Brown, 1974. Rev. by H. Hamilton, HRNB,
2(Jl 1974):191; N. E. Cunningham, Jr. , JAH, 61(Dec 1974):
774-5.

Malone, Joseph J. The Arab Lands of Western Asia. Englewood
Cliffs, N. J. : Prentice-Hall, 1973. Rev. by H. L. Bodman,
Jr. , AHR, 79(Oct 1974):1226.

Mamatey, Victor S. and Radomír Luza, eds. A History of Czechoslovak Republic, 1918-1948. Princeton, N. J. : Prin U Press,
1973. Rev. by B. M. Garver, AHR, 79(Oct 1974):1213-14;
S. Z. Pech, EEQ, 8(Fall 1974):388-91.

Mancall, Mark. Russia and China: Their Diplomatic Relations to
1728. Cambridge, Mass. : Har U Press, 1971. Rev. by
H. J. Beattie, MAS, 8(Apr 1974):266-7.

Mandelbaum, David G. Society in India. 2 vols. Berkeley: U
Cal Press, 1970. Rev. by M. Naidis, AHR, 79(Oct 1974):
1234-5.

Mangione, Jerre. The Dream and the Deal: The Federal Writers'
Project 1935-1943. Boston: Little, Brown, 1972. Rev. by
B. A. Weisberger, AH, 25(Feb 1974):98-100.

Mangua, Charles. A Tail in the Mouth. Nairobi: East Africa Publishing House, 1972. Rev. by H. Dinwiddy, AfAf, 73(Jl 1974):
379-81.

Mann, Arthur, ed. Immigrants in American Life. Boston: Houghton Mifflin, 1973. Rev. by R. J. Wechman, HT, 7(Aug 1974):
638.

_____, Neil Harris, and Sam Bass Warner, Jr. History and the
Role of the City in American Life. Indianapolis: Ind Historical Society, 1972. Rev. by P. A. Kalisch, JISHS, 67(Sep
1974):456-7.

Manning, Brian, ed. Politics, Religion and the English Civil War.
New York: St. Martin's, 1974. Rev. by J. W. Ferguson,
HRNB, 2(Sep 1974):234.

MANSCHRECK 234

Manschreck, Clyde L.   A History of Christianity in the World:
From Persecution to Uncertainty.   Englewood Cliffs, N. J. :
Prentice-Hall, 1974.   Rev. by J. T. McNeill, CH, 43(Dec
1974):529; S. J. Simon, HRNB, 2(Sep 1974):248.

Mansergh, Nicholas, ed.   The Transfer of Power, 1942-47.   Vol.
III.   London: H. M. S. O. , 1971.   Rev. by W. Golant, History, 59(Je 1974):319.

Mansfield, Peter.   The Ottoman Empire and Its Successors.   New
York: St. Martin's, 1973.   Rev. by L. E. Meyer, HRNB, 2
(Apr 1974):147.

Mantell, Martin E.   Johnson, Grant, and the Politics of Reconstruc-
tion.   New York: Columbia U Press, 1973.   Rev. by S. H.
Strom, AHR, 79(Oct 1974):1268-70; G. Linden, CWH, 20(Mar
1974):84-7; A. Craven, Historian, 36(May 1974):566-7; K. I.
Polakoff, JAH, 61(Sep 1974):496-7; R. D. Bridges, JSH, 40
(May 1974):324-5.

Mantran, Robert.   L'Expansion Musulmane (7-11 siècles).   Paris:
Presses Universitaires de France, 1969.   Rev. by B. Lewis,
History, 59(Je 1974):314-15.

Manuel, George and Michael Posluns.   The Fourth World: An Indian Reality.   New York: Free Press, n. d.   Rev. by Staff,
InH, 7(Sum 1974):58.

Manypenny, George W.   Our Indian Wards.   New York: Da Capo,
1972.   Rev. by R. N. Ellis, JISHS, 67(Je 1974):343-4.

Mara, M. G.   Evangile de Pierre.   Paris: Editions du Cerf, 1973.
Rev. by B. M. Metzger, CH, 43(Dec 1974):529-30.

Maravall, José Antonio.   Estado Moderno y Mentalidad social: Siglos XV a XVII.   Vol. I.   Madrid: Revista de Occidente, 1972.
Rev. by H. Kamen, History, 59(Je 1974):264.

Marbut, F. B.   News from the Capital: The Story of Washington
Reporting.   Carbondale: S Ill U Press, 1971.   Rev. by J. E.
Walsh, AHR, 79(Je 1974):856-7.

Marcell, David W.   Progress and Pragmatism: James, Dewey,
Beard, and the American Idea of Progress.   Westport, Conn. :
Greenwood, 1974.   Rev. by J. T. Gay, HRNB, 2(Jl 1974):
194; J. B. Quandt, JAH, 61(Dec 1974):810-12.

Marchal, Guy P. , ed.   Die Statuten des weltlichen Kollegiatstifts
St. Peter in Basel.   Basel: Kommissionsverlag Friedrich
Reinhardt, 1972.   Rev. by G. R. Potter, EHR, 89(Jl 1974):
659-60.

Marchand, C. Roland.   The American Peace Movement and Social

Reform, 1898-1918. Princeton, N. J.: Prin U Press, 1972.
Rev. by S. J. Kneeshaw, Historian, 36(Aug 1974):786-7;
A. W. Thurner, JISHS, 67(Sep 1974):454-5.

Marchand, Leslie A. Alas! The Love of Women. Byron's Letters
and Journals. Volume 3, 1813-1814. n. p.: Murray, n. d.
Rev. by J. Richardson, HTo, 24(Oct 1974):728-9.

Marcillo, Maria-Luiza. La ville de São Paulo. Peuplement et
population, 1750-1850, d'après les registres paroissiaux et les
recensements anciens. Paris: Presses Universitaires de
France, 1973. Rev. by B. Orlove, HAHR, 54(Nov 1974):707-8.

Marcus, Jacob R. and Stanley F. Chyet, eds. Historical Essay on
the Colony of Surinam 1788. New York: KTAV, 1974. Rev.
by R. I. Rotberg, HRNB, 3(Nov/Dec 1974):41.

Marcus, Sheldon. Father Coughlin: The Tumultuous Life of the
Priest of the Little Flower. Boston: Little, Brown, 1973.
Rev. by O. L. Graham, Jr., AHR, 79(Je 1974):899-901;
G. Q. Flynn, JAH, 60(Mar 1974):1176-7.

Marcus, Steven. Engels, Manchester, and the Working Class. New
York: Random House, n. d. Rev. by W. J. Dannhauser, Commentary, 58(Nov 1974):96-8.

Mardock, Robert Winston. The Reformers and the American Indian.
Columbia, Mo.: U Mo Press, 1971. Rev. by F. Nicklason,
AHR, 79(Je 1974):875-6.

Mares, F. H., ed. The Memoirs of Robert Carey. Oxford: Clarendon Press, 1972. Rev. by A. L. Rowse, EHR, 89(Apr
1974):430; J. M. Rodney, Historian, 36(Feb 1974):317-18.

Marett, W. P., ed. A Calendar of the Register of Henry Wake-
field, Bishop of Worcester, 1375-95. Worcester: Worcester
Historical Society ... 1972. Rev. by R. L. Storey, EHR, 89
(Apr 1974):378-80.

Margolin, Jean-Claude, ed. Colloquia Erasmiana Turoneusia. Toronto: U Tor Press, 1972. Rev. by A. Rabil, Jr., RQ, 27
(Sum 1974):198-201.

Marie, Jean-Jacques see Haupt, Georges

Maring, Esther G. and Joel M. Historical and Cultural Dictionary
of the Philippines. Metuchen, N.J.: Scarecrow, 1973. Rev.
by C. O. Houston, JAS, 33(May 1974):506-7.

Markesinis, B. S. The Theory and Practice of Dissolution of Par-
liament. New York: Cam U Press, 1972. Rev. by G. D.
Frangos, AHR, 79(Feb 1974):137-8; D. E. C. Yale, EHR, 89
(Ja 1974):205-6; D. Southgate, History, 59(Je 1974):332.

Markowitz, Norman D. The Rise and Fall of the People's Century: Henry A. Wallace and American Liberalism 1941-1948. New York: Free Press, 1973. Rev. by P. J. Wilkinson, AI, 42 (Win 1974):227-8; D. W. Detzer, MiA, 56(Ja 1974):64-5; A. Yarnell, PNQ, 65(Ja 1974):44-5.

Marks, Frederick W., III. Independence on Trial: Foreign Affairs and the Making of the Constitution. Baton Rouge: LSU Press, 1973. Rev. by G. L. Browne, BHR, 48(Sum 1974): 248-9; D. Higginbotham, FHQ, 53(Oct 1974):210-11; J. May, HRNB, 2(May/Je 1974):165; D. M. Pletcher, IMH, 70(Dec 1974):347-9; L. S. Kaplan, JAH, 61(Sep 1974):470-1; G. L. Seligmann, Jr., JSH, 40(Aug 1974):469-70; R. Leffler, WMH, 57(Spr 1974):243-4; P. A. Varg, WMQ-3, 31(Jl 1974):517.

Marks, Geoffrey and William K. Beatty. The Story of Medicine in America. New York: Scribner's, 1973. Rev. by R. P. Howard, ChOk, 52(Fall 1974):379-80.

Marlow, John. Cecil Rhodes: The Anatomy of Empire. London: Elek, 1972. Rev. by S. Marks, History, 59(Je 1974):313.

Marlowe, John. Perfidious Albion: The Origins of Anglo-French Rivalry in the Levant. London: Elek, 1971. Rev. by J. M. J. Rogister, History, 59(Feb 1974):113-14.

Márquez, Edgar Gabaldón. El México virreinal y la "Sublevación" de Caracas, 1810. Caracas: Archivo General de la Nación, 1971. Rev. by C. D. Ameringer, AHR, 79(Oct 1974):1297.

Marquis, Thomas B., comp.; Ronald H. Limbaugh, ed. Cheyenne and Sioux: The Reminiscences of Four Indians and a White Soldier. Stockton, Cal.: U Pacific Press, 1973. Rev. by F. M. Spindler, HRNB, 2(Ja 1974):69; R. N. Ellis, NMHR, 49(Jl 1974):263.

Marrin, Albert. The Last Crusade: The Church of England in the First World War. Durham, N.C.: Duke U Press, 1974. Rev. by A. Tobriner, HRNB, 2(Apr 1974):138.

Marsh, Andrew J. Letters from Nevada Territory, 1861-1862. Reno, Nev.: Legislative Counsel Bureau, 1972. Rev. by V. Westphall, JAH, 61(Je 1974):209-10; R. E. Smith, JOW, 13 (Apr 1974):125.

_____, Samuel L. Clemens, and Amos Bowman. Reports of the 1863 Constitutional Convention of the Territory of Nevada. Reno: Legislative Counsel Bureau, State of Nevada, 1972. Rev. by R. E. Smith, JOW, 13(Apr 1974):125.

Marsh, Henry. The Caesars: The Roman Empire and Its Rulers. New York: St. Martin's, 1972. Rev. by J. R. Fears, AHR, 79(Je 1974):766-7.

Marshall, Dorothy. Industrial England, 1776-1851. New York:
    Scribner's, 1973. Rev. by R. G. Eaves, Historian, 36(Feb
    1974):321-2; N. McCord, History, 59(Je 1974):284-5.

_____. The Life and Times of Victoria. New York: Praeger,
    1974. Rev. by R. A. Rempel, HRNB, 2(Sep 1974):244-5.

Marshall, Helen E. Mary Adelaide Nutting: Pioneer of Modern
    Nursing. Baltimore: JHU, 1972. Rev. by S. Benison, AHR,
    79(Feb 1974):241-2; J. A. Carrigan, JAH, 60(Mar 1974):1149-
    50.

Marshall, S. L. A. Crimsoned Prairie: The Wars Between the
    United States and the Plains Indians During the Winning of the
    West. New York: Scribner's, 1972. Rev. by M. Koury,
    A & W, 16(Spr 1974):67-8; G. Chappell, CoMag, 51(Sum 1974):
    255-7; D. A. Walker, NKH, 41(Fall 1974):33.

Marshall-Cornwall, Sir James. Haig as Military Commander. New
    York: Crane, Russak, 1973. Rev. by R. J. Maddox, HRNB,
    2(May/Je 1974):185.

Marszalek, John F., Jr. Court-Martial: A Black Man in America.
    New York: Scribner's, 1972. Rev. by R. W. Logan, AHR,
    79(Apr 1974):592-3; N. E. Williams, ChOk, 52(Sum 1974):252-
    3; R. M. Johnson, CWH, 20(Sep 1974):283-5; J. M. Elliot,
    NHB, 37(Oct/Nov 1974):318.

Martienssen, Anthony. Queen Katherine Parr. New York: Mc-
    Graw-Hill, 1973. Rev. by C. B. Cone, RKHS, 72(Oct 1974):
    415-17.

Martin, A. Lynn. Henry III and the Jesuit Politicians. Geneva:
    Librairie Droz, 1973. Rev. by J. Crawford, CH, 43(Sep
    1974):407.

Martin, Albro. Enterprise Denied: Origins of the Decline of Amer-
    ican Railroads, 1897-1917. New York: Columbia U Press,
    1971. Rev. by T. K. McCraw, BHR, 48(Sum 1974):268-71.

Martin, E. W., ed. Comparative Development in Social Welfare.
    London: George Allen and Unwin, 1972. Rev. by D. Hay,
    CHR, 55(Je 1974):218-20.

Martin, Edward C. see Sandler, Martin W.

Martin, Ged. The Durham Report and British Policy: A Critical
    Essay. Cambridge: Cam U Press, 1972. Rev. by P. Bur-
    roughs, CHR, 55(Sep 1974):320-2; T. Reese, EHR, 89(Jl 1974):
    680-2; R. L. Jones, Historian, 36(Feb 1974):323-4.

Martin, Harold H. Ralph McGill, Reporter. Boston: Little, Brown,
    1973. Rev. by J. Spalding, GHQ, 58(Spr 1974):121-2; J. R.

Skates, JSH, 40(Feb 1974):163-4.

Martin, James Kirby. Men in Rebellion: Higher Governmental
Leaders and the Coming of the American Revolution. New
Brunswick, N.J.: Rutgers U Press, 1973. Rev. by J. P.
Greene, JAH, 61(Je 1974):164-5; R. M. Weir, JSH, 40(Feb
1974):123-5; D. Higginbotham, MHM, 69(Sum 1974):228-30;
V. L. Johnson, PH, 41(Oct 1974):464-5; J. J. Waters, WMQ-
3, 31(Ja 1974):149-50.

Martin, Josephine Bacon, ed. Life on a Liberty County Plantation:
The Journal of Cornelia Jones Pond. Darien, Ga.: Darien
News, 1974. Rev. by E. Paris, GHQ, 58(Fall 1974):268-70.

Martin, Paul and Fred Plog. The Archaeology of Arizona: A Study
of the Southwest Region. Garden City, N.Y.: Doubleday, 1973.
Rev. by R. H. Lister, Archaeology, 27(Jl 1974):220.

Martinage-Baranger, Renée. Bourjon et le code civil. Paris: Editions Klincksieck, 1971. Rev. by W. F. Church, AHR, 79(Je
1974):789-90.

Martines, Lauro, ed. Violence and Civil Disorder in Italian Cities
1200-1500. Berkeley: U Cal Press, 1972. Rev. by M. Mallett, EHR, 89(Jl 1974):658-9; A. V. Antonovics, History, 59
(Feb 1974):97-8.

Martinez-Alier, Verena. Marriage, Class and Colour in Nineteenth-
Century Cuba: A Study of Racial Attitudes and Sexual Values
in a Slave Society. New York: Cam U Press, 1974. Rev.
by T. E. Skidmore, HRNB, 3(Nov/Dec 1974):42.

Martínez Peláez, Severo. La patria del criollo. Ensayo de inter-
pretación de la realidad colonial guatemalteca. Guatemala:
Editorial Universitaria, 1971. Rev. by M. J. MacLeod,
HAHR, 54(May 1974):317-19.

Martz, John D. Ecuador: Conflicting Political Culture and the
Quest for Progress. Boston: Allyn and Bacon, 1972. Rev.
by R. Landmann, HAHR, 54(May 1974):349-50.

Marx, Robert F. The Lure of Sunken Treasure. New York: David
McKay, 1973. Rev. by L. S. de Camp, T & C, 15(Jl 1974):
538-9.

Masaryk, Tomás G. The Meaning of Czech History. Chapel Hill:
UNC Press, 1974. Rev. by J. Hajda, HRNB, 2(Jl 1974):208-
9.

Maser, Werner. Hitler: Legend, Myth and Reality. New York:
Harper and Row, 1973. Rev. by H. W. Gatzke, AHR, 79(Oct
1974):1205-6.

Mason, Elizabeth B. and Louis M. Starr, eds.   The Oral History
   Collection of Columbia University.   New York: Oral History
   Research Office, 1973.   Rev. by A. M. Campbell, AmArc,
   37(Ja 1974):91-3.

Mason, Herbert Malloy, Jr.   The Rise of the Luftwaffe: Forging
   the Secret German Air Weapon, 1918-1940.   New York: Dial,
   1973.   Rev. by E. F. Ziemke, HRNB, 2(Feb 1974):110-11.

Massachusetts Historical Society.   Proceedings.   Volumes LXXXII
   (1970); Volume LXXXIII (1971).   Boston: Mass. Hist. Soc.,
   1971, 1972.   Rev. by R. E. Welsh, Jr., NEQ, 47(Mar 1974):
   150-3.

Massachusetts.   House of Representatives.   Journals of the House
   of Representatives of Massachusetts, 1765-1766 and 1766.
   Volumes XLII and XLIII.   Ed. by Malcolm Freiberg.   Boston:
   Mass. Historical Society, 1972 and 1973.   Rev. by J. A.
   Schutz, NEQ, 47(Mar 1974):165-8.

Masson, Olivier and Maurice Sznycer.   Recherches sur les Phéni-
   ciens à Chypre.   Geneva: Librairie Droz, 1972.   Rev. by
   C. G. Starr, AHR, 79(Je 1974):761-2; J. Teixidor, AJA, 78
   (Apr 1974):189-90.

Mastny, Vojtech.   The Czechs under Nazi Rule: The Failure of
   National Resistance, 1939-1942.   New York: Columbia U
   Press, 1971.   Rev. by J. Anderle, JMH, 46(Je 1974):362-5.

Mather, Cotton.   The Angel of Bethesda.   Barre, Mass.: ... American Antiquarian Society, 1972.   Rev. by B. R. Burg, AmArc,
   37(Apr 1974):296-7; J. H. Cassedy, WMQ-3, 31(Ja 1974):162-
   3.

Mathes, W. Michael, tr. and ed.   The Conquistador in California:
   1535.   The Voyage of Fernando Cortes to Baja California in
   Chronicles and Documents.   Los Angeles: Dawson's Book Shop,
   1973.   Rev. by H. P. Hinton, SCQ, 56(Fall 1974):319-21.

Matheson, Peter.   Cardinal Contarini at Regensburg.   Oxford: Clarendon Press, 1972.   Rev. by J. Bossy, EHR, 89(Ja 1974):169.

Mathias, Peter, ed.   Science and Society 1600-1900.   Cambridge:
   Cam U Press, 1972.   Rev. by C. Webster, EHR, 89(Apr 1974):
   435-6.

Mathieu, Jacques.   La Construction navale royale à Québec 1739-
   1759.   Quebec: La Société historique de Québec, 1971.   Rev.
   by J. Pritchard, CHR, 55(Mar 1974):81-2.

Mathis, G. Ray, ed.   College Life in the Reconstruction South:
   Walter B. Hill's Student Correspondence, 1869-1871.   Athens,
   Ga.:   U Ga Press, 1974.   Rev. by J. E. Talmadge, GHQ, 58

(Fall 1974):366-8; W. Smith, HRNB, 2(Sep 1974):261-2.

Mathur, L. P. Indian Revolutionary Movement in the United States
of America. New Delhi: S. Chand, 1970. Rev. by B. R.
Babu, AHR, 79(Oct 1974):1285-6.

Matson, A. T. Nandi Resistance to British Rule 1890-1906. Nairobi: East African Pub. House, 1972. Rev. by G. H. Mun-
geam, JAfH, 15(Num 1 1974):162-3.

Mattelart, Armand, Carmin Castillo and Leonardo Castillo. La
ideología de la dominación en una sociedad dependiente. Buenos
Aires: Ediciones Signos, 1970. Rev. by S. Collier, JLAS, 6
(May 1974):182-5.

Matthew, H. C. G. The Liberal Imperialists: The Ideas and Politics of a Post-Gladstonian Elite. New York: Ox U Press,
1973. Rev. by B. Semmel, AHR, 79(Feb 1974):152-3; M.
Hurst, HJ, 17(Num 3 1974):665-8.

Matthews, Joseph F. George W. Smalley: Forty Years a Foreign
Correspondent. Chapel Hill: UNC Press, 1973. Rev. by
R. J. Amundson, CWH, 20(Sep 1974):272-3; R. R. Grask,
HRNB, 2(May/Je 1974):159; B. K. Zobrist, JAH, 61(Dec 1974):
786-7.

Matthews, Noel. Materials for West African History in the Archives
of the United Kingdom. London: Athlone, 1973. Rev. by
J. D. Fage, History, 59(Je 1974):303-4.

Matthews, William see Latham, Robert

Matthias, Erich see Nicholls, Anthony

Mattila, Walter. Indians, Finns, and Their Thunderbirds. Portland, Ore.: Published by Author, 1973. Rev. by E. Niska,
OrHQ, 75(Mar 1974):83-4.

Mauriac, Claude. The Other de Gaulle, 1944-1954. New York:
John Day, 1973. Rev. by M. F. Goldman, HRNB, 2(Feb
1974):106.

Mauro, Frédéric. Des produits et des hommes: Essais historiques.
latino-américains XVIe-XXe siècles. Paris: Mouton, 1972.
Rev. by K. R. Maxwell, JIH, 5(Aut 1974):348-50.

Mauss, Marcel. A General Theory of Magic. London: Routledge
and Kegan Paul, 1972. Rev. by W. James, AfAf, 73(Apr
1974):234-5.

Maves, Carl. Sensuous Pessimism: Italy in the Work of Henry
James. Bloomington and London: Indiana U Press, 1973.
Rev. by D. K. Kirby, NEQ, 47(Mar 1974):173-5.

Max- Planck Institut fur Geschichte, ed.   Festschrift fur Hermann
Hempel. Göttingen: Vandenhoeck and Ruprecht, 1972. Rev.
by W. Ullmann, History, 59(Je 1974):328-9.

Maxwell, Hu and H. L. Swisher. History of Hampshire County,
West Virginia, From Its Earliest Settlement to the Present.
Parsons, W. Va.: McClain, 1972. Rev. by O. K. Rice,
WVH, 36(Oct 1974):67-8.

Maxwell, Kenneth R.   Conflicts and Conspiracies: Brazil and Portugal, 1750-1808. New York: Cam U Press, 1973. Rev. by
S. B. Schwartz, HAHR, 54(Aug 1974):516-20; P. E. Kuhl,
HRNB, 2(Ja 1974):70; E. Viotti da Costa, TAm, 31(Oct 1974):
221-2.

Maxwell, William, ed. The Virginia Historical Register. 6 vols.
Spartanburg, S. C.: n. p. (Reprint), 1973. Rev. by O. K.
Rice, WVH, 35(Jl 1974):323-4.

Maxwell-Hyslop, K. R.   Western Asiatic Jewellery c. 3000- 612
B. C. London: Methuen, 1971. Rev. by W. W. Rudolph,
AJA, 78(Apr 1974):191-2.

May, Ernest R. "Lessons" of the Past: The Use and Misuse of
History in American Foreign Policy. New York: Ox U Press,
1973. Rev. by A. M. Schlesinger, Jr., JAH, 61(Sep 1974):
443-4; D. S. Patterson, JSH, 40(Aug 1974):511-12; L. J. Gray-
bar, MiA, 56(Jl 1974):205; A. Rappaport, PHR, 43(Aug 1974):
410-12; W. B. Fowler, PNQ, 65(Oct 1974):193-4.

_____ and James C. Thomson, Jr., eds.   American-East Asian
Relations: A Survey. Cambridge, Mass.: Har U Press, 1972.
Rev. by J. Israel, AHR, 79(Feb 1974):219-20.

May, George W.   Charles E. Duryea--Automaker.   Ann Arbor,
Mich.: Edwards Bros., 1973. Rev. by J. B. Rae, JAH, 61
(Dec 1974):808-9; D. L. Lewis, JISHS, 67(Nov 1974):566-7.

May, Robert E.   The Southern Dream of a Caribbean Empire, 1854-
1861. Baton Rouge: LSU Press, 1973. Rev. by S. A. Chan-
ning, CWH, 20(Je 1974):171-3; R. C. Harris, FHQ, 53(Jl
1974):87-9; N. D. Brown, GHQ, 58(Sum 1974):289-91; R. E.
Shalhope, JAH, 61(Dec 1974):781-2; J. C. Kiger, JMiH, 36
(Nov 1974):389-90; R. F. Broussard, JSH, 40(Aug 1974):479-
80; A. B. Pearson, Jr., NCHR, 51(Sum 1974):343-4; J. G.
Tregle, Jr., LaH, 15(Spr 1974):203-4; L. D. Langley, SWHQ,
78(Jl 1974):95-6.

May, Rollo. Paulus. Reminiscences of a Friendship. New York:
Harper & Row, n. d. Rev. by A. Cardona-Hine, Mankind, 4
(Apr 1974):8, 62.

Mayer, H. E.   Marseilles Levantehandel und ein akkonensisches

Fälscheratelier des 13. Jahrhunderts. Tubingen: Niemeyer, 1972. Rev. by T. A. Reuter, EHR, 89(Ja 1974):156.

Mayer, Hans Eberhard. The Crusades. New York: Ox U Press, 1972. Rev. by C. L. Tipton, AHR, 79(Feb 1974):131-2.

Mayer, Harold M. and Richard C. Wade. Chicago: Growth of a Metropolis. Chicago: U Chi Press, 1969. Rev. by D. R. Colburn, HT, 7(Aug 1974):637-8.

Mayfield, James B. Rural Politics in Nasser's Egypt: A Quest for Legitimacy. Austin: U Tx Press, 1971. Rev. by N. R. Keddie, AHR, 79(Feb 1974):207-8.

Mayhew, Alan. Rural Settlement and Farming in Germany. New York: Barnes and Noble, 1973. Rev. by H. S. Snellgrove, Historian, 36(Feb 1974):315-16; L. Schofer, JEH, 34(Je 1974): 511.

Mayr-Harting, Henry. The Coming of Christianity to Anglo-Saxon England. London: Batsford, 1972. Rev. by P. H. Blair, EHR, 89(Ja 1974):146-7.

Mays, Benjamin E. Born to Rebel: An Autobiography. New York: Scribner's, 1971. Rev. by A. Buni, AHR, 79(Je 1974):909.

Mazar (Maisler), Benjamin. Beth She'arim: Report on the Excavations During 1936-1940. Volume I, Catacombs 1-4. New Brunswick, N.J.: Rutgers U Press, 1973. Rev. by R. Brilliant, HRNB, 2(Aug 1974):226.

Mazlish, Bruce. The Riddle of History: The Great Speculators from Vico to Freud. New York: Minerva, 1968. Rev. by C. G. Ryant, HT, 7(Feb 1974):308-9.

Mazzaro, Jerome. William Carlos Williams: The Later Poems. Ithaca, N.Y.: Cornell U Press, 1973. Rev. by A. T. K. Crozier, JAmS, 8(Aug 1974):279-80.

Mbiti, John S. African Religions and Philosophy. London: Heinemann, 1969. Rev. by G. O. M. Tasie, JMAS, 12(Je 1974): 326-9.

_____. Concepts of God in Africa. London: S. P. C. K., 1970. Rev. by G. O. M. Tasie, JMAS, 12(Je 1974):326-9.

Mead, Howard, Jill Dean, and Susan Smith. Portrait of the Past: A Photographic Journey Through Wisconsin. Madison: Wis Tales and Trails, 1971. Rev. by J. J. Newman, IMH, 70(Dec 1974):363-5.

Medick, Hans. Naturzand und Naturgeschichte der bürgerlichen Gesellschaft: Die Ursprünge der bürgerlichen Sozialtheorie

als Geschichtsphilosophie und Sozialwissenschaft bei Samuel
Pufendorf, John Locke und Adam Smith. Göttingen: Vandenhoeck and Ruprecht, 1973. Rev. by L. Krieger, AHR, 79(Apr
1974):483-4.

Medlicott, W. N., D. Dakin and M. E. Lambert, eds. Documents
on British Foreign Policy, 1919-1939. London: H. M. S. O.,
1972. Rev. by D. Dilks, EHR, 89(Ja 1974):237-8.

Meek, R. L., ed. Turgot on Progress, Sociology and Economics.
Cambridge: Cam U Press, 1973. Rev. by J. M. Roberts,
EHR, 89(Ja 1974):200-1.

Megaw, J. V. S. Archaeology from Down Under: A Personal View.
Leicester: Leicester U Press, 1973. Rev. by P. Gathercole,
Antiquity, 48(Je 1974):160-1.

Mehlinger, Howard D. and John M. Thompson. Count Witte and
the Tsarist Government in the 1905 Revolution. Bloomington:
Ind U Press, 1972. Rev. by E. C. Thaden, AHR, 79(Apr
1974):540-1.

Mehnert, Klaus. China Today. London: Thames and Hudson,
1972. Rev. by C. Chintamani, CR, 10(Ja-Apr 1974):71-2.

Meier, August. The Rise of the Ghetto. see Bracey, John H., Jr.

_____ and Elliott Rudwick. CORE: A Study in the Civil Rights
Movement, 1942-1968. New York: Ox U Press, 1973. Rev.
by J. M. McPherson, AHR, 79(Feb 1974):248-9; P. Borden,
HT, 7(Feb 1974):319-20; R. M. Dalfiume, JAH, 60(Mar 1974):
1186-7; J. S. Reed, JSH, 40(Feb 1974):158-60; W. Toll, PNQ,
65(Ja 1974):44.

Meier, Heinz K., ed. Memoirs of a Swiss Officer in the American
Civil War. Bern, Switzerland: Herbert Lang, 1972. Rev.
by J. K. Folmar, CWH, 20(Mar 1974):74-6; T. L. Connelly,
MHM, 69(Spr 1974):108-9.

Meier, Matt S. and Feliciano Rivera. The Chicanos: A History of
Mexican-Americans. New York: Hill and Wang, 1972. Rev.
by A. Hoffman, JOW, 13(Jl 1974):133; M. T. Garcia, PHR,
43(Feb 1974):123-5.

Meier-Dörnberg, Wilhelm. Die Ölversorgung der Kriegsmarine
1935 bis 1945. Freiburg: Verlag Rombach, 1973. Rev. by
A. Norman, AHR, 79(Apr 1974):526-7.

Meighan, Clement W. and Francis A. Riddell. The Maru Cult of
the Pomo Indians: A California Ghost Dance Survival. Los
Angeles: Southwest Museum, 1972. Rev. by H. F. Dobyns,
A & W, 16(Spr 1974):66-7; H. A. Howard, JOW, 13(Ja 1974):
144-5.

Meigs, John, ed. The Cowboy in American Prints. Chicago: Sage
    Books, Swallow Press, 1972. Rev. by C. W. Black, JOW,
    13(Ja 1974):156.

Meinecke, Friedrich. Historism. The Rise of a New Historical
    Outlook. New York: Herder and Herder, 1972. Rev. by
    F. Gilbert, H & T, 13(Num 1 1974):59-64; H. White, PHR,
    43(Nov 1974):597-8.

Meinig, D. W. Southwest: Three Peoples in Geographical Change,
    1600-1970. New York: Ox U Press, 1971. Rev. by H. R.
    Lamar, AHR, 79(Feb 1974):220-1.

Meissner, Boris, ed. Social Change in the Soviet Union: Russia's
    Path Toward an Industrial Society. Notre Dame, Ind.: U
    Notre Dame Press, 1972. Rev. by R. A. Roosa, AHR, 79
    (Apr 1974):537-9.

Mekheda, M. I., et al., eds. History of the Cities and Villages
    of the Ukranian SSR--Khmel'nitsky Province. Kiev: Institut
    Istorii Akademii Nauk URSR, 1971. Rev. by J. Armstrong,
    AHR, 79(Feb 1974):193-4.

Melendy, H. Brett. The Oriental Americans. New York: Twayne,
    1972. Rev. by A. Hoffman, JOW, 13(Jl 1974):132; H. H.
    Sugimoto, PNQ, 65(Ja 1974):42.

Meleski, Patricia F. Echoes of the Past: New Mexico's Ghost
    Towns. Albuquerque: U NM Press, 1972. Rev. by C. E.
    Trafzer, GPJ, 13(Spr 1974):212; F. D. Almaraz, Jr., JOW,
    13(Ja 1974):153.

Melgunov, S. P. The Bolshevik Seizure of Power. Santa Barbara,
    ABC-Clio, 1972. Rev. by R. C. Williams, AHR, 79(Apr 1974)
    546-9.

Melville, Dorothy Sutherland. Tyler-Browns of Brattleboro. Jeri-
    cho, N. Y.: Exposition Press, 1973. Rev. by R. C. Harris,
    CWH, 20(Je 1974):180-2; L. S. Brigham, VH, 42(Win 1974):
    72.

Menchi, S. S., ed. see Guicciardini, Francesco

Mendelson, Robert E. see Judd, Dennis R.

Mennel, Robert M. Thorns and Thistles: Juvenile Delinquents in
    the United States, 1825-1940. Hanover, N. H.: U Press New
    England ..., 1973. Rev. by D. J. Rothman, AHR, 79(Feb
    1974):224-5; C. E. Larsen, JAH, 60(Mar 1974):1110-11.

Menżeńska, Sister Mary Jane. Archives and Other Special Collec-
    tions: A Library Handbook. New York: Columbia U School
    of Library Service, 1973. Rev. by M. I. Crawford, AmArc,
    37(Apr 1974):289-90.

Merino, Hugo Zemelman see Petras, James

Merk, Frederick. Economic History of Wisconsin During the Civil
   War Decade. Madison: The State Historical Society of Wisconsin, 1971. Rev. by R. P. Swierenga, CWH, 20(Sep 1974):
   278-9.

_____. Slavery and the Annexation of Texas. New York: Knopf,
   1972. Rev. by R. V. Haynes, AHR, 79(Apr 1974):578-9;
   W. R. Brock, EHR, 89(Jl 1974):682-4; R. Tyler, JNH, 59(Ja
   1974):89-90; V. B. Howard, JNH, 59(Ja 1974):90-1; J. H.
   Schroeder, NEQ, 47(Je 1974):324-6.

Merley, Jean. L'Industrie en Haute-Loire de la fin de la Monarchie
   de Juillet aux débuts de la Troisieme Republique. Lyon: Centre d'histoire economique et sociale de la region lyonnaise,
   1972. Rev. by C. Lucas, EHR, 89(Ja 1974):211-12.

Merli, Frank J. and Theodore A. Wilson, eds. Makers of American Diplomacy: From Benjamin Franklin to Henry Kissinger.
   New York: Scribner's, 1974. Rev. by G. E. Thurow, HRNB,
   2(Sep 1974):260.

Merrill, Charles E. The Old Guide's Story of the Northern Adiron-
   dacks: Reminiscences of Charles E. Merrill. Saranac Lake,
   N.Y.: Adirondack Yesteryears, 1973. Rev. by E. J. Winslow, NYH, 55(Apr 1974):238-9.

Merrill, Walter M., ed. The Letters of William Lloyd Garrison.
   Volume III: No Union with Slaveholders, 1841-1849. Cambridge, Mass.: Belknap Press of Har U Press, 1973. Rev.
   by R. F. Durden, HRNB, 2(May/Je 1974):160; M. L. Dillon,
   JSH, 40(Nov 1974):659-60.

Mertz, Henriette. Pale Ink: Two Ancient Records of Chinese Exploration in America. Chicago: Swallow, 1972. Rev. by
   B. M. Gough, JOW, 13(Jl 1974):120.

Merwick, Donna. Boston Priests, 1848-1910: A Study of Social
   and Intellectual Change. Cambridge, Mass.: Har U Press,
   1973. Rev. by J. T. Ellis, AHR, 79(Feb 1974):228; T.
   Joyce, CH, 43(Mar 1974):123-4; A. Mann, JAH, 60(Mar 1974):
   1120-1.

Merzagora, Lucia. I Vasi a Vernice Nera Della Collezione H. A.
   di Milano. Milano: Amilcare Pizzi Editore, 1971. Rev. by
   J. G. Szilágyi, AJA, 78(Apr 1974):202-3.

Meskill, John, ed. An Introduction to Chinese Civilization. New
   York: Columbia U Press, 1973. Rev. by C. Dietrich, AHR,
   79(Feb 1974):209-10.

Messbarger, Paul R. Fiction with a Parochial Purpose: Social

Uses of American Catholic Literature, 1884-1900. Boston: Boston U Press, 1971. Rev. by R. M. Miller, AHR, 79(Je 1974):883-4.

Messerli, Jonathan. Horace Mann: A Biography. New York: Knopf, 1972. Rev. by W. R. Hutchison, AHR, 79(Feb 1974): 226-7.

Metz, Leon G. Pat Garrett: The Story of a Western Lawman. Norman: U Ok Press, 1974. Rev. by W. Rundell, Jr., AmArc, 37(Oct 1974):598-9.

Metzger, Thomas A. The Internal Organization of Ch'ing Bureaucracy: Legal, Normative, and Communication Aspects. Cambridge, Mass.: Har U Press, 1973. Rev. by C. T. Hu, HRNB, 2(May/Je 1974):174-5.

Meyer, Carl S., ed. Sixteenth-Century Essays and Studies. Vol. 2. St. Louis: Foundation for Reformation Research, 1971. Rev. by F. D. Price, EHR, 89(Ja 1974):168.

Meyer, D. H. The Instructed Conscience: The Shaping of the American National Ethic. Philadelphia: U Pa Press, 1972. Rev. by G. H. Hinkle, CH, 43(Sep 1974):422.

Meyer, Howard N. The Amendment That Refused to Die--XIV. Radnor, Pa.: Chilton, 1973. Rev. by M. Schwartz, Crisis, 81 (May 1974):176-7.

Meyer, Isidore S., ed. The Hebrew Exercises of Governor William Bradford. Plymouth: The Pilgrim Society, 1973. Rev. by N. Pettit, NEQ, 47(Je 1974):321-2.

Meyer, Jean. La Noblesse Bretonne au XVIIIieme Siecle. Paris: S. E. V. P. E. N., 1970. Rev. by B. Behrens, HJ, 17 (Num 3 1974):631-43.

Meyer, Michael C. Huerta: A Political Portrait. Lincoln: U Neb Press, 1972. Rev. by P. Calvert, JLAS, 6(May 1974):177-9; J. Secrest, NMHR, 49(Jl 1974):256-8.

Michael, Franz with Chung-Li Chang. The Taiping Rebellion: History and Documents. Volumes II and III: Documents and Comments. Seattle: U Wash Press, 1971. Rev. by C. M. Wilbur, MAS, 8(Jl 1974):422-4.

Michel, Antoine. Le Conseil royal des Finances au XVIIIe siecle et le registre E 3569 des Archives nationales. Geneva: Librairie Droz, 1973. Rev. by W. F. Church, AHR, 79(Feb 1974):163-4.

Michel, Marc. La Mission Marchand. Paris: Mouton, 1972. Rev. by A. S. Kanya-Forstner, JAfH, 15(Num 1 1974):160-1.

Michelman, Irving S.   The Crisis Meeters: Business Response to Social Crisis.   Clifton, N. J.:   Augustus M. Kelley, 1973. Rev. by M. Heald, BHR, 48(Sum 1974):273-4.

Michels, Joseph W.   Dating Methods in Archaeology.   New York: Seminar Press, 1973.   Rev. by R. E. Taylor, AmAnt, 39(Oct 1974):645-6.

Michio, Hirao.   A History of the Boshin War.   Tokyo: Misaki Shobo, 1971.   Rev. by C. D. Sheldon, JAS, 33(Feb 1974):314-16.

Middlemas, Keith.   Diplomacy of Illusion.   The British Government and Germany, 1937-39.   London: Weidenfeld and Nicolson, 1972.   Rev. by P. J. Rolo, EHR, 89(Apr 1974):468-9.

Middleton, Drew.   Where Has Last July Gone?   Memoirs.   New York: Quadrangle/N.Y. Times Book Co., 1974.   Rev. by R. N. Stromberg, HRNB, 2(Apr 1974):150.

Middleton, W. E. Knowles.   The Experimenters: A Study of the Accademia del Cimento.   Baltimore: JHU Press, 1971.   Rev. by R. S. Westman, RQ, 27(Sum 1974):221-3.

Midelfort, H. C. Erik.   Witch-Hunting in Southwestern Germany 1562-1684:   The Social and Intellectual Foundations.   Stanford, Cal.:   Stan U Press, 1972.   Rev. by R. J. W. Evans, History, 59(Je 1974):276-7.

Miers, Earl Schenck.   The Last Campaign: Grant Saves the Union. Philadelphia: Lippincott, 1972.   Rev. by R. E. Beringer, Historian, 36(Feb 1974):342-3.

Mihailovic, Kosta.   Regional Development Experiences and Prospects in Eastern Europe.   The Hague: Mouton, 1972.   Rev. by G. W. Hoffman, EEQ, 8(Fall 1974):374-5.

Mihalyi, Gabor, et al., eds.   Index of the English Column of Nagyvilag--1956-1972.   Budapest: n. p., 1973.   Rev. by I. Sanders, EEQ, 8(Fall 1974):387-9.

Miles, David see Benson, Don

Milic, Louis T., ed.   The Modernity of the Eighteenth Century. Cleveland: Press, C-WRU, 1971.   Rev. by I. Wade, JIH, 5 (Sum 1974):151-5.

Milichar, Herbert see Kaneko, Erika

Miller, Alfred J. and Michael Bell.   Braves and Buffalo: Plains Indian Life in 1837.   Toronto: U Tor Press, 1973.   Rev. by C. E. Tigue, JOW, 13(Jl 1974):118; J. C. Ewers, NDH, 41 (Spr 1974):31; D. S. Gaus, TAm, 31(Jl 1974):109-10.

Miller, Charles. Battle for the Bundu: The First World War in East Africa. New York: Macmillan, 1974. Rev. by B. Fetter, HRNB, 3(Oct 1974):16-17.

Miller, David E. , ed. The Golden Spike. Salt Lake City: U Utah Press, 1973. Rev. by R. A. Bartlett, HRNB, 2(Mar 1974): 127; L. Carranco, JOW, 13(Jl 1974):126.

Miller, Edward. That Noble Cabinet: A History of the British Museum. n. p. : Deutsch, n. d. Rev. by M. Greenhalgh, HTo, 24(Je 1974):435-7.

Miller, Elaine K. , ed. Mexican Folk Narrative from the Los Angeles Area. Austin: U of Tex Press, 1973. Rev. by J. Sobrino, HAHR, 54(Nov 1974):738-9.

Miller, Elinor and Eugene D. Genovese, eds. Plantation, Town, and Country: Essays on the Local History of American Slave Society. Urbana: U Ill Press, 1974. Rev. by J. Burt, THQ, 33(Win 1974):455-6.

Miller, Frances Pickens. Man from the Valley: Memoirs of a 20th-Century Virginian. Chapel Hill: UNC Press, 1971. Rev. by G. Osborn, AHR, 79(Oct 1974):1282-3.

Miller, J. D. B. Survey of Commonwealth Affairs: Problems of Expansion and Attrition 1953-1969. New York: Ox U Press, 1974. Rev. by P. H. Scherer, HRNB, 2(Sep 1974):248-9.

Miller, John. Popery and Politics in England, 1660-1688. Cambridge: Cam U Press, 1973. Rev. by J. C. H. Aveling, HJ, 17(Num 3 1974):660-2; R. Howell, Jr. , HRNB, 2(Ja 1974): 86.

Miller, John C. This New Man, the American: The Beginnings of the American People. New York: McGraw-Hill, 1974. Rev. by P. C. Nagel, HRNB, 3(Nov/Dec 1974):45-6.

Miller, Lillian B. , Walter T. K. Nugent, and H. Wayne Morgan. Indiana Historical Society Lectures, 1972-1973: The Centennial Year. Indianapolis: Ind Historical Society, 1973. Rev. by C. W. Smith, IMH, 70(Sep 1974):254-5.

Miller, Molly. The Thalassocracies. Albany: S U N Y Press, 1971. Rev. by G. Downey, AHR, 79(Oct 1974):1152.

Miller, Nathan. Sea of Glory: The Continental Navy Fights for Independence, 1775-1783. New York: David McKay, 1974. Rev. by R. G. O'Connor, HRNB, 2(May/Je 1974):166.

Miller, Peggy. James. London: Allen and Unwin, 1971. Rev. by E. Gregg, ESR, 4(Jl 1974):269-74.

Miller, Robert Moats. How Shall They Hear Without a Preacher?
The Life of Ernest Fremont Tittle. Chapel Hill: UNC Press,
1971. Rev. by T. L. Agnew, AHR, 79(Oct 1974):1282.

Miller, Sally M. Victor Berger and the Promise of Constructive
Socialism, 1910-1920. Westport, Conn.: Greenwood, 1973.
Rev. by D. J. Humes, AHR, 79(Oct 1974):1278-9; G. Adams,
Jr., CHR, 55(Je 1974):226-7; H. H. Quint, JAH, 61(Je 1974):
238-9; L. L. Athey, MiA, 56(Ja 1974):69; R. C. Haney, WMH,
57(Spr 1974):234-5.

Miller, Thomas Lloyd. The Public Lands of Texas, 1519-1970.
Norman: U Ok Press, 1972. Rev. by W. A. Beck, AHR,
79(Je 1974):842-3.

Miller, Townsend. Henry IV of Castile 1425-1474. London: Gollancz, 1972. Rev. by A. Mackay, History, 59(Feb 1974):96.

Miller, William C. see Marsh, Andrew J. Reports....

Miller, Wright. Who Are the Russians? A History of the Russian
People. n. p.: Taplinger Publishing Co., n. d. Rev. by D.
Pfeil, Mankind, 4(Feb 1974):58, 65.

Miller, Zane L. The Urbanization of Modern America: A Brief
History. New York: Harcourt Brace Jovanovich, 1973. Rev.
by D. R. Coleman, HT, 7(Aug 1974):637-8; H. S. Nelli, JAH,
61(Je 1974):149-50.

Millward, Roy and Adrian Robinson. Landscapes of England....
London: Macmillan, 1973. Rev. by D. Thomas, History, 59
(Je 1974):329-30.

Milton, John R., ed. Conversations with Frank Waters. Chicago:
Swallow, 1971. Rev. by O. C. Stewart, CoMag, 51(Sum 1974):
238-40.

Milton, Ohmer. Alternatives to the Traditional: How Professors
Teach and How Students Learn. San Francisco: Jossey-Bass,
1973. Rev. by F. P. Lynch, HT, 7(Aug 1974):641-2.

Milward, A. and S. B. Saul. The Economic Development of Continental Europe, 1780-1870. London: George Allen and Unwin,
1973. Rev. by R. R. Locke, JEH, 34(Sep 1974):796-7.

Milward, Alan S. The New Order and the French Economy. Oxford: Clarendon Press, 1970. Rev. by R. Tilly, JEH, 34
(Je 1974):512-14.

Mims, Sam. Toledo Bend. Gretna, La.: Pelican, 1972. Rev. by
C. Stokes, ETHJ, 12(Spr 1974):60; T. Stacey, LaH, 15(Sum
1974):318.

Minchinton, W. E., ed. Wage Regulation in Pre-Industrial England. Newton Abbot: David and Charles, 1972. Rev. by N. B. Harte, History, 59(Feb 1974):103.

Minear, Richard H. Victors' Justice: The Tokyo War Crimes Trial. Princeton, N.J.: Prin U Press, 1971. Rev. by B. F. Beers, JAH, 61(Dec 1974):836-7.

Miner, Earl. The Cavalier Mode from Jonson to Cotton. Princeton, N.J.: Prin U Press, 1971. Rev. by T. Clayton, RQ, 27(Spr 1974):110-14.

_____, ed. English Criticism in Japan: Essays by Younger Japanese Scholars on English and American Literature. Tokyo: U Tokyo Press, 1973. Rev. by W. Jackson, JAS, 33 (Feb 1974):316-17.

Miners, N. J. The Nigerian Army, 1956-1966. London: Methuen, 1971. Rev. by S. C. Sarkesian, JMAS, 12(Je 1974):338-41.

Minerva Handbücher, Archive. Archive im deutschsprachigen Raum. 2 vols. Berlin: Walter de Gruyter, 1974. Rev. by J. Mendelsohn, AmArc, 37(Oct 1974):591-2.

Ministerio de Relaciones Exteriores. Centenario del Fallecimiento de Don Antonio José de Irisarri. Guatemala: Editorial del Ejercito, 1971. Rev. by T. Schoonover, TAm, 30(Apr 1974): 551-2.

Minor, Joseph E. see Baker, Lindsay T.

Minter, William. Portuguese Africa and the West. New York: Monthly Review Press, 1972. Rev. by J. C. Miller, AfAf, 73(Jl 1974):370-1; W. C. Opello, Jr., JMAS, 12(Sep 1974): 487-91.

Mints, I. I., et al., eds. The Victory of Soviet Power in the Transcaucasus. Tbilisi: Izdatel'stvo "Metsniereba," 1971. Rev. by M. K. Matossian, AHR, 79(Je 1974):824-5.

Miquel, Pierre. La paix de Versailles et l'opinion publique française. Paris: Flammarion, Editeur, 1972. Rev. by P. C. Sorum, AHR, 79(Oct 1974):1192-3.

Miscellanea Wilbouriana. Brooklyn, N.Y.: Brooklyn Museum, 1972. Rev. by H. Goedicke, AJA, 78(Ja 1974):81-2.

La misión La Torre en Bolivia, 1831-1835. Lima: Ministerio de Exteriores del Perú, 1971. Rev. by R. W. Delaney, HAHR, 54(Aug 1974):531-3.

Misra, G. S. P. The Age of Vinaya. New Delhi: Munshiram Manoharlal, 1972. Rev. by C. S. Prebish, JAS, 33(Feb 1974): 324-5.

Mitchell, Allan. Bismarck and the French Nation 1848-1890. New York: Pegasus, 1972. Rev. by R. Bullen, EHR, 89(Ja 1974): 220-1.

Mitchell, Bonner. Rome in the High Renaissance: The Age of Leo X. Norman: U Ok Press, 1973. Rev. by J. W. O'Malley, CH, 43(Je 1974):270-1; DeL. Jensen, HRNB, 2(Ja 1974):80.

Mitchell, Broadus. The Price of Independence: A Realistic View of the American Revolution. New York: Ox U Press, 1974. Rev. by R. F. Detweiler, JSH, 40(Nov 1974):651-2.

Mitchell, Joseph B. Military Leaders in the Civil War. New York: Putnam's, 1972. Rev. by R. D. Hofsommer, CWTI, 13(May 1974):47.

Mitchell, L. G., ed. The Purefoy Letters, 1735-1753. New York: St. Martin's, 1973. Rev. by B. McGill, HRNB, 2(Feb 1974): 108-9.

Mitchell, Otis C., ed. Nazism and the Common Man: Essays in German History (1929-1939). Minneapolis: Burgess, 1972. Rev. by K. R. Nelson, HT, 8(Nov 1974):140-1.

Mitford, Nancy. Frederick the Great. London: Hamish Hamilton, 1970. Rev. by P. Doran, ESR, 4(Jl 1974):276-9.

Mitzman, Arthur. Sociology and Estrangement: Three Sociologists of Imperial Germany. New York: Knopf, 1973. Rev. by J. J. Sheehan, JMH, 46(Sep 1974):556-7.

Miyakawa, T. Scott see Conroy, Hilary

Mizushima, Keiko see Keyes, Roger S.

Modell, John, ed. The Kikuchi Diary: Chronicle from an American Concentration Camp: The Tanforan Journals of Charles Kikuchi. Urbana: U Ill Press, 1973. Rev. by M. Dubofsky, HRNB, 2(Ja 1974):60; D. Hata, JAH, 61(Dec 1974):835-6; R. A. Wilson, PHR, 43(Nov 1974):621-2.

Moeller, B. B. Phil Swing and the Boulder Dam. Berkeley: U Cal Press, 1971. Rev. by A. J. Badger, EHR, 89(Apr 1974): 467.

Moevs, Maria Teresa Marabini. The Roman Thin-Walled Pottery from Cosa (1948-1954). Rome: American Academy in Rome, 1973. Rev. by H. Comfort, AJA, 78(Jl 1974):313-14.

Moggridge, D. E. British Monetary Policy 1924-1931: The Norman Conquest of $4.86. Cambridge: Cam U Press, 1972. Rev. by D. H. Aldcroft, History, 59(Feb 1974):147.

Mohler, Stanley R. and Bobby H. Johnson. Wiley Post, His "Winnie Mae" and the World's First Pressure Suit. Washington: Smithsonian Institution Press, 1971. Rev. by G. E. Hopkins, SWHQ, 78(Oct 1974):229-30.

Mohr, James C. The Radical Republicans and Reform in New York During Reconstruction. Ithaca, N.Y.: Cornell U Press, 1973. Rev. by A. D. Donald, AHR, 79(Je 1974):870-1; W. Gillette, CWH, 20(Mar 1974):82-4; L. Cox, JAH, 60(Mar 1974):1135-6; B. M. Stave, NYH, 55(Apr 1974):240-2; R. E. Ziebarth, NYHSQ, 58(Apr 1974):160-1.

Mohr, Nicholaus. Excursion Through America. Chicago: Lakeside Press, 1973. Rev. by J. J. Weisert, FCHQ, 48(Jl 1974):290-1.

Moir, John S. The Church in the British Era. Toronto: McGraw-Hill Ryerson, 1972. Rev. by G. S. French, CHR, 55(Je 1974): 199-201.

Molella, Arthur P. see Reingold, Nathan

Molho, Anthony. Florentine Public Finances in the Early Renaissance, 1400-1433. Cambridge, Mass.: Har U Press, 1972. Rev. by P. Burke, EHR, 89(Jl 1974):662-3; C. R. Byerly, Historian, 36(Feb 1974):314-15.

Moline, Norman T. Mobility and the Small Town, 1900-1930: Transportation Change in Oregon, Illinois. Chicago: U Chi Press, 1971. Rev. by R. D. Gray, JISHS, 67(Apr 1974):246-7.

Mollat, Michel, ed. Sociétés et compagnies de commerce en Orient et dans l'Ocean Indien. Paris: S. E. V. P. E. N., 1970. Rev. by P. C. Nair, JEH, 34(Je 1974):514-5.

Möller, Birger. Employment Approaches to Economic Planning in Developing Countries. Stockholm: Tryckeri Balder AB, 1972. Rev. by D. R. Snodgrass, JAS, 33(Aug 1974):726-7.

Molnar, Amedeo. Jan Hus: Testimone della verità. Turin: Editrice Claudiana, 1973. Rev. by L. B. Pascoe, CH, 43(Dec 1974):538.

Moltmann, Günter. Atlantische Blockpolitik im 19. Jahrhundert: Die Vereinigten Staaten und der deutsche Liberalismus während der Revolution von 1848/49. Düsseldorf: Droste, 1973. Rev. by H. F. Young, JAH, 61(Sep 1974):484-5.

Monaghan, Jay. Chile, Peru, and the California Gold Rush of 1849. Berkeley: U Cal Press, 1974. Rev. by A. P. Nasatir, CHQ, 53(Spr 1974):89-90; T. Bader, HAHR, 54(May 1974):332-4; J. A. McGowan, JAH, 61(Je 1974):192-3; V. C. Dahl, JOW,

253   MONAHAN

13(Jl 1974):124-5; F. O. Gatell, PHR, 43(May 1974):271-2;
N. A. Bailey, TAm, 30(Apr 1974):553-4; C. Wood, WHQ, 5
(Jl 1974):355.

Monahan, Arthur P. John of Paris on Royal and Papal Power.
New York: Columbia U Press, 1974. Rev. by E. C. Tatnall,
CH, 43(Dec 1974):535-6; B. Nischan, HRNB, 2(Sep 1974):239-
40.

Monroe, Elizabeth. Philby of Arabia. London: Faber and Faber,
n. d. Rev. by A. Jacob, HTo, 24(Ja 1974):63-5.

Monroe, Wilbur F. Japan: Financial Markets and The World Economy. New York: Praeger, 1973. Rev. by R. Evans, Jr.,
JAS, 33(May 1974):486-7.

Montagu, Ashley, ed. Man and Aggression. New York: Ox U
Press, 1973. Rev. by R. Stevenson, HT, 7(Aug 1974):642.

Montenegro, João Alfredo de Sousa. Evolucão do Catolicismo no
Brasil. Petropólis, Brazil: Editora Vozes, 1972. Rev. by
D. Warren, Jr., HAHR, 54(May 1974):308-9.

Montgomery, Charles F. A History of American Pewter. New
York: Praeger, 1973. Rev. by J. Fairbanks, NYHSQ, 58
(Oct 1974):323-5.

Monti, Laura V., comp. A Calendar of Rochambeau Papers at the
University of Florida Libraries. Gainesville: U Fla Libraries,
1972. Rev. by H. C. Rice, Jr., AmArc, 37(Ja 1974):79-81.

Monticone, Alberto. La Germania e la neutralità italiana: 1914-
15. Bologna: Il Mulino, 1971. Rev. by J. Whittam, ESR,
4(Apr 1974):190-1.

Moody, Robert E. The Saltonstall Papers, 1607-1815: Selected
and Edited and with Biographies of Ten Members of the Saltonstall Family in Six Generations. Vol. I: 1607-1789. Boston: Mass Historical Society, 1972. Rev. by A. T. Vaughan,
JAH, 61(Sep 1974):437-8; R. S. Dunn, NEQ, 47(Mar 1974):
137-40.

Moody, T. W. and J. G. Simms, eds. The Bishopric of Derry and
the Irish Society of London, 1602-1705. Vol. I, 1602-70.
Dublin: Stationery Office for Irish Manuscripts Commission,
1968. Rev. by F. G. James, AHR, 79(Oct 1974):1186-7.

Mooney, Chase C. William H. Crawford, 1772-1834. Lexington,
Ky.: U Press Ky, 1974. Rev. by S. Gurr, GHQ, 58(Fall
1974):364-6; R. J. Chaffin, HRNB, 2(Sep 1974):262; J. S.
Chase, HRNB, 3(Nov/Dec 1974):44-5; R. V. Remini, IMH,
70(Dec 1974):351-3.

Moore, Doris Langley. Lord Byron: Accounts Rendered. n. p. :
     Murray, n. d. Rev. by J. Richardson, HTo, 24(Jl 1974):511-
     12.

Moore, Jackson W. , Jr. Bent's Old Fort: An Archaeological Study.
     Boulder, Colo.: Pruett, 1973. Rev. by O. E. Young, Jr. ,
     JAH, 61(Dec 1974):779-80; F. J. Johnston, JOW, 13(Apr 1974):
     134.

Moore, Joe see Livingston, Jon

Moore, John Norton. Law and the Indo-China War. Princeton,
     N. J. : Prin U Press, 1972. Rev. by B. D. Meyers, PHR,
     43(Feb 1974):140-2.

Moore, Richard R. West Texas After the Discovery of Oil: A
     Modern Frontier. Austin: Jenkins, 1971. Rev. by P. H.
     Giddens, JAH, 61(Dec 1974):791-2.

Moore, William Howard. The Kefauver Committee and the Politics
     of Crime, 1950-1952. Columbia, Mo. : U Mo Press, 1974.
     Rev. by T. V. DiBacco, HRNB, 2(Sep 1974):255.

Moortgat-Correus, Ursula. Die Bildwerke vom Djebelet el Beda in
     ihrer räumlichen und zeitlichen Umwelt. New York: Walter
     de Gruyter, 1972. Rev. by W. G. Guterbock, AJA, 78(Jl
     1974):289.

Moquin, Wayne and Charles Van Doren, eds. A Documentary His-
     tory of the Italian Americans. New York: Praeger, 1974.
     Rev. by J. L. Susskind, HRNB, 3(Oct 1974):6; R. Martinez,
     WHQ, 5(Jl 1974):360-1.

     _____, _____, eds. Great Documents in American Indian
     History. New York: Praeger, 1973. Rev. by Staff, InH, 7
     (Win 1974):51; W. R. Jacobs, WHQ, 5(Ja 1974):81-3.

Moran, James. Printing Presses: History and Development from
     the Fifteenth Century to Modern Times. Berkeley: U Cal
     Press, 1973. Rev. by C. R. Schindler, T & C, 15(Ja 1974):
     92-4.

Morenz, Siegfried. Egyptian Religion. Ithaca, N. Y. : Cornell U
     Press, 1973. Rev. by S. J. Simon, HRNB, 2(May/Je 1974):
     172.

Moretti, Mario see Wetter, Erik

Morgan, H. Wayne. Essays on the Gilded Age. see Boren, Car-
     ter E.

     _____, ed. Victorian Culture in America. Itasca, Ill. : F. E.
     Peacock, 1973. Rev. by J. Waksmundski, HT, 7(Aug 1974):
     635-6.

————. Indiana Historical Society Lectures. see Miller, Lillian
        B.

Morgan, Kenneth O. The Age of Lloyd George: The Liberal Party
        and British Politics, 1890-1929. London: Allen and Unwin,
        1971. Rev. by J. Howarth, History, 59(Feb 1974):140-1.

————, ed. Lloyd George Family Letters, 1885-1936. New York:
        Ox U Press, 1973. Rev. by M. Kinnear, AHR, 79(Oct 1974):
        1182-3; M. Bentley, History, 59(Je 1974):296-7.

Morgan, M. C. Lenin. Athens, Ohio: Ohio U Press, 1971. Rev.
        by R. Thompson, AHR, 79(Apr 1974):543-5.

Morgan, M. R. The Chronicle of Ernoul and the Continuations of
        William of Tyre. London: Ox U Press, 1974. Rev. by J.
        Muldoon, HRNB, 2(Jl 1974):211.

Morgan, Roger. Western European Politics Since 1945: The Shap-
        ing of the European Community. London: Batsford, 1972.
        Rev. by D. J. Wenden, History, 59(Feb 1974):158.

Morgan, William James, ed. Naval Documents of the American
        Revolution. Volume 6.... Washington: U. S. Government
        Printing Office, 1972. Rev. by W. B. Kennedy, GHQ, 58(Spr
        1974):129; C. Ubbelohde, NCHR, 51(Sum 1974):349-50; R. K.
        MacMaster, VMNB, 82(Oct 1974):497-9.

Morison, Samuel Eliot. Samuel de Champlain: Father of New
        France. Boston: Little, Brown, 1972. Rev. by J. F. Ban-
        non, JISHS, 67(Je 1974):347-8.

Mørkholm, Otto see Thompson, Margaret

Morlang, F. Missione in Africa Centrale: Diario 1855-1863. Bo-
        logna: Editrice Nigrizia, 1973. Rev. by R. Gray, JAfH, 15
        (Num 3 1974):497-8.

Morley, James William, ed. Dilemmas of Growth in Prewar Japan.
        Princeton, N. J.: Prin U Press, 1971. Rev. by S. Broad-
        bridge, MAS, 8(Jl 1974):424-9.

————, ed. Japan's Foreign Policy 1868-1941: A Research
        Guide. New York: Columbia U Press, 1974. Rev. by J.
        Israel, HRNB, 2(Jl 1974):202-3; W. I. Cohen, HRNB, 2(Sep
        1974):249-50.

Morrill, J. S. Cheshire, 1630-1660: County Government and Soci-
        ety During the English Revolution. New York: Ox U Press,
        1974. Rev. by B. McGill, HRNB, 2(Sep 1974):236; A. L.
        Rowse, HTo, 24(Jl 1974):509.

Morris, C. B. Surrealism and Spain, 1920-1936. New York:

Cam U Press, 1972.   Rev. by A. Balakian, GR, 28(Sum 1974):
335-7.

Morris, Colin. The Discovery of the Individual, 1050-1200.   London: S. P. C. K., 1972.   Rev. by C. N. L. Brooke, History, 59(Feb 1974):88.

Morris, H. F. and James S. Read.   Indirect Rule and the Search
for Justice: Essays in East African Legal History.   Oxford:
Clarendon Press, 1972.   Rev. by R. Martin, JMAS, 12(Je
1974):321-3.

Morris, James.   The Preachers.   New York: St. Martin's, 1973.
Rev. by R. L. Moellering, CH, 43(Mar 1974):126-7.

Morris, John.   The Age of Arthur: A History of the British Isles
from 350 to 650.   New York: Scribner's, 1973.   Rev. by
D. A. White, AHR, 79(Je 1974):768-70.

Morris, Paul C.   American Sailing Coasters of the North Atlantic.
Chardon, Ohio: Block and Osborn, 1973.   Rev. by A. A.
Fahrner, NCHR, 51(Spr 1974):233-4.

Morris, Richard B.   Seven Who Shaped Our Destiny: The Founding
Fathers as Revolutionaries.   New York: Harper and Row,
1973.   Rev. by L. R. Gerlach, JSH, 40(May 1974):300-1;
J. H. Broussard, NEQ, 47(Sep 1974):480-2; R. Ketcham,
VMHB, 82(Apr 1974):198-200; T. J. Archdeacon, WMH, 57(Spr
1974):239-40.

Morris, Robert.   The Papers of Robert Morris, 1781-1784.   Volume I: February 7-July 31, 1781.   Pittsburgh: U Pittsburgh
Press, 1973.   Rev. by R. A. Ryerson, BHR, 48(Sum 1974):
246-8; L. Maganzin, HRNB, 2(Apr 1974):152; S. Bruchey,
JAH, 61(Dec 1974):745-6; C. F. Hobson, NCHR, 51(Spr 1974):
234-5; J. A. Ernst, WMQ-3, 31(Jl 1974):514-16; R. E. Brown,
WVH, 35(Apr 1974):237-8.

Morris, Thomas D.   Free Men All: The Personal Liberty Laws of
the North, 1780-1861.   Baltimore: JHU Press, 1974.   Rev.
by L. Filler, HRNB, 2(Aug 1974):217-18; D. Roper, JNH, 59
(Jl 1974):297-8.

Morrissey, Brenda C., ed. see Hemenway, Abby Maria

Morrison, James L., Jr., ed.   The Memoirs of Henry Heth.   Westport, Conn.: Greenwood, 1974.   Rev. by E. M. Coffman,
HRNB, 3(Nov/Dec 1974):46.

Morrison, Joseph L.   Governor O. Max Gardner: A Power in
North Carolina and New Deal Washington.   Chapel Hill: UNC
Press, 1971.   Rev. by O. L. Graham, Jr., AHR, 79(Je 1974)
899-901.

Mortimer, Rex. Indonesian Communism Under Sukarno: Ideology and Politics, 1959-1965. Ithaca, N.Y.: Cornell U Press, 1974. Rev. by G. R. Hess, HRNB, 3(Oct 1974):18.

Morton, Catherine and Hope Muntz, eds. The Carmen de Hastingae Proelio of Guy, Bishop of Amiens. Oxford: Ox U Press, 1972. Rev. by R. A. Brown, History, 59(Je 1974):251-2.

Morton, Desmond. The Last War Drum: The North West Campaign of 1885. Toronto: Hakkert, 1972. Rev. by P. B. Waite, CHR, 55(Je 1974):194-7; W. O. Beck, NDH, 41(Sum 1974):37-8.

_____ and Reginald H. Roy, eds. Telegrams of the North-West Campaign, 1885. Toronto: Champlain Society, 1972. Rev. by J. E. Sunder, JAH, 60(Mar 1974):1189-90.

Morton, Marian J. The Terrors of Ideological Politics: Liberal Historians in a Conservative Mood. Cleveland, Ohio: Press CWRU, 1972. Rev. by J. P. Diggins, JAH, 61(Je 1974):251-3; R. Reinitz, WMQ-3, 31(Ja 1974):156-8.

Morton, Oren F. A History of Monroe County, West Virginia. Baltimore: Regional Publishing, 1974. Rev. by O. K. Rice, WVH, 35(Jl 1974):323-4.

_____. A History of Pendleton County, West Virginia. Baltimore: Regional Publishing, 1974. Rev. by O. K. Rice, WVH, 35(Jl 1974):323-4.

Moscotti, Albert D. British Policy and the Nationalist Movement in Burma, 1917-1937. Honolulu: U Press Hawaii, 1974. Rev. by W. R. Rock, HRNB, 2(Sep 1974):244.

Moskowitz, Ira see Collier, John

Mosley, Leonard. Backs to the Wall. The Heroic Story of the People of London During World War II. New York: Random House, 1971. Rev. by R. L. Blanco, Historian, 36(May 1974):550-1.

Moss, William W. Oral History Program Manual. New York: Praeger, 1974. Rev. by W. Baum and A. Fry, AmArc, 37(Oct 1974):583-6; P. C. Nagel, HRNB, 2(Sep 1974):248.

Mosse, Werner E., ed. Deutsches Judentum in Krieg und Revolution, 1916-1923. Tübingen: J. C. B. Mohr (Paul Siebeck), 1971. Rev. by G. G. Field, AHR, 79(Je 1974):805-6.

Moulton, Harland B. From Superiority to Parity: The United States and the Strategic Arms Race, 1961-1971. Westport, Conn.: Greenwood, 1973. Rev. by R. M. Slusser, JAH, 61(Je 1974):256-7.

Moulton, Philip P.   The Journal and Major Essays of John Woolman.
New York: Ox U Press, 1971.   Rev. by S. W. Gilley, EHR,
89(Ja 1974):178.

Mousnier, Roland.   The Assassination of Henry IV: The Tyrannicide Problem and the Consolidation of the French Absolute
Monarchy in the Early Seventeenth Century.   New York: Scribner's, 1973.   Rev. by W. Roosen, HRNB, 2(Ja 1974):79.

_____. Social Hierarchies: 1450 to the Present.   New York:
Schocken, 1973.   Rev. by T. K. Rabb, AHR, 79(Apr 1974):
484-6; C. Tilly, JMH, 46(Dec 1974):706-7.

Mowry, George E.   Another Look at the Twentieth-Century South.
Baton Rouge: LSU Press, 1973.   Rev. by T. D. Clarke, AHR,
79(Oct 1974):1275; J. Leonard Bates, Historian, 36(Feb 1974):
349-50; J. Rabun, JISHS, 67(Sep 1974):451-2; V. P. DeSantis,
NCHR, 51(Jan 1974):108-9.

Muelenbrock, B. L.   Briefwisseling van Hugo Grotius.   Vol. 8,
1637.   The Hague: Martinus Nijhoff, 1971.   Rev. by J. L.
Price, EHR, 89(Apr 1974):440-1.

Mueller, John E.   War, Presidents and Public Opinion.   New York:
Wiley, 1973.   Rev. by N. Thorburn, Historian, 36(May 1974):
582-3.

Muench, David and Donald G. Pike.   Anasazi: Ancient People of
the Rock.   Palo Alto, Cal.:   American West, 1974.   Rev. by
H. W. Basehart, JAriH, 15(Win 1974):392-3; G. J. Gumeran,
UHQ, 42(Fall 1974):387-8.

_____ and Hartt Wixom.   Utah.   Portland, Ore.:   C. H. Belding,
1973.   Rev. by L. Kapaloski, UHQ, 42(Win 1974):86-7; E. L.
Cooley, WHQ, 5(Jl 1974):349-50.

Mugot, Hazel.   Black Night of Quiloa.   Nairobi: East African Publishing House, 1972.   Rev. by H. Dinwiddy, AfAf, 73(Jl 1974):
379-81.

Muhly, James David.   Copper and Tin.   The Distribution of Mineral
Resources and the Nature of the Metals Trade in Bronze Age.
Hamden, Conn.:   Archon, 1973.   Rev. by E. R. Caley, AJA,
78(Ja 1974):83-4.

Muise, Del and John Taylor, eds.   Urban History Review, Nos. 1-
3, Feb.-Nov., 1972.   Ottawa: History Division, National
Museum of Man, 1972.   Rev. by M. B. Katz, CHR, 55(Sep
1974):312-13.

Mulder, J. A. Niels.   Monks, Merit, and Motivation: Buddhism
and National Development in Thailand.   Dekalb: N Ill U Press,
1973.   Rev. by J. Bilmes, JAS, 33(Aug 1974):738-9.

Mulder, John M. see Link, Arthur S.

Mull, Donald. Henry James's "Sublime Economy": Money as Symbolic Center in the Fiction. Middletown, Conn.: Wesleyan U Press, 1973. Rev. by D. K. Kirby, NEQ, 47(June 1974):342-4.

Mullan, John. Miners' and Travelers' Guide to Oregon, Washington, Idaho, Montana, Wyoming, and Colorado. n. p.: 1865 (reprint). Rev. by D. A. Smith, CoMag, 51(Spr 1974):157-9.

Muller, Alexander V., ed. and trans. The Spiritual Regulation of Peter the Great. Seattle: U Wash Press, 1972. Rev. by P. Mojzes, CH, 43(Sep 1974):410-11.

Mullins, Marion Day. Republic of Texas: Poll Lists for 1846. Baltimore: Genealogical Publishing Co., 1974. Rev. by C. R. Ericson, ETHJ, 12(Fall 1974):79; L. Anderson, RKHS, 72(Jl 1974):297.

Muncy, Raymond Lee. Sex and Marriage in Utopian Communities: Nineteenth-Century America. Bloomington: Ind U Press, 1973. Rev. by T. K. Hareven, AHR, 79(Feb 1974):223; C. Albanese, CH, 43(Mar 1974):124-5.

Mundy, John H. Europe in the High Middle Ages 1150-1309. London: Longman, 1973. Rev. by C. Morris, EHR, 89(Jl 1974): 618-20.

Munro, Dana G. The United States and the Caribbean Republics, 1921-1933. Princeton, N.J.: Prin U Press, 1974. Rev. by E. D. Fitchen, HRNB, 3(Nov/Dec 1974):43.

Munro, John A. and Alex I. Inglis, eds. Mike: The Memoirs of the Right Honourable Lester B. Pearson, Volume 2, 1948-1957. Toronto: U Tor Press, 1973. Rev. by N. Ward, CHR, 55(Sep 1974):307-12; J. Boudreau, HRNB, 2(May/Je 1974):185-6.

Munro, John H. A. Wool, Cloth, and Gold: The Struggle for Bullion in Anglo-Burgundian Trade, 1340-1478. Toronto: U Tor Press, 1973. Rev. by K. G. Madison, HRNB, 2(May/Je 1974):183.

Munroe, John A. Louis McLane: Federalist and Jacksonian. New Brunswick, N.J.: Rutgers U Press, 1973. Rev. by E. J. Perkins, BHR, 48(Sum 1974):253-4; J. H. Broussard, GHQ, 58 (Sum 1974):300-1; N. S. Cohen, HRNB, 2(Apr 1974):150-1; T. P. Govan, JSH, 40(Aug 1974):475-6; H. Hamilton, RKHS, 72(Jl 1974):280-1; S. W. Higginbotham, MHM, 69(Fall 1974): 330-2; R. E. Welsh, Jr., NYHSQ, 58(Oct 1974):326-7; J. G. Tregle, Jr., WMH, 57(Sum 1974):320-1.

Muntz, Hope see Morton, Catherine

Murdock, Eugene C. One Million Men: The Civil War Draft in the North. Madison: St Historical Society, Wis., 1971. Rev. by H. M. Hyman, AHR, 79(Apr 1974):586-7.

Muriuki, Godfrey. A History of the Kikuyu 1500-1900. New York: Ox U Press, 1974. Rev. by F. J. Berg, HRNB, 3(Nov/Dec 1974):38.

Murphey, Murray G. Our Knowledge of the Historical Past. Indianapolis: Bobbs-Merrill, 1973. Rev. by L. O. Mink, AHR, 79(Apr 1974):482-3; R. A. Skotheim, JAH, 61(Sep 1974):444-6.

Murphy, James B. L. Q. C. Lamar: Pragmatic Patriot. Baton Rouge: LSU Press, 1973. Rev. by P. P. Van Riper, AHR, 79(Oct 1974):1272-3; J. P. Harahan, CWH, 20(Mar 1974):70-1.

Murphy, Lawrence R. Frontier Crusader--William F. M. Arny. Tucson: U Ariz Press, 1972. Rev. by D. Zachert, JISHS, 67(Apr 1974):241-2; C. H. Scott, JOW, 13(Ja 1974):150-1.

_____. Philmont: A History of New Mexico's Cimarron County. Albuquerque: U NM Press, 1974. Rev. by O. L. Jones, Jr., JOW, 13(Apr 1974):116.

Murphy, Paul L. The Constitution in Crisis Times, 1918-1969. New York: Harper and Row, 1972. Rev. by A. M. Paul, AHR, 79(Feb 1974):244-6.

_____. The Meaning of Freedom of Speech: First Amendment Freedoms from Wilson to FDR. Westport, Conn.: Greenwood, 1972. Rev. by B. C. Hardy, AHR, 79(Oct 1974):1283-4; J. P. Roche, JAH, 60(Mar 1974):1169-70; A. A. Marris, PNQ, 65 (Ja 1974):45.

Murray, Lois Smith. Baylor at Independence. Waco, Tx.: Baylor U Press, 1972. Rev. by J. M. Self, ETHJ, 12(Spr 1974):58-9.

Murray, Robert K. The Politics of Normalcy: Governmental Theor and Practice in the Harding-Coolidge Era. New York: Norton 1973. Rev. by C. Lloyd, AHR, 79(Apr 1974):605-6; J. L. Bates, JAH, 60(Mar 1974):1173-4; B. K. Johnpoll, NYH, 55 (Jl 1974):358-60; H. A. Dewitt, OH, 83(Spr 1974):148-9.

Murray-Brown, Jeremy. Kenyatta. New York: Dutton, 1973. Rev by B. Ray, CH, 43(Mar 1974):129-30.

Musca, Giosue. Il Venerabile Beda, storico dell'alto Medioevo. Bari: Dedals, 1973. Rev. by D. W. Robertson, Jr., AHR, 79(Apr 1974):493-4.

Muscatine, Charles. Poetry and Crisis in the Age of Chaucer. Notre Dame, Ind.: U Notre Dame Press, 1972. Rev. by W. Provost, GR, 28(Sum 1974):361-5.

Mussche, H. F., et al. Thorikos V, 1968 and VI, 1969. Brussels: Comité des Fouilles Belges en Grèce, 1973. Rev. by D. G. Mitten, AJA, 78(Apr 1974):198-9.

Musset, L. see Folz, R.

Mussulman, Joseph A. Music in the Cultured Generation: A Social History of Music in America, 1870-1900. Evanston, Ill.: Northwestern U Press, 1971. Rev. by C. Covey, AHR, 79 (Je 1974):879-80.

Musto, David. The American Disease: Origins of Narcotic Control. New Haven, Conn.: Yale U Press, 1973. Rev. by C. O. Jackson, AmArc, 37(Jl 1974):465-6; L. E. Ziewacz, HT, 8 (Nov 1974):143-4; M. H. Haller, JAH, 60(Mar 1974):1153-4; J. W. Ormsby, PNQ, 65(Oct 1974):186-7; R. J. Halstead, WMH, 57(Spr 1974):237-8.

Musulin, Stella. Austria and the Austrians. New York: Praeger, 1972. Rev. by M. E. Riedlsperger, EEQ, 8(Sum 1974):238-40.

Mutharika, B. W. T. Toward Multinational Cooperation in Africa. New York: Praeger, 1972. Rev. by S. Aganda Ochola, JMAS, 12(Mar 1974):150-1.

Muthesius, Stefan. The High Victorian Movement in Architecture, 1850-1870. London: Routledge and Kegan Paul, 1972. Rev. by M. H. Port, History, 59(Feb 1974):124.

Myer, Dillon S. Uprooted Americans: The Japanese Americans and the War Relocation Authority During World War II. Tucson: U Ariz Press, 1971. Rev. by J. Modell, WHQ, 5(Ja 1974):87-8.

Myers, A. R. London in the Age of Chaucer. Norman: U Ok Press, 1972. Rev. by C. M. Barron, History, 59(Je 1974):256-7.

Myers, Robert Manson, ed. The Children of Pride: A True Story of Georgia and the Civil War. New Haven, Conn.: Yale U Press, 1972. Rev. by T. B. Alexander, AHR, 79(Je 1974):868; R. Bellflower, JAmS, 8(Apr 1974):120-1; C. Bolt, JAmS, 8(Apr 1974):121-2; F. C. McLaughlin, WPHM, 57(Apr 1974):221-5.

Myers, William Starr, ed. The Mexican War Diary of General George B. McClellan. New York: Da Capo, 1972. Rev. by

D. E. Livingston-Little, JOW, 13(Apr 1974):108.

Myllyniemi, Seppo. Die Neuordnung der baltischen Länder, 1941-
1944: zum nationalsozialistischen Inhalt der deutschen Besat-
zungspolitik. Helsinki: Suomen Historiallinen Seura, 1973.
Rev. by M. H. Haltzel, AHR, 79(Oct 1974):1202-3.

Myrans, C. B. see Willcox, William B.

Myres, J. N. L. and Barbara Green. The Anglo-Saxon Cemeteries
of Caistor-by-Norwich and Markshall, Norfolk. London:
Thames and Hudson, 1973. Rev. by H. R. Roosens, Antiquity,
48(Sep 1974):248-9.

Nabokov, V. D. The Provisional Government. New York: Wiley,
1970. Rev. by R. C. Williams, AHR, 79(Apr 1974):546-9;
C. M. Foust, Historian, 36(Aug 1974):761-2.

Nada, Narciso, ed. Le relazioni diplomatiche fra l'Austria e il
Regno di Sardegna.... Rome: Instituto Storico Italiano per
l'Età Moderna e Contemporanea, 1972. Rev. by W. A. Jenks,
AHR, 79(Apr 1974):528.

_____, ed. La Révolution Piémontaise de 1821 ed altri scritti.
Turin: Centro Studi Piemontesi, 1972. Rev. by G. T. Romani, AHR, 79(Apr 1974):529-30; A. Ramm, EHR, 89(Jl
1974):675-6; R. J. Rath, JMH, 46(Dec 1974):725-6.

Nagel, Paul C. This Sacred Trust: American Nationality, 1798-
1898. New York: Ox U Press, 1971. Rev. by B. C. Shafer,
AHR, 79(Je 1974):855-6.

Nahm, Andrew C., ed. Korea Under Japanese Colonial Rule. Kalamazoo: W Mich U, 1973. Rev. by J. K. Oh, JAS, 34(Nov
1974):236-7.

Nahrstedt, Wolfgang. Die Entstehung der Freizeit: Dargestelt am
Beispiel Hamburgs; ein Beitrag zur Strukturgeschichte und zur
geschichtlichen Grundlegung der Freizeitpädagogiks. Göttingen:
Vandenhoeck and Ruprecht, 1972. Rev. by E. Tenner, JMH,
46(Je 1974):358-60.

Naidis, Mark. The Second British Empire, 1783-1965: A Short History. Reading, Mass.: Addison-Wesley, 1970. Rev. by
R. D. Fiala, HT, 8(Nov 1974):113-14.

Naim, C. M. see Coppola, Carlo

Nakamura, Kyoko Motomochi, trans. and ed. Miraculous Stories
from the Japanese Buddhist Tradition: The Nihon Ryōiki of
the Monk Kyōkai. Cambridge, Mass.: Har U Press, 1973.
Rev. by K. Brazell, JAS, 34(Nov 1974):241-2.

Nanton, Paul. Arctic Breakthrough: Franklin's Expeditions, 1819-
1847. Toronto, Vancouver: Clarke, Irwin, 1970. Rev. by
M. Zaslow, CHR, 55(Mar 1974):82-4.

Narain, Virendra see Varma, S. P.

Nash, Gary B. Red, White, and Black: The Peoples of Early
America. Englewood Cliffs, N.J.: Prentice-Hall, 1974.
Rev. by N. S. Cohen, HRNB, 2(Sep 1974):261.

Nash, Gerald D. The American West in the Twentieth Century: A
Short History of an Urban Oasis. Englewood Cliffs, N.J.:
Prentice-Hall, 1973. Rev. by L. W. Dorsett, CoMag, 51(Spr
1974):171-2; L. J. Arrington, JAH, 61(Je 1974):233-4; B. M.
Fireman, JAriH, 15(Sum 1974):185-6; R. W. Larson, NMHR,
49(Apr 1974):173-5; J. Wickens, PHR, 43(May 1974):281-2;
T. G. Alexander, WHQ, 5(Apr 1974):196-7.

Nash, Howard P., Jr. Andrew Johnson: Congress and Reconstruction. Rutherford, N.J.: Fairleigh Dickinson U Press, 1972.
Rev. by R. F. Durden, AHR, 79(Je 1974):871-2.

_____. A Naval History of the Civil War. South Brunswick,
N.J.: A. S. Barnes, 1972. Rev. by B. F. Cooling, AHR,
79(Apr 1974):585-6; M. Melton, CWTI, 13(May 1974):46-7.

Nash, Roderick, ed. The Call of the Wild, 1900-1916. New York:
George Braziller, 1970. Rev. by H. Segal, HT, 8(Nov 1974):
129-30.

_____. Wilderness and the American Mind. New Haven, Conn.:
Yale U Press, 1973. Rev. by R. Scheidenhelm, CoMag, 51
(Sum 1974):247-9; A. S. Brown, HT, 7(Aug 1974):638-9.

Naske, Claus-M. An Interpretative History of Alaskan Statehood.
Anchorage, Alaska: Northwest Publishing, 1973. Rev. by
T. G. Smith, JOW, 13(Oct 1974):123; W. H. Wilson, PHR,
43(Feb 1974):128-9; T. C. Hinckley, PNQ, 65(Apr 1974):91;
M. Sherwood, WHQ, 5(Apr 1974):207-9.

Nathan, Andrew J. Modern China, 1840-1972: An Introduction to
Sources and Research Aids. Ann Arbor: U Mich Center for
Chinese Studies ... 1973. Rev. by J. L. Price, JAS, 33(Feb
1974):309-10.

Nathans, Sydney. Daniel Webster and Jacksonian Democracy. Balti-
more: JHU Press, 1973. Rev. by A. D. Aberbach, CHR, 55
(Sep 1974):345-6; K. T. Phillips, CWH, 20(Je 1974):176-7;
J. H. Schroeder, Historian, 36(May 1974):560-1; M. L. Wil-
son, JAH, 60(Mar 1974):1111-12; J. A. Andrew, III, MiA, 56
(Ja 1974):58-9; E. A. Miles, NCHR, 51(Win 1974):115-16; S.
Penney, NYHSQ, 58(Apr 1974):156-8.

National Council of Jewish Women, Pittsburgh Section. By Myself,
   I'm a Book: An Oral History of the Immigrant Jewish Ex-
   perience in Pittsburgh. Waltham, Mass.: American Jewish
   Historical Society, 1972. Rev. by M. A. Rockland, PH, 41
   (Apr 1974):237-8.

Naumov, V. P. A Chronicle of the Heroic Struggle: Soviet Historiography of the Civil War and Imperialist Intervention in
   the USSR. Moscow: Izdatel'stvo "Mysl," 1972. Rev. by
   J. A. White, AHR, 79(Apr 1974):549-51.

Navarro Ledesma, Francisco. Cervantes: The Man and the Genius.
   New York: Charterhouse, 1973. Rev. by T. Niehaus, HAHR,
   54(Feb 1974):161-2.

Navasky, Victor S. Kennedy Justice. New York: Atheneum, 1971.
   Rev. by H. F. Bedford, AHR, 79(Je 1974):910-11.

Naylor, Maria, comp. The National Academy of Design Exhibition
   Record: 1861-1900. New York: Kennedy Galleries, 1973.
   Rev. by M. B. Cowdrey, NYHSQ, 58(Oct 1974):335-6.

Neale, R. S. Class and Ideology in the Nineteenth Century. London: Routledge and Kegan Paul, 1972. Rev. by H. Perkin,
   EHR, 89(Jl 1974):676; P. F. Clarke, History, 59(Feb 1974):
   115.

Neale, Robert E. The Art of Dying. New York: Harper & Row,
   n.d. Rev. by B. Hughes, Mankind, 4(Apr 1974):65-6.

Neatby, Hilda. The Quebec Act: Protest and Policy. Toronto:
   Prentice-Hall, 1972. Rev. by M. Brunet, CHR, 55(Je 1974):
   188-9; J. Sosin, JAH, 60(Mar 1974):1100-1.

Neatby, L. H. Discovery in Russian and Siberian Waters. Athens,
   Ohio: Ohio U Press, 1973. Rev. by J. W. Long, HRNB, 2
   (Mar 1974):115-16.

Neatby, Leslie H. The Search for Franklin. Edmonton: Hurtig,
   1970. Rev. by M. Zaslow, CHR, 55(Mar 1974):82-4.

Nee, Victor G. and Brett DeBary Nee. Longtime Californ': A
   Documentary Study of an American Chinatown. New York:
   Pantheon, 1973. Rev. by P. P. Choy, CHQ, 53(Spr 1974):
   87-8; L. B. Chan, PHR, 43(May 1974):285.

Neelson, John Peter. Student Unrest in India: A Typology and a
   Socio-Structural Analysis. München: Weltforum Verlag, 1973.
   Rev. by P. Altbach, JAAS, 9(Ja & Apr 1974):98.

Neely, James A. see MacNeish, Richard S. The Prehistory of
   the Tehuacan Valley, Volume Four.

Nef, John U.   Search for Meaning: The Autobiography of a Noncom-
      formist. Washington, D. C.: Public Affairs Press, 1973.
      Rev. by M. N. Dobkowski, JISHS, 67(Nov 1974):564-5.

Neighbours, Kenneth F. Indian Exodus: Texas Indian Affairs, 1835-
      1859. Quanah, Tx.: Nortex Press, 1973. Rev. by E. J.
      Gum, ETHJ, 12(Spr 1974):67.

Neihardt, John G. All is But a Beginning: Youth Remembered,
      1881-1901. New York: Harcourt Brace Jovanovich, 1972.
      Rev. by J. Wunder, PNQ, 65(Apr 1974):88.

Neill, Wilfred T. Twentieth-Century Indonesia. New York: Colum-
      bia U Press, 1973. Rev. by W. H. Frederick, JAS, 33(Aug
      1974):741-2.

Nelson, Clifford L. German-American Political Behavior in Nebras-
      ka and Wisconsin, 1916-1920. Lincoln: U Neb Publication,
      1972. Rev. by P. H. Argersinger, MiA, 56(Jl 1974):204-5.

Nelson, E. Clifford. Lutheranism in North America, 1914-1970.
      Minneapolis: Augsburg, 1972. Rev. by J. W. Stewart, AHR,
      79(Oct 1974):1281-2.

Nelson, Herbert B. and Preston E. Onstad, eds. A Webfoot Volun-
      teer: The Diary of William M. Hilleary, 1864-1866. Corval-
      lis, Ore.: Ore St U Press, 1965. Rev. by J. I. Robertson,
      CWH, 20(Sep 1974):279-81.

Nelson, James, ed. General Eisenhower on the Military Churchill:
      A Conversation with Alistair Cooke. New York: Norton, 1970.
      Rev. by R. W. Leopold, AHR, 79(Apr 1974):609-10.

Nelson, Michael. The Development of Tropical Lands: Policy Is-
      sues in Latin America. Baltimore: ... JHU Press, 1973.
      Rev. by H. J. Bruton, HAHR, 54(Nov 1974):733-5.

Nelson, Richard K. Hunters of the Northern Forest: Designs for
      Survival Among the Alaskan Kutchin. Chicago: U Chi Press,
      1973. Rev. by H. A. Howard, JOW, 13(Ja 1974):147-8; F. X.
      Grollig, MiA, 56(Jl 1974):207; E. Gunther, PNQ, 65(Jl 1974):
      149-50; W. B. Workman, WHQ, 5(Oct 1974):472-4.

Nelson, Russell S., Jr. see Wrone, David

Nelson, Truman. The Old Man: John Brown at Harper's Ferry.
      New York: Holt, Rinehart and Winston, 1973. Rev. by J. L.
      Thomas, AHR, 79(Feb 1974):231-3; J. J. Cordoso, CWH, 20
      (Je 1974):159-63; B. L. Turpen, JOW, 13(Oct 1974):126; V. B.
      Howard, VMHB, 82(Oct 1974):506-7.

Neme, Mário. Fórmulas políticas no Brasil Holandês. São Paulo,
      Brazil: n. p., 1971. Rev. by A. J. R. Russell-Wood, HAHR,

54(Feb 1974):131-2.

Nepveux, Ethel S.   George Alfred Trenholm and the Company That
Went to War.   n.p.:   Privately published, n.d.   Rev. by J.
Leland, SCHM, 75(Oct 1974):252.

Neruda, Pablo.   New Poems, 1968-1970.   New York: Grove, 1972.
Rev. by D. A. Yates, HAHR, 54(Aug 1974):550-1.

Nesbit, Robert C.   Wisconsin: A History.   Madison: U Wis Press,
1973.   Rev. by M. Wyman, JAH, 61(Dec 1974):796; P. W.
Gates, PHR, 43(Nov 1974):602-4; M. Curti, WMH, 57(Win
1973-74):155-7.

Netboy, Anthony.   The Salmon: Their Fight for Survival.   Boston:
Houghton Mifflin, 1974.   Rev. by E. H. Eby, PNQ, 65(Oct
1974):192-3.

Nethers, John L.   Simeon D. Fess: Educator and Politician.
Brooklyn, N. Y.:   Pageant-Poseidon, 1973.   Rev. by D. C.
Brown, HRNB, 2(Jl 1974):194; J. A. Brennan, JAH, 61(Dec
1974):819-20.

Neuenschwander, John A.   The Middle Colonies and the Coming of
the American Revolution.   Port Washington, N. Y.:   Kennikat,
1974.   Rev. by J. B. Whisker, HRNB, 2(Aug 1974):220; R. C.
Detweiler, WPHM, 57(Jl 1974):319-21.

Neusner, Jacob.   Invitation to the Talmud: A Teaching Book.   New
York: Harper and Row, n.d.   Rev. by J. Marsh, Commentary,
58(Sep 1974):86-8.

Neve, Peter.   Regenkult--Aflagen in Bogazköy--Hattusa.   Tübingen:
Wasmuth, 1971.   Rev. by P. Z. Spanos, AJA, 78(Ja 1974):
79-80.

Nevins, Allan.   Ordeal of the Union: Selected Chapters.   New York:
Scribner's, 1973.   Rev. by A. Peskin, HT, 7(Feb 1974):301;
B. F. Cooling, PH, 41(Oct 1974):472-3.

Newbury, C. W.   British Policy Towards West Africa: Select Documents, 1875-1914.   Oxford: Ox U Press, 1971.   Rev. by
A. S. Trickett, Historian, 36(Aug 1974):745-8.

Newby, I. A.   Black Carolinians: A History of Blacks in South
Carolina from 1895 to 1968.   Columbia, S. C.:   U SCar Press,
1973.   Rev. by G. B. Tindall, JNH, 59(Ja 1974):87-9.

Newcomb, Benjamin H.   Franklin and Galloway: A Political Partnership.   New Haven, Conn.:   Yale U Press, 1972.   Rev. by
J. H. Hutson, AHR, 79(Je 1974):847-8; R. D. Duncan, PH,
41(Apr 1974):225-6.

Newitt, M. D. D. Portuguese Settlement on the Zambesi: Exploration, Land Tenure and Colonial Rule in East Africa. London:
Longmans, 1973. Rev. by D. Birmingham, AfAf, 73(Jl 1974):
372-4; G. Liesegang, JAfH, 15(Num 2 1974):336-8.

Newmark, Leo. California Family Newmark: An Intimate History.
Santa Maria: N. B. Stern, 1970. Rev. by M. Rischin, PHR,
43(Aug 1974):429-30.

Newsome, Albert Ray see Lefler, Hugh Talmage

Newton, Robert R. Medieval Chronicles and the Rotation of the
Earth. Baltimore: JHU Press, 1972. Rev. by K. Harrison,
EHR, 89(Apr 1974):412.

Nicholas, D. M. Town and Countryside: Social, Economic and Po-
litical Tensions in Fourteenth-Century Flanders. Bruges:
Rijksuniversiteit te Gent, 1971. Rev. by J. R. Maddicott,
EHR, 89(Ja 1974):164.

Nicholls, Anthony see Wheeler-Bennett, Sir John

_____ and Erich Matthias, ed. German Democracy and the Triumph of Hitler: Essays in Recent German History. New York:
St. Martin's, 1971. Rev. by R. Zerner, AHR, 79(Oct 1974):
1206-7.

Nicholls, C. S. The Swahili Coast: Politics, Diplomacy and Trade
on the East African Littoral, 1798-1856. London: Allen and
Unwin, 1971. Rev. by H. J. Fisher, EHR, 89(Ja 1974):203-4;
M. Twaddle, JAfH, 15(Num 1 1974):170-1.

Nichols, Irby C. , Jr. The European Pentarchy and the Congress of
Verona, 1822. The Hague: Martinus Nijhoff, 1971. Rev. by
L. M. Case, AHR, 79(Oct 1974):1174-5.

Nicholson, Robert Lawrence. Joscelyn III and the Fall of the Crusader States, 1134-1199. Leiden: E. J. Brill, 1973. Rev.
by J. A. Brundage, AHR, 79(Oct 1974):1171-2.

Nicol, Donald M. The Last Centuries of Byzantium, 1261-1453.
London: Hart Davis, 1971. Rev. by S. Runciman, EHR, 89
(Ja 1974):116-18.

Nicolson, Nigel. Alex: The Life of Field Marshal Earl Alexander
of Tunis. New York: Atheneum, 1973. Rev. by P. W. Wark-
en, Historian, 36(Aug 1974):762-3.

Niederer, Frances J. Hollins College, an Illustrated History.
Charlottesville: U Press Va, 1973. Rev. by A. H. Freeman,
VMHB, 82(Apr 1974):216-18.

Nieman, Charles L. Spanish Times and Boom Times: Toward an

Architectural History of Socorro, New Mexico. Socorro,
N. M.: Socorro County Hist. Soc., 1972. Rev. by R. F.
Dickey, NMHR, 49(Apr 1974):177-8.

Niemeyer, E. V., Jr. Revolution at Queretaro: The Mexican Constitutional Convention of 1916-1917. Austin: U Tx Press,
1974. Rev. by S. R. Ross, HRNB, 3(Oct 1974):7-8.

Nightingale, Pamela see Skrine, C. P.

Nikolaou, Ino. Cypriot Inscribed Stones. Nicosia: Dept of Antiquities, 1971. Rev. by H. W. Catling, AJA, 78(Apr 1974):
190.

Nimmo, H. Arlo. The Sea People of Sulu: A Study of Social
Change in the Philippines. San Francisco: Chandler, 1972.
Rev. by J. Beckett, JAS, 33(Feb 1974):343-4.

Nish, Ian H. Alliance in Decline. A Study in Anglo-Japanese Relations, 1908-1923. London: Athlone, 1972. Rev. by P. Kennedy, EHR, 89(Ja 1974):135-7; E. W. Edwards, History, 59
(Feb 1974):144.

Nishimura, Eshin. Unsui: A Diary of Zen Monastic Life. Honolulu: U Press Hawaii, 1973. Rev. by R. J. Corless, JAS,
33(May 1974):490-1.

Nissenbaum, Stephen see Boyer, Paul

Nitske, W. Robert see Wilhelm, Paul, Duke of Wurttemberg

Niven, John. Gideon Welles: Lincoln's Secretary of the Navy.
New York: Ox U Press, 1973. Rev. by H. P. Hinton, CWH,
20(Sep 1974):261-2; J. A. Huston, HRNB, 2(Feb 1974):94;
R. N. Current, JAH, 61(Sep 1974):489-90; R. L. Bloom, JSH,
40(May 1974):313-14; B. D. Ledbetter, MiA, 56(Apr 1974):
127-8; J. J. Heslin, NYHSQ, 58(Oct 1974):333-4; H. Hamilton,
SWHQ, 78(Jl 1974):96-7.

Nock, O. S. Railways in the Formative Years. New York: Macmillan, 1973. Rev. by W. H. Becker, HRNB, 2(Feb 1974):
103.

Noer, Deliar. The Modernist Muslim Movement in Indonesia 1900-
1942. London and Kuala Lumpur: Ox U Press, 1973. Rev.
by J. L. Peacock, JAS, 33(Feb 1974):342-3.

Noggle, Burl. Into the Twenties: The United States from Armistice
to Normalcy. Urbana: U Ill Press, 1974. Rev. by T. Di-
Bacco, HRNB, 3(Oct 1974):2.

Nogueira, Octaciano, ed. Obra política de José Bonifácio. 2 vols.
Brasilia: Centro Gráfico do Senado Federal. Rev. by R.

d'Eça, HAHR, 54(Aug 1974):520-1.

Nordmann, Claude. Grandeur et liberté de la Suède (1660-1792).
Paris: Nauwelaerts, 1971. Rev. by M. Roberts, EHR, 89
(Jl 1974):635-40; F. D. Scott, JMH, 46(Mar 1974):132-3.

Nordstrom, Carl. Frontier Elements in a Hudson River Village.
Port Washington, N. J.: Kennikat, 1973. Rev. by M. A. Berger, HT, 7(Feb 1974):313-14; B. Graymont, NYH, 55(Jl 1974):
337-8; P. B. Hensley, WHQ, 5(Apr 1974):192-3.

Norris, John, ed. Strangers Entertained: A History of Ethnic
Groups in British Columbia. Vancouver: Evergreen, 1971.
Rev. by H. Palmer, CHR, 55(Mar 1974):94-6.

Northcott, Cecil. David Livingstone: His Triumph, Decline and
Fall. Philadelphia: Westminster Press, 1973. Rev. by
C. F. Allison, CH, 43(Dec 1974):556-7.

Norton, Mary Beth. The British Americans: The Loyalist Exiles
in England 1774-1789. London: Constable, 1972. Rev. by
W. Brown, HTo, 24(Aug 1974):575; M. W. Hamilton, NYH, 55
(Ja 1974):109-10.

Nosov, N. E., et al., eds. Problems in the History of International Relations: A Collection of Articles in Memory of Academ-
ician E. V. Tarle. Leningrad: Izdatel'stvo "Nauka," 1972.
Rev. by W. W. Kulski, AHR, 79(Feb 1974):108-9.

Notebaart, Jannis C. Windmühlen: Der Stand der Forschung über
das Vorkommen und den Ursprung. The Hague: Mouton Verlag, 1972. Rev. by J. K. Major, T & C, 15(Oct 1974):630-1.

Novak, Maximillian E. see Dudley, Edward

Novak, Michael. Choosing Our King: Powerful Symbols in Presidential Politics. New York: Macmillan, n. d. Rev. by P. H.
Weaver, Commentary, 58(Jl 1974):89-92.

_____. The Rise of the Unmeltable Ethnics. New York: Mac-
millan, 1973. Rev. by R. H. Vigil, NMHR, 49(Apr 1974):
164-7.

Novosel'tsev, A. P., et al. Ways of the Development of Feudalism
(The Caucasus, Middle Asia, Rus', the Baltic States). Moscow: Izdatel'stvo "Nauka," 1972. Rev. by R. Hellie, AHR,
79(Apr 1974):532-3.

Nowlan, Kevin B. and T. Desmond Wilson, eds. Ireland in the
War Years and After, 1939-51. Notre Dame, Ind.: Notre
Dame U Press, 1970. Rev. by R. T. Reilly, E-I, 9(Spr
1974):150-2.

Nuechterlein, Donald E. United States National Interests in a Changing World. Lexington, Ky.: U Press, Ky, 1973. Rev. by M. N. Dobkowski, FCHQ, 48(Apr 1974):197-8.

Nugent, Donald. Ecumenism in the Age of the Reformation: The Colloquy of Poissy. Cambridge, Mass.: Har U Press, 1974. Rev. by K. H. Dannenfeldt, HRNB, 2(Sep 1974):242-3.

Nugent, Walter T. K. see Miller, Lillian B.

Núñez del Prado, Oscar. Kuyo Chico: Applied Anthropology in an Indian Community. Chicago: U Chi Press, 1973. Rev. by J. V. Murra, TAm, 31(Oct 1974):226-7.

Nunis, Doyce B., Jr. The Drawings of Ignacio Tirsch, a Jesuit Missionary in Baja California. Los Angeles: Dawson's, 1972. Rev. by H. P. Hinton, SCQ, 56(Sum 1974):200.

Nunnerley, David. President Kennedy and Britain. New York: St. Martin's, 1972. Rev. by R. H. Heindel, AHR, 79(Je 1974): 759.

Nwabueze, B. O. Constitutionalism in the Emerging States. n. p.: Hurst, 1973. Rev. by J. F. Bayart, AfAf, 73(Apr 1974):233-4.

Nye, Nelson C. Speed and the Quarter Horse: A Payload of Sprinters. Caldwell, Ida.: Caxton, 1973. Rev. by L. J. Kruse, JOW, 13(Oct 1974):131.

Nye, Russel Blaine. Society and culture in America, 1830-1860. New York: Harper and Row, 1974. Rev. by E. Pessen, NYHSQ, 58(Oct 1974):328-9.

Nyerere, Julius K. Freedom and Development. New York: Ox U Press, 1974. Rev. by C. P. Potholm, HRNB, 2(Aug 1974): 226.

Oates, Stephen B., ed. Portrait of America. Volumes 1 and 2. Boston: Houghton Mifflin, 1973. Rev. by B. L. Turpen, JOW, 13(Jl 1974):118.

Oates, William C. The War Between the Union and the Confederacy. Dayton: Morningside Bookshop, 1974. Rev. by H. B. Simpson, Texana, 11(Win 1974):89-90.

Oberländer, Erwin, et al., eds. Russia Enters the Twentieth Century, 1894-1917. New York: Schocken, 1971. Rev. by R. A. Roosa, AHR, 79(Apr 1974):537-9.

Obichere, B. I. West African States and European Expansion: The Dahomey-Niger Hinterland, 1885-1898. New Haven, Conn.: Yale U Press, 1971. Rev. by A. S. Trickett, Historian, 36

(Aug 1974):745-8; M. A. Klein, JAAS, 9(Ja & Apr 1974):127-8.

Obiechina, Emmanuel N. An African Popular Literature: A Study of Onitsha Market Pamphlets. Cambridge: Cam U Press, 1973. Rev. by A. Ricard, JMAS, 12(Mar 1974):163-5.

————. Literature for the Masses: An Analytical Study of Popular Pamphleteering in Nigeria. Enugu: Nwankwo-Ifejika, 1971. Rev. by A. Ricard, JMAS, 12(Mar 1974):163-5.

————, ed. Onitsha Market Literature. New York: Africana, 1972. Rev. by A. Ricard, JMAS, 12(Mar 1974):163-5.

El obispado de Michoacán en el siglo XVII. Informe inedito de beneficios, pueblos y lenguas. Morelia, Mexico: Fimax, 1973. Rev. by P. Gerhard, HAHR, 54(May 1974):316-17.

O'Boyle, Lenore. The European Middle Class in the 19th Century. St. Charles, Mo.: Forum Press, 1973. Rev. by M. P. McCarthy, HT, 8(Nov 1974):109-10.

O'Brien, David J. The Renewal of American Catholicism. New York: Ox U Press, 1972. Rev. by P. W. Williams, CH, 43 (Sep 1974):430.

O'Brien, Francis William, ed. The Hoover-Wilson Wartime Correspondence: September 24, 1914 to November 11, 1918. Ames: Ia St U Press, 1974. Rev. by J. S. Olson, AI, 42(Fall 1974): 459-60; W. B. Fowler, HRNB, 3(Nov/Dec 1974):43.

O'Brien, James H. Liam O'Flaherty. Lewisburg, Pa.: Bucknell U Press, 1973. Rev. by T. C. Ware, E-I, 9(Spr 1974):155-7.

O'Connell, Marvin R. The Counter Reformation, 1559-1610. New York: Harper and Row, 1974. Rev. by B. Nischan, HRNB, 2(May/Je 1974):184.

O'Connor, Raymond G. Diplomacy for Victory: FDR and Unconditional Surrender. New York: Norton, 1971. Rev. by S. Adler, AHR, 79(Apr 1974):610-11.

O'Connor, Stanley J., Jr. Hindu Gods of Peninsular Siam. Ascona, Switzerland: Artibus Asiae, 1971. Rev. by R. M. Bernier, JAS, 33(Aug 1974):732-3.

O'Conor, John F., trans. and comm. The Sokolov Investigation of the Alleged Murder of the Russian Imperial Family: A Translation of Sections of Nicholas A. Sokolov's The Murder of the Imperial Family. New York: Robert Speller, 1971. Rev. by R. C. Williams, AHR, 79(Apr 1974):546-9.

O'Corrain, Donncha. Ireland Before the Normans. Dublin: Gill
    and Macmillan, 1972. Rev. by P. Wormald, EHR, 89(Ja 1974):
    147.

Odell, Peter R. and David A. Preston. Economies and Societies in
    Latin America: A Geographical Interpretation. New York ...:
    Wiley, 1973. Rev. by S. L. Barraclough, HAHR, 54(Nov
    1974):731-2.

O'Donnell, James H., III. Southern Indians in the American Revo-
    lution. Knoxville: U Tenn Press, 1973. Rev. by A. H. De-
    Rosier, Jr., FHQ, 53(Oct 1974):208-9; H. H. Jackson, GHQ,
    58(Sum 1974):292-4; R. Thornton, HRNB, 2(Apr 1974):150; B.
    Graymont, JAH, 61(Dec 1974):767-8; J. D. L. Holmes, JMiH,
    36(May 1974):199-200; L. R. Gerlach, RKHS, 72(Jl 1974):284-
    5; J. Burt, THQ, 33(Spr 1974):109-10; D. H. Corkran, WMQ-
    3, 31(Jl 1974):509-10.

Ofari, Earl. "Let Your Motto Be Resistance": The Life and
    Thought of Henry Highland Garnet. Boston: Beacon, 1972.
    Rev. by R. L. Harris, Jr., CWH, 20(Sep 1974):273-4.

O'Farrell, Patrick. Ireland's English Queen. New York: Schocken,
    1971. Rev. by F. E. Higgins, HT, 7(Feb 1974):292.

O'Gorman, Frank. Edmund Burke: His Political Philosophy. Bloom-
    ington: Ind U Press, 1973. Rev. by R. Howell, Jr., HRNB,
    2(Mar 1974):120-1.

Ogunsanwo, Alaba. China's Policy in Africa, 1958-71. New York:
    Cam U Press, 1974. Rev. by F. E. Rogers, HRNB, 3(Nov/
    Dec 1974):36.

Ohkawa, Kazushi and Rosovsky. Japanese Economic Growth: Trend
    Acceleration in the Twentieth Century. Stanford, Cal.: Stan
    U Press, 1973. Rev. by T. Kobayashi, T & C, 15(Apr 1974):
    347-9.

Ohlendorf, Sheila M., tr. see Torres, Elias L.

Ohly, Dieter. Glyptothek München. Griechische und Romische
    Skulpturen. Ein Kürzer Führer. Munich: C. H. Beck, 1972.
    Rev. by M. C. Sturgeon, AJA, 78(Oct 1974):441-2.

Okafor, Nduka. The Development of Universities in Nigeria. Lon-
    don: Longman, 1971. Rev. by A. H. M. Kirk-Greene, Afri-
    ca, 44(Apr 1974):203-4.

Okamoto, Shumpei see Borg, Dorothy

Okazaki, Hisahiko. A Japanese View of Détente. Lexington, Mass.:
    D. C. Heath, 1974. Rev. by J. Israel, HRNB, 2(Sep 1974):
    249.

Oksenberg, Michael, ed. China's Developmental Experience. New
   York: Praeger, 1973. Rev. by D. M. Lowe, Historian, 36
   (May 1974):554; C. A. Weiss, JAS, 33(Feb 1974):313-14.

Okuma, J. see Hyden, G.

Oldfather, Felicia. see Livingston, Jon

O'Leary, Peter. My Own Story. Dublin: Gill and Macmillan, 1973.
   Rev. by T. C. Ware, E-I, 9(Spr 1974):157-9.

Oliinyk, A. F., et al., eds. History of the Cities and Villages of
   the Ukrainian S S R--Vinnitsa Province. Kiev: Institut Istorii Akademii Nauk URSR, 1972. Rev. by J. Armstrong,
   AHR, 79(Feb 1974):193-4.

Oliva, Leo E. Soldiers on the Santa Fe Trail. Norman, Okla: U
   Okla Press, 1967. Rev. by J. W. Goodrich, NH, 55(Spr 1974):
   160-2.

Oliver, Andrew, ed. The Journal of Samuel Curwen, Loyalist. 2
   vols. Cambridge, Mass.: Har U Press, 1972. Rev. by
   D. J. Keep, Archives, 11(Spr 1974):183-4; R. M. Calhoon,
   JAH, 60(Mar 1974):1104-5.

Oliver, Douglas. Bougainville: A Personal History. Honolulu:
   U Press Hawaii, 1973. Rev. by L. C. Duly, HRNB, 2(Apr
   1974):146.

Ollard, Richard. Pepys: A Biography. London: Hodder and
   Stoughton, n.d. Rev. by B. Pool, HTo, 24(Oct 1974):729-30.

Ollman, Bertell. Alienation: Marx's Conception of Man in Capitalist Society. Cambridge: Cam U Press, 1971. Rev. by
   J. Lively, History, 59(Feb 1974):165-6.

Olney, R. J. Lincolnshire Politics, 1832-1885. New York: Ox
   U Press, 1973. Rev. by D. F. Schafer, HRNB, 2(Mar 1974):
   121.

Olsen, V. Norskon. John Foxe and the Elizabethan Church. Berkeley: U Cal Press, 1973. Rev. by W. M. Southgate, AHR,
   79(Feb 1974):142.

Olson, Alison Gilbert. Anglo-American Politics, 1660-1775: The
   Relationship Between Parties in England and Colonial America.
   New York: Ox U Press, 1973. Rev. by B. H. Newcomb, His-
   torian, 36(Aug 1974):770-1; W. M. Billings, JAH, 61(Sep 1974):
   463-4; R. C. Simmons, JAmS, 8(Apr 1974):115-16; E. M.
   Cook, Jr., JMH, 46(Sep 1974):546-7; T. Archdeacon, NYHSQ,
   58(Jl 1974):234-5; W. R. Smith, PH, 41(Oct 1974):465-7;
   E. R. Sheridan, WMQ-3, 31(Apr 1974):324-5.

Olson, James C. J. Sterling Morton. Lincoln: U Neb Press,
    1972. Rev. by K. C. Watt, JISHS, 67(Sep 1974):462-3.

Olson, Keith W. The G. I. Bill, the Veterans, and the Colleges.
    Lexington, Ky.: U Press Ky, 1974. Rev. by D. R. Warriner,
    IMH, 70(Sep 1974):267-9; D. R. B. Ross, JAH, 61(Dec 1974):
    840-1; E. M. Coffman, WMH, 57(Spr 1974):240-1.

Olson, Ted. Ranch on the Laramie: A Memoir of an American
    Boyhood. Boston: Little, Brown, 1973. Rev. by H. Mother-
    shead, A & W, 16(Spr 1974):82-4; R. Beach, JOW, 13(Jl
    1974):128.

Olusanya, G. O. The Second World War and Politics in Nigeria,
    1939-1953. Lagos and London: Evans, 1973. Rev. by
    A. H. M. Kirk-Greene, JAfH, 15(Num 2 1974):334-6; D. A.
    Offiong, JMAS, 12(Sep 1974):498-500.

O'Malley, J. Steven. Pilgrimage of Faith: The Legacy of the Ot-
    terbeins. Metuchen, N. J.: Scarecrow, 1973. Rev. by K. R.
    Maurer, CH, 43(Sep 1974):417.

O'Neil, Floyd A., ed. see Jefferson, James

O'Neill, William L., ed. Insights and Parallels: Problems and
    Issues of American Social History. Minneapolis: Burgess,
    1973. Rev. by C. Crowe, JAH, 61(Dec 1974):754-5.

Onon, Urgunge. My Childhood in Mongolia. London: Ox U Press,
    1972. Rev. by R. Ante, JAS, 33(Feb 1974):323-4.

Onorato, Michael P. A Brief Review of American Interest in Philip-
    pine Development and Other Essays. Manila: M C S Enter-
    prises, 1972. Rev. by F. L. Jenista, JAAS, 9(Ja & Apr
    1974):108.

Onstad, Preston E. see Nelson, Herbert B.

Onuf, Peter S., ed. Maryland and the Empire, 1773: The Antilon
    --First Citizen Letters. Baltimore: JHU Press, 1974. Rev.
    by R. A. Gleissner, HRNB, 3(Oct 1974):6.

Opler, Morris E., ed. Grenville Goodwin Among the Western
    Apache: Letters from the Field. Tucson: U Ariz Press,
    1974. Rev. by D. J. Berthrong, HRNB, 2(Aug 1974):222;
    F. J. Johnston, JOW, 13(Jl 1974):113; A. H. Schroeder,
    NMHR, 49(Jl 1974):262.

Orantes, Isaac C. Regional Integration in Central America. Lon-
    don: D. C. Heath, 1972. Rev. by D. Browning, JLAS, 6
    (May 1974):161-8.

Oren, Nissan. Bulgarian Communism: The Road to Power, 1934-

<u>1944</u>. New York: Columbia U Press, 1971. Rev. by
<u>L. A.</u> D. Dellin, EEQ, 8(Mar 1974):112-15.

————. Revolution Administered: Agrarianism and Communism
in Bulgaria. Baltimore: JHU Press, 1973. Rev. by F. B.
Chary, AHR, 79(Feb 1974):188-9.

Orieux, Jean. Talleyrand: The Art of Survival. New York:
Knopf, 1974. Rev. by E. I. Perry, HRNB, 2(Jl 1974):209.

Orleans, Leo A. Every Fifth Child: The Population of China.
Stanford, Cal.: Stan U Press, 1972. Rev. by I. B. Taeuber,
JAAS, 9(Ja & Apr 1974):117-18.

Orlow, Dietrich. The History of the Nazi Party: 1933-1945. Pittsburgh: U Pittsburgh Press, 1973. Rev. by H. W. Gatzke,
AHR, 79(Apr 1974):525-6; D. M. Douglas, Historian, 36(Feb
1974):332-3.

Orren, Karen. Corporate Power and Social Change: The Politics
of the Life Insurance Industry. Baltimore: JHU Press, 1974.
Rev. by M. Keller, BHR, 48(Win 1974):575-6.

Osborn, Eric Francis. Justin Martyr. Tubingen: J. C. B. Mohr,
1973. Rev. by G. S. Bebis, CH, 43(Sep 1974):386-7.

Osborn, James M. Young Philip Sidney 1572-1577. New Haven,
Conn.: Yale U Press, 1972. Rev. by P. McGrath, EHR, 89
(Ja 1974):173-4; D. M. Loades, History, 59(Je 1974):274.

Osborne, John. The Naturalist Drama in Germany. Manchester:
Manchester U Press, 1971. Rev. by M. C. Ives, ESR, 4(Ja
1974):93-5.

Osborne, John W. John Cartwright. Cambridge: Cam U Press,
1972. Rev. by D. Read, History, 59(Feb 1974):121.

Osborne, Milton. Politics and Power in Cambodia: the Sihanouk
Years. Melbourne: Longmans Australia, 1973. Rev. by
D. P. Chandler, JAS, 33(Aug 1974):742-3.

Oschinsky, Dorothea. Walter of Henley and Other Treatises on
Estate Management and Accounting. Oxford: Ox U Press,
1971. Rev. by J. Z. Titow, History, 59(Feb 1974):93-4.

Ostaszewski, Jan, ed. Modern Poland Between East and West.
London: The Polish School of Political and Social Science,
1971. Rev. by W. J. Wagner, EEQ, 7(Ja 1974):475-9.

Östenberg, Carl-Eric see Wetter, Erik

Osterweis, Rollin G. The Myth of the Lost Cause, 1865-1900.
Hamden, Conn.: Archon, 1973. Rev. by R. E. Paulson,

AHR, 79(Oct 1974):1268; J. T. Kirby, JAH, 60(Mar 1974):
1134-5; M. L. Wilson, JSH, 40(Feb 1974):148-9.

Oswalt, Wendell H. This Land Was Theirs: A Study of the North
American Indian. New York: Wiley, 1966. Rev. by J. A.
Greene, JOW, 13(Apr 1974):136.

Otis, D. S. The Dawes Act and the Allotment of Indian Lands.
Norman: U Ok Press, 1973. Rev. by J. L. Grabill, JAH,
61(Sep 1974):531-3; D. R. Wrone, JEH, 34(Sep 1974):797-8;
R. L. Munkres, JOW, 13(Apr 1974):130-1; H. R. Grant, NDH,
41(Spr 1974):32; J. T. King, NH, 55(Spr 1974):162-4; H. E.
Fritz, PHR, 43(Nov 1974):606-8.

Ott, Thomas O. The Haitian Revolution, 1789-1804. Knoxville:
U of Tenn Press, 1973. Rev. by H. Cole, HAHR, 54(Aug
1974):510; D. D. Joyce, JSH, 40(Aug 1974):471-2.

Ou, Tsuin-Chen see Clopton, Robert W.

Outland, Charles. Stagecoaching on the El Camino Real, Los Angeles to San Francisco, 1861-1901. Glendale, Cal.: Arthur
H. Clark, 1973. Rev. by E. W. Holland, SCQ, 56(Fall 1974):
312-13.

Överland, Orm. The Making and Meaning of an American Classic:
James Fenimore Cooper's The Prairie. New York: Humanities, 1973. Rev. by J. P. McWilliams, Jr., JAH, 61(Je
1974):175-6.

Owens, William A. Impressions of the Big Thicket. Austin: U
Tx Press, 1973. Rev. by R. Kennedy, ETHJ, 12(Fall 1974):
90.

Oxe, August, comp., Howard Comfort, ed. Corpus Vasorum Arretinorum. Bonn: Rudolf Habelt Verlag, 1968. Rev. by E.
Ettlinger, AJA, 78(Jl 1974):314-15.

Oz, Amos. Elsewhere, Perhaps. New York: Harcourt Brace
Jovanovich, n. d. Rev. by D. Stern, Commentary, 58(Jl 1974):
100-1.

Ozment, Steven E. Mysticism and Dissent: Religious Ideology and
Social Protest in the Sixteenth Century. New Haven, Conn.:
Yale U Press, 1973. Rev. by L. W. Spitz, AHR, 79(Feb
1974):134-5; C. Krahn, CH, 43(Mar 1974):109-10.

Pachai, Bridglal. Malawi: The History of a Nation. London:
Longman, 1973. Rev. by J. McCracken, JAfH, 15(Num 2
1974):338-9.

_____, ed. Livingstone: Man of Africa. Memorial Essays,
1873-1973. New York: Longman, 1973. Rev. by R. P.

Beaver, CH, 43(Dec 1974):557-8; H. J. Fisher, History, 59
(Je 1974):312.

Pächt, Ott and J. J. G. Alexander, eds. Illuminated Manuscripts
in the Bodleian Library, Oxford. Vol. 3. Oxford: Clarendon
Press, 1973. Rev. by L. Yeandle, AmArc, 37(Apr 1974):293-
5.

Packard, Sidney R. Twelfth-Century Europe: An Interpretative
Essay. Amherst: U Mass Press, 1973. Rev. by G. A.
Zinn, Jr., CH, 43(Dec 1974):534-5; B. B. Blaine, T & C, 15
(Oct 1974):631-2.

Packer, James E. The Insulae of Imperial Ostia. Rome: American Academy, 1971. Rev. by H. Bloch, AJA, 78(Ja 1974):
102-3.

Pagden, A. R., ed. Hernan Cortés: Letters from Mexico. New
York: Grossman, 1971. Rev. by C. R. Boxer, EHR, 89(Ja
1974):166-7.

Page, R. I. An Introduction to English Runes. London: Methuen,
1973. Rev. by B. Dickens, Antiquity, 48(Je 1974):152-3.

Pagliaro, Harold E. Irrationalism in the Eighteenth Century.
Cleveland, Ohio: Press CWRU, 1972. Rev. by J. H. Mid-
dendorf, AHR, 79(Feb 1974):112-14.

Paher, Stanley W. Death Valley Ghost Towns. Las Vegas: Nevada
Publications, 1973. Rev. by N. E. Ramirez, JOW, 13(Apr
1974):119.

Pairault, Françoise-Hélène. Recherches sur Quelques Séries
d'Urnes de Volterra à Representations Mythologiques. Paris:
Editions E. de Boccard, 1972. Rev. by M. A. Del Chiaro,
AJA, 78(Apr 1974):204-5.

Paley, Grace. Enormous Changes at the Last Minute. New York:
Farrar, Straus, and Giroux, n.d. Rev. by J. L. Crain, Commentary, 58(Jl 1974):92-3.

Palmer, Alan. Alexander I. Tsar of War and Peace. London:
Weidenfeld and Nicolson, n.d. Rev. by I. Grey, HTo, 24
(Jl 1974):513.

_____. Metternich. London: Weidenfeld and Nicolson, 1972.
Rev. by H. M. Scott, History, 59(Feb 1974):138.

Palsson, Mary Dale see Dinnerstein, Leonard

Palyi, Melchoir. The Twilight of Gold, 1914-1936: Myths and
Realities. Chicago: H. Regnery, 1972. Rev. by T. Grennes,
AHR, 79(Oct 1974):1145-6.

Paolino, Ernest N. The Foundations of the American Empire: William Henry Seward and U. S. Foreign Policy. Ithaca, N. Y.: Cornell U Press, 1973. Rev. by J. Davids, HRNB, 2(Feb 1974):97-8; C. Vevier, JAH, 61(Sep 1974):488-9; A. B. Pearson, Jr., JSH, 40(Aug 1974):495-6; W. G. Sharrow, NYHSQ, 58(Oct 1974):331-3.

Papahatzes, Nicholas see Andronicos, Emmanuel

Papanek, Gustav F. see Falcon, Walter P.

Paredes, Américo, ed. and trans. Folktales of Mexico. Chicago: U Chi Press, 1970. Rev. by J. Sobrino, HAHR, 54(Nov 1974):738-9.

Paret, Peter, ed. Frederick the Great. London: Macmillan, 1972. Rev. by R. M. Hatton, History, 59(Je 1974):279; J. Richardson, HTo, 24(Ja 1974):67.

Pargeter, Edith. The Bloody Field. New York: Viking, 1973. Rev. by S. Curry, HT, 7(Aug 1974):645.

Parker, Donald Dean. Gabriel Renville: Young Sioux Warrior. Jericho, N. Y.: Exposition, 1973. Rev. by J. Poseley, NDH, 41(Fall 1974):33-5.

Parker, Franklin. George Peabody. Nashville: Van U Press, 1971. Rev. by D. K. Adams, EHR, 89(Apr 1974):447-8.

Parker, Gail Thain. Mind Cure in New England: From the Civil War to World War I. Hanover, N. H.: U Press New England, 1973. Rev. by C. Griffen, AHR, 79(Feb 1974):230-1; L. Perry, JAH, 60(Mar 1974):1152-3.

Parker, Geoffrey. The Army of Flanders and the Spanish Road 1567-1659. Cambridge: Cam U Press, 1972. Rev. by R. J. W. Evans, History, 59(Feb 1974):105.

Parker, J. M. An Aged Wanderer: A Life Sketch of J. M. Parker. Bryan, Tx.: Fred White, Jr., 1969. Rev. by C. R. McClure, ETHJ, 12(Spr 1974):65.

Parkinson, Roger. A Day's March Nearer Home: The War History From Alamein to VE Day Based on the War Cabinet Papers of 1942 to 1945. New York: David McKay, 1974. Rev. by A. F Peterson, HRNB, 3(Nov/Dec 1974):26.

Parks, Robert J. Democracy's Railroads: Public Enterprise in Jacksonian Michigan. Port Washington, N. Y.: Kennikat, 1972. Rev. by R. M. Sutton, JAH, 61(Je 1974):181-2.

Parmet, Herbert S. Eisenhower and the American Crusades. New York: Macmillan, 1972. Rev. by M. P. Burg, PNQ, 65(Apr 1971):90-1.

Parris, Guichard and Lester Brooks. Blacks in the City: A History of the National Urban League. Boston: Little, Brown, 1971. Rev. by L. R. Harlan, AHR, 79(Je 1974):890-1; E. Noyes, JISHS, 67(Apr 1974):243-4.

Parrish, William E. A History of Missouri. Volume III, 1860-1875. Columbia, Mo.: U Mo Press, 1973. Rev. by R. E. Shalhope, A & W, 16(Spr 1974):79; J. V. Mering, CWH, 20 (Je 1974):166-7; M. F. Holt, HRNB, 2(Mar 1974):129-30; D. Carmony, JAH, 61(Dec 1974):787-8; K. E. St. Clair, JSH, 40 (May 1974):317-18; L. Anders, MHR, 68(Ja 1974):261-2; W. H. Lyon, PHR, 43(Nov 1974):604-5.

Parsons, R. T. Windows on Africa: A Symposium. Leiden: E. J. Brill; New York: Humanities, 1971. Rev. by J. M. Janzen, JAAS, 9(Ja & Apr 1974):122-3.

Parsons, Stanley B. The Populist Context: Rural versus Urban Power on a Great Plains Frontier. Westport, Conn.: Greenwood, 1973. Rev. by W. T. K. Nugent, AHR, 79(Je 1974): 882-3; H. W. Morgan, Historian, 36(May 1974):579-80; M. Walsh, JAmS, 8(Aug 1974):267-70; P. H. Argersinger, MiA, 56(Jl 1974):203; T. Saloutos, PHR, 43(May 1974):277-8; K. D. Bicha, WHQ, 5(Apr 1974):195-6; B. L. Jones, WMH, 57(Sum 1974):314.

Partner, Peter. The Lands of St. Peter. Berkeley: U Cal, 1972. Rev. by D. S. Chambers, RQ, 27(Sum 1974):203-5.

Partridge, William. A Practical Treatise on Dyeing of Woolen, Cotton, and Skein Silk with the Manufacture of Broadcloth and Cassimere, Including the Most Improved Methods in the West of England. Edington, Wilts., England, 1973: Pasold Research Fund, 1973. Rev. by K. H. Wolff, BHR, 48(Win 1974):586-8.

Pascoe, Louis B. Jean Gerson: Principles of Church Reform. Leiden: E. J. Brill, 1973. Rev. by C. W. Brockwell, Jr., CH, 43(Sep 1974):395.

Pasley, Malcolm, ed. Germany: A Companion to German Studies. New York: Barnes and Noble, 1972. Rev. by J. Donohoe, Historian, 36(Feb 1972):333-5.

Pasternak, Burton. Kinship and Community in Two Chinese Villages. Stanford, Cal.: Stan U Press, 1972. Rev. by H. G. Rohsenow, JAS, 33(May 1974):476-8.

Paterson, Stanley see Seaburg, Carl

Paterson, Thomas G. Soviet-American Confrontation: Postwar Reconstruction and the Origins of the Cold War. Baltimore ...: JHU Press, 1973. Rev. by D. J. Mrozek, BHR, 48(Win 1974): 571-3; W. Lerner, HRNB, 2(Aug 1974):216; A. Theoharis,

JAH, 61(Sep 1974):536-7; M. A. Stoler, WMH, 57(Spr 1974):
245-6.

Paton, Alan. Apartheid and the Archbishop: The Life and Times
of Geoffrey Clayton. New York: Scribner's, 1974. Rev. by
D. G. Baker, HRNB, 2(May/Je 1974):171.

Patrick, Alison. The Men of the First French Republic: Political
Alignments in the National Convention of 1792. Baltimore:
JHU Press, 1972. Rev. by J. P. McLaughlin, CHR, 55(Sep
1974):350-2; W. Doyle, EHR, 89(Ja 1974):201-2.

Patterson, Daniel W. and John W. Garst, eds. The Social Harp.
Athens, Ga.: U Ga Press, 1973. Rev. by M. P. Farmer,
GHQ, 58(Sum 1974):297-8.

Patterson, James T. Mr. Republican: A Biography of Robert A.
Taft. Boston: Houghton Mifflin, 1972. Rev. by G. W.
Reichard, AHR, 79(Oct 1974):1291; R. T. Ruetten, IMH, 70
(Mar 1974):86-7; E. Richardson, PNQ, 65(Spr 1974):89-90.

Patterson, Stephen E. Political Parties in Revolutionary Massachusetts. Madison: U Wis Press, 1973. Rev. by V. Sapio,
HRNB, 2(May/Je 1974):167; H. J. Henderson, JAH, 60(Mar
1974):1101-3; G. A. Billias, WMQ-3, 31(Apr 1974):320-2.

Patterson, Thomas G. America's Past: A New World Archaeology.
Glenview, Ill.: Scott, Foresman, 1973. Rev. by T. B. Hinton, JAriH, 15(Win 1974):393-4.

Paul, Rodman W., ed. A Victorian Gentlewoman in the Far West:
The Reminiscences of Mary Hallock Foote. San Marino, Cal.:
The Huntington Library, 1972. Rev. by L. B. Donovan, CHQ,
53(Sum 1974):181-2; H. L. Carter, JAH, 60(Mar 1974):1142-
3; M. W. Wells, PNQ, 65(Apr 1974):87.

Paul, Roland A. American Military Commitments Abroad. New
Brunswick, N.J.: Rutgers U Press, 1973. Rev. by T. G.
Smith, JOW, 13(Oct 1974):133-4.

Paul, Sherman. Hart's Bridge. Urbana: U Ill Press, 1972. Rev.
by H. Butterfield, JAmS, 8(Apr 1974):127-8.

Paul, Virginia. This Was Cattle Ranching: Yesterday and Today.
Seattle: Superior, 1973. Rev. by C. W. Black, JOW, 13(Jl
1974):127; A. C. McGregor, PNQ, 65(Oct 1974):191-2.

Pauley, Bruce F. Hahnenschwanz und Hakenkreuz: Der Steirische
Heimatschutz und der österreichische Nationalsozialismus,
1918-1934. Vienna: Europaverlag, 1972. Rev. by K. von
Klemperer, AHR, 79(Feb 1974):180-1.

Paulson, Ross Evans. Women's Suffrage and Prohibition: A Comparative Study of Equality and Social Control. Glenview, Ill.: Scott, Foresman, 1973. Rev. by K. Xidis, HT, 8(Nov 1974): 124-5; S. H. Strom, JAH, 61(Sep 1974):478-9.

Pavlowitch, Stevan K. Yugoslavia. New York: Praeger, 1971. Rev. by W. R. Roberts, AHR, 79(Je 1974):811-12.

Paxton, Robert O. Vichy France: Old Guard and New Order, 1940-1944. New York: Knopf, 1972. Rev. by S. Jessner, Historian, 36(Feb 1974):336.

Payne, Robert. The Life and Death of Adolf Hitler. New York: Praeger, 1973. Rev. by H. W. Gatzke, AHR, 79(Feb 1974): 178-9; G. D. Drummond, Historian, 36(Feb 1974):331-2.

Payne, Stanley G. A History of Spain and Portugal. Vol. I and II. Madison: U Wis Press, 1973. Rev. by G. Addy, AHR, 79 (Oct 1974):1199-1201; G. Tortella-Casares, HAHR, 54(Nov 1974):699-702; J. F. Ramsey, Historian, 36(Aug 1974):752-3.

Peabody, James Bishop, ed. The Founding Fathers: John Adams, A Biography in His Own Words. New York: Newsweek, 1973. Rev. by P. H. Smith, NEQ, 47(Mar 1974):163-5; R. Ketchum, VMHB, 82(Ja 1974):119-20.

Peacock, Mary Reynolds see Cutten, George Barton

Pease, Jane H. and William H. Bound With Them in Chains: A Biographical History of the Antislavery Movement. Westport, Conn.: Greenwood, 1972. Rev. by L. Filler, AHR, 79(Apr 1974):579-80; R. Ginger, CHR, 55(Je 1974):223-4; G. Lerner, JAH, 60(Mar 1974):1118-19; J. E. Mooney, NEQ, 47(Je 1974): 318-21; R. Trendel, NYHSQ, 58(Oct 1974):329-31.

Peccorini Letona, Francisco. La Voluntad del pueblo en la emancipación de El Salvador. Un estudio sobre las relaciones del pueblo con los próceres en la independencia y en la anexión a México. San Salvador: El Salvador: Ministerio de Educación, 1972. Rev. by J. W. Gardner, HAHR, 54(Feb 1974):132-3.

Pedersen, James F. and Kenneth D. Wald. Shall the People Rule? A History of the Democratic Party in Nebraska Politics, 1854-1972. Lincoln, Neb.: Jacob North, 1972. Rev. by J. C. Livingston, CoMag, 51(Sum 1974):262-4; J. T. Doyle, JAH, 60(Mar 1974):1127-8; K. L. Brown, JOW, 13(Oct 1974):136; L. S. Theisen, MiA, 56(Apr 1974):125-7; W. D. Aeschbacher, WHQ, 5(Ja 1974):62-3.

Pedretti, Carlo. Leonardo da Vinci: The Royal Palace at Romorantin. Cambridge, Mass.: Har U Press, 1972. Rev. by C. W. Condit, T & C, 15(Oct 1974):634-5.

Peirce, Neal R. The Deep South States of America: People, Poli-

tics and Power in the Seven Deep South States. New York:
Norton, 1974. Rev. by W. B. Gatewood, Jr., JSH, 40(Nov
1974):639-41.

_____. The Mountain States of America: People, Politics, and
Power in the Eight Rocky Mountain States. New York: Norton, 1972. Rev. by W. H. Lyon, JOW, 13(Apr 1974):117.

Pekáry, Thomas. Die Fundmunzen von Vindonissa von Hadrian bis
zum Ausgang der Romerherrschaft. Brugg: Gesellschaft Pro
Vindonissa, 1971. Rev. by T. V. Buttrey, AJA, 78(Ja 1974):
103.

Pelekides, Chryses see Andronicos, Emmanuel

Pelet, Jean Jacques. The French Campaign in Portugal, 1810-1811.
Minneapolis: U Minn Press, 1973. Rev. by J. Bowditch,
AHR, 79(Apr 1973):521-2.

Pelikán, Jirí, ed. The Czechoslovak Political Trials, 1950-1954:
The Suppressed Report of the Dubcek Government's Commis-
sion of Inquiry, 1968. Stanford, Cal.: Stan U Press, 1971.
Rev. by J. Anderle, JMH, 46(Je 1974):365-6.

Pells, Richard H. Radical Visions and American Dreams: Culture
and Social Thought in the Depression Years. New York: Harper and Row, 1973. Rev. by A. A. Ekirch, Jr., AHR, 79
(Feb 1974):247-8; R. L. Buroker, JAH, 61(Je 1974):241-2;
A. R. Raucher, JSH, 40(May 1974):333-4.

Pelto, Pertti J., ed. see Bernard, H. Russell

Pelz, Stephen E. Race to Pearl Harbor: The Failure of the Sec-
ond London Naval Conference and the Onset of World War II.
Cambridge, Mass.: Har U Press, 1974. Rev. by J. Lukacs,
HRNB, 3(Nov/Dec 1974):44.

Penelea, Georgeta. Les foires de la Valachie pendant in période
1774-1848. Bucharest: Editions de l'Académie de la République Socialiste de Roumanie. 1973. Rev. by P. N. Hehn,
AHR, 79(Je 1974):812-13.

Penlington, Norman. The Alaska Boundary Dispute: A Critical
Reappraisal. Toronto: McGraw-Hill, Ryerson, 1972. Rev.
by R. M. Logan, JOW, 13(Apr 1974):110; E. A. Crownhart-
Vaughan, OrHQ, 75(Mar 1974):85; T. C. Hinckley, PHR, 43
(May 1974):286.

Pennington, M. Basil, ed. Contemplative Community: An Interdisciplinary Symposium. Washington, D.C.: Consortium
Press, 1972. Rev. by B. K. Lackner, CH, 43(Mar 1974):
104.

283   PERCELL

Percell, Edward A., Jr. The Crisis of Democratic Theory: Scientific Naturalism and the Problem of Value. Lexington, Ky.:
  U Press Ky, 1973. Rev. by R. A. Skotheim, JSH, 40(Feb
  1974):117-18.

Perdue, Robert E. The Negro in Savannah, 1865-1900. Jericho,
  N. Y.: Exposition Press, 1973. Rev. by D. R. Colburn,
  FHQ, 53(Oct 1974):216-17; M. S. Miller, JNH, 59(Ja 1974):
  99-101.

Peretz, Merhav. La Gauche Israelienne. Paris: Editions An-
  thropos, 1973. Rev. by M. Nahumi, NO, 17(Ja 1974):74-7.

Pericoli, Ugo. 1815: The Armies at Waterloo. New York: Scribner's, 1974. Rev. by A. R. Sunseri, HRNB, 2(Apr 1974):143.

Perkins, Ann. The Art of Dura-Europos. Oxford: Clarendon
  Press, 1973. Rev. by M. A. R. Colledge, AJA, 78(Oct 1974):
  442.

Perloff, Marjorie G. The Poetic Art of Robert Lowell. Ithaca,
  N. Y.: Cornell U Press, 1972. Rev. by S. Fender, JAmS,
  8(Apr 1974):129.

Perman, Michael. Reunion Without Compromise: The South and
  Reconstruction, 1865-1868. New York: Cam U Press, 1973.
  Rev. by R. J. Roske, AHR, 79(Je 1974):870; E. Everly,
  AmArc, 37(Oct 1974):599-600; B. Procter, FHQ, 53(Oct 1974):
  213-14; J. E. Sefton, GHQ, 58(Supp 1974):211-12; P. Kolchin,
  JAH, 61(Sep 1974):494-5; D. L. Winters, JAH, 61(Sep 1974):
  519-20; F. A. Dennis, JMiH, 36(May 1974):200-3; W. Suttles,
  JNH, 59(Oct 1974):401-2; H. L. Trefouse, JSH, 40(May 1974):
  322-3; W. C. Harris, NCHR, 51(Ja 1974):105-7; J. H. Schroe-
  der, SCHM, 75(Ja 1974):57-8.

Perouse de Montclos, Jean-Marie. Etienne-Louis Boullée (1728-
  1799): Theoretician of Revolutionary Architecture. New York:
  George Braziller, 1974. Rev. by R. M. Isherwood, HRNB,
  2(Apr 1974):145.

Perrett, Geoffrey. Days of Sadness, Years of Triumph: The American People, 1939-1945. New York: Coward, McCann and
  Geoghegan, 1973. Rev. by T. A. Krueger, AHR, 79(Je 1974):
  904-5.

Perry, Lewis. Radical Abolitionism: Anarchy and the Government
  of God in Antislavery Thought. Ithaca, N. Y.: Cornell U
  Press, 1973. Rev. by D. J. MacLeod, AHR, 79(Apr 1974):
  580; G. M. Frederickson, CHR, 55(Sep 1974):343-5; C. R.
  Osthaus, CWH, 20(Je 1974):169-70; J. B. Scroggs, Historian,
  36(Feb 1974):340-1; S. Persons, JAH, 60(Mar 1974):1117-18;
  B. Wyatt-Brown, MHM, 69(Spr 1974):107-8; G. Sorin, NYH,
  55(Jl 1974):354-6.

Perry, P. J. British Farming in the Great Depression, 1870-1914:
An Historical Geography. North Pomfret, Vt. : David and
Charles, 1974. Rev. by G. E. Fussell, T & C, 15(Oct 1974):
645-6.

Persons, Stow. The Decline of American Gentility. New York:
Columbia U Press, 1973. Rev. by W. E. Davies, AHR, 79
(Oct 1974):1237-8; R. Berthoff, CWH, 20(Mar 1974):48-9;
H. F. May, JAH, 61(Je 1974):150-2; R. P. Sutton, JSH, 40
(May 1974):289-90; D. D. Hall, NEQ, 47(Je 1974):328-30.

Pescatello, Ann, ed. Female and Male in Latin America. Essays.
Pittsburgh: U Pittsburgh Press, 1973. Rev. by A. M. Gal-
lagher, TAm, 30(Apr 1974):541-2.

Peshtich, S. L. Russian Historiography of the 18th Century. Leningrad: Izdatel'stvo Leningradskogo Universiteta, 1971. Rev.
by M. J. Okenfuss, AHR, 79(Je 1974):815-16.

_____, et al., eds. Problems in the History of Feudal Russia:
Collected Articles for the 60th Birthday of Prof. V. V. Mavrodin. Leningrad: Izdatel'stvo Leningradskogo Universiteta,
1971. Rev. by R. Hellie, AHR, 79(Apr 1974):532-3.

Pessen, Edward. Riches, Class, and Power Before the Civil War.
Lexington, Mass.: D. C. Heath, 1973. Rev. by G. L. Main,
BHR, 48(Sum 1974):251-3; W. J. Gilmore, HRNB, 2(Feb 1974):
90-1; R. Jensen, IMH, 70(Je 1974):185-7; R. Doherty, JAH,
61(Dec 1974):778-9; E. A. Miles, JSH, 40(Aug 1974):476-8;
R. A. Mohl, MiA, 56(Apr 1974):124-5; J. F. Richardson,
NYHSQ, 58(Oct 1974):337-8.

Peters, J. T. and H. B. Carden. History of Fayette County, West
Virginia. Parsons, W.Va.: McClain, 1972. Rev. by O. K.
Rice, WVH, 36(Oct 1974):67-8.

Petersen, Jens. Hitler-Mussolini: Die Entstehung der Achse Berlin-Rom, 1933-1936. Tübingen: Max Niemeyer Verlag, 1973.
Rev. by H. W. Gatzke, AHR, 79(Je 1974):779.

Petersen, Karen Daniels. Plains Indian Art From Fort Marion.
Norman: U Okla Press, 1971. Rev. by G. Metcalf, N H,
55(Sum 1974):308-9.

Peterson, Charles S. Take up Your Mission: Mormon Colonizing
Along the Little Colorado River, 1870-1900. Tucson: U Ariz
Press, 1973. Rev. by G. T. Box, AHR, 79(Je 1974):878;
A. C. Cochran, CH, 43(Mar 1974):121-2; D. Tyler, Historian,
36(Aug 1974):785-6; JAH, 61(Je 1974):214-15; E. L. Schaps-
meier, JOW, 13(Apr 1974):124; J. Brooks, NMHR, 49(Apr
1974):179-80; W. S. Greever, PHR, 43(May 1974):274-5; A. K.
Larson, WHQ, 5(Jl 1974):353-4.

Peterson, Douglas L. Time, Tide, and Tempest: A Study of
    Shakespeare's Romances. San Marino, Cal. : Huntington Li-
    brary, 1973. Rev. by C. Gesner, RQ, 27(Fall 1974):365-6.

Peterson, F. Ross. Prophet Without Honor: Glen H. Taylor and
    the Fight for American Liberalism. Lexington, Ky. : U Press
    Ky, 1974. Rev. by O. L. Graham, Jr. , HRNB, 2(May/Je
    1974):161-2; A. Yarnell, JAH, 61(Sep 1974):542-3.

Peterson, Frank Ross see Rodnitzky, Jerome L.

Peterson, Frederick A. see MacNeish, Richard S.   The Prehis-
    tory of the Tehuacan Valley, Volume Three.

Peterson, Guy L. Fort Collins: The Post--the Town. Fort Col-
    lins, Colo. : Old Army, 1972. Rev. by J. Albright, CoMag,
    51(Sum 1974):250.

Peterson, Merrill D. , ed. James Madison: A Biography in His
    Own Words. New York: Harper and Row, 1974. Rev. by
    D. O. Dewey, HRNB, 2(Apr 1974):151; N. E. Cunningham,
    Jr. , VMHB, 82(Oct 1974):500-1.

Pethybridge, Roger. The Spread of the Russian Revolution: Es-
    says on 1917. New York: St. Martin's, 1972. Rev. by
    R. C. Williams, AHR, 79(Apr 1974):546-9; P. Dukes, History,
    59(Feb 1974):148-9.

Petras, James and Hugo Zemelman Merino. Peasants in Revolt:
    A Chilean Case Study, 1965-1971. Austin: U Tx Press, 1972.
    Rev. by P. E. Sigmund, HAHR, 54(Feb 1974):151-3.

Petropoulos, Demetri see Andronicos, Emmanuel

Petrov, Vladimir. Escape from the Future: The Incredible Adven-
    tures of a Young Russian. Bloomington: Ind U Press, 1973.
    Rev. by P. H. Silfen, HRNB, 2(Feb 1974):106.

Pettitt, George A. Berkeley: The Town and Gown of It. Berkeley:
    Howell-North, 1973. Rev. by C. Wollenberg, CHQ, 53(Sum
    1974):184.

Petz, Weldon, comp. In the Presence of Abraham Lincoln. Har-
    rogate, Tenn. : Lincoln Memorial U Press, 1973. Rev. by
    Mrs. J. S. Huff, FCHQ, 48(Jl 1974):286-8.

Pevsner, Nikolaus. The Buildings of England: Oxfordshire. see
    Sherwood, Jennifer

_____ . The Buildings of England: Staffordshire. London: Pen-
    guin, n.d. Rev. by M. Greenhalgh, HTo, 24(Oct 1974):725-6.

Pfaltzgraff, Robert L. , Jr. see Kintner, William R.

Pfurtscheller, Friedrich. Die Privilegierung des Zisterzienserordens im Rahmen der allgemeinen Schutzund Exemtionsgeschichte vom Anfang bis zur Bulle "Parvus Fons' (1265). Ein Uberblick unter besonderer Berücksichtigung von Schreibers "Kurie und Kloster im 12. Jahrhundert." Bern: Herbert Lang; Frankfurt/M: Peter Lang, 1972. Rev. by L. J. Lekai, CH, 43 (Mar 1974):103-4.

Phelan, Mary Kay. Mr. Lincoln's Inaugural Journey. New York: Crowell, 1972. Rev. by P. Connolly, JISHS, 67(Je 1974):359.

Philip, Kenneth R. see Rodnitzky, Jerome L.

Philip, Lotte Brand. The Ghent Altarpiece and the Art of Jan Van Eyck. Princeton, N.J.: Prin U Press, 1971. Rev. by J. Snyder, RQ, 27(Spr 1974):49-53.

Philipp, Emanuel L. Political Reform in Wisconsin: A Historical Review of the Subjects of Primary Election, Taxation, and Railway Regulation. Madison: State Historical Society Wis., 1973. Rev. by J. Penick, Jr., IMH, 70(Sep 1974):263-4; R. C. Nesbit, WMH, 57(Win 1973-74):158-9.

Phillips, Hazel Spencer. Richard the Shaker. Oxford, Ohio: Typoprint, 1972. Rev. by M. L. Young, FCHQ, 48(Ja 1974):62-3.

Phillips, J. R. S. Aymer de Valence: Earl of Pembroke, 1307-1324: Baronial Politics in the Reign of Edward II. Oxford: Ox U Press (Clarendon), 1972. Rev. by M. Prestwich, EHR, 89(Apr 1974):419-20; J. Taylor, History, 59(Feb 1974):94-5.

Phillips, James W. Alaska-Yukon Place Names. Seattle: U Wash Press, 1973. Rev. by C.-N. Naske, PNQ, 65(Jl 1974):149.

Phillips, John. The Reformation of Images: Destruction of Art in England, 1535-1660. Berkeley: U Cal Press, 1974. Rev. by L. P. Fairfield, CH, 43(Sep 1974):401.

Phong, Nguyen van. La Societe Vietnamienne de 1882 a 1902. Paris: P. U. F., 1971. Rev. by R. B. Smith, EHR, 89(Ja 1974):225-6.

Picker, Henry and Heinrich Hoffman. Hitler Close-Up. New York: Macmillan, 1974. Rev. by J. Remak, HRNB, 2(Apr 1974): 142-3.

Piérard, Christiane. Le Plus Anciens Comptes de la ville de Mons (1279-1356). Brussels: Académie royale de Belgique, 1971. Rev. by P. S. Lewis, EHR, 89(Ja 1974):160.

Pierce, Richard A. see Lantzeff, George V.

Pierson, George W. The Moving American. New York: Knopf,

287   PIERSON

1973. Rev. by W. H. Goetzmann, AHR, 79(Feb 1974):213-14.

Pierson, Stuart see Reingold, Nathan

Pihl, Marshall R., ed. Listening to Korea: A Korean Anthology.
New York: Praeger, 1973. Rev. by Yong-Chol Kim, JAS,
33(May 1974):495-6.

Pike, Donald G. see Muench, David

Pilain, Mary Ann Calkins. Technical and Vocational Teacher Education and Training. New York: Unipub, 1973. Rev. by P.
De Vore, T & C, 15(Jl 1974):520-2.

Pilkington, William T. My Blood's Country: Studies in Southwestern Literature. Fort Worth, Tx.: TCU Press, 1973. Rev.
by E. Speck, ETHJ, 12(Fall 1974):93; J. W. Lee, SWHQ, 78
(Jl 1974):106-7.

Pill, David H. The English Reformation, 1529-58. Totowa, N.J.:
Rowman and Littlefield, 1973. Rev. by W. M. Southgate,
AHR, 79(Apr 1974):511.

Pinchbeck, Ivy and Margaret Hewett. Children in English Society.
Volume 2. London: Routledge and Kegan Paul, n.d. Rev.
by R. O'Day, HTo, 24(Mar 1974):213-14.

Pinchot, Gifford. Breaking New Ground. Seattle: U Wash Press,
1972. Rev. by G. B. Dodds, PNQ, 65(Ja 1974):43.

Pinchuk, Ben-Cion. The Octobrists in the Third Duma, 1907-1912.
Seattle: U Wash Press, 1974. Rev. by S. A. Zenkovsky,
HRNB, 3(Nov/Dec 1974):33.

Pinckney, Elise, ed. The Register of St. Philip's Church, Charleston, S.C., 1810-1822. Charleston, S.C.: Colonial Dames,
n.d. Rev. by S. T. Cobb, SCHM, 75(Jl 1974):190.

Pineas, Rainer. Tudor and Early Stuart Anti-Catholic Drama.
Nieuwkoop, Netherlands: B. De Graaf, 1972. Rev. by J.
Carr, RQ, 27(Fall 1974):366-70.

Pinelo, Adalberto J. The Multinational Corporation as a Force in
Latin American Politics: A Case Study of the International
Petroleum Company in Peru. New York: Praeger, 1973.
Rev. by J. L. Payne, HAHR, 54(Feb 1974):186-8.

Pinkerton, Allan. The Molly Maguires and the Detectives. New
York: Dover, 1973. Rev. by A. E. Barbeau, WPHM, 57(Ja
1974):110-12.

Pinkney, David H. The French Revolution of 1830. Princeton, N.J.:
Prin U Press, 1972. Rev. by E. Newman, Historian, 36(Aug
1974):754-6.

Pinkney, Robert. Ghana Under Military Rule, 1966-1969. London:
Methuen, 1972. Rev. by J. Dunn, EHR, 89(Apr 1974):474;
S. C. Sarkesian, JMAS, 12(Je 1974):338-41.

Pinney, Thomas, ed. The Letters of Thomas Babington Macaulay:
Volume I, 1807-February 1831; Volume II, March 1831-De-
cember 1833. New York: Cam U Press, 1974. Rev. by
H. D. Andrews, HRNB, 3(Nov/Dec 1974):27.

Piper, Henry Don see Horrell, C. William

Pippidi, D. M., ed. Nicolas Iorga: L'homme et l'oeuvre. Bucharest: Editions de l'Academie de la République Socialiste de
Roumanie, 1972. Rev. by S. D. Spector, AHR, 79(Feb 1974):
189-90.

Pitkin, Thomas M. The Captain Departs: Ulysses S. Grant's Last
Campaign. Carbondale: S Ill U Press, 1973. Rev. by J.
Barnett, CWH, 20(Sep 1974):281-3; H. Hattaway, ETHJ, 12
(Fall 1974):84; L. R. Thomas, FCHQ, 48(Jl 1974):277-8;
H. W. Morgan, IMH, 70(Mar 1974):85-6; J. T. Marszalek,
Jr., JAH, 61(Je 1974):204; E. B. Long, RKHS, 72(Apr 1974):
180-1; B. D. Ledbetter, MiA, 56(Jl 1974):202.

Pitzer, Donald E., ed. Robert Owen's American Legacy. Indianapolis: Ind Historical Society, 1972. Rev. by W. E. Wilson,
JISHS, 67(Sep 1974):458-9.

Pivar, David J. Purity Crusade: Sexual Morality and Social Control, 1868-1900. Westport, Conn.: Greenwood, 1973. Rev.
by D. M. Kennedy, AHR, 79(Apr 1974):590-1; E. Cassara,
CH, 43(Mar 1974):125; G. T. McJimsey, Historian, 36(Aug
1974):777-8; J. F. Gardner, Jr., JAH, 61(Je 1974):227; L. W.
Banner, JSH, 40(Feb 1974):151-3; J. A. Andrew, III, MiA,
56(Apr 1974):128-9.

Plank, Will. Banners and Bugles. Marlborough, N.Y.: Centennial
Press, 1972. Rev. by J. Barnett, CWH, 20(Sep 1974):281-3.

Platt, Colin. Medieval Southampton: The Port and Trading Community, A.D. 1000-1600. London: Routledge and Kegan Paul,
1973. Rev. by M. Biddle, Antiquity, 48(Sep 1974):247-8.

Platt, D. C. M. Latin America and British Trade, 1806-1914.
New York: Harper and Row, 1973. Rev. by N. H. Leff,
BHR, 48(Win 1974):589-90; F. Safford, HAHR, 54(Feb 1974):
133-6.

Plesur, Milton. America's Outward Thrust. Approaches to Foreign
Affairs, 1865-1890. De Kalb, Ill.: N Ill U Press, 1971. Rev.
by A. E. Campbell, HJ, 17(Num 2 1974):443-7.

Pletcher, David M. The Diplomacy of Annexation: Texas, Oregon,

and the Mexican War. Columbia, Mo.: U Mo Press, 1973.
Rev. by K. J. Brauer, AHR, 79(Oct 1974):1262; M. A. Graebner, JAH, 61(Je 1974):189-90; R. A. Brent, JSH, 40(Feb 1974):
138-40; C. B. Garcia, TAm, 30(Apr 1974):546-7; M. T. Gilderhus, NMHR, 49(Apr 1974):172-3; A. P. Nasatir, WHQ, 5
(Oct 1974):474-5.

Plog, Fred see Martin, Paul

Plommer, Hugh. Vitruvius and Later Roman Building Manuals.
New York: Cam U Press, 1973. Rev. by J. E. Parker, T
& C, 15(Ja 1974):89-91.

Plongeron, Bernard. Théologie et politique au siècle des Lumières
(1770-1820). Geneva: Librairie Droz, 1973. Rev. by R. R.
Palmer, AHR, 79(Apr 1974):520-1; N. Ravitch, CH, 43(Sep
1974):411.

Plowden, David. Floor of the Sky: The Great Plains. San Francisco: Sierra Book Club, 1972. Rev. by C. E. Trafzer,
GPJ, 13(Spr 1974):209; H. E. Socolofsky, JOW, 13(Apr 1974):
135-6.

Plum, Dorothy A. see Adirondack Bibliography

Plumb, J. H. In the Light of History. Boston: Houghton Mifflin,
1973. Rev. by H. P. Liebel, Historian, 36(Aug 1974):736;
G. Best, History, 59(Feb 1974):159-60; M. Kammen, JIH, 5
(Sum 1974):109-18.

Plummer, Alfred. The London Weavers' Company, 1600-1970. London: Routledge and Kegan Paul, 1972. Rev. by S. D. Chapman, BHR, 48(Spr 1974):117-18; N. B. Harte, EHR, 89(Ja
1974):175-6; P. Corfield, History, 59(Je 1974):334.

Plummer, Mark A. Frontier Governor: Samuel J. Crawford of
Kansas. Lawrence: U Press Kan, 1971. Rev. by F. P.
Prucha, AHR, 79(Je 1974):874.

Plümper, Hans-Dieter. Die Gütergemeinschaft bei den Täufern des
16. Jahrhunderts. Göppingen: Verlag Alfred Kümmerle, 1972.
Rev. by R. S. Armour, 406-7.

Poddar, Arabinda, ed. Indian Literature. Simla: Indian Institute
of Advanced Study, 1972. Rev. by S. Mukherjee, JAS, 33(Aug
1974):719-20.

Pogue, Forrest C. George C. Marshall: Organizer of Victory
(1943-1945). New York: Viking, 1973. Rev. by A. Rappaport, PHR, 43(May 1974):288-9.

Pohl, Frederick J. The Viking Settlements of North America.
New York: Clarkson N. Potter, 1972. Rev. by A. R. Lewis,

AHR, 79(Oct 1974):1247-8.

Polakoff, Keith Ian. The Politics of Inertia: The Election of 1876 and the End of Reconstruction. Baton Rouge: LSU Press, 1973. Rev. by W. P. Vaughn, CWH, 20(Mar 1974):87-8; J. H. Kitchens, GHQ, 58(Spr 1974):127-8; J. H. Schroeder, IMH, 70(Sep 1974):260-1; J. H. Cox, JAH, 61(Je 1974):202-4; J. H. Shofner, JSH, 40(May 1974):328-9; A. Peskin, MiA, 56 (Ja 1974):68; J. F. Steelman, NCHR, 51(Spr 1974):236-7; P. W. Kennedy, PNQ, 65(Jl 1974):152.

Polaschek, Karin. Porträttypen einer clandischen Kaiserin. Rome: "L'Erma" di Bretschneider, 1973. Rev. by D. E. E. and F. S. Kleiner, AJA, 78(Oct 1974):443-4.

_____. Studien zur Ikonographie der Antonia Minor. Rome: "L'Erma" di Bretschneider, 1973. Rev. by D. E. E. and F. S. Kleiner, AJA, 78(Oct 1974):443-4.

Pole, Frederick J. The Viking Settlements of North America. New York: Clarkson N. Potter, 1972. Rev. by A. R. Lewis, AHR, 79(Oct 1974):1247-8.

Polenberg, Richard. War and Society: The United States, 1941-1945. Philadelphia: Lippincott, 1972. Rev. by T. A. Krueger, AHR, 79(Je 1974):904-5.

Polishook, Irwin H. see Judd, Jacob

Pollard, Sidney and Colin Holmes, eds. Documents of European Economic History. 3 vols. New York: St. Martin's, 1972. Rev. by R. Knauerhase, JEH, 34(Je 1974):516.

Pollett, J. V., ed. Julius Pflug, Correspondance. Volume 1: 1510-1539. Volume 2: 1539-1541. Leiden: E. J. Brill, 1969, 1973. Rev. by R. H. Bainton, CH, 43(Sep 1974):402-3.

Pollis, Carol A. see Khare, Ravindra S.

Pollitt, J. J. The Ancient View of Greek Art: Criticism, History, and Terminology. n.p.: 1974. Rev. by J. E. Seaver, HRNB, 3(Nov/Dec 1974):37-8.

Pollock, David H. and Arch R. M. Ritter, eds. Latin American Prospects for the 1970's: What Kinds of Revolutions? New York: Praeger, 1973. Rev. by J. Hodara, HAHR, 54(Feb 1974):168-9.

Pollock, Norman H., Jr. Nyasaland and Northern Rhodesia: Corridor to the North. Pittsburgh: Duquesne U Press, 1971. Rev. by A. D. R., JAfH, 15(Num 3 1974):523.

Polonsky, Antony. Politics in Independent Poland: The Crisis of

Constitutional Government. London: Ox U Press, 1972. Rev.
by T. Hunczak, EEQ, 8(Mar 1974):116-17.

Pomfret, John E. Colonial New Jersey. New York: Scribner's,
1973. Rev. by C. P. Nettels, Historian, 36(Aug 1974):771-2;
S. S. Cohen, PH, 41(Jl 1974):359-60; D. L. Kemmerer, WMQ-
3, 31(Jl 1974):505-7.

Pomper, Philip. Peter Lavrov and the Russian Revolutionary Movement. Chicago: U Chi Press, 1972. Rev. by J. P. Scan-
lan, H & T, 13(Num 1 1974):65-78; W. F. Woehrlin, JMH,
46(Mar 1974):149-50.

Ponomarev, B., et al., eds. Histoire de la politique extérieure
de l'U.R.S.S., 1917-1945. Moscow: Éditions du Progrès,
1971. Rev. by H. S. Robinson, AHR, 79(Apr 1974):553.

Pontal, Odette, ed. and trans. Les statuts synodaux français du
XIIIe siècle, précédés de l'histoire du synode diocèsain depuis
ses origines. Volume 1, Les statuts de Paris et le synodal
de l'Ouest (XIIIe siècle). Paris: Bibliothèque Nationale, 1971.
Rev. by S. Kuttner, AHR, 79(Apr 1974):497-8.

Pool, P. A. S. The History of the Town and Borough of Penzance.
Penzance: Corporation of Penzance, n.d. Rev. by A. L.
Rowse, HTo, 24(Aug 1974):657-8.

Pool, William C. Eugene C. Barker: Historian. Austin: Texas
State Historical Assn., 1971. Rev. by T. L. Miller, AHR,
79(Je 1974):892.

Pop, I. I. Czechoslovak-Hungarian Relations (1935-1939). Moscow:
Izdatel'stvo "Nauka," 1972. Rev. by C. M. Novak, AHR, 79
(Oct 1974):1215-16.

Pope, Thomas H. The History of Newberry County, South Carolina.
Vol. I: 1749-1860. Columbia, S.C.: U SCar Press, 1973.
Rev. by R. K. Macmaster, AHR, 79(Oct 1974):1251-2; W. J.
Cooper, Jr., CWH, 20(Je 1974):188-9; W. W. Abbot, JAH,
60(Mar 1974):1096; E. R. Lacy, JSH, 40(May 1974):341-3;
D. W. Hollis, SCHM, 75(Ja 1974):53-5.

Poppi, Antonino. La dottrina della scienza in Giacomo Zabarella.
Padova: Antenore, 1972. Rev. by W. F. Edwards, RQ, 27
(Fall 1974):330-4.

Poppino, Rollie E. Brazil: The Land and the People. New York:
Ox U Press, 1973. Rev. by L. E. Aguilar, HRNB, 2(Aug
1974):223-4; N. T. Strauss, HT, 8(Nov 1974):114-15; R. H.
Mattoon, Jr., T & C, 15(Jl 1974):510-11.

Popple, Charles S. see Larson, Henrietta M.

Popple, Henry. A Map of the British Empire in America with the French and Spanish Settlements Adjacent Thereto. Kent, England: H. H. Margary, 1972. Rev. by C. F. W. Coker, NCHR, 51(Win 1974):110-11.

Population Research in Thailand, a Review and Bibliography. Honolulu: East-West Center, 1973. Rev. by J. A. Hafner, JAS, 33(May 1974):501-2.

Porch, Douglas. Army and Revolution. France 1815-1848. London: Routledge and Kegan Paul, 1974. Rev. by R. Price, HJ, 17(Num 3 1974):663-5.

Porter, Andrew. A Musical Season. New York: Viking, n.d. Rev. by B. H. Haggin, Commentary, 58(Oct 1974):82-6.

Porter, Glenn. The Rise of Big Business, 1860-1910. New York: Crowell, 1973. Rev. by A. S. Eichner, JAH, 61(Je 1974): 221-2.

_____ and Harold Livesay. Merchants and Manufacturers: Studies in the Changing Structure of Nineteenth-Century Marketing. Baltimore: JHU Press, 1971. Rev. by J. L. Bernardi, JEH, 34(Je 1974):517.

Porter, H. C., ed. Puritanism in Tudor England. Columbia, S. C.: USCar Press, 1971. Rev. by G. B. Martin, GR, 28(Sum 1974):352-3.

Porter, Jack Nusan. Student Protest and the Technocratic Society: The Case of ROTC. Milwaukee: Zalonka, 1973. Rev. by W. L. O'Neill, AHR, 79(Je 1974):911-12.

Posluns, Michael see Manuel, George

Pospielovsky, Dimitry. Russian Police Trade Unionism: Experiment or Provocation? London: Weidenfeld and Nicolson, 1971. Rev. by W. McClellan, AHR, 79(Apr 1974):539-50.

Post, Gaines, Jr. The Civil-Military Fabric of Weimar Foreign Policy. Princeton, N. J.: Prin U Press, 1973. Rev. by A. Dorpalen, AHR, 79(Je 1974):804-5.

Post, Kenneth W. J. and George D. Jenkins. The Price of Liberty: Personality and Politics in Colonial Nigeria. Cambridge: Cam U Press, 1973. Rev. by D. H. Jones, History, 59(Je 1974): 307-8; B. Nkemdirim, JMAS, 12(Mar 1974):144-5.

Post, Kenneth and Michael Vickers. Structure and Conflict in Nigeria, 1960-1966. Madison: U Wis Press, 1974. Rev. by W. W. Schmokel, HRNB, 2(May/Je 1974):172; S. E. Oyovbaire JMAS, 12(Je 1974):336-8.

Postan, M. M. Essays on Medieval Agriculture and General Problems of the Medieval Economy. New York: Cam U Press,
1973. Rev. by D. Knowles, AHR, 79(Oct 1974):1165-7.

_____ . The Medieval Economy and Society: An Economic History of Britain, 1100-1500. Berkeley: U Cal Press, 1972.
Rev. by W. M. Bowsky, JEH, 34(Je 1974):517-19.

_____ . Medieval Trade and Finance. New York: Cam U Press,
1973. Rev. by D. Knowles, AHR, 79(Oct 1974):1165-7.

Potichnyj, Peter J. Soviet Agricultural Trade Unions, 1917-70.
Toronto: U Tor Press, 1972. Rev. by G. D. Jackson, Jr.,
AHR, 79(Apr 1974):551-2.

Potier, René. Le génie militaire de Vercingétorix et le mythe
Alise-Alésia. Clermont Ferrand: Editions Volcans, 1973.
Rev. by D. Fishwick, AHR, 79(Oct 1974):1160.

Potter, David M. The South and the Concurrent Majority. Baton
Rouge: LSU Press, 1973. Rev. by J. Rabun, JISHS, 67(Sep
1974):451-2.

Potter, J. G. see Faber, M. L. O.

Poulton, Helen J. The Historian's Handbook: A Descriptive Guide
to Reference Works. Norman: U Ok Press, 1972. Rev. by
D. F. Walle, JISHS, 67(Sep 1974):457-8.

Poulton, Ron. The Paper Tyrant: John Ross Robertson of the
Toronto Telegram. Toronto/Vancouver: Clarke, Irwin, 1971.
Rev. by P. Rutherford, CHR, 55(Mar 1974):91-2.

Poumarede, Jacques. Les successions dans le sud-ouest de la
France au Moyen Age. Paris: Presses Universitaires de
France, 1972. Rev. by J. R. Strayer, AHR, 79(Feb 1974):
127-8.

Pourade, Richard F. The Sign of the Eagle: A View of Mexico--
1830-1855. San Diego: Union-Tribune, 1970. Rev. by
M. M. Sibley, ETHJ, 12(Fall 1974):76-7.

Powell, Anthony. Temporary Kings. Boston: Little, Brown, 1973.
Rev. by L. Stanton, GR, 28(Sum 1974):371-4.

Powell, Geoffrey. The Kandyan Wars. n. p.: Les Cooper, n. d.
Rev. by A. H., HTo, 24(Apr 1974):291.

Powell, John Wesley. The Exploration of the Colorado River. Chicago: U Chi Press, 1973. Rev. by M. B. Hudson, JOW, 13
(Apr 1974):126.

Powell, Philip Wayne. Tree of Hate: Propaganda and Prejudices

POWELL   294

Affecting United States Relations with the Hispanic World.
New York: Basic Books, 1971. Rev. by A. P. Whitaker,
AHR, 79(Je 1974):841-2.

Powell, William S. see Lefler, Hugh T.

Powers, Thomas. The War at Home: Vietnam and the American
People, 1964-1968. New York: Grossman, 1973. Rev. by
J. M. Harrison, HRNB, 2(Mar 1974):131-2.

Powley, Edward B. The Naval Side of King William's War. London: John Baker, 1972. Rev. by J. S. Bromley, EHR, 89
(Ja 1974):188-9; J. R. Jones, History, 59(Feb 1974):110.

Poznanskii, V. V. Essays on the History of Russian Culture in
the First Half of the 19th Century. Moscow: Izdatel'stvo
Prosveshchenie, 1970. Rev. by R. E. McGrew, AHR, 79(Feb
1974):199-200.

Prachowny, M. F. J., A. K. L. Acheson, and J. F. Chant, eds.
Bretton Woods Revisited. see Acheson, A. K. L., J. F.
Chant, and M. F. J. Prachowny, eds. Bretton Woods Re-
visited.

Prachuabmoh, Visid., et al. The Rural and Urban Population of
Thailand: Comparative Profiles. Bangkok: ... Chulalongkorn
U, 1972. Rev. by J. A. Hafner, JAS, 33(May 1974):502.

Prall, Stuart E. The Bloodless Revolution: England, 1688. Garden City, N.Y.: Doubleday, 1972. Rev. by R. J. Sinner,
Historian, 36(May 1974):540-1.

Prassel, Frank Richard. The Western Peace Officer: A Legacy
of Law and Order. Norman: U Ok Press, 1972. Rev. by
E. West, Historian, 36(Feb 1974):356-7; P. D. Jordan, NDH,
41(Win 1974):27-8; R. F. Cardenas, WHQ, 5(Apr 1974):214-15.

Prawer, Joshua. The Latin Kingdom of Jerusalem. London: Weidenfeld and Nicolson, 1972. Rev. by H. E. J. Cowdrey, History, 59(Je 1974):253-4.

_____. The World of the Crusaders. New York: Quadrangle,
1972. Rev. by M. W. Baldwin, AHR, 79(Feb 1974):131;
J. A. Brundage, CH, 43(Mar 1974):101-2.

Pre-Archival Records Control Operation Manual. n. p.: East Sus-
sex County Council, 1973. Rev. by F. L. Williams, AmArc,
37(Jl 1974):462-3.

Pred, Allan R. Urban Growth and the Circulation of Information.
The United States System of Cities, 1790-1840. Cambridge,
Mass.: Har U Press, 1973. Rev. by F. X. Blouin, Jr.,
BHR, 48(Win 1974):554-5; F. I. Olson, HRNB, 2(Mar 1974):

126; G. R. Taylor, JEH, 34(Sep 1974):799-801.

Prelinger, Catharine M. see Willcox, William B.

Prest, John. Lord John Russell. Columbia, S. C.: USCar Press, 1972. Rev. by J. Winter, CHR, 55(Je 1974):215-17; J. B. Conacher, JMH, 46(Mar 1974):139-141.

Preston, David A. and Peter R. Odell. Economies and Societies in Latin America: A Geographical Interpretation. see Odell, Peter R. and David A. Preston. Economies and Societies....

Preston, Richard A., ed. The Influence of the United States on Canadian Development: Eleven Case Studies. Durham, N. C.: Duke U Press, 1972. Rev. by C. Armstrong, BHR, 48(Spr 1974):141-2; M. Wade, CHR, 55(Je 1974):185-6; D. M. L. Farr, Historian, 36(Feb 1974):358-9.

Prewitt, Audra L. see Boren, Carter E.

Price, Edna Calkins. Burro Bill and Me. Idyllwild, Cal.: Strawberry Valley Press, 1973. Rev. by G. Gardner, JAriH, 15 (Spr 1974):88-90.

Price, J. L. Culture and Society in the Dutch Republic During the 17th Century. New York: Scribner's, 1974. Rev. by S. B. Baxter, HRNB, 3(Oct 1974):9.

Price, Jacob M. The Dimensions of the Past. see Lorwin, Val R.

_____. France and the Chesapeake: A History of the French Tobacco Monopoly, 1674-1791, and of Its Relationship to the British and American Tobacco Trades. 2 vols. Ann Arbor: U Mich Press, 1973. Rev. by W. E. Minchinton, BHR, 48 (Spr 1974):115-17; E. J. Ferguson, JAH, 60(Mar 1974):1093-6; E. Fox-Genovese, JMH, 46(Dec 1974):691-701; R. P. Thomson, JSH, 40(May 1974):295-7; J. J. McCusker, WMQ-3, 31 (Ja 1974):142-3.

Price, John A. Tijuana: Urbanization in a Border Culture. Notre Dame, Ind.: U Notre Dame Press, 1973. Rev. by E. K. Chamberlin, PHR, 43(Aug 1974):432.

Price, Raye Carleson. Diggings and Doing in Park City. Salt Lake City: U Utah Press, 1972. Rev. by L. P. James, JOW, 13(Apr 1974):115.

Prieto, Carlos. Mining in the New World. New York: McGraw-Hill, 1973. Rev. by L. R. Arana, FHQ, 53(Jl 1974):80-1; R. H. Vigil, Historian, 36(Feb 1974):310; W. D. Raat, WHQ, 5(Apr 1974):219-20.

Pringle, Robert. Rajahs and Rebels: The Ibans of Sarawak under
    Brooke Rule, 1841-1941. London: Macmillan, 1970. Rev.
    by A. J. N. Richards, MAS, 8(Oct 1974):555-7.

Prisco, Salvatore III. John Barrett, Progressive Era Diplomat:
    A Study of a Commercial Expansionist, 1887-1920. University,
    Ala.: U Ala Press, 1973. Rev. by S. C. Topik, BHR, 48
    (Win 1974):560-1; W. B. Fowler, GHQ, 58(Supp 1974):208-9;
    R. B. Welch, Jr., HRNB, 2(Ja 1974):59; B. I. Kaufman, JAH,
    61(Sep 1974):509-10; P. S. Holbo, PNQ, 65(Oct 1974):188;
    M. M. True, VH, 42(Win 1974):67-8; G. T. Brown, WHQ, 5
    (Jl 1974):338-9.

Proby, Kathryn Hall. Audubon in Florida: With Selections From
    the Writings of John James Audubon. Coral Gables, Fla.:
    U Miami Press, 1974. Rev. by E. A. Hammond, FHQ, 53
    (Oct 1974):198-9.

Proctor, Raymond. Agonia de un neutral (Las relaciones hispano-
    alemanas durante la segunda guerra mundial y la División
    Azul). Madrid: Editora Nacional, 1972. Rev. by G. Jack-
    son, AHR, 79(Apr 1974):621-2.

Prodan, David. Supplex Libellus Valachorum. Bucharest: Publish-
    ing House of the Academy of the Socialist Republic of Rou-
    mania, 1971. Rev. by R. J. W. Evans, EHR, 89(Ja 1974):
    195-6.

Proudfoot, Mary. British Politics and Government, 1951-1970: A
    Study of an Affluent Society. London: Faber, n. d., Rev. by
    J. Richards, HTo, 24(Sep 1974):664-6.

Provencher, Jean. Québec sous la loi des mesures de guerre 1918.
    Montréal: Boréal Express, 1971. Rev. by J.-Y. Gravel, CHR,
    55(Sep 1974):317-18.

Prucha, Francis Paul, ed. Americanizing the American Indians:
    Writings by the "Friends of the Indian," 1880-1900. Cam-
    bridge, Mass.: Har U Press, 1973. Rev. by R. N. Ellis,
    CoMag, 51(Sum 1974):260-1; T. C. Hinckley, IMH, 70(Dec
    1974):357-8; M. E. F. Mathur, InH, 7(Spr 1974):49-50; D. L.
    Smith, JAriH, 15(Aut 1974):299-300; C. Reese, JOW, 13(Oct
    1974):130; S. D. Youngkin, NH, 55(Sum 1974):301-3; R. L.
    Whitner, PNQ, 65(Oct 1974):191.

_____, ed. see Otis, D. S.

Pruitt, Ruth. see Rogers, William Warren. Stephen S. Renfroe.

Prusek, Janoslav. Chinese Statelets and the Northern Barbarians
    in the Period 1400-300 B. C. Dordrecht: W. Reidel, 1971.
    Rev. by O. Lattimore, MAS, 8(Oct 1974):560-3.

Pullan, Brian. A History of Early Renaissance Italy: From the
Mid-Thirteenth to the Mid-Fifteenth Century. New York: St.
Martin's, 1973. Rev. by D. Herlihy, AHR, 79(Je 1974):774-5.

_____ . Rich and Poor in Renaissance Venice. Oxford: Basil
Blackwell, 1971. Rev. by A. L. Beier, ESR, 4(Apr 1974):
182-4.

Purcell, Edward A., Jr. The Crisis of Democratic Theory: Sci-
entific Naturalism and the Problem of Value. Lexington, Ky.:
U Press Ky, 1973. Rev. by R. W. Etulain, Historian, 36
(May 1974):572-3; R. A. Skotheim, JSH, 40(Feb 1974):117-18;
E. V. Mittlebeeler, RKHS, 72(Apr 1974):192-4.

Purcell, Theodore V. and Gerald F. Cavanagh. Blacks in the Industrial World: Issues for the Manager. New York: Free
Press, 1972. Rev. by L. I. Donnelly, JNH, 59(Ja 1974):94-
6.

Purdue, Howell and Elizabeth. Patrick Cleburne: Confederate General. Hillsboro, Tx.: Hill Jr. Coll Press, 1973. Rev. by
J. C. Harsh, CWH, 20(Je 1974):185-6; T. L. Connelly, JSH,
40(Aug 1974):491-3.

Purves, J. G. and D. A. West, eds. War and Society in the Nineteenth-Century Russian Empire. Toronto: New Review Press,
1972. Rev. by J. L. Black, CHR, 55(Mar 1974):116-17.

Pye, Lucian W. Warlord Politics: Conflict and Coalition in the
Modernization of Republican China. New York: Praeger, 1971.
Rev. by R. A. Kapp, MAS, 8(Apr 1974):271-3.

Quaife, M. M., ed. Yellowstone Kelly: The Memoirs of Luther S.
Kelly. Lincoln: U Neb Press, 1973. Rev. by R. L. Munkres,
JOW, 13(Ja 1974):154.

Quam, Alvina, trans. The Zuñis--Self Portrayals. Albuquerque:
U NM Press, 1972. Rev. by D. M. Brugge, A & W, 16(Spr
1974):75-6; R. Brogan, JOW, 13(Apr 1974):132.

Quance, C. Leroy see Johnson, Glenn L.

Quarles, Benjamin. Allies for Freedom: Blacks and John Brown.
New York: Ox U Press, 1974. Rev. by J. A. Rawley, HRNB,
3(Oct 1974):2.

_____ , ed. Blacks on John Brown. Urbana: U Ill Press, 1972.
Rev. by J. J. Cardoso, CWH, 20(Je 1974):159-63; E. H.
Berwanger, Historian, 36(Feb 1974):344-5; L. C. Lamon, HT,
7(Feb 1974):300.

Quazza, Guido. La Decadenza Italiana nella Storia Europea: Saggi
sul Sei-Settecento. Turin: Einaudi, 1971. Rev. by A. D.

Wright, EHR, 89(Apr 1974):438-9.

The Queen v. Louis Riel: Canada's Greatest Trial.   Toronto: U
    Tor Press, 1974.   Rev. by J. A. Casada, HRNB, 2(Sep 1974):
    253.

Quimby, Ian M. G. , ed.   Ceramics in America.   Charlottesville:
    U Press Va, 1973.   Rev. by R. J. Cox, MHM, 69(Spr 1974):
    112-15.

_____, ed.   Winterthur Portfolio 8.   Charlottesville: U Press
    Va, 1973.   Rev. by E. De Jonge, PH, 41(Ja 1974):108-10.

Quinn, Charles Russell.   History of Downey.   The Life Story of a
    Pioneer Community, And of the Man Who Founded It--California
    Governor John Gately Downey--From Covered Wagon to the
    Space Shuttle.   Downey: Elena Quinn, 1973.   Rev. by W. E.
    Kittell, SCQ, 56(Fall 1974):314-15.

Quinn, Charlotte A.   Mandingo Kingdoms of the Senegambia: Tradi-
    tionalism, Islam, and European Expansion.   Evanston, Ill.:
    Northwestern U Press, 1972.   Rev. by C. Fyfe, History, 59
    (Je 1974):308-9; H. J. Fisher, JAfH, 15(Num 3 1974):499-500.

Quinn, D. B. and N. M. Cheshire, eds. and trans.   The New
    Found Land of Stephen Parmenius.   Toronto: U Tor Press,
    1972.   Rev. by A. L. Rowse, EHR, 89(Apr 1974):431.

Quinn, David Beers.   England and the Discovery of America, 1481-
    1620: From the Bristol Voyages of the Fifteenth Century to
    the Pilgrim Settlement at Plymouth: The Exploration, Exploita-
    tion, and Trial-and-Error Colonization of North America by
    the English.   New York: Knopf, 1974.   Rev. by T. K. Rabb,
    JAH, 61(Dec 1974):758-8; C. L. Ver Steeg, JSH, 40(Nov 1974):
    642-3.

Quinn, Michael A. and Mauricio Solaún.   Sinners and Heretics:
    The Politics of Military Intervention in Latin America.   see
    Solaún, Mauricio and Michael A. Quinn.   Sinners and Here-
    tics. . . .

Quirino, Carlos.   Quezon: Paladin of Philippine Freedom.   Manila:
    Filipiniana Book Guild, 1971.   Rev. by M. P. Onorato, JAAS,
    9(Ja & Apr 1974):112-13.

Quirk, Robert E.   The Mexican Revolution and the Catholic Church,
    1910-1929.   Bloomington: Ind U Press, 1973.   Rev. by J.
    Meyer, HAHR, 54(May 1974):324-6; J. W. Knudson, HRNB, 2
    (Ja 1974):71; F. Morales, TAm, 31(Oct 1974):233-4.

Quitslund, Sonya A.   Beauduin: A Prophet Vindicated.   New York:
    Newman, 1973.   Rev. by J. T. Ellis, AHR, 79(Je 1974):797-
    8; F. J. Murphy, CH, 43(Mar 1974):130-1.

Quotations from Premier Chou En-lai. New York: Crowell, n. d.
Rev. by E. Lubot, HT, 8(Nov 1974):138-9.

RCHM (England). An Inventory of the Historical Monuments in the
City of York, vol. 2: The Defences. London: HMSO, 1972.
Rev. by M. W. Thompson, Antiquity, 48(Mar 1974):67-8.

Rabe, H. Reichsbund und Interim. Koln-Wien: Bohlau, 1971. Rev.
by J. W. Stoye, EHR, 89(Ja 1974):169-70.

Rabie, Hassanein. The Financial System of Egypt A. H. 564-741/
A. D. 1169-1341. London: Ox U Press, 1972. Rev. by R.
B. Serjeant, History, 59(Je 1974):253.

Rabinowitch, Alexander and Janet, eds. Revolution and Politics in
Russia: Essays in Memory of B. I. Nicolaevsky. Blooming-
ton: Ind U Press, 1972. Rev. by T. H. von Laue, AHR, 79
(Apr 1974):542-3.

Rachal, William M. E. see Hutchinson, William T.; Robert A.
Rutland.

Rachocki, Janusz, ed. Poland--West Germany: The Premises and
Process of Normalizing Relations. Poznań: Instytut Zachodni,
1972. Rev. by C. Morley, AHR, 79(Je 1974):780-1.

Radvany, Egon. Metternich's Projects for Reform in Austria. The
Hague: Martinus Nijhoff, 1972. Rev. by C. A. Macartney,
EHR, 89(Ja 1974):212-13.

Rae, John. Conscience and Politics: The British Government and
the Conscientous Objector to Military Service 1916-1919. Oxford: Ox U Press, 1970. Rev. by E. David, History, 59(Feb
1974):144-5.

Rae, Steven R. see Baker, Lindsay T.

Raeff, Marc, ed. Catherine the Great. London: Macmillan, 1972.
Rev. by R. M. Hatton, History, 59(Je 1974):279; J. Richardson, HTo, 24(Ja 1974):67.

Rainbolt, John C. From Prescription to Persuasion: Manipulation
of Seventeenth-Century Virginia Economy. Port Washington,
N. Y.: Kennikat, 1974. Rev. by J. F. Sefcik, HRNB, 2(Aug
1974):220-1; D. B. Rutman, WVH, 36(Oct 1974):70-2.

Rainey, Anne. Mosaics in Roman Britain. Totowa, N. J.: Rowman
and Littlefield, 1973. Rev. by G. Webster, Archaeology, 27
(Jl 1974):215.

Rainsford, George N. Congress and Higher Education in the Nineteenth Century. Knoxville: U Tenn Press, 1972. Rev. by
P. R. Rulon, Historian, 36(Feb 1974):353-4.

Rajan, Mohini see Lynton, Harriet Ronken

Ramm, Agatha. Sir Robert Morier: Envoy and Ambassador in the
    Age of Imperialism, 1876-1893. New York: Ox U Press,
    1973. Rev. by C. J. Lowe, AHR, 79(Je 1974):785-6.

Ramsey, John Fraser. Spain: The Rise of the First World Power.
    University, Ala.: U Ala Press, 1974. Rev. by R. Pike,
    HRNB, 2(Apr 1974):144.

Ramsey, Russell W. Revolución campesina, 1950-1954. Colombia:
    Ediciones Libros de Colombia, n. d. Rev. by P. Gilhodes,
    HAHR, 54(May 1974):339-41.

Randall, Henry S. The Life of Thomas Jefferson. New York: Da
    Capo Press, 1972. Rev. by M. D. Peterson, VMHB, 82(Ja
    1974):121-2.

Randolph, F. Ralph. British Travelers Among Southern Indians,
    1660-1763. Norman: U Ok Press, 1973. Rev. by H. S.
    Marks, JOW, 13(Apr 1974):126; L. R. Gerlach, PHR, 43(Feb
    1974):120-1; D. E. Schab, WHQ, 5(Ja 1974):86-7; D. E.
    Leach, WVH, 35(Ja 1974):167-8.

Rands, Robert L. see Greene, Merle

Ranger, T. O., ed. Aspects of Central African History. London:
    Heinemann, 1968. Rev. by G. Shepperson, Africa, 44(Apr
    1974):219-20.

_____ and I. Kimambo, eds. The Historical Study of African
    Religion. London: Heinemann, 1972. Rev. by E. E. Evans-
    Pritchard, EHR, 89(Ja 1974):109-11; W. E. Phipps, JMAS,
    12(Je 1974):329-31.

Ranke, Leopold von. The Theory and Practice of History. Indi-
    anapolis: Bobbs-Merrill, 1973. Rev. by D. Nicholl, History,
    59(Je 1974):326-7.

Ránki, György see Berend, Ivan T.

Rankin, Hugh F. Francis Marion: The Swamp Fox. New York:
    Crowell, 1973. Rev. by P. D. Nelson, JSH, 40(Aug 1974):
    468-9.

_____. The North Carolina Continentals. Chapel Hill: UNC
    Press, 1971. Rev. by W. M. Wallace, AHR, 79(Feb 1974):
    221-2.

Ransome, Mary, ed. Wiltshire Returns to the Bishop's Visitation
    Queries, 1783. Devizes: Wiltshire Record Society, 1972.
    Rev. by W. R. Ward, EHR, 89(Jl 1974):672.

Rao, V. K. R. V., ed. Bangla Desh Economy: Problems and Prospects. Delhi: Vikas Publications, 1972. Rev. by A. Robinson, MAS, 8(Ja 1974):139-41.

Rapant, Daniel. Slovenské povstanie roku 1848-49: Dejiny a doku-menty. Volume 5. Doplny, opravy, súhrny, mena a veci. 2 parts. Bratislava: Vydavatel'stvo Slovenskej akademie vied., 1967, 1972. Rev. by L. D. Orton, JMH, 46(Je 1974):366-8.

Rasila, Viljo. The Solution of the Crofter Problem: The Crofter Problem in Finland, 1909-1918. Helsinki: Kirjahtymä, 1970. Rev. by P. K. Hamalainen, AHR, 79(Apr 1974):522-3.

Rathjen, Frederick W. The Texas Panhandle Frontier. Austin: U Tx Press, 1973. Rev. by J. B. Pearson, HRNB, 2(Sep 1974):255; G. R. Cruz, JOW, 13(Oct 1974):138-9; W. H. Leckie, JSH, 40(Nov 1974):680-1.

Ratner, Sidney. The Tariff in American History. New York: D. Van Nostrand, 1972. Rev. by G. D. Nash, JAH, 60(Mar 1974):1086-7; B. Baack, JEH, 34(Sep 1974):801-2.

Raubitschek, A. E. see Hoffmann, Herbert

Raulston, J. Leonard and James W. Livingood. Sequatchie, A Story of the Southern Cumberlands. Knoxville: U Tenn Press, 1974. Rev. by J. Fuller, GHQ, 58(Sum 1974):298-9; H. S. Marks, HRNB, 2(May/Je 1974):163; J. H. De Berry, JSH, 40(Nov 1974):682-3; P. H. Bergeron, NCHR, 51(Sum 1974):339-40; R. E. Smith, RKHS, 72(Jl 1974):287-9; T. C. Mercer, THQ, 33(Spr 1974):101-2.

Ravitch, Diane. The Great School Wars. New York: Basic Books, n.d. Rev. by E. Abrams, Commentary, 58(Aug 1974):86-8.

Rawick, George P., ed. From Sundown to Sunup: The Making of the Black Community. Westport, Conn.: Greenwood, 1972. Rev. by F. N. Boney, GR, 28(Spr 1974):147-50.

Rawson, Marion see Blegen, Carl W.

Ray, Jayanta Kumar. Portraits of Thai Politics. New Delhi: Ori-ent Longman, 1972. Rev. by A. Howard, JAS, 33(Aug 1974): 739-40.

Rayback, Joseph G. Free Soil: The Election of 1848. Lexington, Ky.: U Press Ky, 1970. Rev. by W. O. Ferree, AHR, 79 (Je 1974):863-4.

Raybould, T. J. The Economic Emergence of the Black Country: A Study of the Dudley Estate. Newton Abbot: David and Charles, 1973. Rev. by W. E. Minchinton, AHR, 79(Oct 1974): 1179-80; W. H. Chaloner, EHR, 89(Jl 1974):677-8.

Raynell, Thomas, tr. see Erasmus

Read, Donald. Edwardian England 1901-1915. London: Harrap,
    1972. Rev. by P. J. Waller, EHR, 89(Ja 1974):230; J. Hin-
    ton, History, 59(Feb 1974):129-30.

Read, James S. see Morris, H. F.

Read, Piers Paul. Alive: The Story of the Andes Survivors. Phil-
    delphia: Lippincott, n. d. Rev. by W. J. Bennett, Commen-
    tary, 58(Aug 1974):78-9, 82.

Reddy, G. Ram and K. Seshadri. The Voter and Panchayati Raj:
    A Study of the Electoral Behavior During Panchayat Elections
    in Warangal District, Andhra Pradesh. Hyderabad: National
    Institute of Community Development, 1972. Rev. by W. G.
    Vanderbok, JAS, 33(Aug 1974):725-6.

Redeker, Martin. Schleiermacher: Life and Thought. Philadelphia:
    Fortress Press, 1973. Rev. by J. F. Dawson, AHR, 79(Feb
    1974):173-4.

Redman, Charles L., ed. Research and Theory in Current Archae-
    ology. New York: Wiley, 1973. Rev. by J. L. Cotter,
    Archaeology, 27(Oct 1974):287-8.

Redmond, Walter Bernard. Bibliography of the Philosophy in the
    Iberian Colonies of America. The Hague: Martinus Nijhoff,
    1972. Rev. by G. Addy, HAHR, 54(May 1974):319-20; M.
    Cardozo, TAm, 31(Oct 1974):217-18.

Reed, Nathaniel. The Life of Texas Jack. Quanah, Tex.: Nortex
    Press, 1973. Rev. by G. Logsdon, ChOk, 52(Spr 1974):118-
    19.

Rees, David. Harry Dexter White: A Study in Paradox. New
    York: Coward, McCann and Geohegan, 1973. Rev. by B. D.
    Karl, HRNB, 2(Aug 1974):214-15.

Rees, G. The Great Slump: Capitalism in Crisis: 1929-1933.
    New York: Harper and Row, 1970. Rev. by R. N. Seidel,
    AHR, 79(Apr 1974):488-9.

Rees, Robert A. and Earl N. Harbert, eds. Fifteen American
    Authors Before 1900: Bibliographic Essays on Research and
    Criticism. Madison: U Wis Press, 1971. Rev. by R. S.
    Moore, GR, 28(Spr 1974):168-70.

Reese, George and Patricia Hickin, ed. Journal of the Senate of
    Virginia; Session of 1802/03. Richmond, Va.: Va St Library,
    1973. Rev. by D. P. Jordan, VMHB, 82(Oct 1974):501-2.

Reese, Jim E. see Fite, Gilbert C.

Reeves, Marjorie and Beatrice Hirsch-Reich. The "Figurae" of
   Joachim of Fiore. Oxford: Ox U Press, 1972. Rev. by B.
   Smalley, History, 59(Feb 1974):91-2.

Rehder, Denny and Cecil Cook. Grass Between the Rails. Des
   Moines: Waukon and Mississippi Press, 1973. Rev. by
   D. L. Hofsommer, AI, 42(Win 1974):232-3.

Reichard, Richard W. Crippled from Birth: German Social Democracy 1844-1870. Ames: Ia St U Press, 1969. Rev. by
   D. S. White, JIH, 5(Sum 1974):158-61.

Reid, Agnes Just. Letters of Long Ago. Salt Lake City: U Utah
   Library, 1973. Rev. by R. W. Paul, PHR, 43(Nov 1974):
   609-10; B. Beeton, UHQ, 42(Sum 1974):296-8.

Reid, Dennis. A Concise History of Canadian Painting. New York:
   Ox U Press, 1974. Rev. by L. B. Miller, HRNB, 2(Sep
   1974):253-4.

Reingold, Nathan, Stuart Pierson, Arthur P. Molella, James M.
   Hobbins, and John R. Kerwood, eds. The Papers of Joseph
   Henry. Vol. 1: December 1797-October 1832: The Albany
   Years. Washington: Smithsonian Institution Press, 1972.
   Rev. by D. Fleming, JAH, 60(Mar 1974):1073-5; K. Birr,
   NYH, 55(Ja 1974):103-4; J. E. Brittain, T & C, 15(Ja 1974):
   103-5.

Reinhardt, Klaus. Die Wende vor Moskau: Das Scheitern der
   Strategie Hitlers im Winter 1941/1942. Stuttgart: Deutsche
   Verlags-Anstalt, 1972. Rev. by A. W. Turney, JMH, 46
   (Mar 1974):161-2.

Reither, James A. see Kennedy, Judith M.

Rekers, B. Benito Arias Montano (1527-1598). London: Warburg
   Inst., 1972. Rev. by P. E. Russell, EHR, 89(Jl 1974):631-3.

Remington, Jesse A. see Fine, Lenore

Rempel, Richard A. Unionists Divided: Arthur Balfour, Joseph
   Chamberlain and the Unionist Free Traders. Hamden, Conn.:
   Archon, 1972. Rev. by B. Semmel, AHR, 79(Apr 1974):515-
   16; P. F. Clarke, EHR, 89(Jl 1974):688-9; G. R. Searle, History, 59(Feb 1974):128.

Rendall, Doris see Tuohy, Donald R.

Renfrew, Colin. Before Civilization: the Radiocarbon Revolution
   and Prehistoric Europe. London: Jonathan Cape, 1973. Rev.
   by S. Piggott, Antiquity, 48(Mar 1974):68-9; W. F. Weakly,
   NH, 55(Sum 1974):319-20.

_____ . The Emergence of Civilization: The Cyclades and the
Aegean in the Third Millennium B. C. London: Methuen,
1972. Rev. by J. E. Coleman, Archaeology, 27(Jl 1974):214.

_____ . Social Archaeology. Southampton: U Southampton, 1973.
Rev. by P. Gathercole, Antiquity, 48(Je 1974):160-1.

Renfrew, Jane M. Palaeoethnobotany: the Prehistoric Food Plants
of the Near East and Europe. London: Methuen, 1973. Rev.
by A. M. Evans, Antiquity, 48(Mar 1974):73-4.

Reno, Edwin A., Jr. League of Nations Documents, 1919-1946.
New Haven, Conn.: Research Publications, 1973. Rev. by
R. Claus, AmArc, 37(Ja 1974):76-9.

Renzulli, L. Marx, Jr. Maryland: The Federalist Years. Ruther-
ford, N. J.: Fairleigh Dickinson U Press, 1972. Rev. by
J. M. Banner, Jr., JSH, 40(May 1974):301-2; J. W. Cox,
MHM, 69(Spr 1974):103.

Reps, John. Tidewater Towns: City Planning in Colonial Virginia
and Maryland. Williamsburg: Colonial Williamsburg Foundation, 1972. Rev. by E. C. Papenfuse, MHM, 69(Spr 1974):
100-1.

Revelle, Roger see Glass, D. V.

Rex, John. Race, Colonialism and the City. London and Boston:
Routledge and Kegan Paul, 1973. Rev. by C. Onwubu, JMAS,
12(Sep 1974):493-6.

Reymond, E. A. E. and J. W. B. Barns. Four Martyrdoms from
the Pierpont Morgan Coptic Codices. New York: Ox U Press,
1973. Rev. by W. E. Kaegi, Jr., CH, 43(Sep 1974):387-8.

Reynolds, Robert. Texas. Portland: Chas. H. Belding, 1973.
Rev. by R. Tyler, WHQ, 5(Jl 1974):350.

Rhodehamel, Josephine DeWitt and Raymund Francis Wood. Ina
Coolbrith: Librarian and Laureate of California. Provo,
Utah: BYU Press, 1973. Rev. by P. T. Nolan, JOW, 13
(Jl 1974):131-2.

Rhodes, Anthony. The Vatican in the Age of the Dictators, 1922-
1945. New York: Holt, Rinehart and Winston, 1973. Rev.
by J. Rubenstein, Commentary, 58(Sep 1974):91,94; J. J.
Hughes, JMH, 46(Dec 1974):726-8.

Riberette, Pierre. Les bibliothèques françaises pendant la Révolution (1789-1795): Recherches sur un essai de catalogue collectif. Paris: Bibliothèque Nationale, 1970. Rev. by N. N.
Barker, AHR, 79(Je 1974):791.

Rice, Eugene F., Jr., ed. The Prefatory Epistles of Jacques Le-
    fèvre d'Etaples and Related Texts. New York: Columbia U
    Press, 1972. Rev. by W. Gilbert, CH, 43(Sep 1974):399-400;
    G. Tootill, RQ, 27(Spr 1974):74-5.

Rice, Howard C., Jr. and Anne S. K. Brown, eds. The American
    Campaigns of Rochambeau's Army, 1780, 1781, 1782, 1783.
    2 vols. Princeton, N.J.: Prin U Press, 1972. Rev. by
    R. W. Coakley, AHR, 79(Oct 1974):1254-5.

Rice, Tamara Talbot. Elizabeth Empress of Russia. London:
    Weidenfeld and Nicolson, 1970. Rev. by I. de Madariaga,
    ESR, 4(Jl 1974):274-6.

Rich, Norman. Hitler's War Aims. Vol. II. The Establishment
    of the New Order. New York: Norton, 1974. Rev. by
    J. M. Block, HRNB, 2(Aug 1974):229.

Richards, Eric. The Leviathan of Wealth: The Sutherland Fortune
    in the Industrial Revolution. London: Routledge and Kegan
    Paul, 1973. Rev. by J. T. Ward, History, 59(Je 1974):285.

Richards, James O. Party Propaganda Under Queen Anne: The
    General Elections of 1702-1713. Athens, Ga.: U Ga Press,
    1972. Rev. by C. C. Martin, Historian, 36(May 1974):545-6.

Richardson, Elmo. Dams, Parks and Politics: Resource Develop-
    ment and Preservation in the Truman-Eisenhower Era. Lex-
    ington, Ky.: U Press Ky, 1973. Rev. by N. L. Dawson,
    FCHQ, 48(Ja 1974):64-5; O. L. Graham, Jr., HRNB, 2(Ja
    1974):67; P. Funigiello, JAH, 61(Sep 1974):539-41; R. C.
    Post, JOW, 13(Oct 1974):139-40; G. D. Nash, PHR, 43(Aug
    1974):433-4; R. C. Sims, PNQ, 65(Oct 1974):193; J. E.
    Reeves, RKHS, 72(Apr 1974):190-2; J. M. Haymond, UHQ,
    42(Fall 1974):391-2.

Richardson, Ivan L. Urban Government for Rio de Janeiro. New
    York: Praeger, 1973. Rev. by N. Evenson, HAHR, 54(May
    1974):344-5.

Richardson, Kenneth. Twentieth-Century Coventry. London: Mac-
    millan, 1972. Rev. by Roger Smith, History, 59(Feb 1974):
    148.

Richardson, R. C. Puritanism in Northwest England: A Regional
    Study of the Diocese of Chester to 1642. Manchester: Man-
    chester U Press, 1972. Rev. by D. Underdown, CHR, 55(Sep
    1974):327-8; C. Russell, EHR, 89(Ja 1974):176-7.

Richey, Elinor. Remain to Be Seen: Historic California Houses
    Open to the Public. Berkeley: Howell-North, 1973. Rev. by
    S. Black, JOW, 13(Ja 1974):148; J. E. Moss, WHQ, 5(Jl 1974):
    358-9.

Richmond, Al. A Long View from the Left: Memoirs of an American Revolutionary. Boston: Houghton-Mifflin, 1973. Rev. by W. Bilderback, PNQ, 65(Apr 1974):91-2.

Richter, Melvin, ed. Essays in Theory and History: An Approach to the Social Sciences. Cambridge, Mass.: Har U Press, 1970. Rev. by S. R. Graubard, H & T, 13(Num 3 1974):335-42.

Riddell, Francis A. see Meighan, Clement W.

Ridgway, Brunilde Sismondo. Catalogue of the Classical Collection: Classical Sculpture. Providence, R.I.: Museum of Art, R.I. School of Design, 1972. Rev. by E. K. Gazda, AJA, 78(Apr 1974):197.

_____. The Severe Style in Greek Sculpture. Princeton, N.J.: Prin U Press, 1970. Rev. by H. L. Schanz, Archaeology, 27(Ja 1974):70.

Ridley, C. P., Paul H. B. Godwin, Dennis J. Doolin. The Making of a Model Citizen in Communist China. Stanford, Cal.: Hoover Institution Press, 1971. Rev. by S. J. Noumoff, JAAS, 9(Ja & Apr 1974):129-30.

Ridley, Charles P. see Doolin, Dennis J.

Rieger, Paul E. Through One Man's Eyes: The Civil War Experiences of a Belmont County Volunteer, Letters of James G. Theaker. Mt. Vernon, Ohio: Printing Arts, 1974. Rev. by J. I. Robertson, CWH, 20(Sep 1974):279-81.

Riggs, William G. The Christian Poet in Paradise Lost. Berkeley/Los Angeles: U Calif Press, 1972. Rev. by F. L. Huntley, RQ, 27(Sum 1974):257-8.

Rigolot, Francois. Etudes Rabelaisiennes. Geneva: Librairie Droz, 1972. Rev. by L. G. Durand, RQ, 27(Fall 1974):342-4.

Riker, Dorothy L. see Thornbrough, Gayle. Diary of Calvin Fletcher.

_____. see Barnhart, John D.

Riley, Carroll L. see Hedrick, Basil C.

Riley, G. Michael. Fernando Cortés and the Marquesado in Morelos, 1522-1547: A Case Study in the Socioeconomic Development of Sixteenth-Century Mexico. Albuquerque: U NM Press, 1973. Rev. by R. E. Greenleaf, HAHR, 54(May 1974):315-16.

Riley-Smith, Jonathan. The Feudal Nobility and the Kingdom of

Jerusalem, 1174-1277. Hamden, Conn.: Archon, 1973. Rev.
by M. W. Baldwin, AHR, 79(Apr 1974):502-3; J. J. LaGrand,
CH, 43(Mar 1974):102; H. E. J. Cowdrey, History, 59(Je
1974):254.

Ringenbach, Paul T. Tramps and Reformers, 1873-1916: The
Discovery of Unemployment in New York. Westport, Conn.:
Greenwood, 1973. Rev. by R. M. Mennel, JAH, 61(Sep 1974):
505-7; J. A. Andrew, III, MiA, 56(Apr 1974):128-9; D. R.
Jamieson, NYH, 55(Jl 1974):343-4; D. A. Ritchie, NYHSQ, 58
(Apr 1974):161-2; J. A. Fleckner, WMH, 57(W 73/74):161-2.

Ringenberg, William C. Taylor University: The First 125 Years.
Grand Rapids, Mich.: Eerdmans, 1974. Rev. by P. F. Erwin, HRNB, 2(Aug 1974):217; R. Nelson, IMH, 70(Dec 1974):
358-60.

Rippy, Merrill. Oil and the Mexican Revolution. Leiden: E. J.
Brill, 1973. Rev. by P. J. Vanderwood, TAm, 31(Oct 1974):
231-2.

Risjord, Norman K. Forging the American Republic, 1760-1815.
Reading, Mass.: Addison-Wesley, 1973. Rev. by R. McColley, JAH, 61(Dec 1974):772.

Ritter, Arch R. M. see Pollock, David H.

Ritter, Gerhard. The Sword and the Scepter: The Problem of
Militarism in Germany. III: The Tragedy of Statesmanship--
Bethmann Hollweg as War Chancellor (1914-1917); IV: The
Reign of German Militarism and the Disaster of 1918. Coral
Gables, Fla.: U Miami Press, 1972-3. Rev. by M. Eksteins,
CHR, 55(Je 1974):235-8.

_____. The Sword and the Scepter: The Problem of Militarism
in Germany. Volume 4, The Reign of German Militarism and
the Disaster of 1918. Coral Gables, Fla.: U Miami Press,
1973. Rev. by G. A. Craig, AHR, 79(Apr 1974):524-5.

Rivera, Feliciano see Meier, Matt S.

Roberge, Earl. Timber Country: Logging in the Great Northwest.
Caldwell, Ida.: Caxton, 1973. Rev. by H. A. Howard, JOW,
13(Jl 1974):115-16.

Roberts, Andrew D. A History of the Bemba: Political Growth and
Change in North-Eastern Zambia Before 1900. Madison: U
Wis Press, 1974. Rev. by J. R. Hooker, HRNB, 2(Sep 1974):
250-1.

Roberts, Arthur O. see Barbour, Hugh

Roberts, Derrell C. Joseph E. Brown and the Politics of Recon-

struction. University, Ala.: U Ala Press, 1973. Rev. by
R. F. Durden, AHR, 79(Je 1974):871-2; S. W. Wiggins, Ala
HQ, 36(Spr 1974):83-5; W. J. McNeill, CWH, 20(Mar 1974):
88-9; M. G. Cox, FHQ, 53(Jl 1974):91-2; W. F. Holmes,
JAH, 60(Mar 1974):1139-40; E. S. Nathans, JSH, 40(Feb 1974):
149-50.

Roberts, J. M. The Mythology of the Secret Societies. London:
Secker and Warburg, 1972. Rev. by N. Hampson, EHR, 89
(Apr 1974):448-9.

Roberts, John. Civilization: The Emergence of Man in Society.
Volume I. Del Mar, Cal.: C R M Books, 1973. Rev. by
J. D. Doenecke, HT, 7(Feb 1974):289-90.

Roberts, Michael, ed. Sweden's Age of Greatness, 1632-1718.
New York: St. Martin's, 1973. Rev. by R. Rinehart, HRNB,
2(May/Je 1974):179.

Roberts, Nancy. The Goodliest Land: North Carolina. New York:
Doubleday, 1973. Rev. by J. G. Zehmer, Jr., NCHR, 51
(Spr 1974):228-9.

Roberts, Walter R. Tito, Mihailovic and the Allies, 1941-1945.
New Brunswick, N. J.: Rutgers U Press, 1973. Rev. by
A. N. Dragnich, AHR, 79(Oct 1974):1216-17.

Robertson, A. F. see Dunn, John. Dependence and Opportunity.

Robertson, Constance Noyes. Oneida Community, The Breakup,
1876-1881. Syracuse, N. Y.: Syracuse U Press, 1972. Rev.
by R. Salisbury, WPHM, 57(Oct 1974):454-6.

Robertson, Jean, ed. see Sidney, Phillip

Robicsek, Francis. Copan: Home of the Mayan Gods. New York:
Museum of the American Indian-Heye Foundation, 1972. Rev.
by D. M. Pendergast, Archaeology, 27(Apr 1974):146-7.

Robins, Benjamin. New Principles of Gunnery (1742). Richmond,
Surrey: Richmond Pub. Co., 1972. Rev. by R. A. Howard,
T & C, 15(Ja 1974):95-7.

_____. see Walter, Richard

Robinson, A. N. R. The Mechanics of Independence: Patterns of
Political and Economic Transformation in Trinidad and Tobago.
Cambridge, Mass.: M I T Press, 1971. Rev. by A. Bryan,
TAm, 30(Ja 1974):423-4.

Robinson, Adrian see Millward, Roy

Robinson, Douglas H. Giants in the Sky: A History of the Rigid

Airship. Seattle: U Wash Press, 1973. Rev. by J. J. Hudson, AHR, 79(Oct 1974):1143-4.

_____. The Dangerous Sky: A History of Aviation Medicine. Seattle: U Wash Press, 1974. Rev. by J. A. Van Voorhis, HRNB, 2(Sep 1974):246.

Robinson, Ian. Chaucer and the English Tradition. Cambridge: Cam U Press, 1972. Rev. by W. Provost, GR, 28(Sum 1974): 361-5.

Robinson, Thomas W. , ed. The Cultural Revolution in China. Berkeley: U Cal Press, 1971. Rev. by P. Van Ness, JAS, 33 (May 1974):472-3.

Robinson, William F. The Pattern of Reform in Hungary: A Political, Economic and Cultural Analysis. New York: Praeger, 1973. Rev. by T. Spira, EEQ, 8(Mar 1974):126-7.

Roby, Yves et Jean Hamelin. Histoire économique du Québec 1851-1896. see Hamelin, Jean and Yves Roby. Histoire économique. . . .

Roche, Jerome. The Madrigal. London: Hutchinson, 1972. Rev. by C. MacClintock, RQ, 27(Sum 1974):227-9.

Roche, John P. Sentenced to Life. New York: Macmillan, 1974. Rev. by M. Cantor, HRNB, 2(Aug 1974):227.

Rochon, Andre, ed. Formes et significations de la 'beffa' dans la Litterature Italienne de la Renaissance. Paris: Universite de la Sorbonne Nouvelle, 1972. Rev. by M. Cottino-Jones, RQ, 27(Fall 1974):324-6.

Rockwell, E., tr. see Grube, Oswald W.

Roditi, Edouard. Magellan of the Pacific. New York: McGraw-Hill, 1972. Rev. by J. Vogt, HAHR, 54(May 1974):310-11.

Rodnitzky, Jerome L. , Frank Ross Peterson, Kenneth R. Philip, and John A. Garraty. Essays on Radicalism in Contemporary America. Austin: U Tx Press, 1972. Rev. by F. Annunziata, JAH, 61(Dec 1974):848-9.

Roe, Daphne A. A Plague of Corn: The Social History of Pellagra. Ithaca, N. Y.: Cornell U Press, 1973. Rev. by M. S. Legan, JSH, 40(May 1974):337-8.

Roe, Francis see Bates, Charles Francis

Roebuck, Janet. The Making of Modern English Society from 1850. New York: Scribner's, 1973. Rev. by H. E. Landry, Historian, 36(Aug 1974):764-5.

Roff, W. R. Bibliography of Malay and Arabic Periodicals Published in the Straits Settlements and Peninsular Malay States,
1876-1941. Oxford: Ox U Press, 1972. Rev. by W. A.
Lockwood, Archives, 11(Spr 1974):188-9.

Rogers, Alan. This Was Their World: Approaches to Local History. n. p.: British Broadcasting Corp., 1972. Rev. by
A. H. Smith, Archives, 11(Spr 1974):184-6.

Rogers, Malcolm J. Early Lithic Industries of the Lower Basin of
the Colorado River and Adjacent Desert Areas. Ramona: Bellena Press, 1973. Rev. by J. D. Hayden, JAriH, 15(Sum
1974):195-7.

_____. Yuman Pottery Making. Ramona: Bellena Press, 1973.
Rev. by J. D. Hayden, JAriH, 15(Sum 1974):195-7.

Rogers, Will. There's Not a Bathing Suit in Russia and Other Bare
Facts. Stillwater: Ok St U Press, 1974. Rev. by K. A.
Franks, ChOk, 52(Fall 1974):383-4.

Rogers, William Warren. Thomas County, 1865-1900. Tallahassee, Fla.: Fla St U Press, 1973. Rev. by W. J. Cooper,
Jr., CWH, 20(Je 1974):188-9; E. S. Nathans, FHQ, 53(Oct
1974) 214-15; D. E. King, JSH, 40(Feb 1974):162-3; K. Coleman, NCHR, 51(Ja 1974):103-4.

_____ and Robert David Ward. August Reckoning: Jack Turner
and Racism in Post-Civil War Alabama. Baton Rouge: LSU
Press, 1973. Rev. by A. J. Going, FHQ, 53(Jl 1974):93-4;
W. C. Harris, JAH, 61(Sep 1974):497-8; P. Daniel, JNH, 59
(Jl 1974):298-9; P. Kolchin, JSH, 40(May 1974):329-30.

_____ and Ruth Pruitt. Stephen S. Renfroe, Alabama's Outlaw
Sheriff. Tallahassee, Fla.: Sentry, 1972. Rev. by A. J.
Going, JAH, 60(Mar 1974):1140-1.

Roider, Karl A., Jr. The Reluctant Ally: Austria's Policy in the
Austro-Turkish War, 1737-1739. Baton Rouge: LSU Press,
1972. Rev. by E. M. Link, AHR, 79(Apr 1974):527-8.

Rojo, Manuel C. Historical Notes on Lower California: With Some
Relative to Upper California Furnished to the Bancroft Library.
Tr. and ed. by Phillip O. Gericke. Los Angeles: Dawson's
Book Shop, 1972. Rev. by T. E. Trentlein, PHR, 43(Aug
1974):426.

Rolle, Andrew F. The American Italians: Their History and Cultures. Belmont, Calif.: Wadsworth Pub. Co., 1972. Rev.
by H. S. Nelli, PHR, 43(Aug 1974):424.

Romano, Ruggiero. Les mecanismes de la conquete coloniale:
les conquistadores. Paris: Flammarion, 1972. Rev. by

J. R. L. Highfield, EHR, 89(Apr 1974):426.

Romanucci-Ross, Lola. Conflict, Violence, and Morality in a Mexican Village. Palo Alto, Cal.: National Press, 1973. Rev. by J. Collier, HAHR, 54(Aug 1974):547-8.

Ronfeldt, David. Atencingo: The Politics of Agrarian Struggle in a Mexican Ejido. Stanford, Cal.: Stan U Press, 1973. Rev. by W. B. Taylor, Historian, 36(Feb 1974):310-12.

Roots, Ivan, ed. Cromwell: A Profile. New York: Hill and Wang, 1973. Rev. by S. E. Prall, HRNB, 2(Mar 1974):119-20.

Roper, Laura Wood. F L O: A Biography of Frederick Law Olmsted. Baltimore: JHU Press, 1973. Rev. by T. Bender, JAH, 61(Dec 1974):797-8; W. S. Powell, JSH, 40(Nov 1974):661-3.

Rosaldo, Renato, Robert A. Calvert, and Gustav L. Seligmann. Chicano: The Evolution of People. Minneapolis: Winston, 1973. Rev. by R. H. Vigil, NMHR, 49(Apr 1974):159-61; A. Hoffman, WHQ, 5(Apr 1974):204-5.

Roscoe, Theodore. On the Seas and in the Skies: A History of the U.S. Navy's Air Power. New York: Hawthorn, 1970. Rev. by W. P. Newton, AHR, 79(Je 1974):903-4.

Rose, Leo E. see Wilcox, Wayne

Rose, Lisle. After Yalta. New York: Scribner's, 1973. Rev. by D. Wrone, HT, 8(Nov 1974):145; A. L. Hamby, PHR, 43 (Aug 1974):437-8; D. R. Millar, PNQ, 65(Ja 1974):45.

Rose, Lisle A. The Coming of the American Age, 1945-1946: Dubious Victory: The United States and the End of World War II. Kent, Ohio: Kent St U Press, 1973. Rev. by T. H. Etzold, JAH, 61(Dec 1974):839-40.

_____. Dubious Victory: The United States and the End of World War II. Kent, Ohio: Kent St U Press, 1974. Rev. by J. J. Tierney, HRNB, 2(Feb 1974):92; D. Lindsey, Mankind, 4(Aug 1974):66.

Roselli, John. Lord William Bentinck: The Making of a Liberal Imperialist 1774-1839. Berkeley: U Cal Press, 1974. Rev. by R. Howell, Jr., HRNB, 3(Oct 1974):18.

Rosen, Charles. The Classical Style: Haydn, Mozart, Beethoven. New York: Viking, 1971. Rev. by E. R. Reilly, GR, 28 (Sum 1974):366-9.

Rosen, Kenneth, ed. The Man to Send Rain Clouds. New York:

Viking, 1973. Rev. by Staff, InH, 7(Win 1974):50; D. Wynn, NMHR, 49(Oct 1974):337-8.

Rosenbaum, Jürgen. Frankreich in Tunesien: Die Anfänge des Protektorates, 1881-1886. Zurich: Atlantis, 1971. Rev. by R. A. Austen, AHR, 79(Feb 1974):170.

Rosenberg, Carroll Smith. Religion and the Rise of the American City: The New York City Mission Movement 1812-1870. Ithaca: Cornell U Press, 1971. Rev. by J. F. Richardson, CWH, 20(Mar 1974):56-7.

Rosenberg, Marvin. The Masks of King Lear. Berkeley: U Calif Press, 1972. Rev. by J. R. Brown, RQ, 27(Sum 1974):244-6.

Rosenberg, Morton M. Iowa on the Eve of the Civil War: A Decade of Frontier Politics. Norman: U Ok Press, 1972. Rev. by D. L. Lendt, AHR, 79(Apr 1974):584-5; D. Crosson, AI, 42(Sum 1974):395-6; R. P. Swierenga, WHQ, 5(Ja 1974):60-1.

Rosenberg, Philip. The Seventh Hero: Thomas Carlyle and the Theory of Radical Activism. Cambridge, Mass.: Har U Press, n.d. Rev. by G. Himmelfarb, Commentary, 58(Sep 1974):96-100.

Rosenberger, Francis Coleman, ed. Records of the Columbia Historical Society of Washington, D.C. 1871-1972. Charlottesville: U Press Va, 1973. Rev. by L. Rapport, HRNB, 2 (Mar 1974):128-9; K. R. Bowling, NCHR, 51(Spr 1974):238-9; R. R. Duncan, VMHB, 82(Apr 1974):218-19; M. K. Bushong, WVH, 35(Apr 1974):239-41.

Rosenbloom, David H. Federal Service and the Constitution: The Development of the Public Employment Relationship. Ithaca, N.Y.: Cornell U Press, 1971. Rev. by J. C. Duram, AHR, 79(Je 1974):836-7.

Rosenblum, Gerald. Immigrant Workers: Their Impact on American Labor Radicalism. New York: Basic Books, 1973. Rev. by R. J. Vecoli, AHR, 79(Oct 1974):1271-2.

Rosenfeld, Alvin H., ed. see Wheelwright, John

Rosenfield, John M., Fumiko E. Cranston and Edwin A. Cranston. The Courtly Tradition in Japanese Art and Literature: Selections from the Hofer and Hyde Collections. Cambridge, Mass.: ... Har U Press, 1973. Rev. by G. T. Webb, JAS, 34(Nov 1974):239-41.

Rosenkrantz, Barbara Gutmann and William A. Koelsch, eds. American Habitat: A Historical Perspective. New York: Free

Press, 1973. Rev. by R. H. Adams, CoMag, 51(Sum 1974):
249-50; D. W. Grantham, RKHS, 72(Ja 1974):61-2.

_____. Public Health and the State: Changing Views in Massa-
chusetts, 1842-1936. Cambridge, Mass.: Har U, 1972. Rev.
by R. Lubove, AHR, 79(Oct 1974):1244-5; J. H. Ellis, Historian, 36(Feb 1974):350.

Rosenthal, Joel T. Angles, Angels, and Conquerors. New York:
Knopf, 1973. Rev. by R. V. Turner, AHR, 79(Apr 1974):
492-3.

Rosenwaike, Ira. Population History of New York City. Syracuse,
N. Y.: Syr U Press, 1972. Rev. by T. J. Archdeacon, JIH,
5(Aut 1974):333-6; S. C. Berrol, NYHSQ, 58(Ja 1974):59-60.

Roskill, Stephen W. Hankey: Man of Secrets: Volume II, 1918-
1931. New York: St. Martin's, 1973. Rev. by J. D. Hill,
HRNB, 2(Feb 1974):109-10.

Ross, B. Joyce. J. E. Spingarn and the Rise of the NAACP, 1911-
1939. New York: Atheneum, 1972. Rev. by A. E. Strickland, JNH, 59(Jl 1974):293-5; J. E. Haney, NYH, 55(Ja 1974):
112-15.

Ross, C. D. see Chrimes, S. B.

Ross, Dorothy. G. Stanley Hall: The Psychologist as Prophet.
Chicago: U Chi Press, 1972. Rev. by D. W. Levy, MiA,
56(Ja 1974):59-60.

Ross, Ian Simpson. Lord Kames and the Scotland of His Day.
Oxford: Clarendon Press, 1972. Rev. by R. Mitchison, EHR,
89(Apr 1974):445; M. T. Phillipson, History, 59(Je 1974):
280-1.

Ross, Ishbel. The President's Wife: Mary Todd Lincoln: A Biography. New York: Putman's, 1973. Rev. by A. Gates,
CWH, 20(Sep 1974):263-4; C. B. Strozier, JISHS, 67(Feb
1974):124-5.

Ross, Stanley R., ed. Latin America in Transition: Problems in
Training and Research. Albany: SUNY Press, 1970. Rev.
by D. S. Chandler, ETHJ, 12(Spr 1974):76-7.

Ross, William M. Oil Pollution as an International Problem: a
Study of Puget Sound and the Strait of Georgia. Seattle: U
Wash Press, 1973. Rev. by K. A. Murray, PNQ, 65(Jl 1974):
154.

Rossiter, Clinton. The American Quest, 1790-1860: An Emerging
Nation in Search of Identity, Unity, and Modernity. New
York: Harcourt Brace Jovanovich, 1971. Rev. by R. B.

Nye, AHR, 79(Je 1974):851-2.

Rostagni, Carla Meneguzzi, ed. Il carteggio Antonelli-Barili, 1859-61. Roma: Instituto per Storia del Risorgimento Italiano, 1973. Rev. by N. Blakiston, EHR, 89(Apr 1974):456-7.

Rostow, W. W. The Diffusion of Power: An Essay in Recent History, 1957-72. New York: Macmillan, 1972. Rev. by R. C. Haney, WMH, 57(Sum 1974):323.

Roth, John K. see Sontag, Frederick

Roth, Philip. My Life as a Man. New York: Holt, Rinehart and Winston, n. d. Rev. by J. W. Aldridge, Commentary, 58(Sep 1974):82-4, 86.

Rothenberg, Beno. Were These King Solomon's Mines? Excavations in the Timna Valley. New York: Stein and Day, 1972. Rev. by P. S. de Jesus, AJA, 78(Jl 1974):299-300.

Rothenberg, Joshua. The Jewish Religion in the Soviet Union. New York: Ktav, 1971. Rev. by B. Sapir, AHR, 79(Apr 1974):530-1.

Rothman, David J. The Discovery of the Asylum: Social Order and Disorder in the New Republic. Boston: Little, Brown, 1971. Rev. by J. M. Banner, Jr., JIH, 5(Sum 1974):167-74.

_____ and Sheila, eds. On Their Own--The Poor in Modern America. Reading, Mass.: Addison-Wesley, 1972. Rev. by F. F. Esposito, HT, 7(Feb 1974):303-4.

Rougerie, Jacques, ed. 1871. Jalons pour une histoire de la Commune de Paris. Paris: Presses Universitaires de France, 1973. Rev. by M. J. M. Larkin, EHR, 89(Apr 1974):404-5.

Rounds, Glen. The Cowboy Trade. New York: Holiday House, 1973. Rev. by C. P. Westermeier, JAriH, 15(Spr 1974):95-6.

Rouschausse, Jean. La Vie et l'Oeuvre de John Fisher. Angers: Editions Moreana; Nieuwkoop: B. DeGraaf, 1972. Rev. by E. G. Schwiebert, RQ, 27(Sum 1974):211-13.

Rouse, Irving. Introduction to Prehistory: A Systematic Approach. New York: McGraw-Hill, 1972. Rev. by C. Renfrew, Antiquity, 48(Sep 1974):244-6.

Rouse, John M. World Cattle III: Cattle of North America. Norman: U Ok Press, 1973. Rev. by J. G. Nordyke, ChOk, 52 (Fall 1974):380-1.

Rouse, Parke, Jr. Cows on the Campus: Williamsburg in Bygone

Days. Richmond, Va.: Dietz, 1973. Rev. by F. J. Niederer, VMHB, 82(Apr 1974):215-16.

_____. The Great Wagon Road from Philadelphia to the South.
New York: McGraw-Hill, 1973. Rev. by J. A. Caruso,
WMQ-3, 31(Ja 1974):158-9.

Roussos, Evangelos see Andronicos, Emmanuel

Routh, Francis. Early English Organ Music from the Middle Ages
to 1837. New York: Barnes and Noble, 1973. Rev. by D. W.
Hadley, AHR, 79(Oct 1974):1175-6.

Rouvier-Jeanlin, Micheline. Les Figurines Gallo-Romaines en Terre
Cuite au Musée des Antiquities Nationales. Paris: Centre de
la recherche scientifique, 1972. Rev. by V. von Gonzenbach,
AJA, 78(Oct 1974):444-5.

Rowell, John W. Yankee Cavalrymen: Through the Civil War With
the Ninth Pennsylvania Cavalry. Knoxville: U Tenn Press,
1971. Rev. by J. Monaghan, AHR, 79(Apr 1974):587-9.

Rowse, A. L. Simon Forman: Sex and Society in Shakespeare's
Age. London: Weidenfeld and Nicolson, n.d. Rev. by A.
Haynes, HTo, 24(Je 1974):435.

_____. Windsor Castle in the History of the Nation. London:
Weidenfeld and Nicolson, n.d. Rev. in HTo, 24(Apr 1974):
291.

Roy, Reginald H. see Morton, Desmond

Royal Commission on Book Publishing: Background Papers. Toronto: Queen's Printer and Publisher, 1972. Rev. by J. M.
Gray, CHR, 55(Mar 1974):97-8.

Rozwenc, Edwin C. The People Make a Nation. see Sandler,
Martin W.

Rubin, Joseph Jay. The Historic Whitman. University Park, Pa.:
Pa St U Press, 1973. Rev. by J. W. Cooke, JAH, 61(Sep
1974):481.

Rubin, Louis D., Jr., ed. The Comic Imagination in American Literature. New Brunswick, N.J.: Rutgers U Press, 1973.
Rev. by L. Hasley, GR, 28(Fall 1974):545-7.

Ruby, Robert H. and John A. Brown. The Cayuse Indians: Imperial Tribesmen of Old Oregon. Norman: U Okla Press, 1972.
Rev. by V. F. Ray, WHQ, 5(Ja 1974):79-81.

Rudé, George. Debate on Europe, 1815-1850. New York: Harper
and Row, 1972. Rev. by P. N. Stearns, JMH, 46(Sep 1974):
536.

_____. Europe in the Eighteenth Century: Aristocracy and the
Bourgeois Challenge. New York: Praeger, 1972. Rev. by
B. Behrens, CHR, 55(Sep 1974):349-50; M. S. Anderson, His-
tory, 59(Feb 1974):111-12.

Rudwick, Elliott see Meier, August

_____. The Rise of the Ghetto. see Bracey, John H., Jr.

Ruetten, Richard T. see McCoy, Donald R.

Ruffner, Budge. All Hell Needs Is Water. Tucson: U Arizona
Press, 1972. Rev. by F. M. Tanner, WHQ, 5(Oct 1974):
481-2.

Rule, John C., ed. Louis XIV. Englewood Cliffs, N.J.: Prentice-
Hall, 1974. Rev. by R. M. Isherwood, HRNB, 2(Apr 1974):
143.

Rumpler, Helmut. Die deutsche Politik des Freiherrn von Beust,
1848-1850. Vienna: Verlag Hermann Böhlau, 1972. Rev. by
D. J. Mattheisen, JMH, 46(Je 1974):360-1.

[Rusk, Howard A.] A World to Care For: The Autobiography of
Howard A. Rusk, M.D. New York: Random House, 1972.
Rev. by R. C. Powell, AHR, 79(Je 1974):905.

Russ, B. Joyce. J. E. Spingarn and the Rise of the N.A.A.C.P.
New York: Atheneum, 1972. Rev. by G. H. Hudson, Historian, 36(Feb 1974):347-8.

Russell, Andy. Horns in the High Country. New York: Knopf,
1973. Rev. by O. W. Young, UHQ, 42(W 1974):90-1.

Russell, Conrad, ed. The Origins of the English Civil War. London: Macmillan, 1973. Rev. by G. R. Elton, HJ, 17(Mar
1974):213-16.

Russell, D. A. Plutarch. New York: Scribner's, 1973. Rev. by
L. J. Simms, AHR, 79(Oct 1974):1155-6; S. Spyridakis, Historian, 36(Feb 1974):306-7.

Russell, Jeffrey B. Witchcraft in the Middle Ages. London: Cornell U Press, 1972. Rev. by R. I. Moore, History, 59(Je
1974):250-1.

Russell, Josiah Cox. Medieval Regions and Their Cities. Bloomington: Ind U Press, 1972. Rev. by C. R. Young, AHR, 79
(Oct 1974):1161-2; P. W. Knoll, BHR, 48(Spr 1974):111-12.

Russell, Robert R. Critical Studies in Antebellum Sectionalism:
Essays in American Political and Economic History. Westport, Conn.: Greenwood, 1970. Rev. by L. T. Balsamo,

JISHS, 67(Je 1974):354-5.

Russett, Bruce M. No Clear and Present Danger: A Skeptical View of the United States Entry into World War II. New York: Harper and Row, 1972. Rev. by T. A. Bailey, AHR, 79(Apr 1974):608-9.

Rutherford, Noel. Shirley Baker and the King of Tonga. Melbourne: Melbourne U Press, 1971. Rev. by C. W. Newbury, EHR, 89(Ja 1974):221.

Rutkowski, Bogdan. Cult Places in the Aegean World. Breslau: Polish Academy of Sciences, 1972. Rev. by N. S. Stavrolakes, AJA, 78(Ja 1974):90.

Rutland, Robert A. The Newsmongers: Journalism in the Life of the Nation, 1690-1972. New York: Dial, 1973. Rev. by A. Bortz, AHR, 79(Oct 1974):1244.

_____ and William M. E. Rachal, eds. The Papers of James Madison. Volume 8, 10 March 1784-28 March 1786. Chicago: U Chi Press, 1973. Rev. by G. G. Van Deusen, AHR, 79(Je 1974):849-50; C. L. Egan, AmArc, 37(Ja 1974):81-2.

Ryder, A. J. Twentieth-Century Germany: From Bismarck to Brandt. New York: Columbia U Press, 1973. Rev. by H. W. Gatzke, Historian, 36(May 1974):551-2.

Rydjord, John. Kansas Place-Names. Norman: U Ok Press, 1972. Rev. by R. J. Loosbrock, JAH, 60(Mar 1974):1143-4.

Rylance, Daniel F. see Tweton, D. Jerome

Sabaliũnas, Leonas. Lithuania in Crisis: Nationalism to Communism, 1939-1940. Bloomington: Ind U Press, 1972. Rev. by V. Kavolis, EEQ, 8(Mar 1974):117-18.

Sachar, Howard M. Europe Leaves the Middle East, 1936-1954. New York: Knopf, 1972. Rev. by T. Naff, AHR, 79(Oct 1974):1147-8; J. Jankowski, Historian, 36(May 1974):548-9.

Sackrey, Charles. The Political Economy of Urban Poverty. New York: Norton, 1973. Rev. by J. L. Arnold, JNH, 59(Apr 1974):196-203.

Sage, Leland L. A History of Iowa. Ames: Ia St U Press, 1974. Rev. by T. H. Peterson, AmArc, 37(Oct 1974):596-8; P. D. Jordan, MinnH, 44(Sum 1974):76-7; P. D. Jordan, NDH, 41 (Fall 1974):30; R. C. Nesbit, WMH, 57(Sum 1974):313-14.

St. Clair, William. That Greece Might Still Be Free: The Philhellenes in the War of Independence. New York: Ox U Press, 1972. Rev. by L. S. Stavorianos, AHR, 79(Feb 1974):190-2;

D. Dakin, EHR, 89(Apr 1974):451-2; D. Dakin, ESR, 4(Apr 1974):184-5; D. Dakin, History, 59(Feb 1974):114-15.

Saint-Lu, André. Condition coloniale et conscience créole au Guatemala (1524-1821). Paris: Universitaires de France, 1970. Rev. by M. J. MacLeod, HAHR, 54(May 1974):317-19.

Saito, Shiro. Philippine Ethnography: A Critically Annotated and Selected Bibliography. Honolulu: U Press Hawaii, 1972. Rev. by R. W. Lieban, JAS, 33(May 1974):507-8.

Sakellariou, Michael see Andronicos, Emmanuel

Sale, Kirkpatrick. SDS. New York: Random House, 1973. Rev. by W. L. O'Neill, AHR, 79(Je 1974):911-12.

Salisbury, Harrison E. To Peking--and Beyond: A Report on the New Asia. New York: Quadrangle, 1973. Rev. by B. D. Larkin, JAS, 33(May 1974):475-6.

Salvatorelli, Luigi. The Risorgimento: Thought and Action. New York: Harper and Row, 1971. Rev. by C. H. Church, ESR, 4(Ja 1974):95-7.

Salvemini, Gaetano. The Origins of Fascism in Italy. New York: Harper and Row, 1973. Rev. by W. R. Tucker, HRNB, 2(May/Je 1974):180.

Salvucci, Pasquale. Adam Ferguson. Urbino: Argalia, 1972. Rev. by W. C. Lehmann, H & T, 13(Num 2 1974):165-81.

Samaha, Joel. Law and Order in Historical Perspective: The Case of Elizabethan Essex. New York ...: Academic Press, 1974. Rev. by K. Wrightson, HJ, 17(Num 3 1974):656-8.

Sambrook, James. William Cobbett. Boston: Routledge and Kegan Paul, 1973. Rev. by J. W. Osborne, AHR, 79(Je 1974):784.

Sampson, William R., ed. John McLoughlin's Business Correspondence, 1847-48. Seattle: U Wash Press, 1973. Rev. by F. H. Schapsmeier, JOW, 13(Jl 1974):122; D. Lavender, PNQ, 65(Apr 1974):86-7; J. D. McLaird, WHQ, 5(Oct 1974):462-3.

Samuels, Michael A. see Abshire, David M.

Sanakoev, M. P. The Activity of the Peasant Land Bank in Georgia, 1906-1917. Tbilisi: Izdatel'stvo "Metsneireba," 1971. Rev. by R. A. Wade, AHR, 79(Oct 1974):1223-4.

Sánchez, José. Anticlericalism: A Brief History. Notre Dame, Ind.: U Notre Dame Press, 1972. Rev. by H. G. J. Beck, AHR, 79(Feb 1974):112.

319   SANCHEZ-ALBORNOZ

Sánchez-Albornoz, Nicolás. The Population of Latin America: A
History. Berkeley: U Cal Press, 1974. Rev. by G. Maty-
oka, HRNB, 3(Nov/Dec 1974):38-9.

Sanchez Lamego, Miguel A. The Second Mexican-Texas War, 1841-
1843. Hillsboro, Tx.: Hill Jr. Coll Press, 1972. Rev. by
S. E. Bell, ETHJ, 12(Spr 1974):57-8.

Sanders, Daniel S. The Impact of Reform Movements on Social
Policy Change: The Case of Social Insurance. Fair Lawn,
N. J.: R. E. Burdick, 1973. Rev. by R. Lubove, JAH, 61
(Je 1974):246.

Sanders, I. J., ed. Documents of the Baronial Movement of Reform and Rebellion, 1258-1267. New York: Ox U Press,
1973. Rev. by J. R. Lander, AHR, 79(Je 1974):772-3.

Sanders, Mary Elizabeth, comp. Selected Annotated Abstracts of
St. Mary Parish, La. Marriage Book I, 1811-1829. N. p.,
1973. Rev. by M. A. Fontenot, LaH, 15(Sum 1974):315-16.

Sandler, Martin W., Edwin C. Rozwenc, and Edward C. Martin.
The People Make a Nation. 2 vols. Boston: Allyn and Ba-
con, 1971. Rev. by W. N. Murphy, HT, 7(Aug 1974):618-19;
B. Kelsey, HT, 7(Aug 1974):619.

Saner, Hans. Kant's Political Thought: Its Origins and Development. Chicago: U Chi Press, 1973. Rev. by F. Nauen,
JMH, 46(Dec 1974):729-31.

San Martín, Marta see Bonachea, Ramón L.

Santerre, Renand. Pe'dagogie musulmane d'Afrique noire: l'école
coranique peule du Cameroun. Montreal: Press de l'Université de Montreal, 1973. Rev. by H. J. Fisher, JAfH, 15
(Num 1 1974):167-8.

Santonen, Arvo. The Question of Small-Farmer Organizations and
the Establishment of Small-Farmers' Unions in Finland: A
Study of the Transition in Small-Farming Policy in Agriculture
up to the Early 1930's. Helsinki: Suomen Historiallinen
Seura, 1971. Rev. by P. K. Hamalainen, AHR, 79(Je 1974):
800.

Sappenfield, James A. A Sweet Instruction: Franklin's Journalism
as a Literary Apprenticeship. Carbondale and Edwardsville:
So Ill U Press, 1973. Rev. by M. Hall, NEQ, 47(June 1974):
337-9; A. O. Aldridge, WMQ-3, 31(Jl 1974):522-4.

Sappington, Roger E. The Brethren in Virginia: The History of
the Church of the Brethren in Virginia. Harrisonburg, Va.:
Committee for Brethren History in Va, 1973. Rev. by M. H.
Schrag, CH, 43(Dec 1974):550-1; E. E. Eminhizer, JSH, 40

(1974):679-80; W. H. Daniel, VMHB, 82(Oct 1974):491-2.

Sarti, Roland. Fascism and the Industrial Leadership in Italy, 1919-
    1940. A Study in the Expansion of Private Power Under Fas-
    cism. Berkeley: U Cal Press, 1971. Rev. by R. Vivarelli,
    HJ, 17(Num 3 1974):644-51.

Sater, William F. The Heroic Image in Chile: Arturo Prat, Secu-
    lar Saint. Berkeley: U Cal Press, 1973. Rev. by J. R.
    Thomas, AHR, 79(Oct 1974):1297-8; D. E. Worcester, HAHR,
    54(May 1974):328-9; S. W. Schmitt, HRNB, 2(Feb 1974):102;
    S. Collier, TAm, 31(Oct 1974):224-5.

Satterfield, Archie. Chilkoot Pass: Then and Now. Anchorage:
    Alaska Northwest Publishing, 1973. Rev. by R. L. Munkres,
    JOW, 13(Apr 1974):131.

Sauer, James A. Heshbon Pottery 1971: A Preliminary Report on
    the Pottery from the 1971 Excavations at Tell Hesbôn. Ber-
    rien Springs, Mich.: Andrews U Press, 1973. Rev. by
    W. E. Rost, AJA, 78(Oct 1974):434-5.

Saul, S. B. see Milward, A.

Sauvage, Odette. L'itineraire erasmien d'Andre de Resende. Paris:
    Centro Cultural Portugues, 1971. Rev. by S. L. Arora, RQ,
    27(Spr 1974):60-2.

Savage, William W., Jr. The Cherokee Strip Live Stock Associa-
    tion: Federal Regulation and the Cattleman's Last Frontier.
    Columbia, Mo.: U Mo Press, 1973. Rev. by H. C. Miner,
    BHR, 48(Win 1974):558-60; G. H. Shirk, ChOk, 52(Fall 1974):
    382-3; J. T. Schlebecker, JAH, 61(Dec 1974):789-90; N. E.
    Ramirez, JOW, 13(Jl 1974):124; W. T. Hagan, PHR, 43(Nov
    1974):610-11; C. Kenner, WHQ, 5(Oct 1974):483-4.

Savary, Louis M. Psychological Themes in the Golden Epistle of
    William of Saint-Thierry to the Carthusians of Mont-Dieu.
    Salzburg: James Hogg, 1973. Rev. by W. O. Paulsell, CH,
    43(Mar 1974):102-3.

Sâve-Soderbergh, T., ed. The Scandinavian Joint Expedition to
    Sudanese Nubia. Odense and Helsinki: Scandinavian Books,
    1970. Rev. by N. B. Millet, AJA, 78(Ja 1974):82-3.

Sawyer, R. McLaran. Centennial History of the University of Ne-
    braska. Volume II, The Modern University, 1920-1969. Lin-
    coln, Neb.: Centennial Press, 1973. Rev. by R. Vassar,
    IMH, 70(Sep 1974):266-7; W. Havighurst, JAH, 61(Sep 1974):
    525-6; T. Knight, JOW, 13(Jl 1974):114; J. F. Paul, N H, 55
    (Sum 1974):296-7.

Saxton, Dean and Lucille. Legends and Lore of the Papago and

Pima Indians. Tucson: U Ariz Press, 1973. Rev. by D. S.
Matson, JAriH, 15(Spr 1974):85-7.

Sayles, G. O. The King's Parliament of England. New York: Norton, 1974. Rev. by W. H. Dunham, Jr., HRNB, 2(Sep 1974):
238.

Scaglione, Aldo. The Classical Theory of Composition from Its Origins to the Present. Chapel Hill: U N C Press, 1972. Rev.
by W. R. Johnson, RQ, 27(Sum 1974):202-5.

Scalf, Henry P. Kentucky's Last Frontier. Pikeville, Ky.: Pikeville Coll. Press, 1972. Rev. by R. E. Smith, WPHM, 57
(Ja 1974):114-15.

Scarborough, William Kauffman, ed. The Diary of Edmund Ruffin.
Volume I-Toward Independence, October 1856-April 1861.
Baton Rouge, La.: La St U Press, n.d. Rev. by C. Simp-
son, WVH, 35(Ja 1974):164-5.

Scarbrough, Clara Stearns. Land of Good Water, Takachue Pouetsu,
a Williamson County, Texas, History. Georgetown, Tx.: Williamson Cty. Sun Pub., 1973. Rev. by H. B. Simpson, Texana, 11(W 1974):89.

Schaar, John H. see Wolin, Sheldon S.

Schalit, Abraham, ed. The World History of the Jewish People
... Vol. 6. New Brunswick, N.J.: Rutgers U Press, n.d.
Rev. by C. H. Gordon, AHR, 79(Apr 1974):489.

Scheips, Paul J. Hold the Fort! The Story of a Song from the
Sawdust Trail to the Picket Line. Washington: Smithsonian
Institution Press, 1971. Rev. by J. H. Keiser, JISHS, 67
(Sep 1974):461.

Schiller, Bradley R. The Economics of Poverty and Discrimination.
Englewood Cliffs, N.J.: Prentice-Hall, 1973. Rev. by J. L.
Arnold, JNH, 59(Apr 1974):196-203.

Schilling, Heinz. Niederländische Exulanten im 16. Jahrhundert:
Ihre Stellung im Sozialgefüge und im religiösen Leben deutscher
und englischer Städte. Gütersloh: Gerd Mohn, 1972. Rev.
by S. M. Wyntjes, JMH, 46(Mar 1974):123-4.

Schioler, Thorkild. Roman and Islamic Water-lifting Wheels. Copenhagen: Odense U Press, 1973. Rev. by D. R. Hill, T & C,
(Oct 1974):628-30.

Schiwetz, E. M., artist. Notes by John Edward Weems. The
Schiwetz Legacy: An Artist's Tribute to Texas, 1910-1971.
Austin: U Tex Press, 1972. Rev. by M. Huff, WHQ, 5(Jl
1974):351-2.

Schlebecker, John T. The Use of the Land: Essays on the History of American Agriculture. Lawrence, Kans.: Coronado Press, 1973. Rev. by W. D. Rasmussen, T & C, 15(Oct 1974):647-8.

Schlesinger, Arthur M., Jr., ed. History of U. S. Political Parties. 4 vols. New York: Chelsea, 1973. Rev. by R. P. McCormick, JAH, 61(Sep 1974):447-9.

_____. The Imperial Presidency. Boston: Houghton Mifflin, 1973. Rev. by R. H. Ferrell, HRNB, 2(Mar 1974):134; H. A. Larrabee, NEQ, 47(Mar 1974):132-5; M. Borden, PHR, 43 (Aug 1974):439-41.

Schlossberg, Edwin. Einstein and Beckett, a Record of an Imaginary Discussion with Albert Einstein and Samuel Beckett. New York: Link Books, n.d. Rev. by A. Cardona-Hine, Mankind, 4(Feb 1974):6.

Schmeckebier, L. F. Catalogue and Index of the Publications of the Hayden, King, Powell, and Wheeler Surveys. Washington: Government Printing Office, 1904; New York: Da Capo, 1971 (reprint). Rev. by J. W. Roberson, ChOk, 52(Fall 1974): 385-6.

Schmidt, Hubert G. Agriculture in New Jersey: A Three-Hundred-Year History. New Brunswick, N. J.: Rutgers U Press, 1973. Rev. by J. T. Schlebacker, JAH, 61(Sep 1974):454.

Schmidt, Martin. John Wesley: A Theological Biography. Nashville: Abingdon Press, 1963, 1972, 1973. Rev. by A. C. Outler, CH, 43(Dec 1974):547-8.

Schmitt, Charles B. Cicero Scepticus: A Study of the Influence of the Academia in the Renaissance. The Hague: Martinus Nijhoff, 1972. Rev. by J. Hutton, RQ, 27(Fall 1974):334-6.

Schmitt, Karl M. Mexico and the United States, 1821-1973: Conflict and Coexistence. New York: Wiley, 1974. Rev. by K. J. Brauer, TAm, 31(Oct 1974):228-9.

Schmitter, Philippe C. Autonomy or Dependence as Regional Integration Outcomes: Central America. Berkeley: U Cal Press, 1972. Rev. by G. W. Wynia, HAHR, 54(May 1974):338-9.

Schmookler, Jacob. Patents, Invention, and Economic Change: Data and Selected Essays. Ed. by Zvi Grilliches and Leonid Hurwicz. Cambridge: Harvard U Press, 1972. Rev. by F. A. Tarpley, Jr., T & C, 15(Ja 1974):138-9.

Schnabel, James F. Policy and Direction: The First Year. Vol. 3: United States Army in the Korean War. Washington: Office of the Chief of Military History, United States Army, 1972. Rev. by T. Ropp, JAH, 61(Dec 1974):843-4.

Schneider, Christian. Prophetisches Sacerdium und heilgeschichtliches Regnum im Dialog 1073-1077. Munich: Wilhelm Fink
Verlag, 1972. Rev. by W. Ullmann, EHR, 89(Ja 1974):152-3.

Schneider, Laurence A. Ku Chieh-kang and China's New History:
Nationalism and the Quest for Alternative Traditions. Berkeley: U Cal Press, 1971. Rev. by D. C. Price, JAS, 33(Aug
1974):692-5.

Schneir, Miriam, ed. Feminism: The Essential Historical Writings.
New York: Vintage, 1973. Rev. by T. Ripmaster, HT, 8(Nov
1974):125-6.

Schnitzer, Martin. East and West Germany: A Comparative Economic Analysis. New York: Praeger, 1972. Rev. by K. H.
Kahrs, EEQ, 8(Sum 1974):248-50.

Schoenbaum, S. and Alan C. Dessen, ed. Renaissance Drama, New
Series IV: Essays Principally on the Playhouse and Staging.
Evanston, Ill.: Northwestern U Press, 1971. Rev. by V.
Hall, RQ, 27(Spr 1974):94-5.

Schoenfeld, Maxwell P. The War Ministry of Winston Churchill.
Ames: Ia St U Press, 1972. Rev. by H. Pelling, History,
59(Feb 1974):145-6.

Schonhorn, Manuel, ed. see Defoe, Daniel

Schönhoven, Klaus. Die Bayerische Volkspartei, 1924-1932. Düsseldorf: Droste Verlag, 1972. Rev. by G. Braunthal, AHR,
79(Feb 1974):175-6; H. J. Gordon, Jr., JMH, 46(Mar 1974):
158-9.

Schraepler, Ernst. Handwerkerbünde und Arbeitervereine 1830-1853.
Berlin: de Gruyter, 1972. Rev. by W. Carr, EHR, 89(Apr
1974):455-6.

Schreiner-Yantis, Netti, ed. Archives of the Pioneers of Tazewell
County, Virginia. Springfield, Va.: Compiler, 1973. Rev.
by J. I. Robertson, Jr., VMHB, 82(Oct 1974):502.

Schroeder, John H. Mr. Polk's War: American Opposition and
Dissent, 1846-1848. Madison: U Wis Press, 1973. Rev. by
R. L. Hatzenbuehler, CWH, 20(Je 1974):167-8; J. A. Ramage,
FCHQ, 48(Jl 1974):280-1; G. M. Capers, FHQ, 53(Jl 1974):
86-7; N. D. Brown, GHQ, 58(Spr 1974):126-7; J. V. Mering,
HRNB, 2(Feb 1974):96-7; J. P. Bloom, IMH, 70(Sep 1974):
257-8; J. B. Stewart, JSH, 40(Aug 1974):478-9; J. Ware,
JOW, 13(Jl 1974):133-4; M. L. Wilson, MHM, 69(Sum 1974):
231-3; W. S. Hoffman, NCHR, 51(Spr 1974):235-6; D. M.
Pletcher, PHR, 43(May 1974):268-70; D. C. Brink, PNQ, 65
(Oct 1974):190-1; E. M. Coffman, RKHS, 72(Apr 1974):182-3;
P. H. Bergeron, THQ, 33(Spr 1974):105-6; R. W. Sadler,

SCHROEDER   324

WHQ, 5(Oct 1974):480-1; O. B. Faulk, WVH, 35(Apr 1974):
242-4.

Schroeder, Paul W. Austria, Great Britain, and the Crimean War:
The Destruction of the European Concert. Ithaca, N.Y.: Cornell U Press, 1973. Rev. by K. F. Helleiner, CHR, 55(Je
1974):217-18; R. F. C. Okey, ESR, 4(Jl 1974):283-6.

Schruben, Francis W. Wee Creek to El Dorado: Oil in Kansas,
1860-1920. Columbia, Mo.: U Mo Press, 1972. Rev. by
H. L. Schamehorn, WHQ, 5(Ja 1974):68-70.

Schuchhardt, Walter-Herwig. Greek Art. New York: Universe
Books, 1971. Rev. by I. K. Raubitschek, AJA, 78(Jan 1974):
95-6.

Schulkind, Eugene. The Paris Commune of 1871: the View from
the Left. London: Cape, 1972. Rev. by J. P. T. Bury,
EHR, 89(Jl 1974):685.

Schullian, Dorothy M., ed. The Baglivi Correspondence from the
Library of Sir William Osler. Ithaca, N.Y.: Cornell U Press,
1974. Rev. by M. H. Saffron, HRNB, 2(Sep 1974):247.

Schults, Raymond L. Crusader in Babylon: W. T. Stead and the
Pall Mall Gazette. Lincoln: U Neb Press, 1972. Rev. by
B. Harrison, AHR, 79(Feb 1974):146-8.

Schultz, George A. An Indian Canaan: Isaac McCoy and the Vision
of an Indian State. Norman: U Ok Press, 1972. Rev. by
H. E. Fritz, AHR, 79(Je 1974):859-60.

Schultz, Stanley K. The Culture Factory: Boston Public Schools,
1789-1860. New York: Ox U Press, 1973. Rev. by K. V.
Lottich, AHR, 79(Oct 1974):1255-6; H. Schwartz, CWH, 20
(Mar 1974):59-60; R. Welter, JAH, 61(Je 1974):163-4; J. D.
Hoeveler, Jr., NEQ, 47(Je 1974):307-9.

Schumacher, Dieter, ed. see Stober, Gerhard J., ed.

Schumacher, John N. Father Jose Burgos: Priest and Nationalist.
Quezon City: Ateneo U Press, 1972. Rev. by D. J. Steinberg, JAS, 33(Feb 1974):344-5.

Schumacher, Martin. Erinnerungen und Dokumente von Joh. Victor
Bredt, 1914-1933. Düsseldorf: Droste Verlag, 1970. Rev.
by K. von Klemperer, JMH, 46(Mar 1974):153-5.

_____. Mittelstandsfront und Republik: Die Wirtschaftspartei--
Reichspartei des deutschen Mittelstandes, 1919-1933. Düssel-
dorf: Droste verlag, 1972. Rev. by K. von Klemperer, 46
(Mar 1974):153-5.

Schuster, Louis A., et al. The Complete Works of St. Thomas
    More. Vol. 8. New Haven, Conn.: Yale U Press, 1973.
    Rev. by G. R. Elton, EHR, 89(Apr 1974):382-7.

Schwaab, Eugene L., ed. Travels in the Old South 1783-1860, Se-
    lected from the Periodicals of the Times. 2 vols. Lexington,
    Ky.: U Press Ky, 1973. Rev. by L. H. Harrison, FCHQ,
    48(Apr 1974):195-7; L. M. Simms, Jr., GHQ, 58(Sum 1974):
    294-5; P. Yoder, IMH, 70(Dec 1974):354-5; G. Moore, JSH,
    40(Nov 1974):652-4; W. C. Gass, NCHR, 51(Sum 1974):342-3;
    B. Milward, RKHS, 72(Jl 1974):297-9; J. I. Waring, SCHM,
    75(Jl 1974):192; C. C. Davis, VMHB, 82(Oct 1974):504-5.

Schwab, Peter. Decision-Making in Ethiopia: A Study of the Po-
    litical Process. n. p.: Hurst, 1972. Rev. by J. M. Cohen,
    AfAf, 73(Apr 1974):240-1.

Schwabedissen, Hermann, gen. ed. Die Anfäuge des Neolithikums
    vom Orient bis Nordeuropa, Part V. Köln-Wien: Böhlau Ver-
    lag, 1972. Rev. by S. Folting, AJA, 78(Jl 1974):301-2.

Schwartz, Bernard. From Confederation to Nation: The American
    Constitution, 1835 to 1877. Baltimore: JHU Press, 1973.
    Rev. by L. G. Lindley, CWH, 20(Mar 1974):57-8; S. N. Katz,
    JAH, 61(Je 1974):180-1; J. S. Schuchman, JSH, 40(May 1974):
    308-9.

Schwartz, Pedro. The New Political Economy of J. S. Mill. Dur-
    ham, N. C.: Duke U Press, 1972. Rev. by J. M. Robson,
    JMH, 46(Mar 1974):138-9.

Schwartz, Stuart B. Sovereignty and Society in Colonial Brazil:
    The High Court of Bahia and Its Judges, 1609-1751. Berkeley:
    U Cal Press, 1973. Rev. by H. B. Johnson, Jr., HAHR, 54
    (Aug 1973):514-16.

Schweinfurth, U., H. Flohn, and M. Domros. Studies in the Clima-
    tology of South Asia. Wiesbaden: Verlag, 1970. Rev. by
    R. W. Bradnock, MAS, 8(Jl 1974):432.

Schwieder, Dorothy, ed. Patterns and Perspectives in Iowa History.
    Ames: Ia St U Press, 1973. Rev. by G. R. McIntosh, AI,
    42(Win 1974):233-4; F. P. Weisenburger, HRNB, 2(Ja 1974):
    63; D. Crosson, MiA, 56(Ja 1974):67-8.

Scott, George. The Rise and Fall of the League of Nations. New
    York: Macmillan, 1974. Rev. by K. J. Brauer, HRNB, 2
    (Jl 1974):206.

Scott, Joan Wallach. The Glassworkers of Carmaux: French Crafts-
    men and Political Action in a Nineteenth-Century City. Cam-
    bridge, Mass.: Har U Press, 1974. Rev. by F. Fox, HRNB,
    2(Sep 1974):241-2.

Scott, John Anthony. Teaching for a Change. New York: Bantam
    Books, 1972. Rev. by G. A. Danzer, HT, 8(Nov 1974):133-4.

Scott, Kenneth see van Laer, Arnold J. F.

Scott, Nathan A., Jr. Three American Moralists: Mailer, Bellow,
    Trilling. Notre Dame, Ind.: U Notre Dame Press, n.d.
    Rev. by J. Romano, Commentary, 58(Oct 1974):92-6.

Scott, Roy V. and J. G. Shoalmire. The Public Career of Cully A.
    Cobb: A Study in Agricultural Leadership. Jackson, Miss.:
    U and Coll Press Miss, 1973. Rev. D. L. Winters, JAH, 61
    (Sep 1974):519-20; D. G. Sansing, JMiH, 36(May 1974):203-4;
    J. H. Stone, LaH, 15(Sum 1974):306-7; R. S. Kirkendall, PNQ,
    65(Jl 1974):152-3; W. D. Aeschbacher, RKHS, 72(Apr 1974):
    171-2; H. C. Dethloff, SWHQ, 78(Jl 1974):110-11.

Scott, William. Terror and Repression in Revolutionary Marseilles.
    London: Macmillan, 1973. Rev. by C. Lucas, EHR, 89(Jl
    1974):673-5.

Scribner, Robert L., ed. see Van Schreeven, William J.

Scully, Arthur, Jr. James Dakin, Architect: His Career in New
    York and the South. Baton Rouge: LSU Press, 1973. Rev.
    by W. Seale, JSH, 40(May 1974):306-8; W. R. Cullison, LaH,
    15(Sum 1974):303-5; J. M. Bryan, NYHSQ, 58(Jl 1974):244-6.

Seaborne, Malcolm. The English School: Its Architecture and Or-
    ganization. London: Routledge and Kegan Paul, 1971. Rev.
    by G. Sutherland, History, 59(Je 1974):336.

Seaburg, Carl and Stanley Paterson. Merchant Prince of Boston:
    Colonel T. H. Perkins, 1764-1854. Cambridge, Mass.: Har
    U Press, 1971. Rev. by F. C. Jaher, AHR, 79(Apr 1974):
    575.

Seager, Robert, II see Decker, Leslie E.

Seaman, L. C. B. Victorian England: Aspects of English and Im-
    perial History 1837-1901. London: Methuen, 1973. Rev. by
    E. G. Collieu, History, 59(Je 1974):289.

Searight, Sarah. New Orleans. New York: Stein and Day, 1973.
    Rev. by L. V. Huber, LaH, 15(Sum 1974):314-5; R. F. Locke
    Mankind, 4(Apr 1974):8.

Searle, G. R. The Quest for National Efficiency, 1899-1914. Ox-
    ford: Basil Blackwell, 1971. Rev. by H. Pelling, HJ, 17
    (Mar 1974):223-4.

Seay, James. Water Tables. Middletown, Conn.: Wes U Press,
    1974. Rev. by D. Huddle, GR, 28(Fall 1974):535-40.

Sebreli, Juan José. Apogeo y ocaso de los Anchorena. Buenos
     Aires: Ediciones Siglo Veinte, 1972. Rev. by M. Falcoff,
     HAHR, 54(Aug 1974):533-5.

Seers, Dudley see Faber, Mike

Seidel, Karl Josef. Frankreich und die deutschen Protestanten: Die
     Bemühungen um eine religiöse Konkordie und die französische
     Bündnispolitik in den Jahren 1534/35. Münster: Aschendorff-
     sche Verlagsbuchhandlung, 1970. Rev. by C. L. Manschreck,
     JMH, 46(Dec 1974):728-9.

Selby, John. Over the Sea to Skye: The Forty-Five. New York:
     St. Martin's, 1973. Rev. by J. W. Ferguson, AHR, 79(Oct
     1974):1185.

Selby, John E. A Chronology of Virginia and the War of Indepen-
     dence 1763-1783. Charlottesville: U Press Va, 1973. Rev.
     by G. G. Shackelford, VMHB, 82(Apr 1974):194-5.

Self, Huber see Socolofsky, Homer

Seligmann, Gustav L. see Rosaldo, Renato

Sellers, Charles Coleman. Dickinson College: A History. Middle-
     town, Conn.: Wes U Press, 1973. Rev. by J. H. Smylie,
     CH, 43(Mar 1974):120; M. H. Hellerich, PH, 41(Apr 1974):
     231-3.

_____ and Martha Calvert Slotten, comp. Archives and Manu-
     script Collections of Dickinson College: A Guide. Carlisle,
     Pa.: Friends of the Dickinson College Library, 1972. Rev.
     by N. G. Boles, MHM, 63(Spr 1974):113.

Sellers, Ian see Briggs, John

Semmel, Bernard. The Rise of Free Trade Imperialism: Classical
     Political Economy and the Empire of Free Trade and Imperi-
     alism, 1750-1850. New York: Cam U Press, 1970. Rev.
     by J. M. Price, JMH, 46(Mar 1974):135-7.

Semmler, E. G., ed. The Engineer and Society. London: Insti-
     tution of Mech. Engineers, 1973. Rev. by J. B. Rae, T & C,
     15(Jl 1974):523-4.

Senior, Hereward. Orangeism: The Canadian Phase. Toronto:
     McGraw-Hill, 1972. Rev. by E. Jones, CHR, 55(Je 1974):
     190-1.

Senn, Alfred see Cardona, George

Senn, Alfred Erich. Diplomacy and Revolution. The Soviet Mis-
     sion to Switzerland, 1918. Notre Dame, Ind.: U Notre Dame

Press, 1974. Rev. by A. E. Adams, HRNB, 3(Oct 1974):
12-13.

Serhienko, H. Ia. Social-Political Movements in the Ukraine After
the Decembrist Uprising, 1826-1850. Kiev: Vydavnytstvo
"Naukova Dumka," 1971. Rev. by B. Dmytryshyn, AHR, 79
(Apr 1974):556.

Serle, Geoffrey. The Rush to be Rich. Melbourne: Melbourne U
Press, 1971. Rev. by D. K. Fieldhouse, EHR, 89(Apr 1974):
462-3.

Seshadri, K. see Reddy, G. Ram

Sewall, Samuel. The Diary of Samuel Sewall, 1674-1729. Ed. by
M. Halsey Thomas. New York: Farrar, Straus, and Giroux,
1973. Rev. by E. S. Morgan, NYHSQ, 58(Jl 1974):235-7.

Seward, Desmond. Prince of the Renaissance: The Golden Life of
François I. New York: Macmillan, 1973. Rev. by L. S.
Van Doren, AHR, 79(Oct 1974):1187.

Seymour, Catryna Ten Eyck. Enjoying the Southwest. Philadelphia:
Lippincott, 1973. Rev. by T. Beatson, JAriH, 15(Aug 1974):
307-8.

Shade, William Gerald. Banks or No Banks: The Money Issue in
Western Politics, 1832-1865. Detroit: Wayne St U Press,
1972. Rev. by R. P. Swierenga, CWH, 20(Mar 1974):534;
W. H. Becker, Historian, 36(May 1974):563-4; F. O. Gatell,
JAH, 60(Mar 1974):1112-13; J. H. Broussard, MiA, 56(Jl
1974):200; J. R. Sharp, PNQ, 65(Apr 1974):86.

Shafer, Boyd C. Faces of Nationalism. New Realities and Old
Myths. New York: Harcourt Brace Jovanovich, 1972. Rev.
by B. B. Frye, Historian, 36(Feb 1974):304.

Shafer, Robert Jones. Mexican Business Organizations: History
and Analysis. Syracuse, N.Y.: Syr U Press, 1973. Rev.
by D. S. Brothers, BHR, 48(Sum 1974):243-5; W. Withers,
HAHR, 54(May 1974):326-8; M. J. McLeod, HRNB, 2(Ja 1974):
68-9; R. N. Sinkin, TAm, 30(Apr 1974):547-9.

Shankland, Robert S., ed. Scientific Papers of Arthur Holly Compton: X-Ray and Other Studies. Chicago: U Chi Press, 1974.
Rev. by F. J. Dobney, HRNB, 2(May/Je 1974):170.

Shapiro, Peter see Barlow, William

Sharma, Baijnath. Harṣa and His Times. Varanasi: Sushma
Prakashan, 1970. Rev. by R. M. Smith, AHR, 79(Oct 1974):
1234.

Sharp, Daniel A. U. S. Foreign Policy and Peru. Austin: U Tx,
    1972. Rev. by B. Wood, JLAS, 6(May 1974):188-9; R. N.
    Seidel, TAm, 30(Ja 1974):417-18.

Sharp, Paul F. Whoop-Up Country: The Canadian-American West,
    1865-1885. Norman: U Ok Press, 1973. Rev. by F. J.
    Athearn, JAH, 61(Je 1974):257-8.

Sharp, Robert L. Big Outfit: Ranching on the Baca Float. Tucson:
    U Ariz Press, 1974. Rev. by J. J. Wagoner, JAriH, 15(Win
    1974):391-2.

Sheehan, Bernard W. Seeds of Extinction: Jeffersonian Philan-
    thropy and the American Indian. Chapel Hill: UNC Press,
    ... 1973. Rev. by D. J. Berthrong, IMH, 70(Mar 1974):81-
    2; D. A. Grinde, Jr., InH, 7(Spr 1974):50-1; R. Ketcham,
    JAH, 60(Mar 1974):1107-8; A. H. DeRosier, Jr., JSH, 40
    (Feb 1974):133-4; R. E. Bieder, MHM, 69(Spr 1974):103-5;
    R. N. Ellis, MiA, 56(Jan 1974):56-7; R. A. Brent, NYH, 55
    (Jl 1974):352-4; K. R. Nodyne, NYHSQ, 58(Apr 1974):155-6;
    R. McColley, PH, 41(Jl 1974):364-5; M. M. Le Breton, WHQ,
    5(Apr 1974):199-200; D. W. Nelson, WMH, 57(W 1974):160-1.

Shelton, Walter James. English Hunger and Industrial Disorders:
    A Study of Social Conflict During the First Decade of George
    III's Reign. Toronto: U Tor Press, 1973. Rev. by R. J.
    Sinner, HRNB, 2(Aug 1974):230-1.

Shepherd, James F. and Gary M. Walton. Shipping, Maritime
    Trade and the Economic Development of Colonial North Amer-
    ica. Cambridge: Cam U Press, 1972. Rev. by C. K. Har-
    ley, CHR, 55(Sep 1974):342-3; W. I. Davisson, NYHSQ, 58(Ja
    1974):60-1; J. L. Anderson, PH, 41(Ja 1974):96-7.

Sheppard, F. H. W. , ed. Survey of London. Vol. XXXVII: North-
    ern Kensington. London: Athlone, 1973. Rev. by J. M.
    Crook, History, 59(Je 1974):334-5.

Sheppard, Francis. London 1808-1870: The Infernal Wen. Berke-
    ley: U Cal Press, 1971. Rev. by B. McGill, JEH, 34(Sep
    1974):802.

Sheppard, Mubin. Taman Indera: A Royal Pleasure Ground: Ma-
    lay Decorative Arts and Pastimes. Kuala Lumpur: Ox U
    Press, 1972. Rev. by A. L. Becker, JAS, 33(Feb 1974):
    331-2.

Sherburne, James. Stand Like Men. Boston: Houghton Mifflin,
    1973. Rev. by Q. B. Keen, RKHS, 72(Ja 1974):67-9.

Sherburne, James Clark. John Ruskin or the Ambiguities of Abun-
    dance: A Study in Social and Economic Criticism. Cambridge,
    Mass. : Har U Press, 1972. Rev. by G. Levine, JMH, 46

(Mar 1974):142-4.

Sheridan, Richard B. Sugar and Slavery: An Economic History of the British West Indies, 1623-1775. Baltimore: JHU Press, 1974. Rev. by S. L. Engerman, BHR, 48(Win 1974):582-3; J. Parker, HRNB, 3(Nov/Dec 1974):42.

Sherlock, Philip. West Indian Nations: A New History. New York: St. Martin's, 1974. Rev. by M. J. MacLeod, HRNB, 2(Jl 1974):200.

Sherman, A. J. Island Refuge: Britain and Refugees from the Third Reich, 1933-1939. Berkeley: U Cal Press, 1974. Rev. by C. E. McClelland, HRNB, 2(May/Je 1974):178.

Sherman, Richard B. The Republican Party and Black America: From McKinley to Hoover, 1896-1933. Charlottesville: U Press Va, 1973. Rev. by T. W. Dillard, ArkHQ, 33(Aut 1974):265-7; D. W. Grantham, FHQ, 52(Jl 1974):97-8; D. Herreshoff, HRNB, 2(Feb 1974):101; N. J. Weiss, JAH, 61(Sep 1974):511-12; B. L. Clayton, JSH, 40(May 1974):330-2; A. Buni, VMHB, 82(Apr 1974):213-15.

Sherrill, Robert. The Saturday Night Special and Other Guns With Which Americans Won the West.... New York: Charter House, 1973. Rev. by R. Gilmore, WMH, 57(Sum 1974):316-17.

Sherwood, Jennifer and Nikolaus Pevsner. The Buildings of England: Oxfordshire. London: Penguin, n.d. Rev. by M. Greenhalgh, HTo, 24(Oct 1974):725-6.

Shettles, Elijah L. Recollections of a Long Life. Nashville: Blue and Gray Press, 1973. Rev. by W. N. Vernon, ETHJ, 12 (Fall 1974):86-7.

Shih, Cung-wen. Injustice to Tou O (Tou O Yüan): A Study and Translation. New York: Cam U Press, ... 1973. Rev. by C. H. Wang, JAS, 33(Feb 1974):297-8.

Shillony, Ben-Ami. Revolt in Japan: The Young Officers and the February 26, 1936 Incident. Princeton, N.J.: Prin U Press, 1973. Rev. by P. Duus, AHR, 79(Je 1974):826-7; G. R. Falconeri, JAS, 33(Aug 1974):710-12.

Shirley, John W., ed. Thomas Harriot: Renaissance Scientist. New York: Ox U Press, 1974. Rev. by P. D. Thomas, HRNB, 3(Nov/Dec 1974):25; A. Haynes, HTo, 24(Oct 1974): 734-5.

Shively, Donald H., ed. Tradition and Modernization in Japanese Culture. Princeton, N.J.: Prin U Press, 1971. Rev. by P. G. Steinhoff, JAAS, 9(Ja and Apr 1974):115-16.

Shoalmire, J. G. see Scott, Roy V.

Short, James F., Jr. and Marvin E. Wolfgang, eds. Collective
    Violence. Chicago: Aldine-Atherton, 1972. Rev. by R.
    Ginger, CHR, 55(Je 1974):178-9.

Shorter, Aylward. African Culture and the Christian Church. Mary-
    knoll, N.Y.: Orbis, 1974. Rev. by R. W. Sales, CH, 43
    (Sep 1974):415; R. Gray, JAfH, 15(Num 3 1974):524-5.

            . Chiefship in Western Tanzania. A Political History of
    the Kimbu. Oxford: Clarendon Press, 1972. Rev. by R. G.
    Abrahams, Africa, 44(Apr 1974):207-8.

Shorter, Edward. The Historian and the Computer: A Practical
    Guide. Englewood Cliffs, N.J.: Prentice-Hall, 1971. Rev.
    by P. Peebles, AHR, 79(Je 1974):751-2.

Shoufani, Elias. Al-Riddah and the Muslim Conquest of Arabia.
    Toronto: U Tor Press, 1973. Rev. by W. B. Bishai, HRNB,
    2(Sep 1974):250.

Shulman, Frank Joseph see Ward, Robert E.

Shurr, William H. The Mystery of Iniquity: Melville as Poet, 1857-
    1891. Lexington, Ky.: U Press Ky, 1972. Rev. by W. R.
    Dillingham, GR, 28(Spr 1974):154-6.

Shyllon, F. O. Black Slaves in Britain. New York: Ox U Press,
    1974. Rev. by N. Lederer, HRNB, 2(Sep 1974):243-4.

Sibley, Marilyn McAdams. George W. Brackenridge: Maverick
    Philanthropist. Austin: U Tx Press, 1973. Rev. by A. J.
    Mayer, BHR, 48(Spr 1974):130-1; B. D. Ledbetter, CWH, 20
    (Je 1974):178-9; J. O. King, ETHJ, 12(Fall 1974):85-6; J. F.
    Wall, JAH, 61(Sep 1974):486-7; R. Holland, JOW, 13(Apr 1974):
    138; R. S. Maxwell, JSH, 40(May 1974):350-1; R. W. Strick-
    land, WHQ, 5(Oct 1974):458-9.

Sidel, Ruth. Women and Child Care in China. Baltimore: Penguin,
    1973. Rev. by L. E. Collins, JAS, 33(Aug 1974):705-6.

Sider, Ronald J. Andreas Bodenstein Von Karlstadt: The Develop-
    ment of His Thought, 1517-1525. Leiden, Netherlands: E. J.
    Brill, 1974. Rev. by K. H. Dannenfeldt, HRNB, 3(Nov/Dec
    1974):31-2.

Sidney, Phillip. The Countess of Pembroke's Arcadia. (The Old
    Arcadia). Ed. by Jean Robertson. Oxford: Clarendon Press,
    1973. Rev. by F. B. Williams, Jr., RQ, 27(Sum 1974):237-
    42.

Sidorsky, David, ed. The Future of the Jewish Community in Amer-

SIEBURG   332

ica. New York: Basic Books, n. d.   Rev. by A. Mintz, Commentary, 58(Aug 1974):74-5.

Sieburg, Hans-Otto, ed. Napoleon und Europa. Cologne: Kiepen-
heuer and Witsch, 1971. Rev. by G. Ellis, EHR, 89(Apr
1974):450-1.

Siedentopf, Heinrich B., et al. Tiryus. Forschungen und Berichte.
Band VI. Mainz am Rhein: Verlag Philipp Von Zabern, 1973.
Rev. by J. Rutter, AJA, 78(Oct 1974):436-8.

Siegel, Bernard J., Alan R. Beals, and Stephen A. Tyler, ed. Annual Review of Anthropology, Vol. 1. Palo Alto, Calif.: Annual Reviews, 1972. Rev. by R. F. G. Spier, T & C, 15(Ja
1974):156.

Siegel, J., ed. see Holt, C., ed.

Sievers, Harry J., ed. Six Presidents from the Empire State.
Tarrytown, N. Y.: Sleepy Hollow Restorations, 1974. Rev.
by K. E. Shewmaker, HRNB, 3(Sep 1974):254-5.

Sigelschiffer, Saul. The American Conscience: The Drama of the
Lincoln-Douglas Debates. New York: Horizon, 1973. Rev.
by R. A. Heckman, CWH, 20(Je 1974):174-6; E. D. Elbert,
IMH, 70(Dec 1974):355-6; W. D. Mallam, JAH, 61(Dec 1974):
782-3; D. Wells, JSH, 40(Aug 1974):483-4.

Sigmann, Jean. 1848: The Romantic and Democratic Revolutions
in Europe. New York: Harper and Row, 1973. Rev. by
W. L. Langer, AHR, 79(Apr 1974):507-8.

Sih, Paul K. T., ed. Taiwan in Modern Times. New York: St.
John's U Press, 1973. Rev. by S. C. Chu, Historian, 36
(May 1974):557-8; N. R. Miner, JAS, 33(Feb 1974):307-9.

Sihanouk, Norodom. My War with the CIA: Cambodia's Fight for
Survival. London: Allen Lane, Penguin, 1973. Rev. by
D. P. Chandler, JAS, 33(Feb 1974):336-7.

Silber, Irwin, comp. and ed. Songs of Independence. Harrisburg,
Pa.: Stackpole, 1973. Rev. by J. W. Molnar, VMHB, 82
(Apr 1974):196-7.

Silberschlag, Elsig. From Renaissance to Renaissance: Hebrew
Literature from 1492-1970. New York: KTAV, 1973. Rev.
by F. Rosenthal, HRNB, 2(Mar 1974):122-3.

Siler, David W., comp. The Eastern Cherokees. n. p.: Polyanthos, n. d. Rev. by Staff, InH, 7(Sum 1974):58-9.

Silet, Charles L. P. see Gottesman, Ronald

Silhouettes on the Shade: Images from the 50's Reexamined. Mun-
cie, Ind.: Ball St. U, 1973. Rev. by G. S. Jowett, JAH,
61(Je 1974):254-5.

Sillery, Anthony. Botswana. A Short Political History. London:
Methuen, 1974. Rev. by Q. N. Parsons, JAfH, 15(Num 3
1974):493-5.

Silva, Hélio. O ciclo de Vargas. Vol. XI. 1939: Véspera de
guerra. Rio de Janeiro: Editôra Civilização Brasileira, 1972.
Rev. by H. H. Keith, HAHR, 54(Nov 1974):722-3; T. S. Ches-
ton, TAm, 31(Oct 1974):223.

_____. O ciclo de Vargas. Vol. XII. 1942. Guerra no con-
tinente. Rio de Janeiro: Editôra Civilização Brasileira. Rev.
by H. H. Keith, HAHR, 54(Nov 1974):722-3.

Silverman, Saul, ed. Lenin. Englewood Cliffs, N. J.: Prentice-
Hall, 1972. Rev. by T. U. Raun, HT, 7(Feb 1974):290-1.

Simmonds, James D. Masques of God: Form and Theme in the
Poetry of Henry Vaughn. Pittsburgh: U Pitt Press, 1972.
Rev. by H. M. Richmond, RQ, 27(Fall 1974):381-2.

Simmons, William Cranton. Cautantowwit's House: An Indian Buri-
al Ground on the Island of Conanicut in Narragansett Bay.
Providence, R.I.: Brown U Press, 1970. Rev. by A. G.
Postron, AmAnt, 39(Jl 1974):516.

Simmons, William Hayne. Notices of East Florida. Gainesville:
U Fla Press, 1973. Rev. by J. F. Smith, GHQ, 58(Supp
1974):217-18.

Simms, J. G. see Moody, T. W.

Simon, John Y., ed. The Papers of Ulysses S. Grant. Volume 4:
January 8-March 31, 1862. Carbondale: S Ill U Press, 1972.
Rev. by E. C. Bearss, RKHS, 72(Apr 1974):178-80.

_____, ed. The Papers of Ulysses S. Grant. Volume 5: April
1-August 31, 1862. Carbondale: S Ill U Press, 1973. Rev.
by F. D. Williams, IMH, 70(Sep 1974):259-60; W. W. Hassler,
Jr., JSH, 40(Nov 1974):666-7.

Simonis, Udo Ernst and Heide, eds. Socio-Economic Development
in Dual Economies: The Example of Zambia. München: Welt-
form Verlag, 1971. Rev. by C. Ehrlich, AfAf, 73(Jl 1974):
378-9.

Simpson, Colin. The Lusitania. Boston: Little, Brown, 1973.
Rev. by T. A. Bailey, AHR, 79(Feb 1974):114-15.

Simpson, John Eddins. Howell Cobb: The Politics of Ambition.

Chicago: Adams, 1973. Rev. by D. E. Meerse, CWH, 20(Je
1974):182-3; J. C. Bonner, GHQ, 58(Spr 1974):119-20; H. C.
Ferrell, Jr., HRNB, 2(Mar 1974):126-7; J. H. Schroeder,
JSH, 40(Nov 1974):663-4.

Simpson, Lewis P. The Man of Letters in New England and the
South: Essays on the History of the Literary Vocation in
America. Baton Rouge: LSU Press, 1973. Rev. by A. C.
Land, AHR, 79(Feb 1974):217-18; E. W. Hirshberg, FHQ, 53
(Oct 1974):219-20; D. Flower, NEQ, 47(Sept 1974):478-80.

Simpson, William Kelly. The Terrace of the Great God at Abydos.
New Haven, Conn.: Yale U, 1974. Rev. by J. D. Cooney,
AJA, 78(Oct 1974):433-4.

_____. see Dunham, Dows

Sinclair-Stevenson, Christopher. Inglorious Rebellion: The Jacobite
Risings of 1708, 1715, and 1719. New York: St. Martin's,
1972. Rev. by J. Collins, Historian, 36(Feb 1974):320.

Sinel, Allen. The Classroom and the Chancellery: State Educational Reform in Russia Under Count Dmitry Tolstoi. Cambridge,
Mass.: Har U Press, 1973. Rev. by T. G. Stavrou, HRNB,
2(Feb 1974):106-7.

Singh, Fauja, ed. History of the Punjab (A. D. 1000-1526). Pa-
tiala: Punjabi U, 1972. Rev. by B. Ramusack, JAS, 33(Aug
1974):721-2.

Singh, S. Nihal. Malaysia--A Commentary. New York: Barnes
and Noble, 1972. Rev. by R. O. Tilman, JAS, 33(Feb 1974):
333-4.

Siracusa, Joseph M. New Left Diplomatic Histories and Historians:
The American Revisionists. Port Washington, N. Y.: Kennikat, 1973. Rev. by F. L. Loewenheim, JAH, 61(Je 1974):
250-1; E. N. Paolino, HT, 8(Nov 1974):147-8; V. A. Lapomarda, MiA, 56(Ja 1974):62-4; R. W. Leopold, PHR, 43(Nov
1974):629-31.

Sirinelli, Jean and Edouard des Places. Eusèbe de Césarée, La
Préparation Evangélique. 1. Paris: Editions du Cerf, 1974.
Rev. by E. TeSellf, CH, 43(Dec 1974):531-2.

Sirsikar, V. M. Sovereigns Without Crowns: A Behavioral Analysis of the Indian Electoral Process. Bombay: Popular Prakashan, 1973. Rev. by W. G. Vanderbok, JAS, 33(Aug 1974):
725-6.

Sisson, Richard. The Congress Party in Rajasthan: Political Integration and Institution Building in an Indian State. Berkeley:
U Cal Press, 1972. Rev. by W. H. Morris-Jones, MAS, 8(Jl
1974):419-22.

Sitney, P. Adams. Visionary Film: the American Avant-Garde.
New York: Oxford U Press, 1974. Rev. by J. Heddle, WMH,
58(Aut 1974):61-3.

Sjöqvist, Erik. Sicily and the Greeks: Studies in the Interrelationship Between the Indigenous Populations and the Greek Colonists. Ann Arbor: U Mich Press, 1973. Rev. by A. P. Miller, AHR, 79(Je 1974):762.

Skaba, A. D. The Paris Peace Conference and Foreign Intervention
in the Country of the Soviets (January-June 1919). Kiev: Izdatel'stvo "Naukova Dumka," 1971. Rev. by J. A. White,
AHR, 79(Apr 1974):549-51.

Skaggs, David Curtis. Roots of Maryland Democracy, 1753-1776.
Westport, Conn.: Greenwood, 1973. Rev. by G. E. Hartda-
gen, JAH, 61(Sep 1974):466-7; B. E. Steiner, JSH, 40(May
1974):298-300; E. C. Papenfuse, MHM, 69(Fall 1974):329-30;
J. A. Nevenschwander, WMH, 57(Sum 1974):314-15; J. Haw,
WMQ-3, 31(Apr 1974):322-3.

Skaggs, Jimmy M. The Cattle-Trailing Industry: Between Supply
and Demand, 1866-1890. Lawrence: U Press Kan, 1973.
Rev. by W. H. Hutchinson, A & W, 16(Spr 1974):76-7; W. T.
Jackson, AHR, 79(Oct 1974):1270; J. L. Bernardi, BHR, 48
(Sum 1974):258-60; P. M. Edwards, CoMag, 51(Sum 1974):
258-60; R. M. Taylor, GPJ, 13(Spr 1974):207-8; J. B. Frantz,
JAH, 61(Je 1974):213-14; M. Walsh, JAmS, 8(Aug 1974):267-
70; G. G. Suggs, Jr., JOW, 13(Jl 1974):127-8; W. H. Lyon,
JSH, 40(May 1974):327-8.

_____, Ferne Downes, and Winifred Vigness, eds. Chronicles
of the Yaqui Expedition. Lubbock, Tx.: West Texas Museum
Assn., 1972. Rev. by F. M. Hillary, A & W, 16(Spr 1974):
72-3; R. L. Beals, NMHR, 49(Apr 1974):181-2.

Skeat, W. O. George Stephenson: the Engineer and His Letters.
London: Institution of Mech. Engineers, 1973. Rev. by
L. T. C. Polt, T & C, 15(Oct 1974):639-41.

Skidmore, Thomas E. Black into White: Race and Nationality in
Brazilian Thought. New York: Ox U Press, 1974. Rev. by
F. Safford, HRNB, 3(Nov/Dec 1974):40.

Sklar, Kathryn Kish. Catherine Beecher: A Study in American
Domesticity. New Haven, Conn.: Yale U Press, 1973. Rev.
by E. S. Godbold, Jr., AHR, 79(Oct 1974):1263-4; S. R.
Bland, HRNB, 3(Nov/Dec 1974):44; J. S. Elamere, IMH, 70
(Je 1974):187-9; W. L. O'Neill, JAH, 61(Je 1974):185-7; J.
Matlack, NYHSQ, 58(Jl 1974):249-50.

Sklar, Robert, ed. The Plastic Age, 1917-1930. New York:
George Braziller, 1971. Rev. by R. Muccigrosso, HT, 8
(Nov 1974):130-1.

Skotheim, Robert Allen see McGiffert, Michael

Skrine, C. P. and Pamela Nightingale. Macartney at Kashgar: New Light on British, Chinese and Russian Activities in Sinkiang, 1890-1918. London: Methuen, 1973. Rev. by G. J. Adler, History, 59(Je 1974):319-20; H. A. McFarlin, JAS, 33 691-2.

Skutch, Alexander F. A Naturalist in Costa Rica. Gainesville: U Fla Press, 1971. Rev. by C. L. Stansifer, HAHR, 54(May 1974):350-1.

Slack, Paul see Clark, Peter

Slaght, Lawrence T. Multiplying the Witness: 150 Years of American Baptist Educational Ministries. Valley Forge, Pa.: Judson Press, 1974. Rev. by A. R. Meredith, CH, 43(Dec 1974): 553-4.

Slate, Sam J. Satan's Back Yard. Garden City, N. Y.: Doubleday, 1974. Rev. by P. E. Borries, RKHS, 72(Oct 1974):407-8.

Slavin, Arthur J., ed. Tudor Men and Institutions. Baton Rouge: La St U Press, 1972. Rev. by J. P. Cooper, RQ, 27(Spr 1974):78-80.

Slaymaker, S. R., II. Captive's Mansion: An American Family Chronicle Covering Nine Generations and 200 Years in a Pennsylvania Rural Manor. New York: Harper & Row, 1973. Rev. by J. A. Andrew, III, PH, 41(Jl 1974):362-4.

Slim, H. Colin. A Gift of Madrigals and Motets. Chicago: U Chi Press, 1972. Rev. by J. Haar, RQ, 27(Sum 1974):225-7.

Sloan, Douglas, ed. The Great Awakening and American Education: A Documentary History. New York: Teachers College, 1973. Rev. by C. C. Goen, JAH, 61(Je 1974):161-2.

Sloane, Eric. School Days. 2 vols. Garden City, N. Y.: Doubleday, 1972. Rev. by E. B. Howard, RKHS, 72(Ja 1974):64-6.

Slotkin, Richard. Regeneration Through Violence: The Mythology of the American Frontier, 1600-1860. Middletown, Conn.: Wes U Press, 1973. Rev. by R. S. Kramer, CoMag, 51(Win 1974):81-3; P. T. Nolan, JOW, 13(Jl 1974):112; I. H. Bartlett, NEQ, 47(Mar 1974):145-8; R. H. Pearce, PHR, 43(Feb 1974):111-12; L. S. Peterson, WHQ, 5(Jl 1974):72-3; D. Grimsted, WMQ-3, 31(Ja 1974):143-6.

Slotten, Martha Calvert see Sellers, Charles Coleman

Slusser, Robert M. The Berlin Crisis of 1961: Soviet-American Relations and the Struggle for Power in the Kremlin, June-

November **1961**. Baltimore: JHU Press, 1973. Rev. by K.
Eubank, JAH, 61(Je 1974):255-6.

Smalley, Beryl. The Becket Conflict and the Schools: A Study of
Intellectuals in Politics. Totowa, N. J.: Rowman and Littlefield, 1973. Rev. by R. B. Patterson, AHR, 79(Apr 1973):
495-6.

Smalley, Orange A. and Frederick D. Sturdivant. The Credit Merchants: A History of Spiegel, Inc. Carbondale: S Ill U
Press, 1973. Rev. by M. G. Blackford, BHR, 48(Spr 1974):
133-5; S. H. Steinberg, JAH, 61(Je 1974):223-4; J. L. Weston,
JISHS, 67(Nov 1974):560-1.

Smiley, Nixon. Crowder Tales. Miami: E. A. Seeman, 1973.
Rev. by W. Blassingame, FHQ, 53(Oct 1974):201-2.

Smith, Alan G. R. Science and Society in the Sixteenth and Seventeenth Centuries. London: Thames and Hudson, 1972. Rev.
by C. Webster, EHR, 89(Apr 1974):435; A. E. Best, History,
59(Je 1974):268-9.

_____, ed. The Reign of James VI and I. London: Macmillan,
1973. Rev. by D. Hirst, HJ, 17(Num 3 1974):658-60; M.
Lee, Jr., HRNB, 2(Apr 1974):139.

Smith, Alan and Henry G. Abbott. The Lancashire Watch Company,
1889-1910.... Fitzwilliam, N. H.: Ken Roberts, 1973. Rev.
by E. H. Parkhurst, Jr., T & C, 15(Jl 1974):505-6.

Smith, Alice E. The History of Wisconsin. Volume I: From Exploration to Statehood. Madison: St Historical Soc., Wisconsin, 1973. Rev. by D. Chaput, CoMag, 51(Sum 1974):242-3;
D. L. Smith, IMH, 70(Mar 1974):78-9; D. F. Carmony, JAH,
61(Je 1974):178-9; D. R. Wrone, JISHS, 67(Sep 1974):448-9;
F. C. Luebke, MiA, 56(Apr 1974):130; P. D. Jordan, NH,
55(Sum 1974):304-6; C. M. Hinsley, Jr., PH, 41(Je 1974):
367-9; G. L. Prescott, PHR, 43(Aug 1974):416-17; K. Richards, PNQ, 65(Oct 1974):189-90.

Smith, B. see Constable, G.

Smith, C. N., ed. see Taille, Jean de la

Smith, Clifford Neal. Federal Land Series. 2 vols. Chicago:
American Library Assn., 1972. Rev. by E. E. Hill, AmArc,
37(Ja 1974):87-9.

Smith, Courtland L. The Salt River Project: A Case Study in Cultural Adaptation to an Urbanizing Community. Tucson: U
Arizona Press, 1972. Rev. by P. A. Kalisch, WHQ, 5(Oct
1974):485-6.

Smith, David C. A History of Lumbering in Maine, 1861-1960.
Orono: U Me Press, 1972. Rev. by G. Porter, AHR, 79
(Apr 1974):594-5.

Smith, David Horton. Latin American Student Activism: Participation in Formal Volunteer Organizations by University Students
in Six Latin Cultures. Lexington, Mass.: Lexington Books,
1973. Rev. by W. S. Tuohy, HAHR, 54(Nov 1974):727-8.

Smith, Denis. Gentle Patriot: A Political Biography of Walter
Gordon. Edmonton, Atla.: Hurtig, 1973. Rev. by N. Ward,
CHR, 55(Sep 1974):307-12.

Smith, Denis Mack. Victor Emmanuel, Cavour, and the Risorgimento. London: Ox U Press, 1971. Rev. by G. Verucci,
JMH, 46(Je 1974):356-8.

Smith, Duane A. Horace Tabor: His Life and the Legend. Boulder, Colo.: Associated U Press, 1973. Rev. by H. Kelsey,
CoMag, 51(Spr 1974):166-8; J. M. Skaggs, Historian, 36(Aug
1974):784-5; R. H. Peterson, JAH, 61(Je 1974):216-17; J. L.
Dodson, JOW, 13(Jl 1974):119; R. W. Larson, NMHR, 49(Jan
1974):85-6; M. Stonehouse, WHQ, 5(Jl 1974):362-4.

_____. Rocky Mountain Mining Camps: The Urban Frontier.
Lincoln: U Neb Press, 1974. Rev. by R. C. Black, JOW,
13(Jl 1974):122.

Smith, Elizabeth Wiley. The History of Hancock County, Georgia.
2 vols. Washington, Ga.: Wilkes, 1974. Rev. by B. D.
Stanley, GHQ, 58(Supp 1974):218-19.

Smith, Elwyn A., ed. The Religion of the Republic. Philadelphia:
Fortress, 1971. Rev. by W. Smith, AHR, 79(Feb 1974):215-
16.

Smith, Eric. Some Versions of the Fall: The Myth of the Fall of
Man in English Literature. Pittsburgh: U Pittsburgh Press,
1973. Rev. by R. H. West, Gr, 28(Sum 1974):374-5.

Smith, Erwin E. see Haley, J. Evetts. Life on the Texas Range.

Smith, Eugenia B. Centreville, Virginia: Its History and Architecture. Fairfax, Va.: Fairfax Office of Planning, 1973. Rev.
by R. A. Murdock, VMHB, 82(Apr 1974):208.

Smith, Gaddis. Dean Acheson. New York: Cooper Square, 1972.
Rev. by R. J. Maddox, CHR, 55(Sep 1974):347-8; F. J. Dobney, PHR, 43(Nov 1974):628-9.

Smith, Gene. The Horns of the Moon: A Short Biography of Adolf
Hitler. New York: Charterhouse, 1974. Rev. by R. W.
Lougee, HRNB, 2(Sep 1974):246.

_____. Maximilian and Carlota, a Tale of Romance and Tragedy. n. p.: William Morrow, n. d. Rev. by M. B. Stiles, Mankind, 4(Aug 1974):63-4.

Smith, Geoffrey S. To Save a Nation: American Countersubversives, the New Deal, and the Coming of World War II. New York: Basic Books, 1973. Rev. by W. F. Kimball, HRNB, 2(Ja 1974):65-6; W. M. Tuttle, Jr., JAH, 61(Sep 1974):533-4; W. S. Cole, JSH, 40(Feb 1974):160-1.

Smith, George L. Religion and Trade in New Netherland: Dutch Origins and American Development. Ithaca, N. Y.: Cornell U Press, 1973. Rev. by P. S. Onuf, BHR, 48(Win 1974): 545-7; G. F. De Jong, CH, 43(Je 1974):278-9; E. Anderson, HRNB, 2(Mar 1974):134; C. R. Boxer, JAH, 61(Sep 1974):457-8; G. Weaver, NYH, 55(Jl 1974):333-4.

Smith, H. Shelton. In His Image, But ...: Racism in Southern Religion, 1780-1910. Durham: Duke U Press, 1972. Rev. by P. M. Hannan, LaH, 15(Sum 1974):311-3.

Smith, Helen C. and George Swetnam. Hannah's Town. Cleveland: Dillon, Liederbach, 1973. Rev. by Str. M. Walsh, WPHM, 57(Ja 1974):109-10.

Smith, Iain R. The Emin Pasha Relief Expedition, 1886-1890. Oxford: Ox U Press, 1972. Rev. by R. Gray, History, 59(Je 1974):312-13; C. Oliver, JAfH, 15(Num 2 1974):350.

Smith, Irving H., ed. Trotsky. Englewood Cliffs, N. J.: Prentice-Hall, 1973. Rev. by J. H. Montemerlo, HT, 7(Feb 1974): 291-2.

Smith, John Holland. Joan of Arc. New York: Scribner's, 1973. Rev. by A. R. Lewis, HRNB, 2(Ja 1974):83.

Smith, Julia Floyd. Slavery and Plantation Growth in Antebellum Florida, 1821-1860. Gainesville: U Fla Press, 1973. Rev. by S. L. Engerman, BHR, 48(Spr 1974):127-8; J. C. Bonner, GHQ, 58(Supp 1974):207-8; J. W. Blassingame, JAH, 61(Je 1974):179-80; J. G. Taylor, JSH, 40(Feb 1974):134-5.

Smith, Mary Elizabeth. Picture Writing from Ancient Southern Mexico: Mixtec Place Signs and Maps. Norman: U Okla Press, 1973. Rev. by C. E. Dibble, WHQ, 5(Oct 1974):470-1.

Smith, Michael Llewellyn. Ionian Vision: Greece in Asia Minor, 1919-1922. New York: St. Martin's, 1973. Rev. by J. E. Rexine, HRNB, 2(Mar 1974):124-5.

Smith, Myron J., Jr. American Civil War Navies: A Bibliography. Metuchen, N. J.: Scarecrow, 1972. Rev. by R. E. Johnson, CWH, 20(Mar 1974):72-3; F. L. Owsley, Jr., JISHS, 67(Je 1974):356-7.

Smith, Paul, ed. Lord Salisbury on Politics: A Selection from His Articles in the Quarterly Review, 1860-1883. Cambridge: Cam U Press, 1972. Rev. by H. H. Winkler, Historian, 36 (Feb 1974):324-5.

Smith, Paul H., comp. English Defenders of American Freedoms, 1774-1778: Six Pamphlets Attacking British Policy. Washington: Library of Congress, 1972. Rev. by J. A. Ernst, CHR, 55(Sep 1974):335-6; J. K. Martin, PH, 41(Apr 1974):226-7.

Smith, Peter H. see Graham, Richard

Smith, Philip Chadwick Foster, ed. see Bowen, Ashley

Smith, Richard K. First Across! The U.S. Navy's Transatlantic Flight of 1919. Annapolis: Naval Institute Press, 1973. Rev. by R. Higham, JAH, 60(Mar 1974):1168-9.

Smith, Roger M., ed. Southeast Asia: Documents of Political Development and Change. Ithaca, N.Y.: Cornell U Press, 1974. Rev. by J. F. Cady, HRNB, 3(Nov/Dec 1974):35.

Smith, Stephen. The City That Was. Metuchen, N.J.: Scarecrow Reprint, 1973. Rev. by D. R. Jamieson, NYHSQ, 58(Jl 1974): 248.

Smith, Susan see Dean, Jill. Wisconsin: A State for all Seasons.

_____. see Mead, Howard. Portrait of the Past.

Smith, Van Mitchell see DeBoe, David C.

Smith, W. H. C. Napoleon III. New York: St. Martin's, 1973. Rev. by G. Wright, AHR, 79(Oct 1974):1191; R. W. Reichert, Historian, 36(Aug 1974):756-7; B. D. Gooch, JMH, 46(Sep 1974):551-2.

Smith, Warren H. Hobart and William Smith: the History of Two Colleges. Geneva, N.Y.: Hobart and William Smith Colleges Press, 1972. Rev. by D. C. Smith, NYH, 55(Jl 1974):341-2.

Smith, William, Jr. The History of the Province of New York. Ed. by Michael Kammen. Volume I: From the First Discovery to the Year 1732. Volume II: A Continuation, 1732-1762. Cambridge: Harvard U Press, 1972. Rev. by S. B. Kim, NYHSQ, 58(Ja 1974):57-8.

Smith, Wilson, ed. Theories of Education in Early America, 1655-1819. Indianapolis: Bobbs-Merrill, 1972. Rev. by C. W. Albers, HT, 7(Feb 1974):314-15.

Smock, Audrey C. Ibo Politics: The Role of Ethnic Unions in Eastern Nigeria. Cambridge, Mass.: Har U Press, 1971.

Rev. by G. L. Jones, Africa, 44(Apr 1974):200-1.

Smock, Raymond W. see Harlan, Louis R. The Booker T. Washington Papers.

Smolansky, Oles M. The Soviet Union and the Arab East Under Khrushchev. Lewisburg, Pa.: Bucknell U Press, 1974. Rev. by S. D. Spector, HRNB, 2(May/Je 1974):182-3.

Smythe, Donald. Guerrilla Warrior: The Early Life of John J. Pershing. New York: Scribner's, 1973. Rev. by T. R. Stone, 79(Oct 1974):1276-7; E. M. Coffman, JAH, 60(Mar 1974):1159-60; M. Van Kekerix, N H, 55(Sum 1974):299-300; F. J. Munch, PHR, 43(Feb 1974):135-6; J. B. Romney, WHQ, 5(Ja 1974):76-7.

Snelling, Lois. Coin Harvey, Prophet of Monte Ne. Point Lookout, Mo.: C of O Press, 1973. Rev. by M. D. Hudgins, ArkHQ, 33(Aug 1974):267-9.

Snetsinger, John. Truman, the Jewish Vote and the Creation of Israel. Stanford, Cal.: Hoover Institution Press, 1974. Rev. by A. Theoharis, HRNB, 2(May/Je 1974):164.

Snodgrass, A. M. The Dark Age of Greece. Edinburgh: Edinburgh U Press, 1971. Rev. by M. I. Finley, EHR, 89(Ja 1974):143.

Snyder, Eugene E. Skidmore's Portland: His Fountain and Its Sculptor. Portland, Ore.: Binfords & Mort, 1973. Rev. by P. Knuth, OrHQ, 75(Mar 1974):83.

Snyder, John P. The Mapping of New Jersey: The Men and the Art. New Brunswick, N.J.: Rutgers U Press, 1973. Rev. by L. De Vorsey, JAH, 61(Je 1974):155-6.

Snyder, Louis, ed. The Dreyfus Case: A Documentary History. New Brunswick, N.J.: Rutgers U Press, 1973. Rev. by R. R. Locke, HT, 7(Aug 1974):643-4.

Sobel, Robert. The Age of Giant Corporations: A Microeconomic History of American Business 1914-1970. Westport, Conn.: Greenwood, 1972. Rev. by A. M. Johnson, JAH, 60(Mar 1974):1164-5; G. Porter, T & C, 15(Ja 1974):119-21.

————. Conquest and Conscience: The 1840's. New York: Crowell, 1971. Rev. by D. T. Zimmer, BHR, 48(Sum 1974): 250-1.

————. The Money Manias: The Eras of Great Speculation in America, 1770-1970. New York: Weybright and Talley, 1974. Rev. by P. F. Erwin, HRNB, 2(Aug 1974):216; F. McDonald, MHM, 69(Sum 1974):240.

Sochen, June. Movers and Shakers: American Woman Thinkers and Activists, 1900-1970. New York: Quadrangle, 1973. Rev. by K. K. Sklar, JAH, 61(Dec 1974):821-2.

_____. The New Woman in Greenwich Village, 1910-1920. New York: Quadrangle, 1972. Rev. by C. N. Degler, CHR, 55 (Je 1974):224-6.

Socolofsky, Homer and Huber Self. Historical Atlas of Kansas. Norman: U Okla Press, 1972. Rev. by L. E. Oliva, PHR, 43(May 1974):275-6.

Soechting, Dirk. Die Porträts des Septimius Severus. Bonn: Rudolf Habelt, 1972. Rev. by A. M. McCann, AJA, 78(Apr 1974):206-8.

Solaún, Mauricio and Michael A. Quinn. Sinners and Heretics: The Politics of Military Intervention in Latin America. Chicago: U Ill Press, 1973. Rev. by D. Ronfeldt, HAHR, 54 (Nov 1974):725-7; K. J. Grieb, TAm, 31(Jl 1974):106-7.

Solomon, Richard H. Mao's Revolution and the Chinese Political Culture. Berkeley: U Cal Press, 1971. Rev. by G. A. de-Vos, MAS, 8(Ja 1974):113-26.

Solow, Mrs. Barbara Lewis. The Land Question and the Irish Economy 1870-1903. Cambridge, Mass.: Har U Press, 1972. Rev. by E. D. Steele, EHR, 89(Ja 1974):226-7.

Solyom, Garrett and Bronwen. Textiles of the Indonesian Archipelago. Honolulu: U Press Hawaii, 1973. Rev. by M. Gittinger, JAS, 33(Aug 1974):740-1.

Somers, Dale A. The Rise of Sports in New Orleans. Baton Rouge: La St U Press, 1972. Rev. by W. H. Adams, LaH, 15(Spr 1974):206.

Somerville, Robert. The Councils of Urban II. Volume 1: Decreta Claromontensia. Amsterdam: Adolf M. Hakkert, 1972. Rev. by R. Luman, CH, 43(Mar 1974):100.

Sonnichsen, C. L. Colonel Greene and the Copper Skyrocket. Tucson: U Ariz Press, 1974. Rev. by R. Lenon, JAriH, 15 (Win 1974):396-7.

Sonnino, Sidney. Diario 1866-1912. Vol. I. Lawrence: U Press Kan, n.d. Rev. by C. F. Delzell, HRNB, 3(Nov/Dec 1974): 28-9.

_____. Diario 1914-1916. Vol. II. Lawrence: U Press Kan, n.d. Rev. by C. F. Delzell, HRNB, 3(Nov/Dec 1974):28-9.

_____. Diario 1916-1922. Vol. III. Lawrence: U Press Kan,

n. d.   Rev. by C. F. Delzell, HRNB, 3(Nov/Dec 1974):28-9.

_____. Scritti E Discorsi Extraparlamentari, 1870-1920.   2 vols.
Lawrence: U Press Kan, n. d.   Rev. by C. F. Delzell, HRNB,
3(Nov/Dec 1974):28-9.

Sontag, Frederick and John K. Roth.   The American Religious Experience: the Roots, Trends, and Future of Theology.   New
York: Harper & Row, 1972.   Rev. by P. A. Carter, NDH,
41(Fall 1974):30-1.

Sorensen, Mary see Brooke, John.   The Prime Ministers' Papers.

Sørensen, Per and Tove Hatting.   Archaeological Excavations in
Thailand.   Vol. II.   Copenhagen: Munksgaard, 1967.   Rev.
by G. de G. Sieveking, Antiquity, 48(Je 1974):149-151.

Sorin, Gerald.   Abolitionism: A New Perspective.   New York:
Praeger, 1972.   Rev. by J. H. Silbey, JAH, 60(Mar 1974):
1119-20.

Sourdel, D. see Folz, R.

Southgate, Donald, ed.   The Conservative Leadership, 1832-1932.
London: Macmillan, n. d.   Rev. by A. O'Day, 24(Dec 1974):
884-5.

Southwell, Robert.   Two Letters and Short Rules of a Good Life.
Charlottesville: U Press Va, 1973.   Rev. by L. D. Snyder,
CH, 43(Mar 1974):112-13.

The Soviet Economy in the Period of the Great Fatherland War,
1941-1945.   (Sovetskaia ekonomika v period Velikoi Otechest-
vennoi voiny 1941-1945.)   Moscow: Nauka, 1970.   Rev. by
S. Lieberstein, T & C, 15(Ja 1974):122-5.

Spadolini, Giovanni, ed.   Il Cardinale Gasparri e la Questione Romans (con brani delle Memorie inedite).   Florence: Le Mon-
nier, 1972.   Rev. by H. Hearder, EHR, 89(Jl 1974):692.

Spae, Joseph J.   Shinto Man.   Tokyo: Oriens Institute for Religious
Research, 1972.   Rev. by H. B. Earhart, JAS, 33(Aug 1974):
706-8.

Spann, Edward K.   Ideals & Politics: New York Intellectuals and
Liberal Democracy, 1820-1880.   Albany: SUNY, Press, 1972.
Rev. by F. Somkin, JAH, 61(Je 1974):176-7.

Spanos, Peter Z.   Untersuchung über den bei Homer "Depas Amphikypellon" Genannten Gefässtypus.   Tübingen: Ernst Wasmuth,
1972.   Rev. by J. D. Carpenter, AJA, 78(Ja 1974):90-2.

Speck, Ernest B., ed.   Mody Boatright, Folklorist: A Collection

of Essays.   Austin: U Tx Press, 1973.   Rev. by C. Potter,
ETHJ, 12(Spr 1974):75-6; A. E. Fife, WHQ, 5(Jl 1974):339-
40.

Spence, Jonathan D.   Emperor of China: Self-Portrait of K'ang-hsi.
New York: Knopf, 1974.   Rev. by J. Dardess, HRNB, 2(Sep
1974):249.

Spence, Mary Lee and Donald Jackson, eds.   The Expeditions of
John Charles Fremont.   Volume 2, The Bear Flag Revolt and
the Court-Martial.   Urbana: U Ill Press, 1973.   Rev. by
W. R. Jacobs, HRNB, 2(Jl 1974):191-2; J. E. Sunder, JAH,
61(Dec 1974):780-1; K. M. Johnson, JOW, 13(Apr 1974):122.

Spencer, Joseph E.   Oriental Asia: Themes Toward a Geography.
Englewood Cliffs, N.J.: Prentice-Hall, 1973.   Rev. by J. A.
Hafner, JAS, 33(Aug 1974):730-2.

Spencer, Romulus Sanderson, Jr.   see   Swindell, Martha Rebecca

Spengler, Joseph J.   Indian Economic Thought: A Preface to Its
History.   Durham, N.C.: Duke U Press, 1971.   Rev. by
M. F. Franda, JAAS, 9(Ja & Apr 1974):105-6.

Spicer, Edward H.   Cycles of Conquest: The Impact of Spain, Mexico and the United States on the Indians of the Southwest, 1533-
1960.   Tucson: U Ariz Press, 1972.   Rev. by P. A. Kalisch,
ChOk, 52(Fall 1974):376.

_____ and Raymond H. Thompson, eds.   Plural Society in the
Southwest.   New York: Interbook, 1972.   Rev. by J. P.
Bloom, A & W, 16(Spr 1974):65-6; B. A. Glasrud, JOW, 13
(Ja 1974):146; M. P. Servin, TAm, 30(Apr 1974):557-9.

Spinner, Thomas J., Jr.   George Joachim Goschen: The Transformation of a Victorian Liberal.   New York: Cam U Press,
1973.   Rev. by B. McGill, AHR, 79(Oct 1974):1181.

Spinolo, Antonio de.   Portugal e o Futuro.   Lisbon: Arcadia, 1974.
Rev. by W. G. Clarence-Smith, AfAf, 73(Jl 1974):374-6.

Spoehr, Alexander.   Zamboanga and Sulu: An Archaeological Approach to Ethnic Diversity.   Pittsburgh: U Pittsburgh, 1973.
Rev. by K. L. Hutterer, JAS, 34(Nov 1974):258-60.

Sprague, Marshall.   So Vast, So Beautiful a Land: Louisiana and
the Purchase.   Boston: Little, Brown, 1974.   Rev. by J.
Levin, HRNB, 2(Jl 1974):193; H. M. Ward, JOW, 13(Oct 1974):
140.

Spriano, Paolo.   Storia del Partito comunista italiano.   3 vols.
Turin: Giulio Einaudi Editore, 1967, 1969, 1970.   Rev. by
R. Wohl, AHR, 79(Feb 1974):183-6.

Spring, Joel H.   Education and the Rise of the Corporate State.
    Boston: Beacon, 1973.   Rev. by S. J. Rosswurm, NDH, 41
    (Sum 1974):38.

Sprunger, Keith L.   The Learned Doctor William Ames: Dutch
    Backgrounds of English and American Puritanism.   Urbana:
    U Ill Press, 1972.   Rev. by T. H. Breen, AHR, 79(Je 1974):
    755-6.

Srivastava, Ashirbadi Lal.   Akbar the Great.   Vol. III.   Society
    and Culture in 16th-Century India.   Agra: Shiva Lal Agarwala,
    1973.   Rev. by B. K. Gupta, AHR, 79(Feb 1974):212-3.

Stackpole, Edouard A.   Whales and Destiny: The Rivalry Between
    America, France, and Britain for Control of the Southern
    Whale Fishery, 1785-1825.   Amherst: U Mass Press, 1972.
    Rev. by G. A. Billias, AHR, 79(Apr 1974):487-8; A. W. Cros-
    by, Jr., Historian, 36(Aug 1974):773-4; W. P. Strauss, JAH,
    60(Mar 1974):1105-6.

Staff, Washington State University Library.   Selected Manuscript Re-
    sources in Washington State University Library.   Pullman:
    Wash St U Library, 1974.   Rev. by D. L. Johnson, AmArc,
    37(Oct 1974):589-90.

Stallman, R. W.   Stephen Crane: A Critical Bibliography.   Ames:
    Ia St U Press, 1972.   Rev. by G. Monteiro, GR, 28(Fall
    1974):532-5.

Stanley, G. F. G.   Manitoba 1870: A Metis Achievement.   Winni-
    peg: U Winnipeg Press, 1972.   Rev. by D. Morton, CHR,
    55(Je 1974):192-3.

Stanley, Peter W.   A Nation in the Making: The Philippines and
    the United States, 1899-1921.   Cambridge, Mass.: Har U
    Press, 1974.   Rev. by P. W. Kennedy, HRNB, 2(Sep 1974):
    259.

Staples, Charles R.   History of Pioneer Lexington.   Lexington:
    Lexington-Fayette Historic Commission, 1974 (reprint).   Rev.
    by B. L. Mastin, RKHS, 72(Jl 1974):276-8.

Stapleton, Margaret L., comp.   The Truman and Eisenhower Years,
    1945-1960: A Selective Bibliography.   Metuchen, N.J.: Scare-
    crow Press, 1973.   Rev. by M. Burg, PNQ, 65(Jl 1974):153-
    4.

Starr, Jerold M.   see Thrall, Charles A.

Starr, Kevin.   Americans and the California Dream, 1850-1915.
    New York: Ox U Press, 1973.   Rev. by S. C. Olin, Jr.,
    A & W, 16(Spr 1974):77-8; C. Pomeroy, AHR, 79(Feb 1974):
    228-30; D. A. Williams, JAH, 60(Mar 1974):1122-3; R. A.

Burchell, JAmS, 8(Aug 1974):271-2; F. Walker, PHR, 43(Aug 1974):427-8; R. W. Etulain, WHQ, 5(Ja 1974):64-6.

Starr, Louis M. The Oral History Collection of Columbia University. New York: Oral History Research Office, 1964. Rev. by A. M. Campbell, AmArc, 37(Ja 1974):91-3.

_____. Oral History 25th Anniversary Report. New York: Oral History Research Office, 1973. Rev. by A. M. Campbell, AmArc, 37(Ja 1974):91-3.

_____. see Mason, Elizabeth B.

Starr, S. Frederick. Decentralization and Self-Government in Russia, 1830-1870. Princeton, N.J.: Prin U Press, 1973. Rev. by R. F. Leslie, History, 59(Je 1974):295-6.

Starr, Stephen Z. Colonel Grenfell's Wars: The Life of a Soldier of Fortune. Baton Rouge: LSU Press, 1971. Rev. by J. Monaghan, AHR, 79(Apr 1974):587-9.

_____. Jennison's Jayhawkers: A Civil War Cavalry Regiment and Its Commander. Baton Rouge: LSU Press, 1973. Rev. by R. F. Weigley, HRNB, 2(Jl 1974):198-9; A. Barr, JSH, 40(Nov 1974):667-8; L. Anders, MHR, 69(Oct 1974):113-15.

Stayer, James M. Anabaptists and the Sword. Lawrence, Kan.: Coronado Press, 1972. Rev. by J. H. Yoder, CH, 43(Je 1974):272-3; R. P. Liebowitz, JMH, 46(Mar 1974):122-3; S. Ozment, RQ, 27(Sum 1974):213-15.

Stearns, Peter N. 1848: The Revolutionary Tide in Europe. New York: Norton, 1974. Rev. by W. B. Kennedy, HRNB, 2(May/Je 1974):181.

Steele, Richard W. The First Offensive, 1942: Roosevelt, Marshall and the Making of American Strategy. Bloomington: Ind U Press, 1973. Rev. by H. K. Meier, HRNB, 2(Ja 1974):65; M. Blumenson, JAH, 61(Je 1974):249-50.

Stefanescu, Stefan see Barnea, Ion

Steffen, Randy. United States Military Saddles. Norman: U Okla Press, 1973. Rev. by V. E. Nelson, N H, 55(Sum 1974):309-11.

Steglich, Wolfgang, ed. Deutsche Reichstagsakten unter Kaiser Karl V. Volume 8, parts 1 and 2. Göttingen: Vandenhoeck and Ruprecht, 1970, 1971. Rev. by S. W. Rowan, AHR, 79 (Je 1974):800-1.

Stegner, Wallace. The Uneasy Chair: A Biography of Bernard DeVoto. Garden City, N.Y.: Doubleday, 1974. Rev. by P. F.

Erwin, HRNB, 2(Jl 1974):190; D. L. Lythgoe, JAH, 61(Dec 1974):825-6; E. H. Linford, UHQ, 42(Sum 1974):298-300; C. L. Sonnichsen, WHQ, 5(Jl 1974):361-2.

Stein, Walter J. California and the Dust Bowl Migration. Westport, Conn.: Greenwood, 1974. Rev. by G. B. Dodds, AHR, 79 (Je 1974):898-9; T. Salontos, A & W, 16(Spr 1974):74-5; C. A. Chambers, CHR, 55(Sep 1974):346; R. A. Burchell, JAmS, 8 (Aug 1974):271-2; E. L. Schapsmeier, JOW, 13(Oct 1974):132; F. W. Schruben, PHR, 43(Nov 1974):618-19; R. Daniels, PNQ, 65(Apr 1974):93-4; L. Leader, SWHQ, 78(Jl 1974):111-12; A. E. Conrad, WHQ, 5(Ja 1974):63-4; R. Street, WMH, 57 (Spr 1974):238-9.

Steinberg, Alfred. The Bosses. New York: Macmillan, 1972. Rev. by A. Hoffman, JOW, 13(Oct 1974):138; N. W. Hickman, LaH, 15(Sum 1974):309-10; J. F. Bauman, PH, 41(Oct 1974): 480-1.

Steiner, Bruce E. Samuel Seabury 1729-1796. A Study in the High Church Tradition. Athens, Ohio: Ohio U Press, 1972. Rev. by W. R. Ward, EHR, 89(Jl 1974):670-1.

Stem, Thad, Jr. The Tar Heel Press. Charlotte, N. C.: Heritage, 1973. Rev. by R. N. Elliott, NCHR, 51(Sum 1974):335-6.

Stensland, Anna Lee. Literature By and About the American Indian. n. p.: National Council of Teachers of English, 1973. Rev. by Staff, InH, 7(Win 1974):50-1.

Stenson, M. R. Industrial Conflict in Malaya: Prelude to the Communist Revolt of 1948. Oxford: Ox U Press, 1970. Rev. by M. Caldwell, History, 59(Je 1974):322-3.

Stephens, J. E. Aubrey on Education: A Hitherto Unpublished Manuscript. London: Routledge and Kegan Paul, 1972. Rev. by R. C. Latham, EHR, 89(Ja 1974):186-7.

Stephens, Robert W., ed. A Texan in the Gold Rush: The Letters of Robert Hunter 1849-1851. Bryan, Tx.: Barnum and White, 1972. Rev. by C. R. McClure, ETHJ, 12(Spr 1974):65.

Sterling, Dorothy, ed. Speak Out in Thunder Tones: Letters and Other Writings by Black Northerners, 1787-1865. Garden City, N. Y.: Doubleday, 1973. Rev. by J. J. Marszalek, Jr., HRNB, 2(Ja 1974):68.

Stern, Fritz. The Failure of Illiberalism: Essays of the Political Culture of Modern Germany. New York: Knopf, 1972. Rev. by J. A. Leopold, Historian, 36(Aug 1974):757-8.

Stern, Harold P. Ukiyo-e Painting. Washington: Smithsonian Institution ... 1973. Rev. by D. Jenkins, JAS, 33(May 1974): 491-3.

Sternfeld, Frederick see Wellesz, Egon

Steshenko, O. L. , et al. , eds. History of the Cities and Villages
of the Ukrainian SSR--Cherkassy Province. Kiev: Institut
Istorii Akademii Nauk URSR, 1972. Rev. by J. Armstrong,
AHR, 79(Feb 1974):193-4.

Steslicke, William E. Doctors in Politics: The Political Life of
the Japan Medical Association. New York: Praeger, 1973.
Rev. by D. W. Plath, JAAS, 9(Ja & Apr 1974):113-14; D. A.
Titus, JAS, 33(Aug 1974):712-13.

Stevens, G. R. History of the Canadian National Railways. New
York: Macmillan, 1973. Rev. by F. F. Coulon, PNQ, 65
(Apr 1974):87-8; C. W. Condit, T & C, 15(Ja 1974):110-12;
B. M. Gough, WHQ, 5(Oct 1974):471-2.

Stevens, Geoffrey. Stanfield. Toronto: McClelland and Stewart,
1973. Rev. by N. Ward, CHR, 55(Sep 1974):307-12.

Stevens, George. Speak for Yourself, John, The Life of John Mason
Brown, With Some of His Letters and Many of His Opinions.
New York: Viking, 1974. Rev. by W. Mootz, FCHQ, 48(Oct
1974):360.

Stevenson, Charles A. The End of Nowhere: American Policy
Toward Laos Since 1954. Boston: Beacon, 1972. Rev. by
J. J. Zasloff, PHR, 43(Aug 1974):438-9.

Stevenson, H. A. see Armstrong, F. H.

Stevenson, Matilda. The Zuñi Indians: Their Mythology, Esoteric
Fraternities and Ceremonies. Glorieta, N. M.: Rio Grande
Press, 1970. Rev. by D. M. Brugge, A & W, 16(Spr 1974):
75-6.

Stevenson, T. H. Politics and Government. Totowa, N. J.: Littlefield, Adams, 1973. Rev. by T. S. Popkewitz, HT, 7(Aug
1974):622-4.

Steward, Julian H. Alfred Kroeber. New York: Columbia U Press,
1973. Rev. by W. R. Jacobs, JAH, 60(Mar 1974):1161-2.

Stewart, C. C. and E. K. Islam and Social Order in Mauritania:
A Case Study from the Nineteenth Century. New York: Ox U
Press, 1973. Rev. by A. G. Gerteing, AHR, 79(Oct 1974):
1227-8; P. F. de Moraes Farias, History, 59(Je 1974):310-11.

Stewart, Mrs. Catesby Willis. The Life of Brigadier General William Woodford of the American Revolution. 2 vols. Richmond, Va.: Whittet and Shepperson, 1973. Rev. by R. W.
Coakley, AHR, 79(Oct 1974):1254-5; J. R. Sellers, JAH, 60
(Mar 1974):1103-4.

Stewart, J. Douglas and Ian E. Wilson. Heritage Kingston. Kingston, Ont.: Queen's U, 1973. Rev. by G. / C. Rogers, Jr.,
AmArc, 37(Apr 1974):298-9.

Stewart, T. D. The People of America. New York: Scribner's,
1973. Rev. by N. Lederer, ChOk, 52(Sum 1974):256-7.

Stickle, Warren E. see Brownell, Blaine A.

Stickler, A. M. Studia Gratiana. Rome: Libreria Ateneo Salesiano, 1972. Rev. by W. Ullmann, EHR, 89(Ja 1974):162-3.

_____. see D'Eercole, G.

Stober, Gerhard J. and Dieter Schumacher, ed. Technology Assessment and Quality of Life. Amsterdam: Elsevier, 1973.
Rev. by V. L. Ferwerda, T & C, 15(Jl 1974):529-34.

Stoeffler, F. Ernest. German Pietism During the Eighteenth Century. Leiden: E. J. Brill, 1973. Rev. by D. W. Brown,
CH, 43(Mar 1974):115-16.

Stoessinger, John G. Why Nations Go to War. New York: St.
Martin's Press, n.d. Rev. by A. MacClane, Mankind, 4(Dec
1974):71-2.

Stoltz, Jack. Terrell, Texas, 1873-1973: From Open Country to
Modern City. San Antonio: Naylor, 1973. Rev. by G. R.
Cruz, JOW, 13(Jl 1974):131.

Stone, Lawrence. The Causes of the English Revolution, 1529-1642.
New York: Harper Torchbooks, 1972. Rev. by S. E. Prall,
BHR, 48(Sum 1974):232-3; R. J. Sinner, Historian, 36(Feb
1974):318-19; H. G. Koenigsberger, JMH, 46(Mar 1974):99-
110.

_____. Family and Fortune. Oxford: Clarendon Press, 1973.
Rev. by M. W. Beresford, RQ, 27(Sum 1974):218-19.

Stones, Bones, and Skin: Ritual and Shamanic Art. n.p.: Arts-
canada, n.d. Rev. by Staff, InH, 7(Spr 1974):51.

Stora-Sandor, Judith. Alexandra Kollontaï: Marxisme et révolution
sexuelle. Paris: François Maspero, 1973. Rev. by B.
Clements, AHR, 79(Apr 1974):554-5.

Storey, R. L. see Bullough, D. A.

Stott, William. Documentary Expression and Thirties America.
New York: Ox U Press, 1973. Rev. by C. T. Morrisey,
AmArc, 37(Jl 1974):459-60; T. A. Krueger, JSH, 40(Aug
1974):506-7.

Stout, J. A. The Liberators: Filibustering Expeditions Into Mexico, 1848-1862, and the Last Thrust of Manifest Destiny. Los Angeles: Westernlore, 1973. Rev. by J. F. Park, A & W, 16(Spr 1974):81-2; N. L. Benson, CoMag, 51(Win 1974):62-3; M. E. Nackman, PHR, 43(May 1974):270-1; H. P. Hewitt, WHQ, 5(Ja 1974):73-4.

Stout, Neil R. The Royal Navy in America, 1760-1775. A Study of Enforcement of British Colonial Policy in the Era of the American Revolution. Annapolis: Navy Institute, 1973. Rev. by F. B. Wickwire, JAH, 61(Sep 1974):469-70; I. D. Gruber, WMQ-3, 31(Jl 1974):503-5.

Stoutamire, Albert. Music of the Old South: Colony to Confederacy. Rutherford, N. J.: Fairleigh Dickinson U Press, 1972. Rev. by C. Covey, AHR, 79(Je 1974):879-80.

Stowe, Harriet Beecher. Palmetto Leaves. Gainesville: U Fla Press, 1968. Rev. by E. C. Williamson, AlaR, 27(Ja 1974): 76-7.

Strage, Mark. Cape to Cairo: Rape of a Continent. New York: Harcourt Brace Jovanovich, 1973. Rev. by L. E. Meyer, HRNB, 2(Mar 1974):125.

Strathern, Andrew. The Rope of Moka: Big-Men and Ceremonial Exchange in Mount Hagen, New Guinea. Cambridge: Cam U Press, 1971. Rev. by J. A. Barnes, MAS, 8(Jl 1974):429-32.

Strayer, Joseph R. Western Europe in the Middle Ages: A Short History. Englewood Cliffs, N. J.: Prentice-Hall, 1974. Rev. by B. W. Scholz, HRNB, 2(Sep 1974):242.

Strayhorn, Martha I., ed. see Architecture of Middle Tennessee.

Strong, Douglas Hillman. "These Happy Grounds": A History of the Lassen Region. n. p.: Loomis Museum Assn and National Park Service, 1973. Rev. by J. M. Haymond, WHQ, 5(Oct 1974):468.

Strong, John W. see Bromke, Adam

Strong, Roy. Splendour at Court: Renaissance Spectacle and Illusion. London: Weidenfeld and Nicolson, n. d. Rev. by A. Haynes, HTo, 24(Feb 1974):137-8.

Strout, Cushing. The New Heavens and New Earth: Political Religion in America. New York: Harper and Row, 1974. Rev. by S. E. Mead and W. D. Tackenberg, CH, 43(Dec 1974):554-5; W. S. Hudson, JAH, 61(Dec 1974):829-30; S. Persons, JSH, 40(Nov 1974):676-7.

Struve, Walter. Elites Against Democracy: Leadership Ideals in

Bourgeois Political Thought in Germany, 1890-1933. Princeton, N. J.: Prin U Press, 1973. Rev. by F. E. Hirsch, HRNB, 2(Feb 1974):111.

Stryker-Rodda, K. see van Laer, Arnold J. F.

Studies in the Fourth General Elections. New Delhi: Allied, 1972. Rev. by W. G. Vanderbok, JAS, 33(Aug 1974):725-6.

Stuhler, Barbara. Ten Men of Minnesota and American Foreign Policy, 1898-1968. St. Paul, Minn.: Minn Historical Society, 1973. Rev. by R. E. Weber, HRNB, 2(Mar 1974):132-3; R. Ferrell, IMH, 70(Dec 1974):362-3; B. L. Larson, JAH, 61 (Dec 1974):831-2; J. A. Zimmerman, MiA, 56(Apr 1974):133-4; J. Israel, NDH, 41(Sum 1974):36.

Stupperich, Martin. Osiander in Preussen 1549-1552. New York: Walter de Gruyter, 1973. Rev. by L. W. Spitz, CH, 43(Sep 1974):403-4.

Sturdivant, Frederick D. see Smalley, Orange A.

Suarez Fernandez, L. Politica Internacional de Isabel la Católica (1494-6). Valladolid: Departmento de Historia Medieval, 1971. Rev. by J. R. L. Highfield, EHR, 89(Ja 1974):166.

Suchlicki, Jaime. Cuba: From Columbus to Castro. New York: Scribner's, 1974. Rev. by L. E. Aguilar, HRNB, 2(Aug 1974):225.

_____, ed. Cuba, Castro, and Revolution. Coral Gables, Fla.: U Miami Press, 1972. Rev. by A. Suárez, HAHR, 54(Feb 1974):156-7.

Suchodolski, Bogdan. Poland, the Land of Copernicus. Wroclaw/Warsaw/Cracow/Gdansk: Polish Academy of Sciences Press, 1973. Rev. by E. Rosen, T & C, 15(Jl 1974):94-5.

Sugar, Peter F., ed. Native Fascism in the Successor States, 1918-1945. Santa Barbara, Cal.: A B C--Clio, 1971. Rev. by R. V. Burks, AHR, 79(Oct 1974):1213.

Sugg, Redding S., Jr. see White, Helen

Suggs, George G., Jr. Colorado's War on Militant Unionism: James H. Peabody and the Western Federation of Miners. Detroit: Wayne St U Press, 1972. Rev. by H. W. Currie, AHR, 79(Apr 1974):593-4; D. A. Smith, Historian, 36(Feb 1974):355-6; B. A. Storey, JOW, 13(Oct 1974):128.

Summersell, Charles G., ed. The Journal of George Townley Fullam: Boarding Officer of the Confederate Sea Raider Alabama. University, Ala.: U Ala Press, 1973. Rev. by W. S. Hoole,

AlaRe, 27(Apr 1974):156-7; G. T. Edwards, CWH, 20(Je 1974): 186-8; G. E. Buker, FHQ, 53(Oct 1974):212-13; R. Lowe, HRNB, 2(Ja 1974):62; C. McKee, JAH, 61(Sep 1974):493-4; F. L. Owsley, Jr., JMiH, 36(Aug 1974):314-15; E. K. Eckert, JSH, 40(Aug 1974):490-1; A. C. Ashcraft, SWHQ, 78(Jl 1974): 98-100; N. C. Delaney, VMHB, 82(Apr 1974):210-11.

Summerson, John. The London Building World of the Eighteen-Sixties. London: Thames and Hudson, n.d. Rev. by A. O'Day, HTo, 24(Jl 1974):515-16.

Suntharalingam, R. Politics and Nationalist Awakening in South India, 1852-1891. Tucson: U Ariz Press, 1974. Rev. by T. R. Metcalf, HRNB, 3(Nov/Dec 1974):35.

Suny, Ronald Grigor. The Baku Commune, 1917-1918: Class and Nationality in the Russian Revolution. Princeton, N.J.: Prin U Press, 1972. Rev. by A. E. Adams, AHR, 79(Apr 1974): 549; P. Dukes, History, 59(Feb 1974):148-9.

Suret-Canale, J. Afrique Noire Occidentale et Centrale. Paris: Editions Sociales, 1972. Rev. by R. W. Johnson, JAfH, 15 (Num 1 1974):163-4.

A Survey of Research in Psychology. Bombay: Popular Prakashan, 1973. Rev. by L. Minturn, JAS, 34(Nov 1974):249-51.

A Survey of Research in Sociology and Social Anthropology. Volume III. Bombay: Popular Prakashan, 1972. Rev. by D. G. Mandelbaum, JAS, 34(Nov 1974):247-9.

Susman, Warren, ed. Culture and Commitment, 1929-1945. New York: Geo Braziller, 1973. Rev. by P. D. DeFroscia, HT, 8(Nov 1974):132-3.

Susskind, Charles. Understanding Technology. Baltimore: Johns Hopkins U Press, 1973. Rev. by P. F. Drucker, T & C, 15 (Ja 1974):80-2.

Sutherland, Gillian, ed. Studies in the Growth of Nineteenth-Century Government. London: Routledge and Kegan Paul, 1972. Rev. by R. A. Lewis, History, 59(Feb 1974):115-16.

Sutherland, N. M. The Massacre of St. Bartholomew and the European Conflict, 1559-1572. New York: Barnes and Noble, 1973. Rev. by N. L. Roelker, AHR, 79(Feb 1974):135-6; P. Sonnino, Historian, 36(May 1974):539-40; K. R. Andrews, History, 59(Je 1974):274-5.

Suval, Stanley. The Anschluss Question in the Weimar Era: A Study of Nationalism in Germany and Austria, 1918-1932. Baltimore: JHU Press, 1974. Rev. by W. Braatz, HRNB, 2 (May/Je 1974):177.

Sutton, Antony C. Western Technology and Soviet Economic Development, 1945-1965. Stanford, Cal.: Hoover Institution Press, 1973. Rev. by J. L. Nogee, HRNB, 2(May/Je 1974):182; S. Lieberstein, T & C, 15(Fall 1974):508-10.

Suzuki, H. and F. Takai, eds. The Amud Man and His Cave Site. Tokyo: U Tokyo, 1970. Rev. by A. J. Jellinek, AmAnt, 39 (Ja 1974):138-9.

Swadesh, Frances Leon. Los Primeros Pobladores: Hispanic Americans of the Ute Frontier. Notre Dame, Ind.: U Notre Dame Press, 1974. Rev. by E. B. McCluney, HRNB, 2(Aug 1974): 223; D. J. Weber, SWHQ, 78(Oct 1974):217-19.

Swainson, Donald, ed. Oliver Mowat's Ontario. Toronto: Macmillan, 1972. Rev. by G. Friesen, CHR, 55(Je 1974):193-4.

Swamy, Subramanian. Economic Growth in China and India, 1952-70: A Comparative Appraisal. Chicago: U Chi Press, 1973. Rev. by W. Malenbaum, JAS, 34(Nov 1974):246-8.

Swan, James G. Almost out of the World: Scenes from Washington Territory, the Strait of Juan de Fuca, 1859-61. Ed. by William A. Katz. Tacoma: Wash St Hist Soc, 1971. Rev. by G. A. Frykman, PNQ, 65(Jl 1974):148.

_____. The Northwest Coast, or Three Years Residence in Washington Territory. Seattle: U Wash Press, 1972. Rev. by G. A. Frykman, PNQ, 65(Jl 1974):148.

Swanberg, W. A. Luce and His Empire. New York: Scribner's, 1972. Rev. by R. A. Rutland, AHR, 79(Apr 1974):611-12.

Swee-Hock, Saw. Singapore: Population in Transition. Philadelphia: U Pa Press, 1970. Rev. by P. Wheatley, MAS, 8(Oct 1974):557-9.

Swetnam, George see Smith, Helen C.

Swindell, Martha Rebecca and Romulus Sanderson Spencer, Jr., ed. In Memory of ...: An Index to Hyde County Cemeteries. Fairfield, N.C.: Hyde History, Inc., 1973. Rev. by G. Stevenson, NCHR, 51(Jan 1974):95-6.

Swingewood, Alan see Laurenson, Diana T.

Swisher, H. L. see Maxwell, Hu

Sylvester, Richard S., ed. St. Thomas More: Action and Contemplation. New Haven, Conn.: Yale U Press, 1972. Rev. by P. McGrath, EHR, 89(Apr 1974):428; J. Youings, History, 59 (Je 1974):270.

Symeonides, Charalampous P. The Tascones and Tasconia: A Contribution to the Meaning of the Terms and of the Byzantine Institution of the Fortress-Garrison of the Same Name. Thessaloniki: Center for Byzantine Studies, 1972. Rev. by P. Charanis, AHR, 79(Feb 1974):134.

Symons, R. D. Where the Wagon Led: One Man's Memories of the Cowboy's Life in the Old West. Garden City, N.Y.: Doubleday, 1973. Rev. by H. Mothershead, A & W, 16(Spr 1974):82-4; D. F. Danker, CoMag, 51(Win 1974):75-6; M. Simmons, NMHR, 49(Oct 1974):346.

Synan, Vinson. The Holiness-Pentecostal Movement in the United States. Grand Rapids, Mich.: Eerdmanns, 1971. Rev. by C. E. Jones, CH, 43(Sep 1974):427-8.

_____. The Old-Time Power. Franklin Springs, Ga.: Advocate Press, 1973. Rev. by C. E. Jones, CH, 43(Sep 1974):427-8.

Syrett, Harold C., ed. The Papers of Alexander Hamilton. Volume 16, February 1794-July 1794; Volume 17, August 1794-December 1794. New York: Columbia U Press, 1972. Rev. by E. P. Douglass, AHR, 79(Je 1974):853-4; J. S. Pancake, NYH, 55(Jl 1974):334-7.

_____, ed. The Papers of Alexander Hamilton. Vol. 18. January 1795-July 1795; Vol. 19. July 1795-December 1795. New York: Columbia U Press, 1973. Rev. by J. B. Whisker, HRNB, 2(Feb 1974):95; E. J. Ferguson, JAH, 61(Sep 1974): 438-40; N. E. Cunningham, Jr., JSH, 40(May 1974):302-3; J. S. Pancake, NYH, 55(Jl 1974):334-7.

Szemler, G. J. The Priests of the Roman Republic: A Study of Interactions Between Priesthoods and Magistracies. Brussels: Latomus: Revue d'Etudes Latines, 1972. Rev. by J. G. Harson, Jr., AHR, 79(Je 1974):765-6.

Sziklai, Oszkar and Laszlo Adamovich. Foresters in Exile: The Sopron Forestry School in Canada. see Adamovich, Laszlo and Oszkar Sziklai. Foresters in Exile....

Sznycer, Maurice see Masson, Olivier

Szpak, Jan. Kierunki produkoji dworskiej w ekonomii malborskiej w XVI wieku. Warsaw: Polska Akademia Nauk, 1972. Rev. by R. F. Leslie, EHR, 89(Ja 1974):167.

Szucs, Jeno. A nemzet historikuma es a tortenelemszemlelet nemzeti latoszoge: hozxaszolas egy vitahoz. Budapest: Akademiai Kiado, 1970. Rev. by G. Handlery, EEQ, 8(Sum 1974):246-7.

Tabler, Edward C. Travels in the Interior of Southern Africa,

1849-1863. Cape Town: A. A. Balkema, 1971. Rev. by K. Ingham, EHR, 89(Apr 1974):457-8.

Tagliaferri, Amelio. Strutture sociali e sistemi economici precapitalistici. Milan: Giuffré, 1972. Rev. by R. A. Goldthwaite, JEH, 34(Je 1974):519-20.

Tainter, Joe. Salvage Excavations at the Fowler Site. Some Aspects of the Social Organization of the Northern Chumash. San Luis Obispo, Cal.: San Luis Obispo County Archaeological Society, 1971. Rev. by T. King, AmAnt, 39(Apr 1974):392-4.

Takai, F. see Suzuki, H.

Talbot, Edmond E. The Big Thicket. Austin, Tx.: Little House Press, 1973. Rev. by L. W. Parker, ETHJ, 12(Fall 1974): 91.

Talman, James J. see Klinck, Carl F.

Tamrat, Taddesse. Church and State in Ethiopia, 1270-1527. Oxford: Clarendon Press, 1972. Rev. by C. F. Beckingham, JAfH, 15(Num 1 1974):137-40.

Tannenbaum, Edward R. The Fascist Experience. Italian Society and Culture: 1922-1945. New York ...: Basic Books, 1972. Rev. by R. Vivarelli, HJ, 17(Num 3 1974):644-51.

_____, ed. A History of World Civilizations. New York: Wiley, 1973. Rev. by T. H. Von Laue, HT, 7(May 1974):481-3.

Tanner, Annie Clark. A Mormon Mother: An Autobiography. Salt Lake City: U Utah Press, 1974. Rev. by P. Bailey, JAriH, 15(Aut 1974):302-4; F. M. Brodie, PHR, 43(Aug 1974):421-2; A. H. Eakle, UHQ, 42(Spr 1974):199-200.

Tannler, Albert M. One in Spirit. Chicago: U Chi Library, 1973. Rev. by E. J. Blendon, AmArc, 37(Jl 1974):464-5.

Tapié, Victor-L. The Rise and Fall of the Habsburg Monarchy. New York: Praeger, 1971. Rev. by W. E. Wright, JMH, 46(Dec 1974):735-6.

Tarr, Joel Arthur. A Study in Boss Politics: William Lorimer of Chicago. Urbana: U Ill Press, 1971. Rev. by S. J. Mandelbaum, AHR, 79(Oct 1974):1279-80.

Tarrade, Jean. Le commerce colonial de la France à la fin de l'Ancien Régime: L'évolution du régime de "l'Exclusif" de 1763 à 1789. 2 vols. Paris: Universitaires de France, 1972. Rev. by G. T. Matthews, AHR, 79(Apr 1974):519-20.

Tassin, Ray. Stanley Vestal: Champion of the Old West. Glendale,

Cal.: Arthur H. Clark, 1973. Rev. by J. Short, ChOk, 52 (Spr 1974):117-18; T. F. Andrews, HRNB, 2(Mar 1974):127; R. A. Billington, SCQ, 56(Fall 1974):321-2; W. E. Hollon, WHQ, 5(Oct 1974):457-8.

Tate, Cecil F. The Search for a Method in American Studies. Minneapolis: U Min Press, 1973. Rev. by M. T. Gilderhus, HRNB, 2(Feb 1974):99; G. N. Grob, HT, 8(Nov 1974):136; H. R. Dieterich, JAH, 61(Dec 1974):750-1.

Taylor, A. J. P. Beaverbrook. London: H. Hamilton, 1972. Rev. by H. V. Welles, CHR, 55(Sep 1974):330-3.

Taylor, Arthur. Laissez-faire and State Intervention in Nineteenth-Century Britain. London: Macmillan, 1972. Rev. by O. Anderson, EHR, 89(Jl 1974):679-80; S. Collini, History, 59 (Feb 1974):116-17.

Taylor, Charles L. and Michael C. Hudson. World Handbook of Political and Social Indicators. New Haven, Conn.: Yale U Press, 1972. Rev. by A. Van Dam, JMAS, 12(Je 1974):352-3.

Taylor, George Rogers and Lucious F. Ellsworth, eds. Approaches to American Economic History. Charlottesville: U Press Va, 1971. Rev. by K. H. Wolff, AHR, 79(Je 1974):835; H. D. Woodman, JIH, 5(Aut 1974):295-301.

Taylor, John. Urban History Review. see Muise, Del

Taylor, John R. M. (Notes and Introduction.) The Philippine Insurrection Against the United States. A Compilation of Documents.... Pasay City, Philippines: Eugenio Lopez Foundation, 1971. Rev. by D. V. Hart, JAS, 33(May 1974):503.

Taylor, Louise B. Aberdeen Shore Work Accounts, 1596-1670. Aberdeen: Aberdeen U Press, 1972. Rev. by R. Davis, EHR, 89(Ja 1974):178-9.

Taylor, Philip. The Distant Magnet: European Emigration to the U.S.A. New York: Harper and Row, 1972. Rev. by J. Rowe, JAmS, 8(Aug 1974):266-7.

Taylor, Ronald B. Sweatshops in the Sun: Child Labor on the Farm. Boston: Beacon, 1973. Rev. by C. E. Daniel, PNQ, 65(Jl 1974):153.

Taylor, Theodore W. The States and Their Indian Citizens. Washington: US Dept Interior, Bureau Indian Affairs, 1972. Rev. by Staff, InH, 7(Spr 1974):51; W. E. Unrau, NH, 55(Sum 1974) 297-9.

Taylor, Tim. The Book of Presidents. New York: Quadrangle,

n. d.   Rev. by C. E. Kramer, FCHQ, 48(Ja 1974):66-7.

Taylor, William B.   Landlord and Peasant in Colonial Oaxaca.
Stanford, Cal.:   Stan U Press, 1972.   Rev. by M. Bernstein,
TAm, 31(Jl 1974):107-8.

Taylour, Lord William see Blegen, Carl W.

Tebbel, John.   A History of Book Publishing in the United States.
Vol. I.   The Creation of an Industry, 1630-1865.   New York:
Bowker, 1972.   Rev. by F. Johnson, NYHSQ, 58(Apr 1974):
153-5.

Technological Innovation and the Decorative Arts.   An Exhibition at
the Hagley Museum Cosponsored by The Henry Francis du Pont
Winterthur Museum, March 29, 1973, through December 30,
1973.   Wilmington, Delaware: Eleutherian Mills-Hagley Foundation, 1973.   Rev. by D. Glidden, MHM, 69(Fall 1974):337.

Teich, Mikulas and Robert Young, eds.   Changing Perspectives in
the History of Science: Essays in Honour of Joseph Needham.
Boston: D. Reidel, 1973.   Rev. by J. Sevier, HRNB, 2(Ja
1974):73.

Teller, Walter see Whitman, Walt

Témine, Emile see Broué, Pierre

Temkin, Owsei.   Galenism: Rise and Decline of a Medical Philosophy.   Ithaca, N. Y.:   Cornell U Press, 1973.   Rev. by G.
Rosen, AHR, 79(Oct 1974):1139-40.

Temperley, Howard.   British Antislavery 1833-1870.   Columbia,
S. C.:   USCar Press, 1972.   Rev. by M. Reckford, CHR, 55
(Je 1974):214-15; J. A. Rawley, CWH, 20(Mar 1974):60-4;
K. Fielden, JMH, 46(Je 1974):348-9.

Temu, A. J.   British Protestant Missions.   New York: Longman,
1972.   Rev. by F. B. Welbourn, Africa, 44(Apr 1974):208-9;
V. H. Rabe, CH, 43(Dec 1974):555-6.

Teperi, J.   Arvon mekin ansaitsemme: Jaakko Juteinin aatemaailman eräät päälinjat.   Helsinki: Historiallisia Tulkimuksia 85,
1972.   Rev. by A. F. Upton, EHR, 89(Apr 1974):452.

Termes, Josep.   Anarquismo y sindicalismo en España: La Primera Internacional, 1864-1881.   Barcelona: Ediciones Ariel,
1972.   Rev. by J. C. Ullman, AHR, 79(Oct 1974):1196-7.

Terrell, John Upton.   American Indian Almanac.   New York:
Crowell, 1974.   Rev. in CurH, 67(Dec 1974):271.

_____.   Apache Chronicle.   New York: Crowell, 1974.   Rev.

in CurH, 67(Dec 1974):271-2.

Terrett, I. B. see Darby, H. C.

Terrill, Ross. R. H. Tawney and His Times: Socialism as Fellowship. Cambridge, Mass.: Har U Press, 1973. Rev. by
P. Stansky, AHR, 79(Oct 1974):1183-4.

Terrill, Tom E. The Tariff, Politics, and American Foreign Policy, 1874-1901. Westport, Conn.: Greenwood, 1973. Rev.
by S. Ratner, BHR, 48(Sum 1974):261-2; K. J. Brauer, HRNB,
2(Mar 1974):133; J. A. Williams, IMH, 70(Sep 1974):262-3;
W. H. Becker, JAH, 61(Dec 1974):800-1; R. H. Zeitlin, WMH,
57(Spr 1974):235-7.

Terry, Adolphine Fletcher. Charlotte Stephens, Little Rock's First
Black Teacher. Little Rock: Academic Press Ark, 1973.
Rev. by T. W. Dillard, ArkHQ, 33(Spr 1974):92-4.

Teunissen, John J. and Evelyn J. Hinz, eds. William, Roger, A
Key Into the Language of America. Detroit: Wayne St U
Press, 1973. Rev. by Staff, InH, 7(Win 1974):50.

Teuteberg, Hans J. and Günter Wiegelmann. Der Wandel der Nah-
rungsgewohnheiten unter dem Einfluss der Industrialisierung.
Göttingen: Vandenhoeck and Ruprecht, 1972. Rev. by H.
Freudenberger, AHR, 79(Je 1974):802-3.

Thackray, Arnold. John Dalton, Critical Assessments of His Life
and Science. Cambridge, Mass.: Har U Press, 1972. Rev.
by R. J. Morris, Jr., T & C, 15(Ja 1974):100-3.

Thatcher, Mary. Cambridge South Asian Archive. London: Mansell, 1973. Rev. by C. Dewey, MAS, 8(Oct 1974):571-3.

Theen, Rolf H. W. Lenin: Genesis and Development of a Revolutionary. Philadelphia: Lippincott, 1973. Rev. by R. Thompson, AHR, 79(Apr 1974):544-5.

Theodoracopoulos, John see Andronicos, Emmanuel

Theoharis, Athan. Seeds of Repression: Harry S. Truman and
the Origins of McCarthyism. Chicago: Quadrangle, 1971.
Rev. by H. Waltzer, AHR, 79(Oct 1974):1291-2.

Thernstrom, Stephan. The Other Bostonians: Poverty and Progress
in the American Metropolis, 1880-1970. Cambridge, Mass.:
Har U Press, 1973. Rev. by R. E. Pumphrey, BHR, 48(Win
1974):555-7; R. Berthoff, HRNB, 2(Ja 1974):59-60; M. Edel,
JEH, 34(Je 1974):520-2; R. M. Johnson, NEQ, 47(Je 1974):
333-7; R. Lane, NYHSQ, 58(Oct 1974):338-9.

Thirsk, Joan and J. P. Cooper, eds. Seventeenth-Century Economi

Documents. New York: Ox U Press, 1972. Rev. by R. G. Lang, AHR, 79(Apr 1974):512-13.

Thomas, Brinley. Migration and Urban Development. London: Methuen, 1972. Rev. by R. Floud, History, 59(Feb 1974):161.

Thomas, Emory M. The American War and Peace, 1860-1877. Englewood Cliffs, N.J.: Prentice Hall, 1973. Rev. by C. P. Roland, CWH, 20(Je 1974):157-9; W. M. Hays, Historian, 36 (May 1974):565-6; R. A. Wooster, JAH, 61(Je 1974):196-7; G. McWhiney, JSH, 40(Feb 1974):145-6.

_____. The Confederate State of Richmond: A Biography of the Capital. Austin: U Tx Press, 1971. Rev. by T. S. Berry, AHR, 79(Feb 1974):231.

Thomas, John N. The Institute of Pacific Relations: Asian Scholars and American Politics. Seattle: U Wash Press, 1974. Rev. by W. H. Kuehl, HRNB, 3(Oct 1974):5.

Thomas, M. Halsey, ed. The Diary of Samuel Sewall, 1674-1729. 2 vols. New York: Farrar, Strauss and Giroux, 1973. Rev. by L. Ziff, JAH, 61(Sep 1974):460-2.

_____. see Link, Arthur S.

_____, ed. see Sewall, Samuel

Thomas, Mary Elizabeth. Jamaica and Voluntary Laborers from Africa, 1840-1856. Gainesville: U Fla Press, 1974. Rev. by John E. Bauer, TAm, 31(Oct 1974):225-6.

Thomas, Samuel W. and James C. The Simple Spirit, A Pictorial Study of the Shaker Community at Pleasant Hill, Kentucky. Pleasant Hill: Pleasant Hill Press, 1973. Rev. by J. Neal, FCHQ, 48(Ja 1974):61.

Thomasson, Bengt E., et al. San Giovenale. Vol. I. Stockholm: Swedish Institute in Rome, 1972. Rev. by R. R. Holloway, AJA, 78(Apr 1974):204.

Thomis, M. I. Luddism in Nottinghamshire. London: Phillimore, 1972. Rev. by D. Read, EHR, 89(Ja 1974):208.

Thompson, Allan. The Dynamics of the Industrial Revolution. New York: St. Martin's, 1973. Rev. by D. Felix, HRNB, 2(May/Je 1974):186-7.

Thompson, Craig R., ed. Translations of Lucian. New Haven, Conn.: Yale U Press, 1974. Rev. by O. T. Hargrave, CH, 43(Dec 1974):541.

Thompson, Ernest Trice. Presbyterians in the South. Vols. 2 and

3. Richmond, Va.: John Knox Press, 1973. Rev. by J. H. Nichols, CH, 43(Dec 1974):549-50; R. M. Miller, JSH, 40 (May 1974):339-41.

Thompson, Gregory Coyne. Southern Ute Lands, 1848-1899: The Creation of a Reservation. Durango, Colo.: Fort Lewis College, 1972. Rev. by I. Sutton, PHR, 43(Feb 1974):121-2.

Thompson, Gregory C. see Jefferson, James

Thompson, Howard A. and R. E. Wycherley. The Agora of Athens: The History, Shape and Uses of an Ancient City Center. Princeton, N. J.: American School of Classical Studies at Athens, 1972. Rev. by M. Robertson, Archaeology, 27(Apr 1974):140-1.

Thompson, Hunter S. Fear and Loathing: On the Campaign Trail, '72. San Francisco: Straightarrow, 1973. Rev. by B. A. Loomis, WMH, 57(Sum 1974):317-19.

Thompson, J. Eric S. A Commentary on the Dresden Codex: A Maya Hieroglyphic Book. Philadelphia: American Philosophical Society, 1972. Rev. by H. von Winning, HAHR, 54(Feb 1974):167-8.

Thompson, Jerry Don. Colonel John Robert Baylor: Texas Indian Fighter and Confederate Soldier. Hillsboro, Tx.: Hill Jr Coll Press, 1971. Rev. by J. F. Marszalek, Jr., CWH, 20 (Mar 1974):69-70.

Thompson, John M. see Mehlinger, Howard D.

Thompson, Margaret, Otto Mørkholm, and Colin Kraay, eds. An Inventory of Greek Coin Hoards. New York: American Numismatic Society, 1973. Rev. by M. Jessop Price, AJA, 78 (Jl 1974):308-9.

Thompson, Paul. William Butterfield. London: Routledge and Kegan Paul, 1971. Rev. by J. M. Crook, EHR, 89(Ja 1974): 131-3.

Thompson, Raymond H. see Spicer, Edward H.

Thompson, Robert Smith. Pledge of Destiny: Charles de Gaulle and the Rise of the Free French. New York: McGraw-Hill, 1974. Rev. by S. C. Tucker, HRNB, 3(Oct 1974):13-14.

Thomson, James C., Jr. see May, Ernest R.

Thomson, R. M., ed. and trans. The Chronicle of the Election of Hugh: Abbot of Bury St. Edmunds and Later Bishop of Ely. New York: Ox U Press, 1974. Rev. by B. W. Scholz, HRNB, 3(Nov/Dec 1974):26-7.

Thomson, W. G. A History of Tapestry. n. p. : E P Publishing, n. d. Rev. by A. Haynes, HTo, 24(Mar 1974):214.

Thoreau, Henry David. The Illustrated Walden. Princeton: Prin U Press, 1973. Rev. by M. I. Lowance, Jr. , NEQ, 47(June 1974):330-1.

Thornbrough, Emma Lou. T. Thomas Fortune: Militant Journalist. Chicago: U Chi Press, 1972. Rev. by B. Quarles, AHR, 79 (Feb 1974):237-8; E. Gertz, JISHS, 67(Sep 1974):455-6.

Thornbrough, Gayle and Dorothy L. Riker, eds. The Diary of Calvin Fletcher. Vol. II ... 1838-1843: Including Letters to and from Calvin Fletcher. Indianapolis: Ind Historical Society, 1973. Rev. by J. H. Madison, IMH, 70(Je 1974):179-80; J. F. Stover, JAH, 61(Sep 1974):481-2.

Thorne, Christopher. The Limits of Foreign Policy: The West, the League and the Far Eastern Crisis of 1931-1933. New York: Putnam's, 1973. Rev. by H. R. Winkler, AHR, 79 (Feb 1974):117-18.

Thorpe, Earl E. The Old South: A Psycho-History. Durham, N. C. : Seeman Printery, 1972. Rev. by G. W. Mullin, CWH, 20(Je 1974):170-1.

Thorpe, Lloyd. Men to Match the Mountains. Seattle: Craftsman and Met Press, 1972. Rev. by J. H. Engbeck, Jr. , CHQ, 53 (Sum 1974):186-7.

Thrall, Charles A. and Jerold M. Starr, eds. Technology, Power, and Social Change. Lexington, Mass. : D. C. Heath, 1972. Rev. by H. J. Muller, T & C, 15(Ja 1974):82-6.

Thrapp, Dan L. Victorio and the Mimbres Apaches. Norman: U Ok Press, 1974. Rev. by C. W. Altshuler, JAriH, 15(Aut 1974):300-1; C. Trafzer, NMHR, 49(Oct 1974):335-7; H. B. Simpson, Texana, 11(Win 1974):90-1; W. E. Unrau, UHQ, 42 (Sum 1974):304-5.

Tien, Hung-mao. Government and Politics in Kuomintang China, 1927-1937. Stanford, Cal. : Stan U Press, 1972. Rev. by I. Nish, History, 59(Je 1974):321; S. C. Chu, JAAS, 9(Ja & Apr 1974):102-3; L. E. Eastman, JIH, 5(Aut 1974):351-4.

Tilia, Ann Britt. Studies and Restorations at Persepolis and Other Sites of Fàrs. Rome: Is MEO, 1972. Rev. by C. Nylander, AJA, 78(Ja 1974):80-1.

Timberlake, Charles E. , ed. Essays on Russian Liberalism. Columbia, Mo. : U Mo Press, 1972. Rev. by P. Call, AHR, 79(Apr 1974):531-2.

Timmen, Fritz. Blow for the Landing: A Hundred Years of Steam Navigation on the Waters of the West. Caldwell, Ida.: Caxton, 1973. Rev. by M. Naab, OrHQ, 75(Mar 1974):82.

Tindall, George Brown. The Disruption of the Solid South. Athens, Ga.: U Ga Press, 1972. Rev. by T. D. Clark, AHR, 79 (Oct 1974):1275.

Tinhorão, José Ramos. Música popular de índios, negros, e mestiços. Petropolis, Brazil: Editora Vozes, 1972. Rev. by G. Béhague, HAHR, 54(May 1974):347-8.

Tinkle, Lon. Mr. De: A Biography of Everette Lee DeGolyer. Boston: Little, Brown, 1970. Rev. by R. C. Cotner, ETHJ, 12(Spr 1974):72-4.

_____. Texas: A Picture Tour. New York: Scribner's, 1973. Rev. by W. E. McFarland, ChOk, 52(Sum 1974):254-5.

Tint, Herbert. French Foreign Policy Since the Second World War. New York: St. Martin's Press, 1972. Rev. by S. A. Schucker, AHR, 79(Oct 1974):1195-6.

Tinto, Alberto. Il corsivo nella tipografia del Cinquecento. Milano: Edizioni Il Polifilo, 1972. Rev. by R. Nash, RQ, 27 (Sum 1974):223-5.

Tipton, Leon, ed. Nationalism in the Middle Ages. New York: Holt, Rinehart and Winston, 1972. Rev. by W. B. Morris, Jr., JOW, 13(Apr 1974):133.

Tishler, Hace Sorel. Self-Reliance and Social Security, 1870-1917. Port Washington, N. Y.: Kennikat, 1971. Rev. by W. I. Trattner, AHR, 79(Je 1974):878-9.

Tite, M. S. Methods of Physical Examination in Archaeology. New York: Seminar Press, 1972. Rev. by F. H. Goodyear, Antiquity, 48(Sep 1974):238-9; S. L. Glass, T & C, 15(Ja 1974): 153-5.

Titiev, Mischa. The Hopi Indians of Old Oraibi: Change and Continuity. Ann Arbor: U Mich Press, 1972. Rev. by F. J. Johnston, JOW, 13(Ja 1974):149.

Titow, J. Z. Winchester Yields: A Study in Medieval Agricultural Productivity. Cambridge: Cam U Press, 1972. Rev. by J. Hatcher, History, 59(Je 1974):255-6.

Tobin, Terence, ed. Letters of George Ade. West Lafayette, Ind.: Purdue U Studies, 1973. Rev. by R. W. Shumaker, IMH, 70 (Mar 1974):73-4.

Todd, Judith. The Right to Say No. London: Sidgwick and Jackson,

1972. Rev. by V. B. Khapoya, JMAS, 12(Mar 1974):165-8.

Todd, Malcolm. The Coritani. London: Duckworth, 1973. Rev.
    by J. S. Wacher, Antiquity, 48(Mar 1974):76-7.

Todd, William. History as Applied Science: A Philosophical Study.
    Detroit: Wayne St U Press, 1972. Rev. by W. Dray, CHR,
    55(Je 1974):176-7; R. F. Berkhofer, Jr., JMH, 46(Je 1974):
    341.

Tomkowitz, Gerhard see Wagner, Dieter

Tommaso Radini Tedeschi, Orazione Contro Filippo Melantone.
    Brescia: Paideia Editrice, 1973. Rev. by J. Tedeschi, CH,
    43(Dec 1974):543.

Toole, K. Ross. Twentieth-Century Montana: A State of Extremes.
    Norman: U Ok Press, 1972. Rev. by R. Roeder, PNQ, 65,
    (Jl 1974):151, G. W. Rollins, WHQ, 5(Apr 1974):210-12.

Toplin, Robert Brent. The Abolition of Slavery in Brazil. New
    York: Atheneum, 1972. Rev. by D. R. Murray, JLAS, 6
    (May 1974):175-7.

Torres, Elias L. Twenty Episodes in the Life of Pancho Villa.
    Tr. by Sheila M. Ohlendorf. Austin: Encino Press, 1973.
    Rev. by W. Collins, SWHQ, 78(Jl 1974):103-4.

Tortella Casares, Gabriel. Los orígenes del capitalismo en España:
    Banca, industria y ferrocarriles en el siglo XIX. Madrid:
    Editorial Tecnos, 1973. Rev. by D. R. Ringrose, AHR, 79
    (Je 1974):796; J. C. La Force, BHR, 48(Spr 1974):106-7.

La Toscana nel regime fascista (1922-1939). Florence: Olschki,
    1971. Rev. by S. J. Woolf, EHR, 89(Ja 1974):238-39.

Tournerie, Jean-André. Le Ministère du Travail (Origines et
    premiers développements). Paris: Editions Cujas, 1971.
    Rev. by V. R. Lorwin, AHR, 79(Oct 1974):1190-1.

Townley, John M. Conquered Provinces: Nevada Moves Southeast,
    1864-1871. Provo, Utah: BYU Press, n.d. Rev. by L. L.
    Morrison, JOW, 13(Apr 1974):106-7.

Toynbee, Arnold. Constantine Porphyrogenitus and His World.
    New York: Ox U Press, 1973. Rev. by C. Mango, AHR, 79
    (Apr 1974):503-4.

Toynbee, Arnold J. and G. R. Urban. Toynbee on Toynbee: A
    Conversation Between Arnold Toynbee and G. R. Urban. New
    York: Ox U Press, 1974. Rev. by M. D. Feld, HRNB, 2
    (Jl 1974):206.

Toynbee, J. M. C. Animals in Roman Life and Art. London: Thames and Hudson, 1973. Rev. by R. G. Austin, Antiquity, 48(Mar 1974):70-2.

Trachtenberg, Alan, ed. Democratic Vistas 1860-1880. New York: George Braziller, 1970. Rev. by D. H. Culbert, HT, 8(Nov 1974):128-9.

Tracy, James D. Erasmus: The Growth of a Mind. Geneva: Librairie Droz, 1972. Rev. by D. F. S. Thomson, RQ, 27 (Fall 1974):341-2.

Trattner, Walter I. From Poor Law to Welfare State: A History of Social Welfare in America. New York: Free Press, 1974. Rev. by J. B. Stewart, HRNB, 2(Mar 1974):130; V. L. Bullough, JAH, 61(Sep 1974):453-4; F. A. Annunziata, JSH, 40 (Nov 1974):675-6.

Treadgold, Donald W. The West in Russia and China: Religious and Secular Thought in Modern Times. Vol. I. Russia, 1472-1917. New York: Cam U Press, 1973. Rev. by N. V. Riasanovsky, AHR, 79(Feb 1974):192-3; R. F. Smylie, CH, 43 (Mar 1974):127-8; J. K. Fairbank, Historian, 36(May 1974): 553-4; J. B. Grieder, JAS, 33(May 1974):462-6; J. M. Meskill, JMH, 46(Sep 1974):532-4.

_____. The West in Russia and China: Religious and Secular Thought in Modern Times. Vol. II. China, 1582-1949. New York: Cam U Press, 1973. Rev. by R. Croinier, AHR, 79 (Apr 1974):486-7; R. F. Smylie, CH, 43(Mar 1974):127-8; J. K. Fairbank, Historian, 36(May 1974):553-4; J. B. Grieder, JAS, 33(May 1974):462-6; J. M. Meskill, JMH, 46(Sep 1974):532-4.

Treasure, G. R. R. Cardinal Richelieu and the Development of Absolutism. London: A & C Black, 1972. Rev. by R. J. Knecht, History, 59(Apr 1974):107.

Tredway, Gilbert R. Democratic Opposition to the Lincoln Administration in Indiana. Indianapolis: Ind Historical Bureau, 1973. Rev. by H. Jones, CWH, 20(Sep 1974):264-5; L. Cox, IMH, 70(Sep 1974):252-4; F. L. Klement, JAH, 61(Je 1974):197-8; W. E. Baringer, JSH, 40(Aug 1974):484-6; C. A. Zenor, RKHS, 72(Jl 1974):291-2.

Trelease, Allen W. Reconstruction: The Great Experiment. New York: Harper and Row, 1971. Rev. by R. F. Durden, AHR, 79(Je 1974):871-2.

_____. White Terror: The Ku Klux Klan Conspiracy and Southern Reconstruction. New York: Harper and Row, 1971. Rev. by S. P. Hirshson, AHR, 79(Apr 1974):589-90.

Tremlett, T. D. see Dunning, R. W.

Trench, Charles Chenevix. George II. London: Allen Lane, n. d.
    Rev. by J. Richardson, HTo, 24(Ja 1974):65-6.

Trenholm, Virginia Cole. The Arapahoes, Our People. Norman:
    U Ok Press, 1970, 1972. Rev. by C. Bolt, JAmS, 8(Apr
    1974):117-19.

Trexler, Richard C. The Spiritual Power. Leiden: E. J. Brill,
    1974. Rev. by J. Kirshner, CH, 43(Dec 1974):539.

Triaud, Jean-Louis. Islam et societes soudanaises au moyen-âge:
    étude historique. Paris: n. p. , 1973. Rev. by H. J. Fisher,
    JAfH, 15(Num 2 1974):325-6.

Tringham, Ruth. Hunters, Fishers and Farmers of Eastern Europe
    6000-3000 B. C. London: Hutchinson, 1971. Rev. by R. W.
    Ehrich, AJA, 78(Oct 1974):435-6.

Trinkaus, Charles, ed. The Pursuit of Holiness in Late Medieval
    and Renaissance Religion: Papers from The University of
    Michigan Conference. Leiden: E. J. Brill, 1974. Rev. by
    H. J. Grimm, CH, 43(Dec 1974):537-8.

Trofimenkoff, S. M. , ed. The Twenties in Western Canada. Ot-
    tawa: History Division, National Museum of Man, 1972. Rev.
    by H. B. Neatby, CHR, 55(Je 1974):203-4.

Troitskii, N. A. "The People's Will" Before the Tsarist Courts
    1880-1891. Saratov: Izdatel'stvo Saratovskogo Universiteta,
    1972. Rev. by D. Senese, AHR, 79(Oct 1974):1222.

Trollope, Thomas Adolphus. What I Remember. n. p. : William
    Kimber, n. d. Rev. by J. A. Hodge, HTo, 24(Apr 1974):288-
    9.

Trommer, Aage. Railway Sabotage in Denmark During the Second
    World War: A Study in Military History. Odense: Odense U
    Press, 1971. Rev. by F. J. Bowman, AHR, 79(Je 1974):798-
    9.

Troper, Harold Martin. Only Farmers Need Apply: Official Cana-
    dian Government Encouragement of Immigration from the
    United States, 1896-1911. Toronto: Griffin House, 1972.
    Rev. by G. A. Stelter, AHR, 79(Oct 1974):1295; D. J. Hall,
    CHR, 55(Sep 1974):318-19; J. A. Boudreau, JAH, 61(Je 1974):
    258-9.

Troup, Freda. South Africa: An Historical Introduction. London:
    Eyre Methuen, 1972. Rev. by C. Bundy, JAfH, 15(Num 2
    1974):339-41.

Trueblood, Elton. Abraham Lincoln: Theologian of American Anguish. New York: Harper and Row, 1973. Rev. by W. G. Eidson, IMH, 70(Je 1974):191-2; V. Hicken, JISHS, 67(Feb 1974):127-8; M. E. Shively, RKHS, 72(Oct 1974):422-3; M. E. Shively, THQ, 33(Fall 1974):351.

Trunk, Isaiah. Judenrat: The Jewish Councils in Eastern Europe Under Nazi Occupation. London: Collier-Macmillan, 1973. Rev. by L. Kochan, History, 59(Je 1974):303.

Trypanis, Constantine see Andronicos, Emmanuel

Tsamutali, A. N. Survey of the Democratic Direction in Russian Historiography in the 1860s and 1870s. Leningrad: Izdatel' stvo "Nauka," 1971. Rev. by J. L. Black, AHR, 79(Je 1974): 818-19.

Tuathaigh, Geróid O. Ireland Before the Famine. Dublin: Gill and Macmillan, 1972. Rev. by J. C. Beckett, History, 59(Feb 1974):130-1.

Tuchman, Barbara W. Notes from China. New York: Macmillan, 1972. Rev. by K. J. Grieb, CoMag, 51(Win 1974):69-71.

Tuck, Anthony J. Richard II and the English Nobility. New York: St. Martin's, 1974. Rev. by M. E. François, HRNB, 2(Aug 1974):230; A. Rogers, HTo, 24(Feb 1974):138-9.

Tucker, G. S. L. see Forster, Colin

Tucker, Robert C. Stalin as Revolutionary, 1879-1929: A Study in History and Personality. New York: Norton, 1973. Rev. by R. M. Slusser, AHR, 79(Je 1974):820-2; M. Latey, HTo, 24 (Jl 1974):511.

Tugwell, Rexford G. In Search of Roosevelt. Cambridge, Mass.: Har U Press, 1972. Rev. by T. H. Buckley, Historian, 36 (Feb 1974):357-8.

Tulchin, Joseph S. The Aftermath of War. World War I and U.S. Policy Toward Latin America. New York: NYU Press, 1971. Rev. by A. E. Campbell, HJ, 17(Num 2 1974):443-7.

_____, ed. Problems in Latin American History: The Modern Period. New York: Harper and Row, 1973. Rev. by T. C. Wright, HAHR, 54(May 1974):320-1.

_____. see Danelski, David J.

Tull, James E. Shapers of Baptist Thought. Valley Forge, Pa.: Judson Press, 1972. Rev. by R. G. Torbet, CH, 43(Sep 1974):416-17.

Tuma, Elias H. Economic History and the Social Sciences: Problems of Methodology. Berkeley: U Cal Press, 1971. Rev.
by H. D. Woodman, JIH, 5(Aut 1974):295-301.

Tuohy, Donald R. , Doris Rendall, and Pamela A. Crowell, eds.
Five Papers on the Archaeology of the Desert West. Carson
City: Nev St Museum, 1970. Rev. by D. H. Thomas, AmAnt,
39(Ja 1974):139-40.

Turnbull, C. M. The Straits Settlement, 1826-67. London: Athlone, 1972. Rev. by M. Caldwell, EHR, 89(Apr 1974):461-2.

Turner, Frank Miller. Between Science and Religion: The Reaction
to Scientific Naturalism in Late Victorian England. New Haven, Conn.: Yale U Press, 1974. Rev. by E. Tuveson, CH,
43(Sep 1974):412-14; W. G. Simon, HRNB, 3(Mar 1974):121.

Turner, Henry Ashby, Jr. Faschismus und Kapitalismus in Deutsch-
land: Studien zum Verhältnis zwischen Nationalsozialismus und
Wirtschaft. Göttingen: Vandenhoeck und Ruprecht, 1972.
Rev. by G. P. Blum, AHR, 79(Oct 1974):1204-5.

Turner, Justin G. and Linda Levitt Turner. Mary Todd Lincoln:
Her Life and Letters. New York: Knopf, 1972. Rev. by
A. K. Baxter, AHR, 79(Je 1974):867-8.

Turner, Martha Anne. William Barrett Travis, His Sword and His
Pen. Waco, Tx.: Texian Press, 1972. Rev. by L. S. Murphy, ETHJ, 12(Spr 1974):57.

Tuttle, William M. , Jr. , ed. W. E. B. DuBois. Englewood Cliffs,
N. J.: Prentice Hall, 1973. Rev. by J. J. Jackson, Historian,
36(Aug 1974):779; M. M. Kranz, HRNB, 2(Feb 1974):98-9;
W. H. Daniel, HT, 8(Nov 1974):131-2.

Twain, Mark. What is Man? And Other Philosophical Writings.
Berkeley: U Cal Press, 1973. Rev. by R. E. Spiller, AHR,
79(Je 1974):836.

Twellmann, Margrit. Die deutsche Frauenbewegung im Spiegel
repräsentativer Frauenzeitschriften: Ihre Anfänge und erste
Entwicklung. 2 vols. Meisenheim am Glan: Anton Hein,
1972. Rev. by C. M. Rose, AHR, 79(Feb 1974):174-5.

Tweton, D. Jerome and Daniel F. Rylance. The Years of Dispair:
North Dakota in the Depression. Grand Forks, N. D.: Oxcart
Press, 1973. Rev. by H. R. Martinson, NDH, 41(Spr 1974):
32-3.

Twitchett, Denis see Wright, Arthur F.

Tyler, Daniel, ed. Western American History in the Seventies:
Selected Papers Presented to the First Western History Con-

ference, Colorado State University, August 10-12, 1972.   Fort
Collins, Colo.: Robinson ... 1973. Rev. by H. A. Dahl-
strom, CoMag, 51(Win 1974):79-80; J. E. Sunder, JAH, 60
(Mar 1974):1141-2; H. A. Fleming, JOW, 13(Apr 1974):107;
D. A. Smith, NMHR, 49(Ja 1974):87.

Tyler, Robert L. Walter Reuther. Grand Rapids, Mich.: Eerdmans, 1973. Rev. by F. L. Grubbs, Jr., JAH, 60(Mar 1974):
1178.

Tyler, Ronnie C. The Mexican War: A Lithographic Record. Austin: Texas State Historical Assn., 1974. Rev. by W. B.
Fowler, HRNB, 2(Jl 1974):200-1.

_____. Santiago Vidaurri and the Southern Confederacy. Austin:
Texas State Historical Assn., 1973. Rev. by T. Schoonover,
ETHJ, 12(Fall 1974):82; R. Broussard, HAHR, 54(Aug 1974):
529-30; E. H. Moseley, JAH, 61(Sep 1974):492-3; J. A. Irby,
JSH, 40(Nov 1974):668-70; J. F. Gentry, TAm, 31(Oct 1974):
229-30; S. B. Brinckerhoff, WHQ, 5(Jl 1974):340-1.

Tyler, Royall see Keene, Donald

Tyler, Stephen A., ed. see Siegel, Bernard J., ed.

Udokang, Okon. Succession of New States to International Treaties.
Dobbs Ferry, N.Y.: Oceana, 1972. Rev. by R. A. Akindele,
JMAS, 12(Je 1974):323-6.

Ulam, Adam B. Expansion and Coexistence: Soviet Foreign Policy,
1917-1973. New York: Praeger, 1974. Rev. by S. D. Spector, HRNB, 2(Sep 1974):237.

_____. Stalin: The Man and His Era. New York: Viking,
1973. Rev. by R. M. Slusser, AHR, 79(Je 1974):820-2; M.
Patoski, HRNB, 2(Ja 1974):79; M. Latey, HTo, 24(Jl 1974):
511.

Ullman, Richard R. Anglo-Soviet Relations, 1917-1921. Volume 3.
The Anglo-Soviet Accord. Princeton, N.J.: Prin U Press,
1972. Rev. by H. Hanak, AHR, 79(Feb 1974):115-17; C. J.
Bartlett, EHR, 89(Jl 1974):646-8.

Ullman, Victor. Martin R. Delaney: The Beginnings of Black Nationalism. Boston: Beacon Press, 1971. Rev. by C. Crowe,
AHR, 79(Apr 1974):581-2.

Ullman, Walter. A Short History of the Papacy in the Middle Ages.
London: Methuen, 1972. Rev. by J. Dahmus, AHR, 79(Feb
1974):123-4.

Underdown, David. Pride's Purge: Politics in the Puritan Revolution. London: Ox U Press, 1971. Rev. by I. Gentles, CHR,

55(Mar 1974):99-101.

Underhill, Ruth. "Here Come the Navajo." Washington: Bureau of
Indian Affairs, 1953. Rev. by Staff, InH, 7(Sum 1974):57.

Underwater Archaeology: A Nascent Discipline. Paris: UNESCO,
1972. Rev. by H. L. Burstyn, T & C, 15(Ja 1974):151-3.

Updyke, John. Buchanan Dying. New York: Knopf, 1974. Rev.
by E. M. Halliday, AH, 25(Je 1974):98-101.

Upton, Martin. Farm Management in Africa--The Principles of
Production and Planning. London: Ox U Press, 1973. Rev.
by I. G. Simpson, JMAS, 12(Je 1974):345-7.

Upton, Richard, comp. and ed. Fort Custer on the Big Horn.
Glendale, Cal.: Arthur H. Clark, 1973. Rev. by W. Parker,
A & W, 16(Spr 1974):91-2; G. Chappell, CoMag, 51(Spr 1974):
173-4.

Urban, G. R. see Toynbee, Arnold J.

Urofsky, Melvin I. A Mind of One Piece: Brandeis and American
Reform. New York: Scribner's, 1971. Rev. by J. E. Semonche, AHR, 79(Feb 1974):235-7.

_____ and David W. Levy, eds. Letters of Louis D. Brandeis.
Vol. I. (1870-1907): Urban Reformer. Albany: SUNY
Press, 1971. Rev. by J. E. Semonche, AHR, 79(Feb 1974):
235-7.

_____, _____, eds. Letters of Louis D. Brandeis. Vol. II.
(1907-1912). People's Attorney. Albany: SUNY Press, 1972.
Rev. by J. E. Semonche, AHR, 79(Feb 1974):235-7; A. H.
Kelly, JAH, 61(Dec 1974):749-50.

_____, _____, eds. Letters of Louis D. Brandeis. Vol. III.
(1913-1915). Progressive and Zionist. SUNY Press, 1973.
Rev. by M. K. B. Tachau, FCHQ, 48(Apr 1974):192-3; A. H.
Kelly, JAH, 61(Je 1974):142-3; M. K. B. Tachau, RKHS, 72
(Apr 1974):198-200.

Uselding, Paul J. see Cain, Louis P.

Usui, Katsumi. History of Sino-Japanese Foreign Relations: The
Northern Expedition. Tokyo: Hanawa shobo, 1971. Rev. by
R. Suleski, JAS, 33(May 1974):484-6.

_____. Japan and China: The Taisho Period. Tokyo: Hara
shobo, 1972. Rev. by R. Suleski, JAS, 33(May 1974):484-6.

Utley, Robert M. Frontier Regulars: The United States Army and
the Indian, 1866-1891. New York: Macmillan, 1973. Rev.

by L. E. Purcell, AI, 42(Sum 1974):390-4; W. H. Leckie, HRNB, 2(May/Je 1974):159-60; R. N. Ellis, JAH, 61(Dec 1974):787-8; J. H. Nottage, JOW, 13(Oct 1974):146; E. B. Long, MinnH, 44(Spr 1974):35-6; M. J. Mattes, NH, 55(Sum 1974):290-2; W. E. Unrau, NMHR, 49(Oct 1974):333-4; R. L. Nichols, PHR, 43(Nov 1974):605-6; K. A. Franks, RKHS, 72 (Jl 1974):295-7.

Vacalopoulos, Apostolos E. Origins of the Greek Nation: The Byzantine Period, 1204-1461. New Brunswick, N. J.: Rutgers U Press, 1970. Rev. by P. J. Alexander, AHR, 79(Je 1974): 777-8.

Vacca, Roberto. The Coming Dark Age. Garden City, N. Y.: Doubleday, 1973. Rev. by H. A. Taylor, AmArc, 37(Apr 1974):287-9.

Valdes, Nelson P. and Rolando E. Bonachea. Che: Selected Works of Ernest Guevara. see Bonachea, Rolando E. and Nelson P. Valdes. Che: Selected Works....

Vale, Vivian. Labour in American Politics. New York: Barnes and Noble, 1971. Rev. by W. R. Van Tine, AHR, 79(Je 1974):836.

Valentinov, N. (Vol'shkii). The New Economic Policy and the Party Crisis After the Death of Lenin: Reminiscences of My Work at the V S N K H During the N E P. Stanford, Cal.: Hoover Institution Press, 1971. Rev. by D. Mulholland, AHR, 79(Oct 1974):1224-5.

Valeri, Nino. Tradizione liberale e fascismo. Florence: Felice Le Monier, 1972. Rev. by E. R. Tannenbaum, AHR, 79(Oct 1974):1209-10.

Valous, Guy de. Le patriciat lyonnais aux XIIIe et XIVe siècles. Paris: Editions A et J Picard, 1973. Rev. by E. A. R. Brown, AHR, 79(Feb 1974):128.

Vambe, Lawrence. An Ill-Fated People: Zimbabwe Before and After Rhodes. London: Heinemann ... 1972. Rev. by V. B. Khapoya, JMAS, 12(Mar 1974):165-8.

Van Alstyne, Richard W. The United States and East Asia. New York: Norton, 1973. Rev. by E. D. Graham, AHR, 79(Oct 1974):1238-9; L. J. Korb, HRNB, 2(Ja 1974):63; E. P. Trani, JAH, 61(Sep 1974):472-3; A. Iriye, JAS, 33(May 1974):459.

Van Caenegem, R. C. The Birth of the English Common Law. New York: Cam U Press, 1973. Rev. by E. G. Kimball, AHR, 79(Je 1974):772.

Van Creveld, Martin L. Hitler's Strategy, 1940-1941: The Balkan

Clue. New York: Cam U Press, 1973. Rev. J. M. Block, HRNB, 2(Feb 1974):111.

Vanden Berghe, Yvan. Jacobins and Traditionalists: The Reactions of the Inhabitants of Bruges in the Revolutionary Period (1780-1794). Brussells: Pro Civitate, 1972. Rev. by R. R. Palmer, AHR, 79(Feb 1974):172-3.

Vandenbroucke, François. Why Monks? Washington, D. C.: Consortium Press, 1972. Rev. by B. K. Lackner, CH, 43(Sep 1974):428-9.

VanDerBeets, Richard, ed. Held Captive by Indians, Selected Narratives 1642-1836. Knoxville: U Tenn Press, 1973. Rev. by J. H. O'Donnell III, FHQ, 53(Oct 1974):206-7; J. H. Thomas, JOW, 13(Apr 1974):121; L. E. Underhill, NYH, 55(Jl 1974): 347-8; W. E. Unrau, WHQ, 5(Jl 1974):343-5.

Van der Poel, Jean, ed. Selections from the Smuts Papers. Vols. 5-6-7. n. p.: n. p., 1973. Rev. by B. L. Lanier, HRNB, 3 (Oct 1974):16.

van der Veen, Klaas W. I Give Thee My Daughter: A Study of Marriage and Hierarchy Among the Anavil Brahmans of South Gujarat. Assen, Netherlands: Van Gorcum, 1972. Rev. by D. Jacobson, JAS, 33(Aug 1974):722-4.

Van der Woude, A. M. Het Noorderkwartier: Een regionaal historisch onderzoek in de demografische en economische geschiedenis van westelijk Nederland van de late middeleeuwen tot het begin van negentiende eeuw. Wageningen, Netherlands: Afdeling Agrarische Geschiedenis, Landbouwhogeschool, 1972. Rev. by R. C. Alltmont, JEH, 34(Sep 1974):803-4.

Van der Zee, Henri and Barbara. William and Mary. New York: Knopf, 1973. Rev. by S. B. Baxter, AHR, 79(Feb 1974):143-4; W. J. Baker, Historian, 36(May 1974):537-8.

Van Doren, Charles. Great Documents in American Indian History. see Moquin, Wayne

_____. Documentary History.... see Moquin, Wayne

van Dülmen, Richard, ed. Johann Valentin Andreae: Theophilus. Stuttgart: Calwer Verlag, 1973. Rev. by F. E. Stoeffler, CH, 43(Mar 1974):114.

van Dyken, Seymour. Samuel Willard, 1640-1707; Preacher of Orthodoxy in an Era of Change. Grand Rapids, Mich.: Eerdmans, 1972. Rev. by D. Kobrin, AHR, 79(Oct 1974):1248-9.

Van Gelder, H. A. Enno. Getemperde Vrijheid. Gronigen: Wolters-Noordhoff, 1972. Rev. by R. L. Jones, EHR, 89(Ja

1974):180-1.

_____, ed. Sources Concerning Real and Movable Property in the Netherlands in the 16th Century. Volume 1. Nobles, Peasants, Commerce and Transport. The Hague: Martinus Nijhoff, 1972. Rev. by J. Devries, AHR, 79(Je 1974):797.

Van Heerkeren, H. R. and Eigil Knuth. Archaeological Excavations in Thailand. Vol. I. Copenhagen: Munksgaard, 1967. Rev. by G. de G. Sieveking, Antiquity, 48(Je 1974):149-50.

van Laer, Arnold J. F., Kenneth Scott, and K. Stryker-Rodda, trans. and eds. New York Historical Manuscripts: Dutch. Baltimore: Genealogical Pub., 1974. Rev. by J. J. Heslin, NYHSQ, 58(Oct 1974):321-2.

Van Noppen, Ina W. and John J. Van Noppen. Western North Carolina Since the Civil War. Boone, N.C.: Appalachian Consortium Press, 1973. Rev. by C. G. Davidson, NCHR, 51(Jan 1974):93-5.

Van Noppen, John J. see Van Noppen, Ina W.

Van Schreeven, William J. and Robert L. Scribner, comp. and ed. Revolutionary Virginia: The Road to Independence. Volume I: Forming Thunderclouds and the First Convention, 1763-1774: A Documentary Record. Charlottesville: ... U Press Va, 1973. Rev. by A. Barnes, AmArc, 37(Apr 1974):299-300; G. M. Curtis, III, FCHQ, 48(Jl 1974):288-9; G. M. Herndon, GHQ, 58(Spr 1974):130; M. Savelle, JAH, 61(Sep 1974):467-9; V. O. Stumpf, JSH, 40(Aug 1974):464-5; T. W. Tate, NCHR, 51(Ja 1974):101-3; W. F. Willingham, RKHS, 72(Apr 1974):185-7; D. Jackson, VMHB, 82(Ja 1974):114-15; J. F. Sefcik, WPHM, 57(Ja 1974):113-14.

Van Slageren, Jaap. Les origines de l'Eglise Evangélique du Cameroun: missions europeénes et christianisme autochtone. Leiden: E. J. Brill, 1972. Rev. by P. R. Dekar, CH, 43(Je 1974):276-7.

Van Stone, James W., ed. V. S. Khromchenko's Coastal Explorations in Southwestern Alaska, 1922. Chicago: Field Museum of Natural History ... 1973. Rev. by M. Sherwood, PNQ, 65(Apr 1974):91.

Van Tine, Warren R. The Making of the Labor Bureaucrat: Union Leadership in the United States, 1870-1920. Amherst: U Mass Press, 1973. Rev. by G. N. Grob, BHR, 48(Win 1974): 552-3; D. Brody, JAH, 61(Dec 1974):815-16; P. Renshaw, JAmS, 8(Aug 1974):270-1.

Varkey, Ouseph. At the Crossroads: The Sino-Indian Border Dispute and the Communist Party of India, 1959-1963. Columbia,

373   VARMA

Mo.: South Asia Books, 1974.   Rev. by W. E. Langley,
HRNB, 3(Nov/Dec 1974):34.

Varma, S. P. and Virendra Narain, eds. Pakistan Political System
in Crisis: Emergence of Bangladesh. Jaipur: South Asia
Studies Center, 1972. Rev. by L. D. Hayes, JAS, 33(Aug
1974):729-30.

Vasil, R. K. The Malaysian General Election of 1969. Kuala Lumpur: Ox U Press, 1972. Rev. by R. O. Tilman, JAS, 33
(Feb 1974):332-3.

Vaughan, Alden T. and George Athan Billias, eds. Perspectives on
Early American History: Essays in Honor of Richard B. Morris. New York: Harper and Row, 1971. Rev. by M. B.
Norton, JAH, 61(Je 1974):154-5; R. M. Bliss, JAmS, 8(Aug
1974):262-4.

Vaughan, John. The English Guide Book c 1780-1870. Newton Abbot: David and Charles, n.d. Rev. by M. Greenhalgh, HTo,
24(Oct 1974):725-6.

Vaughan, Michaline and Margaret Scotford Archer. Social Conflict
and Educational Change in England and France 1789-1848.
Cambridge: Cam U Press, 1971. Rev. by G. Sutherland,
EHR, 89(Ja 1974):202-3.

Vaughan, R. Charles the Bold. London: Longman, n.d. Rev.
by A. R. Myers, HTo, 24(Mar 1974):210-11.

Vella, Walter F., ed. Aspects of Vietnamese History. Honolulu:
U Press Hawaii, 1973. Rev. by A. Woodside, AHR, 79(Je
1974):831; M. P. Onorato, HT, 8(Nov 1974):139-40.

Ventris, Michael and John Chadwick. Documents in Mycenean
Greek. Cambridge: Cam U Press, 1973. Rev. by M. L.
Lang, AJA, 78(Oct 1974):438.

Venturi, Franco. Italy and the Enlightenment: Studies in a Cosmopolitan Century. London: Longman, 1972. Rev. by H.
Hearder, History, 59(Je 1974):280.

Verardo, Denzil. Big Basin. Los Altos: Sempervirens Fund,
1973. Rev. by J. H. Engbeck, Jr., CHQ, 53(Sum 1974):186-
7.

Verlinden, Charles and E. Scholliers. Dokumenten voor de Geschiedenis van Prijzen en Lonen in Vlaanderen en Brabant, Deel
III (XVIe-XIXe eeuw). Ghent: Ryksuniversiteit, 1972. Rev.
by R. C. Altmont, JEH, 34(Je 1974):522-4.

Vermasern, J. M., ed. Etudes Préliminaires aux religions orientales dans l'empire Romain. Leiden: E. J. Brill, 1972.

Rev. by R. I. Hicks, AJA, 78(Jl 1974):315-16.

Vermeule, Cornelius see Comstock, Mary

Vernadsky, George, et al., eds. A Sourcebook for Russian History from Earliest Times to 1917. 3 vols. New Haven, Conn.: Yale U Press, 1972. Rev. by A. Springer, HT, 7(May 1974): 485-6.

Ver Steeg, Clarence L. and Richard Hofstadter. A People and a Nation. New York: Harper and Row, 1973. Rev. by D. C. Brink, HT, 7(Aug 1974):619-21; F. D. Metcalf, HT, 7(Aug 1974):621-2.

Veysey, Laurence. The Communal Experience: Anarchist and Mystical Counter-Cultures in America. New York: Harper and Row, 1973. Rev. by W. O. Reichert, JAH, 61(Sep 1974): 524-5.

Vickers, Michael see Post, Kenneth

Vidal, Gore. Burr: A Novel. New York: Random House, 1973. Rev. by E. M. Halliday, AH, 25(Je 1974):98-101.

Vien, Nguyen Khac. Tradition and Revolution in Vietnam. Berkeley, Cal.: Indochina Resource Center, 1974. Rev. by J. K. Whitmore, JAS, 34(Nov 1974):261-2.

Vierhaus, Rudolf. Der Adel vor der Revolution: zur sozialen und politischen Funktion des adels im vor-revolutionärem Europa. Göttingen: Vandenhoeck and Rupprecht, 1971. Rev. by J. M. Rogister, EHR, 89(Ja 1974):195.

Vigness, Winifred see Skaggs, Jimmy M. Chronicles.

Villamarina, Emanuele Pes di see Nada, Narciso, ed. La Révolution Piemontaise....

Villeré, Sidney Louis. The Canary Islands Migration to Louisiana, 1778-1783: The History and Passenger Lists of the Islenos Volunteer Recruits and their Families. Baltimore: Genealogical Pub. Co., 1972. Rev. by P. M. Segura, LaH, 15(W 1974):86-7.

Vinay, Valdo. Ecclesiologia ed etica politica in Giovanni Calvino. Brescia: Paideia editrice, 1973. Rev. by J. P. Donnelly, CH, 43(Sep 1974):404-5.

Vishwanathan, Savitri. Normalization of Japanese-Soviet Relations, 1945-1970. Tallahassee, Fla.: Diplomatic Press, 1973. Rev. by J. J. Stephan, AHR, 79(Je 1974):758-9; P. Hyer, HRNB, 2(Ja 1974):76.

Visser 't Hooft, W. A.   Memoirs.   Philadelphia: Westminster
     Press, 1973.   Rev. by W. Nijenhuis, CH, 43(Mar 1974):131.

Vlasto, A. P.   The Entry of the Slavs into Christendom: An Intro-
     duction to the Medieval History of the Slavs.   New York: Cam
     U Press, 1970.   Rev. by P. W. Knoll, AHR, 79(Apr 1974):
     500-1.

Vogel, Barbara.   Deutsche Russlandpolitik.   Dusseldorf: Bertels-
     mann Universitatsverlag, 1973.   Rev. by A. J. P. Taylor,
     EHR, 89(Jl 1974):687.

Vogel, Lise.   The Column of Antoninus Pius.   Cambridge, Mass.:
     Har U Press, 1973.   Rev. by D. L. Thompson, AJA, 78(Apr
     1974):208.

Vogel, Robert M. , ed.   A Report of the Mohawk-Hudson Area Sur-
     vey.   Washington: Smithsonian Inst. Press, 1973.   Rev. by
     J. R. Harris, T & C, 15(Jl 1974):534-6.

Vogel, Virgil J.   This Country Was Ours: A Documentary History
     of the American Indian.   New York: Harper and Row, 1972.
     Rev. by F. B. Prucha, JISHS, 67(Je 1974):345-6; D. F. Bi-
     beau, NDH, 41(Sum 1974):38-9.

Vohra, Ranbir, ed.   The Chinese Revolution, 1900-1950.   Boston:
     Houghton Mifflin, 1974.   Rev. by E. Rhoads, HRNB, 2(Aug
     1974):225-6.

Voight, John W.   see   Horrell, C. William

von Bothmer, Dietrich.   Greek Vase Painting: An Introduction.
     New York: Metropolitan Museum of Art, n. d.   Rev. by C. G.
     Boulter, AJA, 78(Oct 1974):441.

von Maltitz, Horst.   The Evolution of Hitler's Germany: The Ide-
     ology, the Personality, the Movement.   New York: McGraw-
     Hill, 1973.   Rev. by R. Zerner, AHR, 79(Oct 1974):1206-7;
     G. P. Blum, Historian, 36(Aug 1974):758-9.

Von Riekhoff, Harald.   German-Polish Relations 1918-33.   Balti-
     more: JHU Press, 1971.   Rev. by A. M. Cienciala, EEQ,
     7(Ja 1974):472-5; A. Polonsky, EHR, 89(Ja 1974):234-5.

von Zinzendorf, Nicholaus Ludwig Count.   Nine Public Lectures on
     Important Subjects in Religion.   Iowa City: U Ia Press, 1973.
     Rev. by J. D. Nelson, CH, 43(Mar 1974):114-15.

Vorg, Paul A.   The Closing of the Door: Sino-American Relations,
     1936-46.   East Lansing: Mich St U Press, 1973.   Rev. by
     P. H. Clyde, PHR, 43(Aug 1974):435-7.

Vorspan, Max and Lloyd P. Gartner.   History of the Jews of Los

Angeles. San Marino: Huntington Library, 1970. Rev. by
M. Rischin, PHR, 43(Aug 1974):429-30.

Vryonis, Speros, Jr. The Decline of Medieval Hellenism in Asia
Minor and the Process of Islamization from the Eleventh
Through the Fifteenth Century. Berkeley: U Cal Press, 1971.
Rev. by G. G. Arnakis, AHR, 79(Feb 1974):203-4.

Vucinich, Wayne S. , ed. Russia and Asia: Essays on the Influence
of Russia on the Asian Peoples. Stanford, Cal. : Hoover Institution Press, 1972. Rev. by J. J. Stephan, JAAS, 9(Ja &
Apr 1974):116-17.

Waagenaar, Sam. The Pope's Jews. n. p. : Library Press, n. d.
Rev. by J. Rubenstein, Commentary, 58(Sep 1974):91,94.

Wade, Mason. Francis Parkman: Heroic Historian. Hamden,
Conn. : Shoe String Press, 1972. Rev. by D. Miquelon, CHR,
55(Mar 1974):86-7.

Wade, Richard C. see Mayer, Harold M.

Wagenknecht, Edward. Ambassadors for Christ: Seven American
Preachers. New York: Ox U Press, 1972. Rev. by C. E.
Clark, Jr. , AHR, 79(Apr 1974):582.

_____. The Personality of Shakespeare. Norman: U Okla
Press, n. d. Rev. by A. Cardona-Hine, Mankind, 4(Apr 1974):
6,8.

_____. Ralph Waldo Emerson: Portrait of a Balanced Soul.
New York: Ox U Press, 1974. Rev. by L. Filler, HRNB,
2(Sep 1974):262.

Wagner, Dieter and Gerhard Tomkowitz. Anschluss: The Week
Hitler Seized Vienna. New York: St. Martin's, 1971. Rev.
by K. von Klemperer, AHR, 79(Feb 1974):180-1.

Wagner, Jean. Black Poets of the United States, from Paul Laurence Dunbar to Langston Hughes. Urbana: U Ill Press,
1973. Rev. by R. E. Lee, Crisis, 81(Ja 1974):31-2; N. L.
Madgett, JNH, 59(Jl 1974):299-301; M. Perry, NHB, 37(Ja
1974):206-7.

Wagner, Stuart L. and Russell H. Bartley. Latin America in
Basic Historical Collections: A Working Guide. see Bartley,
Russell H. and Stuart L. Wagner. Latin America in Basic
Historical Collections....

Wai, Dunstan M. , ed. The Southern Sudan--The Problem of National Integration. London: Frank Cass, 1973. Rev. by L.
Sanderson, JAfH, 15(Num 3 1974):517-18.

Wakefield, David, ed. Stendhal and the Arts. New York: Phaidon, 1973. Rev. by R. Brilliant, HRNB, 2(Mar 1974):123.

Wakelyn, Jon L. The Politics of a Literary Man: William Gilmore Simms. Westport, Conn.: Greenwood, 1973. Rev. by D. Aaron, AHR, 79(Oct 1974):1264; J. B. Boles, CWH, 20(Sep 1974):268-9; E. A. Miles, JAH, 61(Je 1974):187-8; A. H. Rose, JAmS, 8(Aug 1974):275-6; H. Cohen, JSH, 40(Feb 1974): 137-8; C. H. Bohner, MHM, 69(Sum 1974):230-1; R. M. Atchison, NCHR, 51(Ja 1974):99-100; W. D. Workman, Jr., SCHM, 75(Ja 1974):55-6.

Wakeman, Frederic, Jr. History and Will: Philosophical Perspectives of Mao Tse-tung's Thought. Berkeley: U Cal Press, 1973. Rev. by J. B. Grieder, JAS, 33(Feb 1974):310-13.

Wakin, Jeanette A., ed. The Function of Documents in Islamic Law; The Chapters on Sales from Tahawi's Kitab al-shurut al-kabir. Albany: SUNY Press, 1972. Rev. by F. J. Ziadeh, AHR, 79(Feb 1974):204-5.

Walbank, F. W. Polybius. Berkeley: U Cal Press, 1972. Rev. by L. Pearson, AHR, 79(Feb 1974):121-2; G. V. Sumner, CHR, 55(Je 1974):179-80.

Wald, Kenneth D. see Pedersen, James F.

Walker, Alice. In Love and Trouble: Stories of Black Women. New York: Harcourt Brace Jovanovich, n.d. Rev. by M. A. Wright, Crisis, 81(Ja 1974):31.

Walker, Barbara, ed. The Firebird Library. 16 vols. Englewood Cliffs, N.J.: Prentice Hall, n.d. Rev. by A. Peterson, HT, 8(Nov 1974):121-2.

Walker, D. D. The Ancient Theology: Studies in Christian Platonism from the 15th to the 18th Century. Ithaca, N.Y.: Cornell U Press, 1972. Rev. by J. A. Devereux, RQ, 27(Sum 1974):205-7.

Walker, Eric C. William Dell, Master Puritan. Cambridge: W. Heffer, 1970. Rev. by S. E. Prall, Historian, 36(Aug 1974): 742-3.

Walker, Franklin. The Seacoast of Bohemia. Santa Barbara: Peregrine, 1973. Rev. by R. W. Etulain, PHR, 43(Aug 1974): 431-2.

Walker, James Blaine. Fifty Years of Rapid Transit, 1864-1917. New York: Arno, 1970. Rev. by C. W. Condit, T & C, 15 (Ja 1974):109-10.

Walker, Kenneth R. A History of the Middle West: From the Be-

ginning to 1970. Russellville, Ark.: Pioneer, 1972. Rev.
by H. Knuth, JAH, 60(Mar 1974):1106-7.

Walker, Mack. German Home Towns: Community, State and General Estate, 1648-1817. Ithaca, N.Y.: Cornell U Press, 1971.
Rev. by T. C. W. Blanning, EHR, 89(Ja 1974):190-1.

Wall, Robert Emmet, Jr. Massachusetts Bay: The Crucial Decade,
1640-1650. New Haven, Conn.: Yale U Press, 1972. Rev.
by R. J. Taylor, AHR, 79(Apr 1974):570; G. Miller, CH, 43
(Je 1974):279-80; J. A. Henretta, JAH, 61(Je 1974):159-60;
R. M. Bliss, JAmS, 8(Aug 1974):262-4.

Wallace, William A. Causality and Scientific Explanation: Vol. II,
Classical and Contemporary Science. Ann Arbor: U Mich
Press, 1974. Rev. by J. Stephens, HRNB, 2(Jl 1974):207.

Wallace-Hadrill, J. M. Early Germanic Kingship in England and
on the Continent. New York: Ox U Press, 1971. Rev. by
B. H. Hill, Jr., 79(Oct 1974):1160-1.

Waller, Charles see Killion, Ronald

Waller, Derek J. The Kiangsi Soviet Republic: Mao and the National Congresses of 1931 and 1934. Berkeley: U Cal Press,
1973. Rev. by L. P. Van Slyke, JAS, 33(Aug 1973):698-701.

Walne, Peter, ed. A Guide to Manuscript Sources for the History
of Latin America and the Caribbean in the British Isles. London: R. A. Humphreys, 1973. Rev. by S. Collier, HAHR,
54(Aug 1974):500-1; C. C. Griffin, JLAS, 6(May 1974):169-70.

Walsh, Margaret. The Manufacturing Frontier: Pioneer Industry
in Antebellum Wisconsin, 1830-1860. Madison: State Historical Society of Wisconsin, 1972. Rev. by T. F. Marburg,
AHR, 79(Je 1974):860-1.

Walshe, Peter. The Rise of African Nationalism in South Africa:
The African National Congress, 1912-1952. Berkeley: U Cal
Press, 1971. Rev. by P. D. Pillay, CHR, 55(Mar 1974):
104-5.

Walter, Richard and Benjamin Robins. A Voyage Round the World
in the Years MDCCXL, I, II, III, IV by George Anson. New
York: Ox U Press, 1974. Rev. by S. Sternlicht, HRNB, 3
(Nov/Dec 1974):25.

Walter-Karydi, Elena. Samos. Band VI. Bonn: Rudolf Habelt
Verlag, 1973. Rev. by J. W. Hayes, AJA, 78(Jl 1974):439-
40.

Walters, Betty Lawson. Furniture Makers of Indiana, 1793-1850.
Indianapolis: Indiana Historical Society ... 1972. Rev. by

J. T. Keene, JISHS, 67(Je 1974):352-3.

Walters, John Bennett. Merchant of Terror: General Sherman and Total War. Indianapolis: Bobbs-Merrill, 1973. Rev. by M. D. Krolick, CWH, 20(Sep 1974):265-6; J. F. Marszalek, Jr., JAH, 61(Dec 1974):784-5; R. M. McMurry, JSH, 40(Aug 1974):493-4.

Walters, Ronald. Primers for Prudery: Sexual Advice to Victorian America. Englewood Cliffs, N.J.: Prentice-Hall, 1974. Rev. by R. Berthoff, HRNB, 2(Apr 1974):148-9.

Walton, Gary M. see Shepherd, James F.

Walton, George. Sentinel of the Plains: Fort Leavenworth and the American West. Englewood Cliffs, N.J.: Prentice-Hall, 1973. Rev. by F. D. Monahan, Jr., CWH, 20(Sep 1974):286-7; O. E. Young, JAH, 61(Je 1974):211-2; D. A. Walker, PHR, 43(Aug 1974):417-18.

Walton, Hanes, Jr. Black Political Parties: An Historical and Political Analysis. New York: Free Press, 1972. Rev. by I. A. Newby, Historian, 36(Feb 1974):346-7; L. R. Harlan, JAH, 61(Dec 1974):846-7; G. H. Hudson, NHB, 37(Apr/May 1974):251-2.

Walvin, James. Black and White: The Negro and English Society 1555-1945. London: Allen Lane, 1973. Rev. by R. I. R., JIH, 5(Sum 1974):161-3.

Walzer, Michael. Regicide and Revolution: Speeches at the Trial of Louis XVI. New York: Cam U Press, 1974. Rev. by D. P. Resnick, HRNB, 2(Aug 1974):228.

Wand, Augustin C., S. J., and Sister M. Lilliana Owens, eds. Nerinckx -- Kentucky -- Loretto. 1804-1851. St. Louis: Khoury, 1972. Rev. by S. S. Boldrick, RKHS, 72(Oct 1974):411-12.

Wandel, Eckhard. Die Bedeutung der Vereinigten Staaten von Amerika für das deutsche Reparationsproblem, 1924-1925. Tübingen: Mohr, 1971. Rev. by U. Sautter, AHR, 79(Feb 1974):247.

Wandrusza, Adam see Lesky, Erna

Wang, William S.-Y. and Anatole Lyovin. CLIBOC: Chinese Linguistics Bibliography on Computer. Cambridge: Cam U Press, 1970. Rev. by J. Lust, MAS, 8(Oct 1974):570-1.

Warch, Richard. School of the Prophets: Yale College, 1701-1740. New Haven, Conn.: Yale U Press, 1973. Rev. by B. M. Kelley, CH, 43(Je 1974):280-1; T. R. Crane, JAH, 61(Je 1974):160-1; J. M. Hoffman, NEQ, 47(Je 1974):311-14; N. S. Fiering, WMQ-3, 31(Apr 1974):314-18.

Warch, Richard and Jonathan Fanton, eds. John Brown. Englewood Cliffs, N. J.: Prentice-Hall, 1973. Rev. by J. J. Cardoso, CWH, 20(Je 1974):159-63; R. M. Johnson, HT, 7(Feb
1974):299-300; V. B. Howard, VMHB, 82(Oct 1974):506-7.

Ward, Harry M. Statism in Plymouth Colony. Port Washington,
N. Y.: Kennikat, 1973. Rev. by F. B. Carr, CH, 43(Mar
1974):117; P. Carroll, HT, 7(Feb 1974):312-13; R. M. Bliss,
JAmS, 8(Aug 1974):262-4; J. D. Krugler, WMQ-3, 31(Jl 1974):
521-2.

Ward, James A. That Man Haupt: A Biography of Herman Haupt.
Baton Rouge: LSU Press, 1973. Rev. by M. Klein, BHR,
48(Sum 1974):255; H. D. Woodman, JSH, 40(Nov 1974):664-5;
K. R. Nodyne, WPHM, 57(Oct 1974):456-8.

Ward, Maisie. The Tragi-Comedy of Pen Browning. New York:
Sheed and Ward, 1972. Rev. by J. E. Talmadge, GR, 28
(Spr 1974):175-7.

Ward, Robert David see Rogers, William Warren. August Reckoning. . . .

Ward, Robert E. and Frank Joseph Shulman, comps. and eds. The
Allied Occupation of Japan, 1945-1952, An Annotated Bibliography of Western-Language Materials. Chicago: American Library Assn., 1974. Rev. by J. J. Hastings, AmArc, 37(Oct
1974):600-2.

Ward, Stephen R., ed. The South Dakota Experience: An Oral History Collection of Its People. Volume I. Pierre and Vermillion: South Dakota Oral History Project, 1972-73. Rev.
by D. McComb, CoMag, 51(Spr 1974):168-9; L. J. Sprunk,
NDH, 41(Win 1974):26-7.

_____. see Julin, Suzanne

Ward, W. R. The Early Correspondence of Jabez Bunting. London:
Royal Historical Society, 1972. Rev. by J. Kent, EHR, 89
(Apr 1974):454.

_____. Religion and Society in England, 1790-1850. London:
Batsford, 1972. Rev. by R. Currie, EHR, 89(Apr 1974):453-
4; B. Harrison, History, 59(Feb 1974):118-19; N. C. Miller,
HT, 7(Aug 1974):646.

Warden, G. B. see Willcox, William B.

Waring, Joseph Frederick. Cerveau's Savannah. Savannah: Ga Historical Society, 1973. Rev. by P. Spalding, GHQ, 58(Sum
1974):288-9.

Warner, Denis and Peggy. The Tide at Sunrise: A History of the Russo-Japanese War, 1904-1905. New York: Charterhouse, 1974. Rev. by J. C. Perry, HRNB, 3(Nov/Dec 1974):35-6.

Warner, Marina. The Dragon Empress: The Life and Times of Tz'u-hsi, Empress Dowager of China, 1835-1908. New York: Macmillan, 1972. Rev. by Michael Gasster, JAS, 33(Feb 1974):304-5.

Warner, Sam Bass, Jr. History and the Role of the City. see Mann, Arthur. History and the Role of the City.

_____. The Urban Wilderness: A History of the American City. New York: Harper and Row, 1972. Rev. by C. V. Harris, JSH, 40(Feb 1974):161-2.

Warnke, Frank J. Versions of Baroque: European Literature in the Seventeenth Century. New Haven, Conn.: Yale U Press, 1972. Rev. by R. T. Petersson, RQ, 27(Sum 1974):264-7.

Warren, G. L. Skeletal Analysis of 4-SLD-406. San Luis Obispo, Cal.: San Luis Obispo County Archaeological Society, 1971. Rev. by T. King, AmAnt, 39(Apr 1974):392-4.

Warren, Peter. Myrtos: An Early Bronze Age Site in Crete. London: Thames and Hudson, 1972. Rev. by K. D. Vitelli, AJA, 78(Apr 1974):192-3.

Warth, Robert D. Lenin. Boston: Twayne, 1973. Rev. by S. M. Horak, HRNB, 2(Mar 1974):115.

Washburn, Wilcomb E., ed. and comp. The American Indian and the United States: A Documentary History. New York: Random House, 1973. Rev. by R. C. Crawford, AmArc, 37(Jl 1974):466-8; W. T. Hagan, JAH, 61(Sep 1974):449-50.

Waswo, Richard. The Fatal Mirror: Themes and Techniques in the Poetry of Fulke Greville. Charlottesville: U Press Va, 1972. Rev. by E. W. Tayler, RQ, 27(Spr 1974):107-10.

Waterfield, Robin E. Christians in Persia: Assyrians, Armenians, Roman Catholics, and Protestants. New York: Barnes and Noble, 1973. Rev. by G. R. G. Hambly, AHR, 79(Oct 1974):1225-6; R. P. Beaver, CH, 43(Mar 1974):129.

Waters, Frank. To Possess the Land: A Biography of Arthur Rochford Manby. Chicago: Swallow, 1973. Rev. by R. E. Smith, JOW, 13(Oct 1974):135; R. W. Larson, PHR, 43(Nov 1974):615-16.

Watkins, Floyd C. and Charles Hubert Watkins. Yesterday in the Hills. Athens, Ga.: U Ga Press, 1973. Rev. by J. E. Talmadge, GHQ, 58(Supp 1974):205-7.

Watkins, Owen C. The Puritan Experience. London: Routledge and Kegan Paul, 1971. Rev. by G. F. Nuttall, EHR, 89(Ja 1974):176.

Watson, Andrew, trans. Transport in Transition: The Evolution of Traditional Shipping in China. Ann Arbor: Mich U Press, 1972. Rev. by S. A. M. Adshead, JAS, 33(Feb 1974):300-1.

Watson, David Robin. Georges Clemenceau: A Political Biography. London: Eyre Methuen, n. d. Rev. by J. Richardson, HTo, 24(Apr 1974):285.

Watson, George. The English Ideology. London: Allen Lane, 1973. Rev. by S. Koss, History, 59(Je 1974):287; M. Freeden, JMH, 46(Sep 1974):549-51.

Watson, Inez. see Biographical Directory of the South Carolina House of Representatives

Watson, Richard L., Jr. see Cartwright, William H.

Watt, J. A., trans. John of Paris: On Royal and Papal Power. Toronto: Pontifical Institute of Medieval Studies, 1972. Rev. by C. Morris, EHR, 89(Apr 1974):421; M. Wilks, History, 59(Feb 1974):90-1.

Wayman, Alex. The Buddhist Tantras: Light on Indo-Tibetan Esotericism. New York: Weiser, 1973. Rev. by R. Ray, JAS, 34(Nov 1974):169-75.

Weare, Walter B. Black Business in the New South: A Social History of the North Carolina Mutual Life Insurance Company. Urbana: U Ill Press, 1973. Rev. by R. Higgs, AHR, 79(Feb 1974):240; T. Cripps, Historian, 36(Aug 1974):781-2; A. E. Strickland, JAH, 61(Dec 1974):820-1; D. W. Bishop, JNH, 59 (Oct 1974):399-400; G. H. Hudson, JSH, 40(May 1974):344-5; R. Gavins, NCHR, 51(Ja 1974):96-7.

Weatherford, Richard M., ed. Stephen Crane: The Critical Heritage. Boston: Routledge and Kegan Paul, 1973. Rev. by D. Clough, JAmS, 8(Aug 1974):278-9.

Weathers, Willis T. see Cox, Virginia D.

Weaver, Herbert and Paul H. Bergeron, eds. Correspondence of James K. Polk. Volume 2, 1833-1834. Nashville: Van U Press, 1972. Rev. by J. G. Rayback, AHR, 79(Apr 1974): 576; L. J. Lasswell, FCHQ, 48(Jl 1974):281-2; L. S. Theisen, MiA, 56(Apr 1974):125-7.

Weaver, P. R. C. Familia Caesaris: A Social Study of the Emperor's Freedmen and Slaves. New York: Cam U Press, 1972. Rev. by M. Hammond, AHR, 79(Je 1974):767.

Weaver, Thomas, ed. Indians of Arizona: A Contemporary Perspective. Tucson: U Ariz Press, 1974. Rev. by E. B.
Danson, JAriH, 15(Win 1974):398-9.

Webb, William and Robert A. Weinstein. Dwellers at the Source:
Southwestern Indian Photographs of A. C. Vroman. New York:
Grossman, 1973. Rev. by A. T. Row, JAriH, 15(Win 1974):
400-1; H. Kelsey, SCQ, 56(Fall 1974):217-18.

Weber, David J., ed. Foreigners in Their Native Land: Historical
Roots of the Mexican Americans. Albuquerque: U NM Press,
1973. Rev. by A. Hoffman, JOW, 13(Oct 1974):127; R. H.
Vigil, NMHR, 49(Apr 1974):155-9; D. C. Cutter, TAm, 31(Jl
118-19; V. Mayer, UHQ, 42(Sum 1974):303-4; M. S. Meier,
WHQ, 5(Oct 1974):468-70.

Weber, Francis J. Joseph Sadoc Alimony. Harbinger of a New
Era. Los Angeles: Dawson's, 1973. Rev. by J. A. Schutz,
SCQ, 56(Fall 1974):308-9.

_____. The Pilgrim Church in California. Los Angeles: Daw-
son's Book Shop, 1973. Rev. by C. M. Drury, SCQ, 56(Fall
1974):313-14.

Webster, Charles, ed. The Intellectual Revolution of the Seventeenth Century. Boston: Routledge and Kegan Paul, 1974.
Rev. by F. Rosenthal, HRNB, 3(Oct 1974):12.

Webster, T. B. L. Athenian Culture and Society. Berkeley: U
Cal Press, 1973. Rev. by R. A. Padgug, AHR, 79(Oct 1974):
1155.

Weddle, Robert S. Wilderness Manhunt: The Spanish Search for
La Salle. Austin: U Tx Express, 1973. Rev. by M. A.
Burkholder, ETHJ, 12(Fall 1974):74-5; W. M. Mathes, HAHR,
54(May 1974):313-14; C. E. O'Neill, JAH, 61(Sep 1974):455-6;
J. H. Nottage, JOW, 13(Apr 1974):135; D. E. Chipman, JSH,
40(May 1974):297-8; G. Avery, LaH, 15(Win 1974):92-3; A.
Nasatir, PHR, 43(Nov 1974):601-2; J. F. Bannon, WHQ, 5
(Apr 1974):188-9.

Weeks, Donald. Corvo: Saint or Madman? New York: McGraw-
Hill, 1972. Rev. by P. A. Makurath, Jr., GR, 28(Sum 1974):
349-52.

Weeks, Kent R. see Harris, James E.

Weems, John Edward. To Conquer a Peace: The War Between
the United States and Mexico. Garden City, N.Y.: Doubleday,
1974. Rev. by N. D. Brown, GHQ, 58(Fall 1974):374-6;
J. A. Stout, Jr., JSH, 40(Nov 1974):660-1; M. Stuart, RKHS,
72(Oct 1974):409-10.

_____. The Schiwetz Legacy. see Schiwetz, E. M.

Weidhorn, Manfred. Sword and Pen: A Survey of the Writings of
    Sir Winston Churchill. Albuquerque: U NM Press, 1974.
    Rev. by C. F. Mullett, HRNB, 2(Sep 1974):234-5.

Weidner, Charles H. Water for a City: A History of New York
    City's Problem from the Beginning to the Delaware River Sys-
    tem. New Brunswick, N.J.: Rutgers U Press, 1974. Rev.
    by N. M. Blake, NYH, 55(Apr 1974):239-40; B. M. Wilken-
    feld, NYHSQ, 58(Oct 1974):325-6.

Weigelt, Horst. Spiritualistische Tradition im Protestantismus:
    Das Schwenckfeldertum in Schlesien. New York: De Gruyter,
    1973. Rev. by W. Klaassen, CH, 43(Dec 1974):545-6.

Weigley, Russell F., ed. The American Military: Readings in the His-
    tory of the Military in American Society. Reading, Mass.: Addi-
    son-Wesley, 1969. Rev. by B. L. Turpen, HT, 7(Feb 1974):296.

_____. The American Way of War: A History of United States
    Military Strategy and Policy. New York: Macmillan, 1973.
    Rev. by E. M. Coffman, JAH, 60(Mar 1974):1090-1; S. R.
    Bright, PH, 41(Jl 1974):365-7; J. Leland, SCHM, 75(Ja 1974):
    58-9.

Weinberg, Julius. Edward Alsworth Ross and the Sociology of Pro-
    gressivism. Madison: State Historical Society of Wis., 1972.
    Rev. by D. W. Grantham, AHR, 79(Oct 1974):1274.

Weinstein, Robert A. see Webb, William

Weisband, Edward. Turkish Foreign Policy, 1943-1945: Small
    State Diplomacy and Great Power Politics. Princeton, N.J.:
    Prin U Press, 1973. Rev. by T. A. Bryson, AHR, 79(Apr
    1974):557-8.

Weisbord, Robert G. Ebony Kinship: Africa, Africans, and the
    Afro-American. Westport, Conn.: Greenwood, 1973. Rev.
    by E. D. Cronon, JAH, 61(Sep 1974):504-5; D. C. Lord, JSH,
    40(May 1974):343-4.

Weiss, Nancy J. The National Urban League, 1910-1940. New
    York: Ox U Press, 1974. Rev. by T. C. Reeves, HRNB, 2
    (Aug 1974):215.

Weiss, Rolf. Chlodwighs Taufe: Reims 508. Bern: Herbert Lang,
    1971. Rev. by J. M. Wallace-Hadrill, EHR, 89(Ja 1974):144-
    5.

Weissman, Stephen R. American Foreign Policy in the Congo, 1960-
    1964. Ithaca, N.Y.: Cornell U Press, 1974. Rev. by E. W.
    Lefever, HRNB, 2(Feb 1974):97; R. A. Mortimer, HRNB, 2

(May/Je 1974):163-4; N. R. Bennett, JAH, 61(Sep 1974):546-7.

Welch, Claude. Protestant Thought in the Nineteenth Century. Volume 1: 1799-1870. New Haven, Conn.: Yale U Press, 1972. Rev. by B. A. Gerrish, JMH, 46(Mar 1974):133-5.

Welch, Edwin. The Peripatetic University: Cambridge Local Lectures, 1873-1973. New York: Cam U Press, 1973. Rev. by J. R. K. Kantor, AmArc, 37(Ja 1974):75-6.

Welch, Fay see Merrill, Charles E.

Welch, Holmes. Buddhism Under Mao. Cambridge, Mass.: Har U Press, 1972. Rev. by J. Strong, JAS, 33(May 1974):474-5.

Welch, June Rayfield. Historic Sites of Texas. Dallas, Tx.: G L A Press, 1972. Rev. by C. Parker, ETHJ, 12(Fall 1974):80.

Welch, Stuart Cary. A Flower From Every Meadow: Indian Paintings From American Collections. New York: Asia Society, 1973. Rev. by N. S. Safrani, JAS, 33(Aug 1974):720-1.

Welcome, Henry see Cole, Martin, ed.

Wellborn, C. A. History of the Red River Controversy. Quanah, Tx.: Nortex Offset, 1973. Rev. by T. F. Ruffin, ETHJ, 12 (Spr 1974):71; E. H. Elam, SWHQ, 78(Jl 1974):104-5.

Wellenreuther, Hermann. Glaube und Politik in Pennsylvania 1681-1776: Die Wandlungen der Obrigkeitsdoktrin und des PEACE TESTIMONY der Quaker. Cologne: Böhlau Verlag, 1972. Rev. by R. W. Gilbert, PH, 41(Ja 1974):94-5; D. Rothermund, WMQ-3, 31(Ja 1974):154-6.

Wellesz, Egon and Frederick Sternfeld, eds. The New Oxford History of Music: Vol. II. New York: Ox U Press, 1974. Rev. by R. M. Isherwood, HRNB, 3(Oct 1974):11.

Wellisch, Hans and Thomas D. Wilson, eds. Subject Retrieval in the Seventies. Westport, Conn.: Greenwood, 1972. Rev. by M. Brichford, AmArc, 37(Ja 1974):90-1.

Wells, J. Gipson see Bryant, Clifton D.

Wells, John A. The Peabody Story: Events in Peabody's History, 1626-1972. Salem, Mass.: Essex Institute, 1972. Rev. by B. F. Tolles, Jr., NEQ, 47(Je 1974):322-4.

Wells, Tom Henderson. The Confederate Navy: A Study in Organization. University, Ala.: U Ala Press, 1971. Rev. by B. F. Cooling, AHR, 79(Apr 1974):585-6.

Wels, C. B., ed.   Documents on Foreign Policy of the Netherlands.
The Hague: Martinus Nijhoff, 1972. Rev. by D. W. Jellema,
AHR, 79(Oct 1974):1201.

Welsh, David.   The Roots of Segregation: Native Policy in Natal,
1845-1910. Cape Town: Ox U Press, 1971. Rev. by L.
Frank, JMAS, 12(Mar 1974):137-41.

Wendell, Charles.   The Evolution of the Egyptian National Image:
From Its Origins to Ahmad Lufti al-Sayyid. Berkeley: U Cal
Press, 1972. Rev. by G. B. Doxsee, Historian, 36(Aug 1974):
748-9; J. S. F. Parker, History, 59(Je 1974):314; C. P. Pot-
ham, HRNB, 2(Feb 1974):103-4.

Wendt, Bernd Jürgen see Geiss, Imanuel

Wenk, Edward, Jr.   The Politics of the Ocean.   Seattle: U Wash
Press, 1972. Rev. by K. A. Murray, PNQ, 65(Ja 1974):45-
6.

Were, Miriam.   The Eighth Wife.   Nairobi: East Africa Pub. House,
1972. Rev. by H. Dinwiddy, AfAf, 73(Jl 1974):379-81.

Wermelinger, Hugo.   Lebensmittelteuerungen, ihre Bekämpfung und
ihre politischen Rückwirkungen in Bern: Vom Ausgehenden 15.
Jahrhundert bis in die zeit der Kappelerkriege. Bern: the
Verein, 1971. Rev. by H. Freudenberger, AHR, 79(Feb 1974):
181.

Werner, Walter see Göttlicher, Arvid

Wessells, John H., Jr.   The Bank of Virginia: A History. Charlottesville: U Press Va, 1973. Rev. by W. O. Wagnon, Jr.,
BHR, 48(Win 1974):568-70; W. G. Ryckman, VMHB, 82(Oct
1974):509-10.

West, C. W. "Dub." Person and Places of Indian Territory.
Muskogee, Ok.: Muskogee Pub. Co., 1974. Rev. by G. H.
Shirk, ChOk, 52(Fall 1974):388.

West, D. A. and J. G. Purves, eds.   War and Society in the Nineteenth-Century Russian Empire. see Purves, J. G. and D. A.
West. War and Society....

West, Elliott see DeBoe, David C.

West, Richard.   Back to Africa: A History of Sierra Leone and
Liberia. London: Jonathan Cape, 1970. Rev. by J. Davidson, History, 59(Je 1974):308.

_____.   Congo. New York: Holt, Rinehart, Winston, 1972. Rev
by P. Mustell, N H B, 37(Feb/Mar 1974):229.

Westphall, Victor. Thomas Benton Catron and His Era. Tucson:
U Ariz Press, 1973. Rev. by D. C. Cutter, HRNB, 2(Ja
1974):66; P. A. Stratton, JAH, 61(Sep 1974):498-9; M. L.
Moore, JAriH, 15(Sum 1974):189-91; M. S. Legan, JOW, 13
(Oct 1974):133; J. S. Goff, SCQ, 56(Sum 1974):202-4.

Westrich, Sal Alexander. The Ormée of Bordeaux: A Revolution
During the Fronde. Baltimore: JHU Press, 1972. Rev. by
J. Dent, JMH, 46(Mar 1974):126-7.

Westwood, J. N. Endurance and Endeavor. Russian History, 1812-
1971. New York: Ox U Press, 1973. Rev. by R. H. Mc-
Neal, AHR, 79(Je 1974):817.

Wetter, Erik, Carl-Eric Östenberg, Mario Moretti. Med Kungen Pa
Acqua Rossa. Allhem: Malmo, 1972. Rev. by R. R. Holloway, AJA, 78(Ja 1974):100-1.

Weymouth, Lally, ed. Thomas Jefferson: The Man ... His World
... His Influence. New York: Putnam's, 1973. Rev. by
N. E. Cunningham, Jr., JSH, 40(Nov 1974):647-8.

Whaley, Barton. Codeword BARBAROSSA. Cambridge, Mass.:
M I T Press, 1973. Rev. by T. J. Uldricks, HT, 7(Aug
1974):644-5; D. Kahn, JIH, 5(Aug 1974):328-9; M. Beloff,
JMH, 46(Sep 1974):540-1.

Wharton, David B. The Alaska Gold Rush. Bloomington: Ind U
Press, 1972. Rev. by W. H. Wilson, AHR, 79(Oct 1974):
1270-71; M. Walsh, JAmS, 8(Aug 1974):267-70; T. G. Smith,
JOW, 13(Jl 1974):126; B. F. Gilbert, WHQ, 5(Ja 1974):66-7.

Wharton, James. Learning from the Indians. Philadelphia: Run-
ning Press, 1973. Rev. by J. L. Gill, JOW, 13(Apr 1974):
130.

Wharton, Mary E. and Roger W. Barbour. Trees and Shrubs of
Kentucky. Lexington, Ky.: U Press Ky, 1973. Rev. by W.
Boebinger, FCHQ, 48(Ja 1974):68; H. P. Riley, RKHS, 72(Apr
1974):194-6.

Wheeler, George. Pierpont Morgan and Friends: The Anatomy of
a Myth. Englewood Cliffs, N. J.: Prentice-Hall, 1973. Rev.
by V. P. Carosso, BHR, 48(Sum 1974):265-7; D. W. Noble,
HRNB, 2(Ja 1974):65.

Wheeler-Bennett, Sir John and Anthony Nicholls. The Semblance of
Peace: The Political Settlement After the Second World War.
New York: St. Martin's, 1972. Rev. by H. L. Coles, His-
torian, 36(Aug 1974):768-9.

Wheelwright, John. Selected Poems of John Wheelwright. Ed. by
Alvin H. Rosenfeld. New York: New Directions, 1971. Rev.

by L. Leary, NEQ, 47(Mar 1974):153-5.

Whetham, Edith H. Agricultural Marketing in Africa. London: Ox
U Press, 1972. Rev. by M. Simpson, JMAS, 12(Sep 1974):
504-5.

White, Hayden. Metahistory: The Historical Imagination in Nineteenth-Century Europe. Baltimore: JHU Press, 1974. Rev.
by W. T. Deininger, HRNB, 2(Mar 1974):122; G. Leff, PHR,
43(Nov 1974):598-600.

White, Helen and Redding S. Sugg, Jr., eds. From the Mountain.
Memphis: Memphis St U Press, 1972. Rev. by H. W. Woelfel, III, GR, 28(Spr 1974):177-80.

White, John H., Jr. American Single Locomotives and the "Pioneer."
Washington: Smithsonian Inst. Press, 1973. Rev. by C. M.
Condit, T & C, 15(Spr 1974):337-8.

White, Lonnie, et al. Hostiles and Horse Soldiers: Indian Battles
and Campaigns in the West. Boulder, Colo.: Pruett, 1972.
Rev. by R. Markman, ChOk, 52(Fall 1974):387-8; M. L. Heyman, Jr., JOW, 13(Apr 1974):123.

White, Mary Thornton. Early Medicine in Rapides Parish. Alexandria, La.: Privately printed, 1970. Rev. by P. K. Barber,
LaH, 15(W 1974):85-6.

White, Theodore H. The Making of the President, 1972. New
York: Atheneum, 1973. Rev. by B. A. Loomis, WMH, 57
(Sum 1974):317-19.

White, William G. see Cummins, D. Duane

Whitehead, John S. The Separation of College and State: Columbia,
Dartmouth, Harvard, and Yale, 1776-1876. New Haven,
Conn.: Yale U Press, 1973. Rev. by R. D. Cohen, HRNB,
2(Ja 1974):58.

Whitehill, Walter Muir and Sinclair Hitchings, eds. Boston Prints
and Printmakers, 1670-1775. Boston: Colonial Society, Mass.
1973. Rev. by P. C. Marzio, JAH, 60(Mar 1974):1092-3;
W. G. Duprey, NYHSQ, 58(Apr 1974):149-51.

Whitford, William Clarke. Colorado Volunteers in the Civil War:
The New Mexico Campaign in 1862. Glorieta, N. M.: Rio
Grande Press, 1971. Rev. by L. C. Rampp, JOW, 13(Jl
1974):115.

Whitman, Walt. Walt Whitman's Camden Conversations. Selected,
arranged and with an intro. by Walter Teller. New Brunswick,
N.J.: Rutgers U Press, n.d. Rev. by A. Cardona-Hine,
Mankind, 4(Aug 1974):66-7.

Whitting, P. D. Byzantine Coins. London: Barrie and Jenkins, 1973. Rev. by M. H. Crawford, Antiquity, 48(Sep 1974):237-8.

Whyte, J. A. Church and State in Modern Ireland, 1923-1970. Dublin: Gill and Macmillan, 1971. Rev. by F. S. L. Lyons, EHR, 89(Ja 1974):239-40.

Whyte, Martin King. Small Groups and Political Rituals in China. Berkeley: U Cal Press, 1974. Rev. by W. L. Parish, Jr., JAS, 34(Nov 1974):229-32.

Wickens, James. Highlights of American History. Chicago: Rand McNally, 1973. Rev. by W. G. Anderson, HT, 8(Nov 1974): 119.

Widick, B. J. Detroit: City of Race and Class Violence. Chicago: Quadrangle, 1972. Rev. by R. Lane, AHR, 79(Je 1974):908-9.

Widstrand, Carl Gosta, ed. Co-operatives and Rural Development in East Africa. New York: Africana, 1970. Rev. by C. Ehrlich, AfAf, 73(Jl 1974):378-9.

Wiecek, William M. The Guarantee Clause of the U. S. Constitution. Ithaca, N. Y.: Cornell U Press, 1972. Rev. by D. Fellman, AHR, 79(Apr 1974):567.

Wiegelmann, Günter see Teuteberg, Hans J.

Wiener, Philip P., gen. ed. Dictionary of the History of Ideas. New York: Scribner's, 1973. Rev. by P. Gay, AHR, 79(1974): 103-4; M. Farquand, Mankind, 4(Aug 1974):41.

Wieruszowski, Helene. Politics and Culture in Medieval Spain and Italy. Rome: Edizioni di storia e letteratura, 1971. Rev. by R. Brentano, RQ, 27(Spr 1974):41-3.

Wiesbrod, B. A., R. L. Andreano, R. E. Balwin, and A. C. Kelley. Disease and Economic Development: The Impact of Parasitic Diseases in St. Lucia. Madison: U Wis Press, 1973. Rev. by E. H. Newell, JEH, 34(Sep 1974):804-6.

Wiesflecker, H. Kaiser Maxmilian I. ... Munich: R. Oldenbourg, 1971. Rev. by J. W. Stoye, EHR, 89(Jl 1974):664.

Wightman, W. P. D. Science in a Renaissance Society. London: Hutchinson, 1972. Rev. by V. L. Bullough, RQ, 27(Sum 1974): 219-21.

Wik, Reynold M. Henry Ford and Grass-roots America. Ann Arbor: U Mich Press, 1972. Rev. by C. Fraser, AHR, 79(Oct 1974):1277; D. W. Noble, CHR, 55(Je 1974):227-8; R. and V.

Ginger, JISHS, 67(Je 1974):351-2.

Wikramanayake, Marina.   A World in Shadow: The Free Black in
Antebellum South Carolina.   Columbia,   S. C.: ... U SCar
Press, 1973.   Rev. by L. Schweninger, CWH, 20(Sep 1974):
274-6; D. J. Flanigan, JSH, 40(Aug 1974):481-2; P. H. Wood,
SCHM,   75(Jl 1974):191.

Wilbert, Johannes.   Survivors of Eldorado.   Four Indian Cultures
of South America.   New York: Praeger, 1972.   Rev. by
O. W. Taylor, TAm, 30(Ja 1974):409-10.

Wilcox, Wayne, Leo E. Rose, and Gavin Boyd, eds.   Asia and the
International System.   Cambridge: Winthrop, 1972.   Rev. by
R. L. Park, JAS, 33(Aug 1974):725.

Wilhelm, Paul.   Travels in North America, 1822-1824.   Norman:
U Ok Press, 1974.   Rev. by J. W. Cooke, HRNB, 2(Jl 1974):
193; J. T. Flanagan, MinnH, 44(Sum 1974):78-9; R. H. Simmons, WVH, 36(Oct 1974):72-4.

Wilhelm, Walter, ed.   Studien zur europäischen Rechtsgeschichte.
Frankfurt am Main: Klostermann, 1972.   Rev. by W. H. Bry-
son, EHR, 89(Apr 1974):416-17.

Wilhoit, Francis M.   The Politics of Massive Resistance.   New
York: George Braziller, 1973.   Rev. by N. Bartlett, ETHJ,
12(Fall 1974):91-2; N. R. McMillen, JSH, 40(Aug 1974):510-
11.

Wilkie, William E.   The Cardinal Protectors of England: Rome
and the Tudors Before the Reformation.   New York: Cam U
Press, 1974.   Rev. by P. L. Hughes, HRNB, 3(Nov/Dec):24.

Wilkins, Burleigh Taylor.   Hegel's Philosophy of History.   Ithaca,
N. Y.:   Cornell U Press, 1974.   Rev. by H. D. Andrews,
HRNB, 2(Jl 1974):206-7.

Wilkinson, Henrietta H.   The Mint Museum of Art at Charlotte: A
Brief History.   Charlotte, N. C.:   Heritage Printers, 1973.
Rev. by B. F. Williams, NCHR, 51(Spr 1974):226-7.

Wilkinson, Henry C.   Bermuda from Sail to Steam: The History of
the Island from 1784 to 1901.   Vols. I and II.   London: Ox
U Press, 1973.   Rev. by R. Callahan, AHR, 79(Feb 1974):
155-6; A. J. G. Knox, HAHR, 54(Aug 1974):535-6.

Willard, Beatrice E.   see   Zwinger, Ann H.

Willcox, William B., ed.   The Papers of Benjamin Franklin.   Vol.
15.   1 January 1768-31 December 1768.   New Haven, Conn.:
Yale U Press, 1972.   Rev. by E. Wright, EHR, 89(Ja 1974):
199.

_____, Dorothy W. Bridgewater, Mary L. Hart, Claude A. Lopez, Catharine M. Prelinger, and G. B. Warden, eds. The Papers of Benjamin Franklin. Vol. 16: January 1 through December 31, 1769. New Haven, Conn.: Yale U Press, 1972. Rev. by A. B. Tourtellot, AHR, 79(Oct 1974):1252-3; E. Wright, EHR, 89(Ja 1974):199; J. May, HRNB, 2(Aug 1974):220; B. Hindle, JAH, 60(Mar 1974):1071-3.

_____, _____, _____, _____, C. A. Myrans, Catharine M. Prelinger, and G. B. Warden, eds. The Papers of Benjamin Franklin. Vol. 17: January 1 through December 31, 1770. New Haven, Conn.: Yale U Press, 1973. Rev. by A. B. Tourtellot, AHR, 79(Oct 1974):1252-3; B. Hindle, JAH, 60(Mar 1974):1071-3.

_____, ed. The Papers of Benjamin Franklin. Vol. 18. January 1 through December 31, 1771. New Haven, Conn.: Yale U Press, 1974. Rev. by J. May, HRNB, 2(Aug 1974):220.

Wille, Lois. Forever Open, Clear and Free: The Historic Struggle for Chicago's Lakefront. Chicago: Henry Regnery, 1972. Rev. by M. P. McCarthy, JISHS, 67(Je 1974):348-9.

Willett, Frank. African Art: An Introduction. New York: Praeger, 1971. Rev. by B. M. Fagan, AHR, 79(Apr 1974):559.

Willey, Gordon R. An Introduction to American Archaeology. Vol. II. South America. Englewood Cliffs, N.J.: Prentice-Hall, 1971. Rev. by C. Morris, HAHR, 54(Feb 1974):164-5.

Williams, David see Fritz, Paul

Williams, Frederick D. see Brown, Harry James

Williams, Glyndwr, ed. London Correspondence Inward from Sir George Simpson, 1841-1842. London: Hudson's Bay Record Society, 1973. Rev. by D. E. Livingston-Little, JOW, 13 (Oct 1974):132; J. W. Scott, PNQ, 65(Oct 1974):189.

_____. see Flint, John E.

Williams, John A., ed. Journals and Proceedings of the General Assembly of the State of Vermont, 1793-1794 and 1795-1796, Papers of Vermont, Volume III: Parts VI and VII (2 vols). Montpelier, Vt.: Secretary of State, 1972. Rev. by J. R. Maguire, VH, 42(Win 1974):53-62.

Williams, Judith Blow. British Commercial Policy and Trade Expansion, 1750-1850. Oxford: Clarendon Press, 1972. Rev. by R. M. Cooke, Historian, 36(Feb 1974):320-1; G. Jackson, History, 59(Feb 1974):114; Z. Steiner, JMH, 46(Je 1974):346-7.

Williams, Max R. and J. G. deRoulhac Hamilton, eds. The Papers of William Alexander Graham. Vol. V. 1857-1863. Raleigh: N C Office of Archives and History, 1973. Rev. by E. L. Hill, AmArc, 37(Ja 1974):83-4; C. H. Smith, JAH, 61(Je 1974): 141-2; J. F. Steelman, JSH, 40(Feb 1974):143-4.

Williams, Philip M. and Martin Harrison. Politics and Society in De Gaulle's Republic. London: Longman, 1971. Rev. by G. Neave, History, 59(Feb 1974):156.

Williams, R. Hal. The Democratic Party and California Politics, 1880-1896. Stanford, Cal.: Stan U Press, 1973. Rev. by W. A. Bullough, CHQ, 53(Sum 1974):182-3; R. Jenson, HRNB, 2(Apr 1974):149; R. Holland, JOW, 13(Oct 1974):145; C. E. Grassman, PHR, 43(Aug 1974):428-9; J. L. Shover, PNQ, 65 (Oct 1974):194.

Williams, Roderick T. The Silver Coinage of the Phokians. Oxford: Ox U Press, 1972. Rev. by N. M. Waggoner, AJA, 78(Ja 1974):97-8.

Williams, Roger L. The Mortal Napoleon III. Princeton, N.J.: Prin U Press, 1972. Rev. by J. M. J. Rogister, History, 59(Feb 1974):135-6.

Williams, Roger M. The Bonds: An American Family. New York: Atheneum, 1971. Rev. by I. V. Brown, AHR, 79(Feb 1974): 225-6.

Williams, William Appleman. History as a Way of Learning. New York: New Viewpoints, 1974. Rev. by T. V. DiBacco, HRNB, 2(Apr 1974):144-5.

_____, ed. From Colony to Empire: Essays in the History of American Foreign Relations. New York: Wiley, 1972. Rev. by R. E. Darilek, HT, 7(Aug 1974):624-6; J. D. Doenecke, HT, 7(Aug 1974):629-31; A. DeConde, JAH, 61(Je 1974):152-3.

The Williamsburg Collection of Antique Furnishings. Williamsburg, Va.: Colonial Williamsburg Foundation, 1973. Rev. by L. L. Olcott, FCHQ, 48(Jl 1974):282-4.

Williamson, Jeffrey G. see Kelley, Allen C.

Willis, Parker B. A History of Investment Banking in New England. Boston: Federal Reserve Bank of Boston, 1973. Rev. by T. P. Kovaleff, BHR, 48(Win 1974):567-8.

Wills, John E., Jr. Pepper, Guns, and Parleys: The Dutch East India Company and China, 1622-1681. Cambridge, Mass.: Har U Press, 1974. Rev. by P. B. Cares, HRNB, 3(Oct 1974):17.

393   WILMSEN

Wilmsen, Edwin N.   Lithic Analysis and Cultural Inference: A
    Paleo Indian Case.   Tucson: U Ariz Press, 1970.   Rev. by
    J. M. Fritz, AmAnt, 39(Apr 1974):387-91.

Wilson, A. Jeyaratnam.   Politics in Sri Lanka, 1947-1973.   New
    York: St. Martin's, 1974.   Rev. by B. N. Schoenfeld, HRNB,
    3(Oct 1974):17-18.

Wilson, Charles Morrow.   Geronimo: The Story of an American
    Indian.   Minneapolis: Dillon, 1973.   Rev. by D. L. Thrapp,
    JAriH, 15(Spr 1974):87-8.

Wilson, Clifford.   Campbell of the Yukon.   Toronto: Macmillan,
    1970.   Rev. by M. Zaslow, CHR, 55(Mar 1974):82-4.

Wilson, Derek.   A Tudor Tapestry: Men, Women and Society in
    Reformation England.   Pittsburgh: U Pittsburgh Press, 1972.
    Rev. by M. Lee, Jr., AHR, 79(Feb 1974):141-2.

Wilson, Dorothy Clarke.   Bright Eyes: The Story of Susette La
    Flesche, an Omaha Indian.   New York: McGraw-Hill, 1974.
    Rev. by M. Young, HRNB, 3(Nov/Dec 1974):45; M. N. Dob-
    kowski, WPHM, 57(Oct 1974):450-1.

Wilson, Elinor.   Jim Beckwourth: Black Mountain Man and War
    Chief of the Crows.   Norman: U Ok Press, 1972.   Rev. by
    N. E. Williams, GPJ, 13(Spr 1974):210-11.

Wilson, Francis.   Labour in the South African Gold Mines, 1911-
    1969.   Cambridge: Cam U Press, 1972.   Rev. by L. Frank,
    JMAS, 12(Mar 1974):137-41.

Wilson, Ian E.   see Stewart, J. Douglas

Wilson, J. D.   see Armstrong, F. H.

Wilson, J. W.   People in the Way: The Human Aspects of the
    Columbia River Project.   Toronto: U Tor Press, 1973.   Rev.
    by J. E. Hendrickson, PNQ, 65(Jl 1974):154.

Wilson, James Q.   Political Organizations.   New York: Basic
    Books, n.d.   Rev. by J. Kirkpatrick, Commentary, 58(Sep
    1974):78-81.

Wilson, Joan Hoff.   American Business and Foreign Policy, 1920-
    1933.   Lexington, Ky.: U Press Ky, 1971.   Rev. by J. P.
    Nichols, AHR, 79(Feb 1974):246-7.

Wilson, LeGrand James.   The Confederate Soldier.   Memphis: Mem-
    phis St U Press, 1973.   Rev. by R. J. Sommers, CWH, 20
    (Je 1974):84-5; M. L. Heyman, Jr., JOW, 13(Jl 1974):114.

Wilson, Richard W.   Learning to be Chinese: The Political Sociali-

zation of Children in Taiwan. Cambridge, Mass.: M I T
Press, 1970. Rev. by Cho-Yee To, JAAS, 9(Ja & Apr 1974):
101-2.

Wilson, Theodore A. see Merli, Frank J.

Wilson, Thomas D. see Wellisch, Hans

Wilson, Woodrow. The Papers of Woodrow Wilson. Volume XIV:
    1902-1903. Ed. by Arthur S. Link. Princeton: Prin U Press,
    1972. Rev. by R. F. Durden, NCHR, 51(Win 1974):116-7.

Windham, Kathryn Tucker. Thirteen Georgia Ghosts and Jeffrey.
    Huntsville, Ala.: Strode, 1973. Rev. by E. Paris, GHQ, 58
    (Spr 1974):122.

Windrow, Martin and Gerry Embleton. Military Dress of North
    America 1665-1970. New York: Scribner's, 1973. Rev. by
    J. B. Reaves, ChOk, 52(Sum 1974):375.

Winkler, H. A. Mittelstand, Demokratic und Nationalsozialismus.
    Koln: Kiepenheuer und Winch, 1972. Rev. by J. Noakes,
    EHR, 89(Ja 1974):233-4.

Winslow, Ola Elizabeth. A Destroying Angel: The Conquest of
    Smallpox in Colonial Boston. Boston: Houghton Mifflin, 1974.
    Rev. by G. H. Brieger, HRNB, 2(Jl 1974):192-3; J. M. Quen,
    NEQ, 47(Sep 1974):488-9.

Winston, Henry. Strategy for a Black Agenda: A Critique of New
    Theories of Liberation in the United States and Africa. New
    York: International, 1973. Rev. by L. Brownstein, JMAS,
    12(Sep 1974):491-3.

Wint, Guy see Calvocoressi, Peter

Winter, J. M. and D. M. Joslin, eds. R. H. Tawney's Common-
    place Book. Cambridge: Cam U Press, 1972. Rev. by D.
    Read, EHR, 89(Ja 1974):232.

Winter, William H. see Johnson, Overton

Winterbottom, Michael, ed. Three Lives of English Saints. Toron-
    to: Center for Medieval Studies, 1972. Rev. by J. F. Kelly,
    CH, 43(Sep 1974):391.

Wise, Gene. American Historical Explanations: A Strategy for
    Grounded Inquiry. Homewood, Ill.: Dorsey, 1973. Rev. by
    M. T. Isenberg, HT, 8(Nov 1974):136-7; R. H. King, JAH,
    60(Mar 1974):1083-4.

Wiseman, T. P. New Men in the Roman Senate, 139 B.C.-A.D. 14.
    New York: Ox U Press, 1971. Rev. by R. E. Mitchell, AHR,
    79(Apr 1974):490.

Wiskenman, E. Italy Since 1945. London: Macmillan, 1971. Rev. by C. H. Church, ESR, 4(Ja 1974):95-7.

Wismer, David C. Obsolete Bank Notes of New England. Boston: Quarterman, 1972. Rev. by A. N. Nuquist, VH, 42(Spr 1974): 177-9.

Witonski, Peter P., ed. Gibbon for Moderns: The History of the Decline and Fall of the Roman Empire with Lessons for America Today. New Rochelle, N. Y.: Arlington House, 1974. Rev. by T. H. von Laue, HRNB, 2(Feb 1974):102-3.

Wittenburg, Sister Mary Ste Therese. The Machados and Rancho La Ballona. Los Angeles: Dawson's, 1973. Rev. by R. E. Northrop, SCQ, 56(Sum 1974):197-8.

Wittfogel, Karl A. see MacNeish, Richard S. The Prehistory of the Tehuacan Valley, Volume Four.

Wittkower, Rudolf. Pallado and English Palladianism. London: Thames and Hudson, n. d. Rev. by P. Q., HTo, 24(Jl 1974): 516.

_____ and Irma Jaffe, eds. Baroque Art: The Jesuit Contribution. New York: Fordham U Press, n. d. Rev. by A. Blunt, RQ, 27(Spr 1974):53-4.

Wittram, Reinhard. Studien zum Selbstverstandnis des 1. und 2. Kabinetts der russischen Provisorischen Regierung (März bis Juli 1917). Göttingen: Vandenhoeck & Ruprecht, 1971. Rev. by R. C. Williams, AHR, 79(Apr 1974):546-9; N. Stone, EHR, 89(Ja 1974):233.

Wittreich, Joseph Anthony, Jr., ed. Calm of Mind: Tercentenary Essays on Paradise Regained and Samson Agonisteo. Cleveland: CWRU Press, 1971. Rev. by G. F. Sensabaugh, RQ, 27(Fall 1974):376-81.

Wittreich, Joseph A. see Curran, Stuart

Wixom, Hartt see Muench, David. Utah.

Wojciechowski, Marian. Die polnisch-deutschen Beziehungen, 1933-1938. Leiden: E. J. Brill, 1971. Rev. by D. H. Perman, AHR, 79(Feb 1974):139-40.

Wolf, J. B., ed. Louis XIV. London: Macmillan, 1972. Rev. by R. M. Hatton, History, 59(Je 1974):279; J. Richardson, HTo, 24(Ja 1974):67.

Wolf, William B. The Basic Barnard: An Introduction to Chester I. Barnard and His Theories of Organization and Management. Ithaca, N. Y.: N Y St School of Industrial and Labor Relations,

1974. Rev. by D. A. Wren, BHR, 48(Win 1974):570-1.

Wolfe, Martin. The Fiscal System of Renaissance France. New
    Haven, Conn.: Yale U Press, 1972. Rev. by R. J. Knecht,
    ESR, 4(Apr 1974):181-2; N. M. Sutherland, History, 59(Feb
    1974):102-3.

Wolff, Michael see Dyos, H. J.

Wolff, Richard D. The Economics of Colonialism: Britain and
    Kenya, 1870-1930. New Haven, Conn.: Yale U Press, 1974.
    Rev. by R. V. Pierard, HRNB, 2(May/Je 1974):172-3.

Wolffe, B. P. The Royal Demesne in English History. Athens,
    Ohio: Ohio U Press, 1971. Rev. by S. A. Burrell, RQ, 27
    (Spr 1974):80-2.

Wolfgang, Marvin E. and James F. Short, Jr., eds. Collective
    Violence. see Short, James F., Jr. and Marvin E. Wolfgang,
    eds. Collective Violence.

Wolfson, Harry Austryn. Studies in the History of Philosophy and
    Religion. Cambridge, Mass.: Har U Press, 1973. Rev. by
    B. D. Jackson, CH, 43(Je 1974):270.

Wolin, Sheldon S. and John H. Schaar. The Berkeley Rebellion and
    Beyond: Essays on Politics and Education in the Technological
    Society. New York: New York Review, 1970. Rev. by W. L.
    O'Neill, AHR, 79(Je 1974):911-12.

Wong, Aline K. The Kaifong Associations and the Society of Hong
    Kong. Taipei: Orient Cultural Service ... 1972. Rev. by
    D. K. Jordan, JAS, 33(May 1974):480-1.

Wood, Catherine M. Palomar From Tepee to Telescope. Ramona,
    Calif.: Ballena Press, 1973. Rev. by D. Meadows, SCQ, 56
    (Fall 1974):315.

Wood, Gordon S., ed. The Rising Glory of America, 1760-1820.
    New York: George Braziller, 1971. Rev. by G. A. Danzer,
    HT, 7(Aug 1974):631-2.

Wood, James Playsted. The Curtis Magazines. New York: Ronald
    Press, 1971. Rev. by L. H. Parsons, AHR, 79(Oct 1974):
    1242-4.

Wood, Peter H. Black Majority: Negroes in Colonial South Caro-
    lina From 1670 Through the Stono Rebellion. New York:
    Knopf, 1974. Rev. by T. H. Breen, HRNB, 2(Sep 1974):262-
    3; R. A. Gerber, HRNB, 2(Sep 1974):263; St. J. Childs,
    SCHM, 75(Oct 1974):252-3.

Wood, Raymund Francis see Rhodehamel, Josephine DeWitt

Wood, Richard Coke. Owens Valley as I Knew It: The Owens Val-
ley and the Los Angeles Water Controversy. Stockton, Cal.:
U Pacific Press, 1973. Rev. by A. Hoffman, A & W, 16
(Spr 1974):71-2.

Woodbury, Richard B. see MacNeish, Richard S. The Prehistory
of the Tehuacan Valley, Volume Four.

Woodcock, George. Who Killed the British Empire? London: Cape,
n. d. Rev. by G. Douds, HTo, 24(Dec 1974):879-81.

Woodhouse, A. S. P. The Heavenly Muse: A Preface to Milton.
Toronto: U Tor Press, 1972. Rev. by B. K. Lewalski, RQ,
27(Sum 1974):261-4.

Woodhouse, C. M. Capodistria: the Founder of Greek Independence.
New York: Ox U Press, 1973. Rev. by L. S. Stavorianos,
AHR, 79(Feb 1974):190-2; A. Ramm, EHR, 89(Apr 1974):397-
400; W. St. Clair, ESR, 4(Apr 1974):185-7.

Woodress, James, ed. Essays Mostly on Periodical Publishing in
America: A Collection in Honor of Clarence Gohdes. Durham,
N. C.: Duke U Press, 1973. Rev. by C. B. Green, GR, 28
(Fall 1974):543-5; M. Allen, JAmS, 8(Aug 1974):274-5.

Woods, Frances Jerome. Marginality and Identity: A Colored
Creole Family Through Ten Generations. Baton Rouge: LSU
Press, 1972. Rev. by D. C. Thompson, JAH, 61(Dec 1974):
763-4; C. F. Oubre, LaH, 15(Sum 1974):310-1.

Woodward, C. Vann. The Strange Career of Jim Crow. New York:
Ox U Press, 1974. Rev. by M. Kranz, HRNB, 2(Aug 1974):
218.

Woodward, Guy H. and Grace Steele Woodward. The Secret of
Sherwood Forest: Oil Production in England During World
War II. Norman: U Ok Press, 1973. Rev. by M. A. Fitz-
simmons, HRNB, 2(Apr 1974):139.

Woodward, Sir Llewellyn. Prelude to Modern Europe, 1815-1914.
London: Methuen, 1972. Rev. by P. Philbeam, History, 59
(Feb 1974):113.

Woolf, S. J., ed. The Rebirth of Italy 1943-50. London: Longman, 1972. Rev. by M. Clark, History, 59(Feb 1974):157.

Worcester, Donald E. Brazil: From Colony to World Power. New
York: Scribner's, 1973. Rev. by R. E. Poppino, HAHR, 54
(Aug 1974):502-3; H. G. Warren, Historian, 36(Aug 1974):751-
2.

Worden, Blair. The Rump Parliament, 1648-1653. New York:
Cam U Press, 1974. Rev. by B. P. Levack, HRNB, 2(Sep

1974):235; A. L. Rowse, HTo, 24(May 1974):361-2.

Wreszin, Michael. The Superfluous Anarchist: Albert Jay Nock.
Providence, R. I.: Brown U Press, 1972. Rev. by C. Resek,
AHR, 79(Je 1974):891.

Wright, Antônia Fernanda Pacca de Almeida. Desafio Americano à
preponderância britânica no Brasil, 1808-1850. Rio de Janeiro: Imprensa Nacional. Rev. by E.-S. Pang, HAHR, 54
(Nov 1974):721-2.

Wright, Arthur F. and Denis Twitchett, eds. Perspectives on the
T'ang. New Haven, Conn.: Yale U Press, 1973. Rev. by
J. W. Dardess, HRNB, 2(Ja 1974):78.

Wright, C. E. Fontes Harleiani: A Study of the Sources of the
Harleian Collection of Manuscripts Preserved in the Department of Manuscripts in the British Museum. London: Trus-
tees of the British Museum, 1972. Rev. by R. M. Southern,
EHR, 89(Ja 1974):113-16.

Wright, Elizabeth. Independence in All Things, Neutrality in Nothing, The Story of a Pioneer Journalist of the American West.
San Francisco: Miller Freeman Publications, Inc., 1973.
Rev. by B. B. Beshoar, N H, 55(Sum 1974):306-7; H. Schind-
ler, UHQ, 42(Spr 1974):203-4.

Wright, G. R. H. Kalabsha: The Preserving of the Temple. Berlin: Gebr. Mann Verlag, 1972. Rev. by H. Goedicke, AJA,
78(Ja 1974):82.

Wright, J. Leitch, Jr. Anglo-Spanish Rivalry in North America.
Athens, Ga.: U Ga Press, 1971. Rev. by J. S. Bromley,
EHR, 89(Ja 1974):193-4.

Wright, L. R. The Origins of British Borneo. Oxford: Ox U
Press, 1970. Rev. by P. Tuck, History, 59(Je 1974):323.

Wright, Monte Duane. Most Probable Position: A History of Aerial
Navigation to 1941. Lawrence: U Press Kan, 1972. Rev. by
J. A. Huston, AHR, 79(Oct 1974):1144-5; E. M. Emme, JAH,
60(Mar 1974):1154-5; R. Perry, T & C, 15(Ja 1974):116-19.

Wright, Nathalia, ed. Letters of Horatio Greenough, American
Sculptor. Madison: U Wis Press, 1972. Rev. by M. Fried-
laender, NEQ, 47(Mar 1974):135-7.

Wright, Vincent see Le Clèrc, Bernard. Les préfets du Second
Empire.

Wright, William C. The Secession Movement in the Middle Atlantic
States. Rutherford, N.J.: Fairleigh Dickinson U Press, 1973.
Rev. by F. J. Blue, JAH, 61(Je 1974):195-6; R. A. Wooster,

JSH, 40(May 1974):316-17; W. H. Longton, NYH, 55(Jl 1974):
356-7.

_____, ed. New Jersey in the American Revolution II. Trenton:
N J Historical Commission, 1973. Rev. by L. R. Gerlach,
JAH, 61(Je 1974):168-70.

_____, ed. New Jersey Since 1860: New Findings and Interpreta-
tions. Trenton: N J Historical Commission, 1972. Rev. by
J. M. Allswang, JAH, 61(Je 1974):219-20.

Wrigley, E. A., ed. Nineteenth-Century Society: Essays in the
Use of Quantitative Methods for the Study of Social Data. Cambridge: Cam U Press, 1972. Rev. by M. R. Haines, JEH,
34(Je 1974):524-5; W. H. Sewell, Jr., JMH, 46(Sep 1974):
530-2.

Wrobel, Sylvia and George Grider. Isaac Shelby: Kentucky's First
Governor and Hero of Three Wars. Danville, Ky.: Cumberland, 1974. Rev. by C. G. Talbert, RHKS, 72(Jl 1974):278-
80.

Wrone, David and Russell S. Nelson, Jr., eds. Who's the Savage?
Greenwich, Conn.: Fawcett, 1973. Rev. by Staff, InH, 7(Win
1974):51.

Wu, Yuan-li, ed. China: A Handbook. New York: Praeger, 1973.
Rev. by J. H. Cole, JAS, 33(May 1974):469-71.

Wu-chi, Liu. Su Man-shu. New York: Twayne ... 1972. Rev. by
J. Sailey, JAS, 33(Feb 1974):305-7.

Wurm, Ted. Hetch Hetchy and Its Dam Railroad. Berkeley, Cal.:
Howell-North, 1973. Rev. by J. B. McGloin, CHQ, 53(Spr
1973):91-2.

Wycherley, R. E. see Thompson, Howard A.

Wylie, Max. 400 Miles from Harlem: Courts, Crime, and Correction. New York: Macmillan, 1972. Rev. by S. F. Ginsberg,
NYH, 55(Jl 1974):344-5.

Wyman, Walker D. Charles Round Low Cloud. see Clark, William Leslie

_____. Frontier Woman: The Life of a Woman Homesteader on
the Dakota Frontier. River Falls, Wis.: U Wis--River Falls
Press, 1972. Rev. by C. H. Morris, GPJ, 13(Spr 1974):211-
12; L. Remele, NDH, 41(Spr 1974):32.

Wynia, Gary W. Politics and Planners/Economic Development Policy in Central America. Madison: U Wis Press, 1972. Rev.
by W. P. Glade, HAHR, 54(Feb 1974):178-81; D. Browning,

JLAS, 6(May 1974):161-8.

Wynot, Edward D., Jr. Polish Politics in Transition: The Camp of National Unity and the Struggle for Power, 1935-1939. Athens, Ga.: U Ga Press, 1974. Rev. by R. Szporluk, HRNB, 3(Nov/Dec 1974):29.

Yakemtchouck, Romain. L'Afrique en Droit international. Paris: R. Pichon et R. Durand-Auzias, 1971. Rev. by Y. El-Ayouty, JAAS, 9(Ja & Apr 1974):130-2.

Yamauchi, Edwin M. Pre-Christian Gnosticism: A Survey of the Proposed Evidences. Grand Rapids, Mich.: Eerdmans, 1973. Rev. by H. Patrick, CH, 43(Mar 1974):97.

Yaney, George L. The Systematization of Russian Government: Social Evolution in the Domestic Administration of Imperial Russia, 1711-1905. Urbana: U Ill Press, 1973. Rev. by N. V. Riasanovsky, AHR, 79(Je 1974):816-17.

Yarnell, Allen. Democrats and Progressives: The 1948 Election as a Test of Postwar Liberalism. Berkeley: U Cal Press, 1974. Rev. by R. S. Kirkendall, HRNB, 2(Aug 1974):214.

Yates, Frances. The Rosicrucian Enlightenment. London: Routledge and Kegan Paul, 1972. Rev. by C. Webster, EHR, 89 (Apr 1974):434-5; J. Redwood, History, 59(Feb 1974):107.

Year Book XVII. London: Secker and Warburg ... 1972. Rev. by J. C. Fout, AHR, 79(Je 1974):803-4.

Yegar, Moshe. The Muslims of Burma: A Study of a Minority Group. Wiesbaden: Verlag Otto Harrassowitz, 1972. Rev. by M. E. Spiro, JAS, 33(Feb 1974):329-31.

Yoder, C. P. "Bill." Delaware Canal Journal: A Definitive History of the Canal and the River Valley Through Which It Flows. Bethlehem, Pa.: Canal Press, 1972. Rev. by E. J. Heydinger, T & C, 15(Ja 1974):101-8.

Yoder, John H., trans. and ed. The Legacy of Michael Sattler. Scottdale, Pa.: Herald Press, 1973. Rev. by J. J. Kiwiet, CH, 43(Dec 1974):545.

Yon, Paul D. Guide to Ohio County and Municipal Government Records for Urban Research. Columbus: Ohio Historical Society, 1973. Rev. by D. East, AmArc, 37(Oct 1974):587-9.

Youings, Joyce. The Dissolution of the Monasteries. New York: Barnes and Noble, 1971. Rev. by L. P. Fairfield, AHR, 79 (Apr 1974):511-12.

Young, Charles R. Hubert Walter: Lord of Canterbury and Lord

of England. Durham, N. C.: Duke U Press, 1968. Rev. by
R. Luman, CH, 43(Mar 1974):105.

Young, David. The Heart's Forest: A Study of Shakespeare's Pastoral Plays. New Haven, Conn.: Yale U Press, 1972. Rev.
by J. H. P. Pafford, RQ, 27(Spr 1974):105-7.

Young, James O. Black Writers of the Thirties. Baton Rouge:
LSU Press, 1974. Rev. by R. Polenberg, HRNB, 2(Jl 1974):
197; J. B. Kirby, JAH, 61(Dec 1974):828-9; S. P. Fullinwider,
JSH, 40(Aug 1974):507-8.

Young, Louise B. Power Over People. New York: Ox U Press,
1973. Rev. by T. A. Comp, T & C, 15(Ja 1974):127-9.

Young, Marilyn B., ed. Women in China. Ann Arbor: ... U Mich
Press, 1973. Rev. by L. E. Collins, JAS, 33(Aug 1974):705-
6.

Young, Marilyn Blatt, ed. American Expansionism: The Critical
Issues. Boston: Little, Brown, 1973. Rev. by R. W. Sel-
len, HT, 7(Aug 1974):636.

Young, Robert see Teich, Mikulas

Young, T. Cullen. Notes on the History of the Tumbuka--Kamanga
Peoples in the Northern Province of Nyasaland. London:
Frank Cass, 1970. Rev. by G. Shepperson, Africa, 44(Apr
1974):219-20.

Youngson, A. J. After the Forty-Five: The Economic Impact on
the Scottish Highlands. Edinburgh: Edinburgh U Press, 1973.
Rev. by M. Lee, Jr., AHR, 79(Oct 1974):1185-6; W. A. Moffett, Historian, 36(May 1974):542-3.

Yourgrau, Wolfgang and Allen D. Breck, eds. Biology, History,
and Natural Philosophy. see Breck, Allen D. and Wolfgang
Yourgrau, eds. Biology, History....

Zacour, Norman P. Petrarch's Book Without a Name. Toronto: Pontifical Institute of Medieval Studies, 1973. Rev. by W. L.
Hine, CH, 43(Sep 1974):394.

Zaghi, Carlo. I Russi in Etiopia. 2 vols. Naples: Guida, 1973.
Rev. by R. A. Caulk, JAfH, 15(Num 3 1974):503-6.

_____. L'Africa nella Coscienza europea e l'imperialismo itali-
ano. Naples: Guida Editori. Rev. by G. Baer, AHR, 79
(Apr 1974):488.

Zahn, Peter. Die Inschriften der Friedhöfe St. Johannis, St. Rochus und Wöhrd zu Nürnberg. München: Alfred Druckenmül-
ler Verlag, 1972. Rev. by D. Wuttke, RQ, 27(Fall 1974):339-
40.

Zane, G. L'industrie roumaine au cours de la seconde moitié du XIXe siècle: Sur les origines historiques de l'industrie de fabrique. Bucharest: Editions de l'Académie de la République Socialiste Roumanie, 1973. Rev. by P. N. Hehn, AHR, 79 (Je 1974):812-13.

Zaslavsky, Claudia. Africa Counts: Number and Pattern in Africa. Boston: Prindle, Weber and Schmidt, 1973. Rev. by S. A. Ekpo, JMAS, 12(Je 1974):347-9.

Zaslow, Morris. The Opening of the Canadian North 1870-1914. Toronto/Montreal: McClelland and Stewart, 1971. Rev. by J. K. Stager, CHR, 55(Mar 1974):89-90.

Zebel, Sydney H. Balfour: A Political Biography. Cambridge: Cam U Press, 1973. Rev. by B. L. Crapster, Historian, 36 (May 1974):546-7; M. Bentley, History, 59(Je 1974):296.

Zegger, Robert E. John Cam Hobhouse: A Political Life, 1819-1852. Columbia, Mo.: U Mo Press, 1973. Rev. by V. Cromwell, AHR, 79(Oct 1974):1180-1; M. R. Robinton, HRNB, 2(May/Je 1974):186.

Zeitlin, Solomon. Studies in the Early History of Judaism, Volume I. New York: KTAV, 1973. Rev. by W. D. Jones, HRNB, 2(Ja 1974):73-4.

Zeldin, Theodore. France, 1848-1945. Volume 1: Ambition, Love, and Politics. Oxford: Ox U Press, 1973. Rev. by M. Larkin, EHR, 89(Jl 1974):640-4; J. W. Scott, JMH, 46(Dec 1974):701-5.

Zelenin, I. E. State Farms in the First Decade of Soviet Power, 1917-1927. Moscow: Izdatel'stvo "Nauka," 1972. Rev. by G. D. Jackson, Jr., AHR, 79(Apr 1974):551-2.

Zenushkina, I. S. Soviet Nationality Policy and Bourgeois Historians: The Establishment of the Soviet Multi-National State (1917-1922): in Contemporary American Historiography. Moscow: Izdatel'stvo "Mysl'," 1971. Rev. by M. K. Matossian, AHR, 79(Je 1974):824.

Zeylanicus. Ceylon: Between Orient and Occident. New York: Fernhill House, 1970. Rev. by C. S. Blackston, AHR, 79(Je 1974):829-30.

Zhelubovskaia, E. A., et al., eds. History of the Paris Commune of 1871. Moscow: Izdatel'stvo "Nauka," 1971. Rev. by R. F. Byrnes, AHR, 79(Je 1974):791-2.

Ziegler, Philip. King William IV. New York: Harper and Row, 1973. Rev. by J. R. Rilling, Historian, 36(May 1974):544-5.

Ziff, Larzer. Puritanism in America: New Culture in a New World. New York: Viking, 1973. Rev. by G. M. Waller, AHR, 79 (Oct 1974):1248; D. B. Rutman, JAH, 61(Je 1974):158-9; C. W. Akers, NYHSQ, 58(Oct 1974):318-21; E. Elliott, WMQ-3, 31(Jl 1974):493-4.

Zimin, A. A. Russia on the Threshold of the Age: Essays on the Political History of Russia in the First Third of the 16th Century. Moscow: Izdatel'stvo "Mysl'," 1972. Rev. by T. Esper, AHR, 79(Oct 1974):1218.

Zimmerman, Gerd. Ordensleben und Lebensstandard. Munster Westfalen: Aschendorff, 1973. Rev. by H. E. J. Cowdrey, EHR, 89(Jl 1974):654-5.

Zinn, Howard. The Politics of History. Boston: Beacon, 1970. Rev. by D. M. Scott, JIH, 5(Aut 1970):343-8.

Zins, Henryk. England and the Baltic in the Elizabethan Era. Manchester: Manchester U Press, 1972. Rev. by M. Finlayson, CHR, 55(Je 1974):211-12; G. D. Ramsay, EHR, 89(Ja 1974): 174-5; R. O'Day, History, 59(Feb 1974):104-5.

Ziolkowski, Theodore. Fictional Transfigurations of Jesus. Princeton, N.J.: Prin U Press, 1972. Rev. by T. Molnar, GR, 28(Spr 1974):166-8.

Zivojinović, Dragan R. America, Italy, and the Birth of Yugoslavia (1917-1919). New York: Columbia U Press, 1973. Rev. by S. K. Pavlowitch, ESR, 4(Apr 1974):191-2; D. F. Trask, JAH, 60(Mar 1974):1167-8; V. S. Mamatey, JMH, 46(Mar 1974): 151-2.

Zophy, Jonathan W. see Buck, Lawrence P.

Zub, Al see Boicu, L.

Zuckerman, A. J. A Jewish Princedom in Feudal France, 768-900. London: Columbia U Press, 1972. Rev. by P. Wormald, EHR, 89(Apr 1974):415-16.

Zwinger, Ann H. and Beatrice E. Willard. Land Above the Trees: A Guide to American Alpine Tundra. New York: Harper and Row, 1972. Rev. by R. E. Smith, JOW, 13(Ja 1974):148.

TITLE INDEX

A. D. Xenopol: Studies in His Life and Works. L. Boicu and Al. Zub, eds.

Abby Hemenway's Vermont. Abby Maria Hemenway.

Aberdeen Shore Work Accounts, 1596-1670. Louise B. Taylor.

Die Abgeordneten der ersten Landtage (1946-1951) und der Nationalsozialismus. Rudolf Billerbeck.

The Abolition of Slavery in Brazil. Robert Brent Toplin.

The Abolition of the Brazilian Slave Trade: Britain, Brazil and the Slave Trade Question, 1807-1869. Leslie Bethell.

Abolitionism: A New Perspective. Gerald Sorin.

Abraham and Mary Todd Lincoln. Margaret Bassett.

Abraham Lincoln: Theologian of American Anguish. Elton Trueblood.

According to Hoole: The Collected Essays and Tales of a Scholar-Librarian and Literary Maverick. W. Stanley Hoole.

Aces High. Alan Clark.

L'Acropole d'Athènes. Jean des Gagniers.

The Activity of the Peasant Land Bank in Georgia, 1906-1917. M. P. Sanakoev.

The Acts of William I, King of Scots, 1165-1214. G. W. S. Barrow, ed.

Adam Ferguson. Pasquale Salvucci.

Adams County. 2 vols. Dorothy Weyer Creigh.

The Adams Papers. Adams Family Correspondence. Vols. 3 and 4. L. H. Butterfield and Marc Friedlander, eds.

Adirondack Bibliography Supplement, 1956-1965. Bibliography Committee, Adirondack Mountain Club, Dorothy A. Plum, chrmn., comp.

Adobes in the Sun: Portraits of a Tranquil Era. Augusta Fink and Amelie Elkinton.

The Advance of American Cooperative Enterprise: 1920-1945. Joseph G. Knapp.

The Adventures of Stickeen in Lower California. John F. Janes.

Afghanistan. Louis Dupree.

Africa and the Development of International Law. T. O. Elias.

Africa and the West: Intellectual Responses to European Culture. Philip D. Curtin, ed.

Africa Counts: Number and Pattern in Africa. Claudia Zaslavsky.

L'Africa nella coscienza europea e l'imperialismo italiano. Carlo Zaghi.

African Art: An Introduction. Frank Willett.

African Art and Leadership. Douglas Fraser and Herbert M. Cole.

African Culture and the Christian Church. Aylward Shorter.

The African Dimensions in Latin American Societies. Franklin W. Knight.

African Liberation Movements: Contemporary Struggles Against White Minority Rule. Richard Gibson.

The African Origin of Civilization: Myth or Reality. Cheikh Anta Diop.

An African Popular Literature: A Study of Onitsha Market Pamphlets. Emmanuel N. Obiechina.

African Religions and Philosophy. John S. Mbiti.

African Revolutionary: The Life and Times of Nigeria's Aminu Kano. Alan Feinstein.

The African Slave in Colonial Peru, 1524-1650. Frederick P. Bowser.

The African Slave Trade and Its Suppression: A Classified and

Annotated Bibliography of Books, Pamphlets, and Periodical Articles. Peter C. Hogg.

L'Afrique en Droit international. Romain Yakemtchouck.

Afrique Noire Occidentale et Centrale. J. Suret-Canale.

After the Forty-Five: The Economic Impact on the Scottish Highlands. A. J. Youngson.

After Yalta. Lisle Rose.

The Aftermath of Revolution in Latin America. Tulio Halperin-Donghi.

The Aftermath of War. World War I and U. S. Policy Toward Latin America. Joseph S. Tulchin.

The Age of Absolutism, 1648-1775. Maurice Ashley.

The Age of Arthur: A History of the British Isles from 350 to 650. John Morris.

The Age of Charlemagne. Donald Bullough.

The Age of Expansion, 1848-1917. Marcus Cunliffe.

The Age of Giant Corporations: A Microeconomic History of American Business 1914-1970. Robert Sobel.

The Age of Humanism and Reformation: Europe in the Fourteenth, Fifteenth and Sixteenth Centuries. A. G. Dickens.

The Age of Lloyd George: The Liberal Party and British Politics, 1890-1929. Kenneth O. Morgan.

The Age of Vinaya. G. S. P. Misra.

An Aged Wanderer: A Life Sketch of J. M. Parker. J. M. Parker.

Aggressive Introvert: A Study of Herbert Hoover and Public Relations Management, 1912-1932. Craig Lloyd.

Agonia de un neutral (Las relaciones hispanoalemanas durante la segunda guerra mundial y la División Azul). Raymond Proctor.

The Agora of Athens: The History, Shape and Uses of an Ancient City Center. Howard A. Thompson and R. E. Wycherley.

The Agrarian History of England and Wales. Vol. 1, Part 2. A. D. 43-1042. H. P. R. Finberg, ed.

Agrarian Relations in Wallachia in the 18th Century. Florin Constantiniu.

Agrarian Revolt in a Mexican Village. Paul Friedrich.

Agrarian Structure in Latin America: A Resume of the CIDA Land Tenure Studies of Argentina, Brazil, Child, Colombia, Ecuador, Guatemala, Peru. Solon Barraclough, ed.

Los agraviados de Cataluña. 4 vols.

Agricultural Marketing in Africa. Edith H. Whetham.

Agriculture in New Jersey: A Three-Hundred-Year History. Hubert G. Schmidt.

The Agunah. Chaim Grade.

Aid to Russia, 1941-1946: Strategy, Diplomacy, the Origins of the Cold War. George C. Herring, Jr.

The Air Plan That Defeated Hitler. Haywood S. Hansell, Jr.

Air Power: A Concise History. Robin Higham.

The Airline Pilots: A Study in Elite Unionization. George E. Hopkins.

Das Akademische Kunstmuseum der Universität Bonn. Nikolaus Himmelmann.

Akbar the Great. Vol. III. Society and Culture in 16th-Century India. Ashirbadi Lal Srivastava.

Akhenaten and Nefertiti. Cyril Aldred.

Alas! The Love of Women. Byron's Letters and Journals. Volume 3, 1813-1814. Leslie A. Marchand.

Alaska and Japan: Perspectives of Past and Present. Tsuguo Arai, ed.

The Alaska Boundary Dispute: A Critical Reappraisal. Norman Penlington.

The Alaska Gold Rush. David B. Wharton.

Alaska-Yukon Place Names. James W. Phillips.

Albert J. Beveridge: American Nationalist. John Braeman.

Alex: The Life of Field Marshal Earl Alexander of Tunis. Nigel Nicolson.

Alexander I. Tsar of War and Peace. Alan Palmer.

Alexander Hamilton: A Biography in His Own Words. Mary-Jo Kline, ed.

Alexander the Great. J. R. Hamilton.

Alexander the Great. Robin Lane Fox.

Alexandra Kollontaï: Marxisme et révolution sexuelle. Judith Stora-Sandor.

Alfred Giles: An English Architect in Texas and Mexico. Mary Carolyn Hollers Jutson.

Alfred Kroeber. Julian H. Steward.

Alfred Rosmer (1877-1964) et le mouvement révolutionnaire international. Christian Gras.

L'Algérie Indépendante. Gérard Chaliand and Juliette Minces.

The Alien Invasion: The Origins of the Aliens Act of 1905. Bernard Gainer.

Alienation: Marx's Conception of Man in Capitalist Society. Bertel Ollman.

Alive: The Story of the Andes Survivors. Piers Paul Read.

All Hell Needs Is Water. Budge Ruffner.

All is But a Beginning: Youth Remembered, 1881-1901. John G. Neihardt.

All Quiet on the Yamhill: The Civil War in Oregon. Royal N. Bensell.

Alliance in Decline: A Study in Anglo-Japanese Relations, 1908-1923. Ian H. Nish.

Alliances and Ententes as Political Weapons: From Bismarck's Alliance System to Present Time. Helge Granfelt.

The Allied Occupation of Japan, 1945-1952, An Annotated Bibliography of Western-Language Materials. Robert E. Ward and Frank Joseph Shulman, comps. and eds.

Allies for Freedom: Blacks and John Brown. Benjamin Quarles.

Almost Out of the World. James G. Swan.

Alphonse in Austin: Being Excerpts from the Official Letters Written to the French Foreign Ministry by Alphonse Duboise de Saligny.... Katherine Hart, trans.

Al-Riddah and the Muslim Conquest of Arabia. Elias Shoufani.

Alternatives to the Traditional: How Professors Teach and How Students Learn. Ohmer Milton.

Ambassadors for Christ: Seven American Preachers. Edward Wagen-knecht.

Ambrose L. (Aqua Fortis) Jordan, Lawyer. Richard H. Levet.

Amending Procedures of the Constituent Instruments of International Organisations. J. N. Saxena.

The Amendment That Refused to Die--XIV. Howard N. Meyer.

America: A Dutch Historian's Vision, From Afar and Near. Johan Huizinga.

America Encounters India, 1941-1947. Gary R. Hess.

America for Americans: Economic Nationalism and Anglophobia in the Late Nineteenth Century. Edward P. Crapol.

America in Legend: Folklore from the Colonial Period to the Present. Richard M. Dorson.

America in the Twenties: The Beginnings of Contemporary America. Paul Goodman and Frank Otto Gatell.

America, Italy and the Birth of Yugoslavia (1917-1919). Dragan R. Zivojinović.

America--1603-1789: Prelude to a Nation. Lawrence H. Leder.

America, the Middle Period: Essays in Honor of Bernard Mayo. John B. Boles, ed.

American Architecture Comes of Age: European Reaction to H. H. Richardson and Louis Sullivan. Leonard K. Eaton.

American Boarding Schools: A Historical Study. James McLachlan.

American Building: The Environmental Forces That Shape It. James Marston Fitch

American Buildings and Their Architects. Volumes 3 and 4. William H. Jordy.

American Business and Foreign Policy, 1920-1933. Joan Hoff Wilson.

American Business in the Twentieth Century. Thomas C. Cochran.

The American Campaigns of Rochambeau's Army, 1780, 1781, 1782, 1783. Howard C. Rice, Jr. and Anne S. K. Brown, eds.

American Civil War Navies: A Bibliography. Myron J. Smith, Jr.

American Communism in Crisis--1943-57. Joseph R. Starobin.

The American Conscience: The Drama of the Lincoln-Douglas Debates. Saul Sigelschiffer.

The American Cowboy. Harold McCracken.

The American Cowboy in Life and Legend. Bart McDowell.

The American Disease: Origins of Narcotic Control. David Musto.

American-East Asian Relations: A Survey. Ernest R. May and James C. Thomson, Jr., eds.

American Economic Growth: An Economist's History of the United States. Lance E. Davis, et al.

American Expansionism: The Critical Issues. Marilyn Blatt Young, ed.

The American Experience. James E. Bruner, Jr.

The American Family in Social-Historical Perspective. Michael Gordon, ed.

American Foreign Policy in the Congo, 1960-1964. Stephen R. Weissman.

The American Frontier. D. Duane Cummins and William Gee White.

American Gunboat Diplomacy and the Old Navy, 1877-1889. Kenneth J. Hagan.

American Habitat: A Historical Perspective. Barbara Gutmann Rosenkrantz and William A. Koelsch, eds.

The American Hegelians: An Intellectual Episode in the History of Western America. William H. Goetzmann, ed.

The American Heritage History of American Business and Industry. Alex Groner, et al.

American Historical Explanations: A Strategy for Grounded Inquiry. Gene Wise.

An American History. Rebecca Brooks Gruner.

American History in American Thought. Christopher Columbus to Henry Adams. Bert James Loewenberg.

The American Idea of Success. Richard M. Huber.

The American Indian: From Pacifism to Activism. Donald T. Berthrong.

American Indian Almanac. John Upton Terrell.

American Indian and Eskimo Authors: A Comprehensive Bibliography.

Arlene B. Hirschfelder, comp.

The American Indian and the United States: A Documentary History. Wilcomb E. Washburn, ed. and comp.

American Indian Ceremonial Dances: Navajo--Pueblo--Apache--Zuni. John Collier and Ira Moskowitz.

American Labor History and Comparative Labor Movements. James C. McBreaty.

The American Left in the Twentieth Century. John P. Diggins.

The American Mail: Enlarger of the Common Life. Wayne E. Fuller.

American Military Commitments Abroad. Roland A. Paul.

The American Military: Readings in the History of the Military in American Society. Russell F. Weigley, ed.

American Pacific Ocean Trade: Its Impact of Foreign Policy and Continental Expansion, 1784-1860. J. Wade Caruthers.

American Patchwork Quilts. Lenice Ingram Bacon.

The American Peace Movement and Social Reform, 1898-1918. C. Roland Marchand.

An American Philosophy of Social Security: Evolution and Issues. J. Douglas Brown.

American Policy Toward Communist China, 1949-1969. Foster Rhea Dulles.

The American Problem in British Diplomacy, 1841-1861. Wilbur Devereux Jones.

The American Quest, 1790-1860: An Emerging Nation in Search of Identity, Unity, and Modernity. Clinton Rossiter.

American Racism. Roger Daniels and Harry H. L. Kitano.

The American Religious Experience: the Roots, Trends, and Future of Theology. Frederick Sontag and John K. Roth.

American Religious Thought: A History. William A. Clebsch.

The American Revolution: A General History, 1763-1790. E. James Ferguson.

The American Revolution and Religion: Maryland 1770-1800. Thomas O'Brien Hanley.

American Roulette: The History and Dilemma of the Vice-Presidency. Donald Young.

American Sailing Coasters of the North Atlantic. Paul C. Morris.

American Single Locomotives and the "Pioneer." John H. White, Jr.

American Social Thought: Sources and Interpretations. 2 vols. Michael McGiffert and Robert Allen Skotheim, eds.

American Space: The Centennial Years, 1865-1876. John Brinckerhoff Jackson.

The American Territorial System. John Porter Bloom, ed.

The American War and Peace, 1860-1877. Emory M. Thomas.

The American Way of War: A History of United States Military Strategy and Policy. Russell F. Weigley.

The American West: An Interpretive History. Robert V. Hine.

The American West in the Twentieth Century: A Short History of an Urban Oasis. Gerald D. Nash.

The American Woman: Her Changing Social, Economic, and Political Roles, 1920-1970. William Henry Chafe.

The Americanization of Alaska, 1867-1897. Ted C. Hinckley.

The Americanization of Dixie: The Southernization of America. John Egerton.

The Americanization of the Gulf Coast: 1803-1850. Lucius F. Ellsworth, ed.

The "Americanization" of Utah for Statehood. Gustive O. Larson.

Americanizing the American Indians: Writings by the "Friends of the Indian," 1880-1900. Francis Paul Prucha, ed.

The Americans: The Democratic Experience. Daniel J. Boorstin.

Americans and the California Dream, 1850-1915. Kevin Starr.

Americans in Antarctica, 1775-1948. Kenneth J. Bertrand.

Americans in Conflict: The Civil War and Reconstruction. David Lindsey.

Americans in Southeast Asia: The Roots of Commitment. Russell H. Fifield.

America's Lighthouses: Their Illustrated History Since 1716. Frances Ross Holland, Jr.

America's Major Wars: Crusaders, Critics, and Scholars. Leslie E. Decker and Robert Seager, II, eds.

America's Outward Thrust. Approaches to Foreign Affairs, 1865-1890. Milton Plesur.

America's Past: A New World Archaeology. Thomas G. Patterson.

America's Response to China: An Interpretative History of Sino-American Relations. Warren I. Cohen.

Among the Mescalero Apaches: The Story of Father Albert Braun, O. F. M. Dorothy Emerson.

The Amud Man and His Cave Site. H. Suzuki and F. Takai, eds.

Anabaptism: Neither Catholic nor Protestant. Walter Klaassen.

Anabaptism, A Social History, 1525-1618: Switzerland, Austria, Moravia, South and Central Germany. Peter-Claus Clasen.

Anabaptists and the Sword. James M. Stayer.

Anarchists and Communists in Brazil, 1900-1935. John W. F. Dulles.

Anarquismo y revolución en la España del XIX. Clara E. Lida.

Anarquismo y sindicalismo en España: La Primera Intercional, 1864-1881. Josep Termes.

Anasazi: Ancient People of the Rock. David Muench and Donald G. Pike.

The Anatomy of the Confederate Congress: A Study of the Influences of Member Characteristics on Legislative Voting Behavior, 1861-1865. Thomas B. Alexander and Richard E. Beringer.

Los Anchorena. Política y negacios en el siglo XIX. Andrés M. Carretero.

L'Ancien Regime. Vols. I and II. Pierre Goubert.

The Ancient American Civilizations. Friedrich Katz.

Ancient and Medieval Jewish History: Essays by Salo Wittmayer Baron. Leon A. Feldman, ed.

The Ancient and Rightful Customs:

A History of the English Customs Service. Edward Carson.

Ancient Athenian Maritime Courts. Edward E. Cohen.

The Ancient Civilization of Byzantium. Antoine Bon.

The Ancient Economy. M. I. Finley.

Ancient Ghana and Mali. Nehemia Levtzion.

Ancient Greece: An Illustrated History. Peter Green.

The Ancient Theology: Studies in Christian Platonism from the 15th to the 18th Century. D. D. Walker.

The Ancient View of Greek Art: Criticism, History, and Terminology. J. J. Pollitt.

Andre Gide and Romain Rolland. Frederick John Harris.

Andreas Bodenstein Von Karlstadt: The Development of His Thought, 1517-1525. Ronald J. Sider.

Andrew Johnson: Congress and Reconstruction. Howard P. Nash, Jr.

Andrew Marvell: the Complete Poems. Elizabeth Story Donno, ed.

Aneurin Bevan: A Biography. Volume II. 1945-1960. Michael Foot.

Die Anfänge des Neolithikums vom Orient bis Nordeuropa, Part V. Hermann Schwabedissen, gen. ed.

The Angel of Bethesda. Cotton Mather.

Angles, Angels, and Conquerors. Joel T. Rosenthal.

Anglo-American Politics 1660-1775: The Relationship Between Parties in England and Colonial America. Alison Gilbert Olson.

Anglo-Japanese Relations During the First World War. R. P. Dua.

The Anglo-Saxon Cemeteries of Caistor-by-Norwich and Marshall, Norfolk. J. N. L. Myres and Barbara Green.

Anglo-Saxon England. 2 vols. Peter Clemoes, ed.

Anglo-Soviet Relations, 1917-1921. Volume III. The Anglo-Soviet Accord. Richard R. Ullman.

Anglo-Spanish Rivalry in North America. J. Leitch Wright, Jr.

Anglo-Vatican Relations, 1914-1939: Confidential Annual Reports of the British Ministers to the Holy See. Thomas E. Hachey, ed.

Animals in Roman Life and Art. J. M. C. Toynbee.

Dé L'Anliquite au Monde Médieval. R. Folz, A. Guillou, L. Musset, and D. Sourdel.

Anna Comnena. Rae Dalven.

Annals of Labour: Autobiographies of British Working-Class People 1820-1920. John Burnett, ed.

Anne Royall's U. S. A. Bessie Rowland James.

An Annotated, Selected Puerto Rican Bibliography. Enrique R. Bravo.

Annual Review of Anthropology, Vol. 1. Bernard J. Siegel, ed. et al.

Annual Studies of America, 1972.

Another Look at the Twentieth-Century South. George E. Mowry.

Another Place: Photographs of a Maya Community. Frank Cancian.

Anschluss: The Week Hitler Seized Vienna. Dieter Wagner and Gerhard Tomkowitz.

The Anschluss Question in the Weimar Era: A Study of Nationalism in Germany and Austria, 1918-1932. Stanley Suval.

Anthropologie du conscrit francais d'aprés les comptes numériques et sommaires du recrutement de l'armée (1819-1826). Jean-Paul Aron, Paul Dumont, Emmanuel Le Roy Ladurie.

Anticlericalism: A Brief History. José Sánchez.

El Antiguo Régimen: Los reyes católicos y los Austrias. Antonio Domínguez Ortiz.

Antiken aus dem Akademischen Kunstmuseum Bonn.

Antoine Marcourt: Réformateur et Pamphlétaire du "Livre des Marchans" aux Placards de 1534. Gabrielle Berthoud.

Apache Chronicle. John Upton Terrell.

Apartheid and the Archbishop: The Life and Times of Geoffrey Clayton. Alan Paton.

Apogeo y ocaso de los Anchorena. Juan José Sebreli.

The Apostle Bas-Relief at Saint-Denis. Sumner McK. Crosby.

The Apothecary in Colonial Virginia. Harold B. Gill, Jr.

Applied Measures for Promoting Technological Growth. Stanley A.
Hetzler.

Approaches to American Economic
History. George Rogers Taylor
and Lucius F. Ellsworth, eds.

Aprismo: The Ideas and Doctrines
of Victor Rául Haya de la Torre.
Robert J. Alexander, ed. and
trans.

The Arab Lands of Western Asia.
Joseph J. Malone.

The Arapahoes, Our People. Virginia Cole Trenholm.

Archaeological Excavations in Thailand. Vol. I. H. R. Van Heerkeren and Eigil Knuth.

Archaeological Excavations in Thailand. Vol. II. Per Sørensen
and Tove Hatting.

An Archaeological Perspective.
Lewis R. Binford.

Archaeological Survey of Mossyrock
Reservoir. William S. Dancey.

Archaeology from Down Under: A
Personal View. J. V. S. Megaw.

The Archaeology of Arizona: A
Study of the Southwest Region.
Paul Martin and Fred Plog.

The Archaeology of Michigan: A
Guide to the Prehistory of the
Great Lakes Region. James E.
Fitting.

The Archaeology of the New Testament: The Life of Jesus and
the Beginning of the Early Church.
Jack Finegan.

Architect Extraordinary: The Life
and Work of John Horbury Hunt,
1838-1904. J. M. Freeland.

Architectural Sculpture in Romanesque
Provence. Alan Borg.

Architectural Space in Ancient Greece.
C. A. Doxiadis.

Architecture for the Poor. Hassan
Fathy.

Architecture in Wood: A History of
Wood Building and Its Techniques
in Europe and North America.
Arne Berg, et al.

Architecture in Wood: A History of
Wood-Building and Its Techniques
in Europe and North America.
Hans Jürgen Hansen, ed.

The Architecture of John Wellborn
Root. Donald Hoffmann.

Architecture of Neel Reid in Georgia.
James Grady.

Archivbeiträge, Volume 9: Mitteilungen der Basler Afrika Bibliographien. Jenkins, Trutenau,
Johanson and Schlettwein, eds.

Archives and Manuscript Collections
of Dickinson College: A Guide.
Charles Coleman Sellers and
Martha Calvert Slotten, comp.

Archives and Manuscript Repositories
in the U S S R, Moscow and
Leningrad. Patricia Kennedy
Grimsted.

Archives and Other Special Collections: A Library Handbook. Sister Mary Jane Menźenska.

Archives of the Pioneers of Tazewell County, Virginia. Netti
Schreiner-Yantis, ed.

Archives Procedural Manual, Washington University School of Medicine Library.

L'Archivo Storico del Banco de
Napoli. Una fonte preziosa per
la storia economica sociale e
artistica del Mezzogiorno d'Italia.

Arctic Breakthrough: Franklin's
Expeditions, 1819-1847. Paul
Nanton.

L'Aria di Fiorenza, id est, Il Ballo
del Gran Duca. Warren Kirkendale.

Armies in Revolution. John Ellis.

The Armies of the Streets: The
New York City Draft Riots of
1863. Adrian Cook.

Arming the Union: Small Arms in
the Civil War. Carl L. Davis.

Arms, Autarky and Aggression: A
Study in German Foreign Policy,
1933-1939. William Carr.

Arms for Empire: A Military History of the British Colonies in
North America, 1607-1763. Douglas Edward Leach.

Arms for Texas. A Study of the
Weapons of the Republic of Texas.
Michael J. Koury.

Army and Revolution. France 1815-
1848. Douglas Porch.

The Army of Flanders and the Spanish Road 1567-1659. Geoffrey
Parker.

The Army of Frederick the Great.
Christopher Duffy.

The Army of the Caesars. Michael
Grant.

Art and Politics: Cartoonists of the

Masses and Liberator. Richard Fitzgerald.

Art and the Future. Douglas Davis.

The Art of Black Africa. Elsy Leuzinger.

The Art of Dura-Europos. Ann Perkins.

The Art of Dying. Robert E. Neale.

The Art of Romare Bearden: The Prevalence of Ritual.

The Art of Walt Disney. Christopher Finch.

The Art of Warfare on Land. David Chandler.

L'arte dell'età classica. Giovanni Becatti.

Arthur H. Bremer. An Assassin's Diary. Arthur H. Bremer.

Arthur's Britain: History and Archaeology, AD 367-634. Leslie Alcock.

Artists on Horseback: The Old West in Illustrated Journalism, 1857-1900.

Arts, Crafts, and Architecture in Early Illinois. Betty I. Madden.

The Arts of Black Africa. Jean Laude.

The Arvilla Complex. Elden Johnson.

Arvon mekin ansaitsemme: Jaakko Juteinin aatemaailman eräät päälinjat. J. Teperi.

The Ascendency of Europe: Aspects of European History, 1815-1914. M. S. Anderson.

Asia and the International System. Wayke Wilcox, Leo E. Rose, and Gavin Boyd, eds.

Aspects de la réforme de l'enseignement en Chine au début du XXe siècle, d'après des écrits de zhang Jian. Marianne Bastid.

Aspects des relations russo-roumaines: Rétrospectives et orientations. Etuces. George Cioranesco, et al.

Aspects des relations soviéto-roumaines, 1967-1971. Sécurité européenne. Etudes. George Cioranesco, et al.

Aspects of Central African History. T. O. Ranger, ed.

Aspects of Early New York Society and Politics. Jacob Judd and Irwin H. Polishook, eds.

Aspects of History and Class Consciousness. Istvan Meszaros, ed.

Aspects of Nineteenth-Century Ontario:

Essays Presented to James J. Talman. F. H. Armstrong, H. A. Stevenson, and J. D. Wilson, eds.

Aspects of Vietnamese History. Walter F. Vella, ed.

Aspetti della Controriforma a Firenze. Arnaldo D'Addario.

Assassination in Vienna. Walter B. Maass.

The Assassination of Henry IV: The Tyrannicide Problem and the Consolidation of the French Absolute Monarchy in the Early Seventeenth Century. Roland Mousnier.

The Astronomical Revolution: Copernicus--Kepler--Borelli. Alexandre Koyré.

At the Crossroads: The Sino-Indian Border Dispute and the Communist Party of India, 1959-1963. Ouseph Varkey.

At War With the Bolsheviks: The Allied Intervention into Russia, 1917-20. Robert Jackson.

Atchafalaya Swamp Life: Settlement and Folk Occupations, Vol. II. Malcolm L. Comeaux.

Atencingo: The Politics of Agrarian Struggle in a Mexican Ejido. David Ronfeldt.

Athenian Culture and Society. T. B. L. Webster.

Athenian Propertied Families, 600-300 B.C. J. K. Davies.

Atlantic Islands; Madeira, The Azores and the Cape Verdes in Seventeenth-Century Commerce and Navigation. T. Bentley Duncan.

Atlantische Blockpolitik im 19. Jahrhundert: Die Vereinigten Staaten und der deutsche Liberalismus während der Revolution von 1848/49. Günter Moltmann.

Atlas d'histoire économique et sociale du Québec, 1851-1896. Jacques Letarte.

Atlas of China. Chiao-Min Hsieh.

The Attack on "Feudalism" in Eighteenth-Century France. J. Q. C. Mackrell.

Aubrey on Education: A Hitherto Unpublished Manuscript. J. E. Stephens.

Audubon in Florida, With Selections From the Writings of John James Audubon. Kathryn Hall Proby.

Auf dem Wege zur Staatssonveräni-
tät: Staatliche Grundbegriffe in
Basler juristischen Doktordisputa-
tionen des 17. und 18. Jahrhunderts. Karl Mommsen.

August Reckoning: Jack Turner and
Racism in Post-Civil War Alabama.
William Warren Rogers and Robert
David Ward.

The Australian-New Zealand Agreement, 1944. Robin Kay, ed.

Austria, Great Britain, and the Crimean War: The Destruction of
the Concert of Europe. Paul W.
Schroeder.

The Autobiographical Notes of
Charles Evans Hughes. David J.
Danelski and Joseph S. Tulchin,
eds.

Austria and the Austrians. Stella
Musulin.

Austria and the Hungarian Republic
of Councils. Sandorne Gabor.

Austria, 1918-1972. Elisabeth
Barker.

The Austrian Mind: An Intellectual
and Social History, 1848-1938.
William M. Johnston.

Autonomy or Dependence as Regional
Integration Outcomes: Central
America. Philippe C. Schmit-
ter.

Autumn of Glory: The Army of Tennessee, 1862-1865. Thomas
Lawrence Connelley.

The Awesome Power: Harry S. Truman as Commander in Chief.
Richard F. Haynes.

Aymer de Valence: Earl of Pembroke, 1307-1324: Baronial Politics in the Reign of Edward II.
J. R. S. Phillips.

The Aztec Image in Western Thought.
Benjamin Kreen.

The Aztecs. Nigel Davies.

-B-

Back to Africa: A History of Sierra
Leone and Liberia. Richard West.

Backs to the Wall. The Heroic Story
of the People of London During
World War II. Leonard Mosley.

The Baglivi Correspondence from the
Library of Sir William Osler.

Dorothy M. Schullian, ed.

The Baku Commune, 1917-1918:
Class and Nationality in the Rus-
sian Revolution. Donald Grigor
Suny.

Baldwin: The Unexpected Prime
Minister. H. Montgomery Hyde.

Balfour: A Political Biography.
Sydney H. Zebel.

Bamboula at Kourion. The Necropolis and the Finds. Excavated by
J. F. Daniel. J. L. Benson.

Bangladesh Economy: Problems and
Prospects. V. K. R. V. Rao,
ed.

A Bangladesh Village: Conflict and
Cohesion. A. K. M. Aminul Islam.

The Bank of Virginia: A History.
John H. Wessells, Jr.

Bankers to the Crown: The Riccardi
of Lucca and Edward I. Richard
W. Kaeuper.

The Banking Crisis of 1933. Susan
Estabrook Kennedy.

Banks or No Banks: The Money Issue in Western Politics, 1832-
1865. William Gerald Shade.

Banners and Bugles. Will Plank.

Baroque Architecture in Classical
Antiquity. Margaret Lyttelton.

Baroque Art: The Jesuit Contribution. Rudolf Wittkower and Irma
Jaffe, eds.

The Basic Barnard: An Introduction
to Chester I. Barnard and His
Theories of Organization and Management. William B. Wolf.

Basic Problems of the History of
the USA in American Historiography from the Colonial Period to
the Civil War, 1861-1865.

Basle and France in the Sixteenth
Century: The Basle Humanists
and Printers in Their Contacts
with Francophone Culture. Peter
G. Bietenholz.

Battle for a Continent: Quebec, 1759.
Gordon Donaldson.

Battle for the Bundu: The First
World War in East Africa.
Charles Miller.

Die Bauornamentik des Trajansfor-
ums und ihre Stellung in der
Früh-und Mittelkaiserzeitlichen
Architekturdekoration Roms.
Christoph F. Leon.

Die Bayerische Volkspartei, 1924-

1932. Klaus Schönhoven.

Baylor at Independence. Lois Smith
Murray.

Beau Sejour: Watercolors of the
Louisiana Plantation Country. Ben
Earl Looney.

Beauduin. A Prophet Vindicated.
Sonya A. Quitslund.

Beaverbrook. A. J. P. Taylor.

The Becket Conflict and the Schools:
A Study of Intellectuals in Politics.
Beryl Smalley.

Die Bedeutung der Vereinigten Staaten
von Amerika für das deutsche
Reparations problem, 1924-1925.
Eckhard Wandel.

Beethoven and the Age of Revolution.
Frida Knight.

Before Civilization: the Radiocarbon
Revolution and Prehistoric Europe.
Colin Renfrew.

Before the Bawdy Court: Selections
from Church Court and Other Records Relating to the Correction of
Moral Offenses in England, Scotland and New England, 1300-1800.
Paul Hair, ed.

Before the Ghetto: Black Detroit in
the Nineteenth Century. David
Katzman.

Before the Revolution: The Vietnamese Peasants Under the French.
Ngo Vinh Long.

The Begetters of Revolution: England's Involvement with France,
1759-1789. Derek Jarrett.

Beginner's Guide to Archaeology....
Louis A. Brennan.

The Beginnings of Japanese Art.
Namio Egami.

Bell: Alexander Graham Bell and
the Conquest of Solitude. Robert
V. Bruce.

Ben Gurion, State-Builder: Principles and Pragmatism 1948-1963.
Avraham Avi-hai.

Ben Jonson. Marie-Therese Jones
Davies.

The Bench and the Ballot: Southern
Federal Judges and Black Voters.
Charles V. Hamilton.

Benedetto da Mantova, Il Beneficio
di Criso con le versioni del
secolo XVI. Documenti e testi-
monianze. Salvatore Caponetto,
ed.

Benedict Arnold: The Dark Eagle.
Brian Richard Boylan.

Il beneficio di Cristo. Salvatore
Caponetto, ed.

Bengal: The Nationalist Movement,
1876-1940. Leonard A. Gordon.

Benito Arias Montano (1527-1598).
B. Rekers.

Benito Juárez. Ivie E. Cadenhead,
Jr.

Benjamin Franklin: a Biography
in His Own Words. Thomas
Fleming, ed.

Benjamin Franklin Tracy: Father
of the Modern American Fighting
Navy. Benjamin Franklin Cooling.

Bent's Old Fort: An Archaeological
Study. Jackson W. Moore, Jr.

Berkeley: The Town and Gown Of
It. George A. Pettitt.

The Berkeley Rebellion and Beyond:
Essays on Politics and Education
in the Technological Society.
Sheldon S. Wolin and John H.
Schaar.

The Berlin Crisis of 1961: Soviet-
American Relations and the Strug-
gle for Power in the Kremlin,
June-November 1961. Robert M.
Slusser.

Berliner Unternehmer während der
fruhen Industrialisierung. Herkunft sozialer Status und politischer Einfluss. Hartmut Kaelble.

Bermuda from Sail to Steam: The
History of the Island from 1784
to 1901. Vols. I and II. Henry
C. Wilkinson.

The Best and the Brightest. David
Halberstam.

Beth She'arim: Report on the Excavations During 1936-1940. Volume I, Catacombs 1-4. Benjamin Mazar (Maisler).

Between Harvard and America: The
Educational Leadership of Charles
W. Eliot. Hugh Hawkins.

Between Science and Religion: The
Reaction to Scientific Naturalism
in Late Victorian England. Frank
Miller Turner.

Beyond Stonehenge. Gerald S.
Hawkins.

Beyond the New Deal: Harry S.
Truman and American Liberalism. Alonzo L. Hamby.

Biblical Archaeology and History.
Paul W. Lapp.

Bibliography of British History.
Stuart Period, 1603-1714. Mary
Frear Keeler, ed.
Bibliography of Malay and Arabic
Periodicals Published in the
Straits Settlements and Peninsular
Malay States, 1876-1941. W. R.
Roff.
Bibliography of the Continental Ref-
ormation: Materials Available
in English. Roland H. Bainton
and Eric W. Gritsch.
Bibliography of the Philosophy in the
Iberian Colonies of America.
Walter Bernard Redmond.
Les bibliothèques françaises pendant
la Révolution (1789-1795): Re-
cherches sur un essai de catalogue
collectif. Pierre Riberette.
Bicentennial USA: Pathways to Cele-
bration. Robert G. Hartje.
Bicycling, a History. Frederick
Alderson.
Big Basin. Denzil Verardo.
The Big Lonesome. Will Bryant.
Big-Men and Business: Entrepreneur-
ship and Economic Growth in the
New Guinea Highlands. Ben R.
Finney.
Big Outfit: Ranching on the Baca
Float. Robert L. Sharp.
The Big Thicket. Edmond E. Talbot.
The Big Thicket: A Challenge to
Conservation. A. Y. Gunter.
Die Bildwerke vom Djebelet el Beda
in ihrer räumlichen und zeitlichen
Umwelt. Ursula Moortgat-Correus.
Bill Bailey Came Home. William A.
Bailey.
Billy Durant, Creator of General
Motors. Lawrence R. Gustin.
Biography of Joseph Neef, Educator
in the Ohio Valley, 1809-1854.
Charles W. Hackensmith.
Biology, History, and Natural Philoso-
phy. Allen D. Breck and Wolfgang
Yourgrau, eds.
Biracial Politics: Conflict and Coali-
tion in the Metropolitan South.
Chandler Davidson.
The Birth and Growth of Industrial
England, 1714-1867. John F. C.
Harrison.
The Birth of Mass Political Parties:
Michigan, 1827-1861. Ronald P.
Fromisano.
The Birth of the English Common
Law. R. C. Van Caenegem.

The Bishopric of Derry and the
Irish Society of London, 1602-
1705. Vol. I, 1602-70. T. W.
Moody and J. G. Simms, eds.
Bismarck and the French Nation
1848-1890. Allan Mitchell.
Bizantini Romani si Bulgari Dunarea
de jos. Ion Barnea and Stefan
Stefanescu.
Black and White: The Negro and
English Society 1555-1945. James
Walvin.
Black Bondage in the North. Edgar
J. McManus.
The Black Book. Middleton Harris.
Black Business in the New South:
A Social History of the North
Carolina Mutual Life Insurance
Company. Walter B. Weare.
Black Carolinians: A History of
Blacks in South Carolina from
1895 to 1968. I. A. Newby.
Black Ghettos, White Ghettos and
Slums. Robert E. Forman.
The Black Image in the White Mind:
The Debate on Afro-American
Character and Destiny, 1817-1914.
George M. Fredrickson.
Black Images in the American The-
atre: NAACP Protest Campaigns
--Stage, Screen, Radio and Tele-
vision. Leonard C. Archer.
The Black Infantry in the West, 1869-
1891. Arlen L. Fowler.
Black into White: Race and Nation-
ality in Brazilian Thought.
Thomas E. Skidmore.
Black Majority: Negroes in Colonial
South Carolina from 1670 Through
the Stono Rebellion. Peter H.
Wood.
Black Men, White Cities: Race,
Politics, and Migration in the
United States, 1900-30, and
Britain, 1948-68. Ira Katznelson.
Black Mesa: The Angel of Death.
Suzanne Gordon.
The Black Migration: The Journey
to Urban America. George Groh.
The Black Military Experience in
the American West. John M.
Carroll, ed.
The Black Muslims in America. C.
Eric Lincoln.
Black New Orleans, 1860-1880.
John W. Blassingame.
Black Night of Quiloa. Hazel Mugot.
Black Poets and Prophets: The

Theory, Practice and Esthetics of the Pan-African Revolution. Woodie King and Earl Anthony, eds.

Black Poets of the United States, from Paul Laurence Dunbar to Langston Hughes. Jean Wagner.

Black Political Life in the United States: A Fist as the Pendulum. Lenneal J. Henderson, Jr. , ed.

Black Political Parties: An Historical and Political Analysis. Hanes Walton, Jr.

Black Politics in Philadelphia. Miriam Ershkowitz and Joseph Zikmund II, eds.

Black Power: Past, Present, and Future. John McCartney.

The Black Presence in the Era of the American Revolution, 1770-1800. Sidney Kaplan.

Black Resistance/White Law: A History of Constitutional Racism in America. Mary Frances Berry.

Black Slaves in Britain. F. O. Shyllon.

Black Song: The Forge and the Flame. John Lovell, Jr.

Black Star: A View of the Life and Times of Kwame Nkrumah. Basil Davidson.

Black Studies: Threat or Challenge? Nick Aaron Ford.

Black Women in White America. A Documentary History. Gerda Lerner, ed.

Black Writers of the Thirties. James O. Young.

Blacks and the Military in American History: A New Perspective. Jack D. Foner.

Blacks in the City: A History of the National Urban League. Guichard Parris and Lester Brooks.

Blacks in the Industrial World: Issues for the Manager. Theodore V. Purcell and Gerald F. Cavanagh.

Blacks on John Brown. Benjamin Quarles, ed.

Blake's Sublime Allegory: Essays on the Four Zoas, Milton, Jerusalem. Stuart Curran and Joseph A. Wittreich, eds.

The Blitzkrieg Era and the German General Staff, 1865-1941. Larry H. Addington.

The Bloodless Revolution: England, 1688. Stuart E. Prall.

The Bloody Bozeman: The Perilous Trail to Montana's Gold. Dorothy M. Johnson.

The Bloody Field. Edith Pargeter.

Bloody Knife! Custer's Favorite Scout. Ben Innis.

Blow for the Landing: A Hundred Years of Steam Navigation on the Waters of the West. Fritz Timmen.

Blue Monday. Calvin Forbes.

The Boer War Diary of Sol T. Plaatje: An African at Mafeking. John L. Comaroff, ed.

The Bolshevik Seizure of Power. S. P. Melgunov.

Bolton Priory: The Economy of a Northern Monastery, 1286-1325. Ian Kershaw.

Bond Men Made Free: Medieval Peasant Movements and the English Rising of 1381. Rodney Hilton.

Bondage and Serfdom (End of the 15th-16th Century). E. I. Kolycheva.

The Bonds: An American Family. Roger M. Williams.

The Bone Hunters. Url Lanham.

Bonizo of Sutri, Leben und Werk. Walter Berschin.

Bonnin and Morris of Philadelphia: The First American Porcelain Factory, 1770-1772. Graham Hood.

The Bonus March: An Episode of the Great Depression. Roger Daniels.   \

The Book of Presidents. Tim Taylor.

The Book, the Ring, and the Poet: A Biography of Robert Browning. William Irvine and Park Honan.

Booker T. Washington--The Making of a Black Leader 1856-1901. Louis T. Harlan.

The Booker T. Washington Papers. Vol. 3: 1889-95. Louis R. Harlan, Stuart B. Kaufman and Raymond W. Smock, eds.

Books for the Millions. Frank E. Comparato.

Boomtown: A Portrait of Burkburnett. Minnie M. Benton.

Bordeaux au XXe Siècle. Joseph Jajugie.

Boris Godunov: The Tragic Tsar. Ian Grey.

Born to Rebel: An Autobiography. Benjamin E. Mays.

The Boshin War. Haraguchi Kiyoshi.

Boso's Life of Alexander III. G. M. Ellis, trans.

The Bosses. Alfred Steinberg.

Bosses and Reformers: Urban Politics in America, 1880-1920. Blaine A. Brownell and Warren E. Stickle, eds.

Boston Priests, 1848-1910: A Study of Social and Intellectual Change. Donna Merwick.

Boston Prints and Printmakers, 1670-1775. Walter Muir Whitehill and Sinclair Hitchings, eds.

Botswana. A Short Political History. Anthony Sillery.

Bougainville: A Personal History. Douglas Oliver.

Bound with Them in Chains: A Biographical History of the Antislavery Movement. Jane H. and William H. Pease.

Bourbon Street Black: The New Orleans Black Jazzman. Jack V. Buerkle and Danny Barker.

Bourjon et le code civil. Renée Martinage-Baranger.

Brain of the Firm: the Managerial Cybernetics of Organization. Stafford Beer.

Brasília, Plan and Reality: A Study of Planned and Spontaneous Urban Development. David G. Epstein.

Braves and Buffalo: Plains Indian Life in 1837. Alfred J. Miller and Michael Bell.

Brazil: From Colony to World Power. Donald E. Worcester.

Brazil: The Land and the People. Rollie E. Poppino.

The Brazilian Communist Party: Conflict and Integration, 1922-1972. Ronald H. Chilcote.

Bread Upon the Waters. A History of the United States Grain Exports. Harry Fornari.

Breaking New Ground. Gifford Pinchot.

The Brethren in Virginia: The History of the Church of the Brethren in Virginia. Roger E. Sappington.

Bretton Woods Revisited. A. K. L. Acheson, J. F. Chant, and M. F. J. Prachowny, eds.

Bride of the Revolution: Krupskaya and Lenin. Robert H. McNeal.

Bridgwater Borough Archives V, 1468-1485. R. W. Dunning and T. D. Tremlett, eds.

A Brief Review of American Interest in Philippine Development and Other Essays. Michael P. Onorato.

Briefwechsel mit deutschen Sozialdemokraten. Vol. 1, 1862-1878. Wilhelm Liebknecht.

Briefwisseling van Hugo Grotius. Vol. 8, 1637. B. L. Muelenbrock.

Bright Eyes: The Story of Susette La Flesche, an Omaha Indian. Dorothy Clarke Wilson.

Britain and the Sino-Japanese War, 1937-1939: A Study in the Dilemmas of British Decline. Bradford A. Lee.

Britain at Bay: Defence Against Napoleon, 1803-14. Richard Glover.

The British Americans: The Loyalist Exiles in England 1774-1789. Mary Beth Norton.

British Antislavery 1833-1970. Howard Temperley.

British Commercial Policy and Trade Expansion, 1750-1850. Judith Blow Williams.

British Drums on the Southern Frontier: The Military Colonization of Georgia, 1733-1749. Larry R. Ivers.

British Economic Fluctuations, 1790-1939. Derek H. Aldcroft and Peter Fearon, eds.

British Economy and Society, 1870-1970: Documents, Descriptions, Statistics. R. W. Breach and R. M. Hartwell, ed.

British Factory--Japanese Factory: The Origins of National Diversity in Industrial Relations. Ronald Dore.

British Farming in the Great Depression, 1870-1914: An Historical Geography. P. J. Perry.

The British in the Caribbean. Cyril Hamshere.

British Investment in American Railways, 1834-1898. Dorothy R. Adler.

British Maps of the American Revolution. Peter J. Guthorn.

British Monetary Policy 1924-1931: The Norman Conquest of $4.86.

D. E. Moggridge.
British Nationalisation, 1945-1973.
R. Kelf-Cohen.
British Nitrates and Chilean Politics
1886-1896: Balmaceda and North.
Harold Blakemore.
British Policy and the Nationalist
Movement in Burma, 1917-1937.
Albert E. Moscotti.
British Policy Towards West Africa:
Select Documents, 1875-1914.
C. W. Newbury.
British Politics and Government
1951-1970: A Study of an Af-
fluent Society.   Mary Proudfoot.
British Power in the Punjab, 1839-
1858.   N. M. Khilnani.
The British Press and Germany 1936-
1939.   Franklin Reid Gannon.
British Protestant Missions.   A. J.
Temu.
The British, Slave Trade, and Slavery
in the Sudan, 1820-1881.   Ibrahim
Muhammad Ali Abbas.
Britain Through American Eyes.
Henry Steele Commager, ed.
British Travelers Among Southern
Indians, 1660-1763.   F. Ralph
Randolph.
Broken Hand: The Life of Thomas
Fitzpatrick: Mountain Man, Guide
and Indian Agent.   LeRoy R.
Hafen.
Brokenburn: The Journal of Kate
Stone.   John Q. Anderson, ed.
Bronze Age Migration in the Aegean.
R. A. Crossland and Ann Birchall,
eds.
The Brothers' War: Biafra and Ni-
geria.   John de St. Jorre.
The Browne Site: Early Milling Stone
Horizon in Southern California.
Roberta S. Greenwood.
Bruno Bauer: Studien und Materialien.
Ernst Barnikol.
Buchanan Dying.   John Updyke.
Buddhism Under Mao.   Holmes Welch.
Buddhist Monk, Buddhist Layman:
A Study of Urban Monastic Organ-
ization in Central Thailand.   Jane
Bunnag.
The Buddhist Tantras: Light on Indo-
Tibetan Esotericism.   Alex Way-
man.
Buffalo Bill: The Noblest Whiteskin.
John Burke.
The Buffalo Head: A Century of Mer-
cantile Pioneering in the Southwest.

Daniel T. Kelly.
Buffalo Soldiers West.   John M.
Carroll.
Building Accounts of King Henry III.
H. M. Colvin.
Building an Austrian Nation: The
Political Integration of a Western
State.   William T. Bluhm.
The Buildings of England.   Nikolaus
Pevsner.
The Buildings of England: Oxford-
shire.   Jennifer Sherwood and
Nikolaus Pevsner.
Bulgarian Communism: The Road
to Power, 1934-1944.   Nissan
Oren.
Bulletin philologie et historique du
comite des travaux historiques et
scientifiques.   2 vols.
Bulozi Under the Luyana Kings.
Mutumba Mainga.
The Bureau of American Ethnology:
A Partial History.   Neil M.
Judd.
Bürgerliche Gesellschaft und Kirche
in Augsburg im Spätmittelalter:
Ein Beitrag zur Strukturanalyse
der oberdeutschen Reichstadt.
Rolf Kiessling.
La burguesía revolucionaria (1808-
1869).   Miguel Artola.
Burnt-Out Fires.   Richard Dillon.
Burr: A Novel.   Gore Vidal.
Burro Bill and Me.   Edna Calkins
Price.
Business and Politics in America
from the Age of Jackson to the
Civil War: The Career Biogra-
phy of W. W. Corcoran.   Henry
Cohen.
Business Enterprise and Economic
Change: Essays in Honor of
Harold F. Williamson.   Louis P.
Cain and Paul J. Uselding, eds.
The Business of Banking, 1891-1914.
C. A. E. Goodhart.
By Myself, I'm a Book: An Oral
History of the Immigrant Jewish
Experience in Pittsburgh.   Nation-
al Council of Jewish Women,
Pittsburgh Section.
'By South Cadbury is That Camelot
....'   Leslie Alcock.
Byzantine Coins.   P. D. Whitting.
The Byzantines and Their World.
Peter Arnott.

-C-

CLIBOC: Chinese Linguistics Bib-
liography on Computer. William
S.-Y. Wang and Anatole Lyovin.
CORE: A Study in the Civil Rights
Movement, 1942-1968. August
Meier and Elliott Rudwick.
C Z: The Story of the California
Zephyr. Karl R. Zimmerman.
The Caciques: Oligarchical Politics
and the System of Caciquismo in
the Luso-Hispanic World. Robert
Kern, ed.
The Caesars: The Roman Empire
and Its Rulers. Henry Marsh.
Caging the Bear: Containment and
the Cold War. Charles Gati, ed.
Les Cahiers des Dix, no. 35.
Cal Alley. Charles W. Crawford, ed.
Calendar of Continental Congress
Papers. Claudia B. Grundiman,
comp.
A Calendar of Rochambeau Papers at
the University of Florida Libraries.
Laura V. Monti, comp.
A Calendar of the Register of Henry
Wakefield, Bishop of Worcester,
1375-95. W. P. Marett, ed.
Calendar of the Shrewsbury and Tal-
bot Papers. Vol. VII. Talbot
Papers in the College of Arms.
G. R. Batho.
California: Where the Twain Did
Meet. Anne Loftis.
California and the Dust Bowl Migra-
tion. Walter J. Stein.
California Calligraphy: Identified
Autographs of Personages Con-
nected with the Conquest and De-
velopment of the Californias. May-
nard Geiger, Intro.
California County Boundaries. Owen
C. Coy.
California Family Newmark. Leo
Newmark.
California's Railroad Era, 1850-1911.
Ward McAfee.
The Call of the Wild, 1900-1916.
Roderick Nash, ed.
Calm of Mind: Tercentenary Essays
on Paradise Regained and Samson
Agonisteo. Joseph Anthony Witt-
reich, Jr., ed.
Calvijn En De Doperse Radikalen.

W. Balke.
Cambodia in the Southeast Asian War.
Malcolm Caldwell and Lek Tan.
The Cambridge Ancient History,
Volume 2, part 1, History of
the Middle East and the Aegean
Region c. 1800-1380 B.C.
I. E. S. Edwards, et al., eds.
The Cambridge History of Iran.
Vol. V. The Seljuq and Mongol
Periods. J. A. Boyle, ed.
Cambridge South Asian Archive.
Mary Thatcher.
Campbell of the Yukon. Clifford
Wilson.
Canaanite Myth and Hebrew Epic:
Essays in the History of the Re-
ligion of Israel. Frank Moore
Cross.
The Canadian Crisis and British
Colonial Policy, 1828-1841. Pet-
er Burroughs.
Canadian Defence Priorities: A
Question of Relevance. C. S.
Gray.
Canadian Public Figures on Tape.
The Canary Islands Migration to
Louisiana, 1778-1783. Sidney
Louis Villeré.
Cannon Smoke. The Letters of Cap-
tain John J. Good, Good-Douglas
Texas Battery, CSA. Lester
Newton Fitzhugh, ed.
Cape to Cairo: Rape of a Continent.
Mark Strage.
Capitalism and Material Life, 1400-
1800. Fernand Braudel.
Capodistria: the Founder of Greek
Independence. C. M. Woodhouse.
The Captain America Complex: The
Dilemma of Zealous Nationalism.
Robert Jewett.
The Captain Departs: Ulysses S.
Grant's Last Campaign. Thomas
M. Pitkin.
The Caption of the Seisin of the
Duchy of Cornwell. P. L. Hull.
The Captive Dreamer. Christian de
la Maziere.
Captive's Mansion. S. R. Slaymak-
er, II.
Cardinal Contarini at Regensburg.
Peter Matheson.
The Cardinal Protectors of England:
Rome and the Tudors Before the
Reformation. William E. Wilkie.
Cardinal Richelieu and the Develop-

ment of Absolutism. G. R. R. Treasure.

Il Cardinale Gasparri e la Questione Romans (con brani delle Memorie inedite). Giovanni Spadolini, ed.

Cardinali di Curia e "familiae" cardinalizie dal 1227 al 1254. Agostino Paravicini Bagliani.

Carl Sandburg. Gay Wilson Allen.

Carlo Cattaneo and the Politics of the Risorgimento, 1820-1860. Clara Maria Lovett.

The Carmen de Hastingae Proelio of Guy, Bishop of Amiens. Catherine Morton and Hope Muntz, eds.

Caroline Courtier: The Life of Lord Cottington. Martin J. Havran.

The Carriage and Harness Museum. Janet Sutherland Guldbeck.

Carry Me Back: Slavery and Servitude in Seventeenth-Century Virginia. Robert S. Cope.

Il carteggio Antonelli-Barili, 1859-61. Carla Meneguzzi Rostagni, ed.

Castle Rock--West of Skyline. Deanne Earnshaw.

Castles of Europe from Charlemagne to the Renaissance. William Anderson.

The Catalan Vengeance. Alfonso Lowe.

Catalogue and Index of the Publications of the Hayden, King, Powell, and Wheeler Surveys. L. F. Schmedkebier.

Catalogue of the Classical Collection: Classical Sculpture. Brunilde Sismondo Ridgway.

Catalogue of the Wardrop Collection and of Other Georgian Books and Manuscripts in the Bodleian Library. David Barrett.

'Le Catechisme de la Revolution Francaise," in Annales (Economies Societes, Civilisations) March to April 1971. Francois Furet.

Categories of Medieval Cultures. A. Ia. Gurevich.

Catherine Beecher: A Study in American Domesticity. Kathryn Kish Sklar.

Catherine the Great. Marc Raeff, ed.

Catholics, Peasants and Chewa Resistance in Nyasaland 1889-1939. Ian and Jane Linden.

The Catskills: From Wilderness to Woodstock. Alf Edwards.

The Cattle-Trailing Industry: Between Supply and Demand, 1866-1890. Jimmy M. Skaggs.

Causality and Scientific Explanation .... William A. Wallace.

The Causes of the English Revolution, 1529-1642. Lawrence Stone.

Cautantowwit's House: An Indian Burial Ground on the Island of Conanicut in Narragansett Bay. William Cranton Simmons.

The Cavalier Mode from Jonson to Cotton. Earl Miner.

The Cayuse Indians: Imperial Tribesmen of Old Oregon.

Cecil Rhodes: The Anatomy of Empire. John Marlowe.

The Cecils of Hatfield House: An English Ruling Family. David Cecil.

Celtic Art: An Introduction. Ian Finlay.

The Celtic Churches: A History, A.D. 200 to 1200. John T. McNeill.

Centenario del Fallecimiento de Don Antonio José de Irisarri. Ministerio de Relacions Exteriores.

Centennial History of the University of Nebraska. Volume II, The Modern University, 1920-1969. R. McLaran Sawyer.

The Central American Common Market. Donald H. McClelland.

Centreville, Virginia. Eugenia B. Smith.

Cervantes: The Man and the Genius. Francisco Navarro Ledesma.

Cervantes' Christian Romance: A Study of Persiles y Sigismunda. Alban K. Forcione.

Cerveau's Savannah. Joseph Frederick Waring.

Ceylon: Between Orient and Occident. Zeylanicus.

Champion of Southern Federalism: Robert Goodloe Harper of South Carolina. Joseph W. Cox.

Change and Conflict in the Indian University. Joseph E. Di Bona.

Change and Continuity in India's Villages. K. Ishwaran, ed.

Un Changeur Florentin du Trecento: Lippo di Fede del Sega (1285 env. 1363 env.). Charles M. de la Roncière.

Changing Perspectives in the History of Science: Essays in Honour of

Joseph Needham. Mikulas Teich and Robert Young, eds.

The Changing Politics of the South. William C. Havard, ed.

Charles Demuth: Behind a Laughing Mask. Emily Farnham.

Charles E. Duryea: Automaker. George W. May.

Charles F. Lummis: Crusader in Corduroy. Dudley Gordon.

Charles Kenneth Leith: Scientific Adviser. Sylvia Wallace McGrath.

Charles Round Low Cloud: Voice of the Winnebago. William Leslie Clark and Walker D. Wyman.

Charles the Bold. R. Vaughan.

Charlie the Mole and Other Droll Souls. Howard Jacobs.

Charlotte Stephens, Little Rock's First Black Teacher. Adolphine Fletcher Terry.

Chaucer and the English Tradition. Ian Robinson.

Che: Selected Works of Ernesto Guevara. Rolando E. Bonachea and Nelson P. Valdés, eds.

Chemical Apparatus. C. R. Hill.

The Cherokee Strip Live Stock Association: Federal Regulation and the Cattleman's Last Frontier. William W. Savage, Jr.

Cheshire 1630-1660. J. S. Morrill.

Cheyenne and Sioux: The Reminiscences of Four Indians and a White Soldier. Thomas B. Marquis, comp. and Ronald H. Limbaugh, ed.

The Cheyenne Indians: Their History and Ways of Life. George Bird Grinnell.

Chicago: A Personal History of America's Most American City. Finis Farr.

Chicago: Growth of a Metropolis. Harold M. Mayer and Richard C. Wade.

Chicago 1910-29: Building, Planning and Technology. C. W. Condit.

Chicago, 1930-70: Building, Planning and Urban Technology. Carl W. Condit.

The Chicanos: A History of Mexican-Americans. Matt S. Meier and Feliciano Rivera.

Chicanos and Native Americans: The Territorial Minorities. Rudolph de la Garza et al, ed.

Chiefship in Western Tanzania. A

Political History of the Kimbu. Aylward Shorter.

A Childhood in Prison. Pyotr Yakir.

Children in English Society. Volume 2. Ivy Pinchbeck and Margaret Hewitt.

The Children of Columbus: An Informal History of the Italians in the New World. Erik Amfitheatrof.

The Children of Pride: A True Story of Georgia and the Civil War. Robert Manson Myers, ed.

Children of the Storm. Andrew Billingsley and Jeanne M. Giovannoni.

Chile: A Historical Interpretation. Jay Kinsbruner.

Chile, Peru, and the California Gold Rush of 1849. Jay Monaghan.

The Chilean Road to Socialism. Dale L. Johnson, ed.

Chilkoot Pass; Then and Now. Archie Satterfield.

China: A Handbook. Yuan-li Wu, ed.

China: Management of a Revolutionary Society. John M. Lindbeck.

China and Africa in the Middle Ages. Teobaldo Filesi.

China and Japan at War, 1937-1945: The Politics of Collaboration. John Hunter Boyle.

A China Passage. John Kenneth Galbraith.

China Today. Klaus Mehnert.

The China Trade: Export Paintings, Furniture, Silver and Other Objects. Carl L. Crossman.

China's Developmental Experience. Michael Oksenberg, ed.

China's Nation-Building Effort, 1927-1937: The Financial and Economic Record. Arthur Young.

China's Policy in Africa, 1958-71. Alaba Ogunsanwo.

China's Three Thousand Years: the Story of a Great Civilization. Louis Heren, C. P. Fitzgerald, Michael Freeberne, Brian Hook, and David Bonavia.

Chinese Communism, 1931-1934: Experience in Civil Government. Trygve Lötveit.

A Chinese-English Dictionary of Communist Chinese Terminology. Dennis J. Doolin and Charles P.

Ridley.

The Chinese Revolution, 1900-1950. Ranbir Vohra, ed.

The Chinese Short Story: Studies in Dating, Authorship, and Composition. Patrick Hanan.

Chinese Statelets and the Northern Barbarians in the Period 1400-300 B. C. Janoslav Prusek.

Chinese Village Plays from the Ting Hsien Region: A Collection of Forty-Eight Rural Plays as Staged by Villagers from Ting Hsien in Northern China. Sidney D. Gamble, ed.

Chinese Villages and Theories of Cooperative Systems. Takashi Hatada.

Chlodwigs Taufe: Reims 508. Rolf Weiss.

Choix d'Etudes Bouddhiques. Paul Demiéville.

Choix d'Etudes Sinologiques. Paul Demiéville.

Choosing Our King: Powerful Symbols in Presidential Politics. Michael Novak.

Chou En-lai. Jules Archer.

A Christian America: Protestant Hopes and Historical Realities. Robert T. Handy.

Christian Marriage in Africa. Adrian Hastings.

Christian Mortalism from Tyndale to Milton. Norman T. Burns.

Christian Political Theory and Church Politics in the Mid-Twelfth Century: The Ecclesiology of Gratian's Decretum. Stanley A. Chodorow.

Christianity, Judaism and Revolution. Wilfried Daim.

Christians in Persia: Assyrians, Armenians, Roman Catholics, and Protestants. Robin E. Waterfield.

Christopher Columbus. Ernle Bradford.

The Chromolithographs of Louis Prang. Katharine Morrison Mc-Clinton.

Chronicle Into History: An Essay on the Interpretation of History in Florentine Fourteenth-Century Chronicles. Louis Green.

The Chronicle of Ernoul and the Continuations of William of Tyre. M. R. Morgan.

The Chronicle of the Election of Hugh: Abbot of Bury St. Edmunds

and Later Bishop of Ely. R. M. Thomson, ed. and trans.

A Chronicle of the Heroic Struggle: Soviet Historiography of the Civil War and Imperialist Intervention in the USSR. V. P. Naumov.

Chronicles of the Yaki Expedition. Jimmy M. Skaggs, Ferne Downs, and Winifred Vigness, eds.

Chronology and Documentary Handbook of the State of Colorado. Mary L. Frech, ed.

Chronology of African History. G. S. P. Freeman-Grenville.

A Chronology of Virginia and the War of Independence, 1763-1783. John E. Selby.

Church and Power in Brazil. Charles Antoine.

Church and State in Ethiopia, 1270-1527. Taddesse Tamrat.

Church and State in France, 1870-1914. John McManners.

Church and State in Modern Ireland, 1923-1970. J. A. Whyte.

Church History in the Age of Science: Historiographical Patterns in the United States, 1876-1918. Henry Warner Bowden.

The Church in the British Era. John S. Moir.

The Church of Ireland: Ecclesiastical Reform and Revolution, 1800-1885. Donald Harmon Akenson.

The Church Reform of Peter the Great. James Cracraft.

Churches in Cultural Captivity: A History of the Social Attitudes of Southern Baptists. John Lee Eighmy.

The Churches Militant: The War of 1812 and American Religion. William Gribbin.

Churchill as Warlord. Ronald Lewin.

Churchmen and the Condition of England, 1832-1885: A Study in the Development of Social Ideas and Practice from the Old Regime to the Modern State. G. Kitson Clark.

Cicero. D. R. Shackleton Bailey.

Cicero Scepticus. Charles B. Schmitt.

The Cincinnati Brewing Industry: A Social and Economic History. William L. Downard.

Cities of the Prairie: The Metropolitan Frontier and the American Politics. Daniel J. Elazar.

The Citizen Soldiers: The Plattsburg Training Camp Movement, 1913-1920. John Garry Clifford.

The Citizens' Council: Organized Resistance to the Second Reconstruction, 1954-64. Neil R. McMillen.

City of the Stargazers: The Rise and Fall of Ancient Alexandria. Kenneth Heuer.

The City of Worcester in the Sixteenth Century. Alan D. Dyer.

The City That Was. Stephen Smith.

Civil Disobedience and After: The American Reaction to Political Developments in India During 1930-1935. Manoranjan Jha.

The Civil Lawyers in England, 1603-1641: A Political Study. Brian P. Levack.

The Civil-Military Fabric of Weimar Foreign Policy. Gaines Post, Jr.

Civil Strife in Latin America. William Everett Kane.

Civil Wars in the Twentieth Century. Robin Higham, ed.

Civilization: The Emergence of Man in Society. Volume I. John Roberts.

The Clamourous Malcontents: Criticisms and Defenses of the Colony of Georgia, 1741-1743.

Class and Ideology in the Nineteenth Century. R. S. Neale.

The Classic British Novel. Howard M. Harper, Jr. and Charles Edge, eds.

The Classic Maya Collapse. T. Patrick Culbert, ed.

The Classic Southwest: Readings in Archaeology, Ethnohistory and Ethnology. Basil C. Hedrick, J. Charles Kelley and Carroll L. Riley, eds.

The Classical Style: Haydn, Mozart, Beethoven. Charles Rosen.

The Classical Theory of Composition from Its Origins to the Present. Aldo Scaglione.

The Classical Tradition in West European Farming. G. E. Fussell.

The Classroom and the Chandellery: State Educational Reform in Russia Under Count Dmitry Tolstoi. Allen Sinel.

Climates of Africa. J. F. Griffiths, ed.

Clio and the Doctors: Psycho-History, Quanto-History, and History. Jacques Barzun.

Clive of India. Mark Bence-Jones.

The Closing of the Door: Sino-American Relations, 1936-46. Paul A. Vorg.

Closing the Open Door: American-Japanese Negotiations, 1936-1941. James H. Herzog.

Cobbler in Congress: The Life of Henry Wilson, 1812-1875. Richard H. Abbott.

The Coconut Girl. Joseph Kabui.

The Cod. Albert C. Jensen.

Code Number 72/Ben Franklin: Patriot or Spy? Cecil B. Curry.

Codeword BARBAROSSA. Barton Whaley.

Codex Vaticanus 3773 (Codex Vaticanus B), Biblioteca Apostólica Vaticana. Vol. XXXVI.

Codices Latini Antiquiores. Part 2: Great Britain and Ireland. E. A. Lowe, ed.

Coin Harvey, Prophet of Monte Ne. Lois Snelling.

Les Colbert avant Colbert: Destin d'une famille marchande. Jean-Louis Bourgeon.

The Cold War in Asia: A Historical Introduction. Akira Iriye.

Colección documental de la Independencia del Perú.

Coleridge's American Disciples: The Selected Correspondence of James Marsh. John J. Duffy, ed.

The Collapse of Orthodoxy: The Intellectual Ordeal of George Frederick Holmes. Neal C. Gillespie.

Collected Poems, 1951-1971. A. R. Ammons.

The Collected Writings of John Maynard Keynes. Vols. 7-10, 13-14.

Collective Violence. James F. Short, Jr. and Marvin E. Wolfgang, eds.

A College for This Community. Walter T. Durham.

College Life in the Reconstruction South: Walter B. Hill's Student Correspondence, 1869-1871. G. Ray Mathis, ed.

Colloquia Erasmiana Turoneusia. Jean-Claude Margolin, ed.

Colonel Greene and the Copper Skyrocket. C. L. Sonnichsen.

Colonel Grenfell's Wars: The Life of a Soldier of Fortune. Stephen Z. Starr.

Colonel House in Paris: A Study of American Policy at the Paris Peace Conference 1919. Inga Floto.

Colonel John Robert Baylor: Texas Indian Fighter and Confederate Soldier. Jerry Don Thompson.

Colonial and State Records in the South Carolina Archives, A Temporary Summary Guide. Marion C. Chandler.

The Colonial Legacy. Volume 1, Loyalist Historians; Volume 2, Some Eighteenth-Century Commentators. Lawrence H. Leder, ed.

The Colonial Legacy: Vols. III and IV. Lawrence H. Leder, ed.

Colonial New Jersey. John E. Pomfret.

Colonial North Carolina: A History. Hugh T. Lefler and William S. Powell.

Colonial Roots of Modern Brazil: Papers of the Newberry Library Conference. Dauril Alden, ed.

Colonialism in Africa, 1870-1960: Volume 5, A Bibliographical Guide to Colonialism in Sub-Saharan Africa. Peter Duignan and L. H. Gann.

Color and Light: The Southwest Canvases of Louis Akin. Bruce E. Babbitt.

Colorado: Its Gold and Silver Mines, Farms, and Stock Ranges, and Health and Pleasure Resorts. Frank Fossett.

Colorado Volunteers in the Civil War: The New Mexico Campaign in 1862. William Clarke Whitford.

Colorado's War on Militant Unionism: James H. Peabody and the Western Federation of Miners. George G. Suggs, Jr.

Le Colportage de librairie en France sous le Second Empire. Jean-Jacques Darmon.

The Columbian Exchange: Biological and Cultural Consequences of 1492. Alfred W. Crosby, Jr.

The Columbus Dynasty in the Caribbean, 1492-1526. Troy S. Floyd.

The Column of Antoninus Pius. Lise Vogel.

Comes et Legatus Siciliae: Sul privilegio di Urbano II e la pretesa Apostolica Legazia dei Normanni di Sicilia. Salvatore Fodale.

The Comic Imagination in American Literature. Louis D. Rubin, Jr., ed.

The Coming Dark Age. Roberto Vacca.

The Coming of Christianity to Anglo-Saxon England. Henry Mayr-Harting.

The Coming of the American Age, 1945-1946: Dubious Victory: The United States and the End of World War II. Lisle A. Rose.

A Commentary on Livy, Books XXXI-XXXIII. John Briscoe.

A Commentary on the Dresden Codex: A Maya Hieroglyphic Book. J. Eric S. Thompson.

Le commerce colonial de la France à la fin de l'Ancien Régime: L'évolution du régime de "l'Exclusif" de 1763 à 1789. Jean Tarrade.

The Commercial Revolution of the Middle Ages, 950-1350. R. S. Lopez.

Commonwealth: A History of the British Commonwealth of Nations. H. Duncan Hall.

The Communal Experience: Anarchist and Mystical Counter-Cultures in America. Laurence Veysey.

Communicational Analysis and Methodology for Historians. L. G. Heller.

Communism in Japan: A Case of Political Naturalization. Paul F. Langer.

The Communist Tide in Latin America: A Selected Treatment. Donald L. Herman, ed.

Community Culture and Natural Change. Richard N. Adams, et al.

The Compact History of the United States Air Force. Carroll V. Glines, Jr.

The Comparation of a Virgin and a Martyr (1523). Erasmus.

Comparative Development in Social

Welfare. E. W. Martin, ed.

Competition and Collective Bargaining in the Needle Trades, 1910-1967. Jesse Thomas Carpenter.

The Complete Works of St. Thomas More. Vol. 8. Louis A. Schuster, et al.

Computers in Anthropology and Archeology [sic]. Robert Chenhall.

Comunidade e sociedade no Brasil. Florestan Fernandes.

Comunione interecclesiale, collegialita, primato ecumenismo. G. D'Ercole and A. M. Stickler, eds.

Concepts of God in Africa. John S. Mbiti.

A Concise History of Canadian Painting. Dennis Reid.

Condition coloniale et conscience créole au Guatemala (1524-1821). André Saint-Lu.

Les conditions de pénétration et de diffusion des cultes Egyptiens en Italie. Michel Malaise.

Confederación Perú-Boliviana, 1835-1839.

The Confederate Navy: A Study in Organization. Tom Henderson Wells.

The Confederate Soldier. LeGrand James Wilson.

The Confederate State of Richmond: A Biography of the Capital. Emory M. Thomas.

Conflict and Political Change in Venezuela. Daniel H. Levine.

Conflict and Transformation: The United States, 1844-1877. William R. Brock.

Conflict, Violence, and Morality in a Mexican Village. Lola Romanucci-Ross.

Conflicts and Conspiracies: Brazil and Portugal, 1750-1808. Kenneth R. Maxwell.

Confrontación transpacífica: El Japón y el Nuevo Mundo hispanico, 1542-1639. Lothar Knauth.

Confrontation at Worms: Martin Luther and the Diet of Worms. De Lamar Jensen.

Congo. Richard West.

Congress and Higher Education in the Nineteenth Century. George N. Rainsford.

The Congress Party in Rajasthan: Political Integration and Institution Building in an Indian State. Richard Sisson.

Conquered Provinces: Nevada Moves Southeast, 1864-1871. John M. Townley.

Conquerors and Confucians: Aspects of Political Change in Late Yüan China. John W. Dardess.

Conquest and Conscience: The 1840's. Robert Sobel.

The Conquistador in California: 1535. W. Michael Mathes, tr. and ed.

Conscience and Politics: The British Government and the Conscientous Objector to Military Service 1916-1919. John Rae.

The Conscience Nationale en France Pendant Les Guerres de Religion, 1559-1598. Myriam Yardeni.

Consecrated Thunderbolt: Father Yorke of San Francisco. Joseph H. Brusher.

Le Conseil du Roi sous le Regne de Louis XV. Michel Antoine.

Le Conseil royal des Finances au XVIIIe siecle et le registre E 3569 des Archives nationales. Antoine Michel.

The Conservative Leadership 1832-1932. Donald Southgate, ed.

The Conservative Party, 1918-1970. T. F. Lindsay and Michael Harrington.

Conservative Politics in France. Malcolm Anderson.

Constantine Porphyrogenitus and His World. Arnold Toynbee.

The Constitution in Crisis Times, 1918-1969. Paul L. Murphy.

Constitutionalism in the Emerging States. B. O. Nwabueze.

The Constitutionalist: Notes on the First Amendment. George Anastaplo.

Constitutionalists of the Ch'ing Period. Chang Yü-Fa.

La Construction navale royale à Québec 1739-1759. Jacques Mathieu.

The Containment of Latin America. David Green.

Contemplative Community: An Interdisciplinary Symposium. M. Basil Pennington, ed.

Contemporary American Indian Leaders. Marion E. Gridley.

The Continental Commitment. Michael Howard.

Contradiction and Dilemma: Orestes Brownson and the American Idea. Leonard Gilhooley.

A Contribution to the Study of Agorakritos. G. I. Despinis.

Contributions of the Florida State Museum, Anthropology and History, Number 18, Excavations on Amelia Island in Northeast Florida. E. Thomas Hemmings and Kathleen A. Deagan.

Conversations with Allende. Socialism in Chile. Régis Debray.

Conversations with Frank Waters. John R. Milton, ed.

Cooperation and the Owenite Socialist Communities in Britain, 1825-45. R. G. Garnett.

Co-operatives and Rural Development in East Africa. Carl Gosta Widstrand, ed.

Coozan Dudley Le Blanc: From Huey Long to Hadacol. Floyd Martin Clay.

Copan: Home of the Mayan Gods. Francis Robicsek.

Copper. Ira Joralemon.

Copper and Tin. The Distribution of Mineral Resources and the Nature of the Metals Trade in the Bronze Age. James David Muhly.

Coriolanus in Context. Clifford Chalmers Huffman.

The Coritani. Malcolm Todd.

Corning Mining: Essays on the Organization of Cornish Mines and the Cornish Mining Economy. Roger Burt, ed.

The Coronation of Charlemagne: December 25, 800. Robert Folz.

Corporate Power and Social Change: The Politics of the Life Insurance Industry. Karen Orren.

Corpus Vasorum Antiquorum, The Netherlands III, Leyden I. M. F. Jongkees-Vos.

Corpus Vasorum Arretinorum. August Oxe, comp.; Howard Comfort, ed.

La correspondance de Pierre Ameilh, archêveque de Naples puis d'Embrun (1363-1369). Henri Bresc, ed.

Correspondance de Théodore de Bèze. Hippolyte Aubert.

Correspondence of James K. Polk. Volume 2, 1833-1834. Herbert Weaver and Paul H. Bergeron, eds.

The Correspondence of Lord Acton and Richard Simpson. Volume 2. Josef L. Altholz, et al., eds.

The Correspondence of W. E. B. DuBois. Volume I: Selections, 1877-1934. Herbert Aptheker, ed.

The Corrupt Kingdom: The Rise and Fall of the United Mine Workers. Joseph E. Finley.

Il corsivo nella tipografia del Cinquecento. Alberto Tinto.

Corvo: Saint or Madman? Donald Weeks.

The Cost of Learning: The Politics of Primary Education in Kenya. L. Gray Cowan.

A Cotton Enterprise 1795-1840: A History of McConnell and Kennedy, Fine Cotton Spinners. C. M. Lee.

The Councils of Urban II. Volume I: Decreta Claromontensia. Robert Somerville.

Count Witte and the Tsarist Government in the 1905 Revolution. Howard D. Mehlinger and John M. Thompson.

The Counter Reformation, 1559-1610. Marvin R. O'Connell.

The Counter-Revolution: Doctrine and Action 1789-1804. Jacques Godechot.

Counterrevolution: The Role of the Spaniards in the Independence of Mexico, 1804-38. Romeo Flores Caballero.

The Countess of Pembroke's Arcadia. Phillip Sidney.

The Country Guide for City People. Chase Collins.

A Country Study: Politics in Venezuela. David Eugene Blank.

County Court Records of Accomack-Northampton, Virginia, 1640-1645. Susie M. Ames, ed.

The County Courts in Antebellum Kentucky. Robert M. Ireland.

Court-Martial: A Black Man in America. John F. Marszalek, Jr.

The Court-Martial of Daniel Boone. Allan W. Eckert.

The Courtly Tradition in Japanese Art and Literature: Selections from the Hofer and Hyde Collections. John M. Rosenfield, and Fumiko E. and Edwin A. Cranston.

Cowboy Capital of the World: The Saga of Dodge City. Samuel Carter III.

The Cowboy in American Prints. John Meigs, ed.

The Cowboy Trade. Glen Rounds.

The Cowboys. William H. Forbis.

The Cowman Says It Salty. Ramon F. Adams.

Cows on the Campus. Parke Rouse, Jr.

Creation of the American Empire: U. S. Diplomatic History. Lloyd C. Gardner, Walter F. La Feber, and Thomas J. McCormick.

The Credit Merchants: A History of Spiegel, Inc. Orange A. Smalley and Frederick D. Sturdivant.

Creole Society in Jamaica 1770-1820. Edward Brathwaite.

Crime and Public Order in England in the Late Middle Ages. John Bellamy.

Crimsoned Prairie: The Wars Between the United States and the Plains Indians During the Winning of the West. S. L. A. Marshall.

Crippled from Birth: German Social Democracy 1844-1870. Richard W. Reichard.

Crisis and Order in English Towns, 1500-1700. Peter Clark and Paul Slack.

Crisis, Escalation, War. Ole R. Holsti.

Crisis in Finance: Crown, Financiers, and Society in Seventeenth-Century France. Julian Dent.

Crisis in Identity and Contemporary Japanese Novels. Arthur G. Kimball.

The Crisis in Planning. 2 vols. Mike Faber and Dudley Seers.

The Crisis Meeters: Business Response to Social Crisis. Irving S. Michelman.

Crisis, 1918: The Leading Actors, Strategies, and Events in the German Gamble for Total Victory on the Western Front. Joseph Gies.

The Crisis of Democratic Theory: Scientific Naturalism and the Problem of Value. Edward A. Percell, Jr.

Critical Essays on the Philosophy of R. G. Collingwood. Michael Krausz, ed.

A Critical Examination of the Written and Archaeological Sources' Evidence Concerning the Norse Settlements in Greenland. Henrik M. Jansen.

Critical Studies in Antebellum Sectionalism: Essays in American Political and Economic History. Robert R. Russell.

Cromwell: A Profile. Ivan Roots, ed.

Crop Nutrition. G. E. Russell.

Cross and Flame in Wisconsin: the Story of United Methodism in the Badger State. William Blake.

Crowder Tales. Nixon Smiley.

Crowfoot, Chief of the Blackfeet. Hugh A. Dempsey.

Crucial American Elections: Symposium Presented at the Autumn General Meeting of the American Philosophical Society, November 10, 1972.

Crusade for Justice: The Autobiography of Ida B. Wells. Alfreda M. Duster, ed.

Crusader in Babylon: W. T. Stead and the Pall Mall Gazette. Raymond L. Schults.

The Crusades. Hans Eberhard Mayer.

Cry of the Thunderbird: The American Indian's Own Story. Charles Hamilton, ed.

Cuba: A Perennial Problem in American Foreign Policy. Lester D. Langley.

Cuba: From Columbus to Castro. Jaime Suchlicki.

Cuba, Castro, and Revolution. Jaime Suchlicki, ed.

Cuba, Castro and the United States. Philip W. Bonsal.

Cuba 1933. Prologue to Revolution. Luis E. Aguilar.

The Cuban Insurrection 1952-1959. Ramón L. Bonachea and Marta San Martín.

The Cuban Missile Crisis. Robert A. Divine, ed.

The Cult of the Dead in a Chinese Village. Emily M. Ahern.

Cult Places in the Aegean World.
Bogdan Rutkowski.
Cultural Development: Experience
and Policies. Augustin Girard.
The Cultural Revolution in China.
Thomas W. Robinson, ed.
Culture and Commitment, 1929-1945.
Warren Susman, ed.
Culture and Politics in Indonesia.
C. Holt, B. R. O'G. Anderson,
J. Siegel, ed.
Culture and Society in Renaissance
Italy, 1420-1540. Peter Burke.
Culture and Society in Seventeenth-
Century France. David Maland.
Culture and Society in the Dutch Re-
public During the 17th Century.
J. L. Price.
Culture and Society in Venice, 1470-
1790: The Renaissance and Its
Heritage. Oliver Logan.
The Culture Factory: Boston Public
Schools, 1789-1860. Stanley K.
Schultz.
The Cumberland. James McCague.
Current Research in Romano-British
Coarse Pottery. Alec Detsicas,
ed.
The Curtis Magazines. James Play-
sted Wood.
Custer Engages the Hostiles.
Charles Francis Bates and Fran-
cis Roe.
Custer's Gold. Donald Jackson.
A Cycle of Power: The Career of
Jersey City Mayor Frank Hague.
Richard J. Connors.
Cycles of Conquest: The Impact of
Spain, Mexico and the United
States on the Indians of the South-
west, 1533-1960. Edward H.
Spicer.
Cylinder of Vision: The Fiction and
Journalistic Writings of Stephen
Crane. Milne Holton.
Cypriot Inscribed Stones. Ino Niko-
laou.
Cypriote Antiquities in the Pierides
Collection, Larnaca, Cyprus. Vas-
sos Karageorghis.
Czechoslovak-Hungarian Relations
(1935-1939). I. I. Pop.
The Czechoslovak Political Trials,
1950-1954: The Suppressed Re-
port of the Dubcek Government's
Commission of Inquiry, 1968.
Jirí Pelikán, ed.
Czechoslovakia Before Munich: The

German Minority Problem and
British Appeasement Policy.
J. W. Bruegel.
The Czechs under Nazi Rule: The
Failure of National Resistance,
1939-1942. Vojtech Mastny.

-D-

D-Day: The Normandy Invasion in
Retrospect.
The Damned Inheritance: The Sovi-
et Union and the Manchurian
Crises, 1924-1935. George
Alexander Lensen.
Dams, Parks, and Politics: Re-
source Development and Preser-
vation in the Truman-Eisenhower
Era. Elmo Richardson.
The Danger of War and the Second
International (1911). J. Jemnitz.
The Dangerous Sky: A History of
Aviation Medicine. Douglas H.
Robinson.
Daniel Lee, Agriculturist: His Life
North and South. E. Merton
Coulter.
Daniel Webster and Jacksonian De-
mocracy. Sydney Nathans.
Daniel Webster and the Trial of
American Nationalism, 1843-1852.
Robert F. Dalzell, Jr.
Dansk neutralpolitik under krigen
1778-1783. Ole Feldback.
The Dark Age of Greece. A. M.
Snodgrass.
The Dark Corner of the Confederacy:
Accounts of Civil War Texas as
Told by Contemporaries. B. P.
Gallaway, comp. and ed.
The Darkest Year: Britain Alone,
June 1940-June 1941. Herbert
Agar.
Dating Methods in Archaeology.
Joseph W. Michels.
David Livingstone: His Triumph,
Decline and Fall. Cecil North-
cott.
The Dawes Act and the Allotment of
Indian Lands. D. S. Otis.
The Dawn's Early Light. Walter
Lord.
A Day's March Nearer Home: The
War History From Alamein to
VE Day Based on the War Cabi-

net Papers of 1942 to 1945.
Roger Parkinson.
Days of Sadness, Years of Triumph:
The American People, 1939-1945.
Geoffrey Perrett.
The Days of the Beloved. Harriet
Ronken Lynton and Mohini Rajan.
The Dean: The Life of Julien C.
Monnet. Dave R. McKown.
Dean Acheson. Gaddis Smith.
Dear Ellen: Two Mormon Women
and Their Letters. S. George
Ellsworth.
Dear General: Eisenhower's Wartime
Letters to Marshall. Joseph
Patrick Hobbs.
Dear Miss Em: General Eichelberg-
er's War in the Pacific, 1942-
1945. Jay Luvaas, ed.
Death Valley Ghost Towns. Stanley
W. Paher.
Debate on Europe, 1815-1850.
George Rudé.
The Debate Over Slavery: Stanley
Elkins and His Critics. Ann J.
Lane, ed.
Debtors and Creditors in America:
Insolvency, Imprisonment for
Debt, and Bankruptcy, 1607-1900.
Peter J. Coleman.
La Decadenza Italiana nella Storia
Europea: Saggi sul Sei-Settecento.
Guido Quazza.
Decentralization and Self-Government
in Russia, 1830-1870.
Decision by Default: Peacetime Con-
scription and British Defence.
Peter Dennis.
Decision-Making in Ethiopia: A Study
of the Political Process. Peter
Schwab.
The Decline of American Gentility.
Stow Persons.
The Decline of Gentility. Stow Per-
sons.
The Decline of Medieval Hellenism
in Asia Minor and the Process of
Islamization from the Eleventh
Through the Fifteenth Century.
Speros Vryonis, Jr.
The Deep South States of America:
People, Politics and Power in the
Seven Deep South States. Neal
R. Peirce.
Delaware Canal Journal: A Definitive
History of the Canal and the River
Valley Through Which It Flows.
C. P. Yoder.

La democracia en Chile. Norbert
Lechner.
Democracy's Railroads: Public En-
terprise in Jacksonian Michigan.
Robert J. Parks.
Democratic Humanism and American
Literature. Harold Kaplan.
The Democratic Left in Exile: The
Antidictatorial Struggle in the
Caribbean, 1945-1959. Charles
D. Ameringer.
Democratic Opposition to the Lin-
coln Administration in Indiana.
Gilbert R. Tredway.
The Democratic Party and California
Politics, 1880-1896. R. Hal
Williams.
Democratic Vistas 1860-1880. Alan
Trachtenberg, ed.
Democrats and Progressives: The
1948 Election as a Test of Post-
war Liberalism. Allen Yarnell.
Democrats of Oregon: The Pattern
of Minority Politics, 1900-1956.
Robert E. Burton.
Denver University Park: Four Walk-
ing Tours. Don D. Etter.
Departing Glory: Theodore Roose-
velt as Ex-President. Joseph L.
Gardner.
Dependence and Opportunity: Po-
litical Change in Ahafo. John
Dunn and A. F. Robertson.
Der adel vor der Revolution: zur
sozialen und politischen Funktion
des adels im vor-revolutionärem
Europa. Rudolf Vierhaus.
Derniers Chefs d'un Empire. Pierre
Gentil, ed.
Desafio Americano à preponderância
britânica no Brasil, 1808-1850.
Antônia Fernanda Pacca de Al-
meida Wright.
Description and Measurement in
Anthropology. H. T. Irwin,
D. J. Hurd, and R. M. La-
jeunesse.
Desert: The American Southwest.
Ruth Kirk.
Design and Aesthetics in Wood.
Eric A. Anderson and George
F. Earle, eds.
The Destiny of a King. Georges
Dumézil.
The Destiny of the Warriors.
Georges Dumézil.
Destiny Road: The Gila Trail and
the Opening of the Southwest.

Odie B. Faulk.
A Destroying Angel: The Conquest
   of Smallpox in Colonial Boston.
   Ola Elizabeth Winslow.
The Destruction of Brazilian Slavery,
   1850-1888. Robert Conrad.
Deténte in Europe: Real or Imagin-
   ary? Josef Korbel.
Detroit: City of Race and Class Vio-
   lence. B. J. Widick.
Deutsch-lateinische Narrenzunft.
   Gunter Hess.
Deutsche Archive in West und Ost:
   Zur Entwicklung des staatlichen
   archivwesens seit 1945. Friedrich
   P. Kahlenberg.
Die deutsche Frauenbewegung im Spie-
   gel repräsentativer Frauenzeit-
   schriften: Ihre Anfänge und erste
   Entwicklung, 1843-1889. 2 vols.
   Margrit Twellmann.
Die deutsche Politik des Freiherrn
   von Beust, 1848-1850. Helmut
   Rumpler.
Deutsche Reichstagsakten unter Kaiser
   Karl V. Volume 8, parts 1 and
   2. Wolfgang Steglich, ed.
Deutsche Russlandpolitik. Barbara
   Vogel.
Deutsches Judentum in Krieg und
   Revolution. Werner E. Mosse,
   ed.
Deutschland in der Weltpolitik des
   19. und 20. Jahrhunderts. . . .
   Imanuel Geiss and Bernd Jürgen
   Wendt, eds.
Deutschland und Brasilien, 1889-
   1914. Gerhard Brunn.
Deutschland und die Reparationen
   1918/19: Die Genesis des Re-
   parationsproblems in Deutschland
   zwischen Waffenstillstand und Ver-
   sailler Friedensschluss. Peter
   Krüger.
Development Administration: the
   Kenyan Experience. G. Hyden,
   R. Jackson and J. Okumu, eds.
The Development of a Revolutionary
   Mentality: Papers Presented at
   the First Symposium, May 5 and
   6, 1972, Library of Congress
   Symposium on the American Revo-
   lution.
The Development of Tropical Lands:
   Policy Issues in Latin America.
   Michael Nelson.
The Development of Universities in
   Nigeria. Nduka Okafor.

Development Policy II: The Pakistan Experience. Walter P. Fal-
   con and Gustav F. Papanek, ed.
Deviancy and the Family. Clifton
   D. Bryant and J. Gipson Wells.
D. H. Lawrence, the Man and His
   Work: The Formative Years,
   1885-1919. Emile Delavenay.
The Dialectical Imagination: A His-
   tory of the Frankfurt School and
   the Institute of Social Research,
   1923-1950. Martin Jay.
The Diaries of Walter Murray Gib-
   son, 1886-1887. Jacob Adler
   and Gwynn Barrett, eds.
Diario 1866-1912. Vol. I. Sidney
   Sonnino.
Diario 1914-1916. Vol. II. Sidney
   Sonnino.
Diario 1916-1922. Vol. III. Sidney
   Sonnino.
The Diary of Calvin Fletcher. Vol.
   II. . . . 1838-1843: Including Let-
   ters to and from Calvin Fletcher.
   Gayle Thornbrough and Dorothy
   L. Riker, eds.
The Diary of Edmund Ruffin. Wil-
   liam Kauffman Scarborough, ed.
The Diary of Edward Walter Hamil-
   ton, 1880-1885. 2 vols. W. R.
   Bahlman Dudley, ed.
The Diary of James A. Garfield.
   Volume III: 1875-1877. Harry
   James Brown and Frederick D.
   Williams, eds.
The Diary of Samuel Pepys. Vol.
   VIII. Robert Latham and Wil-
   liam Matthews, eds.
The Diary of Samuel Sewall, 1674-
   1729. M. Halsey Thomas, ed.
Dickinson College: A History.
   Charles Coleman Sellers.
Dictionary of Canadian Biography.
   X: 1871-1880. Marc La Ter-
   reur, ed.
Dictionary of Prehistoric Indian Arti-
   facts of the American Southwest.
   Franklin Barnett.
Dictionary of the History of Ideas.
   Philip P. Wiener, gen. ed.
The Diffusion of Power. W. W.
   Rostow.
Diggings and Doing in Park City.
   Raye Carleson Price.
Diktierte Option: Die Umsiedlung
   der Deutsch-Balten aus Estland
   und Lettland, 1939-1941. Die-
   trich A. Loeber, ed.

Dilemmas of Growth in Prewar
Japan.   James William Morley,
ed.
Dilemmas of Statehood in Southeast
Asia.   Michael Leifer.
Dimensions of a New Identity: The
1973 Jefferson Lectures in the
Humanities.   Erik H. Erikson.
The Dimensions of Quantitative Re-
search in History.   William O.
Aydelotte, Allan G. Bogue, and
Robert William Fogel, eds.
The Dimensions of the Past: Materi-
als, Problems and Opportunities for
Quantitative Work in History.   Val
R. Lorwin and Jacob M. Price,
eds.
The Dinka and Their Songs.   Fran-
cis Mading Deng.
Dionysian Art and Populist Politics
in Austria.   William J. McGrath.
Diplomacy and Revolution.   The
Soviet Mission to Switzerland,
1918.   Alfred Erich Senn.
Diplomacy for Victory: FDR and Un-
conditional Surrender.   Raymond
G. O'Connor.
The Diplomacy of Annexation: Texas,
Oregon, and the Mexican War.
David M. Pletcher.
Diplomacy of Illusion.   The British
Government and Germany, 1937-
39.   Keith Middlemas.
The Diplomacy of the Mexican Em-
pire, 1863-1867.   Arnold Blum-
berg.
A Diplomatic History of the First
World War.   Z. A. B. Zeman.
Discovering Archaeology in Denmark.
James Dyer.
Discovery in Russian and Siberian
Waters.   L. H. Neatby.
The Discovery of the Asylum: Social
Order and Disorder in the New Re-
public.   David J. Rothman.
The Discovery of the Individual, 1050-
1200.   Colin Morris.
Disease and Economic Development:
The Impact of Parasitic Diseases
in St. Lucia.   B. A. Wiesbrod,
R. L. Andreano, R. E. Balwin,
and A. C. Kelley.
Dispossessing the American Indian:
Indians and Whites on the Colonial
Frontier.   Wilbur R. Jacobs.
The Dispute of the New World: The
History of a Polemic, 1750-1900.
Antonello Gerbi.

Disrupted Decades: The Civil War
and Reconstruction Years.
Robert H. Jones.
The Disruption of the Solid South.
George Brown Tindall.
Dissent in American Religion.   Ed-
win Scott Gaustad.
The Dissolution of the Monasteries.
Joyce Youings.
The Distant Magnet: European Emi-
gration to the U. S. A.   Philip
Taylor.
The Distribution of Population Aggre-
gates.   George J. Gumerman, ed.
Dr. Hyde and Mr. Stevenson: The
Life of the Rev. Dr. Charles Mc-
Ewan Hyde, Including a Discussion
of the Open Letter of Robert
Louis Stevenson.   Harold Winfield
Kent.
Dr. Robert Broom: Palaeontologist
and Physician, 1866-1951.
George Findlay.
Doctors in Politics: The Political
Life of the Japan Medical Asso-
ciation.   William E. Steslicke.
Documentary Expression and Thirties
America.   William Stott.
A Documentary History of the Italian
Americans.   Wayne Moquin and
Charles Van Doren.
Documents in Mycenean Greek.
Michael Ventris and John Chad-
wick.
Documents of European Economic
History.   3 vols.   Sidney Pollard
and Colin Holmes, eds.
Documents of the American Revolu-
tion, 1770-1783 (Colonial Office
Series).   3 vols.   K. G. Davies,
ed.
Documents of the Baronial Move-
ment of Reform and Rebellion,
1258-1267.   I. J. Sanders, ed.
Documents on British Foreign Policy,
1919-1939.   W. N. Medlicott, D.
Dakin and M. E. Lambert, eds.
Documents on Foreign Policy of
the Netherlands.   C. B. Wels, ed.
Dog Soldiers, Bear Men and Buffalo
Women: A Study of the Societies
and Cults of the Plains Indians.
Thomas E. Mails.
Dokumenten voor de Geschiedenis
van Prijzen en Lonen in Vlaander-
en en Brabant, Deel III (XVIe-
XIXe eeuw).   Charles Verlinden
and E. Scholliers.

De domeingoederen van de vorst in de Nederlanden omstreeks het midden van de zestiende eeuw, 1551-1559. Baelde.

The Domesday Geography of Midland England. H. C. Darby and I. B. Terrett, eds.

The Dominican Intervention. Abraham F. Lowenthal.

Don Francisco de Paula Marin: A Biography. Ross H. Gast.

Don Pio Pico's Historical Narrative. Martin Cole and Henry Welcome, eds.

Donne at Sermons. Gale H. Carrithers, Jr.

Donne's Anniversaries and the Poetry of Praise. Barbara Kiefer Lewalski.

Donoso Cortés: Utopian Romanticist and Political Realist. John T. Graham.

The Dorr Rebellion: A Study in American Revolution: 1833-1849. Marvin E. Gettleman.

Dos Passos' Path to U.S.A.: A Political Biography, 1912-1936. Melvin Landsberg.

La dottrina della scienza in Giacomo Zanbarella. Antonino Poppi.

The Douglas Diary: Student Days at Franklin and Marshall College. Henry Kyd Douglas.

The Dragon Empress: The Life and Times of Tz'u-hsi, Empress Dowager of China, 1835-1908. Marina Warner.

Dramatic Works. Jean de la Taille.

The Drawings of Ignacio Tirsch, a Jesuit Missionary in Baja California. Doyce B. Nunis, Jr.

The Dream and the Deal: The Federal Writers' Project 1935-1943. Jerre Mangione.

The Dream of the Red Chamber, A Critical Study. Jeanne Knoerle.

Drew Pearson: Diaries, 1949-1959. Tyler Abell, ed.

The Dreyfus Case: A Documentary History. Louis Snyder, ed.

Drie eeuwen Friesland: economische en sociale onluukkelingen van 1500 lot 1800. 2 vols. J. A. Faber.

The Driskill Hotel. Joe B. Frantz.

Dualistic Economic Development: Theory and History. Allen C. Kelley, Jeffrey G. Williamson and Russell J. Cheetham.

Dubious Victory: The United States and the End of World War II. Lisle A. Rose.

Dubrovnik in the 14th and 15th Centuries: A City Between East and West. Barisa Krekic.

Dubrovnik (Ragusa) A Classic City-State. Francis W. Carter.

Le duc de Saint-Simon et la monarchie. Jean-Pierre Brancourt.

Dudley Carleton to John Chamberlain 1603-1624. Maurice Lee, Jr., ed.

Dumbarton Oaks Papers, Number 26.

The Dura-Europos Synagogue: A Re-evaluation (1932-1972). Joseph Gutmann, ed.

Durham Priory, 1400-1450. R. B. Dobson.

The Durham Report and British Policy: A Critical Essay. Ged Martin.

A Dutch Homesteader on the Prairies. Herman Ganzevoort, tr.

The Dutch in the Seventeenth Century. K. H. D. Haley.

The Dutch Republic in Europe in the Seven Years' War. Alice Clare Carter.

Dwellers at the Source: Southwestern Indian Photographs of A. C. Vroman. William Webb and Robert A. Weinstein.

Dwight David Eisenhower: Antimilitarist in the White House. Blanche Wiesen Cook.

The Dynamics of the Industrial Revolution. Allan Thompson.

-E-

The Eager Immigrants. David M. Zielonka and Robert J. Wechman.

The Earliest European Helmets. Bronze Age and Early Iron Age. Hugh Hencken.

The Early American City. Lyle W. Dorsett.

Early Burma--Old Siam: A Comparative Commentary. H. G. Quaritch Wales.

Early Christian Ireland: Introduction to the Sources. Kathleen Hughes.

The Early Correspondence of Jabez Bunting. W. R. Ward.

Early Cretan Armorers. Herbert Hoffmann and A. E. Raubitschek.

Early English Organ Music from the Middle Ages to 1837. Francis Routh.

Early Germanic Kingship in England and on the Continent. J. M. Wallace-Hadrill.

Early Greek Warfare: Horseman and Chariots in the Homeric and Archaic Ages. P. A. L. Greenhalgh.

The Early Growth of the European Economy. Warriors and Peasants from the Seventh to the Twelfth Century. Georges Duby.

Early Lithic Industries of the Lower Basin of the Colorado River and Adjacent Desert Areas. Malcolm J. Rogers.

Early Medicine in Rapides Parish. Mary Thornton White.

Early Quaker Writings, 1650-1700. Hugh Barbour and Arthur O. Roberts, eds.

The Early Sunset Magazine, 1898-1928. Paul C. Johnson, ed.

East Across the Pacific: Historical and Sociological Studies of Japanese Immigration and Assimilation. Hilary Conroy and T. Scott Miyakawa, eds.

East and West Germany: A Comparative Economic Analysis. Martin Schnitzer.

East Carolina Railway: Route of the Yellow-hammer. Henry C. Bridgers, Jr.

The Eastern Cherokees. David W. Siler, comp.

Eastward to Empire: Exploration and Conquest on the Russian Open Frontier, to 1750. George V. Lantzeff and Richard A. Pierce.

Ebony Kinship: Africa, Africans, and the Afro-American. Robert G. Weisbord.

The Ecclesiastical History of Orderic Vitalis. Volume 3: Books, 5 and 6; Volume 4: Books 7 and 8. Marjorie Chibnall, ed. and trans.

Ecclesiologia ed etica politica in Giovanni Calvino. Valdo Vinay.

Echoes of the Past: New Mexico's Ghost Towns. Patricia F. Meleski.

L'Economia lombarda durante la Restaurazione (1814-1859). Bruno Caizzi.

Economic Beginnings in Colonial South Carolina, 1670-1730. Converse D. Clowse.

Economic Change in Thailand, 1850-1970. James C. Ingram.

Economic Development in East-Central Europe in the 19th and 20th Centuries. Iván T. Berend and György Ránki.

The Economic Development of Continental Europe, 1780-1870. A. Milward and S. B. Saul.

The Economic Emergence of the Black Country: A Study of the Dudley Estate. T. J. Raybould.

Economic Forces in French History: An Essay on the Development of the French Economy, 1760-1914. Tom Kemp.

Economic Growth in China and India, 1952-70: A Comparative Appraisal. Subramanian Swamy.

Economic Growth in History: Survey and Analysis. J. D. Gould.

Economic History and the Social Sciences: Problems of Methodology. Elias H. Tuma.

An Economic History of Ireland Since 1660. L. M. Cullen.

An Economic History of Nigeria, 1860-1960. R. Olufemi Ekundare.

An Economic History of the United States. Gilbert C. Fite and Jim E. Reese.

An Economic History of West Africa. A. G. Hopkins.

Economic History of Wisconsin During the Civil War Decade. Frederick Merk.

Economic Institutional Change in Tokugawa Japan: Osaka and the Kinai Cotton Trade. William B. Hauser.

Economic Maturity and Entrepreneurial Decline: British Iron and Steel, 1870-1913. Donald M. McCloskey.

Economic Opportunity and White American Fertility Ratios. Colin Forster and G. S. L. Tucker.

Economic Policy in Socialist Yugoslavia. Rudolf Bicanic.

Economics and Empire, 1830-1914. D. K. Fieldhouse.

The Economics of Colonialism:

Britain and Kenya, 1870-1930.
Richard D. Wolff.
The Economics of Latin America:
Development Problems in Per-
spective. Rawle Farley.
The Economics of Poverty and Dis-
crimination. Bradley B. Schiller.
Economies and Societies in Latin
America: A Geographical Inter-
pretation. Peter R. Odell and
David A. Preston.
The Economy of Bangladesh. Azizur
Rahman Khan.
The Economy of the Roman Empire:
Quantitative Studies. Richard Dun-
can-Jones.
The Economy of the USSR in the
Years of the Great Fatherland
War (1941-1945). G. S. Krav-
chenko.
Ecuador: Conflicting Political Culture
and the Quest for Progress. John
D. Martz.
Ecumenism in the Age of the Refor-
mation: The Colloquy of Poissy.
Donald Nugent.
Edmund Burke: His Political Philos-
ophy. Frank O'Gorman.
Education: Ontario's Preoccupation.
W. G. Fleming.
Education and Enmity: The Control
of Schooling in Northern Ireland,
1920-50. Donald Harman Akenson.
Education and the Rise of the Cor-
porate State. Joel H. Spring.
Education, Development and Nation-
Building in Independent Africa.
H. F. Makulu.
Education in American History: Read-
ings on the Social Issues. Michael
B. Katz, ed.
Edward Alsworth Ross and the So-
ciology of Progressivism. Julius
Weinberg.
Edward Porter Alexander. Maury
Klein.
Edward Preble: A Naval Biography
1761-1807. Christopher McKee.
Edwardian England 1901-1915. Don-
ald Read.
Egyptian Religion. Siegfried Morenz.
1815: The Armies at Waterloo. Ugo
Pericoli.
1848: The Romantic and Democratic
Revolutions in Europe. Jean Sig-
mann.
1848: The Revolutionary Tide in
Europe. Peter N. Stearns.

1871: Jalons pour une histoire de
la Commune de Paris. Jacques
Rougerie, ed.
The Eighteenth Century in Russia.
J. G. Garrard, ed.
The Eighth Wife. Miriam Were.
Einstein and Becket, a Record of an
Imaginary Discussion with Albert
Einstein and Samuel Becket. Ed-
win Schlossberg.
Eisenhower: Portrait of the Hero.
Peter Lyon.
Eisenhower and the American Cru-
sades. Herbert S. Parmet.
Elecciones y partidos políticos en
la Argentina. Historia, inter-
pretación y balance: 1910-1966.
Dario Canton.
The Electric Telegraph in the U. K. :
A Social and Economic History.
Jeffrey Kieve.
Elites Against Democracy: Leader-
ship Ideals in Bourgeois Political
Thought in Germany, 1890-1933.
Walter Struve.
Elizabeth: A Study in Power and
Intellect. Paul Johnson.
Elizabeth Empress of Russia.
Tamara Talbot Rice.
Elizabeth of York: The Mother of
Henry VIII. Nancy Lenz Harvey.
Ellen Glasgow and the Woman With-
in. E. Stanley Godbold, Jr.
Elsewhere, Perhaps. Amos Oz.
The Emancipation of the Russian No-
bility, 1762-1785. Robert E.
Jones.
Emblem of Liberty: The Image of
Lafayette in the American Mind.
Anne C. Loveland.
The Emergence of African Fiction.
Charles R. Larson.
The Emergence of Black Politics in
Senegal: The Struggle for Power
in the Four Communes, 1900-
1920. G. Wesley Johnson, Jr.
The Emergence of Christian Science
in American Religious Life.
Stephen Gottschalk.
The Emergence of Civilization: The
Cyclades and the Aegean in the
Third Millennium B. C. Colin
Renfrew.
The Emergence of Richard Wright:
A Study in Literature and Society.
Kenneth Kinnamon.
The Emergence of the Presidential
Nominating Convention, 1789-1832.

James S. Chase.
The Emin Pasha Relief Expedition, 1886-1890. Iain R. Smith.
Eminent Domain: The Louisiana Purchase and the Making of America. John Keats.
Emissaries to a Revolution: Woodrow Wilson's Executive Agents in Mexico. Larry D. Hill.
The Emperor Maximilian I and Music. Louise Cuyler.
Emperor of China: Self-Portrait of K'ang-hsi. Jonathan D. Spence.
Employment and Economic Growth in Urban China 1949-1957. C. Howe.
Employment Approaches to Economic Planning in Developing Countries. Birger Möller.
The Encyclopedia of American Facts and Dates. Gorton Carruth and Associates, eds.
Encyclopedia of Indians of the Americas. Volume I: Conspectus and Chronology. Keith Irvine, ed.
The End of Nowhere. Charles A. Stevenson.
End of the Trail: Odyssey of a Statue. Dean Krakel.
An End to Silence: The San Francisco State College Student Movement in the '60s. William Barlow and Peter Shapiro.
Endurance and Endeavor: Russian History, 1812-1971. J. N. Westwood.
The Enduring Ghetto: Sources and Readings. David R. Goldfield and James B. Lane, eds.
Engels, Manchester, and the Working Class. Steven Marcus.
The Engineer and Society. E. G. Semmler, ed.
England and the Baltic in the Elizabethan Era. Henryk Zins.
England and the Discovery of America, 1481-1620: From the Bristol Voyages of the Fifteenth Century to the Pilgrim Settlement at Plymouth: The Exploration, Exploitation, and Trial and Error Colonization of North America by the English. Daniel Beers Quinn.
England in the Later Middle Ages: A Political History. M. H. Keen.
England's Mission: The Imperial Idea in the Age of Gladstone and Disraeli, 1868-1880. C. C.

Eldridge.
England's Trade Policy in the Levant and Her Exchange of Goods with the Romanian Countries under the Latter Stuarts (1660-1714). P. Cernovodeanu.
Der Englische Bauernaufstand von 1381 und der Deutsche Bauernkrieg: Ein vergleich. Horst Gerlach.
The English and Immigration, 1880-1910. John A. Garrard.
The English Bishops and the First Vatican Council. Frederick J. Cwiekowski.
English Criticism in Japan: Essays by Younger Japanese Scholars on English and American Literature. Earl Miner, ed.
English Defenders of American Freedoms, 1774-1778: Six Pamphlets Attacking British Policy. Paul H. Smith, comp.
English Diplomacy, 1422-61. John Ferguson.
English Diplomatic Administration, 1259-1339. G. P. Cuttino.
The English Guide Book c 1780-1870. John Vaughan.
English Hunger and Industrial Disorders: A Study of Social Conflict During the First Decade of George III's Reign. Walter James Shelton.
The English Ideology. George Watson.
English Local Administration in the Middle Ages. Helen M. Jewell.
English Money and Irish Land. The Adventurers in the Cromwellian Settlement of Ireland. K. S. Bottigheimer.
The English Novel in the Nineteenth Century: Essays on the Literary Mediation of Human Values. George Goodin, ed.
The English Reformation, 1529-58. David H. Pill.
English Roman Catholics and Higher Education, 1830-1903. Vincent A. McClelland.
The English School: Its Architecture and Organization. Malcolm Seaborne.
English Tin Production and Trade Before 1550. John Hatcher.
An Englishman in the American Civil War: The Diaries of Henry Yates

Thompson, 1863. Sir Christopher Chancellor, ed.

Englishmen and Irish Troubles: British Public Opinion and the Making of Irish Policy, 1918-1922. D. G. Boyce.

The Enigmatic Chancellor: Bethmann and the Hubris of Imperial Germany. Konrad K. Jarausch.

Enjoying the Southwest. Catryna Ten Eyck Seymour.

The Enlightenment: A Comprehensive Anthology. Peter Gay, ed.

Enormous Changes at the Last Minute. Grace Paley.

Enserfment and Military Change in Muscovy. Richard Hellie.

"Entangling Alliances with None": An Essay on the Individual in the American Twenties. Robert H. Elias.

Enterprise Denied: Origins of the Decline of American Railroads, 1897-1917. Albro Martin.

The Enterprising Americans: A Business History of the United States. John Chamberlain.

The Entry of the Slavs into Christendom: An Introduction to the Medieval History of the Slavs. A. P. Vlasto.

Die Entstehung der Freizeit: Dargestellt am Beispiel Hamburgs; ein Beitrag zur Strukturgeschichte und zur geschichtlichen Grundlegung der Freizeitpädagogiks. Wolfgang Nahrstedt.

Die Entstehung der modernen Jahrhundertrechnung. Johannes Burkhardt.

Environmental Quality and Social Responsibility. Ravindra S. Khare, James W. Kolka, and Carol A. Pollis, eds.

The Epistolae Vagantes of Pope Gregory VII. H. E. J. Cowdrey.

L'Epoque pré-Urbaine en Palestine. Pierre R. de Miroschedji.

Les époux bordelais, 1450-1550: Régimes matrimoniaux et mutations sociales. Jacques Lafon.

Erasmus: The Growth of a Mind. James D. Tracy.

Erinnerungen und Dokumente von John Victor Bredt, 1914-1933. Martin Schumacher.

Ernst Brandes, 1758-1810. Carl Haase.

Die Ersten Fünfzig Jahre der Song-Dynastie in China: Beitrag zu einer Analyse der sozial-ökonomischen Formation während der ersten fünfzig Jahre der chinesischen Song-Dynastie (960-ca. 1010). Günter Lewin.

Escape from the Future: The Incredible Adventures of a Young Russian. Vladimir Petrov.

Eskimos. Kaj Birket-Smith.

Espaces et réseaux du haut Moyen Age. Maurice Lombard.

L'Espagne de Charles Quint. 2 vols. Pierre Chaunu.

Essays and Assays: California History Reappraised. George H. Knoles, ed.

Essays in European Economic History, 1500-1800. Peter Earle, ed.

Essays in Population History: Mexico and the Caribbean. Sherburne F. Cook and Woodrow Borah.

Essays in Quantitative Economic History. Roderick Floud, ed.

Essays in Theory and History. An Approach to the Social Sciences. Melvin Richter, ed.

Essays Mostly on Periodical Publishing in America: A Collection in Honor of Clarence Gohdes. James L. Woodress, ed.

Essays on a Mature Economy: Britain After 1840. Donald N. McCloskey.

Essays on American Foreign Policy. David C. DeBoe, Van Mitchell Smith, Elliott West, and Norman A. Graebner.

Essays on Medieval Agriculture and General Problems of the Medieval Economy. M. M. Postan

Essays on Radicalism in Contemporary America. Jerome L. Rodnitzky, Kenneth R. Philip, Frank Ross Peterson, and John A. Garraty.

Essays on Russian Liberalism. Charles E. Timberlake, ed.

Essays on the American Revolution. Stephen G. Kurtz and James H.

Hutson, eds.

Essays on the American West, 1972-73. Thomas G. Alexander, ed.

Essays on the Economic History of Latvia, 1860-1900. M. I. Kozin, ed.

Essays on the Economic History of the Argentine Republic. Carlos F. Diaz-Alejandro.

Essays on the Gilded Age. Carter E. Boren, Robert W. Amsler, Audra L. Prewitt, and H. Wayne Morgan.

Essays on the History of American Foreign Relations. Lawrence E. Gelfand, ed.

Essays on the History of Russian Culture in the First Half of the 19th Century. V. V. Poznanskii.

Essence of Decision: Explaining the Cuban Missile Crisis. Graham T. Allison.

Estado Moderno y Mentalidad social: Siglos XV a XVII. Vol. I. José Antonio Maravall.

Estructura Economica del Sociedad Mexica. Victor M. Castillo F.

The Ethics of Jonathan Edwards: Morality and Aesthetics. Clyde A. Holbrook.

Ethnic Conflict and Political Development. Cynthia H. Enloe.

The Ethnic Experience in Pennsylvania. John E. Bodnar, ed.

Ethnic Groups of Insular Southeast Asia. Volume 1: Indonesia, Andaman Islands and Madagascar. Frank M. LeBar, ed. and comp.

Ethnobotany of Western Washington: The Knowledge and Use of Indigenous Plants by Native Americans. Erna Gunther.

Ethnohistory in Southwestern Alaska and the Southern Yukon: Method and Content. Margaret Lantis.

Etienne-Louis Boullée (1728-1799): Theoretician of Revolutionary Architecture. Jean-Marie Perouse de Montclos.

The Etruscans. Werner Keller.

Etudes Préliminaires aux religions orientales dans l'empire Romain. J. M. Vermasern, ed.

Eugene C. Barker: Historian. William C. Pool.

Die Europaische stadt des mittelalters. Edith Ennen.

Europe in the Eighteenth Century: Aristocracy and the Bourgeois Challenge. George Rudé.

Europe in the High Middle Ages 1150-1309. John H. Mundy.

Europe in the Twentieth Century. George Lichtheim.

Europe Leaves the Middle East, 1936-1954. Howard M. Sachar.

Europe: Mother of Revolutions. Friedrich Heer.

Europe Since 1870. James Joll.

European and Muscovite: Ivan Kireevsky and the Origins of Slavophilism. Abbott Gleason.

European Imperialism in Asia. Michael Adas.

The European Middle Class in the 19th Century. Lenore O'Boyle.

The European Pentarchy and the Congress of Verona, 1822. Irby C. Nichols, Jr.

Eusèbe de Césarée, La Préparation Evangélique 1. Jean Sirinelli and Edouard des Places.

Evangile de Pierre. M. G. Mara.

Every Fifth Child: The Population of China. Leo A. Orleans.

Everyday Life of the Etruscans. Ellen Macnamara.

Evolucão do Catolicismo no Brasil. João Alfredo de Sousa Montenegro.

The Evolution of American Society, 1700-1815: An Interdisciplinary Analysis. James A. Henretta.

The Evolution of an Urban School System: New York City, 1750-1850. Carl F. Kaestle.

The Evolution of Hitler's Germany: The Ideology, the Personality, the Movement. Horst von Maltitz.

The Evolution of the British Welfare State: A History of Social Policy Since the Industrial Revolution. Derek Fraser.

The Evolution of the Egyptian National Image: From Its Origins to Ahmad Lufti al-Sayyid. Charles Wendell.

Excursion Through America. Nicholaus Mohr.

Executive Agreements and Treaties, 1946-1973. Framework of the Foreign Policy of the Period. Amy M. Gilbert.

The Exercise of Judicial Power, 1789-1864. David Marshall

Billikopf.

Exiles and Citizens: Spanish Republicans in Mexico. Patricia W. Fagan.

Expansion and Coexistence: Soviet Foreign Policy, 1917-1973. Adam B. Ulam.

L'Expansion Musulmane (7-11 siècles). Robert Mantran.

The Expatriate Perspective: American Novelists and the Idea of America. Harold T. McCarthy.

The Expeditions of John Charles Fremont: Volume 2, The Bear Flag Revolt and the Court-Martial. Mary Lee Spence and Donald Jackson, eds.

The Experimenters: A Study of the Accademia del Cimento. W. E. Knowles Middleton.

Exploration Archeologique de Délos Faite par L'Ecole Française d'Athens. Philippe Bruneau.

Exploration of Kamchatka-North Pacific Scimitar: Opisanie Zemi Kamchatki: Report of a Journey Made to Explore Eastern Siberia in 1735-1741, by Order of the Russian Imperial Government. Stepan Petrovich Krasheninnokov.

The Exploration of the Colorado River. John Wesley Powell.

Explorations in Managerial Economics. Bela Gold.

The Exposure of Luxury: Radical Themes in Thackeray. Barbara Hardy.

Eye-Witnesses to Wagon Trains West. James Hewitt, ed.

- F -

F L O: A Biography of Frederick Law Olmsted. Laura Wood Roper.

Faces in Clay: The Archaeology and Early History of the Red Man in the Upper Delaware Valley. Vernon E. Leslie.

Faces of Nationalism. New Realities and Old Myths. Boyd C. Shafer.

Faces of the Wilderness. Harvey Broome.

La Factoría de Tobacos de Costa Rica. Marco Antonio Fallas.

Failure of a Dream? Essays in History of American Socialism. John H. M. Laslett and Seymour Martin Lipset, eds.

Failure of a Revolution: Germany, 1918-19. Sebastian Haffner.

The Failure of Illiberalism: Essays of the Political Culture of Modern Germany. Fritz Stern.

The Failure of South African Expansion, 1908-1948. Ronald Hyam.

The Fall of Lloyd George: The Political Crisis of 1922. Michael Kinnear.

The Fall of the House of Borgia. E. R. Chamberlin.

Fame and the Founding Fathers. Douglass Adair.

Familia Caesaris: A Social Study of the Emperor's Freedmen and Slaves. P. R. C. Weaver.

Family and Fortune. Lawrence Stone.

The Family in Renaissance Italy. David Herlihy.

Family, Lineage and Civil Society ... in the Durham Region, 1500-1640. Mervyn James.

Famine 'in China and the Missionary: Timothy Richard as Relief Administrator and Advocate of National Reform, 1876-1884. Paul Richard Bohr.

Fanon. Pierre Bouvier.

Far Eastern Trade, 1860-1914. Francis E. Hyde.

Faraday as a Natural Philosopher. Joseph Agassi.

Farewell to Manzanar: A True Story of Japanese American Experience During and After the World War II Internment. Jeanne Wakatsuki Houston and James D. Houston.

Farm Management in Africa--The Principles of Production and Planning. Martin Upton.

The Farmers' Movement in the USA: From the Grangers to the Populists, 1867-1896. G. P. Kuropiatnik.

Faschismus und Kapitalismus in Deutschland: Studien zum Verhältnis zwischen Nationalsozialismus und Wirtschaft. Henry Ashby Turner, Jr.

Fascism and the Industrial Leadership in Italy, 1919-1940. A Study in the Expansion of Private

Power Under Fascism. Roland
Sarti.
The Fascist Experience. Italian
Society and Culture: 1922-1945.
Edward R. Tannenbaum.
The Fatal Mirror: Themes and Tech-
niques in the Poetry of Fulke
Greville. Richard Waswo.
Father Coughlin: The Tumultuous
Life of the Priest of the Little
Flower. Sheldon Marcus.
Father Jose Burgos: Priest and
Nationalist. John H. Schumacher.
Fear and Loathing: On the Campaign
Trail, '72. Hunter S. Thompson.
The Feast of Kingship: Accession
Ceremonies in Ancient Japan.
Robert S. Ellwood.
Feasting and Social Oscillation: Re-
ligion and Society in Upland
Southeast Asia. A. Thomas
Kirsch.
Federal Land Series. 2 vols. Clif-
ford Neal Smith.
Federal Service and the Constitution:
The Development of the Public Em-
ployment Relationship. David H.
Rosenbloom.
Female and Male in Latin America.
Essays. Ann Pescatello, ed.
Feminism: The Essential Historical
Writings. Miriam Schneir, ed.
Fenimore Cooper: The Critical
Heritage. George Dekker and
John P. McWilliams, eds.
Le Fermiers Generaux au Dix-
huiteme Siecle. Yves Durand.
Fermin Francisco de Lausén (1736-
1803): A Biography. Francis
F. Guest, O. F. M.
Fernando Cortés and the Marquesado
in Morelos, 1522-1547: A Case
Study in the Socioeconomic De-
velopment of Sixteenth-Century
Mexico. G. Michael Riley.
Festschrift Bernhard Bischoff. Jo-
hanne Autenrieth and Franz Brun-
holzl, eds.
Festschrift fur Hermann Hempel.
Max-Planck Institut fur Geschichte,
ed.
The Feudal Nobility and the Kingdom
of Jerusalem, 1174-1277. Jona-
than Riley-Smith.
Fiction with a Parochial Purpose:
Social Uses of American Catholic
Literature, 1884-1900. Paul R.
Messbarger.

Fictional Transfigurations of Jesus.
Theodore Ziolkowski.
Fifteen American Authors Before
1900: Bibliographic Essays on
Research and Criticism. Robert
A. Rees and Earl N. Harbert,
eds.
Fifteenth-Century England 1399-1509.
S. B. Chrimes, C. D. Ross,
and R. A. Griffiths, eds.
The Fifth Monarchy Men. B. S.
Capps.
The Fifth World of Forster Bennett:
Portrait of a Navajo. Vincent
Crapanzano, comp.
Fifty Years of Rapid Transit, 1864-
1917. James Blaine Walker.
Fighting Ships and Prisons: The
Mediterranean Galleys of France
in the Age of Louis XIV. Paul
W. Bamford.
Fighting Tuscarora: The Autobi-
ography of Chief Clinton Rickard.
Barbara Graymont, ed.
The "Figurae" of Joachim of Fiore.
Marjorie Reeves and Beatrice
Hirsch-Reich.
Les Figurines Gallo-Romaines en
Terre Cuite au Musée des An-
tiquities Nationales. Micheline
Rouvier-Jeanlin.
A Financial History of the New
Japan. T. F. M. Adams and
Iwao Hoshii.
The Financial System of Egypt A. H.
564-741/A. D. 1169-1341. Has-
sanein Rabie.
Fire and Blood: A History of Mex-
ico. T. R. Fehrenbach.
The Firebird Library. 16 vols.
Barbara Walker, ed.
First Across! The U. S. Navy's
Transatlantic Flight of 1919.
Richard K. Smith.
The First Americans: A Story of
North American Archaeology.
C. W. Ceram.
The First Book of Discipline.
James K. Cameron, ed.
First Freedom: The Responses of
Alabama's Blacks to Emancipa-
tion and Reconstruction. Peter
Kolchin.
The First Henry Ford: A Study in
Personality and Business Leader-
ship. Anne Jardim.
The First Great Civilizations: Life
in Mesopotamia, the Indus Valley

and Egypt. The History of Hu-
man Society. Jacquetta Hawkes.
The First Offensive, 1942: Roosevelt,
Marshal and the Making of Amer-
can Strategy. Richard W. Steele.
The First Rockingham Administra-
tion, 1765-1766. Paul Langford.
The First West. Ruby Addison Henry.
The Fiscal System of Renaissance
France. Martin Wolfe.
Fisher of Kilverstone. Ruddock F.
Mackay.
Fit and Proper Persons: Ideal and
Reality in Nineteenth-Century Ur-
ban Government. E. P. Hennock.
Five Papers on the Archaeology of
the Desert West. Donald R.
Tuohy, Doris Rendall, and Pamela
A. Crowell, eds.
The Flamboyant Judge, James D.
Hamlin: A Biography. J. Evetts
Haley and William Curry Holden.
Fleet Street Radical: A. G. Gardiner
and the Daily Press. Stephen
Koss.
The Flint Mammoth Cave System,
Mammoth Cave National Park,
Kentucky, U. S. A.
Flood Tide of Empire: Spain and
the Pacific Northwest, 1543-1819.
Warren L. Cook.
Floor of the Sky: The Great Plains.
David Plowden.
Florence in the Forgotten Centuries,
1527-1800: Florence and the
Florentines in the Age of the Grand
Dukes. Eric Cochrane.
Florentine Public Finances in the
Early Renaissance, 1400-1433.
Anthony Molho.
Florida: Its Scenery, Climate, and
History. Sidney Lanier.
Florida History: A Bibliography.
Michael H. Harris, comp.
The Florida Phosphate Industry: A
History of the Development and
Use of a Vital Mineral. Arch
Frederic Blakey.
A Flower From Every Meadow: In-
dian Paintings From American
Collections. Stuart Cary Welch.
Les Fluctuations du produit de la
dîme: Conjoncture décimale et
domainiale de la fin du Moyen Age
au XViiie siècle. Josepn Goy et
Emmanuel Le Roy Ladurie.
Les foires de la Valachie pendant in
période 1774-1848. Georgeta

Penelea.
Folklore: From the Working Folk
of America. Tristram P. Cof-
fin and Henning Cohen, eds.
Folklore and Folklife. Richard M.
Dorson, ed.
Folklore in the Writings of Rowland
E. Robinson. Ronald L. Baker.
Folktales of Mexico. Américo
Paredes, ed. and trans.
The Fontana Economic History of
Europe. Carlo M. Cipolla, ed.
Fontes Harleiani: A Study of the
Sources of the Harleian Collec-
tion of Manuscripts Preserved in
the Department of Manuscripts in
the British Museum. C. E.
Wright.
For Peace and Justice. Pacificism
in America, 1914-1941. Charles
Chatfield.
For the First Hours of Tomorrow:
The New Illinois Bill of Rights.
Elmer Gertz.
Foreign Aid and Industrial Develop-
ment in Pakistan. Irving Brecher
and S. A. Abbas.
The Foreign Policy of Col. McCor-
mick's Tribune, 1929-1941.
Jerome E. Edwards.
The Foreign Policy of the Third
Reich. Klaus Hildebrand.
The Foreign Relations of the People's
Republic of China. Winberg
Chai, ed.
Foreign Relations of the United
States: The Conference at Que-
bec, 1944.
Foreign Relations of the United
States, 1946. Volume 1, Gen-
eral; The United Nations.
Foreign Relations of the United
States, 1946, volume 8, The
Far East; 1947, volume 6, The
Far East.
Foreign Relations of the United
States, 1947. Vol. I. General;
The United Nations.
Foreign Relations of the United
States, 1947. Volume 4, Eastern
Europe; The Soviet Union.
Foreign Relations of the United
States, 1947. Volume 8, The
American Republics.
Foreigners in Their Native Land:
Historical Roots of the Mexican
Americans. David J. Weber, ed.
Foresters in Exile: The Sopron

Forestry School in Canada. Laszlo Adamovich and Oszkar Sziklai.

Forever Open, Clear and Free: The Historic Struggle for Chicago's Lakefront. Lois Wille.

Forging Accounting Principles in Five Countries: A History and an Analysis of Trends. Stephen A. Zeff.

The Forging of the American Empire. Sidney Lens.

Forging the American Republic, 1760-1815. Norman K. Risjord.

The Forgotten Americans: A Survey of Values, Beliefs, and Concerns of the Majority. Frank E. Armbruster and Doris Yokelson.

The Formation of Islamic Art. Oleg Grabar.

Fórmulas políticas no Brasil Holandês. Mário Neme.

Forrest, 1847-1918. Volume 1, 1847-91: Apprenticeship to Premiership. F. K. Crowley.

Fort Collins: The Post--the Town. Guy L. Peterson.

Fort Custer on the Big Horn. Richard Upton, comp. and ed.

Fort Worth: A Frontier Triumph. Julia Kathryn Garrett.

Forward in the Second Century of MacMurray College: A History of 125 Years. Walter B. Hendrickson.

Fouché: The Unprincipled Patriot. Hubert Cole.

1. Foundation of the Cape. 2. About the Bechuanas. W. H. C. Lichtenstein.

The Foundations of American Economic Freedom: Government and Enterprise in the Age of Washington. E. A. J. Johnson.

Foundations of Colonial America: A Documentary History. 3 vols. W. Keith Kavenagh, ed.

The Foundations of Palatial Crete: A Survey of Crete in the Early Bronze Age. Keith Branigan.

The Foundations of the American Empire: William Henry Seward and U. S. Foreign Policy. Ernest N. Paolino.

The Founding Fathers: John Adams, A Biography in His Own Words. James Bishop Peabody, ed.

Foundlings on the Frontier: Racial and Religious Conflict in Arizona Territory, 1904-1905. A. Blake Brophy.

400 Miles from Harlem: Courts, Crime and Correction. Max Wylie.

Four Martyrdoms from the Pierpont Morgan Coptic Codices. E. A. E. Reymond and J. W. B. Barns.

The Fourteenth Chronicle: Letters and Diaries of John Dos Passos. Townsend Luddington, ed.

The Fourth World: An Indian Reality. George Manuel and Michael Posluns.

France and Britain in Africa: Imperial Rivalry and Colonial Rule. Prosser Gifford and William Roger Louis, eds.

France and North America: Over Three Hundred Years of Dialogue. Mathé Allain and Glenn R. Conrad, ed.

France and Poland After the Versailles Treaty. Jósef Kulka.

France and the Chesapeake: A History of the French Tobacco Monopoly, 1674-1791, and Its Relationship to the British and American Tobacco Trades. Jacob M. Price.

France, 1848-1945. Volume 1: Ambition, Love and Politics. Theodore Zeldin.

France in America. W. J. Eccles.

France in Revolution, 1848. Anthony Denholm.

Frances Warde: American Founder of the Sisters of Mercy. Kathleen Healy.

Francesco Vettori: Florentine Citizen and Medici Servant. Rosemary Devonshire Jones.

Francis Drake; Privateer: Contemporary Narratives and Documents. John Hampden, ed.

Francis Lee Jaques: Art of the Wilderness. Florence Page Jaques.

Francis Marion: The Swamp Fox. Hugh F. Rankin.

Francis Parkman: Heroic Historian. Mason Wade.

Francisco de Quevedo and the Neostoic Movement. Henry Ettinghausen.

Francogallia. François Hotman.

Franklin and Galloway: A Political Partnership. Benjamin H. Newcomb.

Franklin D. Roosevelt: Launching the New Deal. Frank Freidel.

Franklin D. Roosevelt and the World Crisis, 1937-1945. Warren Kimball, ed.

Frankreich in Gunesien: Die Anfänge des Protektorates, 1881-1886. Jürgen Rosenbaum.

Frankreich und die deutschen Protestanten: Die Bemühungen um eine religiöse Konkordie und die französische Bündnispolitik in den Jahren 1534/35. Karl Josef Seidel.

Frankreichs Ruhrpolitik: Von Versailles bis zum Daewsplan. Ludwig Zimmerman.

Frantz Fanon: A Critical Study. Irene Gendzier.

Französischer Imperialismus in Vietnam. Die koloniale Expansion und die Errichtung des Protektorates Annam-Tongking 1880-1885. D. Brötel.

Frederic Augustus James' Civil War Diary: Sumter to Andersonville. Jefferson J. Hammer, ed.

Frederic Remington. Peter H. Hassrick.

Frederick Denison Maurice: Rebellious Conformist. Olive J. Brose.

Frederick Jackson Turner: Historian, Scholar, Teacher. Ray Allen Billington.

Frederick the Great. Nancy Mitford.

Frederick the Great. Peter Paret, ed.

Free at Last: The Life of Frederick Douglass. Arna Bontemps.

Free Men All: The Personal Liberty Laws of the North, 1780-1861. Thomas D. Morris.

The Free Peasantry of Feudal Norway. A. Ia. Gurevich.

Free Soil: The Election of 1848. Joseph G. Rayback.

The Free Soilers: Third Party Politics, 1848-54. Frederick J. Blue.

Freedom and Development. Julius K. Nyerere.

Freedom and the Court: Civil Rights and Liberties in the United States. Henry J. Abraham.

The French Campaign in Portugal, 1810-1811. Jean Jacques Pelet.

French Foreign Policy Since the Second World War. Herbert Tint.

French Government and Society 1500-1850. J. F. Bosher, ed.

The French Legation in Texas. Vol. II. Mission Miscarried. Nancy Nichols Barker, trans. and ed.

French Legitimists and the Politics of Moral Order in the Early Third Republic. Robert R. Locke.

The French Revolution and Napoleon Collection at Florida State University: A Bibliographical Guide. Donald D. Horward.

The French Revolution of 1830. David H. Pinkney.

Freud and the Americans: The Beginnings of Psychoanalysis in the United States, 1876-1917. Nathan G. Hale, Jr.

The Freud/Jung Letters: The Correspondence Between Sigmund Freud and C. G. Jung. William McGuire, ed.

Friedrich Engels on Ukraine. I. Hurzhii.

From Colony to Empire: Essays in the History of American Foreign Relations. William Appleman Williams, ed.

From Confederation to Nations: The American Constitution, 1835 to 1877. Bernard Schwartz.

From Contraband to Freedman: Federal Policy Toward Southern Blacks, 1861-1865. Louis S. Gerteis.

From Myth to Fiction: The Saga of Hadingus. Georges Dumézil.

From Ottomanism to Arabism, Essays on the Origins of Arab Nationalism. C. Ernest Dawn.

From Paris to Sèvres: The Partition of the Ottoman Empire at the Peace Conference of 1919-1920. Paul C. Helmreich.

From Personal to Territorial Law: Aspects of the History and Structure of Western Legal-Constitutional Tradition. Simeon L. Guterman.

From Poor Law to Welfare State: A History of Social Welfare in America. Walter I. Trattner.

From Prescription to Persuasion: Manipulation of Seventeenth-Century Virginia Economy. John C. Rainbolt.

From Renaissance to Renaissance: Hebrew Literature from 1492-1970. Elsig Siberschlag.

From Resistance to Revolution:

Colonial Radicals and the Development of American Opposition to Britain, 1765-1776. Pauline Maier.

From Revolution to Rapprochement: The United States and Great Britain, 1783-1900. Charles S. Campbell.

From Revolution to Revolution: England, 1688-1776. John Carswell.

From Sadowa to Sarajevo. The Foreign Policy of Austria-Hungary, 1866-1914. F. R. Bridge.

From Shelter to Self-Reliance: A History of the Illinois Braille and Sight Saving School. Walter B. Hendrickson.

From Spanish Court to Italian Ghetto. Isaac Cardoso: A Study in Seventeenth-Century Marranism and Jewish Apologetics. Yosef Hayim Yerusalmi.

From Sundown to Sunup: The Making of the Black Community. George P. Rawick, ed.

From Superiority to Parity: The United States and the Strategic Arms Race, 1961-1971. Harland B. Moulton.

From the Missouri to the Great Salt Lake; An Account of Overland Freighting. William E. Lass.

From the Molly Maguires to the United Mine Workers: The Social Ecology of an Industrial Union, 1869-1897. Harold W. Aurand.

From the Mountain. Helen White and Redding S. Sugg, Jr., eds.

From the Revolution Through the Age of Jackson: Innocence and Empire in the Young Republic. John R. Howe.

From Union Stars to Top Hat: A Biography of the Extraordinary General James Harrison Wilson. Edward G. Longacre.

Frontier Crusader--William F. M. Arny. Lawrence R. Murphy.

Frontier Defense and the Open Door: Manchuria in Chinese-American Relations, 1895-1911. Michael H. Hunt.

Frontier Elements in a Hudson River Village. Carl Nordstrom.

Frontier Governor: Samuel J. Crawford of Kansas. Mark A. Plummer.

The Frontier Merchant in Mid-America. Lewis E. Atherton.

Frontier Regulars: The United States Army and the Indian, 1866-1890. Robert M. Utley.

Frontier Tales: True Stories of Real People. Juanita Brooks.

Frontier Violence: Another Look. W. Eugene Hollon.

Frontier Woman: The Life of a Woman Homesteader on the Dakota Frontier. Walker D. Wyman.

Frustrated Patriots: North Carolina and the War of 1812. Sarah McCulloh Lemmon.

The Function of Documents in Islamic Law: The Chapters on Sales from Tahawi's Kitab al-shurut al-kabir. Jeanette A. Wakin, ed.

Fundamental Testaments of the American Revolution. Elizabeth Hamer Kegan, ed.

Die Fundmunzen von Vindonissa von Hadrian bis zum Ausgang der Romerherrschaft. Thomas Pekáry.

Furia y Muerte: Los Bandidos Chicanos. Pedro Castillo and Albert Camarillo, ed.

Furniture Makers of Indiana, 1793-1850. Betty Lawson Walters.

Future Builders. George Bush.

The Future of the Jewish Community in America. David Sidorsky, ed.

-G-

G. D. H. Cole: An Intellectual Biography. L. P. Carpenter.

G. K. Chesterton: A Biography. Dudley Barker.

G. Stanley Hall: The Psychologist as Prophet. Dorothy Ross.

Gabriel Renville: Young Sioux Warrior. Donald Dean Parker.

Galenism: Rise and Decline of a Medical Philosophy. Owsei Temkin.

Gambetta and the Making of the Third Republic. J. P. T. Bury.

Gandhi's Rise to Power: Indian Politics 1915-1922. Judith M.

Brown.

Gandhi's Social Philosophy: Perspective and Relevance. B. N. Ganguli.

Le Gauche Israelienne. Merhav Peretz.

Gaullism: The Rise and Fall of a Political Movement. Anthony Hartley.

Gazetteers of the Northern Provinces of Nigeria. 4 vols. A. H. M. Kirk-Greene, ed.

Genealogical Research--A Jurisdictional Approach. Vincent L. Jones, Arlene H. Eakle, and Mildred H. Christensen.

General Eisenhower on the Military Churchill: A Conversation with Alistair Cooke. James Nelson, ed.

A General History of the Pyrates. Daniel Defoe.

General Stilwell in China, 1942-1944: The Full Story. Chin-Tung Liang.

A General Theory of Magic. Marcel Mauss.

The Generation Classes of the Zanaki (Tanzania). Otto Bischoffberger.

The Genet Mission. Harry Ammon.

Genetics and American Society: A Historical Appraisal. Kenneth M. Ludmerer.

Le génie militaire de Vercingétorix et le mythe Alise-Alésia. René Potier.

Les Gens de coleur libres du Fort Royal 1679-1823. Emile Hayot.

Genteel Partisan: Manton Marble, 1834-1917. George T. McJimsey.

Gentle Patriot: A Political Biography of Walter Gordon. Denis Smith.

George II. Charles Chenevix Trench.

George the Third. Stanley Ayling.

George III and Lord Bute: The Leicester House Years. James Lee McKelvey.

George IV: Prince of Wales, 1762-1811. Christopher Hibbert.

George Alfred Trenholm and the Company That Went to War. Ethel S. Nepveux.

George C. Marshall: Organizer of Victory (1943-1945). Forrest C. Pogue.

George Joachim Goschen: The Transformation of a Victorian Liberal. Thomas J. Spinner, Jr.

George Peabody. Franklin Parker.

George Stephenson: the Engineer and His Letters. W. O. Skeat.

George W. Brackenridge: Maverick Philanthropist. Marilyn McAdams Sibley.

George W. Norris: The Persistence of a Progressive, 1913-1933. Richard Lowitt.

George W. P. Hunt and His Arizona. John S. Goff.

George W. Smalley: Forty Years a Foreign Correspondent. Joseph F. Matthews.

George Washington: A Biography in His Own Words. Ralph K. Andrist, ed.

George Washington: Soldier and Man. North Callahan.

Georges Clemenceau: A Political Biography. David Robin Watson.

Georgia's Last Frontier: The Development of Carroll County. James C. Bonner.

Gerard van Swieten und seine zeit .... Erna Lesky and Adam Wandrusza, eds.

German-American Political Behavior in Nebraska and Wisconsin, 1916-1920. Clifford L. Nelson.

German Antiquity in Renaissance Myth. Frank L. Borchardt.

The German Church Struggle and the Holocaust. Franklin H. Littell and Hubert G. Locke, eds.

German Democracy and the Triumph of Hitler: Essays in Recent German History. Anthony Nicholls and Erich Matthias, eds.

German Home Towns: Community, State, and General Estate, 1648-1817. Mack Walker.

German Literature: A Critical Survey. Bruno Boesch, ed.

The German Naval Officer Corps: A Social and Political History, 1890-1918. Holger H. Herwig.

German "Pest Ships." Alice D. Forsyth and Earlene L. Zerinque, comps. and trans.

German Pietism During the Eighteenth Century. F. Ernest Stoeffler.

German-Polish Relations 1918-33. Harald Von Riekhoff.

German Strategy Against Russia, 1939-1941. Barry A. Leach.

La Germania e la neutralità italiana: 1914-15. Alberto Monticone.

The Germans. Erich Kahler.
Germany: A Companion to German Studies. Malcolm Pasley, ed.
Germany and the Approach of War in 1914. V. R. Berghahn.
Germany Since 1918. David Childs.
Geronimo: A Biography. Alexander B. Adams.
Geronimo: The Story of an American Indian. Charles Morrow Wilson.
Geschiedenis van de Vroegere Quakergemeenschap te Amsterdam, 1656 tot begin negentiende eeuw. J. Z. Kannegieter.
Getemperde Vrijheid. H. A. Enno Van Gelder.
Gettysburg: The Final Fury. Bruce Catton.
Ghana Under Military Rule, 1966-1969. Robert Pinkney.
The Ghent Altarpiece and the Art of Jan Van Eyck. Lotte Brand Philip.
The G. I. Bill, the Veterans, and the Colleges. Keith W. Olson.
Giants in the Sky: A History of the Rigid Airship. Douglas H. Robinson.
Gibbon for Moderns: The History of the Decline and Fall of the Roman Empire with Lessons for America Today. Peter P. Witonski, ed.
Gideon Welles: Lincoln's Secretary of the Navy. John Niven.
Gierek's Poland. Adam Bromke and John W. Strong, eds.
A Gift of Madrigals and Motets. H. Colin Slim.
Gilbert Haven, Methodist Abolitionist: A Study in Race, Religion and Reform, 1850-1880. William Gravely.
The Gilded Age and After. John A. DeNovo, ed.
Gilles Aycelin: The Servant of Two Masters. Jo Ann McNamara.
Il giovane Machiavelli banchiere con Berto Berti a Roma. Domenico Maffei.
Giovanni Pico della Mirandola: Conclusiones sive theses DCCCC Romae anno 1486 publice disputandae, sed non admissae. Bohdan Kieszkowski, ed.
Give Me Combat: The Memoirs of Julio Alvarez del Vayo. Julio Alvarea del Vayo.
Give Me the Wind. Jan Jordan.
Give Your Heart to the Hawks: a Tribute to the Mountain Men. Winfred Blevins.
The Gladstones: A Family Biography, 1764-1851. S. G. Checkland.
The Glassworkers of Carmaux: French Craftsmen and Political Action in a Nineteenth-Century City. Joan Wallach Scott.
Glaube und Politik in Pennsylvania 1681-1776: Die Wandlungen der Obrigkeitsdoktrin und des PEACE TESTIMONY der Quaker. Hermann Wellenreuther.
Gloriana: The Years of Elizabeth I. Mary M. Lucke.
The Glorious Enterprise: The Centennial Exhibition of 1876 and H. J. Schwarzmann, Architect-in-Chief. John Maass.
The Glorious Failure: Black Congressman Robert Brown Elliott and the Reconstruction in South Carolina. Peggy Lamson.
The Glorious Revolution in America. David S. Lovejoy.
Glyptique Susienne, des Origines à l'Epoque des Perses Achéménides Cachets, Sceaux-Cylindres et Empreintes Antiques Decouvertes a Suse de 1913 à 1967. Vols. I-II. Pierre Amiet.
Glyptothek München. Griechische und Romische Skulpturen. Ein Kürzer Führer. Dieter Ohly.
God Men of India. Peter Brent.
"God Save This Honorable Court!" Louis M. Kohlmeier, Jr.
The Gods and Goddesses of Old Europe: 7000 to 3500 B. C.: Myths, Legends and Cult Images. Marija Gimbutas.
Gods, Ghosts, and Ancestors: The Folk Religion of a Taiwanese Village. David K. Jordan.
God's Plot: The Paradoxes of Puritan Piety. Being the Autobiography and Journal of Thomas Shepard. Michael McGiffert, ed.
Going to America. Terry Coleman.
Gold Camp Drifter, 1906-1910. Emmett L. Arnold.
The Golden Age of Spain, 1516-1659. Antonio Domínguez Ortiz.

The Golden Legacy: A Folk History of J. Golden Kimball. Thomas E. Cheney.

The Golden Spike. David E. Miller, ed.

Good Old Modern: An Intimate Portrait of the Museum of Modern Art. Russell Lynes.

The Good Provider: H. J. Heinz and His 57 Varieties. Robert C. Alberts.

Good Times: An Oral History of America in the Nineteen Sixties. Peter Joseph.

The Goodliest Land: North Carolina. Nancy Roberts.

The Gospel of Nicodemus. H. C. Kim, ed.

Government and Politics in Kuomintang China, 1927-1937. Hung-mao Tien.

Governor O. Max Gardner: A Power in North Carolina and New Deal Washington. Joseph L. Morrison.

Grace King of New Orleans: A Selection of Her Writings. Robert Bush, ed.

Grand commerce et vie urbaine au XVIe siecle: Lyon et ses marchands.... Richard Gascon.

Un grand préfet de la Côte-d'Or sous Louis-Philippe: La Correspondance d'Achille Chaper (1831-1840). Paul Gonnet.

Grand Strategy. Vol. IV. August 1942-September 1943. Michael Howard.

Grandeur et liberté de la Suède (1660-1792). Claude Nordmann.

The Grasping Imagination: The American Writings of Henry James. Peter Buitenhuis.

Grass Between the Rails. Denny Rehder and Cecil Cook.

Grassroots of America--A Computerized Index to the American State Papers.... Phillip W. McMullin, ed.

The Gray and the Black: The Confederate Debate on Emancipation. Robert F. Durden.

The Great Awakening and American Education: A Documentary History. Douglas Sloan, ed.

Great Britain and Austria-Hungry, 1906-1914: A Diplomatic History. F. R. Bridge.

Great Britain's Woodyard: British

America and the Timber Trade, 1763-1867. Arthur R. M. Lower.

The Great Campaigns: Reform and War in America, 1900-1928. Otis L. Graham, Jr.

Great Contemporaries. Winston S. Churchill.

Great Documents in American Indian History. Wayne Moquin and Charles Van Doren, eds.

The Great Gamble: The Boeing 747. Laurence S. Kuter.

Great Lives Observed: Marcus Garvey. E. David Cronon, ed.

The Great Nixon Turnabout. Lloyd Gardner, ed.

The Great Northwest: the Story of a Land and Its People. American West.

The Great School Wars. Diane Ravitch.

The Great Slump: Capitalism in Crisis: 1929-1933. G. Rees.

The Great Terror: Stalin's Purge of the Thirties. Robert Conquest.

The Great Wagon Road from Philadelphia to the South. Parke Rouse, Jr.

The Great White Lie: Slavery, Emancipation and Changing Racial Attitudes. Jack Gratus.

Great Zimbabwe. P. S. Garlake.

Greedy Institutions: Patterns of Undivided Commitment. Lewis A. Coser.

Greek Art. Walter-Herwig Schuchhardt.

Greek Art: Its Development, Character and Influence. Robert M. Cook.

The Greek Dark Ages. V. R. D'A. Desborough.

Greek, Etruscan and Roman Bronzes in the Museum of Fine Arts, Boston. Mary Comstock and Cornelius Vermeule.

The Greek Historians. Truesdell S. Brown.

Greek Myths: A Vase Painter's Notebook. Jane Henle.

The Greek Struggle for Independence, 1821-1833. Douglas Dakin.

Greek Vase Painting: An Introduction. Dietrich von Bothmer.

Greeks, Celts and Romans: Studies in Venture and Resistance. Christopher and Sonia Hawkes, eds.

The Green Flag: A History of Irish

Nationalism. Robert Kee.

Grenville Goodwin Among the Western Apache: Letters From the Field. Morris E. Opler, ed.

Die Grimanische Figurengruppe in Venedig. Renate Kabus-Jahn.

Die Grossen Registerserien im Vatikanischen Archiv (1378-1523). Hermann Diener.

The Growth and Structure of Human Populations: A Mathematical Investigation. Ansley J. Coale.

The Guarantee Clause of the U.S. Constitution. William M. Wiecek.

Guerrilla Warrior: The Early Life of John J. Pershing. Donald Smythe.

Guida delle Fonti per la Storia dell' Africa a Sud del Sahara esistenti in Italia. Vol. I. Carlo Giglio and Elio Lodolini, eds.

A Guide for the Writing of Local History. John Cumming.

A Guide to Baltimore Architecture. John Dorsey and James D. Dilts.

A Guide to Manuscript Sources for the History of Latin America and the Caribbean in the British Isles. Peter Walne, ed.

Guide to Manuscripts. Katherine Harris, comp.

Guide to Manuscripts and Archives in the West Virginia Collection. James W. Hess.

A Guide to Manuscripts at the Ohio Historical Society. Andrea D. Lentz and Sara S. Fuller, eds.

Guide to Ohio County and Municipal Government Records for Urban Research. Paul D. Yon.

Guide to Research and Reference Works on Sub-Saharan Africa. Peter Duignan, ed.

A Guide to Source Materials for the Study of Barbados History, 1627-1834. Jerome S. Handler.

A Guide to the Historical Geography of New Spain. Peter Gerhard.

A Guide to the Manuscript Collections of the Bancroft Library. Vol. II. George P. Hammond, ed.

A Guide to the Study of the Holiness Movement. Charles Edwin Jones.

Guru Nanak in History. J. S. Grewal.

Die Gütergemeinschaft bei den Täufern des 16. Jahrhunderts. Hans-Dieter Plümper.

-H-

Hahnenschwanz und Hakenkreuz: Der Steirische Heimatschutz und der österreichische Nationalsozialismus, 1918-1934. Bruce F. Pauley.

Haig as Military Commander. Sir James Marshall-Cornwall.

The Haitian Revolution, 1789-1804. Thomas O. Ott.

Hall's Breechloaders: John H. Hall's Invention and Development of a Breechloading Rifle with Precision-Made Interchangeable Parts, and Its Introduction into the United States Service. R. T. Huntington.

Die Haltung der englischen Regierung wahrend der mandschurischen Krise (1931-1933). Christian Blickenstorfer.

Hama. Fouilles et Recherches de la Fondation Carlsberg, 1931-1938, II, 2.... Aristéa Papanicolaou Christensen and Charlotte Friis Johansen.

Handbook of Latin American Studies, 32: Humanities. Henry E. Adams, ed.

Handbook to the Gold Fields of Nebraska and Kansas: Being a Complete Guide to the Gold Regions of the North and South Platte, and Cherry Creek. William H. Byers and John E. Kellom.

Handwerderbünde und Arbeitervereine 1830-1853. Ernst Schraepler.

The Handwriting of Italian Humanists, Vol. 1, fascicule 1. A. C. de la Mare.

Hankey: Man of Secrets; Volume II, 1918-1931. Stephen W. Roskill.

Hannah's Town. Helen C. Smith and George Swetnam.

Hap Arnold: Architect of American Air Power. Flint Dupre.

Harry Dexter White: A Study in Paradox. David Rees.

Harsa and His Times. Baijnath Sharma.

Hart's Bridge. Sherman Paul.

The Heart's Forest: A Study of Shakespeare's Pastoral Plays. David Young.

The Heavenly Muse: A Preface to Milton. A. S. P. Woodhouse.

The Hebrew Exercises of Governor William Bradford. Isidore S. Meyer, ed.

Hegel's Philosophy of History. Burleigh Taylor Wilkins.

Held Captive by Indians, Selected Narratives, 1642-1836. Richard VanDerBeets, ed.

Hellenistic Art: The Art of the Classical World from the Death of Alexander the Great to the Battle of Actium. Christine Mitchell Havelock.

The Hellenistic Kingdoms: Portrait Coins and History. Norman Davis and Colin M. Kraay.

Hellenistische Bildwerke auf Samos. Rudolf Horn.

Hello, Goodbye. Lynn Klamkin.

Helm Bruce, Public Defender: Breaking Louisville's Gothic Political Ring, 1905. Thomas D. Clark.

Helmuth von Moltke: A Leader Against Hitler. Michael Balfour and Julian Frisby.

Helvetia Sacra. Albert Bruckner, ed.

Henri Mercier and the American Civil War. Daniel B. Carroll.

Henry III and the Jesuit Politicians. A. Lynn Martin.

Henry IV of Castile 1425-1474. Townsend Miller.

Henry Alline. J. M. Bumsted.

Henry Ford and Grass-roots America. Reynold M. Wik.

Henry Home, Lord Kames and the Scottish Englightenment: A Study in National Character and in the History of Ideas. William C. Lehmann.

Henry James's "Sublime Economy": Money as Symbolic Center in the Fiction. Donald Mull.

Henry Labouchere and the Empire, 1880-1905. R. J. Hind.

Henry Ward Beecher, the Indiana Years, 1837-1847. Jane Shaffer Elsmere.

Henry Wilson: Practical Radical. A Portrait of a Politician. Ernest McKay.

Henry Winter Davis: Antebellum and Civil War Congressman from Maryland. Gerald S. Henig.

"Here Come the Navajo!" Ruth Underhill.

Herefordshire Militia Assessments of 1663. M. A. Faraday.

Heresy and Obedience in Tridentine Italy: Cardinal Pole and the Counter Reformation. Dermot Fenlon.

The Heresy of the Free Spirit in the Later Middle Ages. Robert E. Lerner.

Heritage Kingston. J. Douglas Stewart and Ian E. Wilson.

The Heritage of the Past: Earliest Times to 1500. Stewart Easton.

Hernan Cortés: Letters from Mexico. A. R. Pagden, ed.

Herod the Great. Michael Grant.

Heroes and Incidents of the Mexican War. Isaac George.

The Heroic Image in Chile: Arturo Prat, Secular Saint. William F. Sater.

Heshbon Pottery 1971: A preliminary Report on the Pottery from the 1971 Excavations at Tell Hesbôn. James A. Sauer.

Het Noorderkwartier: Een regional historisch onderzoek in de demografisch en economische geschiedenis van westalijk Nederland van de late middeleeuwen tot het begin van de negentiende eeuw. A. M. Van der Woude.

Hetch Hetchy and Its Dam Railroad. Ted Wurm.

Heur et malheur du guerrier: Aspects mythiques de la fonction guerrière chez les Indo-Européens. Georges Dumézil.

The High Victorian Movement in Architecture, 1850-1870. Stefan Muthesius.

Highlights of American History. James Wickens.

Hillbilly Women: Mountain Women Speak of Struggle and Joy in Southern Appalachia. Kathy Kahn.

Hindu Gods of Peninsular Siam. Stanley J. O'Connor, Jr.

Hippocrates in a Red Vest: The Biography of a Frontier Doctor. Barron B. Beshoar.

Hiram Martin Chittenden: His Public Career. Gordon B. Dodds.

Histoire de l'Afrique contemporaine de la deuxième guerre mondiale à nos jours. Marianne Cornevin.

Histoire de l'Afrique Noire. Joseph Ki-Zerbo.

Histoire de la politique extérieure de l'U. R. S. S., 1917-1945. B. Ponomarev, et al., eds.

Histoire de Louis XI. Volume V. Thomas Basin.

Histoire des Juifs en France. Roger Berg, et al.

Histoire des usines Renault. Volume 1: Naissance de la grande entreprise. Patrick Fridenson.

Histoire documentaire de la Congrégation des Missionnaires Oblats de Marie-Immaculée dans l'Est du Canada. 2e Partie: Dans la Seconde Moitié du XIXe Siècle (1861-1900). Gaston Carrière.

Histoire économique du Québec 1851-1896. Jean Hamelin et Yves Roby.

Histoire et Dialectique de la Violence. Raymond Aron.

Histoire générale de la presses française. Vol. III. De 1871 a 1940. Claude Bellanger, et al., eds.

Histoire, générale du socialisme. Volume I. Des origines à 1875. Jacques Droz, ed.

Historia de España Alfaguara. Vol. II: La época medieval. J. A. García de Cortázar.

Historia de la iglesia en America Latina. Enrique D. Dussel.

Historia Destructionis Troiae. Guido delle Colonne.

Historia Magistra Vitae.... Rüdiger Landfester.

The Historian and the Computer: A Practical Guide. Edward Shorter.

Historian's Guide to Statistics: Quantitative Analysis and Historical Research. Charles M. Dollar and Richard J. Jensen.

The Historian's Handbook: A Descriptive Guide to Reference Works. Helen J. Poulton.

Historic Architecture in Mississippi. Mary Wallace Crocker.

Historic Denver: the Architects and the Architecture, 1858-1893. Richard R. Brettell.

Historic Sites of Texas. June Rayfield Welch.

The Historic Whitman. Joseph Jay Rubin.

Historical and Cultural Dictionary of the Philippines. Esther G. and Joel M. Maring.

Historical Atlas of Early Oregon. Judith A. Farmer, et al.

Historical Atlas of Kansas. Homer Socolofsky and Huber Self.

Historical Dictionary of Ecuador. Albert William Bork and Georg Maier.

Historical Dictionary of Paraguay. Charles J. Kolinski.

Historical-Economic Studies of Western Poland. Janusz Deresiewicz, ed.

Historical Essay on the Colony of Surinam 1788. Jacob R. Marcus and Stanley F. Chyet, eds.

Historical Farm Records. J. A. Edwards, comp.

Historical Interpretation. Volume 1, Sources of English Medieval History, 1066-1540; volume 2, Sources of English History, 1540 to the Present Day. J. J. Bagley.

Historical Memoirs, Volume III, 1715-1723. Duc de San-Simon.

Historical Notes on Lower California .... Philip O. Gericke, tr. and ed.

Historical Notes on the Wet-Processing Industry. Sidney M. Edelstein.

A Historical, Political, and Natural Description of California. Pedro Fages.

Historical Statistics of the South, 1790-1970. Donald B. and Wynelle S. Dodd.

Historical Studies Today. Felix Gilbert and Stephen R. Graubard, eds.

The Historical Study of African Religion. T. O. Ranger and I. N. Kimambo, eds.

Historical Thought in America: Postwar Patterns. Timothy Paul Donovan.

The Historical Tradition of Busaga. David William Cohen.

Historism. The Rise of a New Historical Outlook. Friedrich Meinecke.

History and American Society: Essays of David M. Potter. Don E. Fehrenbacher, ed.

The History and the Saga. A. Ia. Gurevich.

History and Will: Philosophical Perspectives of Mao Tse-tung's Thought. Frederic Wakeman, Jr.

History as a Way of Learning. William Appleman Williams.

History as Applied Science: A Philosophical Study. William Todd.

The History of a Family and a Community in Northeast Brazil, 1700-1930. Billy Jaynes Chandler.

A History of Alberta. James A. McGregor.

A History of American City Government: The Conspicuous Failure 1870-1900. Ernest S. Griffith.

A History of American City Government: The Progressive Years and Their Aftermath 1900-1920. Ernest S. Griffith.

A History of American Law. Lawrence M. Friedman.

A History of American Pewter. Charles F. Montgomery.

A History of Baltimore Yearly Meeting of Friends. Three Hundred Years of Quakerism in Maryland, Virginia, the District of Columbia, and Central Pennsylvania. Bliss Forbush.

A History of Belize. Narda Dobson.

A History of Book Publishing in the United States. Vol. I: The Creation of an Industry, 1630-1865. John Tebbel.

A History of Buganda from the Foundation of the Kingdom to 1900. M. S. M. Semakula Kiwanuka.

A History of Christianity in the World: From Persecution to Uncertainty. Clyde L. Manschreck.

The History of Converse College. Lillian Adele Kibler.

History of Downey. Charles Russell Quinn.

A History of Early Renaissance Italy: From the Mid-Thirteenth to the Mid-Fifteenth Century. Brian Pullan.

A History of Eastern Civilizations. Guilford A. Dudley.

The History of Eastern Europe in the First Half of the 19th Century. Endre Arató.

A History of English Assizes, 1558-1714. J. S. Cockburn.

History of Fayette County, West Virginia. J. T. Peters and H. B. Carden.

A History of French Louisiana. Volume I. The Reign of Louis XIV, 1698-1715. Marcel Giraud.

A History of Fundamentalism in America. George W. Dollar.

History of Hampshire County, West Virginia, From Its Earliest Settlement to the Present. Hu Maxwell and H. L. Swisher.

The History of Hancock County, Georgia. 2 vols. Elizabeth Wiley Smith.

History of Harrison County, West Virginia, from the Earliest Days of Northwestern Virginia to the Present. Henry Haymond.

History of Indonesia in the Twentieth Century. Bernard Dahm.

A History of Investment Banking in New England. Parker B. Willis.

A History of Iowa. Leland L. Sage.

History of Latin American Civilization. Lewis Hanke, ed.

A History of Lumbering in Maine, 1861-1960. David C. Smith.

A History of Malayalam Literature. Krishna Chaitanya.

A History of Mining on the Kenai Peninsula. Mary J. Barry.

A History of Medieval Philosophy. F. C. Copleston.

History of Mineola. Lucille Jones.

A History of Mississippi. 2 vols. Richard Aubrey McLemore, ed.

A History of Missouri. Vol. I, 1673 to 1820. William E. Foley.

A History of Missouri: Volume II, 1820-1860. Perry McCandless.

A History of Missouri. Volume III. 1860-1875. William E. Parrish.

History of Modern Architecture. 2 vols. Leonardo Benevolo.

A History of Modern Norway. T. K. Derry.

A History of Monroe County, West Virginia. Oren F. Morton.

The History of My Contemporary. V. G. Korolenko.

History of Nevada. Russell R. Elliott.

The History of Newberry County, South Carolina. Vol. I: 1749-1860. Thomas H. Pope.

A History of Nigerian Higher Education. A. Babs Fafunwa.

A History of Pendleton County, West Virginia. Oren F. Morton.

History of Pioneer Lexington. Charles R. Staples.

History of Portugal. Vol. II: From

Empire to Corporate State. A. H. de Oliveira Marques.

A History of Prices in Sweden, 1732-1914. Vol. I and II. Lennart Jorberg.

A History of Regulatory Taxation. R. Alton Lee.

History of Sino-Japanese Foreign Relations: The Northern Expedition. Katsumi Usui.

A History of South Asia. Robert I. Crane.

A History of Spain and Portugal. Vols. I and II. Stanley G. Payne.

History of Standard Oil Company (New Jersey). Vol. III: New Horizons, 1927-1950. Henrietta M. Larson, Evelyn H. Knowlton, and Charles S. Popple.

A History of Tapestry. W. G. Thomson.

A History of the African People. Robert W. July.

A History of the Alans in the West: From Their First Appearance in the Sources of Classical Antiquity through the Early Middle Ages. Bernard S. Bachrach.

A History of the Bemba: Political Growth and Change in North-Eastern Zambia Before 1900. Andrew D. Roberts.

A History of the Boshin War. Hirao Michio.

History of the Church of God, from the Creation to A. D. 1885; Including Especially the History of the Kehukee Primitive Baptist Association. Cushing Biggs Hassell and Sylvester Hassell.

History of the Cities and Villages of the Ukrainian S S R -- Cherkassy Province. O. L. Steshenko, et al., eds.

History of the Cities and Villages of the Ukrainian SSR--Chernigov Province. O. I. Derykolenko, et al., eds.

History of the Cities and Villages of the Ukrainian SSR--Khmel' nitsky Province. M. I. Mekheda, et al., eds.

History of the Cities and Villages of the Ukrainian S S R--Vinnitsa Province. A. F. Oliinyk, et al., eds.

A History of the Czechoslovak Republic, 1918-1948. Victor S.

Mamatey and Radomír Luza, eds.

A History of the Diocese of Cork from the Earliest Times to the Reformation. Evelyn Bolster (Sister Mary Angela).

The History of the Dominican Order. Volume 2: Intellectual and Cultural Life to 1500. William A. Hinnebusch.

History of the Elementary School Contest in England. Francis Adams.

A History of the Greek States. Emmanuel Andronicos, et al.

History of the Jews of Los Angeles. Max Vorspan and Lloyd P. Gartner.

A History of the Kikuyu 1500-1900. Godfrey Muriuki.

History of the Louisville and Nashville Railroad. Maury Klein.

A History of the Middle West: From the Beginning to 1970: Kenneth R. Walker.

A History of the National Intelligencer. William E. Ames.

The History of the Nazi Party, 1933-1945. Dietrich Orlow.

History of the Paris Commune of 1871. E. A. Zhelubovskaia, et al., eds.

The History of the Province of New York. 2 vols. Michael Kammen, ed.

The History of the Province of New York. William Smith, Jr.

History of the Punjab (A. D. 1000-1526). Fauja Singh, ed.

History of the Red River Controversy: The Western Boundary of the Louisiana Purchase. C. A. Welborn.

History of the Role of the City in American Life. Arthur Mann, Neil Harris, and Sam Bass Warner, Jr.

A History of the Royal College of Physicians of London. A. M. Cooke.

A History of the Society of Jesus. William V. Bangert.

The History of the South Tyrol Question. A. E. Alcock.

History of the Supreme Court of the United States. Vol. I. Antecedents and Beginnings to 1801.

The History of the Tenth Cavalry, 1866-1921. E. L. N. Glass, comp. and ed.

The History of the Town and Borough of Penzance. P. A. S. Pool.

History of the Town of Glen Burnie. Ruth P. Eason.

A History of the University of Canterbury, 1873-1973. W. J. Gardner, et al.

A History of the Vikings. Gwyn Jones.

History of U.S. Political Parties. 4 vols. Arthur M. Schlesinger, Jr., ed.

History of West Africa. 2 vols. J. F. A. Ajayi and Michael Crowder, eds.

The History of Wisconsin. Volume I, From Exploration to Statehood. Alice E. Smith.

A History of World Civilizations. Edward R. Tannenbaum, ed.

Hitler: Legend, Myth and Reality. Werner Maser.

Hitler and His Generals: The Hidden Crises, January-June 1938. Harold C. Deutsch.

Hitler and the Beer Hall Putsch. Harold J. Gordon, Jr.

Hitler Close-Up. Henry Picker and Heinrich Hoffman.

Hitler, Horthy and Hungary.... Mario Fenyo.

Hitler-Mussolini: Die Entstehung der Achse Berlin-Rom, 1933-1936. Jens Petersen.

Hitler's Free City: A History of the Nazi Party in Danzig, 1925-39. Herbert S. Levine.

Hitler's Strategy, 1940-1941: The Balkan Clue. Martin L. Van Creveld.

Hitler's War Aims. Vol. II. The Establishment of the New Order. Norman Rich.

Hitler's Weltanshauung: A Blueprint for Power. Eberhard Jäckel.

Hobart and William Smith: the History of Two Colleges. Warren H. Smith.

The Hofstadter Aegis: A Memorial. Stanley Elkins and Eric McKitrick, eds.

Hog Meat and Hoecake: Food Supply in the Old South, 1840-1860. Sam Bowers Hilliard.

Hold the Fort! The Story of a Song from the Sawdust Trail to the Picket Line. Paul J. Scheips.

The Holiness-Pentecostal Movement in the United States. Vinson Synan.

Hollins College, an Illustrated History. Frances J. Niederer.

Holy Man: Father Damien of Molokai. Gavan Daws.

Homage to the American Indians. Ernesto Cardenal.

Homerische Helme. Helmformen der Ägäis in ihren Beziehungen in der Bronze-und Frühen Eisenzeit. Jürgen Borchhardt.

Honor, Commerce and Industry in Eighteenth-Century Spain. William J. Callahan.

The Hoover-Wilson Wartime Correspondence: September 24, 1914 to November 11, 1918. Francis William O'Brien, ed.

Horace Mann: A Biography. Jonathan Messerli.

Horace Tabor: His Life and the Legend. Duane A. Smith.

Horace White, Nineteenth-Century Liberal. Joseph Logsdon.

Horns in the High Country. Andy Russell.

The Horns of the Moon: A Short Biography of Adolf Hitler. Gene Smith.

The Hopi Indians of Old Oraibi: Change and Continuity. Mischa Titiev.

The Hopi People. Robert C. Euler and Henry F. Dobyns.

The Horizon Concise History of Mexico. Victor Alba.

Hostiles and Horse Soldiers: Indian Battles and Campaigns in the West. Lonnie White, et al.

Household and Family in Past Time. Peter Laslett, ed.

The Housewares Story--A History of the Housewares Industry. Earl Lifshey.

How Edison's Lamp Helped Light the West. John Dierdorff.

How It All Began: Origins of the Christian Church. O. C. Edwards, Jr.

How Shall They Hear a Preacher? The Life of Ernest Fremont Tittle. Robert Moats Miller.

How the U.S. Cavalry Saved Our National Parks. H. Duane Hampton.

The Howe Brothers and the American Revolution. Ira D. Gruber.

Howell Cobb: The Politics of Ambition. John Eddins Simpson.

Hsi-Liang and the Chinese National Revolution. Roger V. Des Forges.

Huberinus-Rhegius-Holbein: Bibliographische und druckergeschichtliche Untersuchungen der verbreitesten Trost-und Erbauungsschriften des 16. Jahrhunderts. Gunther Franz.

Hubert Walter: Lord of Canterbury and Lord of England. Charles R. Young.

Huerta: A Political Portrait. Michael C. Meyer.

Hugh Gaine, a Colonial Printer's Odyssey to Loyalism. Alfred Lawrence Lorenz.

Hugo Black: The Alabama Years. Virginia Van der Veer Hamilton.

The Huks: Philippine Agrarian Society in Revolt. Eduardo Lachica.

Hull in the Eighteenth Century: A Study in Economic and Social History. Gordon Jackson.

Humanism and the Rise of Science in Tudor England. Antonia McLean.

Hunters, Fishers and Farmers of Eastern Europe 6000-3000 B.C. Ruth Tringham.

Hunters of the Northern Forest: Designs for Survival Among the Alaskan Kutchin. Richard K. Nelson.

-I-

I Give Thee My Daughter: A Study of Marriage and Hierarchy Among the Anavil Brahmans of South Gujarat. Klaas W. van der Veen.

I Have Spoken: American History Through the Voices of the Indians. Virginia Irving Armstrong, comp.

I Russi in Ethiopia. 2 vols. Carlo Zaghi.

I Vasi a Vernice Nera Della Collezione H. A. di Milano. Lucia Merzagora.

The Ibo People and the Europeans: The Genesis of a Relationship--to 1906. Elizabeth Isichei.

Ibo Politics: The Role of Ethnic

Unions in Eastern Nigeria. C. Audrey Smock.

The Idea of Fraternity in America. Wilson Carey McWilliams.

The Idea of Peace in Antiquity. Gerardo Zampaglione.

Ideals and Politics: New York Intellectuals and Liberal Democracy, 1820-1880. Edward K. Spann.

La ideología de la dominación en una sociedad dependiente. Armand Mattelart, Carmin Castillo, and Leonard Castillo.

La ideología de la Revolución Mexicana. Arnaldo Córdova.

Idéologies des Indépendances Africaines. Yves Bénot.

Ideology and Politics in Contemporary China. Chalmers Johnson, ed.

Ignaz Seipel: Christian Statesman in a Time of Crisis. Klemens von Klemperer.

An Ill-Fated People: Zimbabwe Before and After Rhodes. Lawrence Vambe.

Illuminated Manuscripts in the Bodleian Library, Oxford. Vol. 3. Otto Pächt and J. J. G. Alexander, eds.

Illusions of Security. North Atlantic Diplomacy, 1918-22. Michael G. Fry.

The Illustrated Walden. Henry David Thoreau.

Ilocano Rice Farmers: A Comparative Study of Two Philippine Barrios. Henry T. Lewis.

The Image of Australia: British Perception of the Australian Economy From the Eighteenth to the Twentieth Century. Craufurd D. W. Goodwin.

The Image of Lincoln in the South. Michael Davis.

Immigrant Workers: Their Impact on American Labor Radicalism. Gerald Rosenblum.

Immigrants: Baptists, and the Protestant Mind in America. Lawrence B. Davis.

Immigrants in American Life. Arthur Mann, ed.

The Impact of Reform Movements on Social Policy Change: The Case of Social Insurance. Daniel S. Sanders.

Impeachment: The Constitutional Problems. Raoul Berger.

Impeachment: Trials and Errors. Irving Brant.

The Impeachment and Trial of Andrew Johnson. Michael Les Benedict.

Imperial Japan, 1800-1945. Jon Livingston, Joe Moore, and Felicia Oldfather, eds.

The Imperial Presidency. Arthur M. Schlesinger, Jr.

Imperialism and Free Trade: Lancashire and India in the Mid-Nineteenth Century. Peter Harnetty.

Imperialism and Revolution in South Asia. Kathleen Gough and Hari P. Sharma, eds.

Impressions of the Big Thicket. William A. Owens.

In Defence of Canada. III. Peace-making and Deterrence. James Eayrs.

In His Image, But...: Racism in Southern Religion, 1780-1910. H. Shelton Smith.

In Hitler's Shadow: The Anatomy of American Nazism. Leland V. Bell.

In Hoc Signo? A Brief History of Catholic Parochial Education in America. Glen Gabert.

In Love and Trouble: Stories of Black Women. Alice Walker.

In Memory...: An Index to Hyde County Cemeteries. Martha Rebecca Swindell and Romulus Sanderson Spencer, Jr., ed.

In Search of America: Community, National Identity, Democracy. 2 vols. David H. Fowler, Eugene D. Levy, John W. Blassingame and Jacquelyn S. Haywood, eds.

In Search of Roosevelt. Rexford G. Tugwell.

In Search of the Maya: The First Archaeologists. Robert L. Brunhouse.

In the Fulness of Time: The Memoirs of Paul H. Douglas.

In the Light of History. J. H. Plumb.

In the Presence of Abraham Lincoln. Weldon Petz, comp.

Ina Coolbrith: Librarian and Laureate of California. Josephine DeWitt Rhodehamel and Raymond Francis Wood.

Income Distribution in Latin America.

The Economic Commission for Latin America, The United Nations.

Independence in All Things: Neutrality in Nothing, The Story of a Pioneer Journalist of the American West. Elizabeth Wright.

Independence on Trial: Foreign Affairs and the Making of the Constitution. Frederick W. Marks, III.

Index of the English Column of Nagyvilag--1956-1972. Gabor Mihalyi, et al., eds.

India and Disarmament: Vol. I, Nehru Era, An Analytical Study. J. P. Jain.

India and East Africa. R. G. Gregory.

India in English Fiction, 1800-1970: An Annotated Bibliography. Brijen K. Gupta.

India-Pakistan: The History of Unsolved Conflicts. Lars Blinkenberg.

An Indian Canaan: Isaac McCoy and the Vision of an Indian State. George A. Schultz.

Indian Economic Thought: A Preface to Its History. Joseph J. Spengler.

Indian Exodus: Texas Indian Affairs 1835-1859. Kenneth F. Neighbours.

Indian Integration in Peru: A Half Century of Experience, 1900-1948. Thomas M. Davies, Jr.

Indian Life on the Northwest Coast of North America: As Seen by the Early Explorers and Fur Traders During the Last Decades of the Eighteenth Century. Erna Gunther.

Indian Literature. Arabinda Poddar, ed.

Indian Revolutionaries Abroad, 1905-1922. A. C. Bose.

Indian Revolutionary Movement in the United States of America. L. P. Mathur.

Indian Silver: Navajo and Pueblo Jewelers. Margery Bedinger.

Indiana Canals. Paul Fatout.

Indiana Historical Society Lectures, 1972-1973: The Centennial Year. Lillian B. Miller, Walter T. K. Nugent and H. Wayne Morgan.

Indiana to 1816: The Colonial Peri¢

John D. Barnhart and Dorothy
L. Riker.
Indiana University: Midwestern
Pioneer. Volume II, In Mid-
Passage. Thomas D. Clark.
Indians, Finns, and Their Thunder-
birds. Walter Mattila.
Indians of Arizona: A Contemporary
Perspective. Thomas Weaver, ed.
Indians of the Southeast: Then and
Now. Jesse Burt and Robert B.
Ferguson.
Indians or Jews? Lynn Glaser.
India's Green Revolution: Economic
Gains and Political Costs. Fran-
cine R. Frankel.
India's Revolution: Ghandi and the
Quit India Movement. Francis
G. Hutchins.
Indice de cuadros estadísticos socio-
políticos sobre América Latina,
1946-1969. Charles W. Johnson.
Indirect Rule and the Search for
Justice: Essays in East African
Legal History. H. F. Morris
and James S. Read.
Indo-European and Indo-Europeans.
George Cardona, Henry M. Hoenigs-
wald, and Alfred Senn, eds.
Indonesian Communism Under Sukar-
no: Ideology and Politics, 1959-
1965. Rex Mortimer.
Indus Waters Treaty: An Exercise
in International Mediation. N. D.
Gulhati.
La industria textil mexicana en el
siglo XIX. Dawn Keremitsis.
Industrial Buildings and Factories.
Oswald W. Grube.
Industrial Conflict in Malaya: Pre-
lude to the Communist Revolt of
1948. M. R. Stenson.
Industrial England, 1776-1851. Dor-
othy Marshall.
Industrial Management in the Soviet
Union. William J. Conyngham.
Industrial Polarization Under Economic
Integration in Latin America.
Christopher Garbacz.
The Industrial Revolution and Eco-
nomic Growth. R. M. Hartwell.
L'industrialisation en Europe au XIXe
siècle: Cartographie et typologie
(Lyon, 7-10 octobre 1970). Pierre
Léon, et al., eds.
L'Industrie en Haute-Loire de la fin
de la Monarchie de Juillet aux
débuts de la Troisieme Republique.

Jean Merley.
L'industrie roumaine au cours de la
seconde moitié du XIXe siècle:
Sur les origines historiques de
l'industrie de fabrique. G. Zane.
Inflation and Economic Development
in Brazil, 1946-1963. Raouf
Kahil.
The Influence of the United States
on Canadian Development: Eleven
Case Studies. Richard A. Pres-
ton, ed.
Information Processing: Applica-
tions in the Social and Behavioral
Sciences. William I. Davisson.
Inglorious Rebellion: The Jacobite
Risings of 1708, 1715 and 1719.
Christopher Sinclair-Stevenson.
Injustice to Tou O (Tou O Yüan):
A Study and Translation. Chung-
wen Shih.
Inquiry: U. S. A. Themes, Issues
and Men in Conflict. Ralph J.
Kane, Jeffrey A. Glover, eds.
An Inquiry into the Human Prospect.
Robert L. Heilbroner.
Die Inschriften der Friedhöfe St.
Johannis, St. Rochus und Wöhrd
zu Nürnberg. Peter Zahn.
Insights and Parallels: Problems
and Issues of American Social
History. William L. O'Neill, ed.
Instability and Political Order: Poli-
tics and Crisis in Nigeria. B. J.
Dudley.
Instauration de la politique des che-
mins de fer France. Jean-Paul
Adams.
The Institute of Pacific Relations:
Asian Scholars and American
Politics. John N. Thomas.
Institutii feudale din Moldava....
N. Grigoras.
Institutional Change and American
Economic Growth. Lance E.
Davis and Douglass C. North.
The Instructed Conscience: The
Shaping of the American Nation-
al Ethic. D. H. Meyer.
Instruction et developpement eco-
nomique au XIXeme siecle. Carlo
Cipolla, ed.
The Insulae of Imperial Ostia.
James E. Packer.
Insurgent Governor: Abraham Gon-
zález and the Mexican Revolution
in Chihuahua. William H. Beez-
ley.

The Intellectual Revolution of the Seventeenth Century. Charles Webster, ed.

The Intelligence of a People. Daniel Calhoun.

The Internal Organization of Ch'ing Bureaucracy: Legal, Normative, and Communication Aspects. Thomas A. Metzger.

The Internal Politics of China, 1949-1972. Jürgen Domes.

International Organization: An Interdisciplinary Bibliography. Michael Haas.

Die internationale Buren-Agitation, 1899-1902. Ulrich Kröll.

An Interpretative History of Alaskan Statehood. Claus-M. Naske.

The Interregnum: The Quest for Settlement, 1646-1660. G. E. Aylmer.

Into the Twenties: The United States from Armistice to Normalcy. Burl Noggle.

Introdução ao estudo da História do Brasil. Américo Jacobina Lacombe.

An Introduction to American Archaeology. Vol. II. South America. Gordon R. Willey.

An Introduction to Chinese Civilization. John Meskill, ed.

An Introduction to Chinese Politics. Harold Hinton.

An Introduction to English Runes. R. I. Page.

Introduction to Newton's "Principia." I. Bernard Cohen.

An Introduction to Nineteenth-Century Russian Slavophilism. A Study in Ideas. Volume 2: I. V. Kireevskij. Peter K. Christoff.

Introduction to Prehistory: A Systematic Approach. Irving Rouse.

An Introduction to Quantitative Methods for Historians. Roderick Floud.

Introduction to Traditional Art of Western Africa. E. V. Asihene.

Inventaire Préliminaire des documents Egyptiens. Michel Malaise.

Inventario delle Fonti manoscritte relative alla Storia dell' Africa del Nord esistenti in Italian. 2 vols. Carlo Giglio, ed.

An Inventory of Greek Coin Hoards. Margaret Thompson, Otto Mørkholm, and Colin Krray, eds.

Invisible Colleges. Diana Crane.

Invisible Immigrants: The Adaptation of English and Scottish Immigrants in Nineteenth-Century America. Charlotte Erickson.

Invitation to the Talmud: A Teaching Book. Jacob Neusner.

Ionian Vision: Greece in Asia Minor, 1919-1922. Michael Llewellyn Smith.

Iowa on the Eve of the Civil War: A Decade of Frontier Politics. Morton M. Rosenberg.

Ireland Before the Famine. Geróid O. Tuathaigh.

Ireland Before the Normans. Donncha O'Corrain.

Ireland in the Empire, 1688-1770: A History of Ireland from the Williamite Wars to the Eve of the American Revolution. Francis Godwin James.

Ireland's English Queen. Patrick O'Farrell.

The Irish: Emigration, Marriage, and Fertility. Robert E. Kennedy, Jr.

The Irish in Philadelphia: Ten Generations of Urban Experience. Dennis Clark.

Irish Unionism, 1885-1922. Patrick Buckland.

Irish Unionism. Volume 1, The Anglo-Irish and the New Ireland, 1885-1922. Patrick Buckland.

Irrationalism in the Eighteenth Century. Harold E. Pagliaro.

Is America Used Up? Judith Mara Gutman.

Isaac Newton's "Philosophiae Naturalis Principia Mathematica." Volumes 1 and 2.... Alexandre Koyré and I. Bernard Cohen, eds.

Isaac Shelby: Kentucky's First Governor and Hero of Three Wars. Sylvia Wrobel and George Grider.

Islam and Social Order in Mauritania: A Case Study from the Nineteenth Century. C. C. and E. K. Stewart.

Islam et sociétés soudanaises au moyen-âge: étude historique. Jean-Louis Triaud.

Islam in History: Ideas Men and Events in the Middle East. Bernard Lewis.

Islam Observed. Clifford Geertz.

Islam Under the Crusaders: Colonial Survival in the Thirteenth-Century Kingdom of Valencia. Robert Ignatius Burns.

Island Refuge: Britain and Refugees from the Third Reich, 1933-1939. A. J. Sherman.

Isthmia, Volume I, Temple of Poseidon. Oscar Broneer.

Italy and the Enlightenment: Studies in a Cosmopolitan Century. Franco Venturi.

Italy--Republic Without Government? P. A. Allum.

Italy Since 1945. E. Wiskenman.

L'itineraire erasmien d'Andre de Resende. Odette Sauvage.

La izquierda en punto muerto. Raúl Ampuero D.

-J-

J. E. Spingarn and the Rise of the NAACP, 1911-1939. B. Joyce Ross.

J. H. M. Salmon. François Francogallia Hotman and Ralph E. Giesey, ed. and trans.

J. Sterling Morton. James C. Olson.

Jacob A. Riis and the American City. James B. Lane.

Jacob Meckel: Sein Leben, sein Wirken in Deutschland und Japan. George Kerst.

Jacobellus de Strîbro: Premier Théologien du Hussitisme. Paul De Vooght.

The Jacobin Club of Marseilles, 1790-1794. Michael L. Kennedy.

Jacobins and Traditionalists: The Reactions of the Inhabitants of Bruges in the Revolutionary Period (1780-1794). Yvan Vanden Berghe.

Jamaica: A Historical Portrait. Samuel J. and Edith F. Hurwitz.

Jamaica and Voluntary Laborers from Africa, 1840-1856. Mary Elizabeth Thomas.

James. Peggy Miller.

James Baldwin: a Critical Study. Stanley Macebuh.

James Dakin, Architect: His Career in New York and the South. Arthur Scully, Jr.

James Madison: A Biography. Ralph Ketcham.

James Madison: A Biography in His Own Words. Merrill D. Peterson, ed.

James Mill on Philosophy and Education. W. H. Burston.

James Patton and the Appalachian Colonists. Patricia Givens Johnson.

James W. Connella, Pioneer Editor. E. R. Fox.

James Weldon Johnson: Black Leader, Black Voice. Eugene Levy.

Jan Hus: Testimone della verità. Amedeo Molnar.

Japan: An Anthropological Introduction. Harumi Befu.

Japan: Financial Markets and the World Economy. Wilbur F. Monroe.

Japan and China: The Taisho Period. Katsumi Usui.

Japanese Blue Collar. The Changing Tradition. Robert E. Cole.

Japanese Economic Growth: Trend Acceleration in the Twentieth Century. Kazushi and Rosovsky Ohkawa.

Japanese Foreign Policy on the Eve of the Pacific War: A Soviet View. Leonid N. Kutakov.

A Japanese View of Détente. Hisahiko Okazaki.

Japan's Foreign Policy. F. C. Langdon.

Japan's Foreign Policy 1868-1941: A Research Guide. James William Morley, ed.

Japan's Militant Teachers: A History of the Left-Wing Teachers' Movement. Benjamin C. Duke.

Japan's Trade Liberalization in the 1960's. Alfred K. Ho.

Java in a Time of Revolution: Occupation and Resistance, 1944-1946. B. R. O'G. Anderson.

Javanese-English Dictionary. Elinor Clark Horne.

Jean Bodin: Verhandlungen der internationalen Bodin Tagung in München. Horst Denzer, ed.

Jean Bodin and the Rise of the Absolutist Theory. Julian H. Franklin.

Jean Gerson: Principles of Church Reform. Louis B. Pascoe.

Jean-Francois. French Revolutionary, Patriot, and Director (1747-

1807).

Jedediah Strong Smith: Fur Trader
from Ohio. D. W. Garber.

Jefferson the President: Second
Term, 1805-1809. Dumas Malone.

Jennison's Jayhawkers: A Civil War
Cavalry Regiment and Its Commander. Stephen Z. Starr.

Jesuits by the Golden Gate: The
Society of Jesus in San Francisco,
1849-1969. John Bernard McGloin.

Jethro Tull. G. E. Fussell.

The Jew in Early American Wit and
Graphic Humor. Rudolf Glanz.

Jewels of the Pharaohs: Egyptian
Jewellery of the Dynastic Period.
Cyril Aldred.

The Jewish Experience in Latin America: Selected Studies from the
Publications of the American Jewish
Historical Society. 2 vols. Martin A. Cohen, ed.

A Jewish Princedom in Feudal France,
768-900. A. J. Zuckerman.

The Jewish Religion in the Soviet
Union. Joshua Rothenberg.

The Jews in the Roman World.
Michael Grant.

Jews in the South. Leonard Dinnerstein and Mary Dale Palsson, eds.

The Jews of San Francisco and the
Greater Bay Area, 1859-1919.
Sara G. Cogan, comp.

The Jicarilla Apaches: A Study in
Survival. Dolores A. Gunnerson.

Jim Beckwourth: Black Mountain
Man and War Chief of the Crows.
Elinor Wilson.

Joan of Arc. John Holland Smith.

Johann Valentin Andreae: Theophilus.
Richard van Dülmen, ed.

John B. Connally: a Portrait in Power. Ann Fears Crawford and Jack
Keever.

John Barrett, Progressive Era Diplo-
mat: A Study of a Commercial
Expansionist, 1887-1920. Salvatore
Prisco, III.

John Beckley: Zealous Partisan in a
Nation Divided. Edmund and Dorothy Smith Berkeley.

John Brown. Richard Warch and
Jonathan Fanton, eds.

John Cam Hobhouse: A Political Life,
1819-1852. Robert E. Zegger.

The John Carter Brown Library,
Brown University: Annual Reports,
1901-1966.

John Cartwright. John W. Osborne.

John D. Rockefeller: The Cleveland
Years. Grace Goulder.

John Dalton, Critical Assessments
of His Life and Science. Arnold
Thackray.

John Dee: The World of an Elizabethan Magus. Peter J. French.

John Dewey: Lectures in China
1919-1920. Robert W. Clopton
and Tsuin-Chen Ou, trans. and
eds.

John Dos Passos' Path to USA: A
Political Biography, 1912-1936.
Melvin Landsberg.

John Foster Dulles: A Statesman
and His Times. Michael A.
Guhin.

John Foxe and the Elizabethan
Church. V. Norskon Olsen.

John McIntosh Kell of the Raider
Alabama. Norman C. Delaney.

John McLoughlin's Business Correspondence, 1847-48. [John
McLoughlin.]

John Marshall: A Life in Law.
Leonard Baker.

John Norden's Manuscript Maps of
Cornwall and Its Nine Hundreds.

John of Paris on Royal and Papal
Power. Arthur P. Monahan.

John Philip Sousa: American Phenomenon. Paul E. Bierley.

John Quincy Adams: A Personal
History of an Independent Man.
Marie B. Hecht.

John Ruskin or the Ambiguities of
Abundance: A Study in Social
and Economic Criticism. James
Clark Sherburne.

John Wesley: A Theological Biography. Martin Schmidt.

Johnson, Grant, and the Politics of
Reconstruction. Martin E. Mantell.

Jonathan Swift as a Tory Pamphleteer. Richard I. Cook.

The Jones and Laughlin Case.
Richard C. Cortner.

Joscelyn III and the Fall of the Crusader States, 1134-1199. Robert
Lawrence Nicholson.

Joseph E. Brown and the Politics
of Reconstruction. Derrell C.
Roberts.

Joseph Eötvös and the Modernization of Hungary, 1840-1870.
Paul Body.

Joseph Sadoc Alimony. Harbinger of a New Era. Francis J. Weber.

Joseph Smith's New England Heritage: Influences of Grandfathers Solomon Mack and Asael Smith. Richard Lloyd Anderson.

Joseph Stalin: Man and Legend. Ronald Hingley.

Josephine Clardy Fox: Traveler, Opera-Goer, Collector of Art, Benefactor. Ruby Burns.

Josiah Quincy 1772-1864: The Last Federalist. Robert A. McCaughey.

Josiah Royce: An Intellectual Biography. Bruce Kuklick.

Journal and Letter Book of Nicholas Buckeridge, 1651-1654. John R. Jensen.

The Journal and Major Essays of John Woolman. Philip P. Moulton.

The Journal of George Townley Fullam: Boarding Officer of the Confederate Sea Raider Alabama. Charles G. Summersell, ed.

Journal of Glass Studies. Vol. 14.

The Journal of Major John Norton, 1816. Carl F. Klinck and James J. Talman, eds.

The Journal of Samuel Curwen, Loyalist. 2 vols. Andrew Oliver, ed.

Journal of South Asian Literature: Fall and Winter, 1973. Carlo Coppola, Surjit S. Dulai and C. M. Naim, eds.

Journal politique, septembre 1939-juillet 1942. Jules Jeanneney.

The Journals and Letters of Fanny Burney. Joyce Hemlow, ed.

Journals and Proceedings of the General Assembly of the State of Vermont, 1793-1794 and 1795-1796, Papers of Vermont, Volume III: Parts VI and VII (2 vols.). John A. Williams, ed.

The Journals of Ashley Bowen (1728-1813) of Marblehead. Ashley Bowen.

Journey Through a Part of the United States of North America in the Years 1844 to 1846. Albert C. Koch.

The Joyous Journey of Le Roy R. and Ann W. Hafen: An Autobiography. Le Roy R. and Ann W. Hafen.

The Joys of Trout. Arnold Gingrich.

Judenrat: The Jewish Councils in Eastern Europe Under Nazi Occupation. Isaiah Trunk.

Judentaufen: Eine historisch- biographisch- psychologisch- soziologische Studie besonders für Berlin und Königsberg. Guido Kisch.

Judge: The Life and Times of Leander Perez. James Conaway.

Judge Learned Hand and the Role of the Federal Judiciary. Kathryn Griffith.

Julius Pflug, Correspondance. (2 volumes.) J. V. Pollet, ed.

Justin Martyr. Eric Francis Osborn.

-K-

The Kaifong Associations and the Society of Hong Kong. Aline K. Wong.

Kaiser Maximilian I.... H. Wiesflecker.

Kaiser Franz Joseph und der Ausbruch des Weltkrieges. Robert A. Kann.

Kalabsha: The Preserving of the Temple. G. R. H. Wright.

Kalambo Falls Prehistoric Site: Vol. II: The Later Prehistoric Cultures. J. Desmond Clark.

The Kandyan Wars. Geoffrey Powell.

Kansas Place-Names. John Rydjord.

Kant's Political Thought: Its Origins and Development. Hans Saner.

Kardinal Giovanni Francesco di Bagno. Politik und Religion im Zeitalter Richelieus. G. Lutz.

Karl Radek: The Last Internationalist. Warren Lerner.

The Kefauver Committee and the Politics of Crime, 1950-1952. William Howard Moore.

Kelet-Europa Története a 19. szazad első felében. Andre Arato.

Kemper County Rebel: The Civil War Diary of Robert Masten Holmes, C. S. A. Frank Allen Dennis, ed.

Kenilworth Tree Stories: History Woven Around Its Trees. Colleen Kilner.

Kennedy Justice. Victor S. Navasky.

The Kennedy Neurosis: A Psychological Portrait of an American Dynasty. Nancy Gager Clinch.

The Kent School, 1922-1972. Michael Churchman.

Kentucky's Last Frontier. Henry P. Scalf.

Kenyatta. Jeremy Murray-Brown.

Key West: The Old and the New. Jefferson B. Browne, ed.

Khrushchev Remembers: The Last Testament. Nikita S. Khrushchev.

The Kiangsi Soviet Republic: Mao and the National Congresses of 1931 and 1934. Derek J. Waller.

Kierunki produkoji dworskiej w ekonomii malborskiej w XVI wieku. Jan Szpak.

The Kikuchi Diary: Chronicle from an American Concentration Camp: The Tanforan Journals of Charles Kikuchi. John Modell, ed.

King George III. John Brooke.

The King in Every Man: Evolutionary Trends in Onitsha Ibo Society and Culture. Richard N. Henderson.

King William IV. Philip Ziegler.

The Kingdom of the Scots: Government, Church and Society from the Eleventh to the Fourteenth Century. G. W. S. Barrow.

Kingdoms and Strongholds of the Crusaders. T. S. R. Boase.

The King's Parliament of England. G. O. Sayles.

Kinship and Community in Two Chinese Villages. Burton Pasternak.

Kirby Smith's Confederacy: The Trans-Mississippi South, 1863-1865. Robert L. Kerby.

Knossos: The Sanctuary of Demeter. J. N. Coldstream.

Koran and Koranexegese. Helmut Gätje.

Korea Under Japanese Colonial Rule. Andrew C. Nahm, ed.

Korean Unification: Problems and Prospects. C. I. Eugene Kim, ed.

A Korean Village, Between Farm and Sea. Vincent Brandt.

Kronstadt 1921. Paul Avrich.

The Kru Mariner in the Nineteenth Century: An Historical Compendium. George E. Brooks, Jr.

Ku Chieh-kang and China's New History: Nationalism and the Quest for Alternative Traditions. Laurence A. Schneider.

Kukai: Major Works, Translated, with an Account of His Life and a Study of His Thought. Yoshita S. Hakeda.

Der Kurfürstenrat: Grundzüge seiner Entwicklung in der Reichsverfassung und seine Stellung auf dem Westfälischen Friedenskongress. Winfried Becker.

Kuyo Chico: Applied Anthropology in an Indian Community. Oscar Núñez del Prado.

-L-

L. Q. C. Lamar: Pragmatic Patriot. James B. Murphy.

Labor and Socialism in America: The Gompers Era. William M. Dick.

Labor and Society in Tsarist Russia: The Factory Workers of St. Petersburg, 1855-1870. Reginald E. Zelnik.

Labor Organizations in the United States and Mexico: A History of Their Relations. Harvey A. Levenstein.

Labor's Search for Political Order: The Political Behavior of the Missouri Labor Movement, 1890-1940. Gary M. Fink.

Labour in American Politics. Vivian Vale.

Labour in the South African Gold Mines, 1911-1969. Francis Wilson.

Labouring Classes and Dangerous Classes in Paris During the First Half of the Nineteenth Century. Louis Chevalier.

Ladies and Gentlemen--Lenny Bruce. Albert Goldman.

Ladurie, Emmanuel Le Roy. Anthropologie du conscrit.... see Jean-Paul Aron.

Laissez-faire and State Intervention in Nineteenth-Century Britain. Arthur Taylor.

The Lancashire Watch Company, 1889-1910. Alan Smith and Henry G. Abbott.

Land Above the Trees: A Guide to American Alpine Tundra. Ann H. Zwinger and Beatrice E. Willard.

Land and People in Holywell-cum-
Needingworth. Edwin Brezette
DeWindt.

The Land and People of Cambodia.
David P. Chandler.

Land Between the Rivers: The South-
ern Illinois Country. C. William
Horrell, Henry Don Piper and
John W. Voight.

The Land of Contrasts, 1880-1902.
Neil Harris, ed.

Land of Good Water.... Clara
Stearns Scarbrough.

Land of the Coyote. Shirley Holmes
Cochell.

Land of the Pilgrim's Pride. Jesse
Hays Baird.

Land of the Underground Rain: Irrigation on the Texas High Plains,
1910-1970. Donald E. Green.

Land or Death: The Peasant Struggle in Peru. Hugo Blanco.

The Land Question and the Irish
Economy 1870-1903. Mrs. Barbara Lewis Solow.

Land Snails in Archaeology. J. G.
Evans.

Land Tenure Among the Amhara of
Ethiopia: The Dynamics of Cognatic Descent. Allan Hoben.

Landlord and Peasant in Colonial
Oaxaca. William B. Taylor.

Landlords and Tenants on the Prairie Frontier: Studies in American
Land Policy. Paul W. Gates.

Landmarks of the American Revolution. Mark A. Boatner, III.

The Lands of St. Peter. Peter Partner.

Landscapes of England.... Roy
Millward and Adrian Robinson.

Languages in Conflict: Richard J.
Joy.

The Last Boom. James A. Clark
and Michel T. Halbouty.

The Last Campaign: Grant Saves the
Union. Earl Schenck Miers.

The Last Centuries of Byzantium,
1261-1453. Donald M. Nicol.

The Last Crusade: The Church of
England in the First World War.
Albert Marrin.

The Last Foray: The South Carolina
Planters of 1860. A Sociological
Study. Chalmers Gaston Davidson.

The Last Free Man: The True Story
Behind the Massacre of Shoshone
Mike and His Band of Indians in

1911. Dayton O. Hyde.

The Last Generation of the Roman
Republic. Erich S. Gruen.

The Last War Drum: The North
West Campaign of 1885. Desmond Morton.

The Last War Trail: The Utes and
the Settlement of Colorado. Robert Emmitt.

Late Fifteenth-Century Carthusian
Rubrics for the Deacon and the
Sacristan from the Ms. Valsainte
42 /T. I. 8. James Hogg, ed.

Later Chinese Porcelain: the Ch'ing
Dynasty (1644-1912). Soame
Jenyns.

Latin America: New World, Third
World. Stephen Clissold.

Latin America and British Trade,
1806-1914. D. C. M. Platt.

Latin America in Basic Historical
Collections: A Working Guide.
Russell H. Bartley and Stuart
L. Wagner.

Latin America in Transition: Problems in Training and Research.
Stanley R. Ross, ed.

Latin American Political Parties.
Robert J. Alexander.

Latin American Prospects for the
1970's: What Kinds of Revolutions? David H. Pollock and
Arch R. M. Ritter, eds.

Latin American Student Activism:
Participation in Formal Volunteer
Organizations by University Stu-
dents in Six Latin Cultures.
David Horton Smith.

Latin American Thought: A Historical Introduction. Harold Eugene Davis.

Latin American Urban Research.
Vol. 2. Regional and Urban
Development Policies: A Latin
American Perspective. Guiller-
mo Geisse and Jorge E. Hardoy,
eds.

The Latin Kingdom of Jerusalem.
Joshua Prawer.

Launceston Bank for Savings, 1835-
1970: A History of Australia's
Oldest Savings Bank. E. A.
Beever.

Law and Justice: The Legal System
in China. Phillip M. Chen.

Law and Order in Historical Perspective: The Case of Elizabethan Essex. Joel Samaha.

Law and Social Change in Zinacantan.
Jane Fishburne Collier.

Law and Society in the Visigothic
Kingdom.   P. D. King.

The Law and the Apocalypse: The
Moral Thought of Luis de Leon
(1527?-1591).   Karl A. Kottman.

Law and the Indo-China War.   John
Norton Moore.

The Law Courts of Medieval England.
Alan Harding.

Lawyer's Lawyer: The Life of John
W. Davis.   William H. Harbaugh.

Leader and Vanguard in Mass Society:
A Study of Peronist Argentina.
Jeanne Kirkpatrick.

Leadership in Crisis: FDR and the
Path to Intervention.   Gloria J.
Barron.

The League of Nations.   Ruth B.
Henig, ed.

League of Nations Documents, 1919-
1946.   Edwin A. Reno, Jr.

The Learned Doctor William Ames:
Dutch Backgrounds of English and
American Puritanism.   Keith L.
Sprunger.

Learning from the Indians.   James
Wharton.

Learning to be Chinese: The Political Socialization of Children in
Taiwan.   Richard W. Wilson.

Lebensmittelteuerungen, ihre Bekämpfung und ihre politischen Rückwirkungen in Bern: Vom Ausgehenden 15. Jahrhundert bis in die zeit
der Kappelerkriege.   Hugo Wermelinger.

The Left Bank Revisited: Selections
from the Paris Tribune, 1917-
1934.   Matthew Josephson, ed.

The Legacy of Josiah Johnson Hawes:
19th-Century Photographs of Boston.
Rachel Johnston Homer, ed.

The Legacy of Michael Sattler.   John
H. Yoder, trans. and ed.

A Legal History of Money in the
United States, 1774-1970.   James
Willard Hurst.

The Legend of John Brown: A Biography and a History.   Richard
O. Boyer.

Legends and Lore of the Papago and
Pima Indians.   Dean and Lucille
Saxton.

Lenin.   M. C. Morgan.

Lenin.   Robert D. Warth.

Lenin.   Saul Silverman, ed.

Lenin: Genesis and Development of
a Revolutionary.   Rolf H. W.
Theen.

Lenin and the Comintern.   Volume I.
Branko Lazitch and Milorad M.
Drachkovitch.

Léon Blum: The Formative Years,
1872-1914.   William Logue.

Leonard Wood and Cuban Independence, 1898-1902.   James H.
Hitchman.

Leonardo da Vinci: The Royal
Palace at Romorantin.   Carlo
Pedretti.

Léopold II et les groupes financiers
belges en Chine: la politique
royale et ses prolongments (1895-
1914).

Leopold Sedar Senghor.   An Intellectual Biography.   J. L. Hymans.

"Lessons" of the Past: The Use
and Misuse of History in American Foreign Policy.   Ernest R.
May.

"Let Your Motto Be Resistance":
The Life and Thought of Henry
Higland Garnet.   Earl Ofari.

The Letters and Journal of Francisco de Paula Marin.   Agnes C.
Conrad, ed.

The Letters and Journal of Francisco de Paula Marin.   Ross H.
Gast.

Letters and Notes on the Manners,
Customs, and Conditions of North
American Indians; Written During Eight Years' Travel (1832-
1839) Amongst the Wildest Tribes
of Indians in North America.   2
vols.   George Catlin.

Letters from Nevada Territory, 1861-
1862.   Andrew J. Marsh.

The Letters of Alfred Robinson to the
De La Guerra Family of Santa
Barbara, 1834-1873.   Maynard
Geiger, tr.

Letters of George Ade.   Terence
Tobin, ed.

Letters of Horatio Greenough, American Sculptor.   Nathalia Wright,
ed.

Letters of Long Ago.   Agnes Just
Reid.

Letters of Louis D. Brandeis.   3
vols.   Melvin I. Urofsky and
David W. Levy, eds.

The Letters of Thomas Babington
Macaulay: Volume I, 1807-

February 1831; Volume II, March
1831-December 1833. Thomas
Pinney, ed.
The Letters of William Lloyd Gar-
rison. Volume III: No Union with
Slaveholders, 1841-1849. Walter
M. Merrill, ed.
Lettres d'Amérique 1831-1832. Gus-
tave de Beaumont.
The Leviathan of Wealth: The Suth-
erland Fortune in the Industrial
Revolution. Eric Richards.
Li Po and Tu Fu. Arthur Cooper,
trans.
Liam O'Flaherty. James H. O'Brien.
Liang Ch-i-ch'ao and Intellectual
Transition in China, 1890-1907.
Hao Chang.
Liber Poenitentialis. J. J. Francis
Firth.
The Liberal Imperialists: The Ideas
and Politics of a Post-Gladstonian
Elite. H. C. G. Matthew.
Liberal Politics in the Age of Glad-
stone and Rosebery. D. A.
Hamer.
Liberalismus und Demokratie am
Anfang der Weimarer Republik:
Eine vergleichende Analyse der
Deutchen Demokratischen Partei
und der Deutschen Volkspartei.
Lothar Albertin.
Liberals, Radicals and Social Poli-
tics, 1892-1914. H. V. Emy.
The Liberation Movement in Russia,
1900-1905. Shmuel Galai.
The Liberators: Filibustering Ex-
peditions Into Mexico, 1848-1862,
and the Last Thrust of Manifest
Destiny. J. A. Stout.
Liberty, Equality, and Revolution in
Alexis de Tocqueville. Irving
M. Zeitlin.
Libraries in the Political Scene:
Georg Leyh and German Librarian-
ship, 1933-1953. Marta L. Dosa.
The Lichauco Paper: Imperialism in
the Philippines. Alejandro Lichauco.
Liège et Bourgogne: Actes du col-
loque tenu à Liège les 28, 29 et
30 Octobre 1968.
Lienzos de Chiepetlan. Manuscrits
pictographiques et manuscrits en
caractères latins de San Miguel
Chiepetlan, Guerrero, Mexique.
Joaquín Galarza.
The Life and Death of a Frontier
Fort: Fort Craig, New Mexico,

1854-1885. Marion C. Grinstead.
The Life and Death of Adolf Hitler.
Robert Payne.
The Life and Mind of John Dewey.
George Dykhuizen.
Life and Times in Colonial Phila-
delphia. Joseph J. Kelley, Jr.
The Life and Times of Victoria.
Dorothy Marshall.
The Life of Brigadier General Wil-
liam Woodford of the American
Revolution. Mrs. Catesby Willis
Stewart.
The Life of Captain James Cook.
J. C. Beaglehole.
The Life of George William Gordon.
Ansell Hart.
The Life of Saladin: From the
Works of 'Imad ad-Din and Baba'
ad-Din. Sir Hamilton Gibb.
The Life of Texas Jack. Nathaniel
Reed.
Life on a Liberty County Planta-
tion: The Journal of Cornelia
Jones Pond. Josephine Bacon
Martin, ed.
Life on the Texas Range. J. Evetts
Haley and E. Erwin Smith.
The Limits of American Isolation:
The United States and the Cri-
mean War. Alan Dowty.
The Limits of Dissent: Clement
L. Valladigham and the Civil
War. Frank L. Klement.
The Limits of Foreign Policy: The
West, the League and the Far
Eastern Crisis of 1931-1933.
Christopher Thorne.
The Limits of Power: The World
and United States Foreign Policy,
1945-1954. Joyce and Gabriel
Kolko.
Lincoln Steffens. Justin Kaplan.
Lincolnshire Politics, 1832-1885.
R. J. Olney.
Lindbergh of Minnesota: A Political
Biography. Bruce L. Larson.
The Lion of Tashkent: The Career
of General M. G. Cherniaev.
David MacKenzie.
The Lions of Marash: Personal
Experiences with American Near
East Relief 1919-1922. Stanley
E. Kerr.
Listening to Japan: A Japanese
Anthology. Jackson H. Bailey,
ed.
Listening to Korea: A Korean An-

thology. Marshall R. Pihl, ed.

A Literary Guide to Ireland. Susan and Thomas Cahill.

A Literary History of Iowa. Clarence A. Andrews.

The Literary Manuscripts of Upton Sinclair. Ronald Gottesman and Charles L. P. Silet.

Literary Transcendentalism: Style and Vision in the American Renaissance. Lawrence Buell.

Literature and Society in Early Virginia, 1608-1840. Richard Beale Davis.

Literature By and About the American Indian. Anna Lee Stensland.

Literature for the Masses: An Analytical Study of Popular Pamphleteering in Nigeria. Emmanuel N. Obiechina.

The Literature of Isolationism: A Guide to Non-Interventionist Scholarship, 1930-1972. Justus D. Doenecke.

The Literature of Vermont. Arthur W. Biddle and Paul A. Escholz, ed.

Lithic Analysis and Cultural Inference: A Paleo Indian Case. Tucson: U Ariz Press, 1970. Edwin N. Wilmsen.

Lithuania in Crisis: Nationalism to Communism, 1939-1940. Leonas Sabaliũnas.

Liturgical Renewal: An Agonizing Reappraisal. George Devine.

Liverpool & Manchester Railway Operations 1831-1845. Thomas J. Donaghy.

Liverpool and the Mersey: An Economic History of a Port 1700-1970. Francis E. Hyde.

The Living Arts of Nigeria. W. Fagg.

Livingstone: Man of Africa. Memorial Essays 1873-1973. Bridglal Pachal, ed.

Lloyd George Family Letters, 1885-1936. Kenneth O. Morgan, ed.

Locarno Diplomacy: Germany and the West, 1925-1929. Jon Jacobson.

The Log of the Centurion: Based on the Original Papers of Captain Philip Saumarez on Board [the] H M S Centurion, Lord Anson's Flagship During His Circumnavigation 1740-44. Leo Heaps.

Logging Along the Denver and Rio Grande: Narrow Gauge Logging Railroads of Southwestern Colorado and Northern New Mexico. Gordon S. Chappell.

The London Building World of the Eighteen-Sixties. John Summerson.

London Correspondence Inward from Sir George Simpson, 1841-1842. Glyndwr Williams, ed.

London 1808-1870: The Infernal Wen. Francis Sheppard.

London in the Age of Chaucer. A. R. Myers.

The London Weavers' Company, 1600-1970. Alfred Plummer.

Die Londoner Weltausstellung von 1851. Utz Haltern.

A Long Day for November. Moffitt Sinclair Henderson.

The Long March to Power. A History of the Chinese Communist Party, 1921-72. James Pinckney Harrison.

Longtime Californ': A Documentary Study of an American Chinatown. Victor G. and Brett DeBary Nee.

Lord Bolingbroke: Historical Writings. Isaac Kramnick, ed.

Lord Byron: Accounts Rendered. Doris Langley Moore.

Lord John Russell. John Prest.

Lord Kames and the Scotland of His Day. Ian Simpson Ross.

Lord Morley's Tryumphes of Fraunces Petrarcke: The First English Translation of the Trionfi. D. D. Carnicelli, ed.

Lord Salisbury on Politics: A Selection from His Articles in the Quarterly Review, 1860-1883. Paul Smith, ed.

Lord William Bentinck: The Making of a Liberal Imperialist 1774-1839. John Roselli.

Lorenzo Valla, umanesimo e teologia. Salvatore I. Camporeale.

The Lost Americans: The Indian in American Culture. William Brandon.

Lost Beasts of Britain. Anthony Dent.

Lost Chance in China: The World War II Despatches of John S. Service. Joseph W. Esherick, ed.

Louis XIV. J. B. Wolf, ed.

Louis XIV. John C. Rule, ed.

Louis XIV and His World. R. M. Hatton.

Louis XV et l'Opposition Parlementaire. Jean Egret.

Louis McLane: Federalist and Jacksonian. John A. Munroe.

The Loyalists in Revolutionary America, 1760-1781. Robert McCluer Calhoon.

Loyalty in the Spirituality of St. Thomas More. Brian Byron.

Luce and His Empire. W. A. Swanberg.

Luddism in Nottinghamshire. M. I. Thomis.

Les Lumières en Hongrie, en Europe centrale et en Europe orientale: Actes du colloque de Mátrafüred, 3-5 novembre 1970. Eduard Bene, ed.

Lumpenbourgeoisie: Lumpendevelopment. Dependence, Class and Politics in Latin America. André Gunder Frank.

The Lure of Sunken Treasure. Robert F. Marx.

The Lusitania. Colin Simpson.

Luther and the Peasants' War: Luther's Actions and Reactions. Robert N. Crossley.

Lutheranism in North America, 1914-1970. E. Clifford Nelson.

-M-

MacArthur and Wainwright: Sacrifice of the Philippines. John Jacob Beck.

Macartney at Kashgar: New Light on British, Chinese and Russian Activities in Sinkiang, 1890-1918. C. P. Skrine and Pamela Nightingale.

Macaulay: The Shaping of the Historian. John Clive.

The Machados and Rancho La Ballona. Sister Mary Ste Therese Wittenburg.

Machiavelli and the Art of Renaissance History. Peter E. Bondanella.

Machiavelli and the Nature of Political Thought. Martin Fleischer, ed.

The McKenney-Hall Portrait Gallery of American Indians. James D. Horan.

Mackinaws Down the Missouri. Glen Barrett, ed.

Mackinnon and East Africa, 1878-1895: A Study in the New Imperialism. J. S. Galbraith.

Madagascar. Nigel Heseltine.

Magellan of the Pacific. Edouard Roditi.

The Magnificent Rockies: Crest of a Continent. American West.

Magnolia Journey: A Union Veteran Revisits the Former Confederate States. Russell H. Conwell.

Make Me a Map of the Valley: The Civil War Journal of Stonewall Jackson's Topographer. Archie P. McDonald, ed.

Makers of American Diplomacy: From Benjamin Franklin to Henry Kissinger. Frank J. Merli and Theodore A. Wilson, eds.

Makers of the Russian Revolution: Biographies of Bolshevik Leaders. Georges Haupt and Jean-Jacques Marie.

The Making and Meaning of an American Classic: James Fenimore Cooper's The Prairie. Orm Overland.

The Making of a Model Citizen in Communist China. C. P. Ridley, Paul H. B. Godwin, Dennis J. Doolin.

The Making of Modern English Society from 1850. Janet Roebuck.

The Making of the Labor Bureaucrat: Union Leadership in the United States, 1870-1920. Warren R. Van Tine.

The Making of the President 1972. Theodore H. White.

The Malatesta of Rimini and the Papal State: A Political History. P. J. Jones.

Malawi: The History of a Nation. Bridglal Pachai.

Malaysia--A Commentary. S. Nihal Singh.

The Malaysian General Election of 1969. R. K. Vasil.

Mallet Du Pan (1749-1800): A Career in Political Journalism. Frances Acomb.

The Mallorys of Mystic: Six Generations in Maritime Enterprise. James P. Baughman.

Malta 1813-1914: A Study in Consti-

tutional and Strategic Development.
Hilda I. Lee.
Mammalian Osteo-archaeology:
North America. B. Miles Gil-
bert.
Man and Aggression. Ashley Mon-
tagu, ed.
Man from the Valley: Memoirs of
a 20th-Century Virginian. Fran-
ces Pickens Miller.
The Man Muzzuchelli: Pioneer
Priest. Jo Bartels Alderson and
J. Michael Alderson.
The Man of Letters in New England
and the South: Essays on the His-
tory of the Literary Vocation in
America. Lewis P. Simpson.
The Man to Send Rain Clouds. Ken-
neth Rosen, ed.
The Man Who Led Columbus to Amer-
ica. Paul H. Chapman.
Mandingo Kingdoms of the Senegam-
bia: Traditionalism, Islam, and
European Expansion. Charlotte
A. Quinn.
Manitoba 1870: A Metis Achievement.
G. F. G. Stanley.
Manuel d'Archéologie Punique, I:
Histoire et Archéologie Comparées;
Chronologie des Tempe Archaiques
de Carthage et des Villes Pheni-
ciennes de l'Quest. Pierre Cintas.
Manuel Gutiérrez Najera: Escritos
inéditos de sabor satirico "Plato
del Día." Boyd G. and Mary
Eileen Carter, eds.
La Manufacture de Toiles Imprimees
de Tourne-Mine-Les-Angers (1752-
1820): Etude d'une Enterprise et
d'une Industrie au XVIIIe siecle.
Serge Chassagne.
The Manufacturing Frontier: Pioneer
Industry in Antebellum Wisconsin,
1830-1860. Margaret Walsh.
Manuscrit Tovar Origines et Croyances
des Indiens du Mexique. Jacques
La Faye.
Mao's Great Revolution. Robert S.
Elegant.
Mao's Revolution and the Chinese
Political Culture. Richard H.
Solomon.
A Map of the British Empire in
America with the French and Span-
ish Settlements Adjacent Thereto.
Henry Popple.
The Mapping of New Jersey: The
Men and the Art. John P. Snyder.

Marathon: The Story of Civiliza-
tions on Collision Course. Alan
Lloyd.
Marcus and Narcissa Whitman and
the Opening of Old Oregon. Vols.
I and II. Clifford M. Drury.
Marcus Garvey. E. David Cronon,
ed.
Margaret of Anjou: Queen of Eng-
land. Philippe Erlanger.
The Marginal Revolution in Eco-
nomics: Interpretation and Evalu-
ation. R. D. Collison Black,
A. W. Coats, and Crauford
D. W. Goodwin, eds.
Marginality and Identity: A Colored
Creole Family Through Ten Gen-
erations. Frances Jerome Woods.
Maria Edgeworth: A Literary Bi-
ography. Marilyn Butler.
Marine Archaeology. D. J. Black-
man, ed.
Mark Huish and the London and
Norh Western Railway: A Study
of Management. T. R. Gourvish.
Marlborough as Military Commander.
David Chandler.
The Marquis: A Study of Lord Rock-
ingham, 1730-1782. Ross J. S.
Hoffman.
Marriage and the Family in Rural
Bukwaya. Hugo Huber.
Marriage, Class and Colour in Nine-
teenth-Century Cuba: A Study of
Racial Attitudes and Sexual Values
in a Slave Society. Verena Mar-
tinez-Alier.
Marriages and Deaths from the Mary-
land Gazette, 1727-1839. Robert
Barnes, comp.
Marseilles, Levantehandel und ein
akkonensiches Fälscheratelier des
13. Jahrhunderts. H. E. Mayer.
Marshall versus Jefferson: The Po-
litical Background of Marbury v.
Madison. Donald O. Dewey.
Marti y su concepcion del mundo.
Roberto D. Agramonte.
Martin R. Delaney: The Beginnings
of Black Nationalism. Victor
Ullman.
The Maru Cult of the Pomo Indians:
A California Ghost Dance Survival.
Clement W. Meighan and Francis
A. Riddell.
Maryland: The Federalist Years.
L. Marx Renzulli, Jr.
Marx and the Marxists: An Outline

of Practice and Theory. David
Childs.
Marxism and History. Helmut
Fleischer.
The Marxism of Che Guevara:
Philosophy, Economics, and
Revolutionary Warfare. Michael
Lowry.
Il marxismo teorico negli USA,
1900-1945. Cristiano Camporesi.
Marx's Paris Writings: An Analysis.
John Maguire.
Mary Adelaide Nutting: Pioneer of
Modern Nursing. Helen E. Mar-
shall.
Mary Todd Lincoln: Her Life and
Letters. Justin G. and Linda
Levitt Turner.
Maryland: The Federalist Years.
L. Marx Renzulli, Jr.
Maryland and the Empire, 1773:
The Antilon-First Citizen Letters.
Peter S. Onuf, ed.
Maryland's Revolution of Government,
1689-1692. Lois Green Carr and
David William Jordan.
The Masks of King Lear. Marvin
Rosenberg.
Masones, comuneros y carbonarios.
Iris M. Zavala.
Masques of God: Form and Theme
in the Poetry of Henry Vaughn.
James D. Simmonds.
Massachusetts Bay: The Crucial
Decade, 1640-1650. Robert Em-
met Wall, Jr.
Massacre: A Survey of Today's In-
dians. Robert Gessner.
The Massacre of St. Bartholomew and
the European Conflict, 1559-1572.
N. M. Sutherland.
Masquerade Peace: America's UN
Policy, 1944-1945. Thomas M.
Campbell.
The Mastaba of Queen Mersyankh III.
Dows Dunham and William Kelly
Simpson.
Matagorda, Early History. Lorraine
Bruce Jeter.
Materials for West African History
in the Archives of the United King-
dom. Noel Matthews.
The Mature Society. Dennis Gabor.
Maximilian and Carlota, a Tale of
Romance and Tragedy. Gene
Smith.
Maya Sculpture. Merle Greene,
Robert L. Rands, and John A.

Graham.
The Maya World. Elizabeth P.
Benson.
Maynard Dixon: Artist of the West.
Wesley M. Burnside.
The Meaning of Czech History.
Tomás G. Masaryk.
The Meaning of Freedom of Speech:
First Amendment Freedoms from
Wilson to FDR. Paul L. Murphy.
The Meaning of the Renaissance and
Reformation. Richard L. De-
Molen, ed.
Meany. Joseph C. Goulden.
The Mechanics of Independence:
Patterns of Political and Eco-
nomic Transformation in Trinidad
and Tobago. A. N. R. Robinson.
Les mechanismes de la conquête
coloniale: les conquistadores.
Ruggiero Romano.
Med Kungen Pa Acqua Rossa. Erik
Wetter, Carl-Eric Östenberg, and
Mario Moretti.
Medical Men at the Siege of Boston,
April, 1775-April, 1776: Prob-
lems of the Massachusetts and
Continental Armies. Philip Cash.
Medicine on the Santa Fe Trail.
Thomas B. Hall.
Médecins, Climat, et epidemies à
la fin du XVIIIe siècle. J.-P.
Desaive, et al.
Medieval Chronicles and the Rota-
tion of the Earth. Robert R.
Newton.
Medieval Church and Society: Col-
lected Essays. Christopher
Brooke.
The Medieval Economy and Society:
An Economic History of Britain,
1100-1500. M. M. Postan.
Medieval Jewry in Northern France:
A Political and Social History.
Robert Chazan.
Medieval Regions and Their Cities.
Josiah Cox Russell.
Medieval Southampton: The Port
and Trading Community, A. D.
1000-1600. Colin Platt.
Medieval Texts and Studies. C. R.
Cheney.
Medieval Trade and Finance.
M. M. Postan.
Medieval Wales. R. Ian Jack.
The Mediterranean and the Mediter-
ranean World in the Age of Philip
II. Vol. 1. Fernand Braudel.

A Mediterranean Society: The Jewish Communities of the Arab World as Portrayed in the Documents of the Cairo Geniza. Volume 2, The Community. S. D. Goitein.

Mediums, and Spirit-Rappers, and Roaring Radicals: Spiritualism in American Literature, 1850-1900. Howard Kerr.

Meet Squire Coleman (J. Winston Coleman, Jr.). Holman Hamilton and Edward T. Houlihan.

Meiji 1868: Revolution and Counter-Revolution in Japan. Paul Akamatsu.

The Meiji Restoration. William G. Beasley.

A Memoir of the Peace Conference, 1919. Agnes Headlam-Morley.

Memoirs. W. A. Visser 't Hooft.

Memoirs: The Reign of Louis XI, 1461-83. Philippe de Commynes.

Memoirs of a Captivity Among the Indians of North America. John Dunn Hunter.

Memoirs of a Russian Diplomat. Outposts of the Empire, 1893-1917. Andrew D. Kalmykow.

Memoirs of a Swiss Officer in the American Civil War. Heinz K. Meier.

The Memoirs of Henry Heth. James L. Morrison, Jr., ed.

The Memoirs of Robert Carey. F. H. Mares, ed.

Memoirs, Official and Personal. Thomas L. McKenney.

The Memphis "Commercial Appeal": The History of a Southern Newspaper. Thomas Harrison Baker.

Men and Brothers: Anglo-American Antislavery Cooperation. Betty Fladeland.

Men & Whales at Scammon's Lagoon. David A. Henderson.

Men in a Developing Society: Geographic and Social Mobility in Monterrey, Mexico. Jorge Bálan, Harley L. Browning and Elizabeth Jelin.

Men in Rebellion: Higher Governmental Leaders and the Coming of the American Revolution. James Kirby Martin.

The Men of Cajamarca: A Social and Biographical Study of the First Conquerors of Peru. James Lockhart.

The Men of the First French Republic: Political Alignments in the National Convention of 1792. Alison Patrick.

Men to Match the Mountains. Lloyd Thorpe.

Men versus Systems: Agriculture in the USSR, Poland, and Czechoslovakia. Arthur E. and Jan S. Adams.

Mental Institutions in America: Social Policy to 1875. Gerald N. Grob.

Mercenaries and Their Masters. Michael Mallett.

Merchant of Terror: General Sherman and Total War. John Bennett Walters.

Merchant Prince of Boston: Colonel T. H. Perkins, 1764-1854. Carl Seaburg and Stanley Paterson.

Merchants and Manufacturers: Studies in the Changing Structure of Nineteenth-Century Marketing. Glenn Porter and Harold Livesay.

Mercury: A History of Quicksilver. Leonard J. Goldwater.

Merovingian Military Organization, 481-751. Bernard S. Bachrach.

Metahistory: The Historical Imagination in Nineteenth-Century Europe. Hayden White.

Metairie: A Tongue of Land to Pasture. Henry C. Bezou.

Methods of Physical Examination in Archaeology. M. S. Tite.

Metternich. Alan Palmer.

Metternich et la France Après le congrès de Vienne. Guillaume de Sauvigny De Bertier.

Metternich und die Frage Ungarns. Erzsebét Andics.

Metternich's Projects for Reform in Austria. Egon Radvany.

Mexican Business Organizations: History and Analysis. Robert Jones Shafer.

Mexican Folk Narrative from the Los Angeles Area. Elaine K. Miller, ed.

Mexican Monetary Policy and Economic Development. B. Griffiths.

Mexican Revolution: The Constitutionalist Years. Charles C. Cumberland.

The Mexican Revolution and the

Catholic Church, 1910-1929. Robert E. Quirk.

The Mexican War: A Lithographic Record. Ronnie C. Tyler.

The Mexican War Diary of General George B. McClellan. William Starr Myers, ed.

Mexico and the United States, 1821-1973: Conflict and Coexistence. Karl M. Schmitt.

El México virreinal y la "Sublevación" de Caracas, 1810. Edgar Gabaldón Márquez.

Mexico's Acción Nacional: A Catholic Alternative to Revolution. Donald Mabry.

Michael Drayton and the Passing of Elizabethan England. Richard F. Hardin.

Michel Bakounine et ses relations avec Sergej Necaev, 1870-1872. Arthur Lehning, ed.

Michigan Labor: A Brief History from 1818 to the Present. Doris B. McLaughlin.

Midcentury America: Life in the 1850's. Carl Bode, comp. and ed.

The Middle Beat: A Correspondent's View of Mexico, Guatemala, and El Salvador. Paul P. Kenedy.

The Middle Colonies and the Coming of the American Revolution. John A. Neuenschwander.

The Middle East: Quest for an American Policy. Willard A. Beling, ed.

The Middleton Family. Beth Bland Engel.

Migration and Urban Development. Brinley Thomas.

Mike: The Memoirs of the Right Honourable Lester B. Pearson, Volume 2, 1948-1957. John A. Munro and Alex I Inglis, eds.

The Military and American Society. Stephen E. Ambrose and James A. Barber, ed.

Military Dress of North America 1665-1970. Martin Windrow and Gerry Embleton.

Military Leaders in the Civil War. Joseph B. Mitchell.

Milligan's Fight Against Lincoln. Darwin Kelley.

Milton's Earthly Paradise: A Historical Study of Eden. Joseph E. Duncan.

Mind Cure in New England: From the Civil War to World War I. Gail Thain Parker.

The Mind of Adolf Hitler: The Secret Wartime Report. Walter C. Langer.

A Mind of One Piece: Brandeis and American Reform. Melvin I. Urofsky.

Miners' and Travelers' Guide to Oregon, Washington, Idaho, Montana, Wyoming, and Colorado. John Mullan.

Minerva Handbücher, Archive. Archive im deutschsprachigen Raum. 2 vols.

The Mines of Colorado. Ovando J. Hollister.

Mining Camps and Ghost Towns: A History of Mining in Arizona and California Along the Lower Colorado. Frank Love.

Mining in the New World. Carlos Prieto.

Le Ministère du Travail (Origines et premiers développements). Jean-André Tournerie.

The Minnesota Messenia Expedition: Reconstructing a Bronze-Age Regional Environment. William A. McDonald and George R. Rapp, Jr., eds.

The Mint Museum of Art at Charlotte: A Brief History. Henrietta H. Wilkinson.

Mints, Dies and Currency: Essays Dedicated to the Memory of Albert Baldwin. R. A. G. Carson, ed.

Miracle on Cherry Creek: An Informal History of the Birth and Rebirth of a Neighborhood. Bill Brenneman.

Miraculous Stories from the Japanese Buddhist Tradition: The Nihon Ryoiki of the Monk Kyokai. Kyoko Motomochi Nakamura, trans. and ed.

Miscellanea Wilbouriana.

La misión La Torre en Bolivia, 1831-1835.

Mission Among the Blackfeet. Howard L. Harrod.

La Mission Marchand. Marc Michel.

Mission on the Fraser. John Cherrington.

Missionaries and Education in Bengal,

1793-1837. M. A. Laird.

Missione in Africa Centrale: Dairio 1855-1863. F. Morlang.

Mr. De.: A Biography of Everette Lee DeGolyer. Lon Tinkle.

Mr. Lincoln's Inaugural Journey. Mary Kay Phelan.

Mr. Piper and His Cubs. Francis Devon.

Mr. Polk's War: American Opposition and Dissent, 1846-1848. John H. Schroeder.

Mr. Republican: A Biography of Robert A. Taft. James T. Patterson.

Die mittelalterlichen Geschichtsschreiber des Pramonstratenserordens. Norbert Backmund.

Mittelstand, Demokratic und Nationalsozialismus. H. A. Winkler.

Mittelstandsfront und Republik: Die Wirtschaftspartei--Reichspartei des deutschen Mittelstandes, 1919-1933. Martin Schumacher.

Miwok Means People: The Life and Fate of the Native Inhabitants of the California Gold Rush Country. Eugene L. Conratto.

Mobility and the Small Town, 1900-1930: Transportation Change in Oregon, Illinois. Norman T. Moline.

Moche Occupation of the Santa Valley, Peru. Christopher B. Donnan.

Models in Archaeology. David L. Clarke, ed.

Modern China, 1840-1972: An Introduction to Sources and Research Aids. Andrew J. Nathan.

Modern History of Turkey. M. A. Gasratian, et al., eds.

Modern Poland Between East and West. Jan Ostaszewski, ed.

Modern Revolutions: An Introduction to the Analysis of a Political Phenomenon. John Dunn.

The Modernisation of Irish Society, 1848-1918. Joseph Lee.

The Modernist Muslim Movement in Indonesia 1900-1942. Deliar Noer.

The Modernity of the Eighteenth Century. Louis T. Milic, ed.

Modernization, Dislocation, and Aprismo: Origins of the Peruvian Aprista Party, 1870-1932. Peter F. Klarén.

Modernizing Racial Domination: South

Africa's Political Dynamics. Heribert Adam.

Modes of Thought; Essays on Thinking in Western and Non-Western Societies. Robin Horton and Ruth Finnegan, eds.

Mody Boatright, Folklorist: A Collection of Essays. Ernest B. Speck, ed.

The Molly Maguires and the Detectives. Allan Pinkerton.

Monarchy in the Emperor's Eyes: Image and Reality in the Ch'ien-lung Reign. Harold L. Khan.

Monasteries of Western Europe: The Architecture of the Orders. Wolfgang Braunfels.

Money and Politics in America 1755-1775: A Study of the Currency Act of 1764 and the Political Economy of Revolution. Joseph Albert Ernst.

The Money Manias: The Eras of Great Speculation in America, 1770-1970. Robert Sobel.

Monks, Merit, and Motivation: Buddhism and National Development in Thailand. J. A. Niels Mulder.

Monnaie et histoire d'Alexandre à Mahomet. Maurice Lombard.

Monterey: The Presence of the Past. Augusta Fink.

Montezuma: Lord of the Aztecs. C. A. Burland.

Das Monument des C. Memmius. Wilhelm Alzinger and Anton Bammer.

Moorfield Storey and the Abolitionist Tradition. William B. Hixson, Jr.

Moorish Culture in Spain. Titus Burckhardt.

The Moral and Political Thought of Mahatma Gandhi. Raghavan N. Iyer.

A More Perfect Union: The Impact of the Civil War and Reconstruction on the Constitution. Harold M. Hyman.

More Than a Century. Jim W. Corder.

Mori Arinori. Ivan Parker Hall.

The Morleys--Young Upstarts on the Southwest Frontier. Norman Cleaveland.

A Mormon Mother: An Autobiography. Annie Clark Tanner.

Mormonism and American Culture.
Marvin S. Hill and James B. Allen, eds.
Morning Without Noon. Memoirs.
Salvador de Madariaga.
Il Moro. Ellis Heywood.
Morocco under Colonial Rule: French
Administration of Tribal Areas,
1912-1956. Robin Bidwell.
The Mortal Napoleon III. Roger L.
Williams.
Mosaics in Roman Britain. Anne
Rainey.
Mosaïques de Delos. Philippe
Bruneau.
Moses Mendelssohn: A Biographical
Study. Alexander Altmann.
Most Probable Position: A History
of Aerial Navigation to 1941.
Monte Duane Wright.
Mother Jones, the Miners' Angel: A
Portrait. Dale Fetherling.
The Mound People: Danish Bronze-
Age Man Preserved. P. V. Glob.
The Mountain Men and the Fur Trade
of the Far West. Le Roy R.
Hafen, ed.
The Mountain States of America:
People, Politics, and Power in the
Eight Rocky Mountain States.
Neal R. Peirce.
Movers and Shakers: American Wo-
men Thinkers and Activists, 1900-
1970. June Sochen.
The Moving American. George W.
Pierson.
Mozambique: The Africanization of
a European Institution, the Zambezi
prazos, 1750-1902. Allen F.
Isaacman.
Muddle of the Middle East. Volumes
I and II. Nikshoy C. Chatterji.
The Multinational Corporation as a
Force in Latin American Politics:
A Case Study of the International
Petroleum Company in Peru. Adal-
berto J. Pinelo.
Multiplying the Witness: 150 Years of
American Baptist Educational Min-
istries. Lawrence T. Slaght.
Music and Society in Scotland in the
Eighteenth Century. David Johnson.
Music in the Cultured Generation: A
Social History of Music in America,
1870-1900. Joseph A. Mussulman.
Music in the Service of the King:
France in the Seventeenth Century.
Robert M. Isherwood.

Music is My Mistress: Edward
Kennedy Ellington.
Music of the Old South: Colony to
Confederacy. Albert Stoutamire.
Música popular de índios, negros,
e mestiços. José Ramos Tin-
horão.
A Musical Season. Andrew Porter.
Muslim Spain: Its History and Cul-
ture. Anwar G. Chejne.
The Muslims of British India. P.
Hardy.
The Muslims of Burma: A Study of
a Minority Group. Moshe Yegar.
My Blood's Country: Studies in
Southwestern Literature. William
T. Pilkington.
My Childhood in Mongolia. Urgunge
Onon.
My Girlhood Among Outlaws. Lily
Klasner.
My Life and Experiences Among
Our Hostile Indians. Oliver O.
Howard.
My Life as a Man. Philip Roth.
My Own Story. Peter O'Leary.
My War with the CIA: Cambodia's
Fight for Survival. Norodom
Sihanouk.
Myrtos: An Early Bronze Age Site
in Crete. Peter Warren.
The Mystery of Iniquity: Melville
as Poet, 1857-1891. William H.
Shurr.
Mysticism and Dissent: Religious
Ideology and Social Protest in
the Sixteenth Century. Steven
E. Ozment.
The Myth Against Myth: A Study of
Yeats' Imagination in Old Age.
Daniel Albright.
The Myth of the Bagre. Jack Goody.
The Myth of the Lost Cause, 1865-
1900. Rollin G. Osterweis.
The Mythology of the Secret Societies.
J. M. Roberts.

-N-

NAACP: A History of the National
Association for the Advancement
of Colored People. Volume I.
1909-1920. Charles Flint Kellogg.
The Names of Kings: The Parisian

Laboring Poor in the Eighteenth Century. Jeffry Kaplow.

Nandi Resistance to British Rule 1890-1906. A. T. Matson.

Napoleon III. W. H. C. Smith.

Napoleon III and Mexico: American Triumph Over Monarchy. Alfred Jackson and Kathryn Abbey Hanna.

Napoleon und Europa. Hans-Otto Sieburg, ed.

Napoleon's Soldiers in America. Simone de la Deléry.

A Narrative of the Life of David Crockett of the State of Tennessee. David Crockett.

Narratives of Shipwrecks and Disasters, 1586-1860. Keith Huntress, ed.

Narrow Gauge to Central and Silver Plume. Cornelius W. Hauck.

Nation Building in Kenya: The Role of Land Reform. John W. Harbeson.

A Nation in the Making: The Philippines and the United States, 1899-1921. Peter W. Stanley.

The National Academy of Design Exhibition Record: 1861-1900. Maria Naylor, comp.

The National Archives and Statistical Research. Meyer H. Fishbein, ed.

The National Urban League, 1910-1940. Nancy J. Weiss.

Die Nationalisierung der deutschen Einwanderer und ihrer Nachkommen in Brasilien als Problem der deutsch-brasilianischen Beziehungen 1930-1938. Kate Harms-Baltzer.

Nationalism and the International System. F. H. Hinsley.

Nationalism, Communism, and Canadian Labour: The CIO, the Communist Party, and the Canadian Congress of Labour, 1936-1956. Irving Martin Abella.

Nationalism in the Middle Ages. Leon Tipton, ed.

The Nationality Question in Soviet Central Asia. Edward Allworth, ed.

Native American Tribalism: Indian Survivals and Renewals. D'Arcy McNickle.

Native Fascism in the Successor States, 1918-1945. Peter F. Sugar, ed.

The Naturalist Drama in Germany. John Osborne.

A Naturalist in Costa Rica. Alexander F. Skutch.

Naturzand und Naturgeschichte der bürgerlichen Gesellschaft: Die Ursprünge der bürgerlichen Sozialtheorie als Geschichtsphilosophie und Sozialwissenschaft bei Samuel Pufendorf, John Locke, und Adam Smith. Hans Medick.

The Navajo People. Henry F. Dobyns and Robert C. Euler.

Navajo Roundup: Selected Correspondence of Kit Carson's Expedition Against the Navajo, 1863-1865. Lawrence C. Kelly.

Naval and Maritime History: An Annotated Bibliography. Robert G. Albion.

Naval Documents of the American Revolution. Volume 6.... William James Morgan, ed.

A Naval History of the Civil War. Howard P. Nash, Jr.

The Naval Side of King William's War. Edward B. Powley.

Navigating the Rapids, 1918-1971: From the Papers of Adolf A. Berle. Beatrice Bishop Berle and Travis Beal Jacobs, eds.

The Navy Department in the War of 1812. Edward K. Eckert.

The Nazi Party Courts: Hitler's Management of Conflict in His Movement, 1921-1945. Donald M. McKale.

Nazism and the Common Man: Essays in German History (1929-1939). Otis C. Mitchell, ed.

Le Nécropole Préromaine d'Aléria (1960-1968). Jean and Laurence Jehasse.

The Necropolis at Kaloriziki Excavated by J. F. Daniel and G. H. McFadden for the University Museum, University of Pennsylvania, Philadelphia. J. L. Benson.

The Necropolis of Anemurium. Elisabeth Alfoldi-Rosenbaum.

Negative Integration und revolutionärer Attentismus. Die deutsche Sozialdemokratie am Vorabend des Ersten Weltkrieges. Dieter Groh.

The Negro in Savannah, 1865-1900. Robert E. Perdue.

Negro Progress in Atlanta, Georgia, 1961-1970. Annie L. McPheeters.

Neither Black nor White: Slavery and Race Relations in Brazil and the United States. Carl Degler.

Neither Slave Nor Free: The Freedman of African Descent in the Slave Societies of the New World. David W. Cohen and Jack P. Greene, eds.

Nelson: The Commander. Geoffrey Bennett.

A nemzet historikuma es a tortenelemszemlelet nemzeti latoszoge: hozxaszolas egy vitahoz. Jeno Szucs.

Nerinckx--Kentucky--Loretto. 1804-1851. Augustin C. Wand, S. J., and Sister Lilliana Owens, eds.

The Nevada Constitution: Origin and Growth. Eleanore Bushnell.

New Approaches to Ezra Pound. Eva Hesse, ed.

New Approaches to Latin American History. Richard Graham and Peter H. Smith, eds.

The New Deal for Artists. Richard D. McKinzie.

The New Deal in the Suburbs: A History of the Greenbelt Town Program, 1935-1954. Joseph L. Arnold.

The New Economic Policy and the Party Crisis After the Death of Lenin: Reminiscences of My Work at the V S N K H During the N E P. N. Valentinov (Vol'-shkii).

The New England Mind in Transition: Samuel Johnson of Connecticut, 1696-1772. Joseph J. Ellis.

New England and the Sea. Robert G. Albion, et al.

The New Found Land of Stephen Parmenius. D. B. Quinn and N. M. Cheshire, eds.

New French Imperialism, 1880-1910: The Third Republic and Colonial Expansion. James J. Cooke.

The New Heavens and New Earth: Political Religion in America. Cushing Strout.

A New Historical Geography of England. H. C. Darby, ed.

New Jersey in the American Revolution, II. William C. Wright, ed.

New Jersey Since 1860: New Findings and Interpretations. William C. Wright, ed.

A New Kind of History: From the Writings of Lucien Febvre. Peter Burke, ed.

The New Left and the Origins of the Cold War. Robert James Maddox.

New Left Diplomatic Histories and Historians: The American Revisionists. Jpseph M. Siracusa.

The New Left in America: Reform to Revolution, 1956-1970. Edward J. Bacciocco, Jr.

New Men in the Roman Senate, 139 B. C. - A. D. 14. T. P. Wiseman.

New Mexico: A Pageant of Three Peoples. Edna Fergusson.

The New Order and the French Economy. Alan S. Milward.

New Orleans. Sarah Searight.

The New Oxford History of Music. Vol. II. Egon Wellesz and Frederick Sternfeld, eds.

The New Oyo Empire: Indirect Rule and Change in Western Nigeria 1894-1934. J. A. Atanda.

New Poems, 1968-1970. Pablo Neruda.

The New Political Economy of J. S. Mill. Pedro Schwartz.

The New Woman in Greenwich Village, 1910-1920. June Sochen.

New York Historical Manuscripts: Dutch. Arnold J. F. van Laer, Kenneth Scott and K. Stryker-Rodda, trans. and eds.

New Zealand and Japan, 1900-41. M. P. Lissington.

Newcastle, a Duke Without Money: Thomas Pelham-Holles, 1693-1768. Ray A. Kelch.

News from the Capital: The Story of Washington Reporting. F. B. Marbut.

The Newsmongers: Journalism in the Life of the Nation, 1690-1972. Robert A. Rutland.

Newton and Russia: The Early Influence, 1698-1796. Valentin Boss.

Newton D. Baker and the American War Effort, 1917-1919. Daniel R. Beaver.

Nez Perce Joseph: An Account of His Ancestors, His Lands, His Confederates, His Enemies, His Murderers, His War, Pursuit and Capture. O. O. Howard.

A Nickel's Worth of Skim Milk: A
Boy's View of the Great Depression. Robert J. Hastings.

Nicolae Iorga: A Romanian Historian
of the Ottoman Empire. Maria
Matilda Alexandrescu-Dersca Bulgaru.

Nicolas Iorga: L'homme et l'oeuvre.
D. M. Pippidi, ed.

Niederländische Exulanten im 16.
Jahrhundert: Ihre Stellung im
Socialgefüge und im religiösen
Leben deutscher und englischer
Städte. Heinz Schilling.

The Nigerian Army, 1956-1966.
N. J. Miners.

The Nigerian Military: A Sociological
Analysis of Authority and Revolt,
1960-67. Robin Luckham.

Nigerian Modernization: The Colonial Legacy. Ukandi Godwin Damachi.

The Nigerian War 1967-1970.
Zdenek Cervenka.

Nikolai Strakhov. Linda Gerstein.

Nine Public Lectures on Important
Subjects in Religion. Nicholaus
Ludwig Count von Zinzendorf.

1971 Brand Book: The Denver
Westerners. Dave Hicks, ed.

Nineteenth-Century Society: Essays
in the Use of Quantitative Methods for the Study of Social Data.
E. A. Wrigley, ed.

Nkrumah: A Biography. Robin
McKown.

No Clear and Present Danger: A
Skeptical View of the United
States Entry into World War II.
Bruce M. Russett.

No Haven for the Oppressed: United
States Policy Toward Jewish Refugees, 1938-1945. Saul S. Friedman.

No Peace Beyond the Line: The English in the Caribbean 1624-1690.
Carl and Roberta Bridenbaugh.

The Nobility of Later Medieval England. K. B. McFarlane.

La Noblesse Bretonne au XVIIIieme
Siecle. Jean Meyer.

Nonconformity in the Nineteenth
Century. David M. Thompson.

Normalization of Japanese-Soviet Relations, 1945-1970. Savitri Vishwanathan.

The North Atlantic World in the
Seventeenth Century. K. G.
Davies.

The North Carolina Continentals.
Hugh F. Rankin.

North Carolina: The History of a
Southern State. Hugh Talmage
Lefler and Albert Ray Newsome.

North Carolina Troops, 1861-1865:
A Roster. Volume IV: Infantry.
Weymouth T. Jordan, Jr., comp.

The North Korean Economy: Structure and Development. Joseph
Sang-Hoon Chung.

Northern Italy Before Rome. Lawrence Barfield.

Northumberland: The Political
Career of John Dudley, Earl of
Warwick and Duke of Northumber-
land. Barrett L. Beer.

The Northwest Coast, or Three
Years Residence in Washington
Territory. James G. Swan.

Not a One-Way Street: The Autobiography of James S. Duncan.
James S. Duncan.

Notable American Women. 3 vols.
Edward T. James, et al., eds.

Notes from China. Barbara W.
Tuchman.

Notes on the History of the Tum-
buka-Kamanga Peoples in the
Northern Province of Nyasaland.
T. Cullen Young.

Notices of East Florida. William
Hayne Simmons.

Notions of the Americans, 1820-
1860. David Grimsted, ed.

Numby, Man of Two Worlds: The
Life and Diaries of Arthur J.
Numby, 1828-1910. Derek Hud-
son.

Nuntiaturberichte aus Deutschland
Nuniatur des Girolamo Muzzarelli,
Sendung des Antonio Augustin
Legation des Scipione Rebiba
(1554-1556). Heinrich Lutz, ed.

Nyasaland and Northern Rhodesia:
Corrider to the North. Norman
H. Pollock, Jr.

-O-

O ciclo de Vargas. Vol. XI.
1939. Véspera de guerra. Hélio Silva.

O ciclo de Vargas. Vol. XIX.

1942. Guerra no continente.
Hélio Silva.
El obispado de Michoacán en el siglo XVII. Informe inedito de beneficios, pueblos y lenguas.
Obra politica de José Bonifácio. 2 vols. Octaciano Nogueira, ed.
Obsolete Bank Notes of New England. David C. Wismer.
Occupied America: The Chicano's Struggle toward Liberation. Rodolfo Acuna.
The October Revolution and the Navy. S. S. Khesin.
The Octobrists in the Third Duma, 1907-1912. Ben-Cion Pinchuk.
The Oder-Neisse Boundary and Poland's Modernization. Anthony Kruszewski.
The Offshore Islanders. Paul Johnson.
Oil and the Mexican Revolution. Merrill Rippy.
Oil Pollution as an International Problem. William M. Ross.
Old Calabar 1600-1891: The Impact of the International Economy Upon a Traditional Society. A. J. H. Latham.
Old Houses of King and Queen County, Virginia. Virginia D. Cox and Willis T. Weathers.
The Old Man: John Brown at Harper's Ferry. Nelson Truman.
The Old Ones of New Mexico. Robert Coles.
The Old South: A Psycho-History. Earl E. Thorpe.
The Old-Time Power. Vinson Synan.
Oldenbarnevelt. 2 vols. Jan den Tex.
Oliver Mowat's Ontario. Donald Swainson, ed.
Die Ölversorgung der Kriegsmarine 1935 bis 1945. Wilhelm Meier-Dörnberg.
On Liberty and Liberalism: The Case of John Stuart Mill. Gertrude Himmelfarb.
On the Ragged Edge: The Life and Times of Dudley Leavitt. Juanita Brooks.
On the Seas and in the Skies: A History of the U. S. Navy's Air Power. Theodore Roscoe.
On Their Own--The Poor in Modern America. David J. and Sheila Rothman, eds.

On Thrones of Gold: Three Javanese Shadow Plays. James R. Brandon, ed.
On Wings of Song. A Biography of Felix Mendelssohn. Wilfrid Blunt.
One Hundred Fifty Years in Pike County, Alabama, 1821-1971. Margaret Pace Farmer.
One in Spirit. Albert M. Tannler.
One Million Men: The Civil War Draft in the North. Eugene C. Murdock.
One Thousand Years: Western Europe in the Middle Ages. Richard L. DeMolen, ed.
Onitsha Market Literature. Emmanuel N. Obiechina, ed.
Only Farmers Need Apply: Official Canadian Government Encouragement of Immigration from the United States, 1896-1911. Harold Martin Troper.
The Only Land I Know: A History of the Lumbee Indians. Adolph Dial and David Eliades.
The Opelousas Post: A Compendium of Church Records Relating to the First Families of Southwest Louisiana, 1776-1806. Gladys deVillier.
Open-Field Farming in Medieval England: A Study of Village By-Laws. Warren O. Ault.
Open Veins of Latin America: Five Centuries of the Pillage of a Continent. Eduardo Galeano.
The Opening of the Canadian North 1870-1914. Morris Zaslow.
Opera Omnia. Odorannus De Sens.
Opinion Publica y Oposicion al Poder en la Espana del Siglo XVIII (1713-1759). Teofanes Egido Lopez.
Opus Geographicum sine "Liber adeorum delectationem qui terras peragrare studeant." Al-Idrisi.
The Oral History Collection of Columbia University. Elizabeth B. Mason and Louis M. Starr, eds.
Oral History Program Manual. William W. Moss.
Oral History 25th Anniversary Report. Louis M. Starr.
Oral Literature in Africa. Ruth Finnegan.
Orangeism: The Canadian Phase.

Hereward Senior.
Ordeal of the Union: Selected Chapters. Allan Nevins.
The Ordeal of Thomas Hutchinson. Bernard Bailyn.
Ordensleben und Lebensstandard. Gerd Zimmerman.
The Orders and Callings of the Church. G. Constable and B. Smith, eds. and trans.
Oregon Trail. Ingvard Henry Eide.
Organization, Conflict, and Innovation: A Study of German Naval Strategic Planning, 1888-1940. Carl-Axel Gemzell.
Organized Labor and the Black Worker, 1619-1973. Philip S. Foner.
Origins of the Chinese Revolution, 1915-1949. Lucien Bianco.
The Oriental Americans. H. Brett Melendy.
Oriental Asia: Themes Toward a Geography. Joseph E. Spencer.
Los orígenes del capitalismo en España: Banca, industria y ferrocarriles en el siglo XIX. Gabriel Tortella Casares.
Los orígenes del nacionalismo mexicano. David A. Brading.
Original Sin in the Roman Liturgy. G. M. Lukken.
Les origines de l'Eglise Evangélique du Cameroun: missions européenes et christianisme autochtone. Jaap Van Slageren.
L'Origines des écoles françaises dans l'Ontario. Arthur Godbout.
The Origins of British Borneo. L. R. Wright.
The Origins of Christian Art. Michael Gough.
Origins of English Feudalism. R. Allen Brown.
The Origins of Fascism in Italy. Gaetano Salvemini.
Origins of Intelligence Services.... Francis Dvornik.
The Origins of Modern Europe. R. Allen Brown.
Origins of New Mexico Families in the Spanish Colonial Period.... Fray Angélico Chávez.
The Origins of Polish Socialism: The History and Ideas of the First Polish Socialist Party, 1878-1886. Lucjan Blit.
The Origins of Spain and Portugal. H. V. Livermore.

The Origins of the Civil War. D. Duane Cummins and William G. White.
The Origins of the English Civil War. Conrad Russell, ed.
The Origins of the Feminist Movement in America. Glenda Riley McIntosh.
Origins of the Greek Nation: The Byzantine Period, 1204-1461. Apostolos E. Vacalopoulos.
The Ormée of Bordeaux: A Revolution During the Fronde. Sal Alexander Westrich.
Osceola: The Unconquered Indian. William and Ellen Hartley.
Osiander in Preussen 1549-1552. Martin Stupperich.
The Other Bostonians: Poverty and Progress in the American Metropolis, 1880-1970. Stephan Thernstrom.
The Other de Gaulle, 1944-1954. Claude Mauriac.
The Other South: Southern Dissenters in the Nineteenth Century. Carl N. Degler.
The Ottoman Empire and Its Successors. Peter Mansfield.
The Ottoman Empire, the Great Powers and the Straits Question, 1870-1887. Barbara Jelavich.
Our Historic Desert: The Story of the Anza-Borrego Desert. Diana Lindsay.
Our Indian Wards. George W. Manypenny.
Our Knowledge of the Historical Past. Murray G. Murphey.
Our New West: Records of Travel Between the Mississippi River and the Pacific Ocean, Over the Plains, Over the Mountains, Through the Great Interior Basin, Over the Sierra Nevadas, to and Up and Down the Pacific Coast. Samuel Bowles.
Our Own Metaphor. Mary Catherine Bateson.
Out of the Blue: U. S. Army Airborne Operations in World War II. James A. Huston.
Out of the Ghetto: The Social Background of Jewish Emancipation, 1770-1870. Jacob Katz.
Out of the Old Rock. J. Frank Dobie.
Over to the Sea to Skye: The Forty-

Five.   John Selby.

The Overland Diary of Wilson Price Hunt.   Hoyt C. Franchere, ed.

The Overproduction Trap in U. S. Agriculture: A Study of Resource Allocation from World War I to the Late 1960's.   Glenn L. Johnson and C. Leroy Quance, eds.

Owens Valley as I Knew It: The Owens Valley and the Los Angeles Water Controversy.   Richard Coke Wood.

Owyhee Trails, the West's Forgotten Corner.   Mike Hanley.

- P -

Pablo Neruda: regresó el caminante (aspectos sobresalientes en la obra y la vida de Pablo Neruda).   Morris E. Carson.

Pacem in Maribus.   Elisabeth Mann Borgese, ed.

Pacific Circle 2: Proceedings of the Third Biennial Conference of the Australian and New Zealand American Studies Association.   Norman Harper, ed.

Pacific Estrangement: Japanese and American Expansion 1897-1911.   Akira Iriye.

Pacifism in Europe to 1914.   Peter Brock.

Padju Epat: the Ma'anyan of Indonesian Borneo.   A. B. Hudson.

A Page From Nashville's History.   Wilbur F. Creighton, Jr.

Paine.   David Freeman Hawke.

The Painful Labour of Mr. Elsyng.   Elizabeth Read Foster.

Painting and Experience in Fifteenth-Century Italy: A Primer in the Social History of Pictorial Style.   Michael Baxendall.

The Paiutes of Pyramid Lake: A Narrative Concerning a Western Nevada Indian Tribe.   Ruth Hermann.

La paix de Versailles et l'opinion publique française.   Pierre Miquel.

Pakistan: Failure in National Integration.   Rounaq Jahan.

Pakistan Political System in Crisis: Emergence of Bangladesh.   S. P. Varma and Virendra Narain, eds.

The Palace of Nestor at Pylos in Western Messenia. Vol. III: Acropolis and Lower Town, Tholoi and Grave Circle, Chamber Tombs. Discoveries Outside the Citadel.   Carl W. Blegen, Marion Rawson, Lord William Taylour and William P. Donovan.

Palaeoethnobotany: the Prehistoric Food Plants of the Near East and Europe.   Jane M. Renfrew.

Palaeographical Papers, 1907-1965.   E. A. Lowe.

Pale Ink: Two Ancient Records of Chinese Exploration in America.   Henriette Mertz.

Pallado and English Palladianism.   Rudolf Wittkower.

Palmetto Leaves.   Harriet Beecher Stowe.

Palomar From Tepee to Telescope.   Catherine M. Wood.

Pan-Africanism and Nationalism in West Africa 1900-1945.   A Study in Ideology and Social Classes.   J. Ayodele Langley.

Pan-Africanism from Within.   Ras Makonnen.

Panoramic Maps of Anglo-American Cities: A Checklist of Maps in the Collections of the Library of Congress.   John R. Hébert, comp.

The Paper Tryant: John Ross Robertson of the Toronto Telegram.   Ron Poulton.

Papers Concerning Robertson's Colony in Texas, Volume I, 1788-1822.   Malcolm D. McLean, comp. and ed.

Papers in Economic Prehistory.   E. S. Higgs, ed.

The Papers of Adlai E. Stevenson, Volume II: Washington to Springfield.   Walter Johnson, ed.

The Papers of Adlai E. Stevenson.   Vol. III.   Walter Johnson and Carol Evans, eds.

The Papers of Alexander Hamilton.   Vols. 16, 17, 18, 19.   Harold C. Syrett, ed.

The Papers of Andrew Johnson: Volume 3: 1858-1860.   LeRoy P. Graf and Ralph W. Haskins, eds.

The Papers of Benjamin Franklin.   Vols. 15, 16, 17, 18.   William B. Willcox, et al., eds.

The Papers of Henry Clay. Vol.
IV. Secretary of State, 1825.
James F. Hopkins, et al., eds.
The Papers of Henry Clay. Vol.
V. Secretary of State, 1826.
James F. Hopkins and Mary W. M.
Hargreaves, eds.
The Papers of James Madison. Vol-
ume 7, 3 May 1783-20 February
1784. William T. Hutchinson and
William M. E. Rachal, eds.
The Papers of James Madison. Vol-
ume 8, 10 March 1784-28 March
1786. Robert A. Rutland and Wil-
liam M. E. Rachal, eds.
The Papers of John C. Calhoun.
Vols. 5-7. W. Edwin Hemphill,
ed.
The Papers of Joseph Henry. Vol.
1: December 1797-October 1832:
The Albany Years. Nathan Rein-
gold, Stuart Pierson, Arthur P.
Molella, James M. Hobbins, and
John R. Kerwood, eds.
The Papers of Robert Morris, 1781-
1784. Volume I: February 7-
July 31, 1781. E. James Fergu-
son, ed.
Papers of the Texas Revolution.
John H. Jenkins, ed.
The Papers of Thomas Jefferson.
Volume 18, 4 November 1790-24
January 1791. Julian P. Boyd,
et al., eds.
The Papers of Thomas Jordan Jarvis.
Vol. I: 1869-1882. W. Buck
Yearns, ed.
The Papers of Ulysses S. Grant.
Volumes 4 and 5. John Y.
Simon, ed.
The Papers of William Alexander
Graham. Vol. V. Max R. Wil-
liams and J. G. deRoulhac Hamil-
ton, eds.
The Papers of Woodrow Wilson.
Vols. 14, 15. Arthur S. Link,
et al., eds.
Papst und Frankenkonig: Studien zu
den papstlich-frankischen Rechts-
beziehungen von 754-824. Wolfgang
H. Fritze.
Paradise Lost: A Context. Gladys
W. Hudson.
Paradise Lost, Introduction. John
Broadbent.
Parents and Children in History:
The Psychology of Family Life in
Early Modern France. David Hunt.

The Paris Commune, 1871. Stew-
art Edwards.
The Paris Commune of 1871: the
View from the Left. Eugene
Schulkind.
The Paris Peace Conference and
Foreign Intervention in the
Country of the Soviets (January-
June 1919). A. D. Skaba.
The Parliament of 1621: A Study
in Constitutional Conflict. Robert
Zaller.
The Parliamentary Diary of Narcis-
sus Luttrell 1691-1693. Henry
Horwitz, ed.
Parliamentary Reform, 1640-1832.
John Cannon.
Party and Faction in American Poli-
tics: The House of Representa-
tives, 1789-1801. Rudolph M.
Bell.
Party Propaganda Under Queen
Anne: The General Elections of
1702-1713. James O. Richards.
The Passion of Claude McKay: Se-
lected Poetry and Prose, 1912-
1948. Wayne Cooper, ed.
Pat Garrett: The Story of a West-
ern Lawman. Leon G. Metz.
Patchwork Poetry. Marj Bennett.
Patents, Invention, and Economic
Change. Jacob Schmookler.
La patria del criollo. Ensayo de
interpretación de la realidad
colonial guatemalteca. Severo
Martínez Peláez.
Le patriciat lyonnais aux XIIIᵉ et
XIVᵉ siècles. Guy de Valous.
Patrick Cleburne: Confederate Gen-
eral. Howell and Elizabeth Pur-
due.
Patrick J. Hurley and American
Foreign Policy. Russell D.
Buhite.
The Pattern of Reform in Hungary:
A Political, Economic and Cul-
tural Analysis. William F. Robin-
son.
The Pattern of Rural Dissent: The
Nineteenth Century. Alan Everitt.
The Pattern of the Chinese Past.
Mark Elvin.
Patterns and Perspectives in Iowa
History. Dorothy Schwieder,
ed.
Patterns of Foreign Influence in the
Caribbean. Emanuel de Kadt,
ed.

Patton: A Study in Command. H.
Essame.
The Patton Papers. Volume 1, 1885-
1950. Martin Blumenson.
Paul Cuffe: Black American and the
African Return. Sheldon H. Har-
ris, ed.
Paul U. Kellogg and the Survey:
Voices for Social Welfare and
Social Justice. Clarke A. Cham-
bers.
Paulus. Reminiscences of a Friend-
ship. Rollo May.
Pavel Axelrod and the Development
of Menshevism. Abraham Ascher.
The Peabody Story: Events in Pea-
body's History, 1626-1972. John
A. Wells.
Peace Movements in America.
Charles Chatfield, ed.
Pearl Harbor as History: Japanese-
American Relations, 1931-1941.
Dorothy Borg and Shumpei Oka-
moto, eds.
Peasant Revolts in China, 1840-1949.
Jean Chesneaux.
Peasants in Revolt: A Chilean Case
Study, 1965-1971. James Petras
and Hugo Zemelman Merino.
The Peasants' Revolt of 1381. R. B.
Dobson, ed.
Pédagogie musulmane d'Afrique
noire: l'ecole coranique peule
du Cameroun. Renand Santerre.
Pedro de la Torre: Doctor to Con-
querors. John Tate Lanning.
The Peelites, 1846-1857. Wilbur
Devereux Jones and Arvel B.
Erickson.
The Peelites and the Party System,
1846-52. J. B. Conacher.
The Peers, the Parties and the Peo-
ple: The General Election of
1910. N. Blewett.
Péguy et le nationalisme français.
Eric Cahm.
Penetration of the Economy of West-
ern Ukraine by Foreign Capital in
the Era of Imperialism (till 1918).
Ia. S. Khonigsman.
The Peninsula War of 1807-1814: A
Concise Military History. Michael
Glover.
Pénitents et francs-maçons de l'an-
cienne Provence. Maurice Agulhon.
Pennsylvania Iron Manufacture in the
Eighteenth Century. Arthur Cecil
Bining.

Pennsylvania Politics 1746-1770.
J. H. Hutson.
Il pensiero cristiano di Lorenzo
Valla nel quadro storico-culturale
del suo ambiente. Mario Fois.
A People and a Nation. Clarence
L. Ver Steeg and Richard Hof-
stadter.
People and Pelts: Selected Papers
of the Second North American
Fur Trade Conference. Malvina
Bolus, ed.
People in the Way: The Human
Aspects of the Columbia River
Project. J. W. Wilson.
The People Make a Nation. Martin
W. Sandler, Edwin C. Rozwenc,
and Edward C. Martin.
The People of America. T. D.
Stewart.
People of Paradox: An Inquiry
Concerning the Origins of Ameri-
can Civilization. Michael Kam-
men.
People of the Plains and Mountains:
Essays in the History of the
West Dedicated to Everett Dick.
Ray Allen Billington, ed.
The People's Liberation Army and
China's Nation Building. Ying-
mao Kau.
The Peoples of Philadelphia: A
History of Ethnic Groups and
Lower-Class Life, 1790-1940.
Allen F. Davis and Mark H.
Haller, eds.
"The People's Will" Before the
Tsarist Courts 1880-1891. N. A.
Troitskii.
Pepper, Guns, and Parleys: The
Dutch East India Company and
China, 1622-1681. John E.
Wills, Jr.
Pepys; A Biography. Richard Ollard.
Perceptions of Works: Variations
within a Factory. H. Beynon
and R. M. Blackburn.
Perfidious Albion: The Origins of
Anglo-French Rivalry in the
Levant. John Marlowe.
Pergamon, Gesammelte Aufsätze.
Erich Boehringer, ed.
The Peripatetic University: Cam-
bridge Local Lectures, 1873-1973.
Edwin Welch.
Perry, Pride of the Prairie. Robert
E. Cunningham.
Person and Places of Indian Terri-

tory. C. W. "Dub" West.

The Personality of Shakespeare. Edward Wagenknecht.

Perspectives in the English Urban History. Alan Everitt, ed.

Perspectives of Empire: Essays Presented to Gerald S. Graham. John E. Flint and Glyndwr Williams, eds.

Perspectives on Early American History: Essays in Honor of Richard B. Morris. Alden T. Vaughan and George Athan Billias, eds.

Perspectives on the T'ang. Arthur F. Wright and Denis Twitchett, eds.

Peter Abelard's Ethics. D. E. Luscombe, D. E., ed. and trans.

Peter Lavrov and the Russian Revolutionary Movement. Philip Pomper.

Peter Parker and the Opening of China. Edward V. Gulick.

Peterborough Abbey, 1086-1310: A Study in the Land Market. Edmund King.

Petrarch's Book Without a Name. Norman P. Zacour.

Phil Swing and the Boulder Dam. B. B. Moeller.

Philby of Arabia. Elizabeth Monroe.

Philippine Ethnography: A Critically Annotated and Selected Bibliography. Shiro Saito.

The Philippine Insurrection Against the United States. A Compilation of Documents.... John R. M. Taylor (Notes and Introduction).

Philmont: A History of New Mexico's Cimarron County. Lawrence R. Murphy.

The Philosophy of the Enlightenment: The Christian Burgess and the Enlightenment. Lucien Goldman.

Philosophy of the Urban Guerrilla: The Revolutionary Writings of Abraham Guillén. Donald C. Hodges, ed.

The Physician and Sexuality in Victorian America. John S. Haller, Jr. and Robin M. Haller.

The Pictorial History of the American Revolution. Rupert Furneaux.

The Pictorial History of the Royal Canadian Mounted Police. Stanley W. Horrall.

Picture Writing from Ancient Southern Mexico: Mixtec Place Signs and Maps. Mary Elizabeth Smith.

Pictures from a Brewery. Asher Barash.

Pierpont Morgan and Friends: The Anatomy of a Myth. George Wheeler.

Pierre Charron. Renée Kogel.

Pilgrim at Tinker Creek. Annie Dillard.

The Pilgrim Church in California. Francis J. Weber.

Pilgrimage of Faith: The Legacy of the Otterbeins. J. Steven O'Malley.

Pinckney Benton Stewart Pinchback. James Haskins.

Pioneer Families of Eastern and Southeastern Kentucky. William G. Kozee.

Pioneers of Yesteryear, Pleasant Mound "Public" Cemetery and Memorial Park, 1848-1973. Stella Bryant Vinson.

Pitselak: Pictures out of my Life. Dorothy Eber, ed.

A Plague of Corn: The Social History of Pellagra. Daphne A. Roe.

The Plain People: Left Wing of the Reformation. Edward E. Liechty.

Plains Indian Art From Fort Marion. Karen Daniels Petersen.

Plantation, Town, and Country: Essays on the Local History of American Slave Society. Elinor Miller and Eugene D. Genovese, eds.

The Plastic Age, 1917-1930. Robert Sklar, ed.

Pledge of Destiny: Charles de Gaulle and the Rise of the Free French. Robert Smith Thompson.

Pleistocene and Recent Environments of the Central Great Plains. Wakefield Dort, Jr. and J. Knox Jones, Jr., eds.

The Plot to Seize the White House. Jules Archer.

Plural Society in the South West. Edward H. Spicer and Raymond H. Thompson, eds.

Les Plus Anciens Comptes de la ville de Mons (1279-1356). Christiane Piérard.

Plutarch. D. A. Russell.

The "Pneumatics" of the Hero of

Alexander: A Facsimile of the 1851 Woodcroft Edition. Marie Boas Hall, intro.

Poems from Korea: A Historical Anthology. Peter H. Lee, comp. and trans.

Poems in Persons: An Introduction to the Psychoanalysis of Literature. Norman N. Holland.

The Poetic Art of Robert Lowell. Marjorie G. Perloff.

Poetry and Crisis in the Age of Chaucer. Charles Muscatine.

The Poetry of Black America: Anthology of the 20th Century. Arnold Adoff, ed.

The Poetry of Grace: Reformation Themes and Structures in English Seventeenth-Century Poetry. William H. Halewood.

The Poetry of the Negro, 1746-1970. Langston Hughes and Arna Bontemps, eds.

Poland Since 1956. Tadeusz N. Cieplak.

Poland, the Land of Copernicus. Bogdan Suchodolski.

Poland--West Germany: The Premises and Process of Normalizing Relations. Janusz Rachocki, ed.

The Polar Rosses: John and James Clark Ross and Their Explorations. Ernest S. Dodge.

Policy and Direction: The First Year. Vol. 3: United States Army in the Korean War. James F. Schnabel.

Policy and Police: The Enforcement of the Reformation in the Age of Thomas Cromwell. G. R. Elton.

Policy by Other Means: Essays in honour of C. P. Stacey. Michael Cross and Robert Bothwell, eds.

Polish Agriculture: Characteristics, Types and Regions. Jerzy Kostrowicki and Roman Szczesny.

Polish Politics in Transition: The Camp of National Unity and the Struggle for Power, 1935-1939. Edward D. Wynot, Jr.

Politica Internacional de Isabel la Católica (1494-6). L. Suarez Fernandez.

The Political and Social Ideas of Jules Verne. Jean Chesneaux.

Political Change and Continuity, 1760-1885: A Buckinghamshire Study. Richard W. Davis.

The Political Dilemma of Popular Education: An African Case. David B. Abernathy.

The Political Economy of Colonialism in Ghana: A Collection of Documents and Statistics, 1900-1960. G. B. Kay, ed.

The Political Economy of Urban Poverty. Charles Sackrey.

The Political Elite and the People: A Study of Politics in Occidental Mindoro. Remigio E. Agpalo.

Political Institutions in Traditional China: Major Issues. James T. C. Liu, ed.

Political Justice in a Republic: James Fenimore Cooper's America. John P. McWilliams, Jr.

Political Organizations. James Q. Wilson.

Political Parties Before the Constitution. Jackson Turner Main.

Political Parties in India. Horst Hartmann.

Political Parties in Revolutionary Massachusetts. Stephen E. Patterson.

Political Prints in the Age of Hogarth: A Study of the Ideographic Representation of Politics. Herbert M. Atherton.

The Political Reaction of the 1880s and Russian Journalism. B. P. Baluev.

Political Reform in Wisconsin: A Historical Review of the Subjects of Primary Election, Taxation, and Railway Regulation. Emanuel L. Philipp.

The Political Status of the Negro in the Age of FDR. Ralph J. Bunche.

The Political Thought of William of Ockham: Personal and Institutional Principles. Arthur Stephen McGrade.

The Political Transformation of the Brazilian Catholic Church. Thomas C. Bruneau.

Politics and Culture in Medieval Spain and Italy. Helene Wieruszowski.

Politics and the Public Conscience: Slave Emancipation and the Abolition Movement in Britain. Edith F. Hurwitz.

Politics in Arkansas: The Constitutional Experience. Calvin R.

Ledbetter, et al.
Politics and Government. T. H.
Stevenson.
Politics and Nationalist Awakening in
South India, 1852-1891. R.
Suntharalingam.
Politics and Planners/Economic De-
velopment Policy in Central Amer-
ica. Gary W. Wynia.
Politics and Power in Cambodia:
The Sihanouk Years. Milton Os-
borne.
Politics and Punishment: The His-
tory of the Louisiana State Penal
System. Mark T. Carleton.
Politics and Society in De Gaulle's
Republic. Philip M. Williams
and Martin Harrison.
Politics and the Labour Movement in
Chile. Alan Angell.
Politics in Ghana, 1946-1960. Austin
Dennis.
Politics in Independent Poland: The
Crisis of Constitutional Govern-
ment. Antony Polonsky.
Politics in Sri Lanka, 1947-1973.
A. Jeyaratnam Wilson.
Politics in War: The Bases of Po-
litical Community in South Viet-
nam. Allan E. Goodman.
The Politics of a Literary Man:
William Gilmore Simms. Jon L.
Wakelyn.
The Politics of Chinese Communism:
Kiangsi under the Soviets. Ilpyong
J. Kim.
The Politics of Command: Factions
and Ideas in Confederate Strategy.
Thomas Lawrence Connelly and
Archer Jones.
The Politics of Continuity: Maryland
Political Parties from 1858 to
1870. Jean H. Baker.
The Politics of Depression: Political
Behavior in the Northeast, 1893-
1896. Samuel T. McSeveney.
The Politics of Federal Judicial Ad-
ministration. Peter Graham Fish.
The Politics of German Protestantism:
The Rise of the Protestant Church
Elite in Prussia, 1815-1848.
Robert M. Bigler.
The Politics of History. Howard
Zinn.
The Politics of Inertia: The Elec-
tion of 1876 and the End of Re-
construction. Keith Ian Polakoff.
The Politics of Jacksonian Finance.

John M. McFaul.
The Politics of Labor Legislation
in Japan. Ehud Harari.
Politics of Land: Ralph Nader's
Study Group Report on Land Use
of California. Robert C. Fell-
meth, et al.
The Politics of Massive Resistance.
Francis M. Wilhoit.
The Politics of Normalcy: Govern-
mental Theory and Practice in
the Harding-Coolidge Era.
Robert K. Murray.
The Politics of Reform 1884. An-
drew Jones.
The Politics of the Ocean. Edward
Wenk, Jr.
The Politics of Urban Planning: The
East St. Louis Experience. Den-
nis R. Judd and Robert E. Men-
delson.
Politics, Religion and the English
Civil War. Brian Manning, ed.
Die Politik des schwedischen Reich-
kanzlers Axel Oxenstierna gegen-
uber Kaiser und Reich. Sigmund
Goetze.
Politiques coloniales au Maghreb.
Charles-Robert Ageron.
Die polnisch-deutschen Beziehungen,
1933-1938. Marian Wojciechowski.
Polybius. F. W. Walbank.
Pont-de-Montvert: Social Structure
and Politics in a French Village,
1700-1914. Patrice L.-R. Higon-
net.
Popery and Politics in England,
1660-1688. John Miller.
The Pope's Jews. Sam Waagenaar.
Popular Archaeology Magazine
(monthly). Jack Hranicky, ed.
Popular Culture of East Africa:
Oral Literature. Taban lo Li-
yong, ed.
The Popular Front in France, 1834-
1938. E. A. Kravchenko.
Popular Recreations in English So-
ciety, 1700-1850. Robert W.
Malcolmson.
Population and Social Change.
D. V. Glass and Roger Revelle,
eds.
Population History of New York
City. Ira Rosenwaike.
The Population of Latin America:
A History. Nicolás Sánchez-
Albornoz.
Population Policies and Growth in

Latin America. David Chaplin, ed.
Population Research in Thailand, a
Review and Bibliography.
The Populist Context: Rural versus
Urban Power on a Great Plains
Frontier. Stanley B. Parsons.
Portrait of a Decision: The Council
of Four and the Treaty of Ver-
sailles. Howard Elcock.
Portrait of America. Stephen B.
Oates, ed.
Portrait of the Past: A Photographic
Journey Through Wisconsin. How-
ard Mead, Jill Dean, and Susan
Smith.
Portraits of Thai Politics. Jayanta
Kumar Ray.
Die Porträts des Septimius Severus.
Dirk Soechting.
Porträttypen einer clandischen
Kaiserin. Karin Polaschek.
Portugal: A Short History. H. V.
Livermore.
Portugal e o Future. Antonio de
Spinolo.
La Portugal et le Congo au XIXe
Siècle. Françoise Latour de
Veiga Pinto.
Portuguese Africa: A Handbook.
David M. Abshire and Michael
A. Samuels, eds.
Portuguese Africa and the West. Wil-
liam Minter.
The Portuguese in Ceylon, 1617-1638.
Chandra Richard de Silva.
Portuguese Plain Architecture Be-
tween Spices and Diamonds, 1521-
1705. George Kubler.
Portuguese Settlement on the Zambesi:
Exploration, Land Tenure, and
Colonial Rule in East Africa.
M. D. D. Newitt.
The Post-Industrial Prophets: Inter-
pretations of Technology. William
Kuhns.
Pourade, Richard F., ed. see
Lindsay, Diana E.
Power and Diplomacy in Northern
Nigeria 1804-1906: The Sokoto
Caliphate and Its Enemies. R. A.
Adeleye.
Power and Politics in Africa. Henry
L. Bretton.
Power and Sexuality: The Emergence
of Canon Law at the Synod of
Elvira. Samuel Laeuchli.
Power Over People. Louise B.
Young.

A Practical Treatise on Dyeing of
Woolen, Cotton, and Skein Silk
with the Manufacture of Broad-
cloth and Cassimere, Including
the Most Improved Methods in
the West of England. William
Partridge.
The Preachers. James Morris.
Pre-Archival Records Control Opera-
tion Manual.
Pre-Christian Gnosticism: A Sur-
vey of the Proposed Evidences.
Edwin M. Yamauchi.
Precious Women: A Feminist
Phenomenon in the Age of Louis
XIV. Dorothy Anne Liot Backer.
Pre-Columbian Cities. Jorge E.
Hardoy.
The Prefatory Epistles of Jacques
Lefèvre d'Etaples and Related
Texts. Eugene F. Rice, Jr.,
ed.
Les préfets du Second Empire.
Bernard Le Clèrc and Vincent
Wright.
Prehistoric Greece and Cyprus: An
Archaeological Handbook. Hans-
Günter Buchholz and Vassos
Karageorghis.
The Prehistory of the Tehuacan Val-
ley. Volume Three: Ceramics.
Richard S. MacNeish, Frederick
A. Peterson, and Kent V. Flan-
nery.
The Prehistory of the Tehuacan Val-
ley. Volume Four: Chronology
and Irrigation. Richard S. Mac-
Neish, Frederick Johnson, Karl
A. Wittfogel, Richard B. Wood-
bury, James A. Neely, Gorgonio
Gil Huerta, and Eva Hunt.
Prelude to Modern Europe: 1815-
1914. Sir Llewellyn Woodward.
Prelude to the Enlightenment. G.
Atkinson and A. C. Keller.
Presbyterians in the South, Volume
2: 1861-1890. Volume 3: 1890-
1972. Ernest Trice Thompson.
Preservation: Metropolitan Preser-
vation Plan, Falls of Ohio Metro-
politan Council of Governments.
Walter E. Langsam.
The Presidency of George Washing-
ton. Forrest McDonald.
The Presidency of Rutherford B.
Hayes. Kenneth E. Davison.
The Presidency of William Howard
Taft. Paolo E. Coletta.

The Presidency on Trial: Robert Kennedy's 1968 Campaign and Afterwards. Stuart Gerry Brown.

The President as Commander in Chief. Warren H. Hassler.

President Kennedy and Britain. David Nunnerley.

Presidential Impeachment: An American Dilemma. Walter Erlich, ed.

The President's Wife: Mary Todd Lincoln: A Biography. Ishbel Ross.

Preussentum und Pietismus: Der Pietismus in Brandenburg-Preussen als religiös-soziale Reformbewegung. Carl Hinrichs.

The Price of Independence: A Realistic View of the American Revolution. Broadus Mitchell.

The Price of Liberty: Personality and Politics in Colonial Nigeria. Kenneth W. J. Post and George D. Jenkins.

The Price of Loyalty: Tory Writings from the Revolutionary Era. Catherine S. Crary, ed.

The Price of Perfect Justice: The Adverse Consequences of the Current Legal Doctrine of the American Courtroom. Macklin Fleming.

The Price of Power. Council on Economic Priorities.

The Price of Vision: The Diary of Henry A. Wallace, 1942-1946. John Morton Blum, ed.

Pride's Purge: Politics in the Puritan Revolution. David Underdown.

Priests and Politicians: Protestant and Catholic Missions in Orthodox Ethiopia, 1830-1868. Donald Crummey.

The Priests of the Roman Republic: A Study of Interactions Between Priesthoods and Magistracies. G. J. Szemler.

The Prime Ministers' Papers: W. E. Gladstone, I. Autobiographical Memoranda. John Brooke and Mary Sorensen, eds.

Los Primeros Pobladores: Hispanic Americans of the Ute Frontier. Frances Leon Swadesh.

Primers for Prudery: Sexual Advice to Victorian America. Ronald Walters.

Prince of the Renaissance: The Golden Life of François I. Desmond Seward.

Principles of Architectural History: The Four Phases of Architectural Style, 1420-1900. Paul Frankl.

Printing Presses: History and Development from the Fifteenth Century to Modern Times. James Moran.

Prisoner of War. Clyde Fillmore.

Private Foreign Investment and the Developing World. Peter Ady, ed.

Private Investment in India 1900-1939. Amiya Kumar Bagchi.

Private Liberal Arts Colleges in Minnesota: Their History and Contributions. Merrill E. Jarchow.

Private Pressure on Public Law: The Legal Career of Justice Thurgood Marshall. Randall W. Bland.

Die Privilegierung des Zisterzienserordens im Rahmen der allgemeinen Schutzund Exemtionsgeschichte vom Anfang bis zur Bulle "Parvus Fons" (1265).... Friedrich Pfurtscheller.

The Problem of Miracle in Primitive Christianity. Anton Fridrichsen.

Problems in Latin American History: The Modern Period. Joseph S. Tulchin, ed.

Problems in the History of Feudal Russia: Collected Articles for the 60th Birthday of Prof. V. V. Mavrodin. S. L. Peshtich, et al. eds.

Problems in the History of International Relations. N. E. Nosov, et al., eds.

The Pro-Boers: The Anatomy of an Antiwar Movement. Stephen Koss, ed.

Proceedings of the Gulf Coast History and Humanities Conference, Volume IV, Gulf Coast Politics in the Twentieth Century. Ted Carageorge and Thomas J. Gilliam, eds.

The Proceedings of the Third International Congress of Medieval Canon Law, Strasbourg, 3-6 September 1968. Stephan Kuttner, ed.

Des produits et des hommes: Essais historiques latino-américains XVIe-XXe siècles. Frédéric

Mauro.

Profiles from the Susquehanna Valley. Paul B. Beers.

Progress and Pragmatism: James, Dewey, Beard, and the American Idea of Progress. David W. Marcell.

Progress in Historical Geography. Alan R. H. Baker, ed.

The Progressive Era. Lewis L. Gould, ed.

Progressives and Prohibitionists: Texas Democrats in the Wilson Era. Lewis L. Gould.

The Proletariat at the Head of the Liberation Movement in Russia (1895-1917). P. I. Kabanov, et al.

Prologue to Liberation. Rodney P. Carlisle.

The Prophet Harris. Gordon M. Haliburton.

Prophet Without Honor: Glen H. Taylor and the Fight for American Liberalism. F. Ross Peterson.

Prophetisches Sacerdium und heilgeschichtliches Regnum im Dialog 1073-1077. Christian Schneider.

Prophets and Patrons: The French University and the Emergence of the Social Sciences. Terry Nichols Clark.

Prosecuting Crime in the Renaissance: England, Germany, France. John H. Langbein.

Protest and Resistance in Angola and Brazil. Ronald H. Chilcote, ed.

Protestant-Catholic Relations in America: World War I through Vatican II. Lerond Curry.

Protestant Thought in the Nineteenth Century. Volume 1: 1799-1870. Claude Welch.

Proteus: His Lies, His Truth. Robert M. Adams.

Provincial Magistrates and Revolutionary Politics in France, 1789-1795. Philip Dawson.

Provincial Politics and Indian Nationalism: Bombay and the Indian National Congress, 1880-1915. Gordon Johnson.

The Provincials: A Personal History of the Jews in the South. Eli N. Evans.

The Provisional Government. V. D. Nabokov.

The Prussian Bureaucracy in Crisis 1840-1860. John R. Gillis.

The Prussian Welfare State Before 1740. Reinhold August Dorwart.

Psychological Themes in the Golden Epistle of William of Saint-Thierry to the Carthusians of Mont-Dieu. Louis M. Savary.

Ptolemaic Alexandria. P. M. Fraser.

The Public Career of Cully A. Cobb: A Study in Agricultural Leadership. Roy V. Scott and J. G. Shoalmire.

Public Diplomacy and Political Change--Four Case Studies: Okinawa, Peru, Czechoslovakia, Guinea. Gregory Henderson, ed.

Public Health and the State: Changing Views in Massachusetts, 1842-1936. Barbara Gutmann Rosenkrantz.

The Public Lands of Texas, 1519-1970. Thomas Lloyd Miller.

The Public Life of Eugene Semple: Promoter and Politician of the Pacific Northwest. Alan Hynding.

Public Papers of the Secretaries-General of the United Nations. Vol. III. Dag Hammarskjöld, 1956-1957. Andrew W. Cordier and Wilder Foote, eds.

Public Policy and Urbanization in the Dominican Republic and Costa Rica. Gustavo A. Antonini, ed.

Publicans and Sinners: Private Enterprise in the Service of the Roman Republic. E. Badian.

The Puerto Rican Experience: A Sociological Sourcebook. Francesco Cordasco and Eugene Bucchioni.

The Puerto Ricans' Spirit: Their History, Life, and Culture. María Teresa Babín.

Puerto Rico: A Socio-Historic Interpretation. Manuel Maldonado-Denis.

The Punjab Tradition: Influence and Authority in Nineteenth-Century India. P. H. M. Dungen.

Pura Mutuzuma: Archaeological Work on Miyako Island, Ryukyus. Erika Kaneko and Herbert Melichar.

The Purefoy Letters, 1735-1753. L. G. Mitchell, ed.

The Puritan Experience. Owen C.

Watkins.
Puritanism in America: New Culture
in a New World. Larzer Ziff.
Puritanism in Northwest England:
A Regional Study of the Diocese
of Chester to 1642. R. C. Rich-
ardson.
Puritanism in Tudor England. H. C.
Porter, ed.
Purity Crusade: Sexual Morality
and Social Control, 1868-1900.
David J. Pivar.
The Pursuit of Holiness in Late
Medieval and Renaissance Religion:
Papers from the University of
Michigan Conference. Charles
Trinkaus, ed.

-Q-

The Quaker Family in Colonial Amer-
ica: A Portrait of the Society of
Friends. J. William Frost.
Quantification in History. W. O.
Aydelotte.
Quarry and Kiln: The Story of
Maine's Lime Industry. Roger L.
Grindle.
The Quebec Act: Protest and Policy.
Hilda Neatby.
Québec sous la loi des mesures de
guerre 1918. Jean Provencher.
Queen Anne. David Green.
Queen Katherine Parr. Anthony
Martienssen.
The Queen v. Louis Riel: Canada's
Greatest Trial.
Quest and Response: Minority Rights
and the Truman Administration.
Donald R. McCoy and Richard T.
Ruetten.
The Quest for National Efficiency,
1899-1914. G. R. Searle.
The Question of Palestine, 1914-1918:
British-Jewish-Arab Relations.
Isaiah Friedman.
The Question of Small-Farmer Or-
ganizations and the Establishment
of Small-Farmers' Unions in Fin-
land: A Study of the Transition
in Small-Farming Policy in Agri-
culture up to the Early 1930's.
Arvo Santonen.
Quezon: Paladin of Philippine Free-
dom. Carlos Quirino.

Quichean Civilization: The Ethnohistoric, Ethnographic, and
Archaeological Sources. Robert
Carmack.
The Quiet Revolution: Grass Roots
of Today's Wilderness Preservation Movement. Donald N. Baldwin.
Quotations from Premier Chou En-
lai.

-R-

RCHM (England): An Inventory of
the Historical Monuments in the
City of York, vol. 2: The De-
fences.
R. H. Tawney and His Times:
Socialism as Fellowship. Ross
Terrill.
R. H. Tawney's Commonplace
Book. J. M. Winter and D. M.
Joslin, eds.
Race, Colonialism and the City.
John Rex.
Race to Pearl Harbor: The Failure
of the Second London Naval Con-
ference and the Onset of World
War II. Stephen E. Pelz.
Radical Abolitionism: Anarchy and
the Government of God in Anti-
slavery Thought. Lewis Perry.
The Radical Brethren: Anabaptism
and the English Reformation to
1558. Irvin Buckwalter Horst.
Radical Paradoxes: Dilemmas of
the American Left, 1945-1970.
Peter Clecak.
Radical Politics in West Bengal.
Marcus F. Franda.
The Radical Republicans and Reform
in New York During Reconstruc-
tion. James C. Mohr.
Radical Visions and American
Dreams: Culture and Social
Thought in the Depression Years.
Richard H. Pells.
Radicalism in Mediterranean France
Its Rise and Decline, 1848-1914.
Leo A. Loubère.
Radio, Television and American
Politics. Edward W. Chester.
The Railway Interest. Geoffrey
Alderman.
Railway Sabotage in Denmark Durin

the Second World War: A Study in Military History. Aage Trommer.

Railways in the Formative Years. O. S. Nock.

A Rain of Darts: The Mexica Aztecs. Burr Cartwright Brundage.

Rajahs and Rebels: The Ibans of Sarawak under Brooke Rule, 1841-1941. Robert Pringle.

Ralph Fitch, Elizabethan in the Indies. Michael Edwardes.

Ralph H. Lutz and the Hoover Institution. Charles B. Burdick.

Ralph McGill, Reporter. Harold H. Martin.

Ralph Waldo Emerson: Portrait of a Balanced Soul. Edward Wagenknecht.

Ramon Lull and Lullism in Fourteenth-Century France. J. N. Hillgarth.

Ramsay MacDonald's Political Writings. Bernard Barker, ed.

Ranch on the Laramie: A Memoir of an American Boyhood. Ted Olson.

Rangeland Management for Livestock Production. Hershel M. Bell.

Rank and File: Personal Histories of Working Class Organizers. Alice and Staughton Lynd, eds.

The Reaction Against Emigration: The Emigration Question in Swedish Discussion and Politics 1901-1904. Ann-Sofie Kälvemark.

Reactions to the French Revolution. Richard Cobb.

Readings in Modern Chinese History. Immanuel C. Y. Hsu, ed.

Rebel! A Biography of Tom Paine. Samuel Edwards.

Rebellion and Its Enemies in Late Imperial China: Militarization and Social Structure, 1796-1864. Philip A. Kuhn.

Rebellion in the University. Seymour Martin Lipset.

The Rebirth of Italy 1943-50. S. J. Woolf, ed.

The Rebirth of Liberty: The Founding of the American Republic, 1760-1800. Clarence B. Carson.

Recherches sur les Phéniciens à Chypre. Olivier Masson and Maurice Sznycer.

Recherches sur Quelques Séries d'Urnes de Volterra à Representa-tions Mythologiques. Françoise-Hélene Pairault.

Recollections of a Long Life. Elijah L. Shettles.

Reconstruction: The Great Experiment. Allen W. Trelease.

Reconstruction in Indian Territory: A Story of Avarice, Discrimination, and Opportunism. M. Thomas Bailey.

Records of the Columbia Historical Society of Washington, D. C., 1871-1972. Francis Coleman Rosenberger, ed.

The Recovery of the Sacred. James Hitchcock.

Le Recueil des inscriptions, 1558. Estienne Jodelle.

The Red Bluecoats: The Indian Scouts. Fairfax Downey and J. N. Jacobsen.

Red Capitalism: An Analysis of the Navajo Economy. Kent Gilbreath.

Red Rising in Bavaria. Richard Grunberger.

Red, White, and Black: The Peoples of Early America. Gary B. Nash.

Reform and Renewal: Thomas Cromwell and the Common Weal. G. R. Elton.

Reform and Revolution in Asia. G. F. Hudson, ed.

Reform and Revolution in Mainz 1743-1803. T. C. W. Blanning.

Reform at Osawatomie State Hospital: Treatment of the Mentally Ill, 1866-1970. Lowell Gish.

The Reform Impulse, 1825-1850. Walter Hugins.

Reform, War, and Reaction, 1912-1932. Stanley Coben, ed.

La Reforma Liberal en Guatemala: Vida Politica y Orden Constitucional. Jorge Mario García Laguardia.

The Reformation of Images: Destruction of Art in England, 1535-1660. John Phillips.

The Reformers and the American Indian. Robert Winston Mardock.

Regeneration Through Violence: The Mythology of the American Frontier, 1600-1860. Richard Slotkin.

Regenkult--Aflagen in Boğazköy--Hattuša. Peter Neve.

Regicide and Revolution: Speeches at the Trial of Louis XVI. Michael Walzer.

La régime modernisateur de Brésil, 1964-1972. Georges-André Fiechter.

Régimes matrimoniaux et mutations sociales: Les époux bordelais, 1450-1550. Jacques Lafon.

Regional Development Experiences and Prospects in Eastern Europe. Kosta Mihailovic.

Regional Integration in Central America. Isaac C. Orantes.

Regions of the United States. John Fraser Hart, ed.

The Register of St. Philip's Church, Charleston, S. C., 1810-1822. Elise Pinckney, ed.

The Registers of Roger Martinal, Bishop of Salisbury, 1315-1330. Vol. II (bis): the Register of Divers Letters. (Second Half). C. R. Elrington.

The Regni. Barry Cunliffe.

Reichsbund und Interim. H. Rabe.

Das Reichslagsprotokoll des kaiserlichen Kommissars Felix Hornung von Ausburger Reichstag 1555. H. Lutz and A. Kohler, eds.

The Reign of James VI and I. Alan G. R. Smith, ed.

The Reinterpretation of American History and Culture. William H. Cartwright and Richard L. Watson, Jr., eds.

Relatile agrare din tara Românească în secolul al XVIII-lea. Florin Constantiniu.

Le relazioni diplomatiche fra il governo provvisorio siciliano e la Francia (31 marzo 1848-18 aprile 1849).... Federico Curato, ed.

Le relazioni diplomatiche fra il governo provvisorio siciliano e la Gran Bretagna (14 aprile 1848-10 aprile 1849).... Federico Curato, ed.

Le relazioni diplomatiche fra la Gran Bretagna e il Regno di Sardegna. First Series, 1814-1830.... Federico Curato, ed.

Le relazioni diplomatiche fra l'Austria e il Regno di Sardegna.... Narciso Nada, ed.

The Relevance of History. Gordon Connell-Smith and Howell A. Lloyd.

Reliefs en Bronze d'Etrurie. Flemming Johansen.

Religion and Revolution. Guenter Lewy.

Religion and Society in England, 1790-1850. W. R. Ward.

Religion and the Rise of the American City: The New York City Mission Movement 1812-1870. Carroll Smith Rosenberg.

Religion and Trade in New Netherland: Dutch Origins and American Development. George L. Smith.

Religion and Witchcraft in Early American Society. Jon Butler.

The Religion of the Republic. Elwyn A. Smith, ed.

A Religious History of the American People. Sydney Ahlstrom.

The Religious Philosophy of Quakerism: The Beliefs of Fox, Barclay, and Penn as Based on the Gospel of John. Howard H. Brinton.

The Reluctant Ally: Austria's Policy in the Austro-Turkish War, 1737-1739. Karl A. Roider, Jr.

Remain to Be Seen: Historic California Houses Open to the Public. Elinor Richey.

Remarkable Providences, 1600-1760. John Demos, ed.

Remembering the Answers: Essays on the American Student Revolt. Nathan Glazer.

Reminiscences of an Active Life: The Autobiography of John Roy Lynch. John Hope Franklin, ed.

Renaissance Concepts of Man and Other Essays. Paul Oskar Kristeller.

Renaissance Drama, New Series, IV: Essays Principally on the Playhouse and Staging. S. Schoenbaum and Alan C. Dessen, ed.

Renaissance Venice. J. R. Hale, ed.

Renée Kogel. Pierre Charron.

The Renewal of American Catholicism. David J. O'Brien.

A Report of the Mohawk-Hudson Area Survey. Robert M. Vogel, ed.

Reports of the 1863 Constitutional Convention of the Territory of Nevada. Andrew J. Marsh, Samuel L. Clemens, and Amos Bowman.

Les Représentations Animales dans la Céramique Mochica. Daniele Lavallée.

The Republic and the Civil War in Spain. Raymond Carr, ed.

Republic of Texas: Poll Lists for 1846. Marion Day Mullins.

The Republican Party and Black America: From McKinley to Hoover, 1896-1933. Richard B. Sherman.

La République au village. Maurice Agulhon.

The Rescue of Emin Pasha. Roger Jones.

Research and Theory in Current Archaeology. Charles L. Redman, ed.

The Researcher's Guide to American Genealogy. Val D. Greenwood.

Resistance at Christiana: The Fugitive Slave Rebellion, Christiana, Pennsylvania, September 11, 1851; A Documentary Account. Jonathan Katz.

Respiration and the Lavoisier Tradition: Theory and Modification, 1777-1850. Charles A. Culotta.

Restatement of African Law: The Law of Marriage and Divorce: Kenya (Vol I). Eugene Cotran.

La Restaurazione Cattolica in Inghilterra sotto Maria Tudor. Carlo De Frede.

The Restoration Movement: Essays in Mormon History. F. Mark McKiernan, Alma R. Blair, and Paul M. Edwards, eds.

Reunion Without Compromise: The South and Reconstruction: 1865-1868. Michael Perman.

Revolt in Bussa: A Study of British "Native Administration" in Nigerian Bargu, 1902-1935. Michael Crowder.

Revolt in Japan: The Young Officers and the February 26, 1936 Incident. Ben-Ami Shillony.

Revolución campesina, 1950-1954. Russell W. Ramsey.

La Revolución de 1868: Historia, literatura. Clara Lida and Iris M. Zavala, eds.

De la révolution à l'annexion: L'Autrich de 1918 à 1938. Félix Kreissler.

Revolution Administered: Agrarianism and Communism in Bulgaria. Nissan Oren.

Revolution and Politics in Russia: Essays in Memory of B. I. Nicolaevsky. Alexander and Janet Rabinowitch, eds.

Revolution and Romanticism. Howard Mumford Jones.

The Revolution and the Civil War in Spain. Pierre Broué and Emile Témine.

Revolution and Tradition in People's Poland. Joseph R. Fiszman.

Revolution at Queretaro: The Mexican Constitutional Convention of 1916-1917. E. V. Niemeyer, Jr.

Revolution in Central Europe, 1918-1919. F. L. Carsten.

The Revolution in the New York Party Systems, 1840-1860. Mark L. Berger.

The Revolution of 1688 in England. J. R. Jones.

La révolution piémontaise de 1821 ed altri scritti. Emanuele Pes di Villamarina.

La Révolution Piémontaise de 1821 ed altri scritti. Narciso Nada, ed.

Revolutionaries. Contemporary Essays. E. J. Hobsbawm.

Revolutionaries, Traditionalists, and Dictators in Latin America. Harold Eugene Davis, et al.

Revolutionary Justice: The Social and Political Theory of P. J. Proudhon. Robert L. Hoffman.

Revolutionary Politics in the Long Parliament. John R. MacCormack.

Revolutionary Virginia: The Road to Independence. Volume I: Forming Thunderclouds and the First Convention, 1763-1774: A Documentary Record. William J. Van Schreeven and Robert L. Scribner, comp. and ed.

Revolutionary War Journals of Henry Dearborn, 1775-1783. Lloyd A. Brown, ed.

Ribelli, Libertini e Ortodossi Nella Storiografia Barocca. Sergio Bertelli.

Rich and Poor in Renaissance Venice. Brian Pullan.

The Rich, the Well-Born, and the Powerful: Elites and Upper Classes in History. Frederic Cople Jaher, ed.

Richard II and the English Nobility.

Anthony J. Tucker.

Richard Irvine Manning and the Progressive Movement in South Carolina. Robert Milton Burts.

Richard Lion Heart. James A. Brundage.

Richard Olney: Evolution of a Statesman. Gerald G. Eggert.

Richard Simpson 1820-1876: A Study in XIXth-Century English Liberal Catholicism. Damian McElrath.

Richard the Shaker. Hazel Spencer Phillips.

Richelieu and Reason of State. William F. Church.

Riches, Class, and Power Before the Civil War. Edward Pessen.

The Riddle of History: The Great Speculators from Vico to Freud. Bruce Mazlish.

Riddles in History. Cyrus H. Gordon.

The Right to Say No. Judith Todd.

Righteous Conquest. Woodrow Wilson and the Evolution of the New Diplomacy. Sidney Bell.

The Rise and Decline of Fidel Castro: An Essay in Contemporary History. Maurice Halperin.

The Rise and Fall of the Habsburg Monarchy. Victor-L. Tapié.

The Rise and Fall of the League of Nations. George Scott.

The Rise and Fall of the People's Century: Henry A. Wallace and American Liberalism 1941-1948. Norman D. Markowitz.

The Rise of a Central Authority for English Education. A. S. Bishop.

The Rise of African Nationalism in South Africa: The African National Congress, 1912-1952. Peter Walshe.

The Rise of an American Architecture. Henry-Russell Hitchcock, et al.

The Rise of Big Business, 1860-1910. Glenn Porter.

The Rise of Free Trade Imperialism: Classical Political Economy and the Empire of Free Trade and Imperialism, 1750-1850. Bernard Semmel.

The Rise of Labor in Japan: The Yuaikai, 1912-19. Stephen S. Large.

The Rise of Modern China. Immanuel C. Y. Hsu.

The Rise of Sports in New Orleans.

Dale A. Somers.

The Rise of the Atlantic Economies. Ralph Davis.

The Rise of the Ghetto. John H. Bracey, Jr., August Meier and Elliott Rudwick, eds.

The Rise of the Labor Movement in Ceylon. Visakha Kumari Jayawardena.

The Rise of the Luftwaffe: Forging the Secret German Air Weapon, 1918-1940. Herbert Malloy Mason, Jr.

The Rise of the Monophysite Movement. W. H. C. Frend.

The Rise of the Unmeltable Ethnics. Michael Novak.

The Rising Glory of America, 1760-1820. Gordon S. Wood, ed.

The Risorgimento: Thought and Action. Luigi Salvatorelli.

The Road to Secession: A New Perspective on the Old South. William L. Barney.

The Road to Wounded Knee. Robert Burnette and John Koster.

The Road to Yalta: Soviet Foreign Relations, 1941-1945. Louis Fischer.

The Roads to Russia: United States Lend-Lease to the Soviet Union. Robert Huhn Jones.

Robert Baillie and the Second Scots Reformation. F. N. McCoy.

Robert Dinwiddie: Servant of the Crown. John Richard Alden.

Robert E. Lee. Peter Earle.

Robert Frost. Elaine Barry.

Robert Frost on Writing. Elaine Barry.

Robert Owen's American Legacy. Donald E. Pitzer, ed.

Robespierre. John Laurence Carr.

Rochester on the Genesee: The Growth of a City. Blake McKelvey.

The Rocky Mountain Bench: Territorial Supreme Courts of Colorado, Montana, and Wyoming, 1861-1890. John D. W. Guice.

Rocky Mountain Mining Camps: The Urban Frontier. Duane A. Smith.

Roger of Salisbury, Viceroy of England. Edward J. Kealey.

Le Role des Experts à la Conference de la Paix de 1919. Dimitri Kitskikis.

The Role of the Yankee in the Old

South. Fletcher M. Green.
Die Rolle des Hofes im Absolutismus.
Jürgen Freiherr von Kruedener.
Roma nel Settecento. Vittorio E.
Giuntella.
Roman and Islamic Water-lifting
Wheels. Thorkild Schioler.
Roman Art: From the Republic to
Constantine. Richard Brilliant.
Roman Century, 1870-1970. G. Bol-
ton.
Roman Construction in Italy from
Nerva through the Antonines.
Marion Elizabeth Blake.
Roman France. Paul Mackendrick.
Roman Glass in Limburg. C. Isings.
Roman Myths. Michael Grant.
Roman Social Relations: 50 B. C.
to A. D. 284. Ramsay MacMullen.
The Roman Thin-Walled Pottery from
Cosa (1948-1954). Maria Teresa
Marabini Moevs.
Romanitatea Românilor: Istoria unei
idei. Adolf Armbruster.
The Romantic Generation of Modern
Chinese Writers. Leo Ou-Fan
Lee.
Rome Before Avignon: A Social
History of Thirteenth-Century
Rome. Robert Brentano.
Rome in the High Renaissance: The
Age of Leo X. Bonner Mitchell.
Rome, Monuments of Civilization.
Filippo Coarelli.
Roosevelt and Batista: Good Neigh-
bor Diplomacy in Cuba, 1933-
1945. Irwin F. Gellman.
Roots of Maryland Democracy, 1753-
1776. David Curtis Skaggs.
The Roots of Segregation: Native
Policy in Natal, 1845-1910. David
Welsh.
Roots of the Republic: A New Per-
spective on Early American Con-
stitutionalism. George Dargo.
Roots of War. Richard J. Barnet.
The Rope of Moka: Big-Men and
Ceremonial Exchange in Mount
Hagen, New Guinea. Andrew
Strathern.
The Rosicrucian Enlightenment.
Frances A. Yates.
The Rouen Campaign, 1590-1592:
Politics, Warfare and the Early
Modern State. Howell A. Lloyd.
Route Across the Rocky Mountains.
Overton Johnson and William H.
Winter.

Royal Commission on Book Publish-
ing: Background Papers.
The Royal Demesne in English His-
tory. B. P. Wolffe.
The Royal Navy in America, 1760-
1775. A Study of Enforcement of
British Colonial Policy in the Era
of the American Revolution. Neil
R. Stout.
Le royaume du Waalo. Le Senegal
avant le conquête. Boubacar
Barry.
Ruanda and Burundi. Rene Le-
marchand.
Rulers of Empire: The French
Colonial Service in Africa.
William B. Cohen.
The Rump Parliament, 1648-1653.
Blair Worden.
The Rural and Urban Population of
Thailand: Comparative Profiles.
Visid. Prachuabmoh, et al.
Rural Credit and the Cooperative
Movement in the Bombay Presi-
dency, 1875-1930. I. J. Cata-
nach.
Rural Hausa: A Village and a
Setting. Polly Hill.
Rural Politics in Nasser's Egypt:
A Quest for Legitimacy. James
B. Mayfield.
Rural Santo Domingo: Settled, Un-
settled, and Resettled. Marlin
D. Clausner.
Rural Settlement and Farming in
Germany. Alan Mayhew.
The Rush to be Rich. Geoffrey
Serle.
Russia and Asia: Essays on the
Influence of Russia on the Asian
Peoples. Wayne S. Vucinich, ed.
Russia and China: Their Diplomat-
ic Relations to 1728. Mark Man-
call.
Russia and the Balkan Question: On
the History of Russian-Balkan
Political Relations in the First
Third of the 19th Century. I. S.
Dostian.
Russia and the Kazakh Khanates in
the 16th to 18th Centuries (Kaza-
khstan and the System of Foreign
Politics of the Russian Empire).
V. I. Basin.
Russia Enters the Twentieth Cen-
tury, 1894-1917. Erwin Ober-
länder, et al., eds.
Russia on the Threshold of the Age:

Essays on the Political History of Russia in the First Third of the 16th Century. A. A. Zimin.

Russia Under Western Eyes, 1517-1825. Anthony Cross, ed.

The Russian and Polish Markets in International Trade, 1500-1650. Artur Attman.

The Russian Army and Navy in the 19th Century: Russia's Military-Economic Potential. D. L. Beskrovnyi.

The Russian Constitutional Experiment: Government and Duma, 1907-1914. Geoffrey A. Hosking.

Russian-German Diplomatic Relations, 1905-1911 (From the Peace of Portsmouth to the Potsdam Agreement). I. I. Astaf'ev.

Russian Historiography of the 18th Century. S. L. Peshtich.

Russian Imperialism From Ivan the Great to the Revolution. Taras Hunczak, ed.

Russian Journalism and Politics, 1861-1881: The Career of Aleksei S. Suvorin. Effie Ambler.

Russian Police Trade Unionism: Experiment or Provocation? Dimitry Pospielovsky.

Russian Prerevolutionary Newspapers 1702-1917: A Brief Essay. B. I. Esin.

Russian Progressive Thought of the 19th Century: From Geographic Determinism to Historical Materialism. M. G. Fedorov.

Russian Rebels 1600-1800. Paul Avrich.

The Russian Revolution of February 1917. Marc Ferro.

Russian Villages During the 1861 Reform: The Black-Soil Center 1861-1895. B. G. Litvak.

-S-

SALT: Implications for Arms Control in the 1970s. William R. Kintner and Robert L. Pfaltzgraff, Jr., ed.

SDS. Kirkpatrick Sale.

Sacajawea. Harold P. Howard.

The Sack of Rome, 1527. Judith Hook.

Sailors, Scientists, and Rockets: Origins of the Navy Rocket Program and of the Naval Ordnance Test Station, Inyokern. Albert B. Christman.

Saint Francis: Nature Mystic. The Derivation and Significance of the Nature Stories in the Franciscan Legend. Edward A. Armstrong.

St. Petersburg and Moscow: Tsarist and Soviet Foreign Policy, 1814-1974. Barbara Jelavich.

Le Saint Siège et la guerra mondiale, novembre 1942-décembre 1943. Pierre Blet, et al., eds.

Le Saint Siège et les victimes de la guerra, mars 1939-décembre 1940. Pierre Blet, et al., eds.

St. Thomas More: Action and Contemplation. Richard S. Sylvester, ed.

Saladin. Andrew S. Ehrenkreutz.

Salem Possessed: The Social Origins of Witchcraft. Paul Boyer and Stephen Nissenbaum.

The Salmon: Their Fight for Survival. Anthony Netboy.

The Salt River Project. Courtland L. Smith.

The Saltonstall Papers, 1607-1815 ... Vol. I: 1607-1789. Robert E. Moody.

"Salutary Neglect": Colonial Administration Under the Duke of Newcastle. James A. Henretta.

Salvage Excavations at the Fowler Site: Some Aspects of the Social Organization of the Northern Chumash. Joe Tainter.

Sam Houston's Texas. Sue Flanagan.

Samos. Band VI. Elena Walter-Karydi.

Samuel Bell Maxey: A Biography. Louise Horton.

Samuel Cooper. Daphne Foskett.

Samuel de Champlain: Father of New France. Samuel Eliot Morison.

Samuel Gompers and the Origins of the American Federation of Labor, 1848-1896. Stuart Bruce Kaufman.

Samuel Seabury 1729-1796. A Study in the High Church Tradition. Bruce E. Steiner.

Samuel Willard, 1640-1707; Preacher of Orthodoxy in an Era of Change. Seymour van Dyken.

San Francisco: A Guide to the Bay
and Its Cities. Gladys Hansen,
ed.
San Francisco, 1846-1856: From
Hamlet to City. Roger W. Lot-
chin.
San Giovenale. Vol. I. Bengt E.
Thomasson, et al.
Sanctity and Secularity: The Church
and the World. Derek Baker, ed.
The Santa Fe's Big Three: The Life
Story of a Trio of the World's
Greatest Locomotives. S. Kip
Farrington, Jr.
Santiago Vidaurri and the Southern
Confederacy. Ronnie C. Tyler.
Satan's Back Yard. Sam J. Slate.
The Saturday Night Special and Oth-
er Guns With Which Americans Won
the West.... Robert Sherrill.
The Savage Ideal: Intolerance and
Intellectual Leadership in the
South, 1890-1914. Bruce Clayton.
Savage Scene: The Life and Times
of James Kirker, Frontier King.
William Cochran McGaw.
Savannah Revisited. Mills Lane.
Sayyid Jamal ad-Din "al-Afghani."
A Political Biography. Nikki R.
Keddie.
The Scandinavians in America 986-
1970: A Chronology and Fact
Book. Howard B. Furer, comp.
and ed.
The Scandinavian Joint Expedition to
Sudanese Nubia. T. Sâve-Soder-
bergh, ed.
Scavi di Ostia VI: Edificio con opus
sectile fuori Porta Marina. Gio-
vanni Becatti.
Scenic Form in Shakespeare. Emrys
Jones.
Schiffsmodelle in alten Ägypten.
Arvid Göttlicher and Walter Wern-
er.
The Schiwetz Legacy. E. M.
Schiwetz.
Schleiermacher: Life and Thought.
Martin Redeker.
Schmuckarbeiten in Edelmetall.
Adolf Greifenhagen.
Scholars, Saints, and Sufis: Muslim
Religious Institutions in the Mid-
dle East since 1500. Nikki R.
Keddie, ed.
The Scholastic Culture of the Middle
Ages, 1000-1300. John W. Bald-
win.

School Days. 2 vols. Eric Sloane.
School of the Prophets: Yale Col-
lege, 1701-1740. Richard Warch.
Schoolbooks and Krags: The United
States Army in the Philippines,
1898-1902. John Morgan Gates.
Schuld und Schicksal bei Origens,
Gnostikern und Platonikern. Paul
Kübel.
Science and Society in the Sixteenth
and Seventeenth Centuries. Alan
G. R. Smith.
Science and Society 1600-1900.
Peter Mathias, ed.
Science in a Renaissance Society.
W. P. D. Wightman.
Science, Medicine and Society in
the Renaissance: Essays to Hon-
or Walter Pagel. 2 vols. Allen
G. Debus, ed.
Scientific Papers of Arthur Holly
Compton: X-Ray and Other
Studies. Robert S. Shankland, ed.
Scout and Ranger: Being the Per-
sonal Adventures of James Pike
of the Texas Rangers. Carl L.
Cannon, ed.
Scritti E Discorsi Extraparlamentari,
1870-1920. 2 vols. Sidney Son-
nino.
The Sculpture of Thailand. Theodore
Bowie, M. C. Subhadradis Dis-
kul, and A. B. Griswold.
The Sculptures of El Tajin. Michael
Edwin Kampen.
Sea of Glory: The Continental Navy
Fights for Independence, 1775-
1783. Nathan Miller.
The Sea People of Sulu: A Study of
Social Change in the Philippines.
H. Arlo Nimmo.
The Seacoast of Bohemia. Franklin
Walker.
The Search for a Method in Ameri-
can Studies. Cecil F. Tate.
The Search for Franklin. Leslie
H. Neatby.
Search for Meaning: The Autobi-
ography of a Nonconformist.
John U. Nef.
A Season in Hell. Michael Ed-
wardes.
A Seat at the Table. E. L. M.
Burns.
The Secession Movement in the
Middle Atlantic States. William
C. Wright.
The Secessionist Impulse: Alabama

and Mississippi in 1860. William
L. Barney.
The Second British Empire, 1783-
1965: A Short History. Mark
Naidis.
A Second Flowering, Works and Days
of the Lost Generation. Malcolm
Cowley.
The Second Mexican-Texas War,
1841-1843. Miguel A. Sanchez-
Lamego.
The Second World War and Politics
in Nigeria, 1939-1953. G. O.
Olusanya.
The Secret of Sherwood Forest: Oil
Production in England During
World War II. Guy H. and Grace
Steele Woodward.
A Secret War: Americans in China,
1944-1945. Oliver J. Caldwell.
Securing the Revolution: Ideology in
American Politics, 1789-1815.
Richard Buel, Jr.
Seduction and Betrayal: Women and
Literature. Elizabeth Hardwick.
Seeds of Extinction: Jeffersonian
Philanthropy and the American In-
dian. Bernard W. Sheehan.
Seeds of Repression: Harry S. Tru-
man and the Origins of McCarthy-
ism. Athan Theoharis.
Segregated Sabbaths: Richard Allen
and the Rise of Independent Black
Churches, 1760-1841. Carol
V. R. George.
The Segregation Factor in the Florida
Democratic Gubernatorial Primary
of 1956. Helen L. Jacobstein.
La segunda Presidencia Roca vista
por los diplomáticos norteameri-
canos. Courtney Letts de Espil.
The Seizure of Power: Fascism in
Italy, 1919-1929. Adrian Lyttel-
ton.
Selected Annotated Abstracts of St.
Mary Parish, La. Mary Eliza-
beth Sanders, comp.
Selected Letters of Horace Walpole.
W. S. Lewis, ed.
Selected Manuscript Resources in the
Washington State University Li-
brary. Staff, Washington State
University Library.
Selected Poems of John Wheelwright.
John Wheelwright.
Selected Works of Jawaharlal Nehru.
S. Gopal, ed.
Selections from the Smuts Papers.

Vols. 5-6-7. Jean Van der Poel,
ed.
Self-Consuming Artifacts: the Ex-
perience of Seventeenth-Century
Literature. Stanley E. Fish.
Self-Reliance and Social Security,
1870-1917. Hace Sorel Tishler.
The Seljuk Vezirate: A Study of
Civil Administration, 1055-1194.
Carla L. Klausner.
The Semblance of Peace: The Po-
litical Settlement After the Sec-
ond World War. Sir John Wheel-
er-Bennett and Anthony Nicholls.
The Senator from Slaughter County.
Harry M. Caudill.
The Sense of Power: Studies in the
Ideas of Canadian Imperialism,
1867-1914. Carl Berger.
Sensuous Pessimism: Italy in the
Work of Henry James. Carl
Maves.
Sentenced to Life. John P. Roche.
Sentinel of the Plains: Fort Leaven-
worth and the American West.
George Walton.
The Separation of College and State:
Columbia, Dartmouth, Harvard
and Yale. John S. Whitehead.
Sequatchie: A Story of the Southern
Cumberlands. J. Leonard Raul-
ston and James W. Livingood.
Serbia, Nikola Pasic, and Yugoslav-
ia. Alex N. Dragnich.
La Serenissima: The Last Flower-
ing of the Venetian Republic.
Alfonso Lowe.
Sermons. Volume 2. Guerric
d'Igny.
Serpent in Eden: H. L. Mencken
and the South. Fred C. Hobson,
Jr.
Seth Eastman's Mississippi: A Lost
Portfolio Recovered. John Fran-
cis McDermott.
Seth Low: The Reformer in an Ur-
ban and Industrial Age. Gerald
Kurland.
Seven French Chroniclers: Witnes-
ses to History. Paul Archam-
bault.
Seven Medieval Queens. Joseph
Dahmus.
Seven Voices: Seven Latin Ameri-
can Writers Talk to Rita Guibert.
Rita Guibert.
Seven Who Shaped Our Destiny: The
Founding Fathers as Revolution-

aries. Richard B. Morris.

Seventeenth-Century Economic Documents. Joan Thirsk and J. P. Cooper, eds.

The Seventh Hero: Thomas Carlyle and the Theory of Radical Activism. Philip Rosenberg.

The Severe Style in Greek Sculpture. Brunilde Sismondo Ridgway.

Sex and Marriage in Utopian Communities: Nineteenth-Century America. Raymond Lee Muncy.

Sex and Society in Nazi Germany. Hans Peter Bleuel.

Shaka: King of the Zulus. A Biography. Daniel Cohen.

Shaker Music: A Manifestation of American Folk Culture. Harold E. Cook.

Shakespeare: the Early Writings. John Arthos.

Shakespeare and Decorum. T. McAlindon.

Shakespeare and the Bawdy Court of Stratford. E. R. C. Brinkworth.

Shakespeare and the Energies of Drama. Michael Goldman.

Shakespearean Romance. Howard Felperin.

Shakespeare's Comedies. Ralph Berry.

Shakespeare's Hidden Life: Shakespeare at Law 1585-1595. W. Nicholas Knight.

Shakyh Ahmad Sirhindi. Yohanan Friedmann.

Shall the People Rule? A History of the Democratic Party in Nebraska, 1854-1972. James F. Pedersen and Kenneth D. Wald.

The Shambaa Kingdom: A History. Steven Feierman.

The Shape of European History. William H. McNeill.

Shapers of Baptist Thought. James E. Tull.

The Shattered Synthesis: New England Puritanism Before the Great Awakening. James W. Jones.

The Sheffield Site: An Oneota Site on the St. Croix River. Guy E. Gibbon.

The Shehus of Kukawa: A History of the Al-Kanemi Dynasty of Bornu. Louis Brenner.

Shem, Ham and Japheth: The Papers of W. O. Tuggle.... Eugene Current-Garcia, ed.

Shinto Man. Joseph J. Spae.

Shipping, Maritime Trade and the Economic Development of Colonial North America. James F. Shepherd and Gary M. Walton.

Ships of the Great Lakes. James P. Barry.

Shirley Baker and the King of Tonga. Noel Rutherford.

A Short History of Mexico. Sir Nicolas Cheetham.

A Short History of the Papacy in the Middle Ages. Walter Ullmann.

Sicily and the Greeks: Studies in the Interrelationship Between the Indigenous Populations and the Greek Colonists. Erik Sjöqvist.

The Siege of Atlanta, 1864. Samuel Carter, III.

The Sign of the Eagle: A View of Mexico--1830-1855. Richard F. Pourade.

Signers of the Declaration: Historic Places Commemorating the Signing of the Declaration of Independence. Robert G. Ferris, ed.

Silhouettes on the Shade: Images from the 50's Reexamined.

The Silver Coinage of the Phokians. Roderick T. Williams.

Silversmiths of North Carolina, 1696-1850. George Barton Cutten.

Simeon D. Fess: Educator and Politician. John L. Nethers.

Simon Forman: Sex and Society in Shakespeare's Age. A. L. Rowse.

The Simple Spirit, A Pictorial Study of the Shaker Community at Pleasant Hill, Kentucky. Samuel W. and James C. Thomas.

Los Sindicatos en América Latina. Boris Goldenberg.

Singapore: Population in Transition. Saw Swee-Hock.

Sinners and Heretics: The Politics of Military Intervention in Latin America. Mauricio Solaún and Michael A. Quinn.

Sino-Soviet Dialogue on the Problem of War. John Yin.

Sir Harry Vane: His Life and Times (1613-1662). J. H. Adamson and H. F. Folland.

Sir Robert Morier: Envoy and Ambassador in the Age of Imperialism, 1876-1893. Agatha Ramm.

Sir Robert Peel: The Life of Sir
Robert Peel after 1830. Norman
Gash.
Sir Walter Raleigh. Robert Lacey.
Sir Walter Raleigh--The Renaissance
Man and His Roles. Stephen
Greenblatt.
Sir William Temple's Observations
Upon the United Provinces of the
Netherlands. Sir George Clark,
ed.
Sitting Bull: An Epic of the Plains.
Alexander B. Adams.
La Situación Actual de los Indígenes
en el Paraguay. Miguel Chase-
Sardi.
Six Presidents from the Empire
State. Harry J. Sievers, ed.
Sixteenth-Century Essays and Studies.
Vol. 2. Carl S. Meyer, ed.
Skeletal Analysis of 4-SLD-406.
G. L. Warren.
Sketches of a Tour to the Lakes, of
the Character and Customs of the
Chippeway Indians, and of Inci-
dents Connected with the Treaty of
Fond du Lac. Thomas L. McKen-
ney.
Skidmore's Portland. Eugene E.
Snyder.
The Slave Community: Plantation
Life in the Antebellum South.
John W. Blassingame.
Slave Life in Georgia: A Narrative
of the Life, Sufferings, and Es-
cape of John Brown, a Fugitive
Slave. F. N. Boney, ed.
Slavery and Annexation of Texas.
Frederick Merk.
Slavery and Jeffersonian Virginia.
Robert McColley.
Slavery and Muslim Society in Africa:
The Institution of Saharan and
Sudanic Africa and the Trans-
Saharan Trade. Allan G. B. and
Humphrey J. Fisher.
Slavery and Plantation Growth in
Antebellum Florida, 1821-1860.
Julia Floyd Smith.
Slavery and the Annexation of Texas.
Frederick Merk.
Slavery and the Politics of Libera-
tion, 1787-1861: A Study of
Liberated African Emigration and
British Anti-Slavery Policy. John-
son U. J. Asiegbu.
Slavery Time When I Was Chillun

Down on Marster's Plantation.
Ronald Killion and Charles Wal-
ler, eds.
The Slavs. Marija Gimbutas.
The Slavs and Russia: For the
70th Birthday of S. A. Nikitin.
I. V. Bromlei, et al., eds.
Slovenské povstanie roku 1848-49:
Dejiny a dokumenty. Volume 5.
Doplny, opravy, súhrny, mena a
veci. 2 parts. Daniel Rapant.
Small Earthquake in Chile: Al-
lende's South America. Alistair
Horne.
Small Groups and Political Rituals
in China. Martin King Whyte.
So Short a Time: a Biography of
John Reed and Louise Bryant.
Barbara S. Gelb.
So Vast So Beautiful a Land: Lou-
isiana and the Purchase. Mar-
shall Sprague.
Social Archaeology. Colin Renfrew.
Social Change in Angola. Franz-
Wilhelm Heimer, ed.
Social Change in the Soviet Union:
Russia's Path Toward an Indus-
trial Society. Boris Meissner,
ed.
Social Conflict and Educational
Change in England and France
1789-1848. Michaline Vaughan
and Margaret Scotford Archer.
The Social Content of Education,
1808-1870: A Study of the
Working Class School Reader in
England and Ireland. J. M.
Goldstrom.
Social Control in Slave Plantation
Societies: A Comparison of
St. Dominique and Cuba. Gwen-
dolyn Mildo Hall.
Social Credit: The English Origins.
John L. Finlay.
The Social Foundations of German
Unification, 1858-1871. Struggles
and Accomplishments. Theodore
S. Hamerow.
Social Groups in Polish Society.
David Laue and George Kolau-
kiewicz, eds.
The Social Harp. Daniel W. Pat-
terson and John W. Garst, eds.
Social Hierarchies: 1450 to the
Present. Roland Mousnier.
A Social History of the Disciples

of Christ. (2 vols.). David Edwin Harrell, Jr.

The Social History of the Reformation. Jonathan W. Zophy and Lawrence P. Buck, eds.

Social-Political Movements in the Ukraine After the Decembrist Uprising, 1826-1850. H. Ia. Serhienko.

The Social Problem in the Philosophy of Rousseau. John Charvet.

Socialization for Achievement: Essays on the Cultural Psychology of the Japanese. George A. De Vos.

La Societe Vietnamienne de 1882 a 1902. Nguyen van Phong.

Sociétés et compagnies de commerce en Orient et dans l'Ocean Indien. Michel Mollat, ed.

Society and Culture in America, 1830-1860. Russel Blaine Nye.

Society and Government 1760-1780: The Power Structure in Massachusetts Townships. Dirk Hoerder.

Society and Politics in Medieval Italy: The Evolution of the Civil Life, 1000-1350. J. K. Hyde.

Society in India. 2 vols. David G. Mandelbaum.

Socio-Economic Development in Dual Economies: The Example of Zambia. Udo Ernst and Heide Simonis, eds.

Sociology and Estrangement: Three Sociologists of Imperial Germany. Arthur Mitzman.

The Sociology of Literature. Diana T. Laurenson and Alan Swingewood.

The Sociology of the Professions. Philip Elliott.

The Soil and Health: A Study of Organic Agriculture. Sir Albert Howard.

The Sokolov Investigation of the Alleged Murder of the Russian Imperial Family: A Translation of Sections of Nicholas A. Sokolov's The Murder of the Imperial Family. John F. O'Conor, trans. and comm.

Soldier in the West: Letters of Theodore Talbot During His Services in California, Mexico, and Oregon, 1845-53. Robert V. Hine and Savoie Lottinville, eds.

A Soldier-Scientist in the American Southwest. Michael J. Brodhaus.

Soldiering and Surveying in East Africa, 1891-1894. J. R. L. Macdonald.

Soldiers and Civilians: The Martial Spirit in America, 1775-1865. Marcus Cunliffe.

Soldiers of Fortune: The Story of the Mamluks. Sir John Bagot Glubb.

Soldiers on the Santa Fe Trail. Leo E. Oliva.

Solitary Star: A Biography of Sam Houston. Donald Braider.

The Solution of the Crofter Problem: The Crofter Problem in Finland, 1900-1918. Viljo Rasila.

Some Versions of the Fall: The Myth of the Fall of Man in English Literature. Eric Smith.

Something Happened. Joseph Heller.

Somos Chicanos: Strangers in Our Own Land. David F. Gomez.

Songs of Independence. Irwin Silber, comp. and ed.

Songs of '76: a Folksinger's History of the Revolution. Oscar Brand.

Sonoran Strong Man: Ignacio Pesqueira and His Times. Rodolfo F. Acuña.

Sophie Dorothea. Ruth Jordan.

Source and Meaning in Spencer's Allegory: A Study of The Faerie Queene. John Erskine Hankins.

A Sourcebook for Russian History from Earliest Times to 1917. 3 vols. George Vernadsky, et al., eds.

Sources Concerning Real and Movable Property in the Netherlands in the 16th Century. Volume 1. Nobles, Peasants, Commerce and Transport. H. A. Enno Van Gelder, ed.

Sources of Yoruba History. S. O. Biobaku, ed.

South Africa: An Historical Introduction. Freda Troup.

The South African Voter: Some Aspects of Voting Behavior.... Henry Lever.

South Africa's Foreign Policy 1945-1970. James Barber.

The South and the Concurrent Majority. David M. Potter.

South Asian Archaeology: Papers from the First International Conference of South Asian Archaeolo-

gists Held in the University of
Cambridge. Norman Hammond,
ed.
The South Dakota Experience: An
Oral History Collection of Its
People. Stephen R. Ward, ed.
The South Dakota Experience: An
Oral History Collection of Its
People. Volume 2. Suzanne Julin
and Stephen R. Ward, eds.
South India: Yesterday, Today and
Tomorrow. T. Scarlett Epstein.
The South Since Reconstruction.
Thomas D. Clark, ed.
Southeast Asia: Documents of Po-
litical Development and Change.
Roger M. Smith, ed.
Southern Africa Since 1800. Donald
Denoon.
The Southern Baptist Convention and
Its People, 1607-1972. Robert
A. Baker.
The Southern Dream of a Caribbean
Empire, 1854-1861. Robert E.
May.
Southern England: An Archaeological
Guide. James Dyer.
Southern Indians in the American
Revolution. James H. O'Donnell,
III.
Southern Italy: An Archaeological
Guide. Margaret Guido.
The Southern Sudan--The Problem of
National Integration. Dunstan M.
Wai, ed.
Southern Ute Lands, 1848-1899: The
Creation of a Reservation. Grego-
ry Coyne Thompson.
The Southern Utes: a Tribal His-
tory. James Jefferson, et al.
Southerners and Other Americans.
Grady McWhiney.
Southwest: Three Peoples in Geo-
graphical Change, 1600-1970.
D. W. Meinig.
The Sovereign Lady. A Life of
Elizabeth, Third Lady Holland,
with Her Family. Sonia Keppel.
Sovereign of the Seas: The Story of
British Sea Power. David Howarth.
The Sovereign States, 1775-1783.
Jackson Turner Main.
The Sovereign Wayfarer: Walker
Percy's Diagnosis of the Malaise.
Martin Luschei.
Sovereignty and Protection: A Study
of British Jurisdictional Imperial-
ism in the Late Nineteenth Cen-

tury. W. Ross Johnston.
Sovereignty and Society in Colonial
Brazil: The High Court of Bahia
and Its Judges, 1609-1751. Stu-
art B. Schwartz.
Sovereigns Without Crowns: A Be-
havioral Analysis of the Indian
Electoral Process. V. M.
Sirsikar.
Soviet Agricultural Trade Unions,
1917-70. Peter J. Potichnyj.
Soviet-American Confrontation:
Postwar Reconstruction and the
Origins of the Cold War. Thom-
as G. Paterson.
The Soviet Intelligentsia. L. G.
Churchward.
Soviet Nationality Policy and Bour-
geois Historians: The Establish-
ment of the Soviet Multi-National
State (1917-1922): in Contem-
porary American Historiography.
I. S. Zenushkina.
Soviet Russia and the Hindustan Sub-
continent. Vijay Sen Budhraj.
The Soviet Union and the Arab East
Under Khrushchev. Oles M.
Smolansky.
The Soviet Union in Asia. Geoffrey
Jukes.
The Soviet Union in World Affairs
--A Documented Analysis, 1964-
1972. W. W. Kulski.
Spain. Richard Herr.
Spain: The Rise of the First World
Power. John Fraser Ramsey.
The Spain of Fernando de Rojas:
The Intellectual and Social Land-
scape of "La Celestina." Stephen
Gilman.
The Spanish American Revolutions,
1808-1826. John Lynch.
Spanish and Mexican Land Grants in
the Chihuahuan Acquisition.
J. J. Bowden.
Spanish Central America: A Socio-
economic History, 1520-1720.
Murdo J. MacLeod.
The Spanish-Cuban-American War
and the Birth of American Im-
perialism, 1895-1902. 2 vols.
Philip S. Foner.
The Spanish in the Mississippi Val-
ley, 1762-1804. John Francis
McDermott, ed.
Spanish Times and Boom Times:
Toward an Architectural History
of Socorro, New Mexico. Charles

L. Nieman.

Spatial Evolution of Manufacturing: Southern Ontario 1851-1891. James M. Gilmour.

Spätrömische Gardehelme. Hans Klumbach, ed.

Speak for Yourself, John, The Life of John Mason Brown, With Some of His Letters and Many of His Opinions. George Stevens.

Speak Out in Thunder Tones: Letters and Other Writings by Black Northerners. Dorothy Sterling, ed.

Spectator of America. Edward Dicey.

Speed and the Quarter Horse: A Payload of Sprinters. Nelson C. Nye.

A Spirit of Dissension: Economics, Politics, and the Revolution in Maryland. Ronald Hoffman.

The Spiritual Crisis of the Gilded Age. Paul A. Carter.

The Spiritual Power. Richard C. Trexler.

The Spiritual Regulation of Peter the Great. Alexander V. Muller, ed. and trans.

Spiritualistische Tradition im Protestantismus: Das Schwenckfeldertum in Schlesien. Horst Weigelt.

Splendour at Court: Renaissance Spectacle and Illusion. Roy Strong.

The Spoils of August. Barbara L. Greenberg.

The Spoils of Progress: Environmental Pollution in the Soviet Union. Marshall I. Goldman.

Spokane Sketchbook. Roland Colliander, et al.

The Spread of the Russian Revolution: Essays on 1917. Roger Pethybridge.

Stadrat und Stadlische Oberschicht von Puebla am enden der Kolonialzeit, 1787-1810. Reinhard Liehr.

Stagecoach Inns of Texas. Kathryn Turner Carter.

Stagecoaching on the El Camino Real, Los Angeles to San Francisco, 1861-1901. Charles Outland.

Stalin: The Man and His Era. Adam B. Ulam.

Stalin as Revolutionary, 1879-1929: A Study in History and Personality. Robert C. Tucker.

The Stalinist Terror in the Thirties:

Documentation from the Soviet Press. Borys Levytsky, comp.

Stamford in the Gilded Age: The Political Life of a Connecticut Town, 1868-1893. Estelle F. Feinstein.

Stand Like Men. James Sherburne.

Stanfield. Geoffrey Stevens.

Stanley Vestal, Champion of the Old West. Ray Tassin.

State Farms in the First Decade of Soviet Power, 1917-1927. I. E. Zelenin.

A State of Disunion: Arthur Griffith, Michael Collins, James Craig, Eamon de Valera. Carlton Younger.

The States and Their Indian Citizens. Theodore W. Taylor.

The State's Servants. G. E. Aylmer.

Stations West, the Story of the Oregon Railways. Edwin D. Culp.

Statism in Plymouth Colony. Harry M. Ward.

Die Statuten des weltlichen Kollegiatstifts St. Peter in Basel. Guy P. Marchal, ed.

Les statuts synodaux français du XIIIe siècle, précédés de l'histoire du synode diocèsain depuis ses origines. Volume 1, Les statuts de Paris et le synodal de l'Ouest (XIIIe siècle). Odette Pontal, ed. and trans.

Steam and Sail in Britain and North America. P. W. Brock and Basil Greehill.

The Steamboat Monopoly: Gibbons v. Ogden, 1824. Maurice G. Baxter.

Stendhal and the Arts. David Wakefield, ed.

Stephen A. Douglas. Robert W. Johannsen.

Stephen Crane: A Critical Bibliography. R. W. Stallman.

Stephen Crane: The Critical Heritage. Richard M. Weatherford, ed.

Stephen S. Renfroe, Alabama's Outlaw Sheriff. William Warren Rogers and Ruth Pruitt.

Sternwheelers, Sandbars and Switchbacks.... Edward Lloyd Affeeck.

Die Stiftungsuniversitat Frankfurt am Main, 1914-1932. Paul Kluke.

Stones, Bones, and Skin: Ritual and
Shamanic Art.
Storia d'Italia.   Grancesco Guicciar-
dini.
Storia del Partito comunista italiano.
3 vols.   Paolo Spriano.
Storia della storiografia moderna:
Il Settecento.   Gioacchino Gargallo
di Castel Lentini.
Stormy Petrel: N. G. Gonzales and
His State.   Lewis Pinckney Jones.
The Story of Medicine in America.
Geoffrey Marks and William K.
Beatty.
The Story of the Anza-Borrego Des-
ert, The Largest State Park in the
United States of America.   Diana
E. Lindsay.
The Straits Settlement, 1826-67.
C. M. Turnbull.
The Strange Career of Jim Crow.
C. Vann Woodward.
The Strange Neutrality: Soviet-
Japanese Relations During the Sec-
ond World War, 1941-1945.
George Alexander Lensen.
Strangers Entertained: A History of
the Ethnic Groups in British
Columbia.   John Norris, ed.
Strategy for a Black Agenda: A
Critique of New Theories of Lib-
eration in the United States and
Africa.   Henry Winston.
The Strategy of Overthrow 1798-1799.
Piers Mackesy.
Streams in a Thirsty Land: A His-
tory of the Turlock Region.   Helen
Hohenthal, et al.
Strife on the Waterfront: The Port
of New York Since 1945.   Vernon
H. Jensen.
Strike! Jeremy Brecher.
Structure and Conflict in Nigeria,
1960-1966.   Kenneth Post and
Michael Vickers.
The Structure of the Terror: The
Example of Javogues and the Loire.
Colin Lucas.
Struggle for a Continent: The Diplo-
matic History of South America
1917-1945.   Glen Barclay.
The Struggle for Bread: The Food
Policy of the Communist Party
and the Soviet State During the
Time of the Civil War (1917-
1920).   M. I. Davydov.
The Struggle for Neutrality: Franco-
American Diplomacy During the

Federalist Era.   Albert Hall Bow-
man.
Strutture sociali e sistemi economici
precapitalistici.   Amelio Taglia-
ferri.
Stuart and Cromwellian Foreign
Policy.   G. M. D. Howat.
Stuart Royal Proclamations: Vol. I,
Royal Proclamations of King James
I, 1603-1625.   James F. Larkin
and Paul L. Hughes, eds.
The Stuarts.   K. H. D. Haley, ed.
Student Protest and the Technocratic
Society: The Case of ROTC.
Jack Nusan Porter.
Student Unrest in India: A Typology
and a Socio-Structural Analysis.
John Peter Neelson.
Studenten und Politik, 1918-1933:
Der Fall Freiburg in Breisgau
Wolfgang Kreutzberger.
Students and Politics: A Compara-
tive Study.   Terry Clay Eakin.
Studi sul linguaggio del Petrarca:
La canzone delle visioni.   Fredi
Chiappelli.
Studia Gratiana.   A. M. Stickler.
Studien zum Selbstverständnis des
1. and 2. Kabinetts der russichen
Provisorischen Regierung (März
bis Juli 1917).   Reinhard Wit-
tram.
Studien zur europäischen Rechts-
geschichte.   Walter Wilhelm, ed.
Studien zur Ikonographie der Antonia
Minor.   Karin Polaschek.
Studies and Restorations at Persepo-
lis and Other Sites of Fars.   Ann
Britt Tilia.
Studies in Development Planning.
H. B. Chenery.
Studies in Fifth-Century Attic Epi-
graphy.   Donald William Bradeen
and Malcolm Francis McGregor.
Studies in Greek History: A Com-
panion Volume to A History of
Greece to 322 B. C.   N. G. L.
Hammond.
Studies in Medieval and Renaissance
History.   Vol. IX.   H. L. Adel-
son, ed.
Studies in Richard Hooker: Essays
Preliminary to an Edition of His
Works.   W. Speed Hill, ed.
Studies in the Climatology of South
Asia.   U. Schweinfurth, H.
Flohn, and M. Domros.
Studies in the Early History of

Judaism, Volume I. Solomon Zeitlin.

Studies in the Fourth General Elections.

Studies in the Growth of Nineteenth-Century Government. Gillian Sutherland, ed.

Studies in the History of Philosophy and Religion. Harry Austryn Wolfson.

Studies in the History of the Near East. P. M. Holt.

Studies in Tudor and Stuart Politics and Government: Papers and Reviews, 1946-1972. G. R. Elton.

Studies of Field Systems in the British Isles. Alan R. H. Baker and Robin A. Butlin, eds.

Studies on Machiavelli. Myron P. Gilmore, ed.

Lo studio teologico e la biblioteca dei Domenicani a Padova nel tre e quattrocento. L. Gargan.

A Study in Boss Politics: William Lorimer of Chicago. Joel Arthur Tarr.

The Study of Animal Bones from Archaeological Sites. Raymond E. Chaplin.

A Study of Basic Standards and Methods in Preservation and Restoration Workshops Applicable to Developing Countries. John Davies.

The Study of Medieval Records: Essays in Honour of Kathleen Major. D. A. Bullough and R. L. Storey, eds.

A Study of the Basic Standards for Equipping, Maintaining, and Operating a Reprographic Laboratory in Archives of Developing Countries. Albert H. Leisinger, Jr.

Su Man-shu. Liu Wu-chi.

Subject Retrieval in the Seventies. Hans Wellisch and Thomas D. Wilson, eds.

The Subordinate Sex: A History of Attitudes Toward Women. Vern L. Bullough.

Succession of New States to International Treaties. Okon Udokang.

Les successions dans le sud-ouest de la France au Moyen Age. Jacques Poumarede.

The Successors of Genghis Khan. Rashid Al-din.

Il Sudan come nazione. Carmelo Conte.

A Sufi Saint of the Twentieth Century: Shaikh Ahmed al-'Alawi. His Spiritual Heritage and Legacy. Martin Lings.

Sufis of Andalusia: The Ruh alquds and al-Durrat al fakhirah of Ibn'Arabi. R. W. J. Austin, trans. and ed.

Sugar and Slavery: An Economic History of the British West Indies, 1623-1775. Richard B. Sheridan.

Sugar Without Slaves: The Political Economy of British Guiana, 1838-1904. Alan H. Adamson.

The Suitcase Farming Frontier: A Study in the Historical Geography of the Central Great Plains. Leslie Hewes.

The Sultans. Noel Barber.

The Summer After the War. James Whitfield Ellison.

The Sun Dance Religion: Power for the Powerless. Joseph G. Jorgenson.

Sun, Soil, and Survival: An Introduction to Soils. Kermit C. Berger.

The Superfluous Anarchist: Albert Jay Nock. Michael Wreszin.

Super Imperialism: The Economic Strategy of American Empire. Michael Hudson.

Supplement to the Sociology of Invention. S. Colum Gilfillan.

Supplex Libellus Valachorum. David Prodan.

Support for Secession: Lancashire and the American Civil War. Mary Ellison.

Surrealism and Spain, 1920-1936. C. B. Morris.

Survey of Commonwealth Affairs: Problems of Expansion and Attrition 1953-1969. J. D. B. Miller.

Survey of London. Vol. XXXVII: Northern Kensington. F. H. W. Sheppard, ed.

A Survey of Research in Psychology.

A Survey of Research in Sociology and Social Anthropology. Volume III.

Survey of the Democratic Direction in Russian Historiography in the 1860s and 1870s. A. N. Tsamutali.

A Survey of the Vatican Archives
and of its Medieval Holdings.
Leonard E. Boyle.

Survivors of Eldorado. Four Indian
Cultures of South America. Johannes Wilbert.

The Swahili Coast: Politics, Diplomacy and Trade on the East African Littoral, 1798-1856. C. S.
Nicholls.

Swan Among the Indians: Life of
James G. Swan, 1818-1900. Lucile McDonald.

Sweatshops in the Sun: Child Labor
on the Farm. Ronald B. Taylor.

Sweden's Age of Greatness, 1632-
1718. Michael Roberts, ed.

Swedes in Chicago: A Demographic
and Social Study of the 1846-1860
Immigration. Ulf Beijbom.

A Sweet Instruction: Franklin's Journalism as a Literary Apprenticeship. James A. Sappenfield.

Sword and Pen: A Survey of the
Writings of Sir Winston Churchill.
Manfred Weidhorn.

The Sword and the Scepter: The
Problem of Militarism in Germany
... Volumes 3 and 4. Gerhard
Ritter.

The Sword of Truth: The Life and
Times of Shehu Usuman dan Fodio.
Mervyn Hiskett.

Swords and Scales: The Development of the Uniform Code of Military Justice. William T. Generous,
Jr.

Sylloge of Coins of the British Isles,
Part 18, National Museum, Copen-
hagen, IV; Anglo-Saxon Coins from
Harold I and Anglo-Norman Coins.
C. E. Blunt and R. H. M. Dolley,
eds.

Symbolic Images. E. H. Gombrich.

Systematics in Prehistory. Robert
C. Dunnell.

The Systematization of Russian Government: Social Evolution in the Domestic Administration of Imperial
Russia, 1711-1905. George L.
Yaney.

Les Systèmes politiques africains.
Vol. 1, L'Evolution, la scène
politique, l'intégration nationale.
P.-F. Gonidec.

Szechwan and the Chinese Republic:
Provincial Militarism and Central
Power, 1911-1938. Robert A. Kapp.

-T-

T. Thomas Fortune: Militant Journalist. Emma Lou Thornbrough.

TVA and the Power Fight, 1933-
1939. Thomas K. McCraw.

Tactics and Ethics: Political Essays, 1919-1929. Georg Lukacs.

A Tail in the Mouth. Charles Mangua.

The Taiping Rebellion: History and
Documents. Volumes II and III:
Documents and Comments. Franz
Michael with Chung-Li Chang.

Taiwan in Modern Times. Paul
K. T. Sih, ed.

Take Up Your Mission: Mormon
Colonizing Along the Little Colo-
rado River, 1870-1900. Charles
S. Peterson.

The Tale of Kieu. Nguyen Du.

A Tale of Two Caves. Francois
Bordes.

Talleyrand: The Art of Survival.
Jean Orieux.

Taman Indera: A Royal Pleasure
Ground: Malay Decorative Arts
and Pastimes. Mubin Sheppard.

The Tapping Revolutionary Movement. Jen Yu-Wen.

The Tar Heel Press. Thad Stem,
Jr.

The Tariff in American History.
Sidney Ratner.

The Tariff, Politics, and American
Foreign Policy, 1874-1901. Tom
E. Terrill.

The Tascones and Tasconia: A
Contribution to the Meaning of
the Terms and of the Byzantine
Institution of the Fortress-Garrison of the Same Name. Charalampous P. Symeonides.

Taylor University: The First 125
Years. William C. Ringenberg.

Teaching for a Change. John Anthony Scott.

Teamster Power. Farrell Dobbs.

Teatri Classici in Asia Minore.
Dibyra, Selge, Hieropolis.
Daris de Bernardi Ferrero.

Technical and Vocational Teacher
Education and Training. Mary
Ann Calkins Pilain.

The Technical Services-the Corps
of Engineers: Construction in
the United States. Lenore Fine

503   Technology

and Jesse A. Remington.
Technology and Social Change. H.
Russell Bernard and Pertti J.
Pelto, eds.
Technology Assessment. John W.
Dickey, et al.
Technology Assessment and Quality
of Life. Gerhard J. Stober and
Dieter Schumacher, ed.
Technology, Power, and Social Change.
Charles A. Thrall and Jerold M.
Starr, eds.
Telegrams of the North-West Campaign, 1885. Desmond Morton and
Reginald H. Roy, eds.
Telling Tongues: Language Policy in
Mexico Colony to Nation. Shirley
Brice Heath.
The Templars in the Corona de Aragon. A. J. Forey.
Temples of the Muses and a History
of Pharmacy Museums. Sami K.
Hamarneh.
Temporary Kings. Anthony Powell.
Ten Men of Minnesota and American
Foreign Policy, 1898-1968. Barbara Stuhler.
Tennant's Stalk: The Story of the
Tennants of the Glen. Nancy
Crathorne.
Tennessee: The Dangerous Example;
Watauga to 1849. Mary French
Caldwell.
The Terrace of the Great God at Abydos. William Kelly Simpson.
Terrell, Texas, 1873-1973: From
Open Country to Modern City.
Jack Stoltz.
Le Territoire de l'Historien. Emmanuel Le Roy Ladurie.
The Territory of Michigan [1805-1837]. Alec R. Gilpin.
Terror and Repression in Revolutionary Marseilles. William Scott.
The Terrors of Ideological Politics:
Liberal Historians in a Conservative Mood. Marian J. Morton.
Tertullian: A Historical and Literary
Study. Timothy David Barnes.
A Texan in the Gold Rush: The Letters of Robert Hunter 1849-1851.
Robert W. Stephens, ed.
Texas: A Picture Tour. Lon Tinkle.
Texas Cities and the Great Depression. Robert C. Cotner, et al.
The Texas Panhandle Frontier. Frederick W. Rathjen.
Textile Conservation. Jentina E.

Leene.
Textiles of the Indonesian Archipelago. Garrett and Bronwen
Solyom.
Thackeray: The Major Novels.
Juliet McMaster.
Thai Titles and Ranks: Including a
Translation of Traditions of
Royal Lineage in Siam by King
Chulalongkorn. Robert B. Jones.
The Thalassocracies. Molly Miller.
"That Disgraceful Affair," The
Black Hawk War. Cecil Eby.
That Greece Might Still Be Free:
The Philhellenes in the War of
Independence. William St. Clair.
That Man Haupt: A Biography of
Herman Haupt. James A. Ward.
That Noble Cabinet: A History of
the British Museum. Edward
Miller.
That Wild Fellow John Neal, and
the American Literary Revolution.
Benjamin Lease.
Das Theater von Milet, Vol. I: Das
Hellenistische Theater der
Romische zuschauerbau. Friedrich Krauss.
The Theatre at Isthmia. Elizabeth
R. Gebhard.
A Theatre for Spencerians. Judith
M. Kennedy and James A. Reither, eds.
The Theatrical World of Osaka
Prints: A Collection of Eighteenth and Nineteenth Century
Japanese Woodblock Prints in the
Philadelphia Museum of Art.
Roger S. Keyes and Keiko Mizushima.
Their Solitary Way: The Puritan
Social Ethic in the First Century
of Settlement in New England.
Stephen Foster.
Theodore Francis Green: The Washington Years, 1937-1960. Erwin
L. Levine.
Theodore Roosevelt. David H. Burton.
Theodore Roosevelt and His English
Correspondents: A Special Relationship of Friends. David H.
Burton.
Théologie et politique au siècle des
Lumières (1770-1820). Bernard
Plongeron.
Theories of Education in Early
America, 1655-1819. Wilson
Smith, ed.

Theory and Practice. Jurgen Habermas.

The Theory and Practice of History. Leopold von Ranke.

The Theory and Practice of the Dissolution of Parliament. B. S. Markesinis.

There's Not a Bathing Suit in Russia and Other Bare Facts. Will Rogers.

Thermodynamics Atlas. Vol. 2: The Evolution of the Heat Engine. Ivo Kolin.

"These Happy Grounds": A History of the Lassen Region. Douglas Hillman Strong.

The Things That Are Caesar's: Memoirs of a Canadian Public Servant. Arnold Heeney.

Third International Conference on Economic History, Munich 1965: Section VII, Demography and Economy. D. C. Eversley, ed.

Third Scholarly Conference on "Society and State in China," Theses and Reports. O. E. Nepomnin and Yu V. Chudodeev, comps.

Thirteen Georgia Ghosts and Jeffrey. Kathryn Tucker Windham.

This Country Was Ours: A Documentary History of the American Indian. Virgil J. Vogel.

This Land Was Theirs: A Study of the North American Indian. Wendell H. Oswalt.

This New Man, the American: The Beginnings of the American People. John C. Miller.

This Sacred Trust: American Nationality, 1798-1898. Paul C. Nagel.

This Vast External Realm. Dean Acheson.

This Was Cattle Ranching: Yesterday and Today. Virginia Paul.

This Was Their World: Approaches to Local History. Alan Rogers.

Thomas Benton Catron and His Era. Victor Westphall.

Thomas Bray's Grand Design: Libraries of the Church of England in America, 1695-1785. Charles T. Laugher.

Thomas County, 1865-1900. William Warren Rogers.

Thomas E. Williams & the Fine Arts Press. Richard D. Curtiss.

Thomas Harriot: Renaissance Scientist. John W. Shirley, ed.

Thomas Jefferson: An Intimate History. Fawn M. Brodie.

Thomas Jefferson and Music. Helen Cripe.

Thomas Jefferson: The Man ... His World ... His Influence. Lally Weymouth, ed.

Thorikos. H. F. Mussche, et al.

Thorns and Thistles: Juvenile Delinquents in the United States, 1825-1940. Robert M. Mennel.

Three American Moralists: Mailer, Bellow, Trilling. Nathan A. Scott, Jr.

The Three Empresses: Catherine I, Anne and Elizabeth of Russia. Philip Longworth.

Three Lives of English Saints. Michael Winterbottom, ed.

Three Ranches West. Clarence S. Adams and Tom E. Brown, Sr.

Throb of Drums in Tennessee, 1862-1865. Jennie Starks McKee.

Through One Man's Eyes: The Civil War Experiences of a Belmont County Volunteer, Letters of James G. Theaker. Paul E. Rieger.

Through "Poverty's Vale": A Hardscrabble Boyhood in Upstate New York, 1832-1862. Henry Conklin.

The Tide at Sunrise: A History of the Russo-Japanese War, 1904-1905. Denis and Peggy Warner.

Tides of Empire: Discursions on the Expansion of Britain Overseas. Gerald S. Graham.

Tidewater Towns: City Planning in Colonial Virginia and Maryland. John Reps.

Tiger in the Court. Paul Hoffman.

Tijuana: Urbanization in a Border Culture. John A. Price.

Timber Country: Logging in the Great Northwest. Earl Roberge.

The Timber Economy of Puritan New England. Charles F. Carroll.

The Time of the Buffalo. Tom McHugh.

Time on the Cross: The Economics of American Negro Slavery. Robert William Fogel and Stanley L. Engerman.

Time, Tide, and Tempest: A Study of Shakespeare's Romances. Douglas L. Peterson.

Tito, Mihailovic and the Allies, 1941-
1945. Walter R. Roberts.
To China With Love: The Lives and
Times of Protestant Missionaries
in China, 1860-1900. Pat Barr.
To Die Game: The Story of the Lowry
Band, Indian Guerrillas of Recon-
struction. W. McKee Evans.
To Judge With Justice: History and
Politics of Illinois Judicial Re-
form. Rubin G. Cohn.
To Peking--and Beyond: A Report on
the New Asia. Harrison E. Salis-
bury.
To Possess the Land: A Biography
of Arthur Rochford Manby.
Frank Waters.
To Save a Nation: American Counter-
subversives, the New Deal, and
the Coming of World War II.
Geoffrey S. Smith.
To the Maginot Line: The Politics
of French Military Preparation in
the 1920's. Judith M. Hughes.
To the Sandwich Islands on H M S
Blonde. Pauline King Joerger.
Toledo Bend. Sam Mims.
Tommaso Radini Tedeschi, Orazione
Contro Filippo Melantone.
Toms, Coons, Mulattoes, Mammies,
and Bucks: An Interpretative His-
tory of Blacks in American Films.
Donald Bogle.
A Topical History of the United
States. Gerald Baydo.
La Toscana nel regime fascista
(1922-1939).
Total War: The Story of World War
II. Peter Calvocoressi and Guy
Wint.
A Touchstone for Greatness: Es-
says, Addresses and Occasional
Pieces About Abraham Lincoln.
Roy P. Basler.
Toward a National Power Policy: The
New Deal and the Electric Utility
Industry, 1933-1941. Philip J.
Funigiello.
Toward Multinational Cooperation in
Africa. B. W. T. Mutharika.
Toward the French Revolution:
Europe and America in the Eight-
eenth-Century World. Louis Gott-
schalk and Donald Lach.
Towards a New Ireland. Garret
FitzGerald.
Towards Economic Independence:
Papers on the Nationalisation of

the Copper Industry in Zambia.
M. L. O. Faber and J. G. Pot-
ter.
Towards Ireland Free. Liam Deasy.
Town and Country: the Archaeology
of Verulamium and the Roman
Chilterns. Keith Branigan.
Town and Countryside: Social, Eco-
nomic and Political Tensions in
Fourteenth-Century Flanders.
D. M. Nicholas.
Town Swamps and Social Bridges.
George Godwin.
Toynbee on Toynbee: A Conversa-
tion Between Arnold Toynbee and
G. R. Urban. Arnold J. Toyn-
bee and G. R. Urban.
Tractatus de Mystica Theologica.
2 volumes. Nicholas Kempf.
Tractor Pioneer: The Life of Har-
ry Ferguson. Colin Fraser.
The Trade Makers: Elder Dempster
in West Africa. P. N. Davies.
The Trade Policy of the Soviet
State After the Transition to
N E P, 1921-1924. V. P.
Dmitrenko.
Trader on the Santa Fe Trail:
Memoirs of Franz Huning.
Franz Huning and Lina Fergus-
son Browne.
Tradition and Modernization in Japan-
ese Culture. Donald H. Shively,
ed.
Tradition and Revolution in Vietnam.
Nguyen Khac Vien.
Tradition for the Future. Mirrit
Boutros Ghali.
La Tradition orale: problématique
et méthodologie des sources des
l'histoire Africaine. Dioulde
Laya, ed.
Traditional Korea: A Cultural His-
tory. Wanne J. Joe.
Tradizione liberale fascismo. Nino
Valeri.
The Tragi-Comedy of Pen Browning.
Maisie Ward.
Tragic Cavalier: Governor Manuel
Salcedo of Texas, 1808-1813.
Felix D. Almaraz, Jr.
Tramps and Reformers, 1873-1916:
The Discovery of Unemployment
in New York. Paul T. Ringen-
bach.
The Transfer of Power, 1942-47.
Nicholas Mansergh, ed.
The Transformation of Communist

Ideology: The Yugoslav Case, 1945-1953. A. Ross Johnson.

The Transformation of the American Economy, 1865-1914: An Essay in Interpretation. Robert Higgs.

Transition and Revolution: Problems and Issues of European Renaissance and Reformation History. Robert M. Kingdon, ed.

Translations of Lucian. Craig R. Thompson, ed.

Transport and Communication in Early Modern Europe, A. D. 500-1100. Albert C. Leighton.

Transport in Transition: The Evolution of Traditional Shipping in China. Andrew Watson, trans.

Los Tratados Internacionales de Honduras. Rafael Leiva Vivas.

Travels in North America, 1922-1824. Paul Wilhelm.

Travels in the Interior of Southern Africa, 1849-1863. Edward C. Tabler.

Travels in the Old South, 1783-1860, Selected from the Periodicals of the Times. 2 vols. Eugene L. Schwaab, ed.

Travels Through North and South Carolina, Georgia, East and West Florida. William Bartram.

The Treasure of the Superstition Mountains. Gary Jennings.

Treasures Among Men: The Fudai Daimyo in Tokugawa Japan. Harold Bolitho.

Treasury of American Design. Clarence P. Hornung.

The Treatment of Head Injuries in the Thirty Years' War (1618-1648); Joannis Scultetus and His Age. L. Bakey.

Treaty Rolls Preserved in the Public Record Office. John Ferguson, ed.

Tree of Hate: Propaganda and Prejudices Affecting United States Relations with the Hispanic World. Philip Wayne Powell.

Trees and Shrubs of Kentucky. Mary E. Wharton and Roger W. Barbour.

Trends in British Society Since 1900: A Guide to the Changing Social Structure of Britain. A. H. Halsey, ed.

The Trial of Doctor Sacheverell. Geoffrey Holmes.

Tribunato e resistenza. Pierangelo Catalano.

Tristes Tropiques. Claude Levi-Strauss.

The Triumph of Culture: 18th-Century Perspectives. Paul Fritz and David Williams, eds.

The Troad. An Archaeological and Topographical Study. J. M. Cook.

Trotsky. Irving H. Smith, ed.

Trotskyism in Latin America. Robert J. Alexander.

The Truman and Eisenhower Years, 1945-1960. Margaret L. Stapleton, comp.

The Truman Period as a Research Field: A Reappraisal, 1972. Richard S. Kirkendall, ed.

Truman, the Jewish Vote and the Creation of Israel. John Snetsinger.

Truth and Historicity. Hans-Georg Gadamer, ed.

Tudor and Early Stuart Anti-Catholic Drama. Rainer Pineas.

Tudor and Stuart Ireland. Margaret MacCurtain.

Tudor Foreign Policy. P. S. Crowson.

Tudor Men and Institutions. Arthur J. Slavin, ed.

A Tudor Tapestry: Men, Women and Society in Reformation England. Derek Wilson.

The Tudors. Joel Hurstfield, ed.

Tumacacori's Yesterdays. Earl Jackson.

Tumble-Down Dick: The Fall of the House of Richard Cromwell. Earl Malcolm Hause.

The Tupamaro Guerrillas. Maria Esther Gilio.

Turgot on Progress, Sociology and Economics. R. L. Meek, ed.

Turkish Foreign Policy, 1943-1945: Small State Diplomacy and Great Power Politics. Edward Weisband.

The Turnpike Road System in England 1663-1840. William Albert.

Tuscan Villas. Harold Acton.

The Tweedmakers: A History of the Scottish Fancy Woolen Industry 1600-1914. Clifford Gulvin.

Twelfth-Century Europe: An Interpretative Essay. Sidney R. Packard.

The Twenties in Western Canada.

S. M. Trofimenkoff, ed.

Twentieth-Century Coventry. Kenneth Richardson.

Twentieth-Century Germany: From Bismarck to Brandt. A. J. Ryder.

Twentieth-Century Indonesia. Wilfred T. Neill.

Twentieth-Century Montana: A State of Extremes. K. Ross Toole.

Twenty Episodes in the Life of Pancho Villa. Elias L. Torres.

Twenty Plays of the No Theatre. Donald Keene, ed. with Royal Tyler.

The Twilight of Gold, 1914-1936: Myths and Realities. Melchoir Palyi.

The Twisted Dream: Capitalist Development in the United States Since 1776. Douglas F. Dowd.

The Two Faces of Janus: The Saga of Deep South Change. J. Oliver Emmerich.

Two Letters and Short Rules of a Good Life. Robert Southwell.

Tyler-Browns of Brattleboro. Dorothy Sutherland Melville.

-U-

U D I: The International Politics of the Rhodesian Rebellion. Robert C. Good.

Ukiyo-e Painting. Harold P. Stern.

Ukraine: A Concise Encyclopedia. Volume 2. Volodymyr Kubijovyc, ed.

Ultraroyalism in Toulouse: From its Origins to the Revolution of 1830. David Higgs.

Un heroe espanol del progreso: Agustin de Betancourt. Aleksee Bogolinbov.

The Unappropriated People: Freedmen in the Slave Society of Barbados. Jerome S. Handler.

The Unbounded Frame: Freedom and Community in Nineteenth-Century American Utopianism. Michael Fellman.

Uncle Bud Long: The Birth of a Kentucky Folk Legend. Kenneth W. Clarke.

Under the Guns: New York: 1775-1776. Bruce Bliven, Jr.

Understanding Technology. Charles Susskind.

Underwater Archaeology: A Nascent Discipline.

Une Enterprise Horlogère du Valde-Travers: Fleurier Watch Co. SA. François Jequier.

The Uneasy Alliance: America, Britain, and Russia, 1941-1943. Robert Beitzell.

The Uneasy Chair: A Biography of Bernard DeVoto. Wallace Stegner.

Unemployment and Politics, a Study in English Social Policy, 1886-1914. José Harris.

Unequal Exchange: A Study of the Imperialism of Trade. Arghiri Emmanuel.

The Unification of Greece, 1770-1923. Douglas Dakin.

Union Catalogue of the Serial Publications of the Indian Government, 1858-1947. Teresa MacDonald.

Union Pacific Country. Robert G. Athearn.

Unionists Divided: Arthur Balfour, Joseph Chamberlain and the Unionist Free Traders. Richard A. Rempel.

The United States and East Asia. Richard W. Van Alystyne.

The United States and India, Pakistan, Bangladesh. W. Norman Brown.

The United States and the Caribbean Republics, 1921-1933. Dana G. Munro.

The United States and the Origins of the Cold War, 1914-1947. John Lewis Gaddis.

U. S. China Policy and the Problem of Taiwan. William M. Bueler.

The U. S. Congress: The Men Who Steered Its Course, 1787-1867. Marjorie G. Fribourg.

United States Documents in the Propaganda Fide Archives: A Calendar. Finbar Kinneally.

U. S. Foreign Policy and Peru. Daniel A. Sharp.

United States Military Saddles. Randy Steffen.

United States National Interests in a Changing World. Donald E. Nuechterlein.

United States Postal Service. Gerald Cullinan.

United States-Spanish Relations, Wolfram and World War II.   James W. Cortada.

Universal Fascism.   The Theory and Practice of the Fascist International: 1928-1936.   Michael A. Ledeen.

Universities in Politics: Case Studies from the Late Middle Ages and Early Modern Period.   J. W. Baldwin and R. A. Goldthwaite, eds.

Unsui: A Diary of Zen Monastic Life.   Eshin Nishimura.

Untersuchung über den bei Homer "Depas Amphikypellon" Genannten Gefässtypus.   Peter Z. Spanos.

Unternehmen Sonnenblume: Der Entschluss zum Afrika-Feldzug. Charles B. Burdick.

The Untouchables in Contemporary India.   J. Michael Mahar, ed.

Unwanted Mexican Americans in the Great Depression: Repatriation Pressures, 1929-1939.   Abraham Hoffman.

The Unwritten War: American Writers and the Civil War.   Daniel Aaron.

The Upper Thames Valley: an Archaeological Survey of the River Gravels.   Don Benson and David Miles.

Uprooted Americans: The Japanese Americans and the War Relocation Authority During World War II. Dillon S. Meyer.

Upton Sinclair: An Annotated Checklist.   Ronald Gottesman.

Urban Government for Rio de Janeiro. Ivan L. Richardson.

Urban Growth and the Circulation of Information: The United States System of Cities, 1790-1840.   Allan R. Pred.

Urban History Review.... Del Muise and John Taylor, eds.

Urban Leadership in Western India: Politics and Communities in Bombay City, 1840-1885.   Christine Dobbin.

Urban Liberalism and Progressive Reform.   John D. Buenker.

Urban Southeast Asia: A Selected Bibliography.   Gerald Breese, ed.

The Urban Wilderness: A History of the American City.   Sam Bass Warner, Jr.

The Urbanization of Modern America: A Brief History.   Zane L. Miller.

Das Urkundenwesen in Österreich vom 8. bis zum früben 13. Jahrhundert.   Heinrich Fichtenau.

The Use Of the Land.   John T. Schlebecker.

Utah.   David Muench and Hartt Wixom.

Utah's Black Hawk War.   Carlton Culmsee.

-V-

V. I. Lenin.   Robert Conquest.

V. S. Khromchenko's Coastal Explorations in Southwestern Alaska, 1922.   James W. Van Stone, ed.

Vanguard: A History.   Constance McLaughlin Green and Milton Lomask.

The Vatican in the Age of the Dictators, 1922-1945.   Anthony Rhodes.

Il Venerabile Beda, storico dell'alto Medioevo.   Giosue Musca.

Venetian Phoenix: Paolo Sarpi and Some of His English Friends. John Leon Lievsay.

The Venezuelan Armed Forces in Politics, 1935-1959.   Winfield J. Burggraaff.

Venice: A Maritime Republic. Frederic C. Lane.

Venice: The Hinge of Europe, 1081-1797.   William H. McNeill.

A Venture in History: The Production, Publication and Sale of the Works of Hubert Howe Bancroft. Harry Clark.

The Verderers and Forest Laws of Dean.   Cyril Hart.

Vermont Obsolete Notes and Script. Wayne Burns Coulter.

Versions of Baroque: European Literature in the Seventeenth Century.   Frank J. Warnke.

The Viceroy's Journal.   Penderel Moon, ed.

Vichy France: Old Guard and New Order, 1940-1944.   Robert O. Paxton.

Victor Berger and the Promise of Constructive Socialism, 1910-1920.

Sally M. Miller.
Victor Emanuel, Cavour, and the Risorgimento. Denis Mack Smith.
The Victorian City: Images and Realities. 2 vols. H. J. Dyos and Michael Wolff, eds.
Victorian Culture in America. H. Wayne Morgan, ed.
Victorian England: Aspects of English and Imperial History. L. C. B. Seaman.
A Victorian Gentlewoman in the Far West: The Reminiscences of Mary Hallock Foote. Rodman W. Paul.
Victorian Ladies at Work: Middle-Class Working Women in England and Wales, 1850-1914. Lee Holcombe.
Victorian Noncomformity. John Briggs and Ian Sellers, ed.
Victorian People: A Reassessment of Persons and Themes, 1851-67. Asa Briggs.
The Victorians and Social Protest: A Symposium. J. Butt and I. F. Clarke, eds.
Victorio and the Mimbres Apaches. Dan L. Thrapp.
Victor's Justice: The Tokyo War Crimes Trial. Richard H. Minear.
The Victory of Soviet Power in the Transcaucasus. I. I. Mints, et al., eds.
La Vie et l'Oeuvre de John Fisher. Jean Rouschausse.
La Vie sociale en Provence intérieure au lendemain de la Révolution. Maurice Agulhon.
Vietnam: A Comprehensive Bibliography. John Hsueh-ming Chen.
Viking America: The Norse Crossings and Their Legacy. James Robert Enterline.
The Viking Settlements of North America. Frederick J. Pohl.
La ville de São Paulo. Peuplement et population, 1750-1850, d'après les registres paroissiaux et les recensements anciens. Maria-Luiza Marcillo.
Une Ville ouvrière au temps du socialisme utopique. Toulon de 1815 à 1851. Maurice Agulhon.
Violence and Civil Disorder in Italian Cities 1200-1500. Lauro Martines, ed.

Violence dans la violence: Le débat Bakounine-Nečaev. Michael Confino.
The Virginia Historical Register. 6 vols. William Maxwell, ed.
The Vision of Politics on the Eve of Reformation: More, Machiavelli, and Seyssel. J. H. Hexter.
Visionary Film: the American Avant-Garde. P. Adams Sitney.
Visions of America: Eleven Literary Historical Essays. Kenneth S. Lynn.
Vitruvius and Later Roman Building Manuals. Hugh Plommer.
¡Viva Cristo Rey! The Cristero Rebellion and the Church-State Conflict in Mexico. David C. Bailey.
The Voice of Black America: Major Speeches by Negroes in the United States. Philip S. Foner.
Voices from the Wilderness: The Frontiersman's Own Story. Thomas Froncek, ed.
Voices of the Prairie Land. Martin Litvin, ed.
Les Voies Romaines. Raymond Chevallier.
La Voluntad del pueblo en la emancipación de El Salvador.... Francisco Peccorini Letona.
The von Richthofen Sisters: The Triumphant and the Tragic Modes of Love. Martin Green.
Voyage aux Régions Equinoxiales du Nouveau Continent. Alexander von Homboldt.
A Voyage Round the World in the Years MDCCXL, I, II, III, IV by George Anson. Richard Walter and Benjamin Robins.
Voyages of Francisco de Ortega, California, 1632-1636. Miguel León-Portilla.
Le Voyageurs français et les relations entre le France et l'Abyssinie de 1835 à 1870. Georges Malecot.

-W-

W. E. B. DuBois. William M. Tuttle, Jr., ed.

Wage Patterns and Wage Policy in Modern China 1919-1972. Christopher Howe.

Wage Regulation in Pre-Industrial England. W. E. Minchinton, ed.

Walt Whitman's Camden Conversations. Walt Whitman. Selected by Walter Teller.

Walter of Henley and Other Treatises on Estate Management and Accounting. Dorothea Oschinsky.

Walter Reuther. Robert L. Tyler.

Der Wandel der Nahrungsgewohnheiten unter dem Einfluss der Industrialisierung. Hans J. Tuteberg and Günter Wiegelmann.

War and Society: The United States, 1941-1945. Richard Polenberg.

War and Society in the Nineteenth-Century Russian Empire. J. G. Purves and D. A. West, eds.

War and Trade in Northern Seas: Anglo-Scandinavian Economic Relations in the Mid-Eighteenth Century. H. S. K. Kent.

The War at Home: Vietnam and the American People, 1964-1968. Thomas Powers.

The War Between the Union and the Confederacy. William C. Oates.

The War Game. Charles Grant.

War in Medieval English Society: Social Values in the Hundred Years War 1337-99. John Barnie.

The War Industries Board: Business-Government Relations During World War I. Robert D. Cuff.

War Machinery and High Policy: Defence Administration in Peacetime Britain, 1902-1914. Nicholas D'Ombrain.

The War Ministry of Winston Churchill. Maxwell P. Schoenfeld.

The War of 1812. John K. Mahon.

War, Presidents and Public Opinion. John E. Mueller.

The War That Never Ended: The American Civil War. Robert Cruden.

Warlord Politics: Conflict and Coalition in the Modernization of Republican China. Lucian W. Pye.

The Warrant Chiefs. Indirect Rule in Southeastern Nigeria 1891-1929. A. E. Afigbo.

The Warren Wagontrain Raid. Benjamin Capps.

The Warsaw Rising of 1944. Jan M. Ciechanowski.

Water for a City: A History of New York City's Problem from the Beginning to the Delaware River System. Charles H. Weidner.

Water for the Southwest: Historical Survey and Guide to Historic Sites. Lindsay T. Baker, Steven R. Rae, Joseph E. Minor, and Seymour V. Connor.

Water Tables. James Seay.

Wavell. The Viceroy's Journal. Penderel Moon, ed.

Ways of the Development of Feudalism (The Caucasus, Middle Asia, Rus', the Baltic States). A. P. Novosel'tsev, et al.

We Have All Gone Away. Curtis Harnack.

The Weaver's Pathway: A Clarification of the "Spirit Trail" in Navajo Weaving. Noël Bennett.

A Webfoot Volunteer: The Diary of William M. Hilleary, 1864-1866. Herbert B. Nelson and Preston E. Onstad, eds.

Wee Creek to El Dorado: Oil in Kansas, 1860-1920. Francis W. Schruben.

Weimar, Hitler und die Marine: Reichspolitik und Flottenbau, 1920-1939. Jost Dülffer.

The Wellesley Index to Victorian Periodicals, 1824-1900. Volume II. Walter E. Houghton, ed.

Wellington: Pilar of State. Elizabeth Longford.

Die Wende vor Moskau: Das Scheitern der Strategie Hitlers im Winter 1941/1942. Klaus Reinhardt.

Wentworth Papers, 1597-1628. J. P. Cooper, ed.

Were These King Solomon's Mines? Excavations in the Timna Valley. Beno Rothenberg.

West African States and European Expansion: The Dahomey-Niger Hinterland, 1885-1898. B. I. Obichere.

West African Travels: A Guide to People and Places. Sylvia Ardyn Boone.

West By East: The American West in the Gilded Age. Gene M. Gressley.

The West in Russia and China: Religious and Secular Thought in

Modern Times. Vol. 1: Russia, 1472-1917 ... Vol. 2: China, 1582-1949. Donald W. Treadgold.

West Indian Nations: A New History. Philip Sherlock.

West Indian Societies. David Lowenthal.

West Texas After the Discovery of Oil: A Modern Frontier. Richard R. Moore.

The West Virginia State Grange: the First Century. William D. Barns.

Western American History in the Seventies: Selected Papers Presented to the First Western History Conference, Colorado State University, August 10-12, 1972. Daniel Tyler, ed.

Western Apache Raiding and Warfare. Grenville Goodwin.

Western Asiatic Jewellery c. 3000-612 B.C. K. R. Maxwell-Hyslop.

Western Europe in the Middle Ages: A Short History. Joseph R. Strayer.

Western European Politics Since 1945: The Shaping of the European Community. Roger Morgan.

Western Expansion: A History of the American Frontier. Ray Allen Billington.

The Western Heritage from Earliest Times to the Present. Stewart C. Easton.

Western Man and the Modern World. 5 vols. Leonard F. James.

Western Mining: An Informal Account of Precious-Metals Prospecting, Placering, Lode Mining, and Milling on the American Frontier From Spanish Times to 1893. Otis E. Young, Jr.

Western North Carolina Since the Civil War. Ina W. Van Noppen and John J. Van Noppen.

The Western Peace Officer: A Legacy of Law and Order. Frank Richard Prassel.

Western Technology and Soviet Economic Development, 1945-1965. Antony C. Sutton.

Das Westtor, Ergebnisse der Augsrabungen, 1964-1968. Clemens Krause.

Whales and Destiny: The Rivalry Between America, France, and Britain for Control of the Southern Whale Fishery, 1785-1825. Edouard A. Stackpole.

What I Remember. Thomas Adolphus Trollope.

What is Man? And Other Philosophical Writings. Mark Twain.

"What is the Good of History?" Selected Letters of Carl L. Becker, 1900-1945. Michael Kammen, ed.

What Makes a Man: The Annie E. Kennedy and John Bidwell Letters, 1866-1868. Chad L. Hoppes.

When Shall They Rest? Peter Collier.

When the Navajos Had Too Many Sheep: the 1940's. George A. Boyce.

Where Has Last July Gone? Memoirs. Drew Middleton.

Where the Wagon Led. One Man's Memories of the Cowboy's Life in the Old West. R. D. Symons.

The Whig Party of Louisiana. William H. Adams.

White Eagle-Red Star: The Polish-Soviet War 1919-1920. Norman Davies.

White Flags of Surrender. Lili Hahn.

The White Generals: An Account of the White Movement and the Russian Civil War. Richard Luckett.

White Into Red: A Study of the Assimilation of White Persons Captured by Indians. J. Norman Heard.

The White Man's Burden: Historical Origins of Racism in the United States. Winthrop D. Jordan.

White Savage: The Case of John Dunn Hunter. Richard Drinnon.

White Silence. Silvia E. Crane.

White Terror: The Ku Klux Klan Conspiracy and Southern Reconstruction. Allen W. Trelease.

Who Are the Russians? A History of the Russian People. Wright Miller.

Who Killed the British Empire? George Woodcock.

Whoop-Up Country: The Canadian-American West, 1865-1885. Paul F. Sharp.

Who's the Savage? David Wrone and Russell S. Nelson, Jr., eds.

Why Don't We Learn From History? B. H. Liddell-Hart.

Why Monks? François Vandenbroucke.

Why Nations Go to War. John G. Stoessinger.

The Wild Man Within. An Image in Western Thought from the Renaissance to Romanticism. Edward Dudley and Maximillian E. Novak, eds.

Wilderness and the American Mind. Roderick Nash.

Wilderness Bonanza: The Tri-State District of Missouri, Kansas, and Oklahoma. Arrell M. Gibson.

Wilderness Manhunt: The Spanish Search for La Salle. Robert S. Weddle.

Wiley Post, His "Winnie Mae," and the World's First Pressure Suit. Stanley R. Mohler and Bobby H. Johnson.

Will Rogers: His Life and Times. Richard M. Ketchum.

The Will Rogers Book. Paula McSpadden Love.

Willamette Landings: Ghost Towns of the River. Howard McKinley Corning.

William and Mary. Henri and Barbara van der Zee.

William Barrett Travis, His Sword and His Pen. Martha Anne Turner.

William Butterfield. Paul Thompson.

William Carlos Williams: The Later Poems. Jerome Mazzaro.

William Caslon: Master of Letters. Johnson Ball.

William Cobbett. James Sambrook.

William Dell, Master Puritan. Eric C. Walker.

William Ellery: a Rhode Island Politico and Lord of Admirality. William M. Fowler, Jr.

William Gibbs McAdoo: A Passion for Change, 1863-1917. John J. Broesamle.

William H. Crawford, 1772-1834. Chase C. Mooney.

William Howard Taft: A Conservative's Conception of the Presidency. Donald F. Anderson.

William Penn and Early Quakerism. Melvin B. Endy, Jr.

William, Roger, A Key Into the Language of America. John J. Teunissen and Evelyn J. Hinz, eds.

William Tatham, 1752-1819: American Versatile. G. Melvin Herndon.

The Williamsburg Collection of Antique Furnishings.

The Wilmington Town Book, 1743-1778. Donald R. Lennon and Ida Brooks Kellam, eds.

Wiltshire Returns to the Bishop's Visitation Queries, 1783. Mary Ransome, ed.

Winchester Yields: A Study in Medieval Agricultural Productivity. J. Z. Titow.

Windmühlen: Der Stand der Forschung über das Vorkommen und den Ursprung. Jannis C. Notebaart.

Windows on Africa: A Symposium. R. T. Parsons.

Windsor Castle in the History of the Nation. A. L. Rowse.

The Wine Trade. A. D. Francis.

Winnebago Clothing Styles. Kathleen M. Danker.

The Winter Soldiers. Richard M. Ketchem.

Winterthur Portfolio 8. Ian M. G. Quimby, ed.

Wiriyami. Adrian Hastings.

Die wirtschaftlichen Beziehungen Deutchlands zu Mexiko und Mittelamerika im 19. Jahrhundert. Hendrik Dane.

Wisconsin: A History. Robert C. Nesbit.

Wisconsin: A State for All Seasons. Jill Dean and Susan Smith, eds.

Wisconsin Death Trip. Michael Lesy.

The Wise Minority. Leon Friedman.

Witch-Hunting in Southwestern Germany 1562-1684: The Social and Intellectual Foundations. H. C. Erik Midelfort.

Witchcraft in the Middle Ages. Jeffrey B. Russell.

With Macdonald in Uganda. Herbert H. Austin.

The Woman Citizen: Social Feminism in the 1920s. J. Stanley Lemons.

The Woman in American History. Gerda Lerner.

Women and Child Care in China. Ruth Sidel.

Women in China. Marilyn B. Young, ed.

Women Who Spied for the Blue and the Gray. Oscar A. Kinchen.

Women Writers in France: Variations on a Theme. Germaine Bree.

The Women's Rights Movement in the United States, 1848-1970. Albert Krichmar.

Women's Suffrage and Prohibition: A Comparative Study of Equality and Social Control. Ross Evans Paulson.

Women's Suffrage in New Zealand. Patricia Grimshaw.

Wool, Cloth, and Gold: The Struggle for Bullion in Anglo-Burgundian Trade, 1340-1478. John H. A. Munro.

The Wool Textile Industry in Great Britain. J. Geraint Jenkins.

A Word-Index to the Poetic Works of Rousard. A. E. Creare.

Workable Design: Action and Situation in the Fiction of Henry James. John P. O'Neill.

Working the Homestake. Joseph H. Cash.

The Works of Sir Roger Williams. John X. Evans, ed.

The World at War. Mark Arnold-Foster.

World Cattle III: Cattle of North America. John M. Rouse.

World Handbook of Political and Social Indicators. Charles L. Taylor and Michael C. Hudson.

The World History of the Jewish People. Abraham Schalit, ed.

The World in Depression, 1929-1939. Charles P. Kindleberger.

A World in Shadow: The Free Black in Antebellum South Carolina. Marina Wikramanayake.

The World of Nations: Reflections on American History, Politics and Culture. Christopher Lasch.

The World of the Crusaders. Joshua Prawer.

The World of the Huns: Studies in Their History and Culture. J. Otto Maenchen-Helfen.

The World of the Reformation. Hans J. Hillerbrand.

The World of Time, Inc.: The Intimate History of a Publishing Enterprise. Volume 2, 1941-1960. Robert T. Elson.

The World of the Urban Working Class. Marc Fried.

The World Petroleum Market. M. A. Adelman.

A World Restored. Henry Kissinger.

A World to Care For: The Autobiography of Howard A. Rusk, M. D.

The World Turned Upside Down. Christopher Hill.

-X-

Xenophon. J. K. Anderson.

X-Raying the Pharaohs. James E. Harris and Kent R. Weeks.

-Y-

Yale: A History. Brooks Mather Kelley.

The Yalta Conference. Richard Fenno, ed.

Yamagata Aritomo in the Rise of Modern Japan, 1838-1922. Roger F. Hackett.

Yankee Cavalrymen: Through the Civil War With the Ninth Pennsylvania Cavalry. John W. Rowell.

The Yankee Doodler: Music, Theater, and Fun in the American Revolution.

Yankee Politics in Rural Vermont. Frank M. Bryan.

Ye Atte Wode Annals. Elijah Francis Atwood.

Year Book XVII.

The Year of Erasmus' Birth. A. C. F. Koch.

Year One of the Empire: A Play of American Politics, War, and Protest Taken from the Historical Record. Elinor Fuchs and Joyce Antler.

The Year They Threw the Rascals Out. Charles Deaton.

The Years of Despair: North Dakota in the Depression. D. Jerome Tweton and Daniel F. Rylance.

Years to Victory. Henry H. Adams.

Yellowstone Kelly: The Memoirs of

Luther S. Kelly. M. M. Quaife,
ed.
Yesterday in the Hills. Floyd C.
and Charles Hubert Watkins.
Yorty: Politics of a Constant Candi-
date. John C. Bollens and Grant
B. Geyer.
Young Mr. Pepys. John Hearsey.
Young Philip Sidney 1572-1577.
James M. Osborn.
Youngers' Fatal Blunder. Dallas
Cantrell.
Yugoslavia. Stevan K. Pavlowitch.
Yugoslavia Before the Roman Con-
quest. John Alexander.
Yuman Pottery Making. Malcolm J.
Rogers.
Yvon Delbos at the Quai d'Orsay:
French Foreign Policy During the
Popular Front, 1936-1938. John
E. Dreifort.

-Z-

A ZBC of Ezra Pound. Christine
Brooke-Rose.
Zagora I. Excavation Season 1967;
Study Season 1968-9. Alexander
Cambitoglou, J. J. Coulton, Judy
Birmingham and J. R. Green.
Zamboanga and Sulu: An Archaeologi-
cal Approach to Ethnic Diversity.
Alexander Spoehr.
Zane Grey. Carlton Jackson.
Das Zeitalter des Hauses Österreich:
Die ersten Jahre der Regierung
Ferdinands I. in Österreich (1520-
1527). Alphons Lhotsky.
The Zionist Movement in Palestine
and World Politics, 1880-1918.
N. Gordon Levin, Jr., ed.
The Zulu War. David Clammer.
The Zuñi Indians: Their Mythology,
Esoteric Fraternities, and Cere-
monies. Matilda Stevenson.
The Zuñis--Self Portrayals. Alvina
Quam, trans.